BUSINESS ETHICS

*A Stakeholder and Issues
Management Approach*

THIRD EDITION

JOSEPH W. WEISS
Bentley College

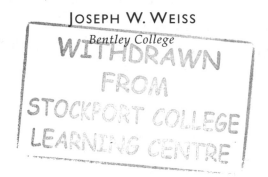
THOMSON
SOUTH-WESTERN

Australia · Canada · Mexico · Singapore · Spain · United Kingdom · United States

Business Ethics: A Stakeholder and Issues Management Approach, 3e
Joseph W. Weiss

VP/Editor-in-Chief:
Jack Calhoun

VP/Team Leader:
Melissa S. Acuña

Executive Editor:
John Szilagyi

Developmental Editor:
Judy O'Neill

Marketing Manager:
Rob Bloom

Production Editor:
Barbara Fuller Jacobsen

Manufacturing Coordinator:
Rhonda Utley

Production House:
Clarinda Publication
Services

Compositor:
The Clarinda Company

Printer:
Transcontinental Printing
Louiseville, Quebec, Canada

Cover Designer:
Chris Miller

**Cover Photographer /
Illustrator:**
Imagebank/Getty Images

Library of Congress
Cataloging-in-Publication
Data

Weiss, Joseph W.
    Business ethics : a
stakeholder and issues
management approach /
Joseph W. Weiss.—3rd ed.
        p. cm.
    Includes bibliographical
references and index.
        ISBN 0-03-018458-4 (pbk.)
        1. Business ethics.
2. Social responsibility of
business. 3. Issues
management. I. Title.

HF5387 .W45 2002
174′4—dc21
                        2001057716

CONTENTS

CHAPTER 4

THE CORPORATION AND INTERNAL STAKEHOLDERS: VALUE-BASED MORAL DIMENSIONS OF LEADERSHIP, STRATEGY, STRUCTURE, CULTURE, AND SELF-REGULATION   101

CHAPTER 5

THE CORPORATION AND EXTERNAL STAKEHOLDERS: MANAGING MORAL RESPONSIBILITY IN THE MARKETPLACE   149

CHAPTER 7

THE GLOBAL ENVIRONMENT, STAKEHOLDER MANAGEMENT, AND MULTINATIONAL CORPORATIONS 255

CHAPTER 8
BUSINESS ETHICS IN THE TWENTY-FIRST CENTURY   305

Cases 337

PREFACE

Read any major newspaper or business journal, turn on any major broadcast network like CNN, or tune into al-Jazeera, if you have satellite, and you will find an event, a crisis, or an issue that relates a corporation's activities to global ethical implications. Questions quickly arise: Who is right? Who is wrong? Who stands to gain or lose? Who is hurt? Who is liable? Who should pay damages? Who acted responsibly? Who did not? Will justice be served?

Business ethics is about the intersection between business and ethics and is fundamental to the relationships between business and society at large. Why does an organization exist in the first place? What is its *raison d'être*? How does it treat its stakeholders? Business ethics engages these essential questions and is also about the purpose, values, and transactions of and among individuals, groups, companies, and their global alliances.

With this in mind, students and professionals need straightforward frameworks to thoughtfully and objectively analyze and then sort through complex issues in order to make decisions that matter—ethically, economically, socially, legally, and spiritually. The global crisis of September 11, 2001 temporarily collapsed—perhaps even for the long term—the ethical, economic, social, legal, human, and spiritual dimensions of the workplace. On that fateful day and in the weeks that followed, owners, managers, and employees acted noticeably more holistically, sharing stakeholder roles not always seen: as human beings with values, as parents, as members of extended families, as leaders literally responsible for the physical safety of employees as well as for their ongoing productivity during times of enormous tragedy, and as people with differing—or perhaps no—religious and spiritual beliefs.

This third edition of *Business Ethics: A Stakeholder and Issues Management Approach* was revised with these concerns in mind and with at least four related goals:

- to cover major contemporary, international, and global topics in business ethics;
- to present stakeholder and issues management frameworks and practical methods for identifying and evaluating news-breaking events in the business world;
- to present the material in a straightforward, "reader-friendly" way; and
- to offer research and business press findings and stories to explain concepts and perspectives.

In addition to providing concrete frameworks for analyzing and discussing a wide range of ethical issues, the third edition of *Business Ethics* also includes a full complement of tools for leading discussions and encouraging student participation:

- Highlighted ethical dilemmas (new to this edition) underscore the fact that difficult business decisions are grounded in ethical dilemmas. Each dilemma asks students not only to make a choice but to defend their decisions and to consider the consequences that inattention to the ethical implications depicted might bring. Plant closings, audit disclosures, and the strategic misrepresentation of facts are among the dilemmas examined in these end-of-chapter cases.
- End-of-chapter questions and exercises have been updated to motivate the reader's active participation in chapter topics.
- Boxed inserts appear throughout the chapters to illustrate current applications of chapter content in a business context. Integrating ethical frameworks with current events provides numerous opportunities to set up problems and deliver the tools to effect solutions at the same time. Businesses face difficult problems every day and the media reports on those problems ceaselessly. *Business Ethics* draws on this vast reservoir to make its points accessible, credible, and relevant.

This edition also expands stakeholder analysis to incorporate values-driven management approaches. For example, Chapter 4, which addresses internal stakeholders, investigates options for assessing an organization's readiness to manage from a values-driven and stakeholder-responsiveness approach.

A PROACTIVE APPROACH

Although business ethics issues change daily, classic ethical principles remain constant. The challenge in writing this book was to devise an effective vehicle that integrates the two. This book presents contemporary and classical business cases and decisions that can be analyzed and interpreted using ethical principles and decision-making negotiation styles. "Hypernorms" and conflict resolution techniques are illustrated along with classical ethical principles.

As earlier editions of this book demonstrated, *Business Ethics* encourages the reader to take on the decision-maker's role. With thought-provoking cases and discussion questions that ask "What would you do if you had to decide a course of action?" *Business Ethics* also encourages readers to articulate and share their decision-making rationales and strategies. Readers will also be able to examine changing ethical issues and business problems with a critical eye. We take a close look at the business reportage of the *Wall Street Journal*, *60 Minutes*, *20/20*, the *New York Times*, *BusinessWeek*, the *Economist*, and other on-line and off-line sources to learn from the challenges, practices, and mistakes of companies and organizations around the world.

STAKEHOLDER AND ISSUES MANAGEMENT ANALYSIS

Stakeholder analysis is one of the most comprehensive orienting approaches for identifying issues, groups, strategies, and outcomes (potential or realized) revolving around complex ethical dilemmas. Stakeholder, issues management, and ethical methods can be used throughout the book. These methods are presented in Chapter 2 alongside an extended discussion of the high-profile Microsoft antitrust case. It offers a useful starting point for mapping the who, what, when, where, why, and how of ethical problems involving organizations and their constituencies. Although issues and crisis management as valuable complements to stakeholder analysis are emphasized, it is important to note that these approaches need not be used to apprehend every ethical dilemma or to solve every crisis or complex moral situation. Several other ethical problem-solving frameworks, quick tests, and negotiation techniques are presented in Chapters 3, 7, and 8.

FEATURES OF THE BOOK

- *Clear and understandable presentations.* Principles, concepts, and examples are written to minimize jargon and maximize meaning. Although intended primarily for the dedicated course in business ethics, this text may also serve as a useful adjunct in other course areas, namely, introduction to business, business law, business and society, and business policy.
- *A variety of cases. Business Ethics* retains and updates its longer end-of-book cases, adding seven new cases to the mix. Shorter cases and assessments are interspersed throughout the chapters.
- *Global scope.* Ethics, advantageously integrated into the world economy, forms the core of Chapter 7, "The Global Environment, Stakeholder Management, and Multinational Corporations."
- *Contemporary approach.* New sections on globalization, international ethics, stakeholder management methods for assessing organizations, and how business ethics has been affected by the September 11, 2001 terrorist attacks are included in this edition. Contemporary individual and professional ethical dilemmas in business are presented throughout the text.
- *Cross-disciplinary reach.* Topics relating to philosophy, law, ethics, business and society, and management enlarge understanding.
- *Emerging perspectives.* Perspectives on business and ethics, as we look to the future, are discussed in detail in Chapter 8, "Business Ethics in the Twenty-First Century," with the events of September 11, 2001 receiving special focus.

OBJECTIVES OF THE BOOK

- To introduce basic ethical concepts, principles, and examples to enhance understanding and use of ethics in solving moral dilemmas;

- To introduce the stakeholder and issues management methods as strategic and practical ways for mapping corporate, group, and individual relationships so readers can understand and apply ethical reasoning in the marketplace and in workplace relationships;
- To expand readers' awareness of what constitutes ethical and unethical practices in business at the individual, group, organizational, and multinational level; and
- To instill a confidence and competence in readers' ability to think and act according to moral principles as they create, manage, and study stakeholder relationships in their own worlds, at the national and international level.

STRUCTURE OF THE BOOK

- Chapter 1 defines business ethics and familiarizes the reader with examples of ethics in business practices, levels of ethical analysis, and what can be expected from a course in business ethics.
- Chapter 2 introduces the stakeholder and issues management methods for studying social responsibility relationships at the individual employee, group, and organizational levels. These methods provide for and encourage the incorporation of ethical principles and concepts from the entire book.
- Chapter 3 contains a discussion of the "micro-level" approach to ethical decision making: moral principles and concepts derived from both classical and more contemporary ways of thinking and acting ethically are presented. Individual styles of moral decision making are also discussed in this section. Although this section is a micro-level approach, these principles can be used to examine and explain corporate strategies and actions as well. (Executives, managers, employees, coalitions, government officials, and other external stakeholder groups are treated as individuals.)
- Chapter 4 presents the corporation as stakeholder and discusses a values-driven stakeholder management approach for organizing corporations internally. Aligning leadership, strategy, structure, culture, and systems is a dominant theme in the chapter, along with how to manage an organization ethically.
- Chapter 5 presents ethical issues and problems that firms face with external consumers, government, and environmental groups. The question "How moral can and should corporations be and act in commercial dealings?" is examined.
- Chapter 6 addresses the individual employee stakeholder and examines the kinds of moral issues and dilemmas individuals face in the contemporary workplace.
- Chapter 7 extends the level of analysis to domestic and multinational corporations (MNCs) and discusses ethical issues between MNCs, host countries, and other groups. International variations of capitalism are

presented. Ethics and industrial competitiveness are also discussed using the United States as an example.

- Chapter 8 discusses the impact of the September 11, 2001 attacks on a number of ethical areas and outlines emerging ethical issues that employees, managers, corporations, and multinational stakeholders must manage in the near future.

CASES

Thirteen cases are included in this edition, seven of which are new:

- Microsoft: Industry Predator or Fierce Competitor? (new)
- Dow Corning Corporation and Silicone Breast Implants
- The "Almost Crisis": Intel's Pentium Chip Problem
- What's Written versus What's Reality: Ethical Dilemmas in a Hi-Tech Public Relations Firm (new)
- Merrill Lynch's Entry into On-Line Trading (new)
- Fleet Bank/BankBoston Merger: Culture Clash: Back to the Future (new)
- In the Beginning, Napster: Killer App or Illegal Weapon? (new)
- Trouble in Paris: EuroDisney's Experiment
- General Motors versus the Media, *Dateline NBC*
- Stella Liebeck versus The McDonald's Corporation: Product (for Judicial System) Liability?
- Colt and the Gun Control Controversy (new)
- Women in Public Accounting (and Other Professions): Gender and Workplace Obstacles
- DoubleClick's Battle over On-Line Privacy (new)

ANCILLARY PACKAGE

The following ancillaries are available to instructors who adopt *Business Ethics: A Stakeholder and Issues Management Approach:*

- *Instructor's Manual with Test Bank* (0030185726). Includes lecture outlines, suggested answers to end-of-chapter discussion questions and ethical dilemmas, case notes, and test questions. Prepared by Amit Shah, Frostburg State University. Available in print or for download at http://weiss.swcollege.com.
- *PowerPoint.* Lecture-support slides. Prepared by Amit Shah, Frostburg State University. Available for download at http://weiss.swcollege.com.
- *ExamView Testing Software* (0030297362). Contains all the questions available in the printed Test Bank. ExamView is an easy-to-use test-creation program available in Windows and Macintosh formats.
- *Turner Learning/CNN Video: Management and Organizations* (0324151799). Features short segments from CNN's Headline News and CNN's finan-

cial network to use as lecture launchers, for discussion, as topical introductions, and more. Includes integration guide, with segment
overviews, suggested discussion questions, and topic keys.

ACKNOWLEDGMENTS

This book has been in the making over the last several years in my teaching
MBA students and executives. My consulting work also pervades this text in
numerous ways. I would like to thank all my students for their questions,
challenges, and class contributions, which have stimulated the research and
presentations in this text. I also thank my colleagues with whom I have met
and worked over the years in the Academy of Management and in the Organizational Behavior Teaching Society. Their suggestions are reflected in the
book. I also thank colleagues at Bentley College who contributed resources,
ideas, and motivation for executing the writing of the text. Kathy Rusiniak,
my graduate assistant, helped enormously with the first edition. Vinamra
Daga and Angela Ding, Bentley College MBA students, helped make the second edition possible with their research and writing assistance. Kristin
Galfetti helped with the original research and construction of the discussion
questions. I also wish to thank Michael Hoffman and his staff at Bentley College's Center for Business Ethics who shared resources and friendship in
helping with research. Aaron Sato and Poojai Pollawait at the Business
Ethics Center were particularly helpful. In addition, I wish to thank Heather
Hogan, of Harcourt College Publishers, and John Szilagyi, my principal editor, who made this edition possible.

I recognize and extend thanks to those who reviewed this book and offered valuable suggestions as this edition and its earlier forms were in preparation:

Albert D. Clark, Southern University

Geri L. Dreiling, Fontbonne University

Robert Giacalone, University of Richmond

John James, University of Florida

Susan Jarvis, University of Texas—Pan
American

Susan Key, University of Alabama at
Birmingham

Tony McAdams, University of Northern Iowa

Michael McCuddy, Valparaiso University

Joan Ryan, Lane Community College

William Wines, Boise State University

Several graduate students, many of whom are not identified here, from
my Management Systems in the Changing Environment course at Bentley
College contributed to the research and writing of the cases. I wish to thank
the following MBA students who authored drafts of the following cases used
in this text: DoubleClick case—Carmen Spear and Joe Rioux; Hi-Tech Public
Relations case—Tim Corbett, Trudy Essember, and Monica McConnell; Fleet
Bank/BankBoston case—Danielle Follett, Erinn O'Boyle, and Soamoya
Rankins; Colt case—Dan Barton, Craig Corsetti, and Aman Datta; and Nap-
ster case—Robert Manning, Leenuta Pola, Kristina Morin, and D. Krachev.

BUSINESS ETHICS, THE CHANGING ENVIRONMENT, AND STAKEHOLDER MANAGEMENT

1.1 BUSINESS ETHICS AND THE CHANGING ENVIRONMENT

Businesses and governments operate in changing technological, legal, economic, social, and political environments with competing stakeholders and power claims. *Stakeholders* are individuals, companies, groups, and nations that cause and respond to external issues, opportunities, and threats. Internet and information technologies, globalization, deregulation, mergers, and wars have accelerated the rate of change and uncertainty in which stakeholders—as professionals, employees, consumers, and members of a community—and even society must make and manage business and moral decisions. Crises concerning questionable ethical and illegal business practices confront organizations, societies, and individuals daily, as the following examples illustrate:

■ The September 11 attacks on the World Trade Center and Pentagon moved the United States to war and realigned international stakeholders. Crises and issues about security, ideologies, cultures, ethics, and national identities are occurring.

■ On August 9, 2000, Firestone recalled 6.5 million defective tires that were used on Ford Explorers. These tires had caused more than 174 deaths and 250 injuries in the U.S. and 50 deaths overseas. Internal documents from Bridgestone/Firestone showed that company officials knew in February, 2000, about possible defects. Bridgestone/Firestone blamed Ford Motor Company, and Ford blamed Bridgestone/Firestone. Ford quit its partnership with the tire companies (*Wall Street Journal*, 15 September 2000, B1; 22 May 2001, A3). William Ford replaced CEO Nasser to rebuild Ford's reputation.

■ DoubleClick's chief executive, Kevin O'Connor, stated that his company would not connect people's names, addresses, and other personal information with data it collects from the web until government and industry set privacy standards. O'Connor did not rule out connecting such data in the future (*Wall Street Journal*, 3 March 2000, B1). (See the DoubleClick case at the end of this book.)

■ Microsoft may win the case on monopoly, but it remains to be seen if government policy can regulate markets that rely on innovation, software, and the Internet. These markets continue to naturally evolve toward consolidations and monopolies. "What balance should be struck between protecting . . . intellectual property and insuring that newcomers get a fair chance to compete?" (*New York Times*, 9 April 2000, 4).

■ Telecommunication, pharmaceutical companies, banks, insurance companies, computer technology companies, and other companies across many industries continue to merge, forming national and global conglomerates, displacing thousands of employees. Combine this trend with a global "war on terrorism" and a declining global economy and the issue emerges, who protects employees who are laid off or unfairly displaced?

■ A new air bag scam was discovered in Los Angeles when police and insurance officials discovered that crooked mechanics were replacing expensive air bags in steering columns of cars that had crashed with junk-foam peanuts, beer cans, or old tennis shoes, while charging customers up to $3,000 for the repair. Air bag repair is big business. It is estimated that about 75,000 air bags are stolen annually. This new type of fraud—installing dummy airbags—is *not* illegal in 49 states (*USA Today*, 6 September 2000, 3A).

*   *   *   *   *

These are a sample of problematic events that occur among stakeholders in rapidly changing business environments. Add the ongoing issues resulting from the effects of disruptive technologies and of increased working hours on professional and personal stress levels and you can see the pressures created on stakeholders. But before discussing stakeholder management, we take a brief look at the broader environmental forces that affect industries, organizations, and individuals.

SEEING THE "BIG PICTURE"

Pulitzer Prize–winning journalist Thomas Friedman, in *The Lexus and the Olive Tree,*[1] has written a vivid account of the accelerating trend toward globalization. A macro environmental perspective provides a first step using stakeholder and issues approaches to map out and analyze interactions between organizations and groups. Friedman notes,

> Like everyone else trying to adjust to this new globalization system and bring it into focus, I had to retrain myself and develop new lenses to see it. . . . Today, more than ever, the traditional boundaries between politics, culture, technology, finance, national security, and ecology are disappearing. You often cannot explain one without referring to the others, and you cannot explain the whole without reference to them all. . . . I wish I could say I understood all this when I began my career, but I didn't. I came to this approach entirely by accident, as successive changes in my career kept forcing me to add one more lens on top of another, just to survive. (pp. 2, 20)

Quoting Murray Gell-Mann, the Nobel laureate and former professor of theoretical physics at Caltech, Friedman continues,

> We need a corpus of people who consider that it is important to take a serious and professional look at the whole system. It has to be a crude look, because you will never master every part or every interconnection. . . . Unfortunately, in a great many places in our society, including academia and most bureaucracies, prestige accrues principally to those who study carefully some [narrow] aspect of a problem, a trade, a technology, or a culture, while discussion of the big picture is relegated to cocktail party conversation. That is crazy. We have to learn not only to have specialists but also people whose specialty is to spot the strong interactions and entanglements of the different dimensions, and then take a crude look at the whole. (p. 28)

ENVIRONMENTAL FORCES AND STAKEHOLDERS

Organizations are embedded in and interact with multiple changing local, national, and international environments, as the excerpts above illustrate. These environments are increasingly moving toward and merging into a global system of dynamically interrelated interactions among local, national

FIGURE 1.1   ENVIRONMENTAL DIMENSIONS AFFECTING INDUSTRIES,
ORGANIZATIONS, AND JOBS

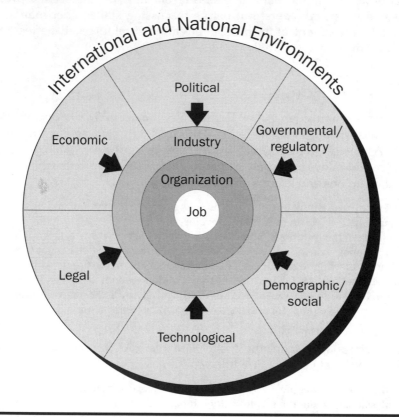

and regional politics, economies, regulations, technologies, demographics, and international law. We must "think globally before acting locally" in many situations. The macrolevel environmental forces shown in Figure 1.1 affect the performance and operation of industries, organizations, and jobs. This framework can be used as a starting point to identify trends, issues, opportunities, and ethical problems that affect industries, companies, professions, and jobs. A first step toward understanding stakeholder issues is to gain an understanding of environmental forces that influence issues and stakes of different groups. As we discuss an overview of these environmental forces here, think of the effects and pressures each of the forces has on your industry, company, profession, career, and job, or education and skill development, if you are a student.

The *economic environment* continues to evolve into a more global context of trade, markets, and resource flows. Large and small U.S. companies are expanding business and products overseas. Stock and bond market volatility and interdependencies across international regions are unprecedented. The European market has consolidated currencies in order to align and facilitate competitiveness and monetary flows. The September attacks have jolted global economic growth.

Technologically, the advent of the Information Age, facilitated by Internet and telecommunications innovations, is also changing economies, industries, companies, jobs, and the way business is conducted. Online technologies facilitate changing corporate "best practices." Company supply chains are becoming virtually integrated on-line. While speed, scope, economy of scale, and efficiency are transforming transactions through information technology, privacy and surveillance issues continue to emerge for employees and consumers. The boundaries between surveillance and convenience continue to blur.

Politically, the fall of communist regimes and the rise of global terrorism are also changing trading and business partners. National and organizational strategic coalitions and political borders and boundaries are blurring. Electronic democracy is changing the way individuals and groups think and act on political issues. Instant web surveys, which are broadcast over CNN and interactive web sites, have created a global chat room on political issues. The transparency of international issues has opened closed systems and ideologies to ubiquitous exposure.

Many *governmental and regulatory* laws and procedures also are changing. Deregulation of industries (utilities, airline, telecommunications, insurance) promotes competitiveness, mergers and acquisitions, consolidations, and even monopolies and oligopolies. Security issues since September 11 compete with civil liberties and rights.

Other federal agencies are also changing standards and rules for corporations. The U.S. Food and Drug Administration (FDA), for example, speeds the required market approval time for new drugs sought after by patients with life-threatening diseases. The September 11 attacks are realigning federal bureaucracies to respond to immediate threats. Public health organizations are also mobilizing to combat bioterrorist attacks on cities.

Regulation over anticompetitive practices is another external influence that affects competition and consumers. Government regulation in the United States is unevenly enforced. Microsoft and some telecommunications firms, but not global banks, have been the focus of the U.S. Department of Justice. Why? How and to what extent are U.S. antitrust laws to be enforced in a fiercely competitive global marketplace? Another major regulatory issue is the government's increasing interest in taxing Internet use. Will Internet use be priced like telephone, fax, and postal services? Who decides? What will the rules be? These issues center on the question: Who is protecting whom and at whose cost and whose benefit?

Legal questions and issues affect all of these environmental dimensions and every stakeholder. To what extent, in a context of global terrorism, should individual privacy be given up for security? Also, who protects the consumer in a free market system? These issues are exemplified in the Firestone defective tire crisis, the Napster recording industry controversy, and the continuing tobacco and gun control debates, all of which question the nature and limits of consumer and corporate law in a free market economy.

Demographically, the workforce has become more diverse. Employers and employees are faced with sexual harassment and discrimination issues and the effects of downsizing on morale, career changes, productivity, and security. How can companies effectively integrate a workforce that is increasingly both younger *and* older, less educated *and* more educated, and technologically sophisticated *and* technologically un-skilled? As these environmental forces continue to press for change and adaption by stakeholders, a stakeholder management approach can benefit all constituencies (individual employees, companies, consumers, environmental groups, government, and communication media) in developing collaborative and socially responsible actions.

STAKEHOLDER MANAGEMENT APPROACH

How do companies, communication media, political groups, consumers, employees, competitors, and other groups respond when they are affected by an issue, dilemma, threat, or opportunity from one or more of the environments just described? The stakeholder management approach is a way of understanding the effects of environmental forces and groups on specific issues that affect real-time stakeholders and their welfare.

The stakeholder approach begins to address these questions by enabling individuals and groups to articulate collaborative, win-win strategies based on:

1. Identifying and prioritizing issues, threats, or opportunities

2. Mapping who the stakeholders are

3. Identifying their stakes, interests, and power sources

4. Showing who the members of coalitions are or may become

5. Showing what each stakeholder's ethics are (and should be)

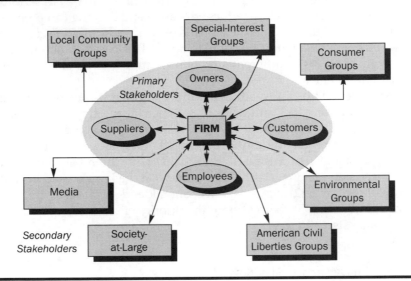

FIGURE 1.2 PRIMARY VS. SECONDARY STAKEHOLDER GROUPS

6. Developing collaborative strategies and dialogue from a "higher ground" perspective to move plans and interactions to the desired closure for all parties

Our underlying aim here is to develop awareness of the ethics and social responsibility of different stakeholders' perceptions, plans, strategies, and actions. As Figure 1.2 illustrates, there can be a wide range of stakeholders in any situation. We turn to a general discussion of "business ethics" in the following section to introduce the subject and motivate you to investigate ethical dimensions of organizational and professional behavior, dilemmas, strategies, and policies.

1.2 WHAT IS BUSINESS ETHICS? WHY DOES IT MATTER?

Business ethicists ask, "What is right and wrong, good and bad, and harmful and beneficial regarding decisions and actions in and around organizational activities?" Ethical "solutions" to business and organizational problems may have more than one right alternative, and sometimes no right solution may seem available.

Learning to think, reason, and act ethically can enable us to first be aware and recognize a potential ethical problem. Then, we can evaluate our own and other's values, assumptions, and judgments regarding the problem before we act. Ultimately, ethical principles alone cannot answer for anyone what the noted theologian Paul Tillich called "the courage to be" in serious ethical dilemmas or crises. At best, ethics education and training can prepare us to be aware of and understand the benefits of acting ethically. We can also learn from business case studies, role playing, and discussions about how our actions affect others in different situations. Acting accountably and responsibly is still a choice.

Laura Nash defined business ethics as "the study of how personal moral norms apply to the activities and goals of commercial enterprise. It is not a separate moral standard, but the study of how the business context poses its own unique problems for the moral person who acts as an agent of this system." Nash stated that business ethics deals with three basic areas of managerial decision making: (1) choices about what the laws should be and whether to follow them; (2) choices about economic and social issues outside the domain of law; and (3) choices about the priority of self-interest over the company's interests.[2]

WHAT ARE UNETHICAL BUSINESS PRACTICES?

Surveys identify prominent everyday ethical issues facing businesses and their stakeholders. Recurring themes include managers lying to employees, office nepotism and favoritism, taking credit for others' work, receiving or offering kickbacks, stealing from the company, firing an employee for whistle-blowing, padding expense accounts to obtain reimbursements for questionable business expenses, divulging confidential information or trade secrets, terminating employment without giving sufficient notice, and using company property and materials for personal use.[3] One study of 148 secretaries who worked for *Fortune 1000* chief executives found that 47% had been asked at some time by their bosses to lie.[4]

The most unethical behavior, one survey showed, happens in the following areas (listed in rank order, starting with the organization that has the most instances of unethical behavior)[5]:

1. Government
2. Sales
3. Law
4. Media
5. Finance
6. Medicine
7. Banking
8. Manufacturing

The sales profession, in particular, is under significant pressure to meet quotas. A survey by Sales & Marketing Management of 200 sales managers showed that 49% reported that their representatives lied on a sales call; 34% said that they heard representatives make unrealistic promises on sales calls; 22% said that their representatives sold products that customers did not need; 30% said that customers demanded a kickback for buying their product; and 54% said that the drive to meet sales goals does a disservice to customers.[6]

These ethical issues in business suggest that any useful definition of business ethics must address a range of social, economic, and organizational problems and pressures in the workplace, including goals, policies, procedures, and relationships among professionals at all organizational levels and between corporate executives and external groups.

Other unethical, illegal, and questionable issues discussed in this book include the effects of *information technology* on the economy, workplace, and workforce (e.g., the "digital divide," rights and justice during transformations); *sexual harassment* (e.g., events at Mitsubishi, Astra USA, and Texaco); *invasion of privacy on the Internet* (e.g., workplace surveillance, individual identity theft, unauthorized use of personal information); limits of a company's *competitiveness* (e.g., the case of Microsoft); the glass ceiling (e.g., women's lack of promotion beyond a certain unspoken barrier and lack of comparable pay for work done in professions and corporations); international human rights and sweatshop labor (e.g., Nike and other large retail firms); the ethics of *diversity* (e.g., the fair and equitable treatment of minorities in the international workforce, the myth and reality of a "level playing field" in businesses); and the future of *capitalism* (e.g., the effects of changes on the so-called "new" and "old" economies and on individuals and groups globally).[7]

WHY DOES ETHICS MATTER IN BUSINESS?

"Doing the right thing" matters to employers, employees, stakeholders, and the public. To companies and employers, acting legally and ethically means saving billions of dollars each year in lawsuits, settlements, and theft. Studies have shown that corporations also have paid significant financial penalties for acting unethically.[8] The tobacco industry discovered that lying about nicotine can be costly to their business. Dow Corning paid heavy penalties for manufacturing and selling unsafe products. It has been estimated that workplace theft costs U.S. businesses $40 billion each year.[9]

Costs to businesses also include deterioration of relationships; damage to reputation; declining employee productivity, creativity, and loyalty; ineffective information flow throughout the organization; and absenteeism.[10] Companies that have a reputation of unethical and uncaring behavior toward employees also have a difficult time recruiting and retaining valued professionals.

For business leaders and managers, managing ethically also means managing with integrity.[11] Integrity cascades throughout an organization. It shapes and influences the values, tone, and culture of the organization; the communications among all members; and the realism, commitment, and imagination of everyone in a company.

WORKING FOR THE BEST COMPANIES

Employees care about ethics because they are attracted to ethically and socially responsible companies.[12] *Fortune* magazine regularly publishes the 100 best companies for which to work (www.fortune.com). While the list continues to change, it is instructive to observe some of the characteristics of good employers that surveyed employees repeatedly cite. The most frequently mentioned characteristics include profit sharing, bonuses, and monetary awards. However, the list also contains policies and benefits that balance work and personal life and those that encourage social responsibility; for example, consider these policies described by employees:

- "When it comes to flextime requests, managers are encouraged to 'do what is right and human.'"
- "An employee hotline to report violations of company values."
- "Will fire clients who don't respect its security officers."
- "Employees donated more than 28,000 hours of volunteer labor last year."

The public and consumers benefit from organizations acting in an ethically and socially responsible manner. Ethics matters in business because all stakeholders stand to gain when organizations, groups, and individuals seek to do the right thing, as well as do things the right way. The following section presents different levels on which ethical issues can occur.

1.3 LEVELS OF BUSINESS ETHICS

Because ethical problems are not only an individual or personal matter, it is helpful to see the different "levels" at which issues originate and how they often move to other levels. Since business leaders and professionals must manage a wide range of stakeholders inside and outside their organizations, understanding the levels of issues that stakeholders face facilitates our understanding of the complex relationships within and among participants involved in solving ethical problems.

Ethical and moral issues in business can be examined from at least five levels. Figure 1.3 illustrates these five levels: *individual, organizational, association, societal,* and *international.*[13] The five levels are explained through the example of issues that surrounded the continuing controversy over the drug RU 486.

RU 486: A STORY

RU 486 is a drug originally manufactured by the French pharmaceutical firm Roussel-Uclaf. Recently the drug, also known as mifepristone, has been made by a less well-known firm—Danco Laboratories LLC (*Wall Street Journal*, 5 September 2000, A1). The drug was known as "the French abortion

FIGURE 1.3	BUSINESS ETHICS LEVELS

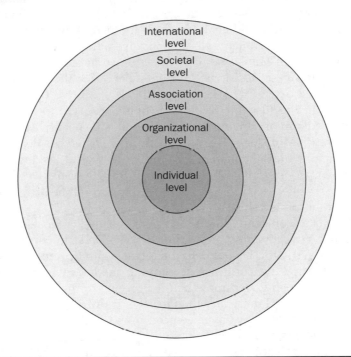

SOURCE: Society for Advancement of Management. (1997). Reframing strategic risk. *SAM Advanced Management Journal*, vol. 62, no. 3: 3. Reprinted with permission from Society for Advancement of Management, Texas A&M University, College of Business, 6300 Ocean Drive, FC111, Corpus Christi, Texas, 78412.

pill," and its use became controversial, especially in the U.S., where it was banned until the year 2000, since it was highly effective in aborting pregnancies if taken during the first five weeks of pregnancy. In the late 1980s, Edouard Sakiz, chairman of Roussel-Uclaf and also a physician, and his top-level management team had to decide whether to market the drug internationally. Dr. Sakiz had helped develop the chemical compound that went into RU 486, and he believed that the drug could particularly help women in poor countries.

Anti-abortion groups opposed distribution of the drug. Controversy also surrounded Roussel-Uclaf's German partner company, Hoechst, and its then chairman, a practicing Roman Catholic. The decision to market RU 486 placed moral and business pressures on Dr. Sakiz. His own beliefs and values were at stake, since he was a medical doctor as well as the head of a profitable firm. At the same time, he advocated for women's right to choose when they would have children.

The issue to market the drug went beyond the French, European, and even U.S. boundaries. China wanted to use RU 486 in its national plan for population control. Also at issue for China and other less developed countries were starvation and health hazards for increasing populations.

The French government was also involved; they owned 36% of Roussel-Uclaf. The French Ministry of Health regulated the company and influenced the firm's business decisions. In September 1988, the French government approved the drug. Dr. Sakiz met with his executive committee a month later. He voted to suspend distribution of the drug. Critics attacked Dr. Sakiz and accused him of denying the public a valuable health benefit.

The French Minister of Health, shortly after Dr. Sakiz's decision, informed the company that the patent for the drug would be given to another company that would distribute RU 486, if Roussel-Uclaf would not comply. Dr. Sakiz reversed his decision and agreed to market the drug. It seemed that he had compromised his personal beliefs to save his job.

It was later conjectured that the entire event—Dr. Sakiz's "no" vote and the French government's pressuring Roussel-Uclaf to concede—may have been contrived. Still, Dr. Sakiz had navigated the firm in a public and bold way by raising the controversy, shaping media coverage, and standing against the French government before agreeing to their demands. The drug was distributed in France and then in other countries. Dr. Sakiz kept his job, although his beliefs may have been compromised.[14]

At the *individual level*, Dr. Sakiz felt pressured to question his own ethics as both as a medical doctor and as an advocate of women's rights. On another level, as a business professional, he had an obligation to help his company earn a profit. It was suggested that he may have had a crisis of conscience and an ethical dilemma because he had to choose between his job and his values. If an ethical issue involves or is limited to an individual's responsibilities, that person may examine his or her own ethical motives and standards before choosing a course of action. In Dr. Sakiz's case, his values became transparent internationally. His eventual decision reflected his choice of his business ethic over his personal ethic.

At the *organizational level*, ethical issues arise when, for example, a person or group is pressured to overlook the wrongdoings of his or her peers in the interest of company harmony or when an employee is asked to perform an unethical or illegal act to earn a division or work unit profit. Sales professionals are sometimes pressured to meet quotas, in which case they, as individuals, may be faced with committing illegal, if not unethical, decisions to offer kickbacks and lie to customers. If an ethical issue arises at the organizational level, the organizational members should examine the firm's policies and procedures and code of ethics, if one exists, before making a decision or taking action. In the case of Roussel-Uclaf, Dr. Sakiz felt responsible as a leader of the company. Representing the company, he had to face a host of questions from his stakeholders: What were the company's obligations to women? To the government laboratory that helped develop the steroid molecule on which RU 486 was based? To the larger medical and research communities? Was he accountable to the unborn around the globe where RU 486 would be available? How would Sakiz justify Roussel-Uclaf's introduction of the drug in China, where women had apparently been coerced into abortions, even near the end of their pregnancies? Dr. Sakiz's decision would define his company's role in society and its relationships with stakeholders.[15]

At the *association level*, Dr. Sakiz had to decide whether he, as a physician, was violating his code to save life, while also acting in the role of a business leader. He was, no doubt, also well aware of the Hippocratic oath and the value it places on human life. Conflicts of interest and conscience—as discussed earlier—can arise in such situations. At the association level, accountants, information technology (IT) professionals, lawyers, physicians, and management consultants can refer to their professional association's charter or code of ethics for guidelines on conducting business before advising a client to deduct questionable items for tax purposes, implementing a questionable or defective software product, offering a plea bargain, risking harmful side effects of prescription drugs, or advising a client to acquire a company that conducts illegal business transactions.

At the *societal level*, laws, norms, customs, and traditions govern the legal and moral acceptability of behaviors. Business activities acceptable in Italy or Turkey may be immoral or illegal in the United States, and vice versa. While RU 486 may have met the Chinese government's needs for population control in 1988, the U.S. government may not have been able to accept the consequences of allowing sales of the drug, given opposing stakeholders' beliefs and political power. The French government was a major force pressuring Dr. Sakiz and his firm to distribute RU 486.

The early history of the RU 486 story illustrates how ethical levels can quickly overlap: what started as a distribution question became an international ethical and moral dilemma. It is interesting to note that, eventually, the FDA approved distribution of RU 486 in the United States. Certain restrictions do apply. Not all stakeholders agreed on this decision. Anti-abortion and pro-life groups strongly opposed the FDA's ruling.

ASKING KEY QUESTIONS

It is helpful for an individual, group, or company to be aware of the ethical levels of a situation and the possible interaction between these levels when confronting a marketing, management, or simple policy question that has moral implications. The following questions can be asked when a problematic decision or action is experienced or perceived (before it becomes an ethical dilemma):

- What are my core values and beliefs?

| FIGURE 1.4 | A FRAMEWORK FOR CLASSIFYING ETHICAL LEVELS |

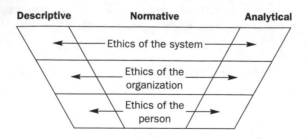

SOURCE: John B. Matthews, Kenneth E. Goodpastor, Laura L. Nash. (1985). *Policies and persons: A casebook in business ethics*, p. 509. New York: McGraw-Hill. Reproduced with permission of The McGraw-Hill Companies.

- What are the core values and beliefs of my organization?
- Whose values, beliefs, and interests may be at risk in this decision? Why?
- Who will be harmed or helped by my decision or by the decision of my organization?
- How will my own and my organization's core values and beliefs be affected or changed by this decision?
- How will I and my organization be affected by the decision?

Figure 1.4 offers a graphic to help separate and identify the ethics of the system (e.g., a country or region's customs, values, and laws), your organization (e.g., the written formal and informal acceptable norms and ways of doing business), and your own ethics, values, and standards. How did these three dimensions of ethics differ in the early history of the RU 486 case? By which level in this figure do you believe Dr. Sakiz's final decision was most influenced? Why? Do you think that Dr. Sakiz was aware of these different levels of influence on him when he made his decision?

In the following section, popular myths about business ethics are presented to challenge conceptions and misconceptions regarding the nature of ethics and business. You may take the "Quick Test of Your Ethical Beliefs" on the following page before reading this section.

1.4 FIVE MYTHS ABOUT BUSINESS ETHICS

Not everyone agrees that ethics is a relevant or necessary subject for business education or dealings. Some have argued that "business ethics" is an *oxymoron*, or a contradiction in terms. Although this book does not advocate or promote a particular ethical position or belief system, it argues that ethics

QUICK TEST OF
YOUR ETHICAL
BELIEFS

Answer each question below with your first reaction. Circle the number, from 1 to 4, that best represents your beliefs if 1 represents "completely agree" and 4 represents "completely disagree."

1. I consider money to be the most important reason for working at a job or in an organization. 1 2 3 4

2. I would hide truthful information about someone or something at work to save my job. 1 2 3 4

3. Lying is usually necessary to succeed in business. 1 2 3 4

4. Cutthroat competition is part of getting ahead in the business world. 1 2 3 4

5. I would do what is needed to promote my own career in a company, short of committing a serious crime. 1 2 3 4

6. Acting ethically at home and with friends is not the same as acting ethically on the job. 1 2 3 4

7. Rules are for people who don't really want to make it to the top of a company. 1 2 3 4

8. I believe that the "Golden Rule" is that the person who has the gold rules. 1 2 3 4

9. Ethics should be taught at home and in the family, not in professional or higher education. 1 2 3 4

10. I consider myself the type of person who does whatever it takes to get a job done, period. 1 2 3 4

Total your scores by adding up the numbers you circled. The *lower* you score, the more questionable your ethical principles regarding business activities. The lowest possible score is 10, the highest score is 40. Be ready to explain and give reasons for your answers in a class discussion.

is relevant to business transactions for the reasons presented throughout the text. However, certain myths persist about business ethics. The more popular myths are presented in Figure 1.5.

A myth is "a belief given uncritical acceptance by the members of a group, especially in support of existing or traditional practices and institutions." Myths regarding the relationship between business and ethics, in this discussion, do not represent truth but, instead, popular and unexamined notions. Which myths have you accepted as unquestioned truth? Do you agree that the following myths are indeed myths? Do you know, work for, or work with anyone who holds any of these myths as true?

MYTH 1: "ETHICS IS A PERSONAL, INDIVIDUAL AFFAIR, NOT A PUBLIC OR DEBATABLE MATTER"

This myth holds that individual ethics is based on personal or religious beliefs and that one decides what is right and wrong in the privacy of one's own conscience. This myth is supported in part by Milton Friedman, a well-known economist, who views "social responsibility," as an expression of business ethics, to be unsuitable for business professionals to address or deal with seriously or professionally, since they are not equipped or trained to do so.[16]

FIGURE 1.5   FIVE BUSINESS ETHICS MYTHS

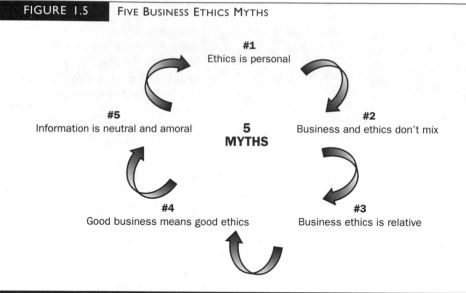

Although it is true that individuals must and do make moral choices in life, including business affairs, it is also true that individuals do not operate in a vacuum. Individual ethical choices are most often made and influenced in discussions, conversations, debates, and group contexts. Individuals often rely on organizations and groups for meaning, direction, and purpose. Moreover, individuals are integral parts of organizational cultures, which have norms, values, rules of conduct, and standards to govern what is acceptable and unacceptable. Therefore, to argue that ethics related to business issues is only or mainly a matter of personal or individual choice is to belittle the role organizations play in shaping and influencing member's attitudes, perceptions, and behavior.

Studies indicate that organizations that act in socially irresponsible ways often pay penalties for unethical behavior.[17] In fact, integrating ethics into the strategic management process is advocated (e.g., "doing well by doing good"). It is argued that integrating ethics into the strategic management process is both the right thing and the profitable thing to do. Corporate social performance has been found to increase financial performance. One study clearly showed that "analysis of corporate failures and disasters strongly suggests that incorporating ethics in before-profit decision making can improve strategy development and implementation and ultimately maximize corporate profits."[18] Moreover, the popularity among *Fortune 500* and *1000* companies regarding books, training, and articles on learning organizations and the habits of highly effective people suggest that organizational leaders and professionals have a need and demand for purposeful, socially responsible management training and practices.[19]

MYTH 2: "BUSINESS AND ETHICS DO NOT MIX"

This popular myth[20] holds that business practices are basically amoral (not necessarily immoral), since businesses operate in a free market. This myth also asserts that management is based on scientific, rather than religious or ethical, principles.

Although this myth might have thrived in an earlier industrializing U.S. society and even in the U.S. during the 1960s, the myth has eroded over the past two decades, given the widespread consequences of computer hacking on individual, commercial, and government systems that affect the public's welfare; identity theft on the Internet (stealing others' social security numbers and using their bank accounts and credit cards); and kickbacks, unsafe products, oil spills, toxic dumping, air and water pollution, and improper use of public funds. The international and national basis for an infatuation with a purely scientific understanding of U.S. business practices, in particular, and of a value-free marketing system has been undermined by these events. As one saying goes, "A little experience can inform a lot of theory."

The ethicist Richard DeGeorge has noted that the myth that business is amoral is a myth because it ignores the business involvement of all of us. Business is a human activity, not simply a scientific one and, as such, can be evaluated from a moral perspective. If everyone in business acted amorally or immorally, as a pseudoscientific notion of business would suggest, businesses would collapse. Employees would openly steal from employers; employers would recklessly fire employees at will; contractors would arrogantly violate obligations; and chaos would prevail. Business and society share the same U.S. values: rugged individualism in a free-enterprise system, pragmatism over abstraction, freedom, and independence. When business practices violate these American values, society and the public are threatened or harmed.

Finally, the belief that businesses operate in totally "free markets" is debatable. Although the value or desirability of the concept and principles of a "free market" is not in question, practices of certain firms in free markets are. At issue are the unjust methods of accumulation and noncompetitive uses of wealth and power in the formation of monopolies and oligopolies (i.e., small numbers of firms dominating the rules and transactions of certain markets). The dominance of AT&T, before the breakup, is an example of how one powerful conglomerate could control the market. Microsoft may be another example. The U.S. market environment can be characterized best as a "mixed economy" based on free-market mechanisms, but not limited to or explained only by them. Mixed economies rely on some governmental policies and laws for control of deficiencies and inequalities. For example, protective laws are still required, such as those governing minimum wage, antitrust situations, layoffs from plant closings, and instances of labor exploitation. In such mixed economies in which injustices thrive, ethics is a viable and lively topic.

MYTH 3: "ETHICS IN BUSINESS IS RELATIVE"

This is one of the more popular myths, and it holds that no right or wrong way of believing or acting exists. Right and wrong are in the eyes of the beholder.

The claim that ethics is not based solely on absolutes has some truth to it. However, to argue that all ethics is relative contradicts everyday experience. For example, the view that because a person or society believes something to be right makes it right is problematic when examined. Many societies believed in and practiced slavery; however, in contemporary individuals' experiences, slavery is historically and morally wrong. When individuals and firms do business in societies that promote slavery, does that mean that the individuals and firms also must condone and practice slavery? The simple logic of relativism, which is discussed in Chapter 3, gets complicated when seen in daily experience. The question that can be asked regarding this myth is, "Relative to whom or what? And why?" The logic of this ethic, which answers that question with "Relative to me, myself, and my interests," as a maxim does not promote community. Also, if ethical relativism were carried to its logical extreme, no one could argue or disagree with anyone about moral issues, since each person's values would be right and true for him or her. Ultimately, this logic would state that no right or wrong exists apart from an individual's or society's principles. How could interactions, communications, transactions, and negotiations be completed if ethical relativism were carried to its limit? Moreover, the U.S. government, in its vigorous pursuit of Microsoft, certainly has not practiced a relativist style of ethics.

MYTH 4: "GOOD BUSINESS MEANS GOOD ETHICS"

The reasoning here[21] is that executives and firms that maintain a good corporate image, practice fair and equitable dealings with customers and employees, and earn profits by legitimate, legal means are de facto ethical. Such firms, therefore, would not have to be concerned explicitly with ethics in the workplace. Just do a hard, fair day's work and that has its own moral goodness and rewards.

The faulty reasoning underlying this logic is that ethics does not always provide solutions to technical business problems in marketing, accounting, finance, research and development, and the like. Moreover, as Buchholz[22] argued, no correlation exists between "goodness" and material success.

It is also argues that "excellent" companies and corporate cultures have created and pursued values and concern for people in the workplace that exceed the profit motive. In these cases, excellence seems to be related more to customer service, to maintenance of meaningful public and employee relationships, and to corporate integrity than just to the profit motive.[23]

The point is that ethics is not something added to business operations; it is integral, necessary, and central to managing successfully. A more accurate, logical statement from business experience would suggest that "good ethics means good business." This is more in line with observations from successful companies that are ethical first and also profitable.

Finally, "What happens, then, if what should be ethically done is not the best thing for business? What happens when good ethics is not good business?"

> The ethical thing to do may not always be in the best interests of the firm. We should promote business ethics, not because good ethics is good business, but because we are morally required to adopt the moral point of view in all our dealings with other people—and business is no exception. In business, as in all other human endeavors, we must be prepared to pay the costs of ethical behavior. The costs may sometimes seem high, but that is the risk we take in valuing and preserving our integrity.[24]

MYTH 5: "INFORMATION AND COMPUTING ARE AMORAL"

This myth holds that information and computing are neither moral nor immoral, but are amoral, i.e., they are in a "gray zone," a questionable area regarding ethics. Information and computing have productive and positive dimensions, such as empowerment and enlightenment through the ubiquitous exposure to information, increased efficiency, and quick access to on-line global communities. It is also true that information and computing have a dark side: information about individuals can be used as "a form of control, power, and manipulation."[25] As mentioned earlier, with open access to information the following issues arise: unlimited and questionable use of databases, violation of privacy, children exposed to pornography and stalking, consumers targeted for fraudulent advertising and selling practices, and pirating of intellectual property.

The point here is to beware of the dark side: the misuse and abuse of information and computing. Ethical implications are present but veiled. Truth and accuracy must be protected and guarded: ". . . falsehood, inaccuracy, lying, deception, disinformation, misleading information are all vices and enemies of the Information Age, for they undermine it. . . . fraud, misrepresentation, and falsehood are inimical to all of them."[26]

Logical problems occur in all five of these myths. In many instances, the myths hold simplistic and even unrealistic notions about ethics in business dealings. In the following sections, the discussion about the nature of business ethics continues by exploring two questions:

- Why use ethical reasoning in business?
- What is the nature of ethical reasoning?

I.5 WHY USE ETHICAL REASONING IN BUSINESS?

Ethical reasoning is required in business for at least three reasons.

First, many times laws are insufficient and do not cover all aspects or "gray areas" of a problem.[27] How could tobacco companies have been protected by the law for decades until the settlement in 1997, when the industry agreed to pay $368.5 billion for the first 25 years and then $15 billion a year indefinitely to compensate states for the costs of health care for tobacco-related illnesses? What gray areas in federal and state laws (or the enforcement of those laws) prevailed for decades? What sources of power or help can people turn to in these situations for truthful information, protection, and compensation when laws are not enough?

Second, free-market and regulated-market mechanisms do not effectively inform owners and managers about how to respond to complex issues and crises that have far-reaching ethical consequences. For example, did Microsoft act unethically while becoming the dominant player in its industry in a free-market environment? Is the Microsoft case really the same as that of AT&T, when the latter was deregulated? Take another historical example: should companies legally prohibit, as American Cyanamid did in the late 1970s, pregnant women from working in toxic areas to protect their unborn fetuses, even though the firm's policy had the effect of pressuring several women into choosing unemployment or sterilization? Later, in the 1980s, the same firm faced unanticipated discrimination charges and lawsuits from several interest groups. In 1991, the Supreme Court ruled, in a six-to-three vote, that such "fetal protection" policies are a form of sex bias prohibited by civil rights law. American Cyanamid may have acted legally in the 1970s, but did it act ethically? Are women and men still coerced to work in unsafe health environments? What reasoning and guidelines help us answer such questions, whether we have enacted laws that provide authoritative guidelines or not?

A third argument holds that ethical reasoning is necessary because complex moral problems require "an intuitive or learned understanding and concern for fairness, justice, due process to people, groups, and communities."[28] Company policies and procedures are limited in scope and detail in covering human, environmental, and social costs of doing business. Judges have had to use intuitive and a kind of learn-as-you-go rulings in the Microsoft case over the years. There have been no clear precedents in the software industry or with a company of Microsoft's size and global scope to offer clear legal direction. Ethics, then, plays a role in business because laws and the enforcement of laws are many times insufficient to guide action.

1.6 CAN BUSINESS ETHICS BE TAUGHT AND TRAINED?

Since laws and legal enforcement are often not always sufficient to help guide or solve complex human problems relating to business situations, the questions arise: Can ethics help? If so, how? And can business ethics, then, be taught? This ongoing debate has no final answer, and studies continue to address the issue. One study, for example, that surveyed 125 graduate and undergraduate students in a business ethics course at the beginning of a semester showed that students did not reorder their *priorities* at the end of the semester on the importance of ten social issues, but they did *change the degree of importance* they placed on the majority of the issues surveyed.[29] What, if any, value can be gained from teaching ethical principles and training people to use them in business?

This discussion begins with what business ethics courses *cannot* or should not, in my judgment, do. Ethics courses should not advocate a set of rules from a single perspective nor offer only one best solution to specific ethical problems. Given the facts and circumstances of situations, more-desirable and less-desirable courses of action may exist. Decisions depend on facts, inferences, and rigorous, logical, ethical reasoning. Neither should ethics courses or training sessions promise superior or absolute ways of thinking and behaving in situations. Rigorous, informed, and conscientious ethical analysis is not the best or only way to reason through moral problems.

Ethics courses and training *can* do the following[30]:

- Provide people with rationales, ideas, and vocabulary to help them participate effectively in ethical decision-making processes
- Help people "make sense" of their environments by abstracting and selecting ethical priorities
- Provide intellectual weapons to do battle with advocates of economic fundamentalism and those who violate ethical standards
- Enable employees to act as alarm systems for company practices that will not meet society's ethical standards
- Enhance conscientiousness and sensitivity to moral issues and commitment to finding moral solutions
- Enhance moral reflectiveness and strengthen moral courage
- Increase people's ability to become morally autonomous ethical dissenters and the conscience of a group
- Improve the moral climate of firms by providing ethical concepts and tools for creating ethical codes and social audits

Other scholars argue that ethical training can add *value* to the moral environment of a firm and to relationships in the workplace in the following ways[31]:

- Finding a match between an employee's and employer's values
- Managing the push-back point, where an employee's values are tested by peers, employees, and supervisors
- Handling an unethical directive from a boss
- Coping with a performance system that encourages cutting ethical corners

Teaching business ethics and training people to use them, then, does not promise to provide answers to complex moral dilemmas; however, thoughtful and resourceful business ethics educators can facilitate the development of *awareness* of what is and is not ethical, help individuals and groups realize that their ethical tolerance and decision-making styles decrease unethical blind spots, and enhance curiosity and concern about discussing moral problems openly in the workplace.

Finally, a useful framework for evaluating ethics training is Lawrence Kohlberg's study[32] of the stages of moral development, as well as studies on the relevance of Kohlberg's study for managers and professionals.[33]

STAGES OF MORAL DEVELOPMENT

Kohlberg's three levels of moral development (which encompass six stages) offer a guide for observing a person's level of moral maturity, especially as he or she engages in different organizational transactions. Whether, and to what extent, ethical education and training contribute to moral development in later years is not known. Most individuals in Kohlberg's 20-year study reached the fourth and fifth stages by adulthood. Only a few attained the sixth stage. Still, this framework is used in ethics classrooms and training centers around the globe.

Level 1: Preconventional Level (Self-Orientation)

☐ Stage 1: Punishment avoidance: avoiding punishment by not breaking rules. The person has little awareness of others' needs.

☐ Stage 2: Reward seeking: acting to receive rewards for oneself. The person has awareness of others' needs but not of right and wrong as abstract concepts.

Level 2: Conventional Level (Others Orientation)

☐ Stage 3: Good person: acting "right" to be a "good person" and to be accepted by family and friends, not to fulfill any moral ideal.

☐ Stage 4: Law and order: acting "right" to comply with law and order and norms in societal institutions.

Level 3: Postconventional, Autonomous, or Principles Level (Universal, Humankind Orientation)

☐ Stage 5: Social contract: acting "right" to reach consensus by due process and agreement. The person is aware of relativity of values and tolerates differing views.

☐ Stage 6: Universal ethical principles: acting "right" according to universal, abstract principles of justice, rights. The person reasons and uses conscience and moral rules to guide actions.

KOHLBERG'S STUDY AND BUSINESS ETHICS

One study of 219 corporate managers working in different companies found that managers typically reason at moral stages 3 or 4, which, the author noted, is "similar to most adults in the Western, urban societies or other business managers."[34] Managers in large- to medium-sized firms, the study discovered, reasoned at lower moral stages than managers who were self-employed or who worked at small firms. Reasons offered for this difference in levels of moral reasoning in firms of different sizes include that larger firms have more complex bureaucracies and layers of structure and more standard policies and procedures and exert more rule-based control over employees. Employees tend to get isolated from other parts of the organization and feel less involved in the central decision-making process.

On the other hand, self-employed professionals and managers in smaller firms tend to interact with people throughout the firm and with external stakeholders. Involvement with and vulnerability to other stakeholders (e.g., customers, clients, competitors, vendors, the public) may cause these managers to adhere to social laws more closely and to reason at stage 4.

This study also found that managers reasoned at a higher level when responding to a presented moral dilemma in which the main character was not a corporate employee. It could be that managers reason at a higher level when moral problems are not associated with the corporation. The author suggested that the influence of the corporation tends to restrict the manager to lower moral reasoning stages, or that it could be that the nature of the moral dilemma may affect the way managers reason, i.e., some dilemmas may, in the managers' thinking, be appropriately addressed with stage 3 or 4 reasoning, other dilemmas may require stage 5 logic. This study raises the question: "How can organizations use these findings in training and managing people?"

Another important study argued that moral decision making is "issue dependent" and, more specifically, that "the moral intensity of the issue itself has a significant effect on moral decision making and behavior at all stages of the process." In fact, the authors argue that "issues of high moral intensity will be recognized as moral issues more frequently than will issues of low moral intensity."[35] The study suggests that people who do not recognize issues as moral will not act morally regarding those issues. This conclusion supports a serious need and justification for business ethics education and training with specific emphasis on identifying stakeholder and issues management.

1.7 PLAN OF THE BOOK

This book focuses on applying stakeholder, issues, and value-based manage-ment approaches along with your own critical reasoning to situations that involve groups and individuals who often have competing demands and in-terpretations of a problem, crisis, or opportunity. Since stakeholders are peo-ple (e.g., individuals, companies, and groups), they generally think and act on beliefs and values as well as from economically and financially motivated strategies. For this reason, ethics is an important part of a stakeholder issues-management approach. It is important to understand why stakeholders act and how they make decisions. The stakeholder management approach ideally aims at having all parties reach win-win outcomes through commu-nication and collaborative efforts. Unfortunately, this does not always happen in reality. If we do not have a systematic approach to understand what happens in complex stakeholder relationships over specific events and issues, we cannot learn from past mistakes or plan for more collaborative, socially responsible future outcomes. A schematic of the book's organization is presented in Figure 1.6.

Chapter 2 provides a systematic approach for structuring and evaluating stakeholder issues, strategies, and options at the outset. Step-by-step methods for collaborating, forming, and evaluating strategies are identified. Chapter 3 provides ethical principles, "quick tests," and scenarios for evaluating motivations for certain decisions and actions. A stakeholder management approach involves knowing and managing different stake-holders' ethics, including your own. Chapter 4 looks at organizations as stakeholders and offers steps for implementing a value-based, collaborative approach for integrating ethics into organizations. Chapter 5 examines an organization's management of external stakeholders, including the envi-ronment. Chapter 6 looks at the 21st-century workforce and discusses rights and obligations of and among employees and employers as stakeholders. Chapter 7 views nations as stakeholders and looks at how multinational corporations operate in and across host countries and different systems of capitalism. Finally, Chapter 8 explores ethical issues of the future.

SUMMARY

Businesses and governments operate in technological, legal, social, economic, and political environments. Understanding the effects of these environmental forces on industries and organizations (professions and jobs) is a first step in identifying stakeholders and the issues that different groups must manage in order to survive and compete. This book explores and illus-trates how stakeholders can manage issues and trends in their changing environments in socially responsible and ethical ways.

| FIGURE 1.6 | PLAN OF THE BOOK |

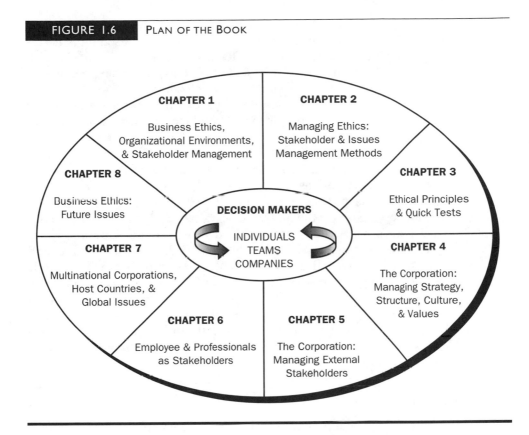

Business ethics deals with what is "right and wrong" in organizational decisions, behavior, and policies. Business ethics provides principles and guidelines that assist people in making informed choices to balance economic interests and social responsibilities.

Business ethics operates at several levels: the individual, organizational, association, societal, and international. These levels illustrate the complexity and linkages of ethical decision making in business transactions. This chapter introduces the stakeholder approach to ethical decision making, which identifies constituencies and their claims at these levels of interaction in business environments.

Stakeholders include corporations, managers, individuals, groups, societal institutions, and nations. The stakeholder approach provides a means for mapping complicated relationships between the focal and other stakeholders, a means of identifying the strategies of each stakeholder, and a means for assessing the moral responsibility of all the constituencies.

Five myths often held about business ethics are discussed. Each myth is illustrated and refuted.

Ethical reasoning in business is explained with steps provided to guide decision making. Three reasons why ethical reasoning is necessary in business are: (1) laws are often insufficient and do not cover all aspects or "gray areas" of a problem; (2) free-market and regulated-market mechanisms do not effectively inform owners and managers about how to respond to complex crises that have far-reaching ethical consequences; and (3) complex moral problems require an intuitive or learned understanding and concern for fairness, justice, and due process for people, groups, and communities. Ethical reasoning helps individuals sort through conflicting opinions and information in order to solve moral dilemmas.

Ethical education and training can be useful for developing a broader awareness of the motivations, values, and consequences of our decisions. Business ethics does not, however, provide superior or universally correct solutions to morally complex dilemmas. Principles and guidelines are provided that can enhance—with case analysis, role playing, and group discussion—a person's insight and self-confidence in resolving moral dilemmas that often have two right (or wrong) solutions. Kohlberg's stages of moral development are presented and discussed as means of assisting professionals and managers with ethical decision making by identifying the basic underlying moral arguments and motivations.

QUESTIONS

1. Characterize some contemporary environmental influences (see Figure 1.1) that organizations must manage in order to survive and compete. Identify three specific environmental influences that the organization for which you work (or study) must address to survive and be competitive. Explain.

2. What are the three major ethical issues that businesses face today? What about the organization in which you work or the college or university you attend? What are the most prominent ethical issues it faces? Explain.

3. Identify some benefits of using a stakeholder approach in ethical decision making. What are the shortcomings of the stakeholder approach? Explain.

4. Which, if any, of the five business myths in the chapter do you *not* accept as a myth, i.e., that you believe is true? Explain.

5. Identify three reasons presented in this chapter for using ethical reasoning in business situations. Do you agree or disagree? Explain.

6. Is the law sufficient to help managers and employees solve ethical dilemmas? Explain and offer an example from your own experiences or from a contemporary event.

7. What are some important distinctive characteristics of ethical problems? What distinguishes an ethical from a legal problem?

8. Briefly describe three or four of the benefits that can be gained from ethics courses and training. In what ways is it impossible to teach ethics? Explain.

EXERCISES

1. Invent and state your own definition of "business ethics." Do you believe that ethics is an important factor in conducting business transactions today? If you were the chief executive officer (CEO) of a corporation, how would you communicate your perspective on the importance of ethics to your employees, customers, and other stakeholder groups?

2. Conduct your own small survey of two people regarding their opinions on the importance of unethical practices in businesses today. Do your interviewees give more importance to economic performance or socially irresponsible behavior? Or do they think other factors are more important? Summarize your results.

3. You are giving a speech at a Rotary Club (or other important community business association) meeting. You are asked to give a presentation called "an introduction to business ethics" for the members. Give an outline of your speech.

4. Explain how a major trend in the environment has affected your profession, job, or skills—as a professional or student. Be specific. Are any ethical consequences involved, and has this trend affected you?

5. Review Kohlberg's levels and stages of moral development. After careful consideration, briefly explain which stage, predominantly or characteristically, defines your ethical level of development. Explain. Has this stage influenced a recent decision you have made or action you have taken? Explain.

6. How can Kohlberg's framework assist professionals in organizations to see, prevent, and solve ethical problems and dilemmas?

7. You are applying to a prestigious organization for an important, highly visible position. The application requires you to describe an ethical dilemma in your history and how you handled it. Describe the dilemma and your ethical position.

ETHICAL DILEMMA

YOU'RE IN THE HOT SEAT

You are a staff associate at a major public accounting firm and graduated from college two years ago. You are working on an audit for a small, non-profit religious publishing firm. After performing tests on the royalty payables system, you discover that for the past five years, the royalty payable system has miscalculated the royalties it owes to authors of their publications. The firm owes almost $100,000 in past due royalties. All of the contracts with each author are negotiated differently. However, each author's royalty percentage will increase at different milestones in books sold (i.e., 2% up to 10,000 and 3% thereafter). The software package did not calculate the increases, and none of the authors ever received their increase in royalty payments. At first you can't believe that none of the authors ever realized they were owed their money. You double-check your calculations and then present your findings to the senior auditor on the job. Much to your surprise, his suggestion is to pass over this finding. He suggests that you sample a few additional royalty contracts and document that you expanded your testing and found nothing wrong. The firm's audit approach is well documented in this area and is firmly based on statistical sampling. Because you had found multiple errors in the small number of royalty contracts tested, the firm's approach suggested testing 100% of the contracts. This would mean: (1) going over the budgeted time/ expense estimated to the client; (2) possibly providing a negative audit finding; and (3) confirming that the person who audited the section in the years past may not have performed procedures correctly.

Based on the prior year's work papers, the senior auditor on the job performed the testing phase in all of these years just before his promotion. For some reason, you get the impression that the senior auditor is frustrated with you. The relationship seems strained. He is very intense, constantly checking staff's progress in the hope of coming in even a half-hour under budget for a designated test/audit area. There's a lot of pressure and you don't know what to do. This person is responsible for writing your review for your personnel file and bonus or promotion review. He is a very popular employee who is "on the fast track" to partnership.

You don't know whether to tell the truth and risk a poor performance review and jeopardize your job and future with this company or to tell the truth, hopefully be exonerated, and be able to live with yourself by "doing the right thing" and facing consequences with a clean conscience.

QUESTIONS

1. What would you do as the staff associate in this situation? Why? What are the risks of telling the truth for you? What are the benefits? Explain.

2. What is the "right" thing to do in this situation? What is the "smart" thing to do for your job and career? What is the difference, if there is one, between the "right" and "smart" thing to do in this situation? Explain.

3. Explain what you would say to the senior auditor, your boss, in this situation if you decided to tell the truth as you know it.

2

STAKEHOLDER AND ISSUES MANAGEMENT APPROACHES

2.1 WHY USE A STAKEHOLDER MANAGEMENT APPROACH FOR BUSINESS ETHICS?

The stakeholder approach is a response to the growth and complexity of understanding and study of the modern corporation and its influence on the environment, the economy, and the public. This chapter explains the stakeholder analysis, which is part of the stakeholder approach. A more familiar way of understanding corporations is the "stockholder approach," which focuses on financial and economic relationships; by contrast, a stakeholder approach is a descriptive method that studies actors.[1] The stakeholder approach includes nonmarket forces that affect organizations and individuals, such as moral, political, legal, and technological interests, as well as economic factors.

Underlying the stakeholder management approach is the ethical imperative that mandates businesses in their fiduciary relationships to their stockholders and shareholders: (1) to act in the best interests of and for the benefit of their customers, employees, suppliers, and stockholders, and (2) to respect and fulfill these stakeholders' rights. One study concluded that ". . . our analysis clearly reveals that multiple objectives—including both economic and social considerations—can be and, in fact, *are* simultaneously and successfully pursued within large and complex organizations that collectively account for a major part of all economic activity within our society."[2]

Among some scholars, there is an ongoing debate regarding the legitimacy of the stakeholder management model.[3] Our view here is grounded in Key's (1999) stakeholder theory of the firm[4] and summarized by Mitchell, Agle, and Wood (1997)[5]:

> We argue that stakeholder theory must account for power and urgency as well as legitimacy, no matter how distasteful or unsettling the results. Managers must know about groups and organizations in their environment that hold power and have the intent to impose their will upon the firm. Power and urgency must be attended to if managers are to serve the legal and moral interests of legitimate stakeholders.

The ethical dimension of this approach is based on the view that profit maximization is constrained by justice, that regard for individual rights should be extended to all constituencies that have a stake in the affairs of a business, and that organizations are not simply or only "economic" in nature but can and do act in socially responsible ways as members of communities. To this end, companies "should" act in socially responsible ways, not only because it's the "right thing to do," but also to ensure their legitimacy.[6]

As an example, the high-profile Microsoft case illustrates how CEO Bill Gates and his executives had to address a host of groups and lawsuits. The number of constituencies and stakeholders with whom Microsoft dealt reflects the complexity of the business environment and the types of economic, market share, ethical, and technological issues and decisions Gates made in the 1990s.

The Microsoft case (see box) illustrates the magnitude of problems and issues that corporations and industries can face in a controversy of this magnitude. This situation provides a window into the combined economic, political, technological, and legal issues leading to and resulting from conflicting stakeholder positions. Moreover, this controversy began as a question about market share regarding software but then migrated to other issues (e.g., bundling, exclusionary agreements, "polluting" other technologies, and monopolizing future technologies' access to the Internet). These issues quickly have accrued to the level of societal and international proportions, since the Internet has become the playing field. (For more on the Microsoft controversy, see the case at the end of this book.)

In this and other complex cases, we ask what methods can best be used to understand and evaluate who is right and who is wrong, and what costs must be incurred by whom in resolving issues of justice, rightness, and fairness? "Rightness" and "wrongness" are not always easy to determine in moral dilemmas. As Abraham Lincoln said, "The true role, in determining to embrace or reject anything . . . is not whether it have any evil in it, but whether it have more evil than of good. There are few things wholly evil or wholly good."

The Microsoft story shows that in a pluralistic, democratic society, power is diffused among groups, individuals, organizations, and institutions. In

MICROSOFT: PREDATOR OR FIERCE COMPETITOR?

In June 2001, the U.S. Court of Appeals in the District of Columbia unanimously found Microsoft guilty of antitrust violations but sent the case back to the (lower) district court to reconsider its recommended remedy to break Microsoft in two after the government conceded not to pursue the breakup. Nine states of eighteen, however, have rejected the Department of Justice's concession. Now U.S. District Judge Collen Kollar-Kotelly will work to settle this case.

On November 5, 1998, Judge Thomas Penfield Jackson of the U.S. District Court of the District of Columbia released his finding of fact that Microsoft has a monopoly in the market for Intel-compatible personal computer (PC) operating systems because: (1) the company's market share has stood at over 90% for the past 10 years and grew to over 95% from 1998 to 2000; (2) significant barriers to market entry prohibit potential competitors from developing operating systems to compete with Windows; and (3) software producers are faced with a lack of viable alternatives, which makes it almost impossible to produce software for any operating system other than Windows.

Although Microsoft maintained that its actions were in the spirit of competition and survival in the fast-moving computer technology industry, several facts in the case suggested that the company employed unethical business practices with the aim of eliminating competitive threats to the dominance of its Windows operating system. The focal stakeholder in the case is Microsoft Corporation (represented by co-founder and current CEO Bill Gates and Microsoft's management team). Other stakeholders include:

- Microsoft's shareholders

- Current and future customers of the Windows operating system and compatible software (by Microsoft or other manufacturers)
- The U.S. government, including the antitrust division of the U.S. Department of Justice, state governments and the 19 State Attorneys General bringing suit against Microsoft, and the U.S. District Court of the District of Columbia
- Microsoft's competitors in operating systems
- Manufacturers of Internet browsers and other software
- Original equipment manufacturers (OEMs)
- Internet content providers (ICPs)
- Internet service providers (ISPs)
- On-line services (OLS)

At stake for this coalition are consumers' access to current technologies without encountering artificially high prices or a business environment that lacks opportunities for innovation.

Competitors form another coalition: Internet browser suppliers, software developers, and operating system developers. Netscape, the Internet browser now owned by AOL, is one of the primary stakeholders involved in bringing the antitrust case against Microsoft. Microsoft perceived Netscape as a potential threat to its dominance of the operating system market because Netscape could be used to develop another platform to compete with Windows. After Netscape refused to enter into a strategic partnership with Microsoft that would have limited its distribution to a niche market, Microsoft developed its own browser, Internet Explorer, and used exclusionary practices to reduce Netscape's market share from over 90% to 40% within 3 years. Another browser, made by Spyglass, was forced out of the browser business when, after Spyglass licensed its technology to Microsoft, Gates' company began bundling Internet Explorer into its Windows operating system and thus gave consumers the technology for free, in effect eliminating consumer need to spend money on a parity product.

Software developers, such as Intel and Apple, also support the government's case against Microsoft because of the company's unfair practices and attempts to prevent competition in the marketplace. Microsoft effectively forced Intel to stop the development of platform-level software that competed with Windows by threatening to withdraw its support for Intel's next generation of microprocessors. Microsoft also tried to stop Apple from producing its QuickTime software, a direct competitor of Microsoft's Direct X multimedia software package, by threatening to enter the authoring business and take Apple's share of the API market.

Developers of alternative operating systems, such as IBM and Apple, also support the government's case against Microsoft. Because of Microsoft's strong-arm tactics, the barriers to market entry are too formidable for alternative operating systems to enter the market, as shown by the failure of IBM's OS/2 and Apple's Mac OS. Software developers are unwilling to write programs for these systems because of Microsoft's market dominance. The subscriber base for any alternative operating system remains low as a result of the limited software available to run on alternative platforms.

Who is right and wrong in this case? What are the central issues? What is the

"harm" (if any) done and to whom? Has there been any harm done to anyone? If harm has been done, who should pay, how much, and why? If you were one of the states holding out of the settlement, what would you want to join?

At stake for all stakeholders in this case are these issues: How will consumer and new competitors be protected against monopoly? To what extent and degree should, or will, justice, rights, the free-market ethic, and social responsibility be changed by the current settlement?

At press time, negotiations regarding the settlement of this case continue to evolve. For more on the controversy, see the case at the end of this book or go to http://weiss.swcollege.com.

SOURCE: Spears, C., MBA student at Bentley College. The material is based on (but not limited to) the following articles, all of which can be found at www.techweb.com: Mosquera, M. Breaking up Microsoft would be tough call. *Technology News,* 25 February 2000; Wilke, J. "Nine States Rebuff U.S.-Microsoft Accord," *Wall Street Journal,* 7 November 2001, A3; Mosquera, M. Microsoft, DOJ to throw final punches. *Technology News,* 23 February 2000; Reuters. Judge compares Microsoft to Rockefeller. *Technology News,* 24 February 2000; Reuters. Lessig skeptical about Microsoft breakup. *Technology News,* 24 February 2000; Rooney, P. Sun ships free Solaris 8. *Computer Reseller News,* 16 March 2000; Taft, D. Microsoft quits group, close to settling. *Computer Reseller News,* 8 March 2000; Taft, D. Microsoft vs. DOJ: Settlement negotiations continue—final arguments on tap in the antitrust case. *Computer Reseller News,* 21 February 2000; Hendren, John, "Company Poised to Deliver New Settlement," *Seattle Times,* 24 October 2001.

fact, no central or absolute source of authority exists to direct, unify, or evaluate competing interests between a company and its stakeholders, especially in a democratic, pluralistic, and capitalist society, such as the United States. Governmental and legal systems often play roles in this process but, more often than not, these entities enter the fray after the fact.

In an open-market system, special interests, lobbyists, and communications media are significant forces that influence corporate decisions. In such a complex, pluralistic society, corporate leaders and those who strive to understand and monitor corporate activities need a method that helps them understand and "keep score" on each of their stakeholders' *strategies and power relationships* in crises and events that affect the public and the business.

The stakeholder analysis is one approach used for these purposes. Just as important, it is a method that can be used to identify the *moral reasoning* of managers and their stakeholders. Stakeholder *welfare, rights, and responsibilities* can be identified and monitored in given situations. "Issues management" and "crises management" frameworks, in addition to (and related to) the stakeholder analysis, can also be used. Issues frameworks are discussed later in the chapter.

2.2 STAKEHOLDER MANAGEMENT APPROACH DEFINED

The *stakeholder approach* provides a framework that enables users to map and, ideally, manage the corporation's relationships (present and potential) with groups to reach "win-win" collaborative outcomes. Here, "win-win" means making moral decisions that benefit all constituencies within the constraints of justice, fairness, and economic interests. In reality, unfortunately, this does not always happen. There are usually winners and losers in complex situations, where there is a perceived zero-sum game, i.e., a situation in which there are limited, scarce resources, and what is gained by one person is necessarily lost by the other.

Scholars and consultants, however, have used the stakeholder approach as a means for planning and implementing collaborative relationships to achieve win-win outcomes among stakeholders.[7] Structured dialogue facilitated by consultants is a major focus in these collaborative communications. The aim in using the stakeholder approach as a collaborative communication strategy is to change perceptions and "rules of engagement" to create win-win outcomes.

A stakeholder approach does not have to result from a crisis or controversial situation, such as in the Microsoft case. It can also be used as a planning method to anticipate and facilitate business decisions, events, and policy outcomes. A stakeholder analysis is also not limited in its use to large enterprises. Business units, teams, and groups can use this approach.

A stakeholder analysis may also begin, as indicated in Chapter 1, by asking what external forces in the general environment are affecting an organization, i.e., the economic, political, technological, legal, and social trends. This context can often provide clues regarding specific issues that lead to responses by stakeholders to opportunities, crises, and extraordinary events. For example, Gates responded, in part, to a perceived threat that

Microsoft's market share would be threatened by certain aggressive competitors. He responded by attempting to form and dominate his strategic alliances with those firms. Other issues then emerged, as did external stakeholder responses. Let's define two major terms before explaining how to do a stakeholder analysis.

STAKEHOLDERS

A *stakeholder* is "any individual or group who can affect or is affected by the actions, decisions, policies, practices, or goals of the organization."[8] We begin by identifying the *focal stakeholder*. This is the company or group that is the center and focus of our analysis. In the Microsoft case, the Microsoft company and its top managers were the focal stakeholder.

The primary stakeholders of a firm include its owners, customers, employees, and suppliers. Also of primary importance to a firm's survival are its stockholders and board of directors. The CEO and other top-level executives can be stakeholders, but in the stakeholder analysis, they are generally considered actors and representatives of the firm.

Secondary stakeholders include all other interested groups, such as the media, consumers, lobbyists, courts, governments, competitors, the public, and society. In the Microsoft case, stockholders also have a stake in the economic consequences of how lawsuits are settled against the company; individual and business users of Microsoft products have personal and professional stakes in the company; local, state, and federal courts had stakes in the legality, liability, and future rulings in this and future similar cases; the New York Stock Exchange (NYSE) and NASDQ have claims, since Microsoft's stock has significant effects on their operation; the U.S. Congress had stakes in serving the competing interests of all companies (past, present, and future) in the software industry; and the President and citizens of the U.S. have a stake in this case, since Microsoft is part of America's global competitiveness. The controversy focuses, in part, on whether or not more parties would be better served if Microsoft would act in a more legal and ethical manner toward its stakeholders.

Stakeholders also have stakeholders. For example, Microsoft's business and strategic partners depend on the company to do business. Think of the suppliers, vendors, and other parties in the value chain that would be affected by Microsoft's not being able to do business. By acknowledging the stakeholders of the stakeholders, we can understand the sources of influence and power for the major interest groups in our analysis.

STAKES

A *stake* is any interest, share, or claim that a group or individual has in the outcome of a corporation's policies, procedures, or actions toward others. Stakes and claims may be based on legal, economic, social, moral, technological, ecological, political, or power interests. The stakes of stakeholders are not always obvious or explicit. The economic viability of competing firms can be at stake when one firm threatens entry into or competition in a market. The physical health of a community can be at stake when a corporation decides to empty toxic waste near residential sites.

Stakes also can be present, past, or future oriented. For example, stakeholders may seek compensation for a firm's past actions, as occurred when lawyers recently argued that certain airlines owed their clients monetary compensation after having threatened their emotional stability when pilots announced an impending disaster (engine failure) that, subsequently, did not occur. Stakeholders may seek future claims; that is, they may seek injunctions against firms that announce plans to drill oil or build nuclear plants in designated areas or to market or bundle certain products in noncompetitive ways.

2.3 HOW TO EXECUTE A STAKEHOLDER ANALYSIS

The stakeholder approach is a pragmatic way of identifying and understanding multiple (often competing) political, social, legal, economic, and moral claims of many constituencies. The aim here is to familiarize yourself with the framework so that you can apply it in the classroom and in newsbreaking events that appear in the press and in other media. Even though you may not be an executive or manager, the framework can enable you to see and understand more clearly the complex corporate dealings, events, and crises in the immediate environment. Former students of mine who are now professional consultants have reported that their having studied the stakeholder approach helped them see the "big picture" and clients differently in their careers and coursework. Although this chapter focuses on upper-level and functional area managers as stakeholders who formulate and direct corporate strategy, Chapter 3 discusses the individual employee as stakeholder. Chapter 3 also provides ethical principles you can use to evaluate the moral criteria of strategies managers use when responding to different stakeholders. Let's begin.

Assume you are the CEO, working with your top managers, in a firm that has just been involved in a major controversy of international proportions. The media, some consumer groups, and several major customers have called you. You want to get a handle on the situation without reverting to unnecessary "firefighting" management methods. A couple of your trusted staff members have advised you to adopt a planning approach quickly, while responding to immediate concerns, to understand the "who, what, where, when, and why" of the situation before jumping to many hasty "hows." Your senior strategic planner suggests you lead and participate in a stakeholder analysis. What is the next step?

The stakeholder analysis is a series of steps aimed at the following tasks (Frederick et al., 1988)[9]:

FIGURE 2.1	SAMPLE QUESTIONS FOR STAKEHOLDER REVIEW

1. Who are our stakeholders currently?
2. Who are our potential stakeholders?
3. How does each stakeholder affect us?
4. How do we affect each stakeholder?
5. For each division and business, who are the stakeholders?
6. What assumptions does our current strategy make about each important stakeholder (at each level)?
7. What are the current "environmental variables" that affect us and our stakeholders (inflation, GNP, prime rate, confidence in business [from polls], corporate identity, media image, and so on)?
8. How do we mesure each of these variables and their impact on us and our stakeholders?
9. How do we keep score with our stakeholders?

SOURCE: R. Edward Freeman. 1984. *Strategic management: A stakeholder approach.* Boston: Pitman, 242. Reproduced with permission of the publisher.

1. Mapping stakeholder relationships
2. Mapping stakeholder coalitions
3. Assessing the nature of each stakeholder's interest
4. Assessing the nature of each stakeholder's power
5. Constructing a matrix of stakeholder moral responsibilities
6. Developing specific strategies and tactics
7. Monitoring shifting coalitions

Each step is described in the following sections. Let us explore each one and then apply them in our continuing scenario example.

STEP 1: MAPPING STAKEHOLDER RELATIONSHIPS

In 1984, R. Edward Freeman offered questions that help begin the analysis of identifying the major stakeholders (Figure 2.1). The first five questions in the figure, in particular, offer a quick jump-start on the analysis. (Questions 6 through 9 may be used in later steps, when you assess the nature of each stakeholder's interest and priorities.)

Let's continue our example with you as CEO. While brainstorming about questions 1 through 5 with employees you have selected who are the most knowledgeable, current, and close to the sources of the problems and issues at hand, you may want to draw a stakeholder map and fill in the blanks. Note that your stakeholder analysis is only as valid and reliable as the sources and processes you use to obtain your information. On a first pass, using only internal staff gets the process going. As more controversial, incomplete, or questionable issues arise, you may wish to go outside your immediate

| FIGURE 2.2 | STAKEHOLDERS MAP OF A LARGE ORGANIZATION |

SOURCE: R. Edward Freeman. 1984. *Strategic management: A stakeholder approach.* Boston: Pitman, 25. Reproduced with permission of the publisher.

core planning group to obtain additional information and perspective. A general picture of an initial stakeholder map is shown in Figure 2.2.

For example, if you were the CEO of one of Microsoft's competitors, your map might resemble the one in Figure 2.3, a hypothetical stakeholder map of Microsoft and its situation regarding monopolistic practices. Note the number and range of stakeholders in this particular depiction. There are other stakeholders; however, this map lists key constituencies. Who else would you include in your map of Microsoft's situation? Why?

STEP 2: MAPPING STAKEHOLDER COALITIONS

After you identify and make a map of the stakeholders who are directly and indirectly involved with your firm in the specific incident you are addressing, the next step is to determine and map any coalitions that have formed. Coalitions among and between stakeholders form around issues and stakes that they have—or seek to have—in common. Interest groups and lobbyists sometimes join forces against a common "enemy." Competitors also may join forces if they see an advantage in numbers. In reference to the Microsoft example in Figure 2.3, notice that the State Attorneys General formed a strategic coalition against Microsoft. What other coalitions formed in this case, with or against Microsoft? Mapping actual and potential coalitions around issues can help you, as the CEO, anticipate and design strategic responses toward these groups before or after they form.

FIGURE 2.3   STAKEHOLDER MAP FOR MICROSOFT

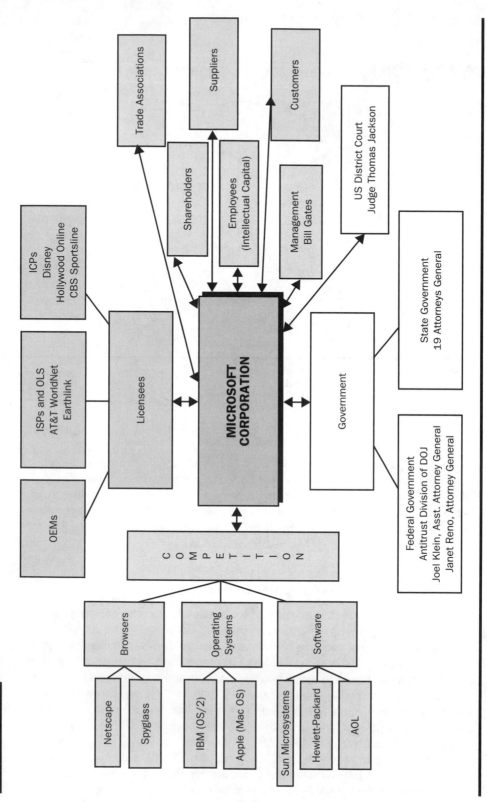

SOURCE: Carmen Spears, MBA student at Bentley College, Waltham, MA.

STEP 3: ASSESSING THE NATURE OF EACH STAKEHOLDER'S INTEREST

Step 3 and step 4, which is assessing the nature of each stakeholder's power, overlap to some extent. By identifying the "supporters" (active and nonactive, or uncommitted) and the active "opposition," as shown in Figure 2.4, you already have begun to assess the relative power of each stakeholder's interests.

In the Microsoft example, a hypothetical CEO, along with his or her staff, might determine that supporters of Microsoft might be some stockholders and employees. The opposition, or those who may seek to disrupt and change Microsoft's ways of doing business, include Netscape, Spyglass, and the U.S. Department of Justice. Who else would you add to those in opposition to Microsoft? By systematically completing this audit through brainstorming about the actions, beliefs, cooperative potential, and stakes of your stakeholders, you, as a CEO in crisis, can create a broader, more objective picture of the situation, the players, and your firm's potential and actual role in the situation.

STEP 4: ASSESSING THE NATURE OF EACH STAKEHOLDER'S POWER

This part of the analysis asks, "What's in it for each stakeholder? Who stands to win, lose, or draw over certain stakes?" Three types of power stakeholders you can use are those with (1) voting power, (2) political power, and (3) economic power (Freeman 1984).[10] For example, owners and stockholders can vote their choices to affect the firm's decisions in the Microsoft case. Federal, state, and local governments can exercise their political power by joining the ongoing lawsuits or by originating new ones. Consumers can exercise their economic power by boycotting Microsoft's products or buying and using other operating systems, browsers, and software. What other sources of stakeholder power exist? Note that you can use specific examples of power that a stakeholder uses in particular situations. Bill Gates apparently tried to exercise his market power when he approached Netscape early on and suggested, according to Netscape officials, that they work together to share the market in the expanding browser domain.

Figure 2.5 provides a series of short questions that assist in identifying and assessing the strategic assumptions of different groups and the power of their stakes. This part of the analysis forces you to attempt to identify the strategies of your your so-called allies and opponents regarding their issues with your firm. It also helps you question your potential strategies toward each stakeholder and asks you to identify the groups with which you wish to cooperate and the groups you wish to neutralize or counteract over particular issues and claims. For example, in the Microsoft case, the hypothetical CEO might discover that a powerful lobbyist group that is organizing a lawsuit against the company could be neutralized if he or she met with its leaders, learned about its grievances, and negotiated demands; negative press coverage could possibly be averted if the CEO faced the issues directly

FIGURE 2.4 A STAKEHOLDER AUDIT

	Supporters (Active)	Uncommitted (Nonactive)	Opposition (Active)
Who Are the Stakeholders?	Currently active? Not active? Potentially active? For or against?		
Actions	What are they doing, e.g., what pressures and procedures are they using, and what actions have they taken to get what they want? What are the thresholds between their indifference and activism? What could trigger their response? What are their sensitive areas? What are they asking for; what will they ask for; what do they want— i.e., what are their objectives?		
Beliefs	What do their executives believe in? Is their knowledge of us accurate or inaccurate? What assumptions do they make about us? What assumptions about them are *implicit* to our strategy? How do they think we affect their success, and they ours? What is their power relative to us? What is our power over them?		
	How do they measure our performance, and we measure theirs? What do we really want? Are these objectives legitimate? Are they satisfied? Are we satisfied? What do they really want? How will time and current trends affect their satisfaction, relative power, and activism?		
Cooperative Potential	With which of our stakeholders sets are they related or dependent? What differences are there between them and us, or our other stakeholders? Are these differences fundamental or superficial? How could they be influenced, and by whom, at what cost?		
Stakes	What is their stake in us, and what is our stake in them? How important are these stakes? What is their real power in our affairs? Is theirs an *equity* interest, or is it economic? Do they seek influence for some other reason? What power do we have in their affairs?		

SOURCE: Kenneth Hatten and Mary Louise Hatten. 1988. *Effective strategic management*. Englewood Cliffs: Prentice Hall, 116. Reproduced with permission of Prentice Hall.

FIGURE 2.5   STAKEHOLDER ANALYSIS

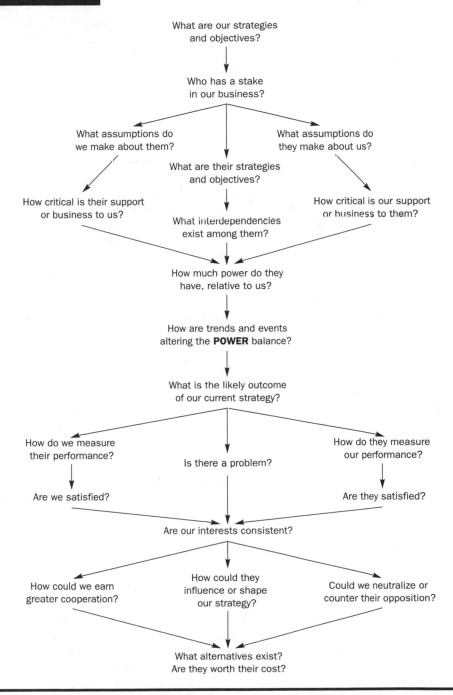

SOURCE: Kenneth Hatten and Mary Louise Hatten. 1988. *Effective strategic management*. Englewood Cliffs: Prentice Hall, 114. Reproduced with permission of Prentice Hall.

FIGURE 2.6	STAKEHOLDER MORAL RESPONSIBILITY MATRIX

Nature of Focal Company Responsibilities

	Legal	Economic	Ethical	Voluntary
Owners				
Customers				
Employees				
Community interest groups				
Public (citizens at large)				

Stakeholders

with two particular stakeholders. Did Bill Gates ever attempt such a strategy? Again, this step asks you to assess the nature of each stakeholder's power. This information enables you to decide later how and when you should respond to these stakeholders and who from your firm should do it.

STEP 5: IDENTIFYING STAKEHOLDER ETHICS AND MORAL RESPONSIBILITIES

After you map stakeholder relationships and coalitions and assess the nature of each stakeholder's interest and power, the next step is to determine the ethics, responsibilities, and moral obligations your company has to each stakeholder. A matrix of stakeholder responsibilities is shown in Figure 2.6. For example, Microsoft's CEO may see the firm's *economic responsibility* to the owners (as stakeholders) as "preventing as many costly lawsuits as possible." *Legally,* the CEO may want to protect the owners and the executive team from corporate as well as personal liability and damage; this would entail proactively negotiating disputes outside the courts, if possible, in a way that is equitable to all. *Ethically,* the CEO may keep the company's stockholders and owners current as to his or her ethical thinking and strategies to show responsibility toward all stakeholders; Chapter 3 explains ethical principles and guidelines that can assist in this type of decision making. *Voluntarily,* the

| FIGURE 2.7 | DIAGNOSTIC TYPOLOGY OF ORGANIZATIONAL STAKEHOLDERS |

Stakeholder's Potential for
Threat to Organization

		High	Low
Stakeholder's Potential for Cooperation with Organization	High	Type 4 **MIXED BLESSING** Strategy: **COLLABORATE**	Type 1 **SUPPORTIVE** Strategy: **INVOLVE**
	Low	Type 3 **NONSUPPORTIVE** Strategy: **DEFEND**	Type 2 **MARGINAL** Strategy: **MONITOR**

SOURCE: G. Savage et al. 1991. Strategies for assessing and managing organizational stakeholders. *The Executive* 5, no. 2 (May): 65.

CEO may advise shareholders to show responsibility by publicly announcing their plans for and roles in resolving the accusations about the firm's "next steps" in more open and conscientious marketing and distribution of products.

This part of the analysis should continue until you have completed matching the economic, legal, ethical, and voluntary responsibilities you have for each stakeholder, so that you can develop strategies toward each stakeholder you have identified.

STEP 6: DEVELOPING SPECIFIC STRATEGIES AND TACTICS

Using your results from the preceding steps, you can now proceed to outline the specific strategies and tactics you wish to use with each stakeholder.

First, you should consider whether to approach each stakeholder directly or indirectly. Second, you need to decide whether to do nothing, monitor, or take an offensive or defensive position with certain stakeholders. Third, you should determine whether to accommodate, negotiate, manipulate, resist, avoid, or "wait and see" with specific stakeholders. Finally, you should decide what combination of strategies you want to employ with each stakeholder.

A useful typology for both identifying and deciding on strategies to employ in a complex situation is shown in Figure 2.7.[11] This diagnostic typology of organizational stakeholders shows two dimensions: potential for threat and potential for cooperation. Note that stakeholders can move among the quadrants, changing positions as situations and stakes change.

The ideal strategic situation for the focal corporation is type 1, the *supportive* stakeholder with a low potential for threat and high potential for cooperation. Here the strategy of the focal company is to *involve* the supportive stakeholder. Think of both internal and external stakeholders who might be supportive and who should be involved in the focal organization's strategy, such as employees, suppliers, board members, the parent company, and vendors.

In contrast, there is type 3, the *nonsupportive* stakeholder who shows a high potential for threat and a low potential for cooperation. The suggested strategy in this situation calls for the focal organization to *defend* its interests and reduce dependence on that stakeholder.

A type 4 stakeholder is a *"mixed blessing,"* with a high potential for both threat and cooperation. This stakeholder calls for a *collaborative* strategy. In this situation, the stakeholder could become supportive or nonsupportive. Collaborative attempts to move the stakeholder to the focal company's interests is the goal.

Finally, type 2 is the *marginal* stakeholder. This stakeholder has a low potential for both threat and cooperation. Such stakeholders may not be interested in the issues of concern. The recommended strategy in this situation is to *monitor* the stakeholder, to "wait and see" and minimize expenditure of resources, unless and until the stakeholder moves to a mixed blessing, supportive, or nonsupportive position.

Figure 2.8 presents an illustration of the typology in Figure 2.7, using the Microsoft case as an example (see box on page 31). The arrows indicate the stakeholders who moved or were influenced to move among quadrants. Using your objective, "third-party perspective" and judgment in reading a case, while observing a series of events, determine the movement among stakeholder positions: who influences whom, by what means, and how. As you look at Figure 2.8, ask yourself: Do I agree with this diagram as it is completed? Did customers and employees move from supportive to mixed blessing stakeholders? Why? How? Critique the logic of this interpretation and add your own.

Microsoft's success hinges greatly on its ability to manage its stakeholders. The company continues to involve its supportive stakeholders by, for example, maintaining its competitive edge and market share to keep shareholders satisfied. Nonsupportive stakeholders include Netscape, Sun, IBM, and Apple, against whom Microsoft must continually defend its position. These companies pose a high-level threat to Microsoft and have low potential for cooperation. Also in this category is the government-led coalition of the U.S. Department of Justice and 18 states' attorneys, who formed to prosecute the government's case. Attorneys for nine states have refused the initial settlement and are likely to pursue tougher remedies.

Within this group, Microsoft had an opportunity to shift some of the nonsupportive stakeholders to a *marginal* position that represents a low potential for threat. Sun Microsystems' development of Java, for example, has the potential to revolutionize the way in which applications are developed, by eliminating the dependence between the application and the operating

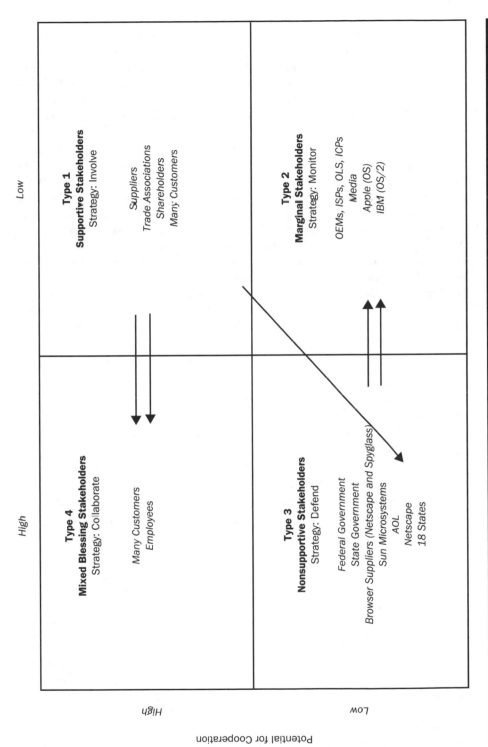

Potential for Threat

| | Low | High |

Type 1
Supportive Stakeholders
Strategy: Involve

Suppliers
Trade Associations
Shareholders
Many Customers

Type 4
Mixed Blessing Stakeholders
Strategy: Collaborate

Many Customers
Employees

Type 2
Marginal Stakeholders
Strategy: Monitor

OEMs, ISPs, OLS, ICPs
Media
Apple (OS)
IBM (OS/2)

Type 3
Nonsupportive Stakeholders
Strategy: Defend

Federal Government
State Government
Browser Suppliers (Netscape and Spyglass)
Sun Microsystems
AOL
Netscape
18 States

Potential for Cooperation

High   Low

SOURCE: Carmen Spears, MBA student at Bentley College, Waltham, MA. Based on G. Savage et al. 1991. Strategies for assessing and managing organizational stakeholders. *The Executive* 5, no. 2 (May): 65.

system. By partnering with Sun, Microsoft could have been the sole distribution channel for the new technology. Instead, Sun partnered with
Netscape to distribute Java and Microsoft had a major threat to both of its
core businesses: operating systems and applications. By not partnering with
Sun, Microsoft lost control over the distribution of Java or future Java development. Instead, Microsoft was forced to develop its own form of Java to
protect its market share.

Supportive Microsoft customers who have used Microsoft operating
systems only because the applications were available and were at first "the
only show in town" are, in actuality, something of a *mixed blessing* for the
corporation. Microsoft needs to collaborate with its customers. Application developers who were partners of Microsoft could potentially expand
into other operating systems and thus shift to a less supportive stakeholder position, such as the mixed blessing group. Netscape's browser
provided the basic operating system commands that were needed to run
applications, thus posing a serious threat to Microsoft's operating system
business. To protect its market domination, Microsoft therefore collaborated
with original equipment manufacturers (OEMs). Managing these stakeholders successfully was key to keeping Microsoft products in front of the
customer.

While you, as the focal stakeholder, are developing specific strategies,
keep the following points in mind:

1. Your goal is to create a win-win set of outcomes, if possible. However,
   this may mean economic costs to your firm if, in fact, members of
   your firm are responsible to certain groups for harm caused as a consequence of your actions.

2. Ask: "What is our business? Who are our customers? What are our responsibilities to the stakeholders, to the public, and to the firm?" Keep
   your mission and responsibilities in mind as you move forward.

3. Consider what the probable consequences of your actions will be. For
   whom? At what costs? Over what period? Ask: "What does a win-win
   situation look like for us?"

4. Keep in mind that the *means* that you use are as important as the ends
   you seek; that is, how you approach and treat each stakeholder can be
   as important as what you do.

Specific strategies now can be articulated and assigned to corporate staff
for review and implementation. Remember, social responsibility is a key
variable; it is as important as the economic and political factors of a decision,
since social responsibility is linked to costs and benefits in other areas. At
this point, you can ask to what extent your strategies are just and fair and
consider the welfare of the stakeholders affected by your decision.

Executives use a range of strategies, especially in long-term crisis situations, to respond to external threats and stakeholders. Their strategies often

are short-sighted and begin in a defensive or reactive mode. In observing and using a stakeholder analysis, question why executives respond to their stakeholders as they do. Following the questions and methods in this chapter systematically helps you understand why key stakeholders respond as they do to critical incidents.

STEP 7: MONITORING SHIFTING COALITIONS

Because time and events can change the stakes and stakeholders, you need to monitor the evolution of the issues and actions of the stakeholders, using Figure 2.7. Media exposure, politics, economics, legal actions, and public reactions change stakeholder strategies and positions on issues. Tracking external trends and events and the resultant stakeholder strategies can help a CEO and his or her team act and react accordingly. How would you evaluate Bill Gates' ability to keep his stakeholders supportive and to move nonsupportive stakeholders to Microsoft's positions?

STAKEHOLDER ANALYSIS AND THE THIRD-PARTY OBJECTIVE OBSERVER ROLE

To explain the process of using a stakeholder analysis, we asked you to assume the role of a CEO or leader of a company. However, another, more objective perspective you may wish to assume to analyze business incidents, crises, opportunities, or cases is that of "third-party observer." In this role, you would not necessarily take, support, or defend the position of the focal company's interests or stakes, nor would you advocate for any one stakeholder's claims or positions. Instead, like a judge, you would be impartial in your research, analysis, and decision regarding the process and outcomes of each constituency. In this regard, you would use the stakeholder methods as means toward exercising independent judgment regarding the moral responsibilities of stakeholders' interests and claims and their uses of power, tactics, and strategies. Your evaluations of the process and outcomes of such an analysis would be impartial.

SUMMARY OF STAKEHOLDER ANALYSIS

You have now completed the basic stakeholder analysis and should be able to proceed with strategy implementation in more realistic, thoughtful, interactive, and responsible ways. The stakeholder approach should involve other decision makers inside and outside the focal organization.

The stakeholder analysis provides a rational, systematic basis for understanding economic, political, social, and moral issues involved in complex relationships between an organization and its constituents. It helps decision-makers guide and structure strategic planning sessions and decide how to meet the moral obligations of all stakeholders. The extent to which the resultant strategies and outcomes are moral and effective for a firm and its stakeholders depends on many factors, including the values of the firm's leaders, the stakeholders' power, the legitimacy of the actions, the uses of available resources, and the exigencies of the changing environment. Many CEOs and top management teams could benefit from managing their constituencies by using this analytical method, with everyone's rights and responsibilities in mind.

2.4 STAKEHOLDER APPROACH AND ETHICAL REASONING

Because the stakeholder analysis is an analytical method, no prescribed ethical principles or responsibility rules are "built in." Ethical reasoning in the stakeholder analysis means asking: "What is equitable, just, fair, and good for those who affect and are affected by business decisions? Who are the weaker stakeholders in terms of power and influence? Who can, who will, and who should help weaker stakeholders make their voices heard and encourage their participation in the decision process and outcomes?" Finally, the stakeholder analysis requires the focal or principal stakeholders to define and fulfill their ethical obligations to the affected constituencies.

Chapter 3 explains major ethical principles that can be used to examine individual motivation for resolving an ethical dilemma. That chapter explains several ethical frameworks and principles, including the following: (1) rights, (2) justice, (3) utilitarianism, (4) relativism, and (5) universalism, all of which can be applied to individual and organizational belief systems, policies, and motives.

2.5 MORAL RESPONSIBILITIES OF FUNCTIONAL AREA PROFESSIONALS

One goal of a stakeholder analysis is to encourage and prepare organizational managers to articulate their own moral responsibility, as well as the responsibilities of their company and their profession, toward their different constituencies. Stakeholder analysis focuses the enterprise's attention and moral decision-making process on external events. The stakeholder approach also applies internally, especially to individual managers in and across traditional functional areas. These managers can be seen as conduits through which other external stakeholders are influenced.

Because our concern is to focus on managing moral responsibility in organizational stakeholder relationships, this section briefly outlines some of the general responsibilities of selected functional area managers to illustrate moral dilemmas that can arise in their work. With the Internet, the trans-

| FIGURE 2.9 | A MANAGER'S STAKEHOLDERS |

R. Edward Freeman. 1984. *Strategic management: A stakeholder approach.* Boston: Pitman, 218. Reproduced with permission of the publisher.

Note: The letters K, L, M, and N are hypothetical designations in place of real department names. Dotted lines refer to hypothetical linkages.

parency and ubiquitous exposure of all organizational actors and internal stakeholders (i.e., owners, managers, employees) increases the risks and stakes of unethical practices. Chat rooms, message boards, and breaking news sites provide instant conduits and platforms for exposing both rumor and truth about companies. (In the tobacco controversy, it was an anti-smoking researcher and advocate who first posted inside information from a whistleblower to the Internet. This action was a first step toward opening the tobacco companies' internal documents to public scrutiny and the resulting lawsuits.)

Figure 2.9 illustrates a manager's stakeholders. The particular functional area you are interested in can be kept in mind while you read the descriptions discussed next. Note that the same procedures, steps 1 through 7, presented in the stakeholder analysis can also be used for this level of analysis.

Traditional functional and expert areas include marketing, research and development (R&D), manufacturing, public relations, and human resource management (HRM). The basic moral dimensions of each of these are discussed. Several other line and staff functions, such as finance, information systems, planning, and legal advice, are not covered here. Even though functional areas are often blurred in some emerging network organizational structures and self-designed teams, many of the responsibilities of these managerial areas remain intact. Understanding these managerial roles from a stakeholder perspective helps to clarify the pressures and moral responsibilities of these job positions. This section can be read and revisited after reading chapter 3, which explains and presents ethical principles and quick ethical tests for professionals.

MARKETING AND SALES PROFESSIONALS AND MANAGERS AS STAKEHOLDERS

Sales professionals and managers are on the "frontline" of a company's interface with its customers, suppliers, and vendors. Sales professionals are also evaluated by measured quotas and quantitative expectations on a weekly, monthly, and quarterly basis. The stress and pressure to meet expectations is always present. Sales professionals must continually balance and evaluate their personal ethics against their professional pressures. The dilemma often becomes: "Who do I represent? What weight do my beliefs and ethics have when measured against my department's and company's performance measures for me?" Another key question for sales professionals, particularly, is: "Where is the line between unethical and ethical practices for me?" Also, because customers are an integral part of business, these professionals must create and maintain customer interest and loyalty. They must be concerned with consumer safety and welfare regarding product use, while increasing revenue and obtaining new accounts. Many marketing and sales professionals also are responsible for determining and managing the firm's advertising and the truthfulness (and legality) of the data and information they issue to the public about products and services. Thus, they must interact with many of the other functional areas and with advertising agencies, customers, and consumer groups. Moral dilemmas can arise for marketing managers, who may be asked to promote unsafe products or to implement advertising campaigns that are untrue or not in the consumer's best interests.

For example, marketing managers at Nestlé, the Swiss conglomerate, were forced decades ago in a now classical business ethics case to battle criticisms for advertising and selling infant formula in developing countries. The criticisms centered on the company's practice of persuading mothers to bottle-feed, instead of breastfeed, their infants. Because of impure water, poor health conditions, and illiteracy, women in these countries used the formula improperly. Executives at Nestlé never imagined the international controversy that this would cause.

A major moral dilemma for marketing managers is having to choose between a profitable decision and a socially responsible one. The stakeholder analysis helps marketing managers in these morally questionable situations by identifying stakeholders and understanding the effects and consequences of profits and services on them. Balancing company profitability with human rights and interests is a moral responsibility of marketers. Companies that have no ethics code or socially responsible policies and procedures—as well as those that do have these, but do not enforce them—increase the personal pressure, pain, and liability of individual professionals. Such tensions can and often do lead to unethical and illegal activities. A case discussed in this text highlights a media, public relations, and marketing company's ethical tensions in dealing with customers and competitors.

R&D Engineering Professionals
and Managers as Stakeholders

R&D managers and engineers are responsible for the safety and reliability of product design. Faulty products can mean public outcry, which can result in increased public attention, unwanted media exposure, and possibly (perhaps justifiably) lawsuits. R&D managers must work and communicate effectively and conscientiously with professionals in manufacturing, marketing, and information systems; senior managers; contractors; and government representatives, to name a few of their stakeholders. As studies and reports on the Challenger space shuttle disaster illustrate, engineers and managers at the National Aeronautics and Space Administration (NASA) and the cooperating company, Thiokol, had different priorities, perceptions, and technical judgments regarding the "go, no-go" decision of that space launch. Lack of individual role responsibility and critical judgment contributed to the miscommunication and resulting disaster.

Moral dilemmas can arise for R&D engineers whose technical judgments and risk assessments conflict with administrative managers seeking profit and time-to-market deadlines. R&D managers also can benefit from doing a stakeholder analysis, before events like the *Challenger* launch occur. The discussion of the "levels of business ethics" in Chapter 1 also provides the individual professional with a way of examining his or her individual ethics and moral responsibilities in the context of both professional and corporate moral standards and codes—or lack thereof.

Public Relations Managers as Stakeholders

Public relations (PR) managers must constantly interact with outside groups and corporate executives, especially in an age when communications media, external relations, and public scrutiny play such vital roles. PR managers are responsible for transmitting, receiving, and interpreting information about employees, products, services, and the company. The firm's public credibility and image depend on how PR professionals manage stakeholders, since PR personnel must often negotiate the boundaries between corporate loyalty and credibility with external groups. These groups often use different criteria than corporate executives do for measuring success and responsibility, especially during crises. Moral dilemmas can arise when PR managers must defend or protect company actions or policies that have possible or known harmful effects on the public or on certain stakeholders. A stakeholder analysis can prepare PR managers and inform them about the situation, the stakes, and the strategies they must address.

HUMAN RESOURCE MANAGERS AS STAKEHOLDERS

Human resource managers (HRMs) are on the frontline of helping other managers recruit, hire, fire, promote, evaluate, reward, discipline, transfer, and counsel employees. They negotiate union settlements and assist the government with enforcing Equal Employment Opportunity Commission (EEOC) standards. Human resource management professionals must translate employee rights and laws into practice. They also research, write, update, and maintain company policies on employee affairs. They face constant ethical pressures and uncertainties over issues about invasion of privacy and violations of employees' individual and constitutional rights. Stakeholders of HRMs include but are not limited to employees, other managers and bosses, unions, community groups, government officials, lobbyists, and competitors.

Moral dilemmas can arise for these managers when affirmative action policies are threatened in favor of corporate decisions to hide biases or protect profits. Human resource managers and professionals also straddle the often fine line between the individual rights of employees and corporate self-interests, especially when downsizing, layoffs, reductions in force (RIFs), and other hiring or firing decisions are involved. As industries restructure, merge, downsize, and expand internationally, the HRM's work becomes even more complicated. Human rights versus corporate profit is always a tightrope these professionals must walk when making decisions.

SUMMARY OF MANAGERIAL MORAL RESPONSIBILITIES

Expert and functional area managers are confronted with balancing operational profit goals with corporate moral obligations toward stakeholders. These pressures are considered "part of the job." Unfortunately, clear corporate directions for resolving dilemmas that involve conflicts between individuals' rights and corporate economic interests generally are not available. Using a stakeholder analysis is a step toward clarifying the issues, stakes, and parties involved in resolving such potential or actual ethical dilemmas. Chapter 3 presents moral decision-making principles and criteria that can help individuals and managers think through these issues and take responsible action.

2.6 THREE ISSUES MANAGEMENT APPROACHES

Most national and international business-related controversies develop around the exposure of a single issue, which then evolves into more serious and costly issues. The Ford Explorer and Bridgestone Firestone tire crisis started with what appeared to be faulty tires. The issue escalated to questions about the design of the Ford vehicle itself, then to questions of how many deaths and accidents over what period of time in how many countries. These issues began to center on who was responsible for what, when, and how. The leadership of these companies was brought into question, as was the relationship between the companies. Every organization and every professional does a balancing act between conscientiously deliberating the possible solutions to a problem and making prompt decisions. In the above example, what may have originally seemed like a few defective tires developed into a more complex set of issues involving a wide range of stakeholders.

This section presents three general issues frameworks and two crisis management methods for mapping and managing issues before and even after they become crises for companies. You can use any of these frameworks with the stakeholder management approach. Issues are caused, affected, and managed by stakeholders.

Some studies argue that moral reasoning is "issue-dependent," that "people generally behave better when the moral issue is important than they do when it is unimportant."[12] Questions regarding issue recognition include: To what extent do people actually recognize moral issues? Is it by the magnitude of the potential or actual consequences of the issue? By the social consensus regarding how serious or important the issue is? How likely is it that the effects of the issue will be felt? How quickly the issue will occur?[13] While these questions continue to be studied, one certainty exists: Companies face issues every day. Some issues have patterns and do lead to serious, sometimes disastrous, consequences—dramatic and tragic oil spills, the loss of millions of lives to the effects of tobacco, intended and unintended violence from use of firearms, or the explosion of a U.S. space shuttle with citizens aboard. Other issues evolve in a way that leads to spectacular outcomes: the invention and commercialization of the Internet, information technology that enables individuals and companies wireless access to anyone at any time in any place, and the capability to network customers, businesses, suppliers, and vendors. Of course, there are always stakeholders who do not benefit or gain from the spectacular events and there are those who gain from the disasters.

TV programs like "60 Minutes," "Dateline," and "Frontline," and other investigative news channels like Al-Jazeera air "issue-breaking" news content that focuses on crises that companies, organizations, governments, leaders, communities, and professionals may face. Approaches such as the stakeholder analysis and issues management frameworks help reveal how significant issues develop and are—or are not—addressed by stakeholders.

By exploring and analyzing the issues that underlie and result from stake-holder strategies and interactions, a window into societies, institutions, power, politics, business, and environmental forces is provided. Any one of the three approaches explained here can be used, along with a stakeholder analysis, to identify how a company or constituency navigated its strate-gies—or was navigated by others' strategies—toward or away from a vision.

Strategic issues management attempts to: (1) detect and address issues that may cause a firm and its stakeholders problems or harm and (2) contain or resolve issues that could become potentially damaging crises. Many firms (e.g., Monsanto, Sears, and Arco) have hired issues management staff who alert top management about controversial trends that could affect operations. The role of identifying and managing strategic issues is often the work of a top-level management team.

FIRST APPROACH: 6-STEP ISSUE MANAGEMENT PROCESS

The first of the three methods is the most straightforward. This approach is more appropriate for companies or groups trying to understand, manage, and control their internal environments. A third-party observer could also use this approach to describe how a company or group acted in retrospect or could act toward an opportunity, impending crisis, or significant trend or event. The process involves the following steps, illustrated in Figure 2.10.[14]

1. Environmental scanning and issues identification
2. Issues analysis
3. Issues ranking and prioritizing
4. Issues resolution strategizing
5. Issues response and implementation
6. Issues evaluation and monitoring

These steps are part of a firm's corporate planning process. In the strategic issues management process, these steps are isolated and a firm uses its spe-cial-issues unit or a selected team to work on emerging trends as they relate to the industry and company. This framework is a first-step, basic approach for mapping, strategizing, and responding to issues before they develop into serious problems or crises. You may want to consider how Microsoft's lead-ership could have used this process to avert the difficulties it faced with the Department of Justice, or using these six steps, you could evaluate how Mi-crosoft did address the issues it created and faced. The following two ap-proaches add additional depth and dimension to this framework.

SECOND APPROACH: 7-PHASE ISSUE DEVELOPMENT PROCESS

Issues also are believed to follow a developmental life cycle. Views differ on the stages and time involved in the life cycle. Steven Fink's method of

FIGURE 2.10   6-STEP ISSUE MANAGEMENT PROCESS

1.
Environmental
scanning and issues
identification

6.
Issues evaluation
and monitoring

2.
Issues
analysis

**6-Step
Issue
Management**

5.
Issues response and
implementation

3.
Issues ranking
and prioritizing

4.
Issues resolution
strategizing

analyzing an 8-year issue's life is illustrated in Figure 2.11. It is instructive to understand some of the life-cycle stages suggested for tracking an issue.[15]

1. A felt need arises (from emerging events, advocacy groups, books, movies).
2. Media coverage is developed (television segments, such as on *60 Minutes* and *20/20*, and radio announcements).
3. Interest group development gains momentum and grows.
4. Policies are adopted by leading political jurisdictions (cities, states, counties).
5. The federal government gives attention to the issue (hearings and studies).
6. Issues and policies evolve into legislation and regulation.
7. Issues and policies enter litigation.

Using Figure 2.11, let's apply this approach to the Microsoft case.

FIGURE 2.11   7-PHASE ISSUE DEVELOPMENT PROCESS

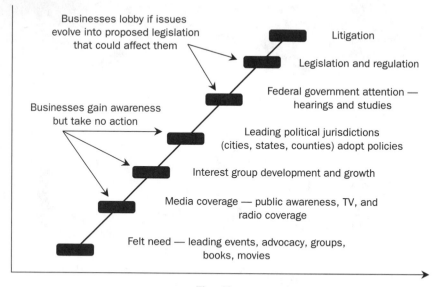

Time Line

A beginning issue of what apparently became part of Microsoft's continued pattern of monopolistic practices can be traced to 1995, when Microsoft began using "strong-arm" tactics with some of its partners to restrict them in growing their business with Microsoft competitors. For example, Microsoft threatened to stop supporting Intel microprocessors if Intel continued to develop platform-related software for graphics and video, which Microsoft viewed as a potential threat. Microsoft also denied beneficial pricing to IBM for Windows operating systems. IBM needed licenses to sell its IBM personal computers. Microsoft apparently did this to try to coerce IBM into stopping development of OS/2 Warp, a direct competitor for Microsoft's operating systems. Intel, IBM, and other Microsoft partners started to feel that some control was needed over Microsoft. This was the genesis of the *felt need* in the case. These stakeholders felt that Microsoft was using its market dominance in operating systems to prevent other applications and products from entering the market. Although many stakeholders were affected, at this point they were not organized to address or exercise their concerns about Microsoft.

Awareness that Microsoft's market power and dominance were growing began in 1997 and was most clearly evident with Microsoft's control of the operating system market. As Microsoft launched its new operating system,

Windows 98, in December 1997, marketing studies revealed that a price of $49.00 would provide reasonable margins for the product. Because the demand was so high and competition was futile, Microsoft introduced the product at $89.00. This is a key point in the issue development process because it makes public Microsoft's ability to command higher prices for products.

Businesses lobby and then escalate concerns into lawsuits. In October 1997, Sun Microsystems filed suit against Microsoft, accusing them of "polluting" the Java technology that it had agreed to distribute for Microsoft. As previously stated, Microsoft viewed the combination of Java and an operating system, such as Netscape, as a serious threat to its core businesses. This was the first significant action a Microsoft competitor had taken in opposition against the "strong-arm" tactics that Microsoft was using. In March 1998, Sun won an injunction preventing Microsoft from altering Java. After this lawsuit, other companies began to take notice. Rather than take on Microsoft individually, Microsoft's competitors elicited the aid of the Department of Justice as well as the State Attorneys General. The two issues raised were Microsoft's business practices in violation of the Sherman Antitrust Act and anti-competitive business practices that threatened damage to the economies of the states.

Once these lawsuits were filed, federal and state governments moved in and *escalated the issues to a regulatory level.* The key difference between the suit filed by Sun and the suit filed by the U.S. Government is that in the earlier suit, one company sued another company. At this legislative and regulatory stage, the U.S. Government sued a company. The ramifications of the latter could lead to government-enforced company restructuring or new legislation preventing similar occurrences in the future.

The issue then moved to *litigation* at the federal level. The suit, *United States of America v. Microsoft Corporation,* was decided, and Microsoft was found guilty of using business practices in violation of the Sherman Antitrust Act. Settlement talks faltered. The Department of Justice under the Bush administration will probably resolve the case. At press time, November 2001, a government-led consensus regarding settlement is expected.

Issues management is a skill involving the *ability to learn about the future.* "Leaders are confronted with a new challenge: to develop the capacity for 'precognition.'" (T. Stewart, "Learning from the Future," *Business 2.0,* Vol. 2, No. 20, Nov. 7, 2001.) As you read these approaches, ask whether or not a company that you are familiar with passed through part or all of these stages. Did issues change in their perceived importance to the focal company or its stakeholders? To society? If the incident or event reached national recognition, as did Microsoft's issues, did the issues gain or lose public legitimacy as they evolved through the different stages? How did the stakes and stakeholders change as the issue evolved?

| FIGURE 2.12 | LIFE CYCLE ISSUE DEVELOPMENT |

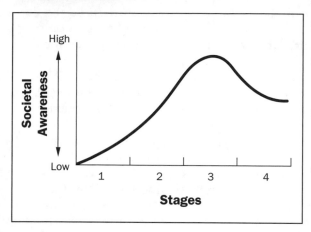

1. Social Expectations and Awareness
   · Social Discussion and Debate
   · Interest Group Attention
2. Political Awareness
   · Media Attention
   · Legislation Initiated
   · Hearings Held
3. Legislative Engagement
   · Law Passed
   · Legal Involvement
   · Regulations Enacted
4. Social Control and Litigation
   · Compliance Issues
   · Legal Conflict
   · Court Rulings

SOURCE: Thomas Marx. 1986. Integrating public affairs and strategic planning. *California Management Review (Fall),* 145.

THIRD APPROACH: 4-STAGE ISSUE LIFE CYCLE

A broader but somewhat related approach is that of Thomas Marx,[16] who of-fered a four-stage issue life cycle. Marx observed that issues evolve from so-cial expectations to social control through the following steps (Figure 2.12).

1. Social expectations
2. Political issues
3. Legislation
4. Social control

Marx illustrated his framework with the automobile safety belt issue. The four stages of this case, according to Marx, were reflected by the following events.

1. Ralph Nader's now-classic book, *Unsafe at Any Speed*, published in 1964, created a social expectation regarding the safe manufacturing of automobiles. The Chevrolet Corvair, later pulled off the market, was the focus of Nader's astute legal and public advocacy work in expos-ing manufacturing defects.

2. The National Traffic and Auto Safety Act and the resulting motor ve-hicle safety hearings in 1966 moved this expectation into the political arena.

3. In 1966, the Motor Vehicle Safety Act was passed, and four states began requiring seat-belt use in 1984.

4. Social control was established in 1967, when all cars were required to have seat belts. Driver fines and penalties, recalls of products, and litigation concerning defective equipment further reinforced the control stage.

Nader's pioneering consumer advocacy and legal work with regard to U.S. automobile manufacturing set an enduring precedent for watchdog congressional and voluntary advocacy groups.

Selecting an issue in the news and tracing its evolution through these different stages provides a window into the social, political, economic, and legislative processes of society. Issues are not static or predetermined commodities. Stakeholder groups' values and interests move or impede an issue's development. To understand how an issue develops or dies is to understand how power works in a political system.

APPLYING MARX'S APPROACH TO THE MICROSOFT CASE. Thomas Marx's 4-stage life-cycle approach to issues management illustrates the series of events in the 1990s that led Microsoft to the courtroom. Figure 2.13 illustrates an adaptation of this model. According to Marx's model, during the first stage of the issue development life cycle, expectations and awareness of the issues are raised. In the case of Microsoft, it quickly became evident that the company's dominance in operating systems presented high-level barriers to market entry, which made it nearly impossible for competitors to break into the market. The failure of both IBM's OS/2 and Apple's Mac OS operating systems support this point. Both systems failed to gain a large position in the market because they were unable to attract software developers to write programs for their platforms, allegedly because of Microsoft's domination of the subscriber base. During this phase, Microsoft used the dependency of its partners and competitors on the Windows licensing agreements to prevent cross-platform software from being developed and to preserve their high-level barriers to market entry.

The *second stage* in Marx's developmental life cycle is the creation of political awareness. During this phase, the communications media turn their attention to the issue and legislation is initiated. After Netscape introduced its Navigator browser and packaged it with Java, Microsoft perceived a threat to the dominance of Windows and attempted to forge an agreement with Netscape that would relegate the Navigator browser to a niche market. When Netscape declined the offer, Microsoft built its own browser, Internet Explorer, and began bundling it into Windows in December of 1995, in an alleged attempt to eliminate a competitive threat and maintain barriers to entry in the market for PC operating systems. At this point, Microsoft's anti-competitive tactics gained both public and media attention. Microsoft allegedly drove Netscape's market share from over 90% in 1995 to

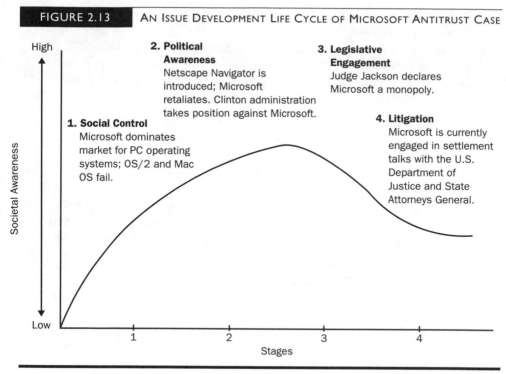

FIGURE 2.13   AN ISSUE DEVELOPMENT LIFE CYCLE OF MICROSOFT ANTITRUST CASE

SOURCE: Dan Walles and Carmen Spears, MBA students at Bentley College, Waltham, MA. Based on Thomas Marx's model.

approximately 40% in mid-1998 by giving away a parity product with its operating system. At stake for Microsoft during this phase was a threat to the company's dominance in the market for PC operating systems, while at stake for Netscape was its unobstructed access to the market for Internet browsers.

Also during this phase, Sun Microsystems charged that Microsoft was in violation of its licensing agreement for Java and had been polluting the technology of the programming language to create an unfair advantage for the introduction of its own product. Sun was granted an injunction to stop Microsoft from altering the technology and a lawsuit was scheduled for 1999. The subsequent antitrust suit against Microsoft was a direct result of the company's mismanagement of its stakeholders.

The *third stage* of Marx's developmental life cycle is legislative engagement, during which there is legal involvement and regulations are enacted. In the Microsoft case, Judge Jackson handed down a statement of fact on November 5, 1998, charging Microsoft with being a monopoly in the market for PC operating systems. The judge ruled that Microsoft's actions, i.e., bundling, strong–arm tactics, and exclusionary agreements with ISPs,

OEMs, and ICPs, constituted illegal anti-competitive and exclusionary practices. Microsoft's competitors were seeking compensatory justice in an effort
to lower the barriers to entry and stop Microsoft's anti-competitive practices.
Microsoft was seeking to preserve its dominant position in the market for
operating systems and therefore took both a defensive stand to deny illegal
practices and an offensive stand to justify its rights.

The *final stage* of Marx's development life cycle is social control and litigation. The antitrust case against Microsoft is currently in this stage: litigation is still pending. Arbitration must be agreed to by Microsoft, the Department of Justice, and the 18 State Attorneys General. Gates and the
Department of Justice want to settle. As a result of litigation, Microsoft has
conducted some organizational restructuring and has shifted its strategy to
diversification outside of PC operating systems. Microsoft's interests have
changed since the first phase of the issue development life cycle because the
case is likely to result in restrictions that level the playing field for operating
systems and threaten Microsoft's dominance. Microsoft's competitors are
currently in a position to gain from the outcome of the case because their
barriers to entry may be lowered. By using this analytical framework to examine the major issues surrounding the antitrust case against Microsoft, it
becomes apparent how the main stakeholders' interests have shifted over
time.

ISSUES MANAGEMENT AND STAKEHOLDER ANALYSIS

The first step of a stakeholder analysis can be the identification of the major
or precipitating issue or issues that a company faces. After the issues are
identified, a stakeholder analysis can be enhanced by asking the following
questions:

- Which stakeholders are affected by the issue?

- Who has an interest in the issue?

- Who is in a position to exert influence on the issue?

- Who has expressed an opinion on the issue?

An issues management approach complements the stakeholder analysis
and can be used to anticipate and resolve corporate issues and crises and to
understand and track newsbreaking incidents that present economic, legal,
social, and moral problems for a company and its stakeholders.

QUICK
ASSESSMENT

You are the president of a manufacturing company (with 550 employees) that has an excellent reputation in the small town in which you work. A newspaper reporter has discovered that two members of your top-level management team have been involved in buying illegal drugs on two occasions from a street-corner dealer. Both employees (a man and woman) have been with the company for more than 7 years, and both have excellent work records and reputations in the community. You really cannot afford to lose them.

The reporter has written a devastating story revealing all the details, has called on you to fire them immediately, and has given the story and an interview to the local television station. You have already received a call from the mayor to act responsibly with regard to the matter. More than 100 of your loyal and conscientious employees have E-mailed you, asking that you *not* fire the two employees and that, if you did fire them, they too would consider leaving the company.

1. Write out your response to this scenario. Describe what you would *do* (not what you would hope to or like to do) in the situation, and explain why.

2. Meet in small groups in your classroom and share your responses. Then make your report to the class, and while the reports are being made, observe the reasoning used and how the responses corresponded to any of the crisis management sections in the chapter.

3. What did you learn from the exercise? Explain.

2.7 TWO CRISIS MANAGEMENT APPROACHES

"Crisis management" methods have evolved from the study of how corporations responded (and should have responded) to crises. Steven Fink (1986) states that a crisis is a "turning point for better or worse," a "decisive moment" or "crucial time," or "a situation that has reached a critical phase." He goes on to say that crisis management ". . . is the art of removing much of the risk and uncertainty to allow you to achieve more control over your destiny."[17] Crises, from a corporation's point of view, can deteriorate if the situation escalates in intensity, comes under closer governmental scrutiny, interferes with normal operations, jeopardizes the positive image of the company or its officers, and damages a firm's bottom line. A turn for the worse also could occur if any of the firm's stakeholders were seriously harmed or if the environment was damaged or destroyed. The following two approaches map and describe ways that organizations can respond to crises.

FIRST APPROACH: PRECRISIS THROUGH RESOLUTION

According to this model, a crisis consists of four stages: (1) prodromal (precrisis), (2) acute, (3) chronic, and (4) resolved. Judgment and observation are required to manage these stages (Figure 2.14). This approach differs from the second one in that a "precrisis stage" is shown.[18]

FIGURE 2.14	FOUR CRISIS MANAGEMENT STAGES

Stage 1	Stage 2	Stage 3	Stage 4
Precrisis	**Crisis occurs**	**Lingering**	**Health restored**
PRODROMAL STAGE	ACUTE STAGE	CHRONIC STAGE	CONFLICT RESOLUTION STAGE
Warning; symptoms	Point of no return	Self-doubt, self-analysis	Return to normalcy

The *prodromal stage* is the warning stage. If this stage is not recognized or does not actually occur, the second stage (acute crisis) can rush in, requiring damage control. Clues in the prodromal stage must be carefully observed. For example, a clue could be verbal, such as a union leader telling upper management that a strike may occur if certain contract conditions are not signed. At Microsoft, did Gates have any warning of a precrisis stage—that some of his actions were inviting lawsuits from disgruntled competitors?

In the second stage, *acute crisis,* damage has been done. The point here is to control as much of the damage as possible. This is most often the shortest of the stages. Can you identify this stage in the Microsoft case?

The third stage, *chronic crisis,* is the clean-up phase. This is a period of recovery, self-analysis, self-doubt, and healing. Congressional investigations, audits, and interviews occur during this stage, which can linger indefinitely, according to Fink. A survey of *Fortune* 500 CEOs reported that companies that did not have a crisis management plan stayed in this stage two and a half times longer than those who had plans. Did Microsoft experience a chronic crisis stage?

The final stage, *crisis resolution,* is the crisis management goal. The key question here is: What can I do to speed up this phase and resolve this crisis once and for all? Has this stage started in the Microsoft case?

SECOND APPROACH: REACTION THROUGH ACCOMMODATION

Matthews, Goodpaster, and Nash[19] have suggested five phases of corporate social response to crises related to unsafe products, or product crisis management. This model is based on the authors' study of how corporations have responded to serious crises. The phases, illustrated in Figure 2.15, are (1) reaction, (2) defense, (3) insight, (4) accommodation, and (5) agency.

Not all executives involved in unsafe product crises respond the same way to the public, media, and other stakeholders. This approach can be used to examine and evaluate the moral responsibility of corporate responses to

---

FIGURE 2.15   CORPORATE SOCIAL RESPONSE PHASES

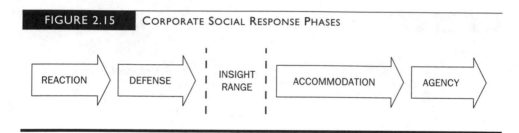

---

crises. These authors studied the classic Firestone 500 radial tire case, the Tylenol tampering case, the Rely tampon case, and the Ford Pinto case. More recent cases, such as the Dow Corning silicon-gel issue and the Ford Explorer and Firestone tire case, exemplify similar phases. It is interesting to observe how some executives continue to deny or avoid responsibility in crises that become disastrous. Knowledge of these stages certainly would be a first step toward corporate awareness. Let's look more closely at each stage.

The *reaction stage* is the first phase when a crisis has occurred. Management lacks complete information and time to analyze the event thoroughly. A public reaction that responds to allegations about the product and the crisis is required. This stage is important to corporations, because the public, the media, and the stakeholders involved see for the first time who the firm selects as its spokesperson, how the firm responds, and what the message is.

The second stage, *defense,* signals that the company is overwhelmed by public attention. The firm's image is at stake. This stage usually involves the company's recoiling under media pressure. But this does not always have to be a negative or reactive situation.

The third stage, *insight,* is the most agonizing time for the firm in the controversy. The stakes are substantial. The firm's existence may be questioned. The company must come to grips with the situation under circumstances that have been generated externally. During this stage, the executives realize and confirm from evidence whether and to what extent their company is at fault in the safety issues of the product in question.

In the fourth stage, *accommodation,* the company either acts to remove the product from the market or refutes the charges against product safety. Addressing public pressure and anxiety is the task in this stage.

During the last stage, *agency,* the company attempts to understand the causes of the safety issue and develop an education program for the public.

To use this approach for analysis, observe newspaper and media reports of industrial crises. Apply this model and compare how company executives and spokespersons handle crises. Take special note of how companies respond morally to their different stakeholders. Observe the relative amounts of attention companies give to consumers, the media, and government stakeholders. Use the frameworks in this chapter to help inform your observations and judgments. Develop a time line as the crisis unfolds. Notice who the company chooses as its spokesperson. Determine how and why the company is assuming or avoiding responsibility.

CRISIS MANAGEMENT RECOMMENDATIONS

A number of suggestions that corporations can follow to respond more effectively to crises are briefly summarized here. More in-depth strategies and tactics can be found in several sources.[20]

- Face the problem: don't avoid or minimize it; tell the truth.
- Take your "lumps" in one big news story rather than in bits and pieces; "no comment" answers imply guilt;
- Recognize that, in the age of instant news, no such thing as a secret or private crisis exists.
- Stage "war games" to observe how your crisis plan holds up under pressure. Train executives to practice press conferences, and train teams to respond to crises that may affect other functional areas or divisions.
- Use the firm's philosophy, motto, or mission statement to respond to a crisis; for example, "We believe in our customer. Service is our business."
- Use the firm's closeness to customers and end users for early feedback on the crisis and to evaluate your effectiveness in responding and addressing the events.

Finally, issues and crisis management methods and preventive techniques are effective in corporations only if[21]:

- Top management is supportive and participates.
- Involvement is cross-departmental.
- The issues management unit fits with the firm's culture.
- Output, instead of process, is the focus.

SUMMARY

Organizations and businesses in the 20th century increased in complexity and power. Because of the numerous economic and noneconomic transactions of corporations with different groups in the environment, a method is required to understand an organization's moral obligations and relationships to its constituencies.

The stakeholder approach provides an analytical method for determining how various constituencies affect and are affected by business activities. The stakeholder model also provides a means for assessing the power, legitimacy, and moral responsibility of managers' strategies in terms of how they meet the needs and obligations of various stakeholders.

CONSULTANTS
SPLIT ON
BRIDGESTONE'S
CRISIS
MANAGEMENT

Experts in crisis management criticized Bridgestone/Firestone for minimizing their tires' problems during the week of August 11. The experts gave the company mixed reviews on its handling of the recall of 6.5 million tires that involved 46 deaths and over 300 incidents involving tires that were allegedly shredded on the highway. The tire maker spokespersons blamed the poor treads on underinflation, improper maintenance, and poor road conditions.

Mark Braverman, principal of CMG Associates—a crisis-management firm in Newton, Mass.—noted that the company blamed the victim and that Bridgestone/Firestone lacked a visible leader for its crisis-management effort. "The CEO should be out there, not executive vice presidents."

Steve Fink, another crisis-management expert, noted, "After they [Bridgestone/Firestone] announced the recall, they were not prepared to deal with it. They were telling consumers they will have to wait up to a year to get tires. And things like busy telephone call lines and overloaded Web sites—these are things that can be anticipated. That's basic crisis management."

Stephen Greyser, professor of marketing and communications at Harvard Business School, stated, "It's about what they didn't do up to now. The fact that the company [Bridgestone/Firestone] is just stepping up to bat tells me they've never really had the consumer as the principal focus of their thinking."

Defending the way Bridgestone/Firestone handled the crisis was Dennis Gioia, professor of organizational behavior at Smeal College of Business Administration at Penn State University: "With hindsight, you can always accuse a company of being too slow, given the history of automotive recalls. Sometimes you can't take hasty action or you would be acting on every hint there's a problem. It can create hysteria."

DISCUSSION QUESTION

Who do you agree or disagree with among these crisis-management consultants? Explain.

SOURCE: "Consultants Split on Bridgestone's Crisis Management," *Wall Street Journal*, 11 August 2000, A6.

A stakeholder analysis is also a strategic management tool that allows firms to map and manage relationships with constituents in any given or projected situation. An individual or group is said to have a "stake" in a corporation if it possesses an interest, share, or claim in the outcome of that corporation's policies, procedures, or actions. A "stakeholder" is defined as an individual or group who can affect or be affected by the actions, policies, practices, or goals of the organization.

Recent studies (Key, 1999) have indicated that profits and stockholder approval may not be the most important driving forces behind management objectives.[22] Job enrichment, concern for employees, and personal well-being are also important objectives.

The implementation of a stakeholder analysis involves a series of steps designed to help a corporation understand the complex economic, political, and moral factors involved in its obligations toward constituencies.

The moral dimensions of managerial, functional, and area expert roles (such as marketing, research and development, manufacturing, public relations, and human resource management) also have a stakeholder perspective. The stakeholder approach can assist functional area managers in resolving difficulties from conflicts over individual rights and corporate objectives. This approach can help managers think through and chart morally responsible decisions in their work for the corporation and its stakeholders.

The use of the stakeholder analysis by an observer or third party is a means for understanding social responsibility issues between a firm and its constituencies. Ethical reasoning can also be analyzed relative to the stakeholder approach.

Issues and crisis management frameworks complement the stakeholder analysis. Understanding what the central issues are for a company and how the issues evolved over time can help explain the changes in stakes and stakeholders. Crisis frameworks help to predict and evaluate an organization's response to emergencies.

QUESTIONS

1. Describe the stakeholder analysis and its steps.
2. Define the term "stakeholder." Give examples of primary and secondary stakeholders.
3. What changes have occurred in the Information Age that have facilitated the need for a stakeholder approach?
4. What are some of the types of power that stakeholders can use to support their positions? Briefly explain these.
5. Describe one of the issues management approaches in the chapter. Explain how you would use it in a current, complex situation in the news or media.
6. Who are some of the principal stakeholders for area and functional managers in companies? Could teams use a stakeholder approach in their project or business environment? Explain.
7. What are the reasons for encouraging expert area and functional managers to use the stakeholder approach? Would these reasons apply to teams?
8. List six common questions and problems that arise when executing a stakeholder analysis.

9. Give a recent example of a corporation that had to manage a crisis in public confidence. Did the company spokesperson respond effectively or ineffectively to stakeholders regarding the crisis? What should the company have done differently in its handling of the crisis?

10. Using a framework from the chapter, identify a controversial societal issue and explain how it evolved and changed. Predict how the issue will evolve. Defend your prediction, using available evidence.

EXERCISES

1. Describe a situation in which you were a stakeholder. What was the issue? What were your stakes? Who were the other stakeholders? What was the outcome? Did you have a win-win resolution? If not, who won, who lost, and why?

2. Recall your personal work history. Who were your manager's most important stakeholders? What, in general, were your manager's major stakes in his or her particular position?

3. In your company, or one in which you have worked, what is the industry? The major external environments? Your product or service? Describe the major influences of each environment on your company (for example, on its competitiveness and ability to survive). Evaluate how well your company is managing its environments strategically, operationally, and technologically, as well as in relation to new and existing products and public reputation and image.

4. Choose one type of functional area manager described in the chapter. Describe a dilemma involving this manager, taken from a recent media report. Discuss how a stakeholder analysis could have helped or would help that manager work effectively with stakeholders.

5. Describe a recent crisis that involved a product. Which crisis management model best explains the crisis and management responses? Explain, using that model.

ETHICAL DILEMMA

WHO IS RESPONSIBLE TO WHOM?

Last year, I worked as a marketing manager in Belgium for a mid-sized engineering company. Total revenues for the company were $120 million. The company had recently gone public and, in two public offerings, had raised over $60 million dollars. The firm was organized into four distinct strategic business units, based on products. The group that I worked in was responsible for over $40 million in sales. We had manufacturing plants in four countries.

Our plant in Belgium manufactured a component that was used in several products, which produced $15 million in revenue. However, these products were old technology and were slowly being replaced in the industry. The overhead associated with the plant in Belgium was hurting the company financially, so they decided to sell the facility. The unions in Belgium are very strong and had approved the final sale agreement. After this sale, the work force was going to be reduced to half its size. Those who were laid off were not going to receive full severance pay, which in Belgium could take several years and then workers would receive only 80% of total payment—a drastic change from what is offered in the United States. I was surprised that our executives in the U.S. had stated that the sales agreement was more than fair—contrary to the union's position. A strike was imminent; the materials manager was told to stock 10 weeks of product.

My ethical dilemma started after the strike began. Originally, the company thought the strike would not last longer than a couple of days. Instead of causing a panic among our customers, management decided to withhold information on the strike from our customers and sales force. I could understand the delay in telling our customers, but to withhold information from our sales force was, I believed, unconscionable. Inevitably, our inside sales representatives became suspicious when they called the Belgium plant to get status on an order, and nobody answered. They called me, and I ignored the corporate request and informed them of the strike. When it became obvious that the strike was going to be longer than anticipated, I asked the vice presidents of marketing and sales about our strategy for informing the affected customers. They looked at me quizzically and told me to keep things quiet ("don't open a can of worms") because the strike should be over soon. In addition, they dictated that customer service should not inform customers of the strike and that excuses should be developed for late shipments.

The strike lasted longer than 12 weeks. In this time, we managed to shut down a production line at Lucent Technologies (a $5-million customer) with only a couple of days' notice and alienated countless other valuable and loyal customers. I did not adhere to the company policy: I informed customers about the strike when they inquired about their order status. I also told customer service to direct any customer calls to me when we were going to miss shipments. This absolved them of the responsibility to tell the customer.

We did not take a proactive stance until 11 weeks into the strike, when the vice president of sales sent a letter informing our customers about the strike—too little and much too late to be of any help. The materials manager was fired because he only stocked 10 weeks of product and management thought he should have been conservative with his estimates. Halfway through this ordeal, I updated my resume and started a search for a new job. It was clear that management was more concerned about their year-end bonus than doing the right thing for the long-term prospects of the company and its customers.

QUESTIONS

1. Do you agree with the writer's decision to inform customers about the strike? Explain.

2. Did management have the right to withhold this information from customers? Explain.

3. Explain what you would have done, and why, if had you been in the writer's situation.

4. What should management have done in this case? When? Why?

3

ETHICAL PRINCIPLES, QUICK TESTS, AND DECISION-MAKING GUIDELINES

3.1 DECISION CRITERIA FOR ETHICAL REASONING

Louise Simms, newly graduated with a master of business administration (MBA) degree, was hired by a prestigious multinational firm based in the United States and sent, with minimal training, to join a company partner to negotiate with a high-ranking Middle Eastern government official. The partner informed Simms that he would introduce her to the government contact and then leave her to "get the job done." Her assignment was to "do whatever it takes to win the contract: it's worth millions to us." The contract would enable Simms' firm to select and manage technology companies that would install a multi-million-dollar computer system for that government. While in the country, Simms was told by the representative government official that Simms' firm had "an excellent chance to get the contract" if the official's nephew, who owned and operated a computer company in that country, could be assured "a good piece of the action."

While discussing details on two different occasions, the official attempted unwelcomed advances toward Simms that offended her. He backed off both times whenever he observed her subtle negative responses. Simms was told that "the deal" would remain a confidential matter and closed by saying, "That's how we do business here; take it or leave it." Simms was frustrated about the terms of the deal and about the advances toward her. She called her superior in Chicago and informed him about the conditions of the deal. She urged the supervisor not to accept these conditions because of the questionable arrangements and also because of the disrespect shown toward her, which she said reflected on the company as well. Simms' supervisor responded, "Take the deal! And don't let your emotions get involved. You're in another culture. Go with the flow. Accept the offer and get the contract groundwork started. Use your best judgment on how to handle the details."

Simms couldn't sleep that night. She now had doubts about her supervisor's and the government administrator's ethics. She felt that she had conflicting priorities. This was her first job and a significant opportunity. At the same time, she had to live with herself.

Complex ethical dilemmas in business situations usually involve tough choices that must be made among conflicting and competing interests. Should Louise Simms move to close the lucrative deal or not? Is the official offering her a bribe? What other personal, as well as professional, obligations would she be committing herself to if she accepted? Is the official's request legal? Is it ethical? Is this a setup? If so, who is setting her up? Would Louise be held individually responsible if something went wrong? Who is going to protect her if legal complications arise? How is she supposed to negotiate such a deal? What message is she sending about herself as well as her company? What if she is asked to return and work with these people if the contract is signed? (She wasn't taught how to handle this in a management class.) What does Louise stand to win and lose if she does or does not accept the official's offer?

Finally, what *should* Louise do to act morally responsible in this situation? Is she acting only on behalf of her company or also from her own integrity and beliefs? What is the right action to take? These are the kinds of questions and issues this chapter addresses. No obvious or easy answers may exist, but understanding principles and guidelines, sharing ethical dilemmas and outcomes, discussing ethical and unethical experiences in depth, and using role-play to analyze situations can help you identify, think, and feel through the issues that underlie ethical dilemmas. Louise might refer to the "My Ethical Motives" assessment in the box on page 73 to gauge her own motives. Refer to this box to assess your ethical motives in general.

The Louise Simms scenario may be complicated by the international context. This is a good starting point for a chapter on ethics, because business transactions now increasingly involve international players, cultures, and different "rules of engagement." Chapter 7, on the global environment and stakeholder issues peculiar to multinational corporations, offers additional guidelines for solving dilemmas in international contexts. Deciding what is right and wrong about an action, policy, or procedure in an international context also involves understanding the laws, customs, and level of economic, social, and technological development of the nation or

MY ETHICAL MOTIVES	Complete the following steps:	moral decision making in this chapter. Describe and explain which principle best describes first your reasoning and then your action(s) in the dilemma you presented in Step 1.

STEP 1

Describe in writing an ethical dilemma that you recently experienced. Be detailed: What was the situation? Who did it involve? Why? What happened? What did you do? What did you *not* do? Describe your reasoning process in taking or not taking action. What did others do to you? What was the result?

STEP 2

Read the descriptions of relativism, utilitarianism, universalism, rights, justice, and

STEP 3

Were you conscious that you were reasoning and acting on these (or other) ethical principles before, during, and after your ethical dilemma? Explain.

STEP 4

After reading this chapter, would you have acted any differently in your dilemma than you did? Explain.

region involved, i.e., do European and U.S. standards of doing business and acting in other countries carry certain legal, cultural, or moral biases? Would these biases result in consequences that are beneficial or harmful to those affected in the local host culture? Answers to these questions may not be easy in specific situations. On the other hand, we should not easily accept stereotypical descriptions of how to do business by means of what may be considered "local customs" in international contexts. Is corruption legal in all Middle Eastern business transactions? Certainly not. In this regard, we may refer back to chapter 2 and distinguish between individual, company, national, and international levels of decision making when doing business internationally. For example, an individual company, owner, or group may have an ethic in doing business that is not legal or acceptable in their own country.

The aim here is to present ethical principles and thinking that can help you evaluate your own and others' moral responsibilities when resolving ethical dilemmas (Figure 3.1). The ethical dilemmas at the end of each chapter and the cases in the text provide opportunity for discussion, debate, role-play, and insight into your own principles and "ethics." Change begins with awareness.

The stakeholder analysis in Chapter 2 illustrated how to map and plan socially responsible strategies between corporate managers and external stakeholders. This chapter introduces and summarizes fundamental ethical principles and decision rules to use when making difficult moral decisions in complex business transactions. It intentionally *does* not offer exhaustive explanations of ethical principles or the philosophical reasoning underlying

FIGURE 3.1   INTENDED EFFECTS OF BUSINESS ETHICS EDUCATION ON STAKEHOLDER BELIEF SYSTEMS AND DECISIONS

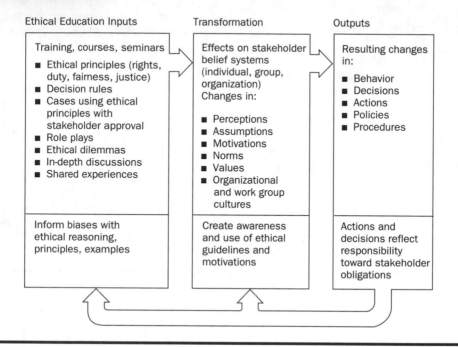

SOURCE: Copyright © Joseph W. Weiss, Bentley College, Waltham, MA, 2002.

these principles. Here our aim is to simplify and briefly present a summary of major ethical principles and guidelines that you can use in your personal and professional life and can apply in a stakeholder analysis framework, i.e., a decisional context that involves business settings. This section begins by presenting ethical reasoning at the individual level. The ethical reasoning processes, principles, and decision rules also are applicable at the corporate policy and group levels.

A first step in addressing ethical dilemmas is to identify the problem and related issues. This is particularly necessary for a stakeholder approach, because the problems and issues depend on who the stakeholders are and what their stakes entail. Before specific ethical principles are discussed, let's begin by considering important decision criteria for ethical reasoning. How would you, as you read these, apply the criteria to Louise Simms' situation?

Twelve questions, developed by Laura Nash,[1] to ask yourself during the decision-making period to help clarify ethical problems are:

1. Have you defined the problem accurately?
2. How would you define the problem if you stood on the other side of the fence?

3. How did this situation occur in the first place?

4. To whom and to what do you give your loyalty as a person and as a member of the corporation?

5. What is your intention in making this decision?

6. How does this intention compare with the probable results?

7. Who could your decision or action injure?

8. Can you discuss the problem with the affected parties before you make your decision?

9. Are you confident that your decision will be as valid over a long period as it seems now?

10. Could you disclose, without qualm, your decision or action to your boss, your chief executive officer, the board of directors, your family, or society as a whole?

11. What is the symbolic potential of your action if understood? If misunderstood?

12. Under what conditions would you allow exceptions to your stand?

These 12 questions can help individuals openly discuss the responsibilities necessary to solve ethical problems. Sharing these questions can facilitate group discussions, build cohesiveness and consensus around shared points, serve as an information source, uncover ethical inconsistencies in a company's values, help a CEO see how senior managers think, and increase the nature and range of choices. The discussion process is cathartic.

To return briefly to the opening case, if Louise Simms considered the first question, she might, for example, define the problem she faces from different levels or perspectives (as discussed in Chapter 1). At the *organizational* level, her firm stands to win a sizable contract if she accepts the government official's conditions. Yet her firm's image and reputation could be jeopardized in the United States if this deal turned out to be a scandal, a controversy arose among competitors, or the media covered the events in a critical way. At the *societal* level, the issues are complicated. In this Middle Eastern country, this type of bargaining might be acceptable. In the United States, however, Louise could have problems with the Foreign Corrupt Practices Act. Is this a bribe? And is she acting officially on behalf of her company or as an individual? At the *individual* level, she must decide if her values and conscience can tolerate the actions and consequences this deal involves. As a woman, she may be at risk, because advances were made toward her. Her self-esteem and integrity have also been jarred. She must consider the economic, political, social, and moral costs and benefits that she will incur from her company if she decides either to accept or reject this assignment. She must decide to whom her loyalty belongs in this situation, as a person and as an employee. Who could her decision potentially injure? Also, does her supervisor or the administrator have any of her interests in mind? As you can see, these questions can serve to help Louise clarify her goal of making a decision and the price she is or is not willing to pay for that decision.

THREE CRITERIA IN ETHICAL REASONING

The following criteria can be used in ethical reasoning. They help to systematize and structure our arguments[2]:

1. Moral reasoning must be logical. Assumptions and premises, both factual and inferred, used to make judgments should be known and made explicit.

2. Factual evidence cited to support a person's judgment should be accurate, relevant, and complete.

3. Ethical standards used in a person's reasoning should be consistent. When inconsistencies among a person's ethical standards in an argument or decision are discovered, one or more of the standards must be modified.

If Louise Simms were to use these three criteria, she would articulate the assumptions underlying her decision. If, for example, she chose to accept the government official's offer, she might reason that she assumed it was not a bribe, that if it were a bribe she assumed she would not get caught, and that even if she or her company did get caught, she would be willing to incur any penalty individually, including loss of her job. Moreover, Louise would want to obtain as many facts as she could about both the U.S. laws and the Middle Eastern country's laws on negotiating practices such as the one she will accept. She also would gather information from her employer and check the accuracy of the information against her decision.

She would have to be consistent in her standards. If she chooses to accept the foreign official's conditions, she must be willing to accept additional contingencies consistent with those conditions. She would not, for example, midway through helping the official's nephew obtain part of the contract, suddenly decide that these actions were "unethical" and then back out. She must think through these contingencies *before* she makes a decision.

Finally, a simple but powerful question can be used throughout your decision-making process in solving ethical dilemmas: "What is my motivation for choosing a course of action?" Examining individual motives and separating these from the known motivations of others provides clarity and perspective. Louise, for example, might ask, "Why did I agree to negotiate with the official on his terms? Was it for money? To keep my job? To impress my boss? For adventure?" She also might ask whether her stated motivation from the outset would carry her commitments through the entire contracting process.

MORAL RESPONSIBILITY

A major aim of ethical reasoning is to gain a clearer and sharper logical focus on problems to facilitate acting in morally responsible ways.

Individuals are morally responsible for the harmful effects of their actions when *(1) they knowingly and freely acted or caused the act to happen and knew that the act was morally wrong or hurtful to others,* and *(2) they knowingly and freely failed to act or prevent a harmful act and they knew it would be morally wrong for a person do this.*[3] Although no universal definition of what constitutes a morally wrong act exists in absolute terms, an act and the consequences of an act can be defined as morally wrong if physical or emotional harm or damage is done to another as a result of the act. The degree of harm and the two conditions previously stated must also be considered.

Two conditions that eliminate a person's moral responsibility for causing injury or harm are *ignorance* and *inability.*[4] Persons, however, who intentionally prevent themselves from understanding or knowing that a harmful action will occur are still responsible. Persons who negligently fail to inform themselves about a potentially harmful matter may still be responsible for the resultant action. Of course, some mitigating circumstances can excuse or lessen a person's moral responsibility in a situation. These include circumstances that show: *(1) a low level of or lack of seriousness to cause harm, (2) uncertainty about knowledge of wrongdoing,* and *(3) the degree to which a harmful injury was caused or averted.* As we know from court trials, proving intent or motive for an alleged illegal act is not an easy matter. Similarly, the extent to which a person is morally irresponsible for complicated harmful actions can be difficult to determine. For example, did Bill Gates knowingly try to set up a monopoly against some of his competitors and alliance partners? Are tobacco executives morally responsible for the deaths cigarette smoking causes to chronic smokers? What principles and standards can we, as well as judges and juries, use to establish moral responsibility for ourselves and others?

In the following sections, five fundamental ethical principles (illustrated in Figure 3.2) that can be used in our ethical reasoning for choosing particular alternatives and justifying difficult decisions and actions are explained and discussed. The principles are: (1) relativism, (2) utilitarianism, (3) universalism, (4) rights, and (5) justice. In addition, four social responsibility modes and four individual styles of ethical reasoning are presented. Finally, some "quick ethical tests" are provided, which you may use to clarify ethical dilemmas.

The intent here is to inform and develop your ethical thinking and decision making by presenting guidelines that you may use to reason through examples of your own actions with others, in order to see and clarify your assumptions. By using this system, your resultant decisions, actions, and policies may better reflect fairness, justice, and responsibility toward those you serve and your own interests. While reading the following sections, think of different stakeholders and situations where individuals, students, managers, owners, suppliers, competitors, government regulators, and interest groups might apply these principles to their actions.

3.2 ETHICAL RELATIVISM: A SELF-INTEREST APPROACH

Ethical relativism holds that no universal standards or rules can be used to guide or evaluate the morality of an act, i.e., what is right for you may be wrong for me. This view argues that people set their own moral standards for judging their actions. Only the individual's self-interest and values are relevant for judging his or her behavior. This form of relativism is also referred to as *naive relativism.*

If Louise Simms were to adopt the principle of ethical relativism for her decision making, she might, for example, choose to accept the government official's offer to promote her own standing in his firm. She might reason that her self-interests would be served best by making any deal that would push her career ahead. But Simms also could use ethical relativism to justify her rejection of the offer. She might say that any possible form of such a questionable negotiation is against her beliefs. The point behind this principle is that individual standards are the basis of moral authority.

The logic of ethical relativism also extends to cultures. *Cultural relativism,* as the position is called, argues that "when in Rome, do as the Romans do." What is morally right for one society or culture may be wrong for another. Moral standards vary from one culture's customs, belief systems, and value structure to another. Cultural relativists would argue that firms and business professionals doing business in a country are obliged to follow that country's laws and moral codes. A criterion that relativists would use to justify their actions would be: "Are my beliefs, moral standards, and customs satisfied with this action or outcome?"

The benefit of ethical and cultural relativism is that they recognize the distinction between individual and social values, customs, and moral standards. These views take seriously the conscientiousness and unique belief systems of individuals and societies. Social norms and mores are seen in a cultural context.

However, ethical and cultural relativism lead to several problems. First, these views imply an underlying laziness.[5] Individuals who justify their morality only from their personal beliefs, without taking into consideration other ethical principles, may use the logic of relativism as an excuse for not having or developing moral standards that can be argued and tested against other claims, opinions, and standards. Second, this view contradicts everyday experience. Moral reasoning is developed from conversation, interaction, and argument. What I believe or perceive as "facts" in a situation may or may not be accurate. How can I validate or disprove my ethical reasoning and moral judgments if I do not communicate, share, and remain open to changing my own standards? Third, ethical relativists can become absolutists, i.e., individuals who claim their moral standards are right—regardless of whether others view the standards as right or wrong—can become closed to outside influence and accept only their beliefs as true. For example: What if my beliefs conflict with yours? Whose relativism is right then? Who decides and on what grounds? In practice, ethical relativism does not effectively or efficiently solve complicated conflicts that involve many parties, because these situations require tolerating doubts and permitting our observations and beliefs to be informed.

Cultural relativism embodies the same problems as ethical relativism. Although the values and moral customs of all cultures should be observed and respected, especially because business professionals are increasingly operating across national boundaries, we must not be lazy or blindly absolute or divorce ourselves from rigorous moral reasoning or laws aimed at protecting individual rights and justice. For example, R. Edward Freeman and Daniel Gilbert Jr. ask, "Must American managers in Saudi Arabia treat women as the Saudis treat them? Must American managers in South Africa treat blacks as white South Africans treat them? Must white South Africans treat blacks in the U.S. as U.S. managers treat them? Must Saudis in the U.S. treat women as U.S. managers treat them?"[6] They continue, "It makes sense to question whether or not the norms of the Nazi society were in fact morally correct."[7] Using rigorous ethical reasoning to solve moral dilemmas is important across cultures.

However, this does not suggest that flexibility, sensitivity, and awareness of individual and cultural moral differences are not necessary; they are. It does mean that upholding principles of rights, justice, and freedom in some situations may conflict with the other person's or culture's belief systems and standards. Depending on the actions taken and decisions made from a person's moral standards, a price may have to be paid for maintaining those moral, and sometimes legal, standards. Often, negotiation agreements and understanding can be reached without overt conflict when different ethical principles or cultural standards clash.

Finally, it could be argued that cultural relativism does provide an argument against cultural imperialism. Why should American laws, customs, and values that are embedded in a U.S. firm's policies be enforced in another country that has opposing, differing, or no laws and values regarding the activities in question?

ETHICAL RELATIVISM AND STAKEHOLDER ANALYSIS

When considering the principles of relativism in a stakeholder analysis, ask the following questions:

1. What are the major moral beliefs and principles at issue for each stakeholder affected by this decision?
2. What are my moral beliefs and principles in this decision?
3. To what extent will my ethical principles clash if a particular course of action is taken? Why?
4. How can conflicting moral beliefs and principles be avoided or resolved in seeking a desirable outcome?

3.3 UTILITARIANISM: A CONSEQUENTIALIST (RESULTS-BASED) APPROACH

Jeremy Bentham (1748–1832) and John Stuart Mill (1806–1873) are acknowledged as founders of the concept of *utilitarianism*. Although various interpretations of the concept exist, the basic utilitarian view holds that an action is judged as right, good, or wrong on the basis of its consequences. The ends of an action justify the means taken to reach those ends. As a *consequentialist principle*, the moral authority that drives utilitarianism is the calculated *consequences*, or results, of an action, regardless of other principles that determine the means or motivations for taking the action. Utilitarianism also includes the following tenets[8]:

1. An action is morally right if it produces the greatest good for the greatest number of people affected by it.

2. An action is morally right if the net benefits over costs are greatest for all affected compared with the net benefits of all other possible choices considered.

3. An action is morally right if its immediate and future direct and indirect benefits are greatest for each individual and if these benefits outweigh the costs and benefits of the other alternatives.

Utilitarian concepts are widely practiced by government policy makers, economists, and business professionals. Utilitarianism is a useful principle for conducting a stakeholder analysis, since it forces decision makers to (1) consider collective as well as particular interests, (2) formulate alternatives based on the greatest good for all parties involved in a decision, and (3) estimate the costs and benefits of alternatives for the affected groups.[9]

Louise Simms of our example would use utilitarian principles in her decision making by identifying each of the stakeholders and groups who would be affected by her decision. She then would calculate the costs and benefits of her decision as it affects each group. Finally, she would decide a course of action based on the greatest good for the greatest number. For example, after identifying all the stakeholders in her decision, including her own interests, Simms might believe that her firms' capabilities were not competitive and may estimate that rejecting the official's offer would produce the greatest good for the people of the country where the contract would be negotiated, because obtaining bids from the most technically qualified companies would best serve the interests of those receiving the services.

Problems with utilitarianism include the following:

1. No agreement exists about the definition of the "good" that is to be maximized for all concerned in the situation. Is it truth, health, peace, profits, pleasure, cost reductions, or national security?[10]

2. No agreement exists about who decides. Who decides what is good for whom? Whose interests are primary in the decisions?

3. The rightness or wrongness of the actions themselves are not judged, but rather their consequences. What if some actions are simply wrong? Should decision makers proceed to take those actions based only on their consequences?

4. How are the costs and benefits of nonmonetary stakes, such as health, safety, and public welfare, measured? Should a monetary value be assigned to nonmarketed benefits and costs, such as safety, health, and the environment?[11] What if the actual or even potentially harmful effects of an action cannot be measured in the short term, but the action is believed to have potentially long-term effects, say in 20 or 30 years? Should that action be chosen?

5. Utilitarianism as a principle does not consider the individual. It is the collective, the aggregate, for whom the greatest good is estimated. Do instances exist when individuals and their interests should be valued in a decision?

6. The principles of justice and rights are ignored in utilitarianism. The principle of justice is concerned with the distribution of good, not the amount of total good in a decision. The principle of rights is concerned with individual entitlements, regardless of the collective calculated benefits.

Even given these problems, the principle of utilitarianism is still valuable under the some conditions: when resources are fixed, lacking, or scarce; when priorities are in conflict; when no clear choice fulfills everyone's needs and goals; and when large or diverse collectives are involved in a zero-sum decision, i.e., when a gain for some corresponds to a loss for others.[12]

UTILITARIANISM AND STAKEHOLDER ANALYSIS

Because businesses use utilitarian principles when conducting a stakeholder analysis, you, as a decision maker, should:

1. Define how costs and benefits will be measured in selecting one course of action over another. Include social, economic, and monetary costs and benefits as well as long-term and short-term costs and benefits.

2. Define what information you will need to determine the costs and benefits for comparisons.

3. Identify the procedures and policies you will use to explain and justify your cost-benefit analysis.

4. State your assumptions when defining and justifying your analysis and conclusions.

5. Ask yourself what moral obligations you have toward each of your stakeholders, after the costs and benefits have been estimated for particular strategies.

3.4 UNIVERSALISM: A DEONOTOLOGICAL (DUTY-BASED) APPROACH

Immanuel Kant (1724–1804) is considered one of the leading founders of the principle of *universalism*. Universalism, which is also called "deontological ethics," holds that the means justify the ends of an action, not the consequences. Universalism, therefore, is also referred to as a *nonconsequentialist* ethic. The term "deontology" is derived from the Greek word *deon*, or duty. Regardless of consequences, this approach is based on universal principles, such as justice, rights, fairness, honesty, and respect.

Kant's principle of the *categorical imperative*, unlike utilitarianism, places the moral authority for taking an action on an individual's duty toward other individuals and humanity. The categorical imperative consists of two parts. The first part states that *a person should choose to act if and only if she or he would be willing to have every person on earth, in that same situation, act exactly that way*. This principle is absolute and allows for no qualifications across situations or circumstances. The second part of the categorical imperative states that, in an ethical dilemma, *a person should act in a way that respects and treats all others involved as ends as well as means to an end*.

Kant's categorical imperative forces decision makers to take into account their duty to act responsibly and respectfully toward all individuals in a situation. Individual human welfare is a primary stake in any decision. Decision makers also must consider formulating their justifications and reasons as principles to be applied to everyone.

In Louise Simms' situation, if she followed deontological principles of universalism, she might ask, "If I accept the government official's offer, could I justify that anyone anywhere would act the same way?" Or, "Since I value my own self-respect and believe my duty is to uphold self-respect for others, I will not accept this assignment because my self-respect has been and may again be violated by these individuals."

The major weaknesses of universalism and Kant's categorical imperative specifically include these criticisms: First, these principles are imprecise and lack practical utility. It is difficult to think of all humanity each time one must make a decision in an ethical dilemma. Second, it is hard to resolve conflicts of interest when using a criterion that states that all individuals must be treated equally. Degrees of differences in stakeholders' interests and relative power exist in certain situations. However, Kant would remind us that the human being and his or her humanity must be considered above the stakes, power bases, or consequences of our actions. Still, it is often impractical not to consider these other elements in a dilemma. Finally, what if a decision maker's duties conflict in an ethical dilemma? The categorical imperative does not allow for prioritizing one's duties. A primary purpose of the stakeholder analysis is to prioritize conflicting duties—toward competitors, customers, employees, suppliers, owners, the media, and the public. It is, again, difficult to take absolute positions when limited resources and time and conflicting values are factors in ethical dilemmas. For more about Kant's ideas, see *Groundwork for the Metaphysics of Morals* (1964, Harper and Row, translated by H. J. Paton).

UNIVERSALISM AND STAKEHOLDER ANALYSIS

The logic underlying universalism and the categorical imperative can be helpful for applying a stakeholder analysis. Even though we may not be able to employ Kant's principles absolutely, we can consider the following as guidelines for using his ethics:

1. Identify individuals as well as groups and their welfare and risks when considering policy decisions and outcomes.

2. Identify the needs of individuals involved in a decision, the choices they have, and the information they need to protect their own welfare.

3. Identify any manipulation, force, coercion, or deceit that might harm individuals involved in a decision.

4. Recognize the duties of respecting and responding to individuals affected by particular decisions before adopting policies and actions that affect them.

5. Ask if the desired action or policy would be acceptable to the individuals involved if they were informed of the policy intentions. Under what conditions would they accept the decision?

6. Ask if individuals in a similar situation would acceptably repeat the designated action or policy as a principle. If not, why not? And would they continue to employ the designated action?

3.5 RIGHTS: AN ENTITLEMENT-BASED APPROACH

The moral authority that drives the ethics of the principle of *rights* is entitlement. Individual rights mean entitlements and unquestionable claims. Every U.S. citizen is guaranteed, in the Declaration of Independence, the right to life, liberty, and the pursuit of happiness. The U.S. Constitution also holds that each citizen is guaranteed certain fundamental rights. These rights are given legality by the U.S. system of legislation and justice. The principle of rights is one of the most powerful concepts that enables and protects individual freedom, dignity, and choice. This principle is the cornerstone of American democracy.

Moral rights are based on legal rights and the principle of duty. My moral right implies that you have certain duties toward aiding—or at least not obstructing—my rights. Moral rights are also based on and viewed from an *individual* perspective, rather than a societal or group point of view. Individual freedom, welfare, safety, health, and happiness are the essential core values of moral rights. Chapter 6 deals with the rights of employees and employers in the workplace.

Rights also can override utilitarian principles. Many times, violations of rights are solved by the criterion of whose rights have precedence in a given situation. Lawsuits are won and lost on the principle of individual rights not being upheld or protected.

Louise Simms might ask what her rights are in her situation. If she believes that her constitutional and moral rights would be violated by accepting the offer or by her firm's pressuring her to accept the offer, she would consider refusing to negotiate on the foreign official's terms.

The limitations of the principle of rights include the following:

1. The entitlement justification of individual rights can be used by certain individuals and groups to disguise and manipulate selfish, unjust political claims and interests.

2. Protection of rights can exaggerate certain entitlements in society at the expense of others. Fairness and equity issues may be raised when rights of certain individuals and groups take precedence over the rights of others in similar situations. Issues of reverse discrimination, for example, have arisen from this reasoning.

3. The limits of rights come into question. To what extent should industrial and governmental practices that may benefit the entire society, but threaten certain individual or group rights, be permitted to occur?

RIGHTS AND STAKEHOLDER ANALYSIS

The principle of rights is particularly useful in a stakeholder analysis when conflicting legal or moral rights of individuals occur or when individual and group rights may be violated if certain courses of action are pursued. The following are guidelines for observing this principle[13]:

1. Identify the individuals who and the rights that may be violated by a particular policy or course of action.

2. Determine the legal and moral bases of these individuals' rights. Does the decision violate these rights on such bases?

3. Determine to what extent the action to be taken has moral justification from utilitarian principles if individual rights may be violated. National crises and emergencies may warrant overriding certain individual rights for the public good.

3.6 JUSTICE: PROCEDURES, COMPENSATION, RETRIBUTION

The principle of *justice* deals with fairness and equality. Here, the moral authority that decides what is right and wrong concerns the fair distribution of opportunities, as well as of hardships or burdens, to all. The principle of justice also pertains to punishment for wrong done to the undeserving. John Rawls (1971), a contemporary philosopher, offers two principles of fairness that are widely recognized as representative of the principle of justice[14]:

1. Each person has an equal right to the most extensive basic liberties that are compatible with similar liberties for others.

2. Social and economic inequalities are arranged so that they are both (a) reasonably expected to be to everyone's advantage and (b) attached to positions and offices open to all.

The first principle states that all individuals should be treated equally. The second principle states that justice is served when all persons have equal opportunities and advantages (through their positions and offices) to society's opportunities and burdens. Equal opportunity or access to opportunity does not guarantee equal distribution of wealth. Society's disadvantaged may not be justly treated, some critics claim, when *only* equal opportunity is offered. The principle of justice also addresses the unfair distribution of wealth and the infliction of harm.

Richard DeGeorge identifies four types of justice:[15]

1. *Compensatory justice* concerns compensating someone for a past harm or injustice. For example, affirmative action programs, discussed in Chapter 6, are justified, in part, as compensation for decades of injustice and injury that minorities have suffered.

2. *Retributive justice* means serving punishment to someone who has inflicted harm on another. A criterion for applying this justice principle is: "Does the punishment fit the crime?"

3. *Distributive justice* refers to the fair distribution of benefits and burdens. Have certain stakeholders received an unfair share of costs accompanying a policy or action? Have others unfairly profited from a policy?

4. *Procedural justice* designates fair decision practices, procedures, and agreements among parties. This criterion asks, "Have the rules and processes that govern the distribution of rewards, punishments, benefits, and costs been fair?"

These four types of justice are part of the larger principle of justice. How they are formulated and applied varies with societies and governmental systems.

Following the principle of justice, Louise Simms might ask whether accepting the government official's offer would provide a fair distribution of goods and services to the recipients of the new technological system to be implemented in that country. Also, are the conditions demanded by the government administrator fair for all parties concerned? If Simms determined that justice would not be served by enabling her company to be awarded the contract without a fair bidding process, she might well recommend that her firm reject the offer.

The obvious practical problems of using the principle of justice include the following: Outside the jurisdiction of the state and its legal judicial systems, where ethical dilemmas are solved by procedure and law, who decides who is right and who is wrong? Who has the moral authority to punish whom? Can opportunities and burdens be fairly distributed to all, when it is not in the interest of those in power to do so?

Even with these shortcomings, the principle of justice adds an essential and unique contribution to the other ethical principles discussed so far. Beyond the utilitarian's calculation of moral responsibility based on consequences, beyond the universalist's absolute duty to treat everyone as a means and not an end, and beyond the principle of rights, which values unquestionable claims, the principle of justice forces us to ask how fairly benefits and costs are distributed to everyone, regardless of power, position, wealth, and station in life.

RIGHTS, POWER, AND "TRANSFORMING JUSTICE"

Justice, rights, and power are really interwined. Rights plus power equals "transforming justice." T. McMahon states, "While natural rights are the basis for justice, rights cannot be realized nor justice become operative without power."[16] Judges and juries exercise power when two opposing parties, both of whom are "right," seek justice from the courts.

Power generally is defined and exercised through inheritance, authority, contracts, competition, manipulation, and force. Power exercised through manipulation cannot be used to obtain justice legitimately. The two steps in exercising "transforming justice" are:

1. Be aware of your rights and power. McMahon states, "It is important to determine what rights and how much legitimate power is necessary to exercise these rights without trampling on other rights. For example, an employer might have the rights and power to fire an insolent employee, but she or he might not have enough to challenge union regulations."[17]

2. Establish legitimate power as a means for obtaining and establishing rights. According to McMahon, "If the legitimacy of transforming justice cannot be established, its exercise may then be reduced to spurious power plays to get what someone wants, rather than a means of fulfilling fights."[18]

This interrelationship of rights, justice, and power is particularly helpful in studying stakeholder management relationships. Since stakeholders exercise power to implement their interests through strategies, the concept of "rights plus power equals transforming justice" adds value in determining justice (procedural, compensatory, and retributive). The question of justice in complex, competitive situations becomes not only "Whose rights are more right?" but also "By what means and end was power exercised?"

JUSTICE AND STAKEHOLDER ANALYSIS

In a stakeholder analysis, the principle of justice can be applied with these questions:

1. How equitable will the distribution of benefits and costs, pleasure and pain, and reward and punishment be among stakeholders if you pursue a particular course of action? Would all stakeholders' self-respect be acknowledged?

2. How clearly have the procedures for distributing the costs and benefits of a course of action or policy been defined and communicated? How fair are these procedures to all affected?

3. What provisions can we make to compensate those who will be unfairly affected by the costs of the decision? What provisions can we make to redistribute benefits among those who have been unfairly or overly compensated by the decision?

Figure 3.2 summarizes the ethical principles presented here. This figure can be used as a reference for applying these principles individually and in a stakeholder analysis with groups.

3.7 IMMORAL, AMORAL, AND MORAL MANAGEMENT

It is possible for owners, managers, and individual stakeholders to relate to their constituencies from at least three broad orientations: immorality, amorality, and morality. *Immoral treatment* of constituencies signifies a minimally ethical, or unethical, approach, such as laying off employees without fair notice or compensation, offering upper-level management undeserved salary increases and perks, and giving "golden parachutes" (attractive payments or settlement contracts to selected employees) when a change in company ownership or control is negotiated (such payments are often made at the expense of shareholders' dividends without their knowledge or consent). Managing immorally means intentionally going against the ethical principles of justice and fair and equitable treatment of other stakeholders.

Amoral management happens when owners, supervisors, and managers treat shareholders, outside stakeholders, and employees negligently or unintentionally, without concern or care for the consequences of their policies or actions. No willful wrong may be intended, but neither is thought given to moral behavior or outcomes. Minimal actions are taken while setting policies that are solely profit-oriented, production-centered, or short-term. Employees and other stakeholders are viewed as instruments for executing the economic interests of the firm. Strategies, control systems, leadership style, and interactions in such organizations also reflect an amoral, minimalist

FIGURE 3.2	SUMMARY OF FIVE ETHICAL DECISION-MAKING PRINCIPLES AND STAKEHOLDER ANALYSIS

Belief Systems	Source of Moral Activity	Stakeholder Analysis Issues
Ethical Relativism (Self-Interest)	Moral authority is determined by individual or cultural self-interests, customs, and religious principles. An act is morally right if it serves one's self-interests and needs.	1. What are the moral beliefs and principles of the individual(s)? 2. If a particular action or policy is chosen, to what extent will ethical principles clash? 3. While seeking a mutually desirable outcome, how can conflicting moral beliefs and principles be avoided or negotiated?
Utilitarianism (Calculation of Costs and Benefits)	Moral authority is determined by the consequences of an act: An act is morally right if the net benefits over costs are greatest for the majority. Also, the greatest good for the greatest number must result from this act.	1. Consider collective as well as particular interests. 2. Formulate alternatives based on the greatest good for all parties involved. 3. Estimate costs and benefits of alternatives for groups affected.
Universalism (Duty)	Moral authority is determined by the extent the intention of an act treats all persons with respect. Includes the requirement that everyone would act this way in the same circumstances.	1. Identify individuals whose needs and welfare are at risk with a given policy or decision. 2. Identify the use or misuse of manipulation, force, coercion, or deceit that may be harmful to individuals. 3. Identify duties to individuals affected by the decision. 4. Determine if the desired action or policy would be acceptable to individuals if the decision were implemented.
Rights (Individual Entitlement)	Moral authority is determined by individual rights guaranteed to all in their pursuit of freedom of speech, choice, happiness, and self-respect.	1. Identify individuals and their rights that may be violated by a particular action. 2. Determine the legal and moral basis of these individual rights. 3. Determine the moral justification from utilitarian principles if individuals' rights are violated.
Justice (Fairness and Equity)	Moral authority is determined by the extent opportunities, wealth, and burdens are fairly distributed among all.	1. If a particular action is chosen, how equally will costs and benefits be distributed to stakeholders? 2. How clear and fair are the procedures for distributing the costs and benefits of the decision? 3. How can those who are unfairly affected by the action be compensated?

SOURCE: Copyright © Joseph W. Weiss, Bentley College, Waltham, MA, 2001.

approach toward stakeholders. Nevertheless, the consequences of unintentional amoral actions are real for the persons affected. Harm is done.

Moral management by owners, upper-level executives, supervisors, and employees places value on equitable, fair, and just concern and treatment of shareholders, employees, customers, and other stakeholders. Ethics codes are established, communicated, and included in training; employee rights are built into visible policies that are enforced; and employees and other stakeholders are treated with respect and trust. The firm's corporate strategy, control and incentive systems, leadership style, and interactions reflect a morally managed organization. Moral management is the preferred mode of acting toward stakeholders, since respect, justice, and fairness are considered in the decisions.

It is helpful to consider these three orientations while observing managers, owners, employees, and coworkers. Have you seen amoral policies, procedures, and decisions in organizations? The next section summarizes four social responsibility roles (see Figure 3.3) that business executives historically have characterized and presently view as moral for decision makers. The model presented complements the five ethical principles by providing a broader orientation for describing individual ethical orientations toward business decisions. You may want to use the following framework to characterize your own moral and responsible roles, those of your boss and colleagues, and even those of contemporary international figures in government or business.

3.8 FOUR SOCIAL RESPONSIBILITY ROLES

What social obligations do businesses and their executives have toward their stockholders and society? The traditional view that the responsibility of corporate owners and managers was to serve only, or primarily, their stockholders' interests has been challenged and modified—but not abandoned—since the turn of this century. The debate continues over whether the roles of businesses and managers include serving social stakeholders along with economic stockholders. Because of changing demographic and educational characteristics of the workplace and the advent of laws, policies, and procedures that recognize greater awareness of employee and other stakeholders' rights, distinctions have been made about the responsibility of the business to its employees and to the larger society.

Four ethical interpretations of the social roles and modes of decision making are discussed and illustrated in Figure 3.3. The four social responsibility modes reflect business roles toward stockholders and a wider audience of stakeholders.[20]

Figure 3.3 illustrates two distinct social responsibility orientations of businesses and managers toward society: the *stockholder model* (the primary

FIGURE 3.3	FOUR SOCIAL RESPONSIBILITY MODES AND ROLES

ORIENTATIONS

		Stockholder Model	Stakeholder Model
MOTIVES	Self-Interest	1 Productivism	2 Progressivism
	Moral Duty	3 Philanthropy	4 Ethical Idealism

SOURCE: Anthony F. Buono and Lawrence T. Nichols. 1990. Stockholders and stakeholder interpretations of business' social rule. In *Business ethics: Readings and cases in corporate morality,* 2d ed., edited by W. Michael Hoffman and Jennifer Moore. New York: McGraw-Hill, 172. Reproduced with permission of Anthony F. Buono.

responsibility of the corporation to its economic stockholders) and the *stakeholder model* (the responsibility of the corporation to its social stakeholders outside the corporation). The two sets of motives underlying these two orientations are "self-interest" and "moral duty."

The stockholder self-interest (box 1 in Figure 3.3) and moral duty (box 3) orientations are discussed first, followed by the stakeholder self-interest (box 2) and moral duty (box 4) orientations. The two stockholder orientations are *productivism* and *philanthropy.*

Productivists (who hold a free-market ethic) view the corporation's social responsibility in terms of rational self-interest and the direct fulfillment of stockholder interests. The free market values the basis of rewards and punishments in the organization. This ethic drives internal and external vision, mission, values, policies, and decisions—including salaries, promotion, and demotions. Productivists believe the major—and, some would say, only—mission of business is to obtain profit. The free market is the best guarantee of moral corporate conduct in this view. Supply-side economists as productivists, for example, argue that the private sector is the vehicle for social improvement. Tax reduction and economic incentives that boost private industry are policies that productivists advocate as socially responsible. Ronald Reagan's "trickle-down" economic policies, i.e., seeking social benefits from private-sector wealth, are a recent example of this view. The economist Milton Friedman is a productivist.

A free-market-based ethic is widely used by owners and managers who must make tough workplace decisions on such questions as: (1) How many and which people are to be laid off because of a market downturn and significantly lowered profits? (2) What constitutes fair notice and compensation to employees who are to be terminated from employment? and (3) How can employees be disciplined fairly in situations in which people's rights have been violated? A company has entitlement to private property rights and responsibilities to shareholders. Robert Nozick, a Libertarian philosopher, is an advocate of a market-based ethic. He makes his case for a market-based principle of justice and entitlement in his book *Anarchy, State, and Utopia* (New York: Basic Books, 1974). Opponents to the market-based ethic argue that the rights of less-advantaged people also count, that property rights are not absolute in all situations, that there are times when the state can be justified in protecting the rights of others in disputes against property owners, and that the distribution of justice depends on the conditions of a situation—if war, illegal entry, fraud, or theft occur, some form of redistribution of wealth can be justified.[20]

Philanthropists, who also have a stockholder view of the corporation, hold that social responsibility is justified in terms of a moral duty toward helping less-advantaged members of society through organized, tax-deductible charity and *stewardship.* Proponents of this view believe that the primary social role or mission of the corporation is still to obtain profits. However, moral duty drives their motives instead of self-interest solely (the productivist view). Advocates of this view are stewards and believe that those who have wealth ought to share some of it with less-advantaged people. As stockholder stewards, philanthropists share profits primarily through their tax-deductible activities. Ted Turner has become a philanthropist: He is contributing $1 billion to the United Nations to offer medical assistance to children internationally.

Progressivism and *ethical idealism* are the two social-responsibility modes in the stakeholder model, the other dominant orientation. *Progressivists* believe corporate behavior is justified from a motive of self-interest, but they also hold that corporations should take a broader view of responsibility toward social change. Enlightened self-interest is a value that characterizes progressivists. Rheinhold Niebuhr, the famous Christian theologian, was a modern example of a progressivist who argued for the involvement of the church in politics to bring about reasoned, orderly reform. He also worked with unions and other groups to improve workers' job conditions and wages. Progressivists support policies such as affirmative action, environmental protection, employee stock option programs (ESOPs), and energy conservation. Did Ben and Jerry's follow a progressivist philosophy for their formerly independent company?

Finally, *ethical idealists* believe that social responsibility is justified when corporate behavior directly supports stakeholder interests from moral duty motives. Ethical idealists, such as Ralph Nader, hold that, to be fully responsible, corporate activity should help transform businesses into institutions where workers can realize their full human potential. Employee ownership, cooperatives, and community-based and community-owned service industries are examples of the type of corporate transformation that ethical idealists advocate. The boundaries between business and society are fluid for ethical idealists. Corporate profits are to be shared for humanitarian purposes—to help bring about a more humane society.

Of course, a spectrum of beliefs exists for each of these four responsibility modes. For example, a variety of ethical idealists profess different visions and programs regarding the obligations of business to society. Some are more radical than others in orientation. One group of ethical idealists calls for the transformation of society to redistribute wealth.

Which orientation best characterizes your current beliefs of business responsibility toward society: productivism, philanthropy, progressivism, or ethical idealism?

3.9 INDIVIDUAL ETHICAL DECISION-MAKING STYLES

In addition to the four social responsibility modes, researchers have defined ethical styles. Stanley Krolick developed a survey that interprets individual primary and secondary ethical decision-making styles.[21] The four styles he found are (1) individualism, (2) altruism, (3) pragmatism, and (4) idealism. These four styles are summarized here to complement the social responsibility modes and the ethical principles we have discussed. Caution must be used when considering any of these schemes to avoid labeling or stereotyping oneself or others. These categories are, at best, guides for further reflection, discussion, and study.

Individualists are driven by natural reason, personal survival, and preservation. The self is the source and justification of all actions and decisions. Individualists believe that "If I don't take care of my own needs, I will never be able to address the concerns of others."[22] The moral authority of individualists is their own reasoning process, based on self-interest. Individualism is related to the principle of naive ethical relativism and to productivism.

Altruists are concerned primarily with other people. Altruists relinquish their own personal security for the good of others. They would, as an extreme, like to ensure the future of the human race. The altruist's moral authority and motivation is to produce the greatest good for the largest number of people. Unlike utilitarians, altruists would not diligently calculate and measure costs and benefits. Providing benefits is their major concern. Altruists justify their actions by upholding the integrity of the community. They enter relationships from a desire to contribute to the common good and to humankind. Altruists are akin to universalists and philanthropists.

Pragmatists are concerned primarily with the situation at hand, not with the self or the other. The pragmatist's bases for moral authority and motivation are the perceived needs of the moment and the potential consequences of a decision in a specific context. The needs of the moment dictate the importance of self-interest, concern for others, rules, and values. Facts and situational information are justifications for the pragmatist's actions. Pragmatists may abandon significant principles and values to produce certain results. They are closest philosophically to utilitarians. Although this style

> ## THE ORGANIZATION GAME

Instructions: Read the following description of the game. Write or type out your working agreement. Then proceed to address the questions.

Assume that you are self-interested in the sense that you are interested in your own welfare, although not necessarily to the exclusion of interest in the welfare of others. Assume that you do not know your age, race, nationality, religion, abilities, or educational background. Assume that you do know that you are not presently employed but will be employed by an entirely new organization that designs, produces, and markets some high-tech product. You also know certain "goods" that you hope to achieve through your employment at the firm. These include security, adequate compensation, safe working conditions, and opportunity for advancement and personal growth. Your task is to devise a working agreement with others in the same circumstances about how the organization will handle:

1. *Purpose.* What is the ultimate purpose of the organization? To maximize profit? Provide customer satisfaction? Provide for the needs of the employees? Something else?
2. *Conflict.* What will be done in the event of conflict or disagreement between persons or groups of persons within the organization?
3. *Authority.* Who, if anyone, is to have authority in the organization, how much are they to have, and how is it to be controlled?
4. *Change.* How can the rules you devise be changed, or can they be changed?

Falling under one or more of the above agreements are some more specific areas of agreement you may want to consider. They largely concern distribution of burdens and benefits and include, but are not limited to:

1. **Employment:** How will you decide who will be employed, the terms of employment, and in what capacity they will be employed?
2. **Termination:** What are the grounds and procedures for terminating an employee?
3. **Promotion:** Under what conditions will someone be promoted and how should the decision be made?
4. **Compensation:** How will pay rates be established? Will there be things like bonuses, and on what grounds will they be awarded? What benefits will be available, if any?
5. **Retirement:** What retirement policies will be in place?

QUESTIONS

1. Evaluate your working agreement (including the specifics in it) using the ethical principles in this chapter (rights, justice, universalism, relativism, duty, others). Consider the employer (owners) and the employees (workers) as you evaluate the ethical terms of your agreement. What parts of your agreement distribute more burden to the employer? To employees? Why? What parts distribute more benefits to the employer? To employees? Why?

2. How "just" is your agreement overall? (Discuss different theories of justice with this exercise.)

3. After sharing your agreement and these questions with the class, what did you learn about your theory of justice in the workplace?

may seem the most objective and appealing, the shifting ethics of pragmatism make this orientation (and the person who espouses it) difficult and unpredictable in a business environment.

Idealists are driven by principles, rules, regulations, and values. Reason, relationships, or the desired consequences of an action do not substitute for the idealist's adherence to principles. Duties are absolute for the idealist. Idealists' moral authority and motivation are commitment to principles and consistency. Values and rules of conduct are the justifications that idealists use to explain their actions. Seen as people with high moral standards, idealists also can be rigid and inflexible. Stanley Krolick states, "This absolute adherence to principles may blind the Idealist to the potential consequences of a decision for oneself, others, or the situation."[23] This style is related to the social responsibility mode of ethical idealism and to the principle of universalism.

Which of the four styles best characterizes your ethical orientation? The orientation of your colleagues? Your supervisor, or "boss"?

COMMUNICATING AND NEGOTIATING ACROSS ETHICAL STYLES

When working or communicating with an ethical style yourself, you also must observe *the other person's ethical style.* According to Krolick, the first step is to "concede that the other person's values and priorities have their own validity in their own terms and try to keep those values in mind to facilitate the process of reaching an agreement."[24] Toward that end, the following guidelines can help when communicating, negotiating, or working with one of the four ethical styles:

- *Individualist:* Point out the benefits to the other person's self-interest.
- *Altruist:* Focus on the benefits for the various constituencies involved.
- *Pragmatist:* Emphasize the facts and potential consequences of an action.
- *Idealist:* Concentrate on the principles or duties at stake.

Learning to recognize and communicate with people who have other ethical styles and being willing to be flexible in accommodating your ethical style to others, without sacrificing your own, are important skills for working effectively with others in organizations.

3.10 QUICK ETHICAL TESTS

In addition to knowing the ethical principles, social responsibility modes, and ethical styles presented in this chapter, businesspeople can take short "ethical tests" before making decisions. Many of these quick rules are based on or reflect the principles discussed in this chapter. These practical, quick guides and "checkpoints," if observed, could change the actions you would automatically take in ethical dilemmas.

The Center for Business Ethics at Bentley College articulated six simple questions for the "practical philosopher." They are used in training programs. Before making a decision or acting, ask the following:

1. Is it right?
2. Is it fair?
3. Who gets hurt?
4. Would you be comfortable if the details of your decision were reported on the front page of your local newspaper?
5. What would you tell your child to do?
6. How does it smell? (How does it feel?)

Other quick ethical tests, some of which are classical, include:

- *The Golden Rule:* "Do unto others as you would have them do unto you." This includes not knowingly doing harm to others.

- *The Intuition Ethic:* We know apart from reason what is right. We have a moral sense about what is right and wrong. We should follow our "gut feeling" about what is right.

- *The Means-Ends Ethic:* We may choose unscrupulous but efficient means to reach an end if the ends are really worthwhile and significant. Be sure the ends are not the means.

- *The Test of Common Sense:* "Does the action I am getting ready to take really make sense?" Think before acting.

- *The Test of One's Best Self:* "Is this action or decision I'm getting ready to take compatible with my concept of myself at my best?"

- *The Test of Ventilation:* Do not isolate yourself with your dilemma. Get others' feedback before acting or deciding.

- *The Test of the Purified Idea:* "Am I thinking this action or decision is right just because someone with appropriate authority or knowledge says it is right?" An action may not be right because someone in a position of power or authority states it is right. You may still be held responsible for taking the action.[25]

Use these principles and guidelines for examining the motivations of stakeholders' strategies, policies, and actions. Why do stakeholders act and talk as they do? What principles drive these actions?

3.11 CONCLUDING COMMENTS

Individual stakeholders have a wide range of ethical principles, orientations, and "quick tests" to draw on before taking action or solving an ethical dilemma. Specifically, if, in a given business situation, decision makers have mapped stakeholders and their stakes (from Chapter 2), this chapter can assist their analysis of the moral dimension of the stakeholder approach by helping them identify what have been called the "ground rules" or "implicit morality" of institutional members. As R. Edward Freeman and Daniel Gilbert Jr. state:

> Think of the implicit morality of an institution as the internal rules that must be followed if the institution is to be a good one of its kind. The rules are often implicit, because the explicit rules of an institution may well be the reason that the institution functions rather badly. Another way to think of the implicit morality of an institution is as the internal logic of the institution. Once this internal logic is clearly understood, we can evaluate its required behaviors against external standards.[26]

In the next chapter, the conceptual basis of the organization as stakeholder is presented, and the moral dimensions of a corporation's strategy, leadership, and culture, as well as issues of corporate self-regulation, are examined.

BACK TO LOUISE SIMMS . . .

Let's return to the scenario in which Louise Simms is trying to decide what to do. Put yourself in Louise's situation. Identify your ethical decision-making style. Are you primarily an idealist, pragmatist, altruist, or individualist? Describe the predominant ethical principles you usually follow in your life. Are you rights-oriented? Do you follow universalist values? Do you seek justice and act in just ways? Are you a relativist? Do you follow what you believe is your duty? What about your company? Describe Louise's organization. Is it characterized as productivist (i.e., market ethics)? Progressive? Philanthropic? Idealist? You may want to consider the steps at the beginning of the chapter for ethical reasoning to address what you would do. What is your moral responsibility? (Check the beginning of the chapter on the criteria for moral reasoning.) Now make Louise's decision. Share your decision with your classmates and see what they said and their reasons for saying it. Do you think that you made the right decision?

SUMMARY

Complex ethical dilemmas in business situations involve making tough choices among conflicting and competing interests. This chapter begins with 12 questions and three decision criteria that can assist individuals in determining the most suitable course of action. These also can be applied at the group and corporate levels of analysis.

Individuals can gain a clearer perspective of their own motivations and actions by distinguishing them from those of others. This perspective can be useful for guiding your own decision-making process. Understanding the ethical reasoning and decision criteria from this chapter can enable you to reason more critically when examining other stakeholders' ethical reasoning.

A primary goal of ethical reasoning is to help individuals act in morally responsible ways. Ignorance and bias are two conditions that blind a person's moral awareness. Five principles of ethical reasoning are presented to expose you to methods of ethical decision making. The five principles are ethical relativism (both naive relativism and cultural relativism), utilitarianism, universalism, rights, and justice. Each principle is discussed in terms of the utility and drawbacks characteristic of it. Guidelines for thinking through and applying each principle in a stakeholder analysis are provided. These principles are not mechanical recipes for selecting a course of action. They are filters or screens to use for clarifying dilemmas.

Three ethical orientations, moral, amoral, and immoral, can be used to evaluate individuals' and organizations' ethics. Moral and immoral orientations are more discernable than amoral motives. Amoral orientations include lack of concern for others' interests and well-being. While no intentional harm or motive may be observed, it is harmful consequences from ignorance or neglect that reflect amoral styles of operating.

Four social responsibility roles or business modes are productivism and philanthropy (influenced by stockholder concerns) and progressivism and ethical idealism (driven by stockholder concerns but also influenced by external stakeholders).

Individuals also have ethical decision-making styles. Four different (but not exclusive) styles are individualism, altruism, pragmatism, and idealism. Another person's ethical decision-making style must be understood when engaging in communication and negotiation. These styles are a starting point for reflecting on and identifying our (and others') predominant decision-making characteristics. Individual styles can change over time.

The final section offers quick "ethical tests" that can be used to provide insight into your decision-making process and actions.

The methods and principles of ethical reasoning discussed in this chapter can enable individuals to better understand moral issues and their own motivations and intentions.

QUESTIONS

1. What is a first step for addressing ethical dilemmas?
2. What are three criteria that can be used in ethical reasoning to help structure our thinking and arguments?
3. What single focal question is often the most powerful for solving ethical dilemmas?
4. What are two conditions that eliminate a person's moral responsibility for causing injury or harm?

5. Briefly explain five fundamental ethical principles that can be used in ethical reasoning.

6. What are some of the problems characteristic of the principle of cultural relativism? What are the benefits?

7. Why is utilitarianism useful for conducting a stakeholder analysis? What are some of the problems we may encounter when using this principle?

8. Briefly explain the categorical imperative. What does it force you, as a decision maker, to do when choosing an action in a moral dilemma?

9. Explain the difference between the principles of rights and justice. What are some of the strengths of each principle? What are some of the weaknesses?

10. What are the four social responsibility modes? How can these be used?

11. Briefly explain each of the individual ethical decision-making styles. Which style do you think most closely matches your own?

12. Which of the ethical "quick tests" do you prefer for yourself? Why?

EXERCISES

1. Describe a serious ethical dilemma that you have experienced. Use the 12 questions developed by Laura Nash to offer a resolution to the problem, even if your resolution is different from the first time. Did you use any of the questions in your original experience? Would any of these questions have helped you? How? What would you have done differently? Why?

2. Identify a real-life example of an instance when you thought ignorance absolved a person, group, or organization from moral responsibility. Then identify an example of a person, group, or organization simply failing to become fully informed about a moral situation. Under what conditions do you think individuals are morally responsible for the effects of their actions? Why?

3. With which of the four social responsibility business modes in the chapter do you most identify? Why? Name a company that reflects this orientation. Explain why. Would you want to work for this company? Would you want to be part of the management team? Explain.

4. Select a company in the news that has acted morally and one that has acted immorally. Using this chapter, characterize the apparent ethics of each company or of its spokespersons or executives.

ETHICAL DILEMMA

NOW WHAT SHOULD I DO?

I was recently employed as a certified public accountant (CPA) for a regional accounting firm, which specialized in the audits of financial institutions and had many local clients. My responsibilities included supervising staff, collecting evidence to support financial statement assertions, and compiling work papers for managers and partners to review. During the audit of a publicly traded bank, I discovered that senior bank executives were under investigation by the FDIC for removing funds from the bank. They were also believed to be using bank funds to pay corporate credit card bills for gas and spouses' expenses. The last allegation noted that the executives were issuing loans to related parties, in this instance, relatives, without proper collateral.

After reviewing the work papers, I found two checks that were selected during a cash count from two tellers. These checks were made payable to one executive of the bank. There were no indications based on our sampling that expenses were being paid for spouses. There were several instances of loans made to related parties that did not have the necessary support. My audit manager and the chief financial officer (CFO) of my firm were aware of these problems.

After the field work for the audit was completed, I was called into the CEO's office. The CEO, along with the chief operating officer (COO), stated that the FDIC examiners wanted to interview the audit manager, two staff accountants, and me. The CEO then asked the following question: "If you were asked by the FDIC regarding a check or checks made payable to bank executives, how would you answer?"

I told them that I would answer the FDIC examiners by stating that, during our audit, we made copies of two checks made payable to an executive of the bank for $8,000 each.

The COO stated that, during his review of the audit work papers, he had not found any copies of checks made payable to executives. He also stated that a better response to the question regarding the checks would be, "I was not aware of reviewing any checks specifically made payable to the executive in question." The COO then said that the examiners would be in the following day to speak with the audit staff. At that time I was dismissed from the meeting.

Neither the CEO nor the COO asked me if that (the suggested "better" response) was the response I would give, and I did not volunteer the information. During the interview, the FDIC investigators never asked me if I knew about the checks. Should I have volunteered this information?

QUESTIONS

1. What would you have done? Volunteered the information or stayed silent? Explain your decision.

2. Was there anything unethical going on in this case? Explain.

3. Describe the "ethics" of the officers of the firm in this case.

4. What, if anything, should the officers have done, and why?

5. What lessons, if any, can you take from this case, as an employee working under company officials who have more power than you do?

4

THE CORPORATION
AND INTERNAL STAKEHOLDERS
VALUE-BASED MORAL DIMENSIONS OF LEADERSHIP, STRATEGY, STRUCTURE, CULTURE, AND SELF-REGULATION

4.1 STAKEHOLDER MANAGEMENT AND VALUE-BASED ORGANIZATIONAL SYSTEMS

An organization's enacted purpose, values, and mission are central to its internal alignment and external market effectiveness. Chester Barnard wrote, in 1939, that effective managers "inspire cooperative personal decisions by creating faith in common understanding, faith in the probability of success, faith in the ultimate satisfaction of personal motives, and faith in the integrity of common purpose."[1] In the now classic book *Built to Last*,[2] authors James Collins and Jerry Porras state, "Purpose is the set of fundamental reasons for a company's existence beyond just making money. Visionary companies get at purpose by asking questions similar to those posed by David Packard [cofounder of Hewlett-Packard] . . . 'I want to discuss *why* a company exists in the first place . . . why are we here? I think many people assume, wrongly, that a company exists simply to make money. While this is an important result of a company's existence, we have to go deeper and find the real reasons for our being.'"

This chapter focuses on the internal stakeholders and systems of an organization from a value-based stakeholder management perspective. This perspective centers on examining the extent to which an organization's leaders—their vision and strategy—and culture, structure, technology, and other measurement systems adopt and reflect an ethical and collaborative orientation toward those served inside and outside the firm.[3] In contrast to the method or tool of stakeholder analysis in Chapter 2, a value-based approach assumes that internal stakeholders' values orientation (i.e., their assumptions, beliefs, intrinsic values, and desired results) influence both the processes and outcomes of an organization's strategies and treatment of its stakeholders. In Chapter 2, we assumed the role of a third party observer and of the CEO. The focal organization's strategies relative to external groups and forces were analyzed. In this chapter, the organization is viewed internally. From this approach, stakeholder-responsive, value-based companies[4] demonstrate collaborative, "win-win," trust-based relationships with their employees, customers, suppliers, investors, and other constituencies in order to succeed. One of an organization's most prized assets is its reputation. Reputations are built through productive and conscientious relationships with stockholders and stakeholders.[5]

A stakeholder management approach examines the extent to which an organization's leadership, systems management, and stakeholder relations[6]:

- Are integrated *or* fragmented
- Manage *or* create and build relationships
- Emphasize buffering and protecting the organization *or* create and generate mutual benefits and opportunities
- Develop and sustain short-term *or* long-term goals and relationships
- Encourage idiosyncratic dependent implementation, based on division, function, business structures, and personal interests and styles, *or* encourage coherent approaches, driven by enterprise, visions, missions, values, and strategies.

This approach argues that organizations succeed in market and nonmarket (i.e., government and other not-for-profit stakeholders) environments through open dialogue and a duty to assist stakeholders. These relationships are based on respect, trust, fairness, fiscal accountability, and responsibility. A company's policies, procedures, operating practices, and business processes should also reflect these values. Taken together, a value-based stakeholder management approach can be used with other management and consulting techniques to review and, where necessary, transform internal organizational practices—ethically and legally—in the marketplace.

BUILT TO LAST OR CREATIVELY DESTRUCT?

The digital information technology revolution has increased pressure on industries and corporations to question to what extent ethical and stakeholder value-based management principles and practices still work. Stated another way, Do ethics and long-term values matter? Part of this debate centers on whether traditionally excellent companies are models or dinosaurs for emerging and existing firms that wish to successfully compete in the changing information and service-based economy. This discussion is relevant to stakeholder and value-based management approaches with regard to beliefs about to what extent value-based stakeholder management principles actually apply to companies in hypercompetitive environments. We briefly review the organizational built-to-last and creative destruction arguments with examples, and then address from studies and company examples how value-based stakeholder management is relevant to organizational market effectiveness.

The visionary built-to-last companies "are premier institutions—the crown jewels—in their industries, widely admired by their peers and having a long track record of making a significant impact on the world around them . . . a visionary company is an *organization*—an institution . . . visionary *companies* prosper over long periods of time, through multiple product life cycles and multiple generations of active leaders."[7] Such companies include 3M, American Express, Boeing, Citicorp, Ford, General Electric, Hewlett-Packard, IBM, Johnson & Johnson, Marriott, Merck, Motorola, Nordstrom, Philip Morris, Procter and Gamble, Sony, Wal-Mart, and Disney. These visionary companies, Collins and Porras discovered, succeeded over their rivals by developing and following a "core ideology" that consisted of core values plus purpose. Core values are "the organization's essential and enduring tenets—a small set of general guiding principles; not to be confused with specific cultural or operational practices; not to be compromised for financial gain or short-term expediency." Purpose is "the organization's fundamental reasons for existence beyond just making money—a perpetual guiding star on the horizon; not to be confused with specific goods or business strategies."[8] Excerpts of core ideologies from some of the visionary companies include[9]:

- Disney: "To bring happiness to millions and to celebrate, nurture, and promulgate wholesome American values."
- Wal-Mart: "We exist to provide value to our customers—to make their lives better via lower prices and greater selection; all else is secondary . . . Be in partnership with employees."
- Sony: "Respecting and encouraging each individual's ability and creativity."
- Motorola: "To honorably serve the community by providing products and services of superior quality at a fair price."

Built-to-last companies "more thoroughly indoctrinate employees into a core ideology than their comparison companies [i.e., similar companies] creating cultures so strong that they are almost cult-like around the ideology."[10] The visionary companies also select and support senior management on the basis of a fit between the core ideology more than other companies. These best-in-class companies also attain more consistent goals, strategy, tactics, and organizational structure alignment with their core ideology than do comparison companies in Collins and Porras's study.[11]

Not all organizations have the characteristics of "built-to-last" companies, nor would all companies agree with or support some of the ideologies, products, and strategies of visionary firms. For example, Philip Morris tobacco products are controversial with many external stakeholders. Teacher/researcher Jim Collins's latest book, *Good to Great*, looks at eleven companies that have achieved greatness over time often from mediocre beginnings. According to Collins, great companies have "Level 5 Executive" leadership, which "blends enduring greatness through a paradoxical blend of personal humility and professional will."[12]

CREATIVE DESTRUCTION

A view that contrasts with those of the authors of *Good to Great* is the argument of Joseph Schumpeter, a noted economist who died in 1950, that "the perennial gale of *creative destruction*" blows in new technologies and ideas that destroy old technologies and ideas. The Darwinian nature of capitalist market systems overwhelms all corporations over time. Richard Foster and Sarah Kaplan, in their book *Creative Destruction*, recently tracked the performance of 1,000 companies in 15 industries over 38 years.[13] They argue that their results confirm Schumpeter's thesis. They concluded that McKinsey Corporation's "long-term studies of corporate birth, survival, and death in America clearly show that the corporate equivalent of El Dorado, the golden company that continually performs better than the markets, *has never existed*. It is a myth. Managing the survival even among the best and most revered corporations does not guarantee strong long-term performance for shareholders. In fact, just the opposite is true. In the long run, markets always win."[14] These authors state that, by the year 2020, over 75% of the S&P 500 will consist of companies unknown to us today. They note that corporations and their operations have been built and managed on the assumption of *continuity*; whereas capital markets are based on assumptions of *discontinuity*. Markets focus on continual creation and destruction.

Foster and Kaplan attribute corporations' failure to survive the creative destruction of capital market waves to several factors. A major cause is "cultural lock-in" of managers, the inability to change the culture even when the market threatens. Corporate control systems also become bureaucratic, lack creativity, and move toward "convergent," instead of "divergent," thinking. Corporations, the authors argue, need to be redesigned around the models of private equity, holding companies, and venture capital firms. Corporations need to think of their businesses as a revolving portfolio of companies in different stages of development and to act accordingly, i.e., design their businesses to evolve at the pace and scale of the market, letting the market control the company wherever possible.

Foster and Kaplan's arguments are not new. Clayton Christensen's *The Innovator's Dilemma: When New Technologies Cause Great Firms to Fail* (Harvard Business Press, 1997) introduced similar themes. The current state of rapid innovative technology development and applications to business processes, coupled with the experience of disruptive technologies and the effects of the Internet on company supply chains—i.e., automating business processes and taking out intermediaries and middle management layers—raises questions about the place and significance of stakeholder value in relationship to marketplace competitiveness. However, Foster and Kaplan do not include visions, missions, or long-term values (other than valuing continual creative destruction) as guiding processes and principles. For that matter, ethics is not explicitly addressed in either *Built to Last* or *Creative Destruction*. Are ethics and stakeholder management relevant in a Darwinian, *creatively destructive*, market-driven environment?

VALUE-BASED ORGANIZATIONAL SYSTEMS AND STAKEHOLDERS

Internal organizations are composed of systems and stakeholders, regardless of the nature of external environments. Corporate leaders, employees, strategy, structure, culture, and other systems (i.e., rewards, human resources, finance, research and development, marketing, production, sales) characterize the internal operating profile of a company. Internal organizational systems are value-based because the values of professionals interpret the environments and determine what works, what doesn't, and what is right and wrong. The skill and value-based decisions and actions of professionals influence the direction and outcomes of the organization. Does ethics matter for an organization's survival and market effectiveness? The "good management hypothesis" in business ethics literature suggests that there is a positive relationship between a corporation's performance outcomes (e.g., financial indicators) and how it treats its stakeholders. Studies confirm this hypothesis.[15] Managing and aligning organizational stakeholders and systems for market performance are related.

Do built-to-last companies manage their stakeholders well? That is, do visionary companies demonstrate ethical treatment of employees, customers, communities, and external stakeholders and the environment? An empirical and statistical study[16] confirmed the hypothesis that the *content* of the values of the built-to-last companies positively correlated to treatment of stakeholders. The study used the visionary companies along with a major rival for comparison to demonstrate that the built-to-last companies' "chosen core ideology must be capable of bringing a range of stakeholders together for a common purpose that goes beyond the trivial or the mere material and provides a common basis for doing this work together."[17]

Foster and Kaplan, researchers at the McKinsey Corporation (a strategy consulting firm), discuss the importance of organizational culture, dialogue, and mental models in their book. However, since their own dominant mental model and research lens focus on capital markets, corporate flexibility, and methods that enable companies to respond to and move with markets, they omit or overlook the role that ethical dimensions of vision, purpose, values, and stakeholder management play. Perhaps they should consider how and to what extent a company can self-destruct without the effects of competitive market forces. What happens when greedy or unethical leaders or outside coalitions destroy or disable the competitiveness of a market-responsive company? What happens when elements in a corporate culture breed illegal activities that eventually bring lawsuits that erode the otherwise market-competitive company? The ethical, value-based, and legal motives and interactions of internal stakeholders of a company cannot be overlooked or minimized in trying to understand the competitiveness of the company.

Creative Reconstruction

An interesting concept, and counterpart to the creative destruction argument, is creative reconstruction.[18] This concept describes some dot-com survivors who used destructive market forces to creatively accelerate their path toward profitability by making significant changes to their plans and with their investors. Can other start-up and mature organizations develop their businesses incrementally and actually use threatening market forces and constraints to evolve different business models, processes, and revenue sources? The notion of creative reconstruction could further be developed to include a value-based stakeholder management approach to argue that start-up and older companies might well succeed in growing and changing their direction, systems, and processes through highly ethical collaborative stakeholder strategies. Can organizations also respond incrementally and in value-driven ways to Darwinian market forces to compete? Evidence validates that organizations, including the built-to-last companies, can and do succeed by using value-based stakeholder management principles to guide and manage change.[19] Internal operations in companies, start-ups included, must resolve human, political, social, and ethical conflicts and dilemmas, as well as economic ones, to survive and thrive.

Balancing Internal Stakeholder Values in the Organization

The internal dimensions of an organization are illustrated in the diagnostic contingency model in Figure 4.1. This model, used here because it offers an organization-wide view of major systems, depicts the customer as a central source of information input, integral to all the organizational systems and dimensions. A company's leadership, environment (including market forces), history, and resources are "input" dimensions and influences.

The purpose and core ideology of organizations are modeled by its leaders and embedded in its enterprise strategy (i.e., the strategy for the entire company). The culture of a company is at the center "spoke" of the wheel of transformation, because it the "glue" that holds together the other internal systems. The vision and strategy, people, systems, structure, technology, and nature of work comprise the internal operations of the organization.

FIGURE 4.1   DIAGNOSTIC CONTINGENCY MODEL

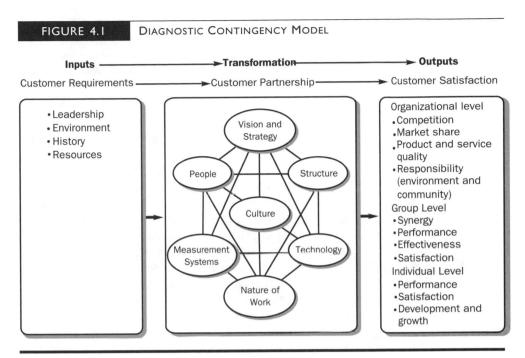

Copyright Joseph W. Weiss, 2002.

Based on contingency theory, these systems and their stakeholders effectively respond to market and environmental forces through their alignment around the corporate purpose, vision, strategy, and core competencies.[20] There are variations to the contingency model. Many companies outsource and broker project work, technology, and even professionals. Customers and strategic alliance partners may also participate in the internal decisions of some companies digitally, through networked "intranets" and "extranets."

According to stakeholder management theory, the organization should also treat its internal and external stakeholders ethically to be effective with its marketplace communities. In practice, however, aligning an organization's dominant values and mission with its internal stakeholders, while treating external groups and organizations ethically, is difficult because of pressures from changing environments (see Chapter 1), innovative and disruptive technologies, Darwinian market competitiveness, and competing values of internal stakeholders. The following quote from Anderson[21] illustrates the diversity among stakeholder values:

> An organization in almost all its phases is a reflection of competing value choices. Owners want a return on their investment. Employees want secure jobs and career development. Managers want growth and industry leadership. Government regulators want minimal pollution, safety, work opportunities for a wide variety of groups, and tax revenues. For top managers, this competition comes to a head

because they must unravel complex problems whose solutions benefit some groups but have negative consequences for others. Framing these decisions inevitably leads to some crucial dilemmas for managers, who must answer the broad question, "What is a convincing balance among competing value choices?"

Ideally, the values of the CEO and other employees are aligned, ethically and operationally. This is not to say that professionals in a company should not disagree. It is a question of having the different professional groups aligned around a common effective and socially responsible purpose and values. This may not always be the case in practice. Even built-to-last companies have their top-level team differences and difficulties.

Balancing internal organizational stakeholder interests can be difficult because of the diversity of functional backgrounds, training, goals, time horizons, and reward systems. These differences are further influenced by organizational politics, the constraints and pressures of other systems, and changing roles and assignments. Figure 4.2 is an example of an organization's internal stakeholders and their competing professional value orientations.

While newer forms of organizational arrangements, such as customer-focused integrated teams, do blur traditional functional roles and relationships, conflicts among team members still occur. For example, function orientations (e.g., marketing, research and development, production, information systems, and finance) have built-in competing values, especially when employees who are under pressure must design, deliver, and service complex products. Marketing and sales people work with short- to medium-term time horizons and are rewarded on the basis of their results. Sales professionals, in particular, have a very short time horizon and depend on the success of individual and team selling ability to satisfy, retain, and attract customers. Research and development (R&D) professionals generally have a longer time horizon and are rewarded for their innovations.

Contrast, for example, the marketing and sales professionals' goals, rewards, time horizons, and backgrounds with those of reasearch and development professionals, as shown in Figure 4.2, and you can see how value differences and role conflicts can occur among these employees and within their cross-functional teams.

From a stakeholder management perspective, it is the role of an organization's leaders, with the support of each professional, to ensure that the integration and market effectiveness of a company is based on the types of relationship and values that embody trust, collaboration, and a "win-win" goal for stakeholders and stockholders. Collaborative stakeholder management strategies for aligning cross-functional teams are discussed in the section on "Culture, Structure, and Systems."

This chapter argues that amorally and unethically led and managed organizations with conflicting internal values can and sometimes do lead to illegal situations. Noted scandals and crises in prestigious multinational corporations (see Chapter 1) that have thousands of employees across the globe cannot afford costly lawsuits and damages from unethical, unsafe, and non-

FIGURE 4.2	A Functional Profile of Internal Organizational Stakeholders: Professional Orientations

Professional Stakeholders

Orientations	Marketing & Sales	Research & Development (R&D)	Production	Finance & Accounting	Information Systems
Background	Liberal arts; social sciences; entrepreneurial; technical	Electrical engineering; technical	Mechanical engineering; operations	Finance; accounting; auditing; tax	Software "engineers;" data management; programming
Goals and "Stakes"	High product mix; revenue and market competitiveness; customer satisfaction	Market dominance, innovation, competitiveness	Product yield; quality control	Low-cost capital; efficient borrowing; accountability	Problem solving; organizational integration; systems functioning
Focus and Rewards	Product or service leadership; creative autonomy; bonuses; equity; career mobility	Next "killer" application; resources to innovate; prestige	Product lifecycle stability; peace with R&D job security; bonuses	Low costs; high yields; data access; accuracy; cooperation; career advancement	Satisfied users; state-of-art technology; career advancement; new skill development
Time Horizon	Short to medium time frame	Medium to long time frame	Short to continuous time frame	Continuous time frame	Continuous time frame

Copyright Joseph W. Weiss, Bentley College, Waltham, MA, 2002.

competitive internal and external business and human relations practices. The Intel case at the end of this book provides an example of what can go wrong when an organization is not aligned to listen and respond to customers. Aligning systems is a necessity, not a luxury.

4.2 A 10-STEP, VALUE-BASED STAKEHOLDER MANAGEMENT ASSESSMENT

A stakeholder management approach that is value-based is argued to be more effective in implementing organizational change programs that include ethics and compliance training.[22] (It should also be recognized that the effectiveness of change management and ethics training programs in global businesses depends on the societal and organizational cultures. We discuss this topic in Chapter 7.) Why? First, people are generally motivated to act and change when they are personally engaged and inspired. Involving employees in implementing an organization's purpose, direction, and values inspires them.

Secondly, people generally want to do "what's right," as well as doing "things the right way." In other words, there is a relationship between acting socially responsibly and acting productively. In fact, legal and ethical compliance programs seem to work best when people are positively motivated and excited to participate in a company's decision-making processes. Compliance-based training programs that instruct only on laws, statutes, and penalties for certain behaviors appear to be less effective.

Third, organizational programs, initiatives, and changes—whether these relate to ethics, strategy, marketing, product development, or information technology—are more likely to be accepted and practiced when introduced with open dialogue and the commitment of top leaders. Fourth, many ethical dilemmas and tough management decisions in organizations involve "gray" (undefined) areas. Dialog through value-based decisions is often required to resolve ethical and even legal dilemmas.

There are many stakeholder management audits and assessment frameworks. Some borrow and are based on literature and practices from management consulting, ethical and legal compliance programs, and industrial, association, and professional codes of conduct. Several of these sources are referred to and used here to create a comprehensive framework, which combines value-based and stakeholder management approaches.[23] Companies use management, human resources, and ethics consultants to design and deliver these types of assessments.

This 10-step assessment framework is designed to:

- Define the problem or opportunity and gain the commitment of the leaders to support the assessment process
- Review and develop the organization's vision, purpose, and guiding values
- Use a value-based, stakeholder management "readiness" checklist
- Develop value-based, stakeholder-responsive performance measures
- Identify the enterprise strategy and determine its stakeholder responsiveness and responsibility capabilities
- Determine the degree of alignment and integration of the organization's systems from value-based stakeholder criteria
- Conduct a baseline assessment and "gap analysis" of the "as is" and desired "future state" of the organization
- Create benchmarks (i.e., best practices and standards)
- Develop a written report with specific recommendations for change
- Review the report and findings with senior management and other stakeholders

The assessment steps are briefly explained here and are presented as if you, the reader, are doing the assessment. The remainder of the chapter expands on defining and aligning organizational systems, discussing best practices and examples from a stakeholder management approach.

STEP 1: DETERMINE THE PROBLEM OR OPPORTUNITY AND GAIN TOP LEADER SUPPORT

The first step in any major or large-scale organizational assessment and change process is to determine the problems and opportunities with involvement from the top leaders. The commitment, support, and participation of leaders are necessary in the process. Key questions at this stage include: How is the company performing with and treating its stakeholders? What are the leaders' assumptions and beliefs about how well or poorly the company is performing? How much better can and should the company perform with its stakeholders? Ideally, the board of directors should be involved, because they govern the CEO's role and responsibilities.

A complete assessment includes the CEO and other senior officers in the audit because they define policy and make key decisions: The buck starts and stops with them. Other top-level officers in large corporations who are responsible for value-based and stakeholder management programs may include the senior vice presidents in human resources, corporate ethics, compliance, organizational effectiveness, business policy, and strategy, as well as ethics officers, if this position exists. BellSouth, Nynex, Sears, Pacific Bell, Texas Instruments, and General Electric are some companies that use this type of assessment with the involvement of senior executives. Small and medium-sized companies may involve their human resources and functional area managers.

STEP 2: REVIEW AND DEVELOP THE VISION, MISSION, VALUES, AND ETHICS CODE

The next step is discovering whether or not an organization has a written vision or mission statement, list of core values, or ethics code. While many large corporations do, a key question is: To what extent are these documents known and used throughout the company for decision making, aligning systems, and resolving disputes between divisions, business units, and functions? Many times a company has one or more of these documents, but the documents are not used or known by employees when they are surveyed regarding these documents. Some companies have different dated iterations of these documents lying around in some offices. The role of the assessing consultants is to determine how contemporary and accurate these statements are and in what ways these statements could be changed and used to focus and integrate the enterprise within its competitive niche and with its key stakeholder relationships. Ethics codes with examples are discussed later in this chapter.

STEP 3: USE A VALUE-BASED STAKEHOLDER READINESS CHECKLIST

A value-based stakeholder readiness checklist mobilizes, educates, and commits top level leaders to proceed with the assessment. The following readiness checklist is an example that can be modified, used as a preliminary questionnaire to start the assessment, and then expanded into a more formal "audit" to plan the assessment:

1. Do the top leaders believe that key stakeholder and stockholder relationship building is important to the company's financial and bottom-line success?

2. What percentage of the CEO's activities are spent in building new and sustaining existing relationships with key stakeholders?

3. Can employees identify the organization's key stakeholders?

4. What percentage of employee activities are spent in building productive stakeholder relationships?

5. Does the organization's vision, mission, and value statements identify stakeholder collaboration and service? If so, do leaders and employees "walk the talk" of these statements?

6. Does the corporate culture value and support participation and open and shared decision making and collaboration across structures and functions?

7. Does the corporate culture treat its employees fairly, openly, and with trust and respect? Are policies employee-friendly? Are training programs on diversity, ethics, and professional development available and used by employees?

8. Is there collaboration and open communication across the organization? Are openness, collaboration, and innovative ideas rewarded?

9. Is there a defined process for employees to report complaints and illegal or unethical company practices without risking their jobs or facing retribution?

10. Does the strategy of the company encourage or discourage stakeholder respect and fair treatment? Is the strategy oriented toward the long or short term?

11. Does the structure of the company facilitate or hinder information sharing and shared problem solving?

12. Are the systems (i.e., human resources, information, rewards, finance, legal) aligned around a common purpose or are they separate and isolated?

13. Do senior managers and employees know what customers want and does the organization meet customer needs and expectations?

STEP 4: DEVELOP PERFORMANCE AND RESPONSIBILITY MEASURES AND GET FEEDBACK

This step involves identifying effective questions with simple qualitative and quantitative instruments to determine what needs to be measured and why. Who is responsible for what? What happens with goals when deadlines are missed? What happens when customers and end-users are dissatisfied? It is important to get feedback from managers and employees who are responsible for implementing and measuring activities and systems.

While most companies have performance measures, many do not have "stakeholder-sensitive" measures to capture, for example, customer satisfaction, feedback, and involvement in product development, safety, and use.

STEP 5: IDENTIFY STAKEHOLDER LEVEL OF RESPONSIVENESS AND RESPONSIBILITY IN THE CORPORATE STRATEGY

The enterprise strategy is the major map used by a company. The strategy is an indicator of the company's interpretation and intended response to its competitive environments. The strategy generates business unit and functional area substrategies and goals that indicate to what extent the company will engage and involve its stakeholders: employees, customers, stockholders, suppliers, and vendors. This part of the assessment aims at discovering to what extent top leaders and employees are aware of, responsive to, and responsible to these stakeholders. Are employees treated as assets or liabilities? Are customers treated as partners or second-class citizens? Elements of this part of the assessment are discussed in the later section on strategy.

STEP 6: DETERMINE THE ORGANIZATION'S SYSTEMS ALIGNMENT

This part of the assessment checks for readiness and gaps in communication, dialog, responsiveness, and integrated resource sharing within and among systems to respond to stakeholders. Each system is then evaluated using the following questions: What changes and improvements need to be made within and between systems? How can integration within and between systems be enhanced? Employee interviews, participant observation, and review of collected information, information flow, and key documents are methods used during this step. Attitudes, habits, mind-sets, and skills (or lack of skills) are also contributors to system integration and effectiveness.

STEP 7: CONDUCT BASELINE AND "GAP ANALYSIS" BETWEEN CURRENT ("AS IS") AND DESIRED FUTURE STATE

During this step, a baseline assessment of where the company currently stands in relation to its stated goals, objectives, relationships with stakeholders, and systems alignment and responsiveness is done. Gaps can appear within or between systems and teams, e.g., core competencies may be lacking, operating procedures may be confusing, integrating mechanisms between teams may not be defined, or goals and objectives may be too aggressive or not aggressive enough. In many cases, lack of alignment results from not having clearly communicated expectations, values, and procedures. From interviews, surveys, direct observation, and a review of policies and procedures, the *as-is* state of the organization can be described. The *desired future state* involves a separate consultative process, which is often inspired from seeing the current state. Figure 4.3 can be used to lead a desired future state discussion.

STEP 8: CREATE BENCHMARKS

Benchmarks, or standards for best practices, can be used in each of the systems and in the vision and values statements, leadership practices, ethics codes, and training. "What works best?" and "Who are examples for us?" are questions used to identify and locate benchmarks.

STEP 9: DEVELOP SUMMARY REPORT WITH RECOMMENDATIONS

Given the major findings to this point, the questions to be addressed include: What needs to be improved, strengthened, eliminated, or changed, and why? What do the results show about leadership, strategy, culture, structure, teams, different systems, positions, and stakeholder management for specific personnel? What specific changes and alignments must be implemented to strengthen, create, and build social performance and productivity with stakeholders?

STEP 10: REVIEW RESULTS AND RECOMMENDATIONS WITH SENIOR MANAGEMENT AND OTHER STAKEHOLDERS

Information sharing, giving and receiving feedback, educating, and deciding if implementation of recommendations are desired characterizes this step. Since leaders are the prime movers of organizations, the following section addresses their role from a value-based stakeholder management perspective. We then discuss strategy, culture, and systems with these assessment questions in mind.

| FIGURE 4.3 | STRATEGIC ALIGNMENT QUESTIONS |

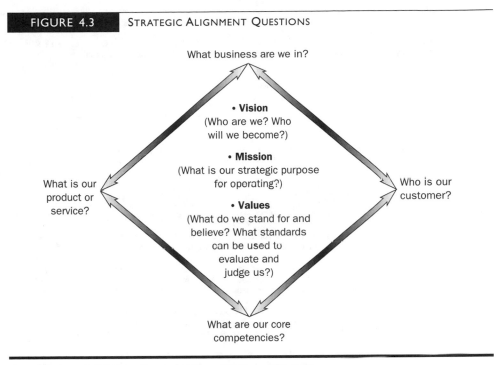

What business are we in?

• **Vision**
(Who are we? Who
will we become?)

• **Mission**
(What is our strategic purpose
for operating?)

What is our
product or
service?

Who is our
customer?

• **Values**
(What do we stand for and
believe? What standards
can be used to
evaluate and
judge us?)

What are our core
competencies?

Copyright Joseph W. Weiss, Bentley College, Waltham, MA, 2002.

4.3 LEADERSHIP AND STRATEGY

LEADERSHIP

Leadership is a shared process, although the values and behaviors of company founders and CEOs often frame and set the cultural tone for organizations. A starting point for identifying a leader's values is the vision and mission statement of a company. Figure 4.4 presents the outstanding example of a values and vision statement for Levi Strauss, extended to include aspiration and leadership statements. Levi Strauss CEOs have "walked the talk" in their stated ethical principles and commitments to their stakeholders. The leaders of Levi Strauss decided to leave China in the 1980s when they had to choose between their company's and that country's conflicting values.

A leader's values can be explicit, i.e., written, seen, and used, and implicit (observed in actions and behaviors). Values can sometimes best be observed during a potential or actual crisis. For example, Ford's CEO Jacques Nasser made damage control the "job one" priority when the Ford and Bridgestone/Firestone crisis erupted. The response was late. The following excerpt demonstrates some of Nasser's responses after the crisis was revealed:

| FIGURE 4.4 | LEVI STRAUSS & CO. VALUES AND VISION STATEMENT |

VALUES

Our values are fundamental to our success. They are the foundation of our company, define who we are and set us apart from the competition. They underlie our vision of the future, our business strategies and our decisions, actions and behaviors. We live by them. They endure.

Four core values are at the heart of Levi Strauss & Co.: Empathy, Originality, Integrity and Courage. These four values are linked. As we look at our history, we see a story of how our core values work together and are the source of our success.

Empathy—Walking in Other People's Shoes

Empathy begins with listening . . . paying close attention to the world around us . . . understanding, appreciating and meeting the needs of those we serve, including consumers, retail customers, shareholders and each other as emloyees.

Levi Strauss and Jacob Davis listened. Jacob was the tailor who in the 1870s first fashioned heavy cotton cloth, thread and metal rivets into sturdy "waist overalls" for miners seeking durable work pants. Levi in turn met Jacob's needs for patenting and mass production of the product, enthusiastically embracing the idea and bringing it to life. The rest is history: The two created what would become the most popular clothing in the world—blue jeans.

Our history is filled with relevant examples of paying attention to the world around us. We listened. We innovated. We responded.

- As early as 1926 in the United States, the company advertised in Spanish, Portuguese and Chinese, reaching out to specific groups of often-neglected consumers.
- In the 1930s, consumers complained that the metal rivets on the back pockets of our jeans tended to scratch furniture, saddles and car seats. So we redesigned the way the pockets were sewn, placing the rivets underneath the fabric.
- In 1982, a group of company employees asked senior management for help in increasing awareness of a new and deadly disease affecting their lives. We quickly became a business leader in promoting AIDS awareness and education.

We believe in empathetic marketing, which means that we walk in our consumers' shoes. In the company's early years, that meant making durable clothes for workers in the American West. Now, it means responding to the casual clothing needs of a broad range of consumers around the world. Understanding and appreciating needs—consumer insight—is central to our commercial success.

Being empathetic also means that we are inclusive. Levi Strauss' sturdy work pants are sold worldwide in more than 80 countries. Their popularity is based on their egalitarian appeal and originality. They transcend cultural boundaries. Levi's® jeans—the pants without pretense—are not just for any one part of society. Everyone wears them.

Inclusiveness underlies our consumer marketing beliefs and way of doing business. We bring our Levi's® and Dockers® brands to consumers of all ages and lifestyles around the world. We reflect the diverse world we serve through the range and relevancy of our products and the way we market them.

Likewise, our company workforce mirrors the marketplace in its diversity, helping us to understand and address differing consumer needs. We value ethnic, cultural and lifestyle diversity. And we depend and draw upon the varying backgrounds, knowledge, points of view and talents of each other.

As colleagues, we also are committed to helping one another succeed. We are sensitive to each other's goals and interests, and we strive to ensure our mutual success through exceptional leadership, career development and supportive workplace practices.

Empathy also means engagement and compassion. Giving back to the people we serve and the communities we operate in is a big part of who we are. Levi Strauss was both a merchant and a philanthropist—a civic-minded leader who believed deeply in community service. His way lives on. The company's long-standing traditions of philanthropy, community involvement and employee volunteerism continue today and contribute to our commercial success.

Originality—Being Authentic and Innovative

Levi Strauss started it and forever earned a place in history. Today, the Levi's® brand is an authentic American icon, known the world over.

Rooted in the rugged American West, Levi's® jeans embody freedom and individuality. They are young at heart. Strong and adaptable, they have been worn by generations of individuals who have made them their own. They are a symbol of frontier independence, democratic idealism, social change and fun. Levi's® jeans are both a work pant and a fashion statement—at once ordinary and extraordinary. Collectively, these attributes and values make the Levi's® brand unlike any other.

Innovation is the hallmark of our history. It started with Levi's® jeans, but that pioneering spirit permeates all aspects of our business—innovation in product and marketing, workplace practices and corporate citizenship. Creating trends. Setting new standards. Continuously improving through change. For example:

- We were the first U.S. apparel company to use radio and television to market our products.
- With the introduction of the Dockers® brand in 1986, we created an entirely new category of casual clothing in the United States, bridging the gap between suits and jeans. A year later, Dockers® khakis had become the fastest growing apparel brand in history. Throughout the 1990s, we were instrumental in changing what office workers wear on the job.
- Our European Levi's® brand team reinvented classic five-pocket jeans in 1999. Inspired by the shape and movement of the human body, Levi's® Engineered JeansTM were the first ergonomically designed jeans.

Now, more than ever, constant and meaningful innovation is critical to our commercial success. The worldwide business environment is fiercely competitive. Global trade, instantaneous communications and the ease of market entry are among the forces putting greater pressure on product and brand differentiation. To be successful, it is imperative that we change, competing in new and different ways that are relevant to the shifting times.

As the "makers and keepers" of Levi Strauss' legacy, we must look at the world with fresh eyes and use the power of ideas to improve everything we do across all dimensions of our business, from modest improvements to total re-inventions. We must create product news that comes from the core qualities of our brands—comfort, style, value and the freedom of self-expression—attributes that consumers love and prefer.

Integrity—Doing the Right Thing

Ethical conduct and social responsibility characterize our way of doing business. We are honest and trustworthy. We do what we say we are going to do.

Integrity includes a willingness to do the right thing for our employees, brands, the company and society as a whole, even when personal, professional and social risks or economic pressures confront us. This principle of responsible commercial success is embedded in the company's experience. It continues to anchor our beliefs and behaviors today, and is one of the reasons consumers trust our brands. Our shareholders expect us to manage the company this way. It strengthens brand equity and drives sustained, profitable growth and superior return on investment. In fact, our experience has shown that our "profits through principles" approach to business is a point of competitive advantage.

This values-based way of working results in innovation:

- Our commitment to equal employment opportunity and diversity predates the U.S. Civil Rights movement and federally mandated desegregation by two decades. We opened integrated factories in California in the 1940s. In the 1950s, we combined our need for more production and our desire to open manufacturing plants in the American South into an opportunity to make change: we led our industry by sending a strong message that we would not locate new plants in Southern towns that imposed segregation. Our approach changed attitudes and helped to open the way for integration in other companies and industries.
- In 1991, we were the first multinational company to develop a comprehensive code of conduct to ensure that individuals making our products anywhere in the world would do so in safe and healthy working conditions and be treated with dignity and respect. Our Terms of Engagement are good for the people working on our behalf and good for the long-term reputation of our brands.

Trust is the most important value of a brand. Consumers feel more comfortable with brands they can trust. Increasingly, they are holding corporations accountable not only for their products but also for how they are made and marketed. Our brands are honest, dependable and trusted, a direct result of how we run our business.

Integrity is woven deeply into the fabric of our company. We have long believed that "Quality Never Goes Out of Style®." Our products are guaranteed to perform. We make them that way. But quality goes beyond products: We put quality in *everything* we do.

Courage—Standing Up For What We Believe

It takes courage to be great. Courage is the willingness to challenge hierarchy, accepted practices and conventional wisdom. Courage includes truth telling and acting resolutely on our beliefs. It means standing by our convictions. For example:

- It took courage to transform the company in the late 1940s. That was when we made the tough decision to shift from dry goods wholesaling, which represented the majority of our business at the time, and to focus instead on making and selling jeans, jean jackets, shirts and Western wear. It was a foresighted—though risky—decision that enabled us to develop and prosper.
- In the 1980s, we took a similar, bold step to expand our U.S. channels of distribution to include two national retail chains, Sears and JCPenney. We wanted to provide consumers with greater access to our products. The move resulted in lost business in the short term because of a backlash from some important retail customers, but it set the stage for substantial growth.
- We also demonstrated courage in our workplace practices. In 1992, Levi Strauss & Co. became the first *Fortune* 500 company to extend full medical benefits to domestic partners of employees. While controversial at the time, this action foreshadowed the widespread acceptance of this benefit and positioned us as a progressive employer with prospective talent.

With courage and dedication, we act on our insights and beliefs, addressing the needs of those we serve in relevant and significant ways. We do this with an unwavering commitment to excellence. We hold ourselves accountable for attaining the high performance standards and results that are inherent in our goals. We learn from our mistakes. We change. This is how we build our brands and business. This is how we determine our own destiny and achieve our vision of the future.

* * *

The story of Levi Strauss & Co. and our brands is filled with examples of the key role our values have played in meeting consumer needs. Likewise, our brands embody many of the core values that our consumers live by. This is why our brands have stood the test of time.

Generations of people have worn our products as a symbol of freedom and self-expression in the face of adversity, challenge and social change. They forged a new territory called the American West. They fought in wars for peace. They instigated counterculture revolutions. They tore down the Berlin Wall. Reverent, irreverent—they all took a stand.

Indeed, it is this special relationship between our values, our consumers and our brands that is the basis of our success and drives our core purpose. It is the foundation of who we are and what we want to become:

VISION

People love our clothes and trust our company.
We will market the most appealing and widely worn casual clothing in the world.
We will clothe the world.

SOURCE: Levi Strauss & Co. Reprinted by permission.

[T]he damage control effort has become nearly a full-time job that promises to make or break his [Nasser's] career. He participates in each daily crisis meeting, even when he's out of town. He arrives armed with information gleaned from outside his usual reporting channels. He has taken to calling dealers, suppliers, and even owners of Ford vehicles who have written or E-mailed him. He has called Ford's own customer hotlines and those of Bridgestone/Firestone, posing as a consumer. . . . [I]n sharp contrast with the more difficult behavior of other CEOs in the midst of corporate crises . . . his [Nasser's] counterparts at Bridgestone/Firestone and its parent, Japan's Bridgestone Corporation, have stayed largely in the background, raising questions in some critics' minds as to whom is in charge.[24]

The lack of effectiveness and late timing of Ford's and Bridgestone/Firestone's organizational responses to this crisis may have later cost Nasser his job, even though $3 billion was spent to replace 10 to 13 million Firestone Wilderness tires as a precautionary measure, and, in the early summer of 2001, Ford terminated its relationship with Bridgestone/Firestone to prevent further accidents and to protect the company's already strained image.

Fast forward to Herb Kelleher, founder and former CEO of Southwest Airlines, one of America's most successful companies. Herb Kelleher cofounded the company in 1966 on a personal $10,000 investment. He retired June 19, 2001, with a $200 million stake in the company. Kelleher's principles of management are straightforward and simple[25]:

- Employees come first, customers second.
- The team is important, not the individual.
- Hire for attitude, train for skills.
- Think like a small company.
- Eschew organizational hierarchy.
- Keep it simple.

Kelleher owned and operated Southwest Airlines on these principles. When asked how the company would survive once he stepped down, Kelleher responded, "The real answer is we have a very strong culture and it has a life of its own that is able to surmount a great deal. If we should, by happenstance, have someone succeed me who is not interested in the culture, I don't think they would last a long time. The place would just rise up."[26] Visitors are immediately exposed to Kelleher's message in white letters on the black elevator glass when they enter the corporate headquarters lobby:

The people of Southwest Airlines are the creators of what we have become—and what we will be. Our people transformed an idea into a legend. That legend will continue to grow only so long as it is nourished—by our people's indomitable spirit, boundless energy, immense goodwill, and burning desire to excel. Our thanks—and our love—to the people of Southwest Airlines for creating a marvelous family and a wondrous airline.[27]

When Herb Kelleher retired, he was replaced by three new executive positions.

Highly ethical companies usually include a "social mission" in their formal mission and values statements. Social missions are commitments by the organization to give back to their communities and external stakeholders who make the organization's existence possible. Ben and Jerry's, Land's End, Southwest Airlines, and many Fortune 500 and smaller companies commit to serving their communities through different types of stewardship outreach, facility sharing (e.g., day care and tutoring programs), and other service-related activities.

LEADERSHIP STAKEHOLDER COMPETENCIES. From a stakeholder management, value based assessment, a CEO and other organizational leaders would demonstrate the following skills:

1. Define and lead the social and ethical, as well as the competitive, mission of organizations. This includes community-based, social, and environmental stewardship goals and objectives, i.e., serving the interests of being a global corporate citizen.
2. Build and sustain relationships with stakeholders.
3. Talk with stakeholders, showing interest and concern for others' needs beyond the economic and utilitarian dimensions.
4. Demonstrate collaboration and trust in shared decision making and strategy sessions.
5. Show awareness and concern for employees and other stakeholders in the policies and practices of the company.

Effective and ethical leaders develop a collaborative approach to setting direction, leading top-level teams, and building relationships with strategic alliance partners and customers. For example, at Johnson & Johnson, one of the seven principles of leadership development states: "People are an asset of the corporation; leadership development is a collaborative, corporation-wide process."[28] The company lives its leadership principles through its Executive Development Program, which brings participants back 90 to 120 days after the main session to discuss the implemented action plans created during the training.

LEADERSHIP RESPONSIBILITY. Organizational leaders, then, are ultimately responsible for the economic viability and profitability of a company. From a value-based, stakeholder management perspective, leaders are also responsible for overseeing and implementing the following activities of an organization:

- Set the vision, mission, and direction.
- Articulate, model, and communicate the dominant values.
- Create and sustain a legal and ethical culture throughout the organization.

■ Articulate and guide the strategy and direction.

■ Build and sustain collaborative stakeholder relationships.

■ Ensure the competitive and ethical alignment of organizational systems.

■ Demonstrate responsibility toward people, processes, and the environment.

Beyond these requirements, leaders who dare to be different and stretch toward some of the built-to-last leadership characteristics might also consider (and be assessed according to) the following leadership responsibilities:

■ Seek to revolutionize every strategy and process for optimal beneficial results, while maintaining the organization's integrity.

■ Empower everyone to achieve and perform beyond stated standards, while maintaining balance of life and personal values.

■ Understand and serve the customer as you would yourself.

■ Create and reward a culture obsessed with fairness and goodwill and toward everyone.

■ Act with compassion and forgiveness in every decision toward every person and group.

■ Do unto your stockholders and stakeholders as you would have them do unto you. They may.

■ Treat the environment as your home. It is.

SPIRITUALITY AND LEADERSHIP. An emerging body of literature and practice describes leadership from a deeper spiritual and value-based perspective.[29] Theological and philosophical literature has helped redefine leadership to include new concepts and vocabulary that capture the human and spiritual domains from which business leaders already work. Spirituality, broadly defined, is the search and outcome for "ultimate meaning and purpose in one's life."[30] The following characteristics and competencies are an example to illustrate the point. Leaders, from a spiritual perspective[31]:

■ Understand and practice reflective "being" as well as "doing"; genuine spirituality must be the willingness to enter into the process of dialogue within oneself and with others, to try to stay with it over a period of time. "Being is the only reality with integrity; obeying one's conscience brings one into communion with this 'integrity of Being.'"[32]

■ Use discernment, prayer, and patience in strategic decision making. Decisions are analyzed within the context of communities.

■ See the leadership role as a calling that reveals its presence by the enjoyment and sense of renewed energies in the practice and results yielded.

■ Seek to *connect* with people and connect people to people with *meaning* and in meaningful ways.

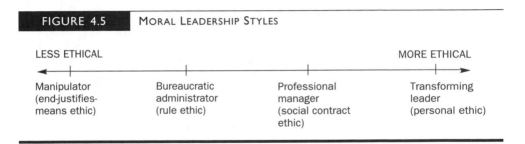

FIGURE 4.5   MORAL LEADERSHIP STYLES

LESS ETHICAL   MORE ETHICAL

Manipulator   Bureaucratic   Professional   Transforming
(end-justifies-   administrator   manager   leader
means ethic)   (rule ethic)   (social contract   (personal ethic)
                                         ethic)

- Create communities, holding environments, and safe havens for empowerment, mobilization, development, spiritual growth, and nourishment.
- Lead with reflection and choice, passion and reason, compassion, humility, vulnerability, and prayer, as well as courage, boldness, and vision.

Aaron Feuersten of Malden Mills Industries, Inc.; Jeffrey Swartz of The Timberland Company; David Steward of World Wide Technology, Inc.; and Krishan Kalra of BioGenex Laboratories, Inc., are a few of a growing number of executives who have used their spiritual beliefs in their professional lives to create and promote strategies and policies involving employees, customers, suppliers, vendors, their communities, and other stakeholders.

The study by Ian Mitroff and Elizabeth Denton[33] interviewed 215 executive officers and managers. A surprising finding in the study was that the leaders desired a way to express their spiritual selves while at work, rather than to "park it at the office door." Leaders and organizations enable the expression of spirituality in different ways: from the *religious firm*, where religious teachings are openly articulated, modeled, and included in business practices, to the *value-based company* (like Ben & Jerry's), where nonreligious, nonspiritual secular values (awareness, consciousness, dignity, honesty, openness, and trust) are policy-setting and decision-making guides in the firm. In these types of firms, the Golden Rule is the major business principle and "the whole person comes to work" and "causes no embarrassment by expressing 'deeply felt emotions' such as love and grieving."[34]

ETHICS OF LEADERSHIP STYLES. A leader's (as well as your own) moral style in organizations can also be observed and evaluated. A leader's, or manager's, source of authority, decision making, and activities can be observed along a continuum (see Figure 4.5).[35]

The *manipulator* leadership style is based on a Machiavellian ethic that views leadership amorally. That is, the end result justifies the means taken to reach it. Power is the driving force behind a manipulator's motives. This is an egotistically and essentially economically motivated moral leadership style. It lacks trust and relationship-building interests and qualities and is oriented toward the short term. Although the motives underlying this style may be amoral, the consequences could prove immoral for those affected. Have you ever worked under someone who used this style?

The *bureaucratic* administrator is a rule-based moral leadership style. Based on the theories of famed German sociologist Max Weber,[36] the bureaucratic administrator acts on the rational principles embodied in an ideal organizational bureaucracy, i.e., fixed rules that explain the purpose and functions of the organization; a hierarchy that shows the chain-of-command control structure; well-defined job descriptions; professional managers who communicate and enforce the rules; and technically qualified employees who are promoted by expertise and rewarded by rank and tenure. The driving force behind this style is *efficiency* ("doing things right," functioning in the least wasteful manner) more than effectiveness (producing the intended result or aim, "doing the right things"). Although this leadership style has an admirable aim of basing decisions only on objective, rational criteria, the moral problem with it lies in the "sin of omission." That is, a leader may follow all the rules exactly but hurt someone unintentionally—amorally—by not attending to legitimate human needs because the option to do so was not prescribed or included in the rules.

For example, a professional bus driver has orders not to stop between two cities for any reason. During one of the bus trips, a bystander is accidentally shot and appears to be fatally wounded by a hunter. The driver sees and recognizes the victim but refuses to stop because of the rules. The bystander dies. Is the bus driver's failure to stop morally justified because he or she followed the rules?

Rules cannot address all problems and needs in what we know are imperfect and political organizations. The well-intentioned bureaucratic administrator may try to act amorally, but his or her efforts could result in immoral and irresponsible consequences to others. Do you recognize this moral leadership style? Have you ever worked for someone who used it?

The *professional* manager aims at effectiveness, "doing things right." The theory about this style is grounded in Peter Drucker's[37] principles and view of managers as professionals who have the expertise and tools for accomplishing work effectively through others. Based on a social contract ethic, this management style relies—like the previous two styles—on amoral techniques and assumptions for getting work done. For example, professional career managers use rational objectives and their training to accomplish the organization's work. The organization's corporate culture and the social contract—implicit and explicit agreements—made between managers and organizational executives set the ground rules and ethics that govern the manager's behavior. However, social contracts are not always ethically justifiable.

An ethical problem with this leadership style lies in the real possibility that the collective corporate culture and dominant governing group may think and act amorally or immorally. *Groupthink* (consensus-dominated decision making, based on uncritical, biased thinking) may occur.[38] The collective may lead itself astray. Professional managers by training and expertise are still prone to unethical behavior. Do you recognize managers or leaders who act amorally or immorally as "professionals"?

Finally, the *transforming* leadership style, based on James Burns'[39] theory, is grounded on a personal ethic. The transformational leader bases his or her effectiveness on relationships with followers. Also, this style focuses on the charisma, energy, and excitement the leader brings to relationships. The transformational leader is involved in the growth and self-actualization of others and views others according to their potential. This type of leader identifies and elevates the values and motives of others. He or she empowers, coaches, and helps promote other leaders. This leadership style is moral in that "it raises the level of human conduct and aspirations of both leaders and led, and thus has a transforming effect on both."[40]

William Hitt[41] moved the continuum of moral leadership one step beyond the transformational leader to what he termed an "encompassing approach to leadership," or "the effective leader-manager." The *encompassing* leader learns from the shortcomings of each of the four leadership styles on the continuum and uses all of their strengths.

For example, manipulative leadership does value the effective use of power. However, this style's deceptive and dysfunctional uses of power should be avoided. The bureaucratic administrator values the effective use of rules, roles, and responsibilities; however, these should not become ends rather than means. The professional manager values results; however, human concerns should be valued more highly than physical and fiscal resources and results. The transformational leader values human empowerment; however, even this characteristic is not the complete job of management.

Socially and morally responsible leaders and managers as individual and organizational stakeholders should, according to a stakeholder management approach, observe their obligations to all stakeholders, including their own conscience, and observe in their business and stakeholder dealings the ethical principles of rights, justice, and duty—in addition to utilitarian logic.

FAILURE OF ETHICAL LEADERSHIP. There are many examples of leaders who have violated their legal and ethical responsibilities to stockholders and stakeholders. Micky Monus, former CEO of the Phar-Mor company (a discount retail drugstore chain), was sentenced to 20 years in prison and fined $1 million on December 12, 1995, when he was "convicted on all counts of a 109-count indictment that charged him with conspiracy to commit mail fraud, wire fraud, bank fraud, and transportation of funds obtained by theft or fraud." Monus was hailed as a community hero in Youngstown, Ohio, when he led Phar-Mor to historical growth. His charismatic, entrepreneurial personality and leadership had a dark side—greed, deceit, and theft. His influence also led his young finance management team into the massive theft, fraud, and cover-up.[42]

There was also "Chainsaw Al" Dunlap, a former CEO of Sunbeam, who was fired following an SEC investigation of accounting fraud under his watch. Dunlap was known, and questioned, for his ability to achieve profits. To meet Sunbeam's profit projections and appease Wall Street analysts in 1997, Dunlap devised a method of selling Sunbeam spare parts (used to fix broken blenders and grills) for $11 million to a company that warehoused the parts. That company valued the parts at $2 million. Dunlap and company pressured the warehouse firm to sign a contract to buy the parts at $11 million, booking $8 million in profit. (The parts were never sold). Dunlap described his other approaches in more detail in a book, *Mean Business: How I Save Bad Companies and Make Good Companies Great.*[43] He was instrumental in laying off large numbers of employees and cutting back organizational operations to achieve profitability.[44]

Seven symptoms of the failure of ethical leadership provide a practical lens to examine a CEO's, team leader's, or professional's (including your own) leadership shortsightedness[45]:

1. Ethical blindness: they do not perceive ethical issues from inattention or inability.
2. Ethical muteness: they do not have or use ethical language or principles. "Talk the talk" but do not "walk the talk" on values.
3. Ethical incoherence: they are not able to see inconsistencies among values they say they follow; e.g., they say they value responsibility but reward performance based only on numbers.
4. Ethical paralysis: they are unable to act on their values from lack of knowledge or fear of the consequences of their actions.
5. Ethical hypocrisy: they are not committed to their espoused values. They delegate things they are unwilling to or cannot do themselves.
6. Ethical schizophrenia: they do not have a set of coherent values; they act at work one way, at home another way.
7. Ethical complacency: they believe they can do no wrong because of who they are. They believe they are immune from being unethical.

How should CEOs be evaluated?

CEO PAY: EXCESSIVE OR EARNED?   CEOs at major U.S. companies received an average total compensation of $36.2 million in 2000, up by 60% from 1999. This does not include perks, which companies are not required to report if the value is below $50,000 a year or less than 10% of an executive's pay.[46]

These are some of the issues. First, many CEOs who have been with the same company most of their career are looking toward retirement and do not need the bonuses and perks (e.g., free loans, corporate jet, company car and allowance, first class air travel) that they could well afford on their own. Second, the salary increases, stock options, and perks are offered even during times when the company's performance is suboptimal and layoffs are occurring. Third, the CEO's pay can be 20, 30, or 50 times higher than the salaries of some first-line managers and supervisors. However, a difference of more than a factor of seven is considered sizable for an average CEO position. Finally, while CEOs certainly bear much greater responsibility, risk, and blame for a company's successes and failures on Wall Street and in its competitive markets, one question remains: Are employees and managers rewarded and punished more unfairly for their individual shortcomings and contributions than CEOs and other company officers? Should such comparisons be made at all?

CEO EVALUATIONS. The board of directors of a company is technically responsible for disciplining and rewarding the CEO. A Korn/Ferry survey of board members found that 72% of the largest U.S. companies do a formal CEO evaluation.[47] Evidence shows that "CEO appraisals require a special commitment from the CEO and from the board members" in order for the process to work well and the results to be meaningful.[48] However, in many instances, it is the CEO who is also president of the company and chairperson of the board.

Two forces influence the popularity of boards of directors evaluating CEOs. The first is the increased recognition of the critical roles CEOs play and the increased compensation levels received for those roles. CEO bonus and salary levels and increases over the past decade have grown, regardless of company or stock performance. The second influential force is pressure from the investment community, which dates back to the beginning of shareholder awareness in the 1980s, when corporate acquisitions and restructuring activities were questioned with regard to the effectiveness of CEOs and their boards, due diligence, and management practices. Still, not all CEOs are formally evaluated with their top-level team members and other employees. For publicly traded companies, i.e., those listed on the New York Stock Exchange, NASDAQ, and other trading companies, industry analysts constantly score and keep pressure on the performance of CEOs and chief financial officers (CFOs)—by the numbers. Market performance is a major evaluator of these officers' financial effectiveness. Annual reports and financial audits available to stockholders are another form of assessing leaders.

CEOs are also evaluated by assessing gaps between their stated and enacted strategies and by using customer and employee surveys. Assessments of the organization's systems (e.g., accounting, human resources, information technology, supply chain, and work flow) are also reflections of the leader's overall effectiveness in directing, aligning, and implementing strategy. Finally, leaders must balance and align stakeholder interests with the dominant mission and values of the company. This requires courage, emotional intelligence, and moral principles.

STRATEGY

We turn next to strategy, which, as a major organizational dimension, influences the goals and objectives of the company and its stakeholders.

Strategy and the strategy development process are part of the domain of organizational leaders. Gary Hamel, a contemporary strategy guru, calls for a "revolution" in leading the strategy innovation process. He states that "you need a set of values that will set you apart from the courtiers and wannabes." Those values include "honesty, compassion, humility, pragmatism, and fearlessness."[49] The strategy-making process also involves stakeholder management. A corporation's strategy is propelled and supported by its people, stakeholders, culture, and moral contributions to its communities, customers, and society. Strategic thinking has evolved from a mechanistic to a more holistic process, which emphasizes innovation, generation of value for stakeholders and stockholders, involvement and learning with stakeholders, and building customer partnerships and relationships.[50] This section and the next discuss the relationships among corporate strategy, structure, culture, systems, and moral responsibility. How do strategy and structure influence the moral behavior of employees?

Corporate leaders are responsible for orchestrating the development and execution of strategy. An organization's strategy influences legality, morality, innovation, and competitiveness in the following ways:

1. Strategy sets the overall direction of business activities. Enterprise strategy, for example, can emphasize revenue and growth over customer satisfaction or product quality. It can drive technical concern over professional development. Corporate strategy can also direct a firm's activities toward social issues, employee rights, and other stakeholder obligations. It can include or exclude stakeholders and employees. It can innovate recklessly for the short term or in long-term ways that benefit society as well as a few market niches.

2. Strategy reflects and models activities that management values and prioritizes. It mirrors management's ethics and morality. It is the message to the messengers. Strategy says: "We care and value your feedback, safety, and concerns," or "we only want your money and participation in our profits."

3. Strategy sets the tone and tenor of business activities and transactions inside the organization. Reward and control systems reflect the emphasis and values of the larger strategic direction. An emphasis on profit at the expense of employee development is usually reflected as rigid and unrealistic incentive and revenue quota systems. Growth and expansion can be made a priority above talent development and contribution.

Enterprise strategy, then, sets and affects corporate expectations, ways of doing business, rewards, motivations, and performance. Strategy influences the types of control systems that govern business activities and the pressures that lead to moral or immoral behavior. All stakeholders have an interest in the strategies and strategy building processes of organizations.

FOUR LEVELS OF STRATEGY. Chapter 2 explained how a stakeholder analysis is used as a strategic method for mapping a firm's social responsibility toward external stakeholders. Here strategy is described from an internal perspective. Corporations formulate at least four levels of strategies: *enterprise, corporate, business,* and *functional.*[51] The enterprise strategy, the broadest level, identifies the corporation's role in society, decides how the firm will be perceived by stakeholders, defines its principles and values, and shows the firm's standards. The corporate strategy identifies goals, objectives, and business areas on which the firm's policies and plans are based. Business strategy translates the corporate strategy into more detailed goals and objectives for specific business activities. Functional strategy takes business strategy into even more detail in marketing, research and development, production, sales, and other functional areas.

At the enterprise strategic level, the CEO and upper-level managers state their social responsibility and stakeholder commitments. Corporate strategy also should reflect ethical considerations. For example, R. Edward Freeman and Daniel Gilbert Jr. argued that we must understand the multiple and competing values underlying stakeholders' actions in order to understand the choices and actions corporations make.[52]

From a value-based stakeholder management approach, the strategy development and implementation process should link to and respect the vision and mission of the organization. As with the Levi Strauss values and vision statement in Figure 4.4, the strategy would be reviewed according, for example, to these statements: "*Integrity—Doing the Right Thing.* Ethical conduct and social responsibility characterize our way of doing business. We are honest and trustworthy. We do what we say we are going to do. Integrity includes a willingness to do the right thing for our employees, brands, the company and society as a whole, even when personal, professional and social risks or economic pressures confront us. This principle of responsible commercial success is embedded in the company's experience. It continues to anchor our beliefs and behaviors today, and is one of the reasons consumers trust our brands. Our shareholders expect us to manage the company this way. It strengthens brand equity and drives sustained, profitable growth and superior return on investment. In fact, our experience has shown that our 'profits through principles' approach to business is a point of competitive advantage."

STRATEGY FORMULATION AND IMPLEMENTATION PROCESS. The strategy management process involves:

1. Formulating goals
2. Formulating strategies
3. Implementing strategies
4. Controlling strategies
5. Evaluating strategies
6. Analyzing the environment

This process is neither linear nor static in practice. Articulating strategies involves iteration, interaction, and collaboration. Analyzing the environment also requires interpretation among various professionals, as does reformulating goals. Stakeholder involvement, then, is an integral part of the strategy management process. Identifying and addressing strategic issues, as discussed in Chapter 2, is also part of the strategy formulation, implementation, and evaluation process. Leaders' and stakeholders' values are significant in this process because these professionals interpret trends and responses to the environment according to their values, expertise, backgrounds, training, and interests.

Economic, political, technological, and environmental goals, strategies, and issues can, as was discussed in Chapter 2, evolve into social and moral problems and dilemmas for corporations, as did Microsoft's dealings with strategic alliance partners and the government. For this reason, at the very outset of the *goal and strategy formulation* stage, priorities for values and moral and social responsibility should be identified, listed in the vision and mission statements, and practiced by the CEO. Strategy is also a reflection of priorities. From a value-based stakeholder perspective, strategic priorities might include enhancing the physical environment, involving and protecting customers and consumers, and building safe workplaces and products in relation to profit and revenue milestones.

The *strategy formulation* stage involves a competitive analysis of the firm's strengths and weaknesses in terms of managerial, financial, and social issues. For social issues, a moral perspective should be articulated at this stage and should reflect a concern for the visibility, vulnerability, and obligations of social issues in a firm's strategies. During this stage, professionals must estimate the firm's risks and opportunities in pursuing specific goals and spell out the organization's obligations to relevant stakeholders (e.g., suppliers, consumers and customers, competitors, government, communities, and society).

During the third stage, *implementing the strategy*, managers and employees from the entire organization should be involved in the process. Social and moral responsibilities play a role in strategy implementation by ensuring that the procedures for putting strategy and resources into action are just, fair, and equitable and that the corporation is morally fulfilling its fiduciary responsibilities for its stakeholders. Responsibilities of the leader, as shown in Figure 4.4, can be monitored: teamwork and trust, diversity, recognition, ethical management practices, communications, and empowerment.

During the fourth stage, *strategy control,* and the fifth stage, *strategy evaluation,* corporate managers set standards to measure the intended performance against the actual performance of their actions. During these stages, managers also assess the moral, social, and economic results with their performance criteria. During the strategy control stage, corrective action should be taken if results are not in line with stated goals. During both of these stages, the "social audit" (explained later in this chapter) can be used for checking, evaluating, and correcting unethical activities.

During the *environmental analysis* stage, the managers scan, identify, monitor, and forecast issues and trends in the technological, political, economic, and social environments to determine the effects of targeted issues on the organization. Research think tanks (such as the Gardner Group and Forester Research), opinion and survey organizations (such as the Yankelovich Group and the Roper Organization) analyze and predict environmental trends that are used by companies to redirect and change strategies.

From a stakeholder perspective, a firm would be interested in identifying issues that affect its stakeholder obligations and relationships. Obtaining accurate information from the environment can help managers estimate risks and costs of an issue that is leading to a crisis. Strategies can then be formulated to proactively prevent harm to the company and its constituencies. From a social and moral perspective, managers would be concerned about fulfilling their internal stakeholder obligations through these strategies. Responsible corporations must be prepared to equitably and justly manage enabling the workforce with new technical skills and integrating aging employees, dual-career families, and new immigrants. Flexible work times, health care programs, and flexible management styles must be implemented to manage this changing workforce responsibly.

4.4 CULTURE, STRUCTURE, AND SYSTEMS

HIGH-ETHICS COMPANIES

What would a highly effective value-based organizational culture look like? Mark Pastin studied 25 "high-ethics, high-profit" firms, which at the time included Motorola, 3M, Cadbury Schweppes, Arco, Hilby Wilson, Northern Chemical, and Apple. While the list of high-ethics firms—like "built-to-last" firms—may change, the four principles that Pastin discovered to describe such firms serve as a benchmark for understanding ethically effective organizations:

> *Principle 1:* High-ethics firms are at ease interacting with diverse internal and external stakeholder groups. The ground rules of these firms make the good of these stakeholder groups part of the firm's own good.
>
> *Principle 2:* High-ethics firms are obsessed with fairness. Their ground rules emphasize that the other person's interests count as much as their own.
>
> *Principle 3:* In high-ethics firms, responsibility is individual rather than collective; individuals assume responsibility for the firm's actions. The ground rules mandate that individuals are responsible to themselves.
>
> *Principle 4:* The high-ethics firm sees its activities as having a purpose, a way of operating that members of the firm value. And purpose ties the firm to its environment.[53]

ORGANIZATIONAL CULTURE DEFINED

Purpose, embodied in corporate culture, is the glue that holds organizations together. A corporation's culture is the shared values and meanings its members hold in common, which are articulated and practiced by an organization's leaders.

Corporate culture is transmitted through: (1) the values and leadership styles that the leaders espouse and practice, (2) the heroes and heroines that the company rewards and holds up as models, (3) the rites, rituals, and symbols that organizations value, and (4) the way that organizational executives and members communicate among themselves and with their stakeholders.

Heroes and heroines in corporations set the moral tone and direction by their present or even remembered examples. They are the role models; they define what is successful and attainable; they symbolize the company to outsiders and insiders; and they preserve the valued qualities of the firm, set standards of excellence, and motivate people. Enduring corporate and organizational cultural heroes include Herb Kelleher at Southwest Airlines, Sam Walton at WalMart, Ben Cohen and Jerry Greenfield at Ben & Jerry's, Mary Kay at Mary Kay, David Packard at Hewlett-Packard, and Bill Gates at Microsoft. Jimmy Carter, an unpopular president during his term, now has higher popularity ratings than when he was in office and will probably be remembered as a highly ethical president and person. Carter still works on housing and inner-city projects to assist the poor and economically disadvantaged. Who are the heroes and heroines in your organization? By what qualities and characteristics are they remembered? Are they moral, immoral, or amoral leaders?

Rituals and communication in companies help define corporate culture and its moral nature. Corporately sanctioned rituals that bring people together, foster openness, and promote cross-functional and integrated hierarchical levels of communication can lower stress and encourage moral behavior. Social gatherings, picnics, recognition ceremonies, and other company outings where corporate leaders are present and where sharing of values, stories, problems, accomplishments, and aspirations occur can lead to cultures that value people and the company's aims.

OBSERVING ORGANIZATIONAL CULTURE

Organizational cultures are both visible and invisible, formal and informal. They can be studied by observation, by listening to and interacting with people in the culture, and also in the following ways:

- Studying the physical setting
- Reading what the company says about its own culture
- Observing and testing how the company greets strangers
- Watching how people spend time
- Understanding career path progressions
- Noting the length of tenure in jobs, especially for middle managers
- Observing anecdotes and stories.

How would you describe your organizational or company culture using these methods?

STRONG CORPORATE CULTURE TRAITS AND VALUES

Strong corporate cultures: (1) have a widely shared philosophy, (2) value the importance of people, (3) have heroes (presidents and products) that symbolize the success of the company, and (4) celebrate rituals, which provide opportunities for caring and sharing, for developing a spirit of "oneness" and "we-ness."[54] From a stakeholder management view, organizational systems are aligned around the purpose, ethical values, and mission of the company. Also, individuals and teams in ethical cultures demonstrate a tolerance and respect for individual differences and diversity, compassion, ability for forgiveness and acceptance, and freedom and courage to do the right thing in questionable situations.

Corporate values statements serve as the economic, political, social, and ethical compasses for employees, stakeholders, and systems. Two classic benchmark values statements are those of Borg-Warner (Figure 4.6) and Johnson & Johnson (Figure 4.7). Seattle-based Boeing Corporation's values were first articulated by its former CEO William Allen. These values still serve as an outstanding example at the individual level. They are[55]:

- Be considerate of my associates' views.
- Don't talk too much . . . let others talk.
- Don't be afraid to admit that you don't know.
- Don't get immersed in detail.
- Make contacts with other people in industry.
- Try to improve feeling around Seattle toward the company.
- Make a sincere effort to understand labor's viewpoint.
- Be definite, don't vacillate.
- Act—get things done—move forward.

CULTURES IN TROUBLE

Companies that reinforce secrecy, hidden agendas, and physical settings that isolate executives from managers and employees and emphasize status over human concern often are cultures in trouble. Troubled corporate and organizational cultures can breed and encourage unethical activities.

Organizations that also stress competition, profit, and economic or introverted self-interests over stakeholder obligations and that have no morally active direction often have cultures in trouble. Signs of cultures in trouble, or weak cultures, include the following[56]:

- An inward focus
- A short-term focus
- Morale and motivational problems
- Emotional outbursts
- Fragmentation and inconsistency (in dress, speech, physical settings, or work habits)

FIGURE 4.6   THE BELIEFS OF BORG-WARNER: TO REACH BEYOND THE MINIMAL

Any business is a member of a social system, entitled to the rights and bound by the responsibilities of that membership. Its freedom to pursue economic goals is constrained by law and channeled by the forces of a free market. But these demands are minimal, requiring only that a business provide wanted goods and services, compete fairly, and cause no obvious harm. For some companies, that is enough. It is not enough for Borg-Warner. We impose upon ourselves an obligation to reach beyond the minimal. We do so convinced that by making a larger contribution to the society that sustains us, we best assure not only its future vitality, but our own.

This is what we believe.

We Believe In the Dignity of the Individual.

However large and complex a business may be, its work is still done by dealing with people. Each person involved is a unique human being, with pride, needs, values, and innate personal worth. For Borg-Warner to succeed, we must operate in a climate of openness and trust, in which each of us freely grants others the same respect, cooperation, and decency we seek for ourselves.

We Believe In Our Responsibility to the Common Good.

Because Borg-Warner is both an economic and social force, our responsibilities to the public are large. The spur of competition and the sanctions of the law give strong guidance to our behavior, but alone do not inspire our best. For that we must heed the voice of our natural concern for others. Our challenge is to supply goods and services that are of superior value to those who use them; to create jobs that provide meaning for those who do them; to honor and enhance human life; and to offer our talents and our wealth to help improve the world we share.

We Believe In the Endless Quest for Excellence.

Though we may be better today than we were yesterday, we are not as good as we must become. Borg-Warner chooses to be a leader—in serving our customers, advancing our technologies, and rewarding all who invest in us their time, money, and trust. None of us can settle for doing less than our best, and we can never stop trying to surpass what already has been achieved.

We Believe In Continuous Renewal.

A corporation endures and prospers only by moving forward. The past has given us the present to build on. But to follow our visions to the future, we must see the difference between traditions that give us continuity and strength and conventions that no longer serve us—and have the courage to act on that knowledge. Most can adapt after change has occurred; we must be among the few who anticipate change, shape it to our purpose, and act as its agents.

We Believe In the Commonwealth of Borg-Warner and Its People.

Borg-Warner is both a federation of businesses and a community of people. Our goal is to preserve the freedom each of us needs to find personal satisfaction while building the strength that comes from unity. True unity is more than a melding of self-interests; it results when values and ideals also are shared. Some of ours are spelled out in these statements of belief. Others include faith in our political, economic, and spiritual heritage; pride in our work and our company; the knowledge that loyalty must flow in many directions; and a conviction that power is strongest when shared. We look to the unifying force of these beliefs as a source of energy to brighten the future of our company and all who depend on it.

SOURCE: Borg-Warner Corp. The beliefs of Borg Warner: to reach beyond the minimal. Reprinted with permission of the Borg-Warner Corporation.

FIGURE 4.7	JOHNSON & JOHNSON CREDO

We believe our first responsibility is to the doctors, nurses, and patients; to mothers and
  fathers; and all others who use our product and services. In meeting their needs,
  everything we do must be of high quality.
We must constantly strive to reduce our costs in order to maintain reasonable prices.
Customers' orders must be serviced promptly and accurately.
Our suppliers and distributors must have an opportunity to make a fair profit.

We are responsible to our employees, the men and women who work with us throughout
  the world.
Everyone must be considered as an individual. We must respect their dignity and
  recognize their merit.
They must have a sense of security in their jobs.
Compensation must be fair and adequate, and working conditions clean, orderly, and
  safe.
We must be mindful of ways to help our employees fulfill their family responsibilities.
Employees must feel free to make suggestions and complaints.
There must be equal opportunity for employment, development, and advancement for
  those qualified.
We must provide competent management, and their actions must be just and ethical.

We are responsible to the communities in which we work and to the world community as
  well.
We must be good citizens—support good works and charities and bear our fair share of
  taxes.
We must encourage civic improvements and better health and education.
We must maintain in good order the property we are privileged to use, protecting the
  environment and natural resources.

Our final responsibility is to our stockholders.
Business must make a sound profit.
We must experiment with new ideas.
Research must be carried on, innovative programs developed, and mistakes paid for.
New equipment must be purchased, new facilities provided, and new products launched.
Reserves must be created to provide for adverse times.
When we operate according to these principles, the stockholders should realize a fair
  return.

SOURCE: Johnson & Johnson. Used by permission of Johnson & Johnson, the copyright owner.

- Clashes among subcultures
- Ingrown subcultures
- Dominance of subculture values over shared company values
- No clear values or beliefs about how to succeed in business
- Many beliefs, with no priorities about which are important
- Different beliefs throughout the company
- Destructive or disruptive cultural heroes, rather than builders of common understanding about what is important
- Disorganized or disruptive daily rituals

A value-based stakeholder management approach would assess an organization's values with these questions: Do the leaders and culture embody "high-ethic" or "in trouble" characteristics in their values, actions, and policies? Are the values written down? Do others know the values? Do the values reflect a concern for and obligation toward the organization's stakeholders? Do the values reflect a utilitarian, just, dutiful, or egotistical ethic? Are the values taken at "face value" only, or are they practiced and implemented by employees? Do the values and communication patterns promote moral, immoral, or amoral behavior?

ORGANIZATIONAL STRUCTURE

Ask to see almost any organization's structure and you will be handed a hierarchical set of top-down ordered boxes connected by lines. This so-called pyramid, or functional structure, is one of the oldest forms of depicting arrangements in companies. Corporations can be structured in several ways and many firms combine some of these types[57]:

- By function (e.g., marketing, sales, production)
- By product (e.g., shoes, sports equipment, formal wear)
- By geographic region (e.g., Asia, Europe, North America)
- By matrix (i.e., a functional area combined with a special project or program manager)

Usually, if the company is international or global, a combination of these forms is used. Corporations also can be organized into the following:

- Strategic business units (SBUs) that perform as independent profit centers
- Networks, in which organizational teams of experts (e.g., from marketing, production, or finance) work with outside suppliers and vendors to satisfy customer demands.

Finally, there are other ad hoc arrangements, which include clustered and virtual teams (a mix of functional areas) targeted for special assignments and modified matrix and self-designed teams, which are designed to increase profit and minimize expenses by flexibly serving the needs of end-users and customers.

Regardless of the type of structure, from a value-based stakeholder management perspective, some key concerns and questions regarding any structure are:

- How centralized or decentralized is the authority, responsibility, communication, and information flow?
- How organic (less structured) or mechanistic (more structured) are the systems managed and controlled?
- How tall (more layers of bureaucracy) or flat are the reporting systems?

- How formal or informal are procedures, rules, and regulations?
- How much autonomy, freedom, and discretion do internal stakeholders and decision makers have?
- How flexible, adaptable, and responsive are systems and professionals to responding to internal and external threats and opportunities, potential crises, and imminent opportunities?

While there are no absolute guidelines regarding which structure is more immune or leads to ethical problems, the following overview provides some evidence for further discussion and consideration. Functionally centralized structures can encourage lack of communication, coordination, and increased conflict, because each area is typically separated by its own boundaries, managers, and systems. Infighting over budgets, "turf," and power increase the likelihood of unethical, and even illegal, activities. On the other hand, highly supervised employees in bureaucratic firms may also act more ethically than employees in entrepreneurial, laissez-faire firms, because employees tend to think through the risk of getting caught in firms with more supervised structures. A study conducted by John Cullen, Bart Victor, and Carrol Stephens[58] reported that a subunit's location in the organizational structure affects its ethical climate: At a savings and loan association and also at a manufacturing plant, the employees at the home offices reported less emphasis on laws, codes, and rules than did the employees at the branch offices. Perhaps control by formal mechanisms becomes more necessary when direct supervision by top management is not feasible.

There is evidence that decentralized structures can encourage more unethical behavior among employees than more supervised, controlled structures. One account of Citicorp's credit-card processing division illustrated the relationships among organizational structure, competitive pressures, and immoral and illegal behavior. The bank fired the president and 11 senior executives of that division because they had fraudulently overstated revenue by $23 million for 2 years. The illegal inflating of revenue by division employees may reflect the problem that employee bonuses were tied to unrealistic revenue targets. Citicorp centralized its organizational functions. Not all decentralized structures promote ethical behavior. In this case, the decentralized structure left the bank susceptible to potential abuse by employees.

Pressures from upper-level managers who overemphasize unrealistic bottom-line quarterly revenue objectives and who give unclear policies and procedures to guide ethical decision making in business transactions may contribute to immoral behavior in more decentralized structures. There is evidence to support the argument that middle- and lower-level managers, in particular, feel pressured to compromise their personal moral standards to meet corporate expectations.[59] Managers in large firms may compromise their personal ethics to meet corporate expectations for several reasons, which include:

1. Decentralized structures with little or no coordination with central policy and procedures encourage a climate for immoral activities when pressures for profit-making increase.

2. Unrealistic, short-term, and bottom-line profit quotas add pressure on employees to commit unethical actions.

3. Overemphasis on numbers-driven financial incentives encourages shortcuts around responsible decisions.

4. Amoral organizational and work-unit cultures can create an environment that condones illegal and immoral actions.

BOUNDARYLESS AND NETWORKED ORGANIZATIONS

The decentralization of organizations has been accelerated with information technologies and the re-engineering of business processes. Software applications and web-enabled intranets and extranets allow the boundaries within organizations and between customers and companies to become more transparent and fluid.[60] Dell computers has eliminated middle layers of its company, supply chain, and industry by enabling individual customers to design, order, and purchase—and even receive, in the case of software—their own customized computer products on-line. These changes are not easy, nor are they isolated from the larger context of the organization. An organizational expert[61] noted that the main reason implementation of major technology changes fails is that "the technology was seen as the solution, without taking into account the complex dynamic of the organization and people. It doesn't matter in which area, whether it's knowledge management or B-to-B. You can't forget that organizations are made of people and technology, and both people and technology will define the success of an organization." From both an ethics and efficiency perspective, care should be taken by companies implementing digital networks, because one study[62] reports that digital networks generate both opportunities for and threats to worker autonomy. Major opportunities include increased communication capabilities, "informedness," and "teleworking." Threats to worker autonomy are electronic monitoring, dependence on third-party operator and managers, and task prestructuring, which can reduce individual responsibility and control. These opportunities and problems depend on the type of organizational structure in place (how open and responsive it is), the particular design features of the network, and the strategies of the company and units—to what extent employee stakeholders can engage and be involved in deciding the choice and use of the technologies.

ORGANIZATIONAL SYSTEMS

A stakeholder management view of organizations supports a holistic, systems view of operations and processes.[63] This view holds that organizational systems operate—or do not operate—effectively together in interdependent ways. To understand an organization, we must learn to see the systems from all of its stakeholders' and stockholders' views. Moreover, internal systems, such as marketing, finance, production, sales, research, and development, depend on mutually shared information. John Rosthorn, a 30-year veteran who

| FIGURE 4.8 | BUSINESS ETHICS ORGANIZATIONAL PROFILE: SEVEN-AXIS PERFORMANCE DISPLAY |

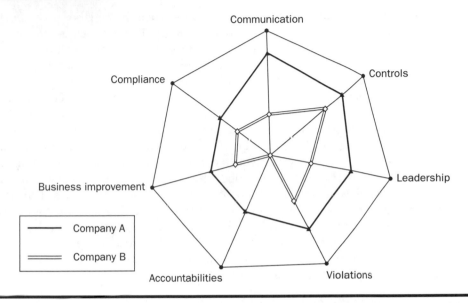

SOURCE: Based on the illustration by J. Rosthorn, Business ethics auditing: More than a stakeholder's toy. *Journal of Business Ethics, 27,* 18, Figure 9. Lower scores are near the center; higher scores are near the border. Company A (black line) scored higher than Company B (white line) in all dimensions.

worked with two transnational corporations, wrote[64]: "The more serious survival issue for top managers and investors is not the 'competition,' but the enemies within the corporation. It was Nick Leeson who sank Barings Bank with fraudulent and misplaced trades. It was Shell managers in Nigeria who caused immense difficulties for the Shell corporation by their blindness toward basic human rights and misplaced loyalties. In the case of British Biotech, where the market capitalization fell by 90% in just a few months, it was about the integrity of its top management team that the deepest concerns existed." Rosthorn describes a seven-axis performance display, which is part of a general business ethics audit and Business Ethics Strategic Survey used by managers, audit committees, and fund managers. Organizations that have been audited with this survey receive results for each of the seven dimensions plotted on the display, as portrayed in Figure 4.8. The process can also be externally verified. Examples of survey questions plotted on the figure are: "Is an independent audit of business conduct done annually? Is there a written, approved business ethics plan for the present financial year? Is there a strategy for the further development of good ethical conduct in the business?" Notice that several general management systems and dimensions are included in Figure 4.8. Financial and corporate auditing is not an isolated function. (This figure is presented here to show an overview of the dimensions included in the audit, not as a measurement tool. Company B shows signs of potential trouble.)

Value and innovation are also created only when the collaborative efforts among an organization's systems create synergy. The organization's vision, values, and mission, which are reinforced by the culture and example of the leader, are the cornerstone for integrating the internal systems. Following this logic, W. Chan Kim and Renee Mauborgne[65] posed the following research question: "What type of organization best unlocks the ideas and creativity of its employees to achieve this end?" They discovered that "when putting value innovation strategies into action, structural conditions create only the potential for individuals to share their best ideas and knowledge. To actualize this potential, a company must cultivate a corporate culture conducive to willing collaboration."[66] The authors describe "the positively reinforcing cycle of fair process" as one which creates innovative outcomes for companies. They describe this process as follows: For each success a group has in implementing a "general value innovation strategy" based on fair process, the result strengthens the group's cohesiveness and their belief in the process. This, in turn, sustains the collaboration and creativity inherent to value innovation. The four components of that process include the following[67]:

1. Engagement, explanation, expectation, clarity
2. Idea sharing and voluntary cooperation
3. Value innovation plans and rapid execution
4. Organizational confidence in and respect for colleagues' intellectual and emotional worth

The voluntary, value-based, and supportive nature of an organization's culture, policies, and processes with regard to its professionals is a necessary ingredient for this type of innovation and value-added productivity.

4.5 CORPORATE SELF-REGULATION: CHALLENGES AND ISSUES

A value-based stakeholder management approach assumes that corporations (owners and management) *ought* to intrinsically value all stakeholders' interests.[68] In practice (and according to some theorists), this is not always the case.[69] Self-regulation in companies is necessary for the protection and implementation of some stakeholders' interests, including employees. Complete your company's "ethical weather report" (Figure 4.9) to identify from your point of view how ethical your company is.

Establishing codes of ethical and legal conduct, implementing stakeholder management assessments, and enacting ethics programs can help a company financially and morally, as the following discussion indicates. The federal sentencing guidelines were established in 1984 by the U.S. Congress,

| FIGURE 4.9 | ETHICAL WEATHER REPORT |

Step 1: Complete the following questionnaire using the organization in which you are working or one in which you have worked. Beside each statement, write the number from the scale that accurately reflects your knowledge and experience with the company.

Completely False	Mostly False	Somewhat False	Somewhat True	Mostly True	Completely True
0	1	2	3	4	5

_____ 1. In this company, people are expected to follow their own personal and moral beliefs.

_____ 2. People are expected to do anything to further the company's interests.

_____ 3. In this company, people look out for each other's good.

_____ 4. It is very important here to follow strictly the company's rules and procedures.

_____ 5. In this company, people protect their own interests above other considerations.

_____ 6. The first consideration is whether a decision violates any law.

_____ 7. Everyone is expected to stick by company rules and procedures.

_____ 8. The most efficient way is always the right way in this company.

_____ 9. Our major consideration is what is best for everyone in the company.

_____ 10. In this company, the law or ethical code of the profession is the major consideration.

_____ 11. It is expected at this company that employees will always do what is right for the customer and the public.

Step 2: Score your answers by adding up your responses to 1, 3, 6, 9, 10, and 11. Write the sum under Subtotal 1 below. Now reverse the scores on questions 2, 4, 5, 7, and 8 (5 = 0, 4 = 1, 3 = 2, 2 = 3, 1 = 4, 0 = 5). Add these reverse scores (i.e., number value) and write the sum in Subtotal number 2. Now add Subtotal 1 with Subtotal 2 for your overall score. The total score ranges between 0 and 55. The higher the score, the more the organization supports ethical behavior.

Subtotal 1 _____ + Subtotal 2 _____ = Overall Score _____

Step 3: Write a paragraph explaining your organization's ethical profile: Why is it the way it is? Offer specific steps you would recommend in your organization's cultural dimensions, leadership, policies, or procedures that would either enhance its already ethical climate or help change the climate.

SOURCE: J. B. Cullen, B. Victor, C. Stephens. An Ethical Weather Report Assessing the Organization's Ethical Climate. Reprinted with permission of publisher, from *Organizational Dynamics,* Autumn/1989, © 1989. American Management Association, New York. All rights reserved.

which passed a crime bill that instituted the U.S. Sentencing Commission. This commission, made up of federal judges, was empowered with sentencing those found in violation and convicted of any of the guidelines, violations of which became federal crimes. In 1987, uniform guidelines were created for sentencing *individuals* in the federal courts. Some federal judges quit the bench in protest to the strictness of the guidelines and sentences they were required to hand down. In 1991, the commission shifted the emphasis from individual wrongdoers to *organizations* that might be found guilty for the illegal actions of their employees. The 1991 guidelines threaten fines of up to $290 million to companies found guilty of violation of the federal guidelines (e.g., money laundering, drug dealing). However, those fines can be substantially reduced if an organization implements an "effective program to prevent and detect violations of law." Corporate interest and participation in ethics programs flourished.[70]

Corporate self-regulation does not seem to work to prevent or lessen illegal and unethical activities—even with the federal sentencing guidelines—without active leadership involvement and integration of and support from other organizational systems.[71] Moreover, agreement on and commitment to "best practices" also enhance effective self-regulation with regard to company and industry.[72] The stakeholder assessments discussed earlier are a first step toward improving an organization's self-regulatory processes. This last section of the chapter discusses the following self-regulatory mechanisms and programs in companies: ethics codes, ombudspersons, peer review, and ethics officer programs.

ETHICS CODES

Ethics codes are value statements that define an organization. Johnson & Johnson's credo (Figure 4.7) is an outstanding example. Major purposes of ethics codes include the following[73]:

- To state corporate leaders' dominant values and beliefs, which are the foundation of the corporate culture
- To define the moral identity of the company inside and outside the firm
- To set the moral tone of the work environment
- To provide a more stable, permanent set of guidelines for right and wrong actions
- To control erratic and autocratic power or whims of employees
- To serve business interests (because unethical practices invite outside government, law enforcement, and media intervention)
- To provide an instructional and motivational basis for training employees regarding ethical guidelines and for integrating ethics into operational policies, procedures, and problems
- To constitute a legitimate source of support for professionals who face improper demands and intrusions on their skills or well-being
- To offer a basis for adjudicating disputes among professionals inside the firm and between those inside and outside the firm
- To provide an added means of socializing professionals, not only in specialized knowledge but also in beliefs and practices the company values and rejects

One survey of U.S. corporate ethics codes found that the most important topics to include were general statements about ethics and philosophy; conflicts of interest; compliance with applicable laws; political contributions; payments to government officials or political parties; inside information; gifts, favors, and entertainment; false entries in books and records; and customer and supplier relations.[74] Notable firms go further in detailing corporate obligations. The examples of Johnson & Johnson and Borg-Warner (Figures 4.6 and 4.7) define their obligations to various stakeholders. Other exemplary codes include those of General Electric, Boeing, General Mills, GTE, Hewlett-Packard, McDonnell Douglas, Xerox, Norton, Chemical Bank, and Champion International.

Companies looking to buy (acquirers) other companies (targets) perform *preacquisition due diligence* on the management, finance, technology, services and products, legality, and ethics of the targets. That is, companies looking to buy other companies need to perform analyses to discover if the targets are telling the truth about their products, finances, and legal records. "Where does one start in uncovering the ethical vulnerability of a target?" The following basic questions are suggested as starting points[75]:

1. Does the target have a written code of conduct or code of ethics?
2. Does the company provide ethics training or ethics awareness-building programs for management and company employees?
3. Are avenues, such as an ethics office or hotline, available for employees to ask questions about ethical issues?

The problems with corporate ethics codes in general are the following[76]:

1. Most codes are too vague to be meaningful, i.e., the codes do not inform employees about how to prioritize among conflicting interests of distributors, customers, and the company. What does being a "good citizen" really mean in practice?
2. Codes do not set priorities among beliefs, values, and norms. Should profit always supersede concern for customers or employees?
3. Codes are not enforced in firms.
4. All employees are not informed of codes in most firms.

Ethics codes are a necessary but not sufficient means of assisting or influencing professionals with managing moral conduct in companies. One study[77] showed that companies that had corporate ethics codes had "less wrongdoing and higher levels of employee commitment." However, the authors explained that "formal ethical codes are one component of a milieu that encourages and supports high standards of ethical behavior; that is, these organizations have formal and informal mechanisms to ensure that ethical conduct becomes 'a way of life.'" Also, employee behavior was not as influenced by the ethics codes because the codes "are not part of the organizational environment." Part of the message here may also be that implementing several organizationally supported and integrated value-based stakeholder management and ethics programs has a better chance of meeting intended goals than does reliance on brochures and printed documents with ethics codes.

OMBUDSPERSONS AND PEER REVIEW PROGRAMS

Ombudspersons and peer review programs are methods that corporations use to manage the legal and moral aspects of potentially problematic activities in the workplace. The ombudsperson approach provides employees with a means of having their grievances heard, reviewed, and resolved. Originating in Sweden, this concept was first tried at Xerox in 1972 and later at General Electric and Boeing. Ombudspersons are third parties inside the corporation to whom employees can take their grievances. At Xerox, employees are encouraged to solve their problems through the chain of command before seeking out the ombudsperson. However, if that process fails, the employee can go to the ombudsperson, who acts as an intermediary. The ombudsperson, with the employee's approval, can go to the employee's manager to discuss the grievance. The ombudsperson can continue through the chain of command, all the way to the president of the corporation, if the problem has not been satisfactorily resolved for the employee. Ombudspersons have no power themselves to solve disputes or override managers' decisions. Complaints usually center on salary disputes, job performance appraisals, layoffs, employee benefits, and job mobility in the firm. At General Electric, ombudspersons report that they handle 150 cases every year.

An example of an effective ombudsperson program is that of the International Franchise Association (IFA). Its board of directors adopted a comprehensive self-regulation program that has a clearly, strongly stated ethics code, an investor awareness and education program, a franchise education compliance and training program, a code enforcement mechanism, and an ombudsperson program, which is described as follows: "The ombudsperson program is designed to enable franchisors and franchisees to identify disputes early and to assist them in taking preventative measures . . . facilitating dispute resolution . . . recommending non-legal methods and approaches to resolving disputes, encourage [both parties] to work together to resolve disputes, provide confidentiality throughout the process, and provide objective and unbiased advice and guidance to all the participants."[78]

A problem with the ombudsperson approach is that managers may feel their authority is threatened. Employees who seek out ombudspersons also might worry about their managers retaliating against them from fear or spite. Confidentiality also has to be observed on the part of ombudspersons. The ombudsperson is as effective as the support of the program by stakeholders (i.e., owners, officers, managers, and employees) allows it to be. An ombudsperson's success is measured by the trust, confidence, and confidentiality he or she can create and sustain with and among the stakeholders. Finally, the ombudsperson's effectiveness depends on the acceptance by managers and employees of the solutions adopted to resolve problems.

Ombudsperson programs have, for example, met with success at IBM, Xerox, General Electric, the U.S. Department of Education, Boeing, and several major U.S. newspaper organizations.[79]

The *peer review panel* is another program that more than 100 large companies have used to enable employees to express and solve grievances and complaints, thus relieving stresses and pressures that could lead to immoral activities. Employees initially use the chain of command whenever a problem exists. If the supervisors or executives do not resolve the problem, the employee can request a peer review panel to hear it and help find a solution. Two randomly selected workers in the same job classification are chosen for the panel along with an executive from another work unit. The selection must be reviewed in reference to company policy. Peer review panels work when top management supports such due process procedures and when these mechanisms are perceived as long-term, permanent programs.

Peer review programs have received positive reviews and have had good results, particularly in the health care and accounting industries. Over 50% of the U.S. state boards of accountancy require certified public accountants (CPAs) to participate in a peer review program to obtain a license to practice.[80] Congress has mandated the use of the Medicare Peer Review Organization (PRO) since 1982.[81] In England, peer review accreditation programs have evolved as external voluntary mechanisms that also provide organizational development of health care providers.[82] Ombudsperson and peer review programs serve as popular mechanisms, not only for solving disputes among stakeholders but also for integrating the interests of diverse stakeholders.

ETHICS PROGRAMS

Ethics departments provide another method for handling moral questions and concerns in the workplace. Among the largest corporations having such departments are Nynex, Pacific Bell, Texas Instruments, General Dynamics, and Dow Corning. Many large companies have organized ethics programs in response to public scandals, potentially harmful misconduct, and competitors' programs.[83]

Ethics programs serve several purposes. Telephone hotlines are the first step toward opening lines of communication in the organization. Professional staff in ethics departments, consisting of two to six full-time employees along with as many as 20 part-time employees, handle personal grievances and complaints, coordinate problem resolution across functional and staff areas, and create, update, and help enforce ethics codes. At General Dynamics, for example, more than 30,000 contacts with ethics officers since 1985 have resulted in 1,419 sanctions, 165 terminations, 58 cases of financial reimbursement receiving financial reimbursement, 26 demotions, and 10 referrals to lawyers for civil lawsuits or to public prosecutors for criminal proceedings.

Some critics of these programs doubt that a full-time ethics department is really necessary. They cite examples of companies, such as IBM and Johnson & Johnson, that have cultivated records of positive ethical conduct by using less formal alternatives. Despite the skepticism about their effectiveness, ethics programs will most likely continue to be created for two reasons: (1) according to federal sentencing guidelines that went into effect November 1,

1991, judges are asked to look more favorably on firms that can provide evidence of a substantial investment in programs and procedures designed to facilitate ethical behavior; and (2) the demise of several of the large Wall Street investment firms has awakened companies to the fact that the unethical conduct of a few employees can have detrimental effects on the entire organization.

Financial concerns factor into the decision of whether or not to set up an ethics program. Many companies, such as Nynex, are investing in these programs in response to a public scandal or known misconduct. Others, such as Texas Instruments (TI), have seen competitors struggling with issues of ethical conduct and have implemented ethics programs to reinforce their previously written company code of ethics. According to Carl Skoogland, TI's first ethics director, "We have had a written code for over 30 years but we wanted a formal focal point for reinforcing what we felt was an already strong culture." Whatever the motivation, ethics programs appear to be an effective means of handling a variety of personnel issues and moral issues in the workplace.

SUMMARY

A stakeholder management, values-based approach is central to organizing and aligning internal systems to respond to all stakeholders. "Built-to-last" companies have a fundamental purpose and a set of core values (ideology) that form a foundation for competitive long-term achievement. In contrast, companies used to illustrate the "creative destruction" argument exemplify survival and success from changing capital markets. These firms continuously reinvent themselves according to changes in the market in order to survive and compete. Firms of the future will look more like holding and venture capital companies according to the creative destruction view. Ethics is not explicitly discussed in either of the "built-to-last" or the "creative destruction" views.

"Creative reconstruction" was discussed as part of a values-based stakeholder approach that can incorporate ethical management and alignment of a company around core values and stakeholder interests in order to compete responsibly in changing markets. Organizations can be economically successful by being socially responsible and ethical with their stakeholders.

Figure 4.1 summarized a contingency approach for understanding the "big picture" of organizational systems alignment. The contingency approach is used here with a value-based stakeholder approach. Internal systems are aligned around core values, leadership, and a company's culture. This approach is compatible with the "built-to-last" view. Customers as key stakeholders are also central to an organization's alignment since they are essential to a firm's success. This argument is, in part, compatible with the creative destruction view.

Figure 4.2 illustrated the challenge of balancing internal organizational and professional stakeholders' values. Professional stakeholders in the classical departments of marketing, R&D (research and development), sales, finance, and production often function within four boundaries: rewards, time horizons, training backgrounds, and resource constraints. A critical task of organizational leaders is to guide internal professionals and focus them on the mission and values of the company.

A ten-step approach for assessing organizational systems alignment from a value-based, stakeholder readiness perspective enables firms to address external stakeholder and market needs. Figure 4.3 illustrated the beginning steps for an alignment and assessment process. Systems such as leadership, strategy, and culture, and subsystems such as rewards, finance, and IT (information technology) are motivated and brought into line with the firm's leaders, culture, strategy, and structure.

Leadership in organizations can be defined from a values-based approach: Leaders define and model the social and ethical as well as the competitive mission of companies. They build and sustain relationships with stakeholders while demonstrating collaboration and trust. Stakeholder management is the basis for strategic alliances. Former president of Southwest Airlines Herb Kelleher, Aaron Feuerstein of Malden Mills, and Jeffrey Swartz of The Timberland Company are a few examples of successful competitive industry leaders who lead ethically and spiritually.

Failure of ethical leadership is evidenced by seven symptoms: ethical blindness, muteness, incoherence, paralysis, hypocrisy, schizophrenia, and complacency. Micky Monus, former CEO of the Phar-Mor company, failed to lead ethically and was sentenced to 20 years in prison for mail fraud, wire fraud, bank fraud, and theft. "Chainsaw Al" Dunlap, former CEO of Sunbeam, was fired after the SEC found fraudulent activities during his tenure.

This leads to a question regarding the reasonableness of CEO pay and performance: Are CEOs paid too much considering the performance (or lack thereof) of their firms? Critics say yes—not for all CEOs, but certainly for enough to question CEO pay with regard to performance. CEO evaluations by boards of directors can be a way to curb and address unfair and unjust pay practices.

Strategy is another major organizational dimension and therefore must be aligned with markets, values and culture, leadership style, and structure to be effective. Strategy serves both a revolutionary role (to be innovatively competitive) and a more classical role at four levels: enterprise, corporate, business, and function. The enterprise strategy (whether revolutionary or evolutionary) must be aligned with the other levels in order to be effectively implemented. Strategies influence ethics by the expectations, pressures, motivation, and rewards they create. Overly aggressive strategies, which may also be unrealistic, can create implementation pressures that in turn lead to unethical activities by sales and other professionals.

Culture, structure, and other subsystems (e.g., finance, rewards, IT) are internal dimensions that enable leaders and professionals to implement strategy. "High-ethics" company cultures can serve as a benchmark (i.e., standard of excellence) for other organizations' cultures. Such cultures are grounded in well-defined purposes that drive operations. These cultures are also modeled by leaders who are devoted to fairness, interaction with all stakeholders, concern for stakeholder interests, and individual responsibility.

Organizational structures that are overly centralized or decentralized may be recipes for ethical problems. While there is not a "one best way" to structure a company, there are advantages and disadvantages to each type of structure. For example, centralized functional structures discourage open communication and sharing and must be integrated to allow for such drawbacks. Decentralized structures, such as networks and project teams with little or no coordination, may create a climate for unethical activities, such as fraud, theft, and pressuring of customers and alliance partners in unfair ways. Having leaders who rely on mission-driven ethical values that are communicated, reflected in the culture, and enforced throughout a firm is a necessary part of structural alignment.

Ethics codes, ombudspersons, peer review, and ethics officers programs are a way in which corporations can attempt to regulate themselves. Johnson & Johnson's "Our Credo" in Figure 4.6 is an example of an outstanding ethics code.

QUESTIONS

1. Do you believe that "built-to-last" or "creatively deconstructing" best describes the way companies should be organized? Explain. For which type of company would you rather work?

2. Do companies have to operate ethically to be financially successful? Explain.

3. Identify some characteristics of a value-based stakeholder management approach to leading and running a company. Do you agree or disagree with these characteristics? Explain.

4. Which of the ten steps in the organizational assessment would you find the easiest to perform in a company (e.g., the one for which you work)? Which one would you find the most difficult? Explain.

5. Do you believe there are pay inequities (with regard to performance) among top, middle, or entry-level positions in U.S. companies? Explain. What pay or performance criteria do you believe should be used for top-level officers in companies?

6. What differences, if any, would a stakeholder management approach make in the formulation and implementation of an organization's strategy? Explain.

7. What differences, if any, would a stakeholder management perspective make in forming and building a new organizational culture? Explain.

8. What clues would you look for in identifying ethical and unethical activities by evaluating an organization's structure? Explain.

9. If you were to evaluate the alignment of an organization's systems from a stakeholder management approach, what kinds of criteria would you use and what are some questions you would ask?

10. Which is most effective for organizational stakeholders: internal self-regulation or government regulation? Explain.

11. Explain the strengths and weaknesses of organizational (a) ethics codes, (b) ombudsperson and peer review programs, (c) ethics departments.

EXERCISES

1. Assume you are an ombudsperson or an ethics officer for a large organization (or the organization in which you work). What problems do you believe you, personally, would experience? Why? What contributions do you think you, personally, could make in this role? Why?

2. Describe the type of training you would need and list specific competencies that would help you in the role of ombudsperson or ethics officer.

3. Draft a brief values statement (or list some major values) of the ideal company for which you would like to work. Compare your list with other students' lists. What similarities and differences did you find? Compare your list to the examples in this chapter. What are the similarities or differences?

4. Briefly describe the leaders (CEO or other top-level person) of an organization in which you work or have worked. Evaluate the moral, amoral, or immoral characteristics of the leader. Refer to the "ethics of leadership styles" and the "seven symptoms of the failure—or success—of leadership" in the chapter.

5. Return to question 4. Suggest specific ways that your leader could improve his or her leadership competencies and ethical style.

6. Briefly describe the culture of an organization in which you work or have worked. Explain how the culture affected the strategy and any of the systems (e.g., human resources, performance measurement, finance, information systems, accounting, reward programs).

7. Return to question 6. Suggest a few ways in which that organization's culture could be strengthened or changed. Offer a suggestion for the way the strategy formulation or implementation could be changed. Offer a way in which one of the practices or management methods of the system could be changed for improvement.

ETHICAL DILEMMA

WHOSE VALUES? WHOSE DECISION?

Jim Howard is a sales manager at a software company that produces a search interface for databases with indexed information. The company is an established vendor and has a good reputation in the market for its high quality of products, fast and personal customer support, and strong loyalty to its customers. Part of the values statement of the company includes, "We will treat our customers with respect and dignity."

In his first year with the company, Jim noticed that the sales force was having difficulties in acquiring new customers and retaining existing ones. The problem was complex: a shrinking market with continuously increasing buying power, increasing competition, and the emergence of free alternative services from the Internet. These problems started to significantly affect the company's revenues. The company's reaction was to drastically decrease the cost of its products, bundle databases into packages, and start to alter product introductions by including several value-added services that were new to the market.

Jim Howard's boss suggested that Jim take over the responsibility for the yearly renewals of customer subscriptions, which previously had been regarded as an easy clerical procedure, from the company's secretary. When he started to check the old accounts and follow up with the renewals, he faced a problem that he thought would never have occurred: unfair treatment of old customers in comparison to new customers in terms of the product pricing. Existing customers were offered renewal at triple the price of the same package and renewals offered to new customers.

When he asked his boss whether he should inform the old customer that the price had changed and whether the old customer could now benefit from the lowered price, the answer was, "Why don't we try to get this price? If the customer refuses to pay it, then we'll negotiate." An additional difficulty was that, in the last few months, information had been disseminated to all customers (old and new) that made the company's new pricing strategy visible to customers. Jim shared the fact that this information was already available to customers with his boss and pointed out the contradiction. His boss remained insistent, to the point of shouting, that Jim follow his previous instructions with the sales force.

Jim felt he was betraying the company, the customer, his sales force, and his own professional values. He didn't want to lose his job and he didn't want to lose any more customer accounts.

QUESTIONS

1. If you were Jim, what would you do in this situation?

2. What are the issues here? For whom?

3. Who stands to be hurt the most from following the advice of Jim's boss?

4. What would a value-based stakeholder management approach suggest that you do, if you were Jim? Lay out an action plan and be ready to role play your suggested approach.

5. Compare what you said in question 1 to your approach in question 5. Any differences? If so, could you still follow what you said in question 4?

THE CORPORATION
AND EXTERNAL STAKEHOLDERS
MANAGING MORAL RESPONSIBILITY IN THE MARKETPLACE

5.1 MANAGING CORPORATE RESPONSIBILITY IN THE MARKETPLACE: CRISES AND OPPORTUNITIES

Managing legal and moral responsibility in the marketplace can be a significant part of a corporation's activities. Even best-in-class and built-to-last
companies must manage new product risks and potential liabilities as well
as successes with their customers—who are also consumers. At stake when
products seriously injure consumers are sizable lawsuits, product boycotts,
image, reputation, name brand loyalty, competitiveness, and even survival.
Managing products and services responsibly requires effective leadership
that aligns companies with stakeholder interests in mind, as discussed in
Chapter 4. Figure 5.1 illustrates a corporation's major external stakeholders,
moral stakes, and responsibilities in these relationships. A major stake for
corporations is obviously profit, and brand name and reputation are linked
to profits. Thus, it is in a company's long-term interest to create and sustain
customer trust by offering safe products, truthfully informing consumers
about product content and use, and treating stakeholders ethically.

Not all leaders and companies, however, demonstrate ethical competencies and due diligence with regard to their stakeholders. With the advent

FIGURE 5.1   EXTERNAL STAKEHOLDERS, MORAL STAKES, AND
CORPORATE RESPONSIBILITIES

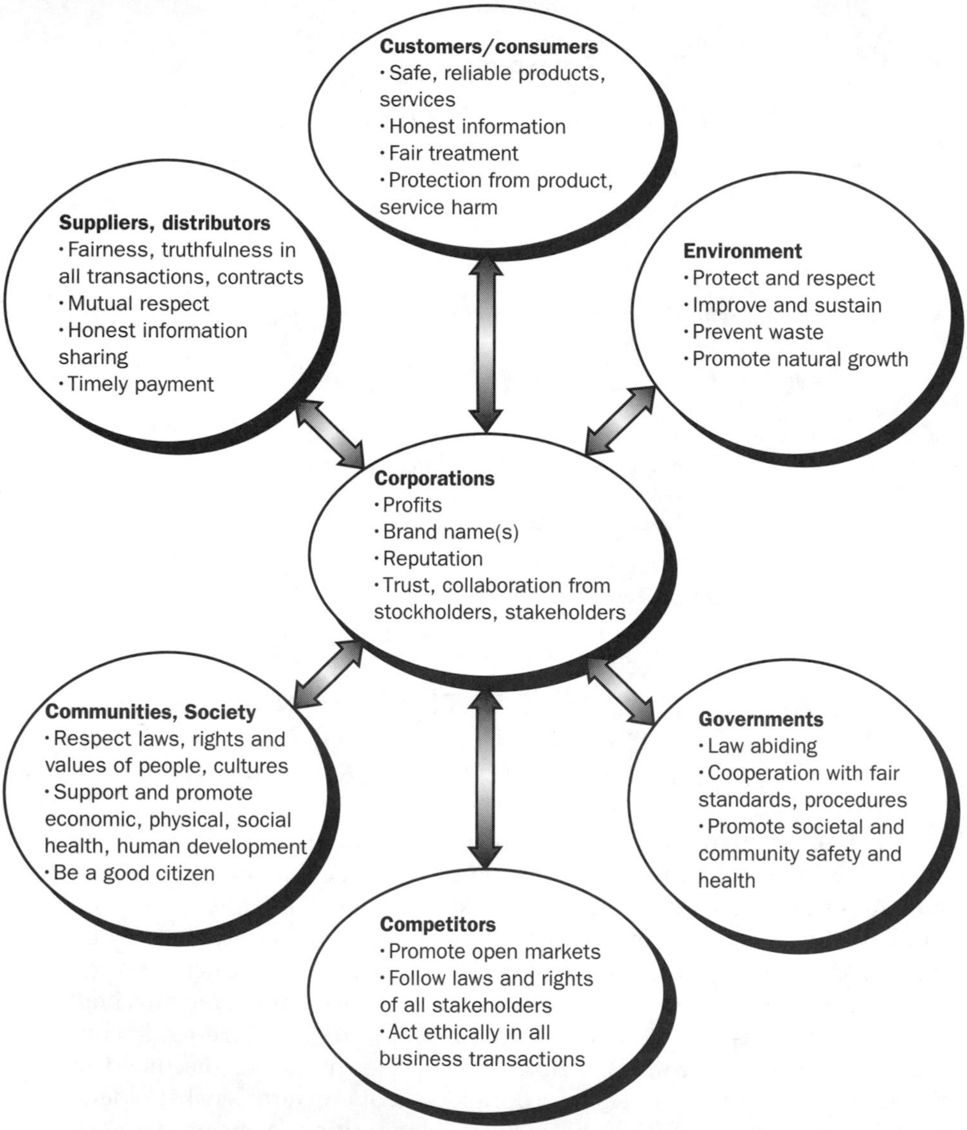

Customers/consumers
· Safe, reliable products,
services
· Honest information
· Fair treatment
· Protection from product,
service harm

Suppliers, distributors
· Fairness, truthfulness in
all transactions, contracts
· Mutual respect
· Honest information
sharing
· Timely payment

Environment
· Protect and respect
· Improve and sustain
· Prevent waste
· Promote natural growth

Corporations
· Profits
· Brand name(s)
· Reputation
· Trust, collaboration from
stockholders, stakeholders

Communities, Society
· Respect laws, rights and
values of people, cultures
· Support and promote
economic, physical, social
health, human development
· Be a good citizen

Governments
· Law abiding
· Cooperation with fair
standards, procedures
· Promote societal and
community safety and
health

Competitors
· Promote open markets
· Follow laws and rights
of all stakeholders
· Act ethically in all
business transactions

SOURCE: Based on the Caux Round Table's Principles for Business. The principles are printed in *Business Ethics* magazine, 52 S. 10th St. #110, Minneapolis, MN 55403.

of the Internet, transparency and speed of information diffusion pressures businesses to acknowledge stakeholder concerns—especially privacy. The DoubleClick company case (see end of text for full case) illustrated that a global Internet advertising solutions firm could legally but perhaps unethically threaten the privacy of customers by creating a database of several billion of its individual catalog shoppers. Consumer groups and privacy advocates nationally and internationally protested and even filed class action lawsuits along with proposed state and federal legislation when they learned of DoubleClick's obtaining and using private information. The lawsuit alleged that the company had used its powerful cookie technology to create a "sophisticated and highly intrusive means of collecting and cross-referencing private personal information without the knowing consent of Internet users." DoubleClick's officers have responded and addressed these concerns. Nevertheless, the issues created by the company live on and have yet to be fully resolved legally and in other on-line businesses' practices.[1]

DoubleClick is not the only company to violate consumers' privacy rights, intentionally or unintentionally. RealNetworks of Seattle, an on-line company that enables customers to listen to music over their computers, apologized in 1999 for its software's unauthorized, secret collection of information about people's listening preferences. Toysmart.com was investigated by the Federal Trade Commission (FTC) in 2000 when it tried to sell its customer database as the firm was going out of business. Then, in July 2001, Eli Lilly Company released on the Internet the e-mail addresses of over six hundred Prozac users. The company's spokesman stated that patients could sign onto a Lilly Website to request automated e-mail reminding them of their Prozac dose. A subsequent reminder message accidentally included the e-mail addresses of all the subscribers in the message header.[2]

CLASSIC CORPORATE CRISES

Several of the now classic product- and consumer-related crises show that companies have responded and reacted slowly and insensitively to injured customers and other stakeholders. (The Internet as a medium of instant global communication may decrease the time executives have to respond to potential and actual crises.[3]) It is important to review some of the major crises from the 1970s to the present, since several of these are only now being resolved. Also, these cases serve to remind corporate leaders and the public that issues and crisis management should be part of a company's management strategy and planning process. The Exxon *Valdez* oil spill disaster and the Manville Corporation's asbestos crisis—two of the most catastrophic— are summarized in the feature boxes on the following pages. The infamous Ford Pinto case is included in the case section at the end of the text. Also, the insightful reflections and lessons of Dennis Gioia, then Ford's vehicle recall

JOHNS-MANVILLE
CORPORATION:
ASBESTOS
LEGACY

"'They'll be following in our footsteps,' said Robert A. Falise, chairman of the Manville Personal Injury Trust, which was created by the bankruptcy court to ensure a steady source of money to pay claims filed against Johns-Manville by workers exposed to asbestos in their workplaces."[1] The company will be responding to outstanding claims by asbestos victims and their families for several future decades. In June 2000, the company was finally sold to Warren Buffett for $1.9 billion in cash and the assumption of $300 million in debt. The asbestos-related trust, created to pay claimants, received $1.5 billion. As of March 2001, the trust had paid over $2.5 billion to 350,000 beneficiaries. There are still over a half million claimants and another half million expected to file. Looking backward, reviews of Manville's social responsibility management of the complex web of issues surrounding its asbestos production are mixed.

Asbestosis, mesothelioma, and lung cancer, all life-threatening diseases, share a common cause: inhalation of microscopic particles of asbestos over an extended period of time. The link between these diseases and enough inhaled asbestos particles is a medical fact. Manville Corporation is a multinational mining and forest product manufacturer, and it was a leading commercial producer of asbestos. As of March 1977, 271 asbestos-related damages suits were filed against the firm by workers. The victims claimed the company did not warn them of the life-threatening dangers of asbestos. Since 1968, Manville has paid over $2.5 billion in such claims. And since the 1950s, Manville has faced hundreds of lawsuits from workers: the estimated value is over $1 billion. By 1982, Manville faced over 500 new asbestos lawsuits filed each month. Consequently, in August 1982, Manville filed for Chapter 11 bankruptcy in order to reorganize and remain solvent in the face of the asbestos-related lawsuits; the firm was losing over half the cases that reached trial. The reorganization was approved, and Manville set up a $2.5 billion trust fund to pay asbestos claimants. Shareholders surrendered half their value in stock, and it was agreed that projected earnings over 25 years would be reduced to support the trust.

Manville devised a settlement that gave the Manville Personal Injury Settlement Trust enough cash to continue meeting claims filed by asbestos victims. Under the settlement, the building products division stated it would give the trust 20 percent of Manville's stock and would pay a special $772 million dividend in exchange for the trust's releasing its right to receive 20 percent of Manville's profits. After the transaction, the trust would own 80 percent of Manville and have $1.2 billion in cash and marketable securities, plus $2.3 billion in assets. This transaction enabled Manville to rectify its balance sheet. Also, it changed its name to Schuller Corp.

The trust was organized in 1988 as a way to pay asbestos claims. After Manville spent several years operating under Chapter 11 of the U.S. Bankruptcy Code, the company emerged with $850 million in cash, 50 percent of its common stock, a claim on 20 percent of the company's consolidated profits, and bonds with a face value of $1.3 billion. Payments to the trust stopped in 1991, but under a plan approved in 1994 by a federal court, payments started again. The trust is expected to pay 10 percent of an estimated $18 billion in present and future asbestos claims to 275,000 victims who already have filed claims.[2]

The extent of Manville's social responsibility toward its workers, the litigants, the communities it serves, and society has, at best, been uneven. Manville, since 1972, has been active and cooperative with the U.S. Department of Labor and the AFL/CIO in developing standards to protect asbestos workers. However, Dr. Kenneth Smith—the medical director of one of the firm's plants in Canada—refused in the 1970s to inform Manville workers that they had asbestosis. Lawsuits ensued.

There is also the complication and confusion of evolving and changing legislation on asbestos. The U.S. Supreme Court, as stakeholder, has not taken a stand on who is liable in these situations: Are insurance firms liable when workers are initially exposed to asbestos and later develop cancer, or are they liable 20 years later? Also, right-to-know laws are not definitive in state legislatures. Does that leave Manville and other corporations liable for government's legal indecision?

Of the original 16,500 personal injury plaintiffs, 2,000 have died since the reorganization in 1982. With Warren Buffet's purchase of the company and the asbestos trust solidified, the management of this issue for the company is over.

Notes

1. Gross, D. (April 29, 2001). Recovery lessons from an industrial phoenix. *New York Times*, 3, 4.

2. Tejada, C. (1996). Manville settlement gives trust enough cash for asbestos claims. *Wall Street Journal*.

Questions

1. Should asbestos victims' claims over these decades be the liability of Manville or of the decision makers who authorized the work policies and orders?

2. Who was or is to blame for the asbestos-related deaths and injuries in the Manville case?

3. Is the declaration of Chapter 11 bankruptcy and the creation of a trust the best or only solution in this case? Who wins and who loses with this type of settlement? Why?

4. What ethical principle(s) did Manville's owners and officers use regarding this type of settlement? What principle(s) do you believe they should have used? Explain.

coordinator, are presented at the end of this chapter. A sample of other crises includes the following[4]:

- Over 18 years ago, someone inserted cyanide into Johnson & Johnson's (J&J's) Extra-Strength Tylenol tablets, killing seven people. J&J's response in this case demonstrates outstanding ethical leadership. The company acted swiftly to remove the product until safety procedures were ensured, a move that cost the firm $125 million. Three months later the company had developed a sealed, tamper-resistant package. The following year Tylenol took back its top spot in its product category. CEO James Burke (also a marketing professional) was

EXXON VALDEZ: WORST OIL SPILL IN UNITED STATES HISTORY

"A year after the Exxon Valdez ripped open its bottom on Bligh Reef [off the Alaskan coast] and dumped 11 million gallons of crude oil, the nation's worst oil spill is not over . . . . Like major spills in the past, this unnatural disaster sparked a frenzy of reactions: congressional hearings, state and federal legislative proposals for new preventive measures, dozens of studies and innumerable lawsuits."[1] The grounding of the tanker on March 24, 1989, spread oil over more than 700 miles. Oil covered 1,300 miles of coastline and killed 250,000 birds, 2,800 sea otters, 300 seals, 250 bald eagles, and billions of salmon and herring eggs, according to the Exxon Valdez Oil Spill Trustee Council, which manages Exxon settlement money. More controversial was Exxon's failure to pay the $5 billion in assessed damages.[2] A grand jury indicted Exxon in February 1990. At that time, the firm faced fines totaling more than $600 million if convicted on the felony counts. More than 150 lawsuits and 30,000 damage claims were reportedly filed against Exxon, and most were not settled by July 1991, when Exxon made a secret agreement with seven Seattle fish processors. Under the arrangement, Exxon agreed to pay $70 million to settle the processors' oil-spill claims against Exxon. However, in return for the relatively quick settlement of those claims, the processors agreed to return to Exxon most of any punitive damages they might be awarded in later Exxon spill-related cases. Exxon paid about $300 million in damages claims in the first few years after the spill. However, ". . . lawyers for people who had been harmed called that a mere down payment on losses that averaged more than $200,000 per fisherman from 1990 to 1994."[3]

The charge that the captain of the Valdez, Joseph Hazelwood, had a blood-alcohol content above 0.04 percent was dropped, but he was convicted of negligently discharging oil and ordered to pay $50,000 as restitution to the state of Alaska and to serve 1,000 hours cleaning up the beaches over five years.[4] Exxon executives and stockholders have been embroiled with courts, environmental groups, the media, and public groups over the crisis. Exxon has paid $300 million to date in nonpunitive damages to 10,000 commercial fishers, business owners, and native Alaskan villages.

In 1996, the grand jury ordered Exxon to pay $5 billion in punitive damages to the victims of the 1989 oil spill. At the time the fish processors had entered the secret agreement with Exxon, they did not know the Alaskan jury would slap the company with the $5 billion punitive damages award. One of the judges claimed that had the jury known about this secret agreement, it would have charged Exxon even more punitive damages.[5] As of 2001, Exxon has not paid any of these damages. It is also estimated that with Exxon's reported rate of return on its investments, it makes $800 million every year on the $5 billion it does not pay. By 2002, the company will make back the $5 billion it refuses to pay with accrued interest.[6] Brian O'Neill, the Minneapolis lawyer who represents 60,000 plaintiffs in the suit against Exxon, stated, "I have had thousands of clients that have gone bankrupt, got divorced, died, or been down on their financial luck" while waiting for the settlement.[7] In the meantime, Captain Hazelwood continues to pick up trash on Alaska state lands. And the November 2001 federal appeals court ruling opens the way for a judge to reduce the $5 billion punitive verdict. (However, the 1994 jury award of $287 million to compensate commercial fishers was not reduced.)[8]

Hosmer, a noted ethicist, stated:

The most basic lesson in accident prevention that can be drawn from the wreck of the Exxon Valdez is that management is much more than just looking at revenues, costs, and profits. Management requires the imagination to understand the full mixture of potential benefits and harms generated by the operations of the firm, the empathy to consider the full range of legitimate interests represented by the constituencies of the firm, and the courage to act when some of the harms are not certain and many of the constituencies are not powerful. The lack of imagination, empathy, and courage at the most senior levels of the company was the true cause of the wreck of the Exxon Valdez.[9]

NOTES

1. Dumanoski, D. (April 2, 1990). One year later—The lessons of Valdez. *Boston Globe*, 29.

2. Allen, S. (March 7, 1999). Deep problems 10 years after Exxon Valdez/Worst oil spill in US has lingering effects for Alaska, industries. *Wall Street Journal*, A1.

3. Ibid.

4. Exxon Valdez, ten years later. (Summer 1999). *Amicus Journal, 21*, 10.

5. McCoy, C. (June 13, 1996). Exxon's secret Valdez deals anger judge. *Wall Street Journal*, A3.

6. Rawlins, R. (Feb. 28, 1990). U.S. indicts Exxon in oil spill. *Miami Herald*, 5.

7. Exxon Valdez, ten years later.

8. Associated Press. Exxon Valdez fine excessive, court says. (Nov. 8, 2001). *USA Today*, 6A.

9. Hosmer, L. (1998). Lessons from the wreck of the Exxon Valdez: The need for imagination, empathy, and courage. *Business Ethics Quarterly*, 122.

QUESTIONS

1. Should Exxon's officers and lawyers pay the agreed-on $5 billion in punitive damages to settle this case? Why or why not?

2. Should Captain Hazelwood have been convicted of criminal drunkenness in this case? If so, how would that have changed the outcome of the settlement? If not, why?

3. Has Captain Hazelwood settled his "debt" in this case by agreeing to serve 1,000 hours in cleanup time in Alaska? Explain.

4. Describe Exxon's ethics toward this disaster.

5. What should be done now, if anything, and who should do it to settle this case?

6. Respond to Hosmer's statement. Do you believe this sentiment applies to all responsibilities of senior executives in corporations; that is, do they need to show imagination, empathy, and courage toward all their constituencies? Explain your answer.

credited with resolving the situation through his proactive, open, and quick response.

■ In June 2001, Katsuhiko Kawasoe, Mitsubishi Motor Company's president, apologized for that firm's 20-year cover-up of consumer safety complaints. (The company also had agreed in 1998 to pay $34 million to settle 300 sexual harassment lawsuits filed by women in its Normal, Illinois plant. This is one of the largest sexual harassment settlements in U.S. history.)

■ By the end of 2001, the American Home Products Corporation paid over $11.2 billion to settle about 50,000 consumer lawsuits related to the fen-phen diet drug combination. In addition, the company put aside $1 billion to cover future medical checkups for former fen-phen users and $2.35 billion to settle individual suits.

■ Between 1971 and 1974, more than 5,000 product liability lawsuits were filed by women who had suffered severe gynecological damage from A. H. Robins Company's Dalkon Shield, an intrauterine contraceptive device. Although the company never recalled its product, it paid more than $314 million to settle 8,300 lawsuits. It also established a $1.75 billion trust to settle ongoing claims. The firm avoided its responsibility toward its customers by not considering a recall or preventing further harm for nine years after the problem was known.

■ Procter & Gamble's Rely tampon was pulled from the market in 1980 after 25 deaths were allegedly associated with toxic shock syndrome caused by tampon use.

■ Firestone's problems first erupted in 1978, when the Center for Auto Safety said it had reports that Firestone's steel-belted radial TPC 500 tire was responsible for 15 deaths and 12 injuries. In October 1978, after attacking the publicity this product received, Firestone executives recalled 10 million of the 500-series tires. Firestone recently paid $7.5 million in addition to $350,000 to settle the first case in the Bridgestone/Firestone-Ford Explorer crisis. Two hundred injury and death suits have been settled since the recall, and $50 million is estimated to settle the lawsuits.

■ A federal bankruptcy judge approved Dow Corning Corporation's $4.5 billion reorganization plan, with $3.2 billion to be used to settle claims from recipients of the company's silicone gel breast implants, and the other $1.3 billion to be paid to its commercial creditors. A jury had already awarded $7.3 million to one woman whose implant burst, causing her illness. The company is alleged to have rushed the product to market in 1975 without completing proper safety tests and to have misled plastic surgeons about the potential for silicone to leak out of the surgically implanted devices. Over 600,000 implants were subsequently performed. (The complete case appears in the case section at the end of the text.)

As discussed in the first two chapters, managing corporate responsibility, issues, and crises in the marketplace is a negotiated process that involves numerous stakeholders. The next section discusses companies that do act in socially responsible ways to serve the interests of consumers and stakeholders.

MANAGING OPPORTUNITIES AND GROWTH RESPONSIBLY

There are incentives for corporations to act socially responsible and ethically toward stakeholders. "Globalization and the information technology revolution have resulted in increased competition, greater shareholder activism and wider access to information worldwide. The result is that many employees, investors and consumers are seeking assurances that the goods and services they are producing, financing or purchasing are not damaging to workers, the environment or communities by whom and where they are made."[5]

Corporate social responsibility refers to a business's attention to and promotion of the welfare and goodwill of stakeholders.[6] There is evidence that socially responsible corporations have a competitive advantage in the following areas:

1. Reputation[7]
2. Successful social investment portfolios[8]
3. Ability to attract quality employees[9]

Business Ethics, a media company, ranks corporations in terms of citizenship, using its own collected data including the Domini 400 Social Index (which also tracks, measures, and publishes information on companies that act socially responsible). The Standard & Poor 500 plus 150 publicly owned companies are ranked on a scale that measures stakeholder ratings. Variables in the ranking include how companies treat stakeholders (customers, employees, stock owners, the community, the environment, minorities, and non-U.S. stakeholders). The March-April 2001 ranking gave first place to Procter and Gamble (P&G), which ranked high on "service to international stakeholders." P&G gave grants and gifts to communities in Japan, China, Romania, Malaysia, and France and earthquake relief in Turkey. Other highly ranked ethical companies included Hewlett-Packard, Fannie Mae, Motorola, IBM, Sun Microsystems, Herman Miller, Polaroid, The St. Paul Companies, and Freddie Mac.[10]

Harris Interactive Inc. and Reputation Institute, a New York-based research group, conducted an on-line nationwide survey of 10,830 people to identify the companies with the best corporate reputations among Americans at the turn of the millennium.[11] The Reputation Quotient (RQ) is a standardized instrument that measures a company's reputation by examining how the public perceives companies based on 20 attributes: for example, emotional appeal; social responsibility; good citizenship in its dealings with communities, employees, and the environment; the quality, innovation, value, and reliability of its products and services; how well the company is

<table>
</table>

RANK YOUR ORGANIZATION'S REPUTATION	Quickly score your present or a previous company (college or university) at which you

worked (or studied) on the following characteristics. Be objective. Answer each question based on your experience and what you objectively know about the company (college or university).

1 = very low; 2 = somewhat low; 3 = average; 4 = very good; 5 = excellent

- Emotional appeal of the organization for me _____
- The social responsibility of the organization _____
- The organization's treatment of employees, community, and environment _____
- The quality, innovation, value, and reliability of the organization's products and/or services _____

- The clarity of vision and strength of the organization's leadership _____
- The organization's profitability, prospects in its market, and handling of risks _____

Total your score _____

Interpretation: Consider 30 a perfect score; 24 very good; 18 average; 12 low; and 6 very low.

1. How did your company do on the ranking? Explain.

2. Explain your scoring on each item; that is, give the specific reasons that led you to score your company on each item as you did.

3. Suggest specific actions your organization could take to increase its Reputation Quotient.

managed; how much the company demonstrates a clear vision and strong leadership; profitability, prospects, and risk. The overall ranking of the companies is as follows:

1. Johnson & Johnson
2. Coca-Cola
3. Hewlett-Packard
4. Intel
5. Ben & Jerry's
6. Xerox
7. Home Depot
8. Gateway
9. Disney
10. Dell
11. General Electric
12. Lucent
13. Anheuser-Busch
14. Microsoft

The executive director of the newly formed Reputation Institute noted, "Reputation is much more than an abstract concept; it's a corporate asset that is a magnet to attract customers, employees and investors."[12] You can score your own company's reputation in the "Rank Your Organization's Reputation" feature box.

FOCUS OF THE CHAPTER

We begin the next section by explaining corporations as economic, value-based stakeholders. The process by which a corporation handles proactive stakeholder and issues management planning and response is then discussed. In doing so, we address a number of questions: How do and should responsible companies plan for and provide responsible advertising and product service in the marketplace? What is the relationship between ethics and advertising? Product safety and liability? Who is liable for unsafe products? What is the price to be paid for the use of products that are unsafe in terms of design and/or use, and who pays it? To what extent are corporations responsible for their industrial use of the environment? Who does the environment belong to anyway? What is the relationship between ethics and ecology? What difference does a value-based stakeholder management approach make regarding an organization's relationship to the environment?

5.2 MANAGING CORPORATE RESPONSIBILITY WITH EXTERNAL STAKEHOLDERS

THE CORPORATION AS SOCIAL AND ECONOMIC STAKEHOLDER

The stakeholder management approach views the corporation as a legal entity and a collective of individuals and groups. The CEO and top-level managers are hired to maximize profits for the owners and shareholders. As discussed in Chapter 4, to accomplish this, corporations must respond to a variety of stakeholders' needs, rights, and legitimate demands. From this perspective, the corporation has primary obligations to the economic mandates of its owners; however, to survive and succeed, it must also respond to legal, social, political, and environmental claims from a host of stakeholders inside and outside its boundaries.

One study argued that ". . . using corporate resources for social issues not related to primary stakeholders may not create value for shareholders."[13] This finding does not suggest that corporations refrain from philanthropic activities; rather, ". . . the emphasis on shareholder value creation today should not be construed as coming at the expense of the interests of other primary stakeholders."[14] Corporations are economic and social stakeholders. This is not a contradiction but a leadership choice that requires balancing economic and moral priorities.

THE SOCIAL CONTRACT

Corporations have an implied social contract with consumers and the public. The contract is based on mutual trust, with the understanding that companies have the interests of consumers in mind. However, even social contracts can vary depending on economic and social changes in society. A

Business Week article entitled "New Economy, New Social Contract, argues that "[t]he neopopulism that abounds today is not about lack of prosperity. Just the opposite. Americans do give credit to Corporate America for innovating, creating jobs, and above all, making profits. People are grumbling about what they see as business' disregard for their safety, the norms of equity, and the absence of responsibility."[15] Almost three-quarters of Americans believe that business has gained substantial power over their lives, according to a *Business Week* poll.[16] The authors report that "[t]he triumph of the market over the state and the high-tech New Economy are changing the boundaries and the balance between work and family, office and home, corporate and private. The result is an uneasiness with the powerful institution held responsible, the corporation."[17]

Four predominant issues underlie this popular sentiment: (1) *Propriety:* There is a sense of corporate invasiveness into people's private lives through computer "cookies," workplace monitoring, employee testing, and pervasive advertising. (2) *Equity:* Productivity is up 13.5 percent since 1992, while real wages and benefits have increased only 7.5 percent. According to the *Business Week* poll, only 4 percent of the public believes the sole purpose of corporations is to make profit for shareholders, while 95 percent feel corporations should do more for employees and communities. (3) *Safety:* People feel increasingly threatened by unsafe products and services. Health maintenance organizations (HMOs) are seen as being operated on a cost basis; crops genetically modified by the Monsanto Company have consumers worried about food safety. The Ford-Bridgestone/Firestone finger-pointing regarding accident causes leads to consumer concern over who is managing their safety. (4) *Responsibility:* While corporations are connecting to customers in more personal, emotional ways, customers expect more from corporations. College students picket Nike and Gap to protest sweatshops in Asia. Child labor and environmental laws abroad are becoming trade issues. Global warming and damage to the environment raise real concerns. Daniel Yankelovich, chairman of pollster DYG, warns, "Executives haven't had to worry about social issues for a generation, but there's a yellow light flashing now and they better pay attention."[18]

The stakeholder management approach of the corporation is grounded in the concept of a social contract. Developed by early political philosophers, a social contract is a set of rules and assumptions about behavior patterns among the various elements of society. Much of the social contract is embedded in the customs of society. Some of the "contract provisions" result from practices between parties. Like a legal contract, the social contract often involves a quid pro quo (something for something) exchange.[19]

The social contract between a corporation and its stakeholders is often based on implicit as well as explicit agreements. For example, it is argued that the success of many businesses is directly related to the public's confidence in those businesses. A loss of public confidence can be detrimental to the firm and to its investors. One way to retain and to reinforce public confidence is by acting in an ethical manner, a manner that shows a concern for the investing public and the customers of the firm.[20]

COVENANTAL ETHIC

The *covenantal ethic* concept is related to the social contract view and is also central to a stakeholder management approach. The covenantal ethic focuses on the importance of *relationships*—social as well as economic—among businesses, customers, and stakeholders. Relationships and social contracts (or covenants) between corporate managers and customers embody a "seller must care" attitude, not only "buyer or seller beware."[21] A manager's understanding of problems is measured not only over the short term, in view of concrete products, specific cost reductions, or even balance sheets (though obviously important to a company's results), but also over the long term, in view of the quality of relationships that are created and sustained by business activity.[22]

PRAGMATIC PRINCIPLES FOR CORPORATE STAKEHOLDER RELATIONSHIPS

At a more general level, it is argued that a corporation's obligations include—in addition to making a profit—acting justly; causing no avoidable, unjustifiable harm; and preventing harm where possible. Norman Bowie and Ronald Duska argue that corporations realistically should be moral according to the criterion of "ought implies can" and according to a "moral minimum" standard.[23] *Ought implies can* means that companies are not ethically required to produce the most safe products if the cost will stop consumers from buying them; consumers also weigh price against safety concerns. Why expect or require firms to produce the safest products if they will not sell? Companies *ought* to do what they reasonably *can* do. The *moral minimum* standard holds that firms should not produce products or services or engage in activities that inflict avoidable harm on others. At a minimum, corporations should design, manufacture, distribute, and sell safe products that will sell while following this standard.

THE MORAL BASIS AND SOCIAL POWER OF CORPORATIONS AS STAKEHOLDERS

Keith Davis reasons that the social responsibility of corporations is based on social power and that "if business has the power, then a just relationship demands that business also bear responsibility for its actions in these areas." He terms this view the "iron law of responsibility." "[I]n the long run, those who do not use power in a manner in which society considers responsible will tend to lose it." Davis discusses five broad guidelines or obligations business professionals should follow to be socially responsible:

1. Businesses have a social role of "trustee for society's resources." Since society entrusts businesses with its resources, businesses must wisely serve the interests of all their stakeholders, not just those of owners, consumers, or labor.

2. "Business shall operate as a two-way open system with open receipt of inputs from society and open disclosure of its operations to the public."

3. "Social costs as well as benefits of an activity, product, or service shall be thoroughly calculated and considered in order to decide whether to proceed with it." Technical and economic criteria must be supplemented with the social effects of business activities, goods, or services before a company proceeds.

4. "The social costs of each activity, product, or service shall be priced into it so that the consumer (user) pays for the effects of his consumption on society."

5. "Business institutions as citizens have responsibilities for social involvement in areas of their competence where major social needs exist."[24]

These five guidelines provide a foundation for creating and reviewing the moral bases of corporate stakeholder relationships.

CORPORATE PHILANTHROPY

A corporation's social responsibility includes philanthropic responsibilities in addition to its economic, legal, and ethical ones.[25] Corporate philanthropy is an important part of a company's role as "good citizen" at the global, national, and local levels. At noted above, Procter & Gamble's reputation has been enhanced because of its global contributions. Some of the largest corporate philanthropists include Ted Turner of Time Warner, who has given over $1 billion to the United Nations; Kathryn Albertson of Albertson's grocery, who has contributed in excess of $600 million to support public education in Idaho; and George Soros, the preeminent global investor, who has donated over $525 million to assist Russian health and education programs and U.S. drug and education programs.[26]

Larger corporations can also act socially responsible by detecting and responding to external issues before they become crises. One of the issues management methods introduced in Chapter 2 is explained here as a strategic method for identifying, predicting, and managing external trends and events in order to prevent crises from occurring and to lessen harm to customers and stakeholders when crises do occur.

ISSUES MANAGEMENT AND CORPORATE RESPONSIBILITY

Several larger companies that operate in high environmental risk industries include issues management processes in their strategic planning function as a proactive way of anticipating and responding to potential crises. Crises discussed earlier, such as the Ford-Firestone/Bridgestone fiasco, the Exxon *Valdez* oil spill, and the Ford Pinto fires, demonstrate the need for issues

FIGURE 5.2   6-STEP ISSUES MANAGEMENT PROCESS

management. Royal Dutch/Shell, Weyerhaeuser, Procter & Gamble, and General Electric are some of the more notable examples of large firms that include issues management in their planning. The September 11, 2001, attack on the U.S. World Trade Center in New York has resulted in more companies and government agencies using issues and crisis planning. The Issues Management Council indicates that there are numerous management consultants who assist companies in this area.

"Issues management" is defined as "developing a systematic process by which the company can identify, evaluate, and respond to strategic issues affecting the company."[27] One of the most generic issues management processes used by corporations is presented in Figure 5.2.

Issues management should be a continuous strategic process that involves all business and functional units. Methods used in this process include *environmental scanning*, which seeks possible issues in any and all sources in the economic, technological, demographic, legal, and political environments of an industry; *brainstorming* with professionals who have first-hand experience with what can go wrong in a company's current operational capabilities; and the use of a *probability and impact matrix* to hypothesize (a) the probability of a crisis occurring along with (b) the impact on the company. On these two dimensions, high, medium and low probability with impact scenarios can be determined; *what-if, worst-case, and best-case scenarios* related to the occurrence of a crisis can be constructed. Then current resources and staffing are assessed in the context of each scenario. After these and other crisis prevention and intervention techniques are completed, a strategic plan with goals, priorities, and deployment of staff and resources should be drafted and integrated with the enterprise planning process. These techniques create awareness and mobilize planning techniques.[28]

Consider the crises identified earlier in this chapter. Which ones could have been prevented and which ones could have been dealt with more responsibly and efficiently after they did occur had any or all of these methods discussed above been used?

WHO MANAGES CORPORATE ISSUES MANAGEMENT?

Who is involved in the issues management process, and where is this process located in an organization? Studies show that issues management can be managed at the corporate, functional, or business unit/operating company level.[29]

Oomens and van den Bosch[30] identify three organizational levels at which companies use issues management, as illustrated in Figure 5.3. At the *corporate level*, the process is more centralized, involves higher-level organizational issues, and has low involvement of the rest of the organization. The authors studied an actual but disguised "Company X" using this approach. At the *functional level*, the issues are local to the organization in nature (e.g., marketing, production), the decision making is also centralized, and there is medium participation across the organization. The *process-oriented* issues management function, exemplified by the actual but also disguised "Company Z" in Figure 5.3, is decentralized to business units and operating companies and deals with corporate, business, and local issues with high involvement across the company. The authors suggest that while there is not one "best way" for a company to organize its approach to issues management planning and response, the process-oriented approach offers more flexibility, proactive attitudes, a strategic (versus reactive) posture, and more response options to issues.

The authors describe the response options a company uses to address issues in terms of three stages: (1) "Gap in expectations," (2) "Controversy (conflict of interests)," and (3) "Impact on the firm." The authors state: "Company Z is supposedly more proactive towards its environment. The line managers are involved in Issue Management at all stages, and they have to be sensitive to signals, developments, and trends in the company's environment. They must pay attention to the outside world and adopt a more open attitude towards various stakeholders in society, and taking this information into account in their decision-making, so the company's ability to

FIGURE 5.3   AN INTEGRATED MANAGERIAL FRAMEWORK

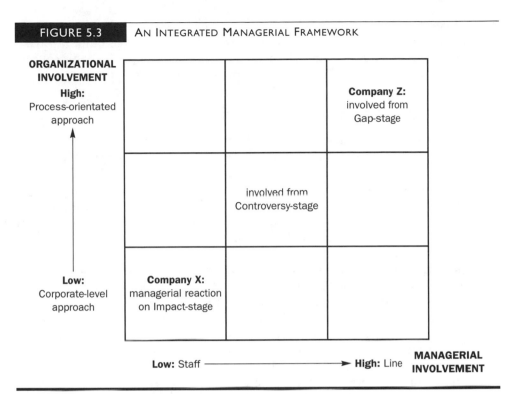

SOURCE: Reprinted with permission. M. Oomens and F. van den Bosch, 1999, "Strategic Issue Management in Major European-Based Companies," *Long Range Planning, 32(1)*, 54.

respond is enhanced. Their actions may help their company reduce or even avoid negative publicity and financial damage."[31]

Had the U.S. CIA (Central Intelligence Agency) and other federal agencies used a Company Z issues identification and response framework for anticipating and addressing global terrorism in the early 1990s, do you believe the attack on the U.S. World Trade Center and Pentagon could have been prevented?

5.3 CORPORATE RESPONSIBILITY TOWARD CONSUMER STAKEHOLDERS

Consumers may be the most important stakeholders of a business. If consumers do not buy, commercial businesses cease to exist. Consumer confidence and spending also are important indicators of economic activity as well as of business prosperity. Consumer interests should be foremost when businesses are designing, delivering, and servicing products. Unfortunately, this often is not the case. As the examples at the beginning of this chapter illustrate, many companies continue to manufacture or distribute unreliable products, placing consumers at risk. Many advertisers continue to make false and misleading claims about products. What, then, is the nature of corporate responsibility toward consumers as stakeholders?

U.S., FRENCH, AND GERMAN CONSUMERS

One study contrasted consumers' views on the social responsibility of organizations in the cultures of their three countries.[32] American individualism was compared to German and French communitarian social values. German consumers were more willing to support businesses that were identified as socially responsible than were U.S. consumers. Germans placed a higher priority on social responsibility attributed to businesses than did Americans. U.S. consumers highly valued the economic aspects of corporations first and the legal responsibilities second, while French and German consumers were concerned more about businesses conforming to legal and ethical standards. The French consumer sample considered ethical responsibilities second in importance to corporations' legal duties. German consumers were most interested in businesses conforming to social norms and less so in corporate economic performance. The study, admittedly based on small sample sizes, indicates regional differences in consumers' expectations of corporations' social responsibility and ". . . points to the difficulty of implementing uniform communication programs about social responsibility across borders."[33] The results also indicate cultural differences in consumers' expectations about corporate responsibility. Are there corporate values and responsibilities toward consumers that should not be limited by geographies and cultural boundaries?

CORPORATE RESPONSIBILITIES AND CONSUMER RIGHTS

Corporations as value-based stakeholder managers have certain responsibilities and duties toward their customers and consumers in society:

- *The duty to inform* consumers truthfully and fully of a product or service's content, purpose, and uses
- *The duty not to misrepresent or withhold information* about a product or service that would hinder consumers' free choice
- *The duty not to force or take undue advantage* of consumer buying and product selection choice through fear or stress or by other means that constrain rational choice
- *The duty to take "due care" to prevent any foreseeable injuries* or mishaps a product (in its design and production or in its use) may inflict on consumers.[34]

While these responsibilities seem reasonable, there are several problems with the last responsibility, known as "due care" theory. First, there is no straightforward method for determining when "due care" has been given. What should a firm do to ensure the safety of its products? How far should it go? A utilitarian principle has been suggested. But the problem arises when use of this method adds costs to products. Also, what health risks should be measured and how? How serious must an injury be? The second problem is that "due care" theory assumes that a manufacturer can know its products' risks before injuries occur. Certainly, testing can be, should be, and is done for most high-risk products; but for most products, *use* generally determines product defects. Also, these questions must still be addressed: Who pays the costs for injuries resulting from product defects unknown beforehand by consumer and manufacturer? Should the manufacturer be the party that determines what is safe and unsafe for consumers? Or is this a form of paternalism? In a free market, who should be able to determine what products will be used at what cost and risk?[35]

Related rights consumers have in their social contract with corporations include the following:

- *The right to safety*—to be protected from harmful commodities that injure
- *The right to free and rational choice*—to be able to select among alternative products
- *The right to know*—to have easy access to truthful information that can help in product selection
- *The right to be heard*—to have available a party who will acknowledge and act on reliable complaints about injustices regarding products and business transactions
- *The right to be compensated*—to have a means to receive compensation for harm done to a person because of faulty products or for damage done in the business transaction[36]

These rights are also constrained by free-market principles and conditions. For example, ". . . products must be as represented: producers must live up to the terms of the sales agreement; and advertising and other information about products must not be deceptive. Except for these restrictions, however, producers are free, according to free-market theory, to operate pretty much as they please."[37]

The "buyer beware" principle plays well according to free-market theory, which we briefly discuss next since this doctrine underlies the topic of corporate responsibility in advertising, product safety, and liability, discussed later in the chapter.

FREE-MARKET THEORY: RELATIONSHIP BETWEEN CONSUMERS AND CORPORATIONS

Free-market theory holds that the primary aim of business is to make a profit. As far as business obligations toward consumers, this view assumes an equal balance of power, knowledge, and sophistication of choice in the buying and selling of products and services between companies and customers. If businesses deliver what customers want, customers buy. Customers have the freedom and wisdom to select what they want and to reject what they do not want. Faulty or undesirable products should not sell. If businesses do not sell their products or services, it is their own fault. The marketplace is an arena of arbitration. Consumers and corporations are protected and regulated, according to this view, by Adam Smith's "invisible hand."

Several scholars argue that Adam Smith's "invisible hand" view is not completely oriented toward stockholders: for example, Szwajkowski argued that "Smith's viewpoint is most accurately positioned squarely between those who contend firms should act out of self-interest and those who believe corporations should be do-gooders. This middle ground is actually the stakeholder perspective. That is, stakeholders are in essence the market in all its forms. They determine what is a fair price, what is a successful product, what is an unacceptable strategy, what is intolerable discrimination . . . . The mechanisms for these determinations include purchase transactions, supplier contracts, government regulation, and public pressure. . . ."[38] The author continues, "Our own empirical research has clearly shown that employee relations and product quality and safety are the most significant and reliable predictors of corporate reputation."[39]

Free markets require certain conditions for business activity to help society. These conditions include (1) minimal moral restraints to enable businesses to operate and prevent illegal activities such as theft, fraud, and blackmail; (2) full competitiveness with entry and exit; (3) relevant information needed to transact business available to everyone; and (4) accurate reflection of all production costs in the prices that consumers and firms pay (including the costs of job-related accidents, injuries from unsafe products, and externalities, which are spillover costs that are not paid by manufacturers or companies, but that consumers and taxpayers often pay, e.g., pollution costs). Legal and ethical problems arise when some or all of these conditions are violated, as the summary of corporate crises illustrated at the beginning of this chapter.

PROBLEMS WITH THE FREE-MARKET THEORY

Although the free-market theory is currently popular and has validity, controversy also exists regarding its assumptions about consumer-business relationships. For example, consider these arguments:

1. Most businesses are not on an equal footing with consumers at large. Large firms spend sizable amounts on research aimed at analyzing, creating, and—some argue—manipulating the demand of targeted buyers. Children, for example, are not aware of the effects of advertising on their buying choices.

2. Whether many firms' advertising activities truthfully inform consumers about product reliability, possible product dangers, and

proper product use is questioned. As discussed in the next section, a thin line exists between deceit and artistic exaggeration in advertising.

3. The "invisible hand" is often nonexistent for consumers in need of protection against questionable advertising and poorly manufactured products released to market. One reason a stakeholder view has become a useful approach for determining moral, legal, and economic responsibility is that the issues surrounding product safety, for example, are complex and controversial. Who is right and who is wrong and who is innocent and who is liable must be examined before informed judgments are made. The question then arises, What are realistic company obligations toward consumers in marketplace relationships and exchanges?

Another important argument against free-market theory is based on what economists refer to as *imperfect markets*, that is, markets in which competition "is flawed by the ability of one or more parties to influence prices."[40] An example of an imperfect market and skewed market power occurs in Africa, ". . . where a few pharmaceutical companies effectively control the availability of several key drugs. In effect, they are beyond the financial means of millions of Africans or their governments. When a few dominating companies cut the prices of several key ingredients of the AIDS cocktail recently, they demonstrated this power. But this also revealed a further imperfection in the real market, where only rickety systems, if any, exist to deliver the drugs to patients requiring sophisticated and continuous follow-up care."[41]

MIXED MARKET ECONOMIES

The debate regarding free markets, imperfect markets, and other forms of social organization (socialism, communism, Marxism) is interesting but not always helpful in describing how these systems actually work in the marketplace. The free-market system has been more accurately described by economist Paul Samuelson as a "mixed economy."[42] Mixed economies include a balance between private property systems and the government laws, policies, and regulations that protect consumers and citizens. In mixed economies, ethics becomes part of legal and business debates. Principles of justice, rights, and duty coexist with utilitarian and market principles, as we see in the next section.

5.4 CORPORATE RESPONSIBILITY IN ADVERTISING, PRODUCT SAFETY, AND LIABILITY

Advertising is big business. In 1991, $126.7 billion was spent on advertising; by 1994, the estimate was $150 billion.[43] The ad business is expected to grow to $249.8 billion in 2001 and to $262 billion by 2002.[44] Advertising expenditures on the Internet were $350 million during the first quarter of 1998, a 271 percent increase over the same period for 1997. It is estimated that almost 2 percent of the gross national product is spent on advertising. Since advertising significantly affects the public and consumers, it is an important topic of study in business ethics.

The purposes of advertising are to inform customers about products and services and to persuade them to purchase. A corporation's ethical responsibility in advertising is to inform and persuade consumer stakeholders in ways that do not lie, deceive, conceal, or withhold the truth. This does not always happen, as the tobacco, diet, and food industries, for example, have shown.

ETHICS AND ADVERTISING

At issue, legally and ethically, for consumers is whether or not advertising is deceptive and creates or contributes to creating harm to consumers. While advertising is supposed to provide information to consumers, a major aim is to sell products and services. As part of a selling process, both buyer and seller are involved. As discussed earlier, "buyer beware" imparts some responsibility for believing and being susceptible to ads to the buyer. Ethical issues arise whenever corporations target ads in manipulative, untruthful, subliminal, and coercive ways to vulnerable buyers such as children, youth, and minorities. Also, inserting harmful chemicals into products without informing the buyer is deceptive advertising. The tobacco industry's use of nicotine and addictive ingredients in cigarettes was deceptive advertising, as we will discuss below.

The American Association of Advertising (AAA) has a code of ethics that helps organizations monitor their own ads. The code cautions against false, distorted, misleading, and exaggerated claims and statements as well as pictures that are offensive to the public and minority groups in the population.

THE FTC AND ADVERTISING

The Federal Trade Commission (FTC) and the Department of Labor (DOL) are the federal agencies appointed and funded to monitor and eliminate false and misleading advertising when corporate self-regulation is not used or fails to control harm done to consumers. Following is a sample of the FTC's guidelines:

> The Federal Trade Commission Act allows the FTC to act in the interest of all consumers to prevent deceptive and unfair acts or practices. In interpreting Section 5 of the Act, the Commission has determined that a representation, omission or practice is *deceptive* if it is likely to:
>
> ■ mislead consumers and
> ■ affect consumers' behavior or decisions about the product or service.
>
> In addition, an act or practice is *unfair* if the injury it causes, or is likely to cause, is:

- substantial,
- not outweighed by other benefits, and
- reasonably avoidable.

The FTC Act prohibits unfair or deceptive advertising in any medium. That is, advertising must tell the truth and not mislead consumers. A claim can be misleading if relevant information is left out or if the claim implies something that's not true. *For example, a lease advertisement for an automobile that promotes "$0 Down" may be misleading if significant and undisclosed charges are due at lease signing.* In addition, claims must be *substantiated*, especially when they concern health, safety, or performance. The type of evidence may depend on the product, the claims, and what experts believe necessary. If your ad specifies a certain level of support for a claim—*"tests show X"*—you must have at least that level of support.

Sellers are responsible for claims they make about their products and services. Third parties—such as advertising agencies or Website designers and catalog marketers—also may be liable for making or disseminating deceptive representations if they participate in the preparation or distribution of the advertising, or know about the deceptive claims.[45]

ADVERTISING AND THE INTERNET

Advertising on the Internet presents new opportunities and problems for consumers. The ubiquity of ads on the Web causes ethical problems, particularly for parents and those wishing to protect youth and minors from a host of pop-up ads as well as exposure to Websites and advertisements dealing with sex, pornography, violence, drinking, and tobacco.

Pop-up and pop-under ads (i.e., ads that open up in a separate, full browser window, underneath whatever site the user is viewing) are available on some of the most visited services (AOL, Microsoft, Yahoo, X10, Terra Lycos, eBay, and others).[46] In addition, marketers are turning to Web films to push their products through "byte-sized movies." In place of TV commercials that confront consumers with 30-second product introductions, the new "advertainment" shorts (also known as "commission content") present product or service information to the viewer in the course of or around a story— for example, Volkswagen's "VW Drive-In" Website features short films; Madonna starred in a BMW-funded film directed by her husband. "You're not using a product-based appeal, you're using an image-based appeal."[47]

At issue ethically is the unlimited availability of and exposure to explicit sexual, pornographic, and other questionable content on ads and Websites, mixed with carefully crafted entertainment that is enhanced by newer technologies. Should youth be able to log on from their own computers, or from computers in libraries and cyber cafes, to Websites showing ads and previews of explicit sexual and pornographic pictures and video clips? The issue centers around how much government protection through censorship you and the public want. While AOL and other servers offer controls for parents, as do private firms through products such as CyberPatrol, CYBER-sitter, and WebTrack, the issue remains one of principle: How much regulation interferes with free speech and exposure to ideas for all? Moreover, the file-sharing technology made popular by Napster provides additional opportunities not only to see and experience provocative and controversial material by anyone, anywhere, anytime, but to also share the content instantly.

Another related ethical issue introduced through the Internet and pioneered by Napster is the blurring of boundaries between advertising and product sampling, which enables people to steal copyrighted songs, movies, and other information on the Web. "What do you tell 40 million kids who know how to turn a product into data that they can trade freely?"[48] Responses to this question from technology chief executives included the following: "You teach them some values. You can walk into any store and steal something, and kids don't do it. We've got to bring up a generation that understands that if you steal a movie over the Net, and it is 'Pearl Harbor,' that is stealing." Another executive: "You've got to make it easier to do something legally than it is to do it illegally."[49] While Napster has been forced to change its on-line copyright violation practices, the ethical questions the technology and practice presented remain relevant areas of ethical inquiry.

Again, the FTC has regulatory guidelines for on-line advertising, dot com disclosures, and information sharing. The following is a sample from the FTC's Website:

> *Dot Com Disclosures: Information About Online Advertising,* an FTC staff paper, provides additional information for online advertisers. The paper discusses the factors used to evaluate the clarity and conspicuousness of required disclosures in online ads. It also discusses how certain FTC rules and guides that use terms like "writing" or "printed" apply to Internet activities and how technologies such as email may be used to comply with certain rules and guides.

PROTECTING CONSUMERS' PRIVACY ONLINE

> The Internet provides unprecedented opportunities for the collection and sharing of information from and about consumers. But studies show that consumers have very strong concerns about the security and confidentiality of their personal information in the online marketplace. Many consumers also report being wary of engaging in online commerce, in part because they fear that their personal information can be misused.

> These consumer concerns present an opportunity for you to build on consumer trust by implementing effective voluntary industry-wide practices to protect consumers' information privacy. The FTC has held a number of workshops for industry, consumer groups and privacy advocates to explore industry guidelines to protect consumers' privacy online.

> In June 1998, the FTC issued *Online Privacy: A Report to Congress.* The Report noted that while over 85 percent of all websites collected personal information from consumers, only 14 percent of the sites in the FTC's random sample of commercial websites provided any notice to consumers of the personal information they collect or how they use it. In May 2000, the FTC issued a follow-up report, *Privacy Online: Fair Information Practices in the Electronic Marketplace.*

While the 2000 survey showed significant improvement in the percent of websites that post at least some privacy disclosures, only 20 percent of the random sample sites were found to have implemented four fair information practices: notice, choice, access and security. Even when the survey looked at the percentage of sites implementing the two critical practices of notice and choice, only 41 percent of the random sample provided such privacy disclosures. You can access the FTC's privacy report at www.ftc.gov.

The _Children's Online Privacy Protection Act (COPPA)_ and the FTC's implementing Rule took effect April 21, 2000. Commercial Websites directed to children less than 13 years old or general audience sites that have actual knowledge that they are collecting information from a child must obtain parental permission before collecting such information. The FTC also launched a special site at www.ftc.gov/kidzprivacy to help children, parents and the operators understand the provisions of COPPA and how the law will affect them.[50]

PATERNALISM OR MANIPULATION?

Moral responsibility for consumers in advertising can be viewed along a continuum. At one end of the spectrum is the control criticism regarding _paternalism_; that is, "Big Brother" (or government, in most cases) regulates the "free market" to control and even ban certain products as well as what consumers can or should be allowed to hear and see. Too much protection can lead to too much control and enforcement over free choice. This is not desirable in a democratic market economy. At the other extreme of the continuum is the illusion of free choice, which is another type of control; that is, corporations manipulate consumers' free choice through cleverly researched ads aimed at deception. This is also undesirable, since it limits consumer choice and knowledge. Ideally, corporations should seek to inform consumers truthfully while using nonmanipulative persuasive techniques to sell their products.

Enforcement of advertising also can be viewed along this continuum. Outright bans on ads can result in court decisions that rule that consumer free choice has been violated and that a party was or could be harmed. At the other end, companies and industry groups can police themselves, as has been the case in the alcohol industry, with the U.S. Brewers Association issuing guidelines against beer ads that promote overindulgence. Where moral and legal disputes over specific ads actually occur on the continuum is a matter of perception and judgment. Therefore, the general debate over the pros and cons of what constitutes ethical advertising continues whether it focuses on claims that women are discriminated against in beer ads; on claims that the general public is being deceived by food labels that show half-truths about fat and cholesterol content; on claims that tobacco ads target youths and unsophisticated buyers by showing smokers as people who live enviable, successful lifestyles; or on claims that jeans and lingerie ads may be too sexually explicit. The following discussion summarizes the major arguments for and against advertising.

ARGUMENTS FOR ADVERTISING

Arguments that justify advertising and the tactics of puffery and exaggeration include the following:

1. Advertising introduces people to and influences them to buy goods and services. Without advertising, consumers would be uninformed about products.

2. Advertising enables companies to be competitive with other firms in domestic and international markets. Firms across the globe use advertisements as competitive weapons.

3. Advertising helps a nation maintain a prosperous economy. Advertising increases consumption and spending, which in turn creates economic growth and jobs, which in turn benefits all. "A rising tide lifts all ships."

4. Advertising helps a nation's balance of trade and debt payments, especially in large industries, such as the food, automobile, alcoholic beverage, and computer technology industries, whose exports help the country's economy.

5. Proponents of advertising argue that customers' lives are enriched by the images and metaphors advertising creates. Customers pay for the illusions as well as the products advertisements promote.

6. Those who defend the general practice of advertising claim consumers are not ignorant. Buyers know the differences among lying, manipulation, and colorful hyperbole aimed at attracting attention. Consumers have freedom of choice. Ads do not coerce anyone to buy anything. Ads try to influence desires already present in people's minds. Companies have a constitutional right to advertise in free and democratic societies. Moreover, studies tend to show that advertising does not effectively cause people to buy products or services. In fact, the effectiveness of advertising in general is questionable.[51]

ARGUMENTS AGAINST (QUESTIONABLE) ADVERTISING

Critics of questionable advertising practices argue that advertising can be harmful for the following reasons. First, advertisements often cross that thin line that exists between puffery and deception. For example, unsophisticated buyers, especially children and youth, are targeted by companies. David Kessler, former commissioner of the Food and Drug Administration (FDA), referred to smoking as a pediatric disease, since 90 percent of lifelong smokers started when they were 18 and half began by the age of 14.[52]

Another argument against questionable advertising is that advertisements tell half-truths, conceal facts, and intentionally deceive with a profit goal, not consumer welfare, in mind. For example, the $300 billion to $400 billion *food industry* is increasingly being watched by the FDA for printing misleading labels that undermine nutritional information. Misleading labels that use terms such as "cholesterol free," "lite," and "all natural" are under attack, with an added push from the Nutritional Education and Labeling Act of 1990. Consumers need understandable information quickly on how much fat (a significant factor in heart disease) is in food, on standard serving sizes, and on the exact nutritional contents of foods.[53] At stake in the short term for food companies is an outlay of between $100 million and $600 million for re-labeling. In the long term, product sales could be at risk.

> One of the great paradoxes of Americans today is that we are obsessed with diet and health and yet have one of the worst diets in the world. Fifty-four percent of adults are considered overweight. Only 2 percent of children eat the recom-mended variety of foods daily. Food industry executives blame the customers, saying they ask for low-fat food but rarely buy it. For many Americans, the problem isn't just that they are consuming so much fat, it is that they don't know what they are eating . . . . To put this in perspective, consider nutrition guide-lines that suggest the 30-year-old male eat a maximum of 2,900 calories and 97 grams of fat per day, and the average 30-year-old female eat no more that 1,900 calories and 73 grams of fat, according to the CSPI [Center for Science in the Public Interest]. Many Americans far exceed those recommendations, in part because of their increasing reliance on restaurant food.[54]

Professionals at the CSPI, who won the battle to require nutrition labels on many grocery items, are lobbying the government to require restaurants to provide similar information on their menus. Subway chain restaurants al-ready aggressively distribute this type of information.

FAST FOOD NATION

Eric Schlosser's book *Fast Food Nation* explores a topic related to advertising and nutrition. Schlosser argues that there is a dark side of the fast food in-dustry, where the best and worst of American marketing and capitalism con-nect, as manifested in the transformation of fast food production globally; the reliance on low-paid, unskilled labor; and alarming health trends. Mc-Donald's has 28,700 outlets in 120 countries. Fast food chains are driving in-dependent restaurants out of business. Almost a quarter of the adult popula-tion in the United States eats at a fast food restaurant daily. Over $110 billion was spent in fast food restaurants in 2000 compared with $6 billion in 1970. In 1960, the average American ate 4 pounds of frozen french fries a year; in 2001, that amount was over 30 pounds. Chicken McNuggets have twice as much fat per once as hamburgers. The typical soda has the equivalent of 10 tablespoons of sugar.[55]

Schlosser traces the growth of the fast food restaurant industry to Ameri-can marketing gurus Ray Kroc, who led the franchising of McDonald's, and Carl Karcher, who set up hot dog stands that grew into a fast food empire. While these businessmen were geniuses in creating advertising innovations and linking them to build franchising empires, the results of the products for consumers are more questionable. Schlosser describes worst-case scenarios such as the slaughterhouses where beef is prepared for fast food chains—and where conditions give rise to food-borne diseases (about 14 people die in the United States each day from Listeria and E. coli). Schlosser's historical arguments and exposé are reminiscent of Upton Sinclair's classic research-based novel, *The Jungle*, in which he described Chicago's slaughterhouses and the working conditions for immigrant employees in the early 1900s.

While *Fast Food Nation* is criticized for its negative bias toward the fast food industry, some of Schlosser's critics agree that his research is "impressive and comprehensive, even if his conclusions are somewhat overstated."[56]

TOBACCO AND ALCOHOL ADVERTISING

Critics argue that tobacco and alcohol companies, in particular, continue to unjustifiably promote products that are dangerously unhealthy and that have effects that endanger others. The tobacco industry spent approximately $8.2 billion in 1999 for traditional magazine direct-to-consumer advertising. Cigarette companies reportedly are targeting ads at low-income women and minorities and focusing less on college-educated consumers. Three thousand new teenagers and youth begin smoking each day. One out of three is predicted to die from tobacco-related illnesses—several when they are middle-aged.[57]

R.J. Reynolds's "trend-influence marketing" and Brown & Williamson's "relationship marketing" have the goal of connecting with customers on a personal level. For example, the "Lucky Strike Force" (teams of attractive twentysomethings) promotes the brands while offering smokers roses and coffee. R.J. Reynolds hosted 700 parties for smokers in 70 U.S. cities. Philip Morris hosted 117 events that featured musicians like Smash Mouth, Violent Femmes, and Afghan Whigs.[58]

The Philip Morris tobacco company told the Czech government that smoking is not a public health menace because the premature deaths save the country money on elder care. The company calculated that in 1999 "the premature demise of smokers saved the Czech government between $24 million and $30 million on health care, housing, and pensions." The company stated that "weighing the costs and benefits," the Czech government actually made $147 million from its smoking policies when considering the care it paid for smokers who were still living and for victims of secondhand smoke.[59] The company later stated, "We're not trying to suggest that there would be a benefit to society from the diseases related to smoking."

Alcohol ads also raise problems for consumers. Critics of alcohol ads argue that youth, in particular, are targeted—enticed by suggestive messages linking drinking to contemporary lifestyles, popularity, and success. The Marlboro man, the infamous and now defunct Old Joe Camel, and other cigarette brands linked adventure, fun, social acceptance, being "cool," and risk taking to smoking. Several popular movie stars are paid by cigarette companies to smoke in films. Consumers, public lobbying groups such as

Mothers Against Drunk Driving (MADD), and state attorneys general have protested against the use of such ads in places that attract teens and youth to smoking and drinking.

ETHICS AND ADVERTISING

Advertising issues related to what is legal or illegal, moral or immoral, are matters of judgment, values, and changing societal standards. As stated earlier, most of these types of issues have been and are argued in and out of courts on a case-by-case basis. Still, corporations and consumers can use the following questions to address the moral responsibility of advertisements:

1. Is the consumer being treated as a means to an end or as an end? What and whose end?
2. Whose rights are being protected or violated intentionally and inadvertently? At what and whose costs?
3. Are consumers being justly and fairly treated?
4. Are the public welfare and good taken into consideration for the effects as well as the intention of advertisements?
5. Has anyone been harmed, and can this harm be proven?

ADVERTISING AND FREE SPEECH

Should certain ads be banned or restricted by courts? The U.S. Supreme Court has differentiated commercial speech from pure speech in the context of the First Amendment. (See *Central Hudson Gas and Electric Corporation v. Public Service Commission,* 1980, and *Posadas de Puerto Rico Associates v. Tourism Company of Puerto Rico,* 54 LW 4960). "Commercial speech" in ads and business transactions has not been as protected in courts as "pure speech." Pure speech is more generalized, relating to political, scientific, and artistic expression in marketplace dealings. Commercial speech refers to language in ads and business dealings. The Supreme Court has balanced both these concepts of speech against the general principle that freedom of speech must be weighed against the public's general welfare. The four-step test developed by Justice Lewis F. Powell Jr. and used to determine whether commercial speech in advertisements could be banned or restricted follows:

1. Is the ad accurate, and does it promote a lawful product?
2. Is the government's interest in banning or restricting the commercial speech important, nontrivial, and substantial?
3. Does the proposed restriction of commercial speech assist the government in obtaining a public policy goal?
4. Is the proposed restriction of commercial speech limited only to achieving the government's purpose?[60]

The commercial speech doctrine is presently controversial and confused. The Supreme Court has turned to the First Amendment to protect commercial speech (which is supposedly based on informational content). Public discourse is protected to ensure the participation and open debate needed to sustain democratic traditions and legitimacy. The Supreme Court has ultimate jurisdiction over decisions regarding the extent to which commercial speech in particular ads and cases meets the above four standards.

Recent judicial decisions regarding casino gambling advertising and dietary supplement labeling (see *Greater New Orleans Broadcasting Association Inc. v. United States* and *Pearson v. Shalala*, respectively) have sent a message that "[t]he government's heretofore generally accepted power to regulate commercial speech in sensitive areas has been restricted." Regulators have prohibited certain advertisements and product claims based on the government's authority to protect public safety and the common good. The court decisions clearly show "[t]he emerging bottom line: regulations must be coherent and consistent, and it is preferable to require disclaimers than to stifle commercial speech altogether." The courts have sent the government (namely, the FDA) "back to the drawing board" to write disclaimers for claims it had argued to be inconclusive. The FDA's regulations and regulatory power have currently been curtailed.[61]

The following section explores corporations' responsibility toward consumer stakeholders with regard to the manufacture, distribution, and sale of products.

PRODUCT SAFETY AND LIABILITY

Managing product safety should be priority number one for corporations. A sign in one engineering facility reads, "Get it right the first time or everyone pays!" Product quality, safety, and liability are interrelated topics, especially when products fail in the marketplace, as the crisis cases summarized at the beginning of the chapter illustrate. As new technologies are used in product development, risks increase for end users. This section discusses the ethics of product safety and the nature of product liability.

HOW SAFE IS SAFE? THE ETHICS OF PRODUCT SAFETY

Each year thousands of people die and millions are injured from the effects of smoking cigarettes, using diet drugs, suffering from silicon breast implants, and using consumer products such as toys, lawn mowers, appliances, power tools, and household chemicals, according to the U.S. Consumer Product Safety Commission. But how safe is safe? Few, if any, products are 100 percent safe. Adding the manufacturing costs to bolster safety features to the sales price would, in many instances, discourage price-sensitive consumers. Just as companies use utilitarian principles when developing products for markets, consumers use this logic when shopping and purchasing. Risks are calculated by both manufacturer and consumer. However, enough serious instances of questionable product quality and lack of manufacturing precautions taken (see the Ford Pinto crisis case in the case section at the end of the text) occur to warrant more than a simple utilitarian ethic for preventing and determining product safety for the consuming public. This is especially the case for commercial products such as air-, sea-, and spacecraft, over which consumers have little, if any, control.

Are cigarettes safe products? Tobacco smoke contains 4,000 chemicals including 40 known carcinogens. Each year 53,000 deaths in the United States are attributed to passive smoking; 37,000 are attributed to heart disease.[62] Are airlines more safe? Open a newspaper and you will find that ValuJet (called Air Tran before 1996) has some of the cheapest airfares available. The ValuJet crisis in 1996 sent a message to airline users: How much are you willing to pay, or not pay, for a safe flight? The fatal ValuJet crash awakened the Federal Aviation Administration (FAA) and resulted in the temporary grounding of that airline until safety requirements were met. The FAA rejected a recommendation, made three years before, that airlines install smoke detectors and fire suppression systems in cargo holds because the installation was too expensive. It is believed that lack of such safety systems may have cost the lives of 110 passengers on ValuJet Flight 592. Investigators believe a fire that raged in the plane's forward cargo hold was fueled by 144 oxygen generators—these generators should not have been on board.

The cost of designing and installing such safety devices has been estimated to be less than $1 for each person per flight. The FAA calculated it would have cost $100,000 (other industrial estimates were as low as $50,000) to upgrade each plane. With 3,500 planes in the United States requiring upgrades, the total bill would be $350 million. For each of the 548 million passengers who flew on U.S. carriers in 1995, the estimated cost would have been 64 cents per passenger. Bill Wadlock at the Aviation Resource Safety Center at Embry-Riddle University in Prescott, Arizona, states: "There's a phrase in the airline business, and it's kind of depressing. 'If it's cheaper to fix something, they'll fix it. If it's cheaper to kill you, they'll kill you.'"

Consumers also value safety and will pay for safe products up to the point where, in their own estimation, the product's *marginal value equals its marginal cost*; that is, people put a cost on the price they are willing to pay for their own lives whether they are rollerblading, sunning, sky diving, drinking, overeating, or driving to work.[63]

PRODUCT SAFETY CRITERIA: WHAT IS THE VALUE OF A HUMAN LIFE? The National Commission on Product Safety (NCPS) notes that product risks should be reasonable. Unreasonable risks are those that could be prevented or that consumers would pay to prevent if they had the knowledge and choice, according to the NCPS. Three steps that firms can use to assess product safety from an ethical perspective follow[64]:

1. How much safety is technically attainable, and how can it be specifically obtained for this product or service?

FIGURE 5.4	THE PRICE OF A HUMAN LIFE?

Assume it would cost $500 per car to put antiskid brakes in each of 10 million cars sold this year—a total of $5 billion. Then assume that installing gadgets on this year's fleet ultimately would save 5,000 lives, or $1 million per life. Next assume that, on average, individuals value their lives at $5 million. Since the $1 million cost of saving a life is less than the $5 million value of life, the safety feature might be worth buying.

If seat belts cost, say, $50 per car and equipping 1 million cars with seat belts will save 1,000 lives, then regulators must assume lives are worth at least $50,000 a piece. Take another example. If smoke detectors cost $20 each and are widely seen as reducing the risk of a death by 1 chance in 10,000, then buyers surely would value their lives for at least 20 times $10,000, or $200,000. Again, if it takes an extra $100,000 in lifetime earnings to persuade miners to cope with 1 extra chance in 100 of premature death underground, then miners implicitly must value their lives at no more than 100 times $100,000, or $10 million.

The following table has estimates of the minimum value of a human life found in a sampling of governmental regulations. The figures take into account the medical and hospital costs avoided if calculated lives are saved, but these figures ignore other benefits of regulations, such as prevention of property damage and injuries that do not result in death. The estimates are based on risk experts' calculations of what a human life is worth considering all costs of installing various lifesaving gadgets. For example, if the government spent $110 million annually on a B-58 bomber ejection system and 5 lives would be saved, then each life is estimated at $22 million ($110 million divided by 5).

Automobiles	Child restraint in cars	$1,221.3 million
	Dual master cylinders for car brakes	$7.8 million
Ejection System	For the B-58 bomber	$22.0 million
Flashing Lights	For railroad crossings	$0.73 million
Sea Walls	For protection against 100-year-storm surges	$96.0 million
Asbestos	Banned in brake linings	$0.23 million
	Banned in automatic transmission parts	$1,200.0 million
Radiation	Safety standards for X-ray equipment	$0.4 million
	Safety standards for uranium mine tailings	$190.0 million

SOURCE: Harvard Center for Risk Analysis.

Who is to say a life is worth $5 million rather than $500 million? Numerous studies calculate the value of life. But these studies do not produce uniform answers, nor do risk analysts claim this. People have very different estimates for risk. But researchers are still willing to generalize. Most middle-income U.S. citizens usually act as if their lives were worth $3 million to $5 million, based on what individuals demand in extra pay for dangerous jobs and what they spend for safety devices.

SOURCE: "How Much for a Life? Try $3 Million to $5 Million" by Peter Passell from *The New York Times*, January 29, 1995, p. F3. Copyright © 1995 by The New York Times Co. Reprinted by permission.

2. What is the acceptable risk level for society, the consumer, and the government regarding this product?

3. Does the product meet societal and consumer standards?

These steps, of course, will not be the same for commercial aircraft as for tennis shoes.

Estimates regarding the monetary value of human life vary. As Figure 5.4 illustrates, these "expert" estimates range from $3 million to $5 million.

REGULATING PRODUCT SAFETY. Because of the number of product-related casualties and injuries annually and because of the growth of the consumer movement in the 1960s and 1970s, Congress passed the 1972 Consumer Product Safety Act, which created the Consumer Product Safety Commission (CPSC: http://www. cpsc.gov). This is the federal agency empowered to protect the public from unreasonable risks of injury and death related to consumer product use. The five members of the commission are appointed by the president. The commission has regional offices across the country. It develops uniform safety standards for consumer products; assists industries in developing safety standards; researches possible product hazards; educates consumers about comparative product safety standards; encourages competitive pricing; and works to recall, repair, and ban dangerous products. Each year the commission targets potentially hazardous products and publishes a list of them with consumer warnings. It recently targeted Cosco for the faulty product design of children's products. Since the mid-1990s, Cosco has made 12 recalls of 7 of 12 products that consumers have complained about. The death of an 11-month-old in July 1988 in a Cosco-designed crib was never reported by the company even though the company began to redesign the product. Cosco was forced to pay a record $1.3 million in civil penalties to settle charges that it violated federal law by failing to report hundreds of injuries and the death.[65]

The CPSC is constrained in part by its enormous mission, limited resources, and critics who argue that the costs for maintaining the agency exceed the results and benefits produced by it.

CONSUMER AFFAIRS DEPARTMENTS AND PRODUCT RECALLS. Many companies actively and responsibly monitor their customers' satisfaction and safety concerns. Companies set up and coordinate consumer affairs departments (CADs) to ensure customer confidence and corporate responsiveness. Procter & Gamble, General Electric, Shell Oil, Federal Express, and Pepsi-Cola, to name only a few, have established such departments. One survey estimated that 80 percent of the 500 largest companies have Websites that enable customers to ask questions and post comments.[66]

Many companies aggressively and voluntarily recall defective products and parts when they discover or are informed about them. When unsafe products are not voluntarily recalled, the Environmental Protection Agency (EPA), National Highway Traffic Safety Administration (NHTSA), Food and Drug Administration (FDA), and Consumer Product Safety Commission (CPSC) have the authority to enforce recalls of known or suspected unsafe products. Recalled products are usually repaired. If not, the product or parts can be replaced or even taken out of service. American autos are not infrequently recalled for replacement and adjustment of defective parts.

PRODUCT LIABILITY DOCTRINES

Who should pay for the effects of unsafe products, and how much should they pay? Who determines who is liable? What are the punitive and compensatory limits of product liability? The payout in 2001 in litigation and settlements in diet pill cases alone totaled $7 billion.[67] Also, 26 major companies have filed for bankruptcy court protection, and several others claim they have paid over $10 billion to settle asbestos liability–related lawsuits from products used in the 1970s.[68] The doctrine of product liability has evolved in the court system since 1916, when the dominant principle of *privity* was used. Until the decision in *Macpherson v. Buick Motor Company*, consumers injured by faulty products could sue and receive damages from a manufacturer if the manufacturer was judged to be negligent regarding a product defect. Manufacturers were not held responsible if consumers purchased a hazardous product from a retailer or wholesaler.[69] In the *Macpherson* case, the defendant was ruled liable for harm done to Mr. Macpherson. A wheel on the car had cracked. Although Macpherson had bought the car from a retailer and although Buick had bought the wheel from a different manufacturer, Buick was charged with negligence. Even though Buick did not intend to deceive the client, the court ruled the company responsible for the finished product (the car) because—the jury claimed—it should have tested its component parts.[70] The doctrine of *negligence* in the area of product liability thus was established. The negligence doctrine meant that all parties, including the manufacturer, wholesaler, distributor, and sales professionals, could be held liable if reasonable care was not observed in producing and selling a product that injured a person.

The doctrine of *strict liability* is an extension of the negligence standard. Strict liability holds that the manufacturer is liable for a person's injury or death if a product that is dangerous because of a known or knowable defect goes to market. A consumer has to prove three things to win the suit: (1) an injury happened, (2) the injury resulted from a product defect, and (3) the defective product was delivered by the manufacturer being sued.[71]

Absolute liability is a further extension of the strict liability doctrine. Absolute liability was used in 1982 in the *Beshada v. Johns-Manville Corporation* case. Employees sued Manville for diseases later found related to exposure to asbestos. The court ruled the manufacturer liable for not warning of product danger even though the danger was scientifically unknown at the time of the production and sale of the product.[72] Medical and chemical companies, in particular, whose products could produce harmful but unknowable side effects years later would be held liable under this doctrine.

LEGAL AND MORAL LIMITS OF PRODUCT LIABILITY

Product liability lawsuits have two broad purposes: first, they provide a level of compensation for injured parties, and second, they act to deter large corporations from negligently marketing dangerous products.[73] When a California jury recently awarded Richard Boeken, a victim who had smoker's lung cancer, a record $3 billion in a suit filed against Philip Morris, it may have overstepped the boundaries of rationality regarding the nature of product liability law. The legal and moral limits of product liability suits evolve historically and are, to a large degree, determined by political as well as legal stakeholder negotiations and settlements. Consumer advocates and stakeholders (for example, the Consumer Federation of America, the National Conference of State Legislators, the Conference of State Supreme Court Justices, and activist groups) argue and lobby for strong liability doctrines and laws to protect consumers against powerful firms that, these stakeholders contend, seek profits over consumer safety. In contrast, advocates of product liability law reform (for example, corporate stockholders, Washington lobbyists for businesses and manufacturers, and the President's Council on Competitiveness) argue that liability laws in the United States have become too costly, excessive, routine, and arbitrary. Liability laws can inhibit companies' competitiveness and willingness to innovate, they claim. Also, insurance companies claim that all insurance-paying citizens are hurt by excessive liability laws that allow juries to award hundreds of millions of dollars in punitive damages because as a result, insurance rates rise.

However, a two-year study of product liability cases concluded that punitive damages are rarely awarded, more rarely paid, and often reduced after the trial.[74] The study, partly funded by the Roscoe Pound Foundation in Washington, D.C., is the most comprehensive effort to date to show the patterns of punitive damages awards in product liability cases over the past 25 years. The results of the study follow:

1. Only 355 punitive damages verdicts were handed down by state and federal court juries during this period. One-fourth of those awards involved a single product—asbestos.

2. In the majority of the 276 cases with complete post-trial information available, punitive damages awards were abandoned or reduced by the judge or the appeals court.

3. The median punitive damages award for all product liability cases paid since 1965 was $625,000—a little above the median compensatory damages award of $500,100. Punitive damages awards were significantly larger than compensatory damages awards in only 25 percent of the cases.

4. The factors that led to significant awards—those that lawyers most frequently cited when interviewed or surveyed—were failure to reduce risk of a known danger and failure to warn consumers of those risks. A Cornell study reported similar findings.[75]

Also, an earlier federal study of product liability suits in five states showed that plaintiffs won less than 50 percent of the cases; a Rand Corporation study that surveyed 26,000 households nationwide found that only 1 in 10 of an estimated 23 million people injured each year thinks about suing; and the National Center for State Courts surveyed 13 state court systems from 1984 to 1989 and found that the 1991 increase in civil caseloads was for real-property rights cases, not suits involving accidents and injuries.[76] Contrary to some expectations, a recent study found that "judges are more than three times as likely as juries to award punitive damages in the cases they hear." Plaintiffs' lawyers apparently mistakenly believe that juries are a soft touch, and "they route their worst cases to juries. But in the end, plaintiffs do no better before juries than they would have before a judge." The study also found that the median punitive damages award made by judges ($75,000) was nearly three times the median award made by juries ($27,000).[77]

PROACTIVE ACTION BY STATES

Thirty-three states have laws in the making to limit liability and reduce damages awards. Seven states already have limited the amount of punitive damages that can be awarded.[78] Several states, including Connecticut and Louisiana, have also introduced reforms to limit and cap punitive damages.[79]

Product liability litigation may change dramatically in the coming years, moving liability back to the injured consumer. Tort reform legislation is predicted to reduce liability to negligence by redefining defective product design to protect manufacturers and by limiting the discovery and disclosure of defectiveness by excluding expert witnesses.[80]

E-COMMERCE AND PRODUCT LIABILITY. Product liability law is largely an undeveloped area in the e-commerce space. As such, ". . . advertisers are advised to assume that what they sow on the Web with intent to sell may generate a presumption of reliance by injured consumers. The risk adverse advertisers must assume that any express warranty is vulnerable to claims by a range of people who have specifically relied on it. If anything, the vastness of the Web environment will expand this field of liability."[81] E-marketers should avoid unqualified safety language, including variations of the word "safe." They also should avoid broad warranty-guarantee language unless such claims can be backed up. Regarding "puffery," it is advised that e-marketers use common sense and precaution and seek counsel's advice on the breadth and limits of selling language.

Product liability laws in the United States are influenced by the political process at both the federal and the state levels. Different stakeholders redraw battle lines on product liability laws depending on a number of factors, including industry interests, power, and political access. As a result, tort reform continues to evolve. In the following section, we ask, Who is responsible for the environment, and how can corporations adopt innovative ways to make profits while protecting the environment?

5.5 CORPORATE RESPONSIBILITY AND THE ENVIRONMENT

A time existed when corporations used the environment as a free and unlimited resource. That time is ending, in terms of international public awareness and increasing legislative control. The magnitude of environmental abuse, not only by industries but also by human activities and nature's processes, has awakened an international awareness of the need to protect and save the environment. At risk is the most valuable stakeholder, the earth itself. The depletion and destruction of air, water, and land are at stake in terms of natural resources. Consider the destruction of the rain forests in Brazil; the thinning of the ozone layer above the earth's atmosphere; climatic warming changes from carbon dioxide accumulations; the smog in Mexico City, Los Angeles, and New York City; the pollution of the seas, lakes, rivers, and groundwater supplies as a result of toxic dumping; and the destruction of Florida's Everglades National Park. At the human level, environmental pollution and damage cause heart and respiratory diseases and lung and skin cancer. Registered voters have stated that the most important environmental problems facing the nation are air pollution (26%), unsafe drinking water (11%), water pollution (11%), and toxic/hazardous waste (10%).[82]

MOST SIGNIFICANT ENVIRONMENTAL PROBLEMS

TOXIC AIR POLLUTION.   More people are killed, it is estimated, by air pollution (automobile exhaust and smokestacks emissions) than by traffic crashes. The so-called greenhouse gases are composed of the pollutants carbon monoxide, ozone, and ultrafine particles called particulates. These pollutants are produced by the combustion of coal, gasoline, and fossil fuels in cars. The American Lung Association ranked the following U.S. metropolitan areas the worst in 2001 in terms of ozone and greenhouse pollution: Los Angeles and three other California sites, the Houston-Galveston area of Texas, and Atlanta. Another study stated that by adopting greenhouse gas abatement technologies that are currently available, 64,000 lives could be saved in Sao Paulo, Brazil; Mexico City, Mexico; Santiago, Chile; and New York City alone in the next 20 years. The same study estimated that 65,000 cases of chronic bronchitis could be avoided and save almost 37 million person-days of lost work.[83]

Air pollution and greenhouse gases are linked to global warming, as evidenced in

- The 5 degree increase in Arctic air temperatures, as the earth becomes warmer today than at any time in the past 125,000 years.

- The snowmelt in northern Alaska, which comes 40 days earlier than it did 40 years ago.

- The sea-level rise, which, coupled with the increased frequency and intensity of storms, could inundate coastal areas, raising groundwater salinity.

- The atmospheric CO_2 levels, which are 31 percent higher than preindustrial levels 250 years ago.[84]

Nationally, carbon dioxide emissions are a major source of air pollution. The "dirtiest dozen" states with the most pollutant emissions from electric power plants are listed in Figure 5.5. Internationally, greenhouse gas

FIGURE 5.5	STATES WITH HIGHEST POLLUTANT EMISSIONS FROM POWER PLANTS	
Rank	**State**	**Pollutant Emissions (millions of pounds)**
1	Ohio	95.2
2	West Virginia	62.3
3	Pennsylvania	58.9
4	Florida	58.0
5	North Carolina	48.4
6	Georgia	47.2
7	Kentucky	44.8
8	Indiana	44.3
9	Michigan	33.8
10	Illinois	32.1
11	Alabama	28.7
12	Tennessee	26.7

SOURCE: U.S. Public Interest Research Group. Adapted from J. Fialka, "Bush Clean-Air Plan Born in Gore's Kyoto Playbook," *Wall Street Journal,* March 12, 2001, A24.

emission statistics show that Spain had the largest increase in emissions, followed by Ireland, the United States, Japan, the Netherlands, Italy, and Denmark. The European Union (EU), Britain, and Germany had emission decreases during this period (Figure 5.6).

To stabilize the climate, global carbon emissions must be cut in half, from the current 6 billion tons a year to under 3 billion tons a year. This reduction can be accomplished by producing more efficient cars and power plants, using mass transit and alternative energy, and improving building and appliance standards. These changes would also help alleviate energy crises as well as global warming and air pollution.[85]

WATER POLLUTION AND THE THREAT OF SCARCITY. Over a billion people—one in every five on earth—have no access to safe drinking water. Sample percentages of the populations who do have access to safe water include Ethiopia (18%), Sudan (45%), Pakistan (56%), Mexico (72%), and the United States (99%).[86]

Water pollution is a result of industrial waste dumping, sewage drainage, and runoff of the byproducts of agricultural chemicals. The combined effects of global water pollution are causing a noticeable scarcity. Water reserves (in major aquifers) are decreasing by an estimated 200 trillion cubic meters each year. The problem stems from the depletion and pollution of the world's

FIGURE 5.6	GREENHOUSE GAS EMISSIONS: UNITED STATES, JAPAN, AND SELECTED EU COUNTRIES	
	Reduction Target Increases by 2008–2012*	**Emission Change 1990–1999**
Spain	15%	23.2%
Ireland	13.0	22.1
United States	−7.0	16.0
Japan	−6.0	7.8
Netherlands	−6.0	6.1
Italy	−6.5	4.4
Denmark	−21.0	4.0
European Union	−8.0	−4.0
Britain	−12.5	−14.0
Germany	−21.0	−18.7

*Kyoto Protocol and E.U. burden sharing

SOURCE: European Commission: European Climate Network. Adapted from G. Winestock, "EU Wrestles with Business over Emissions," *Wall Street Journal*, July 13, 2001, A9.

groundwater. "In Bangladesh, for instance, perhaps half the country's population is drinking groundwater containing unsafe levels of arsenic. . . . By inadvertently poisoning groundwater, we may turn what is essentially a renewable resource into one that cannot be recharged or purified within human scales, rendering it unusable."[87] It is estimated that the United States will have to spend $1 trillion over the next 30 years to begin to purify thousands of sites of polluted groundwater. An EPA report estimated that it could cost $900 million to $4.3 billion dollars annually to implement one of the tools under the Clean Water Act for cleaning up the nation's waters.[88] It will require an integrated global effort of public and private groups, of individuals and corporations to begin planning and implementing massive recycling, including agricultural, chemical, and other pollution controls to address water protection and control. Many companies have already begun conservation efforts. Xerox has halved its use of dichloromethane, a solvent used to make photoreceptors. The firm also reuses 97 percent of the solvent and will replace it with a nontoxic solvent. The Netherlands has a national goal of cutting wastes between 70 and 90 percent.

HAZARDOUS WASTE AND LAND POLLUTION. The United States produces an estimated 212 million tons of hazardous waste each year—about a ton for each man, woman, and child in this nation. The vast bulk of this is refinery or chemical waste. Output of hazardous waste is estimated to be growing at the rate of about 3 percent per year.[89]

In the United States, individuals and industries throw out 400,000 tons of solid waste—trash—each day. Landfills are overflowing, while communities are fighting the addition of dump and incineration sites in their areas. NIMBY ("Not in My Back Yard") groups are protesting site proposals due to the side effects of air and underground water pollution from trash dumping.[90] Cleaning up dumps has been and continues to be the goal of the EPA and its Superfund toxic waste law—now 20 years old. This Congress-backed fund has restored 220 dangerous sites. Now the EPA has proposed a $460 million plan to dredge "hot spots" in a 40-mile stretch of the Hudson River in New York in order to take out 1 million pounds of toxic chemicals. General Electric (GE) is reportedly fighting the EPA effort. The EPA claims GE dumped polychlorinated biphenyls (PCBs) over 30 years and is now trying to shirk its responsibility.[91]

The U.S. military is a major source of international pollution. Hazardous waste generated by the Air Force, including pesticides, chemical residues, insecticides, gasoline, mercury, and bacteria, has, according to a Pentagon report, caused serious environmental problems at bases in Greenland, Spain, Japan, Panama, Italy, Iceland, and the United Kingdom. The Pentagon spent approximately $165 million on environmental projects internationally in 1999. Domestically, the military spends $1.72 billion annually to clean up contamination at its sites.[92]

CAUSES OF ENVIRONMENTAL POLLUTION

Some of the most pervasive factors that have contributed to the depletion of resources and damage to the environment are as follows:

1. *Consumer affluence.* Increased wealth—as measured by real personal per capita income—has led to increased spending, consumption, and waste.

2. *Materialistic cultural values.* Values have evolved to emphasize consumption over conservation—a mentality that believes in "bigger is better," "me first," and a throwaway ethic.

3. *Urbanization.* Concentrations of people in cities increase pollution, as illustrated by the examples of Los Angeles; New York City; Mexico City, Mexico; Sao Paulo, Brazil; and Santiago, Chile, to name a few.

4. *Population explosion.* Population growth means more industrialization, product use, waste, and pollution.

5. *New and uncontrolled technologies.* Technologies are produced by firms that prioritize profits, convenience, and consumption over environmental protection. While this belief system is changing, the environmental protection viewpoint is still not mainstream.

6. *Industrial activities.* Industrial activities that, as stated earlier, have emphasized depletion of natural resources and destructive uses of the environment for economic reasons have significantly caused environmental decay.[93]

ENFORCEMENT OF ENVIRONMENTAL LAWS

A number of governmental regulatory agencies have been created to develop and enforce policies and laws to protect the general and workplace environments. The Occupational Safety and Health Administration (OSHA), the Consumer Product Safety Commission, the Environmental Protection Agency, and the Council on Environmental Quality (CEQ) are among the more active agencies that regulate environmental standards. The EPA, in particular, has been a leading organization in regulating environmental abuses by industrial firms.

In 1970, the EPA's mission and activities concentrated on controlling and decreasing toxic substances, radiation, air pollution, water pollution, solid waste (trash), and pesticides. The EPA has since that time used its regulatory powers to enforce several important environmental laws:*The Clean Air Act of 1970, 1977, 1989, and 1990:* The latest revision of this law includes provisions for regulating urban smog, greenhouse gas emissions, and acid rain and for slowing ozone reduction. Alternative fuels were promoted and companies were authorized to sell or transfer their right to pollute within same-state boundaries—before, pollution rights could be bought, sold, managed, and brokered like securities.

- *The Federal Water Pollution Control Act of 1972:* Revised in 1977, this law controls the discharge of toxic pollutants into the water.
- *The Safe Drinking Water Act of 1974 and 1996:* It established standards nationally for drinking water.
- *The Toxic Substances Control Act of 1976.* It created a national policy on regulating, controlling and banning toxic chemicals where necessary.
- *The Resource Conservation and Recovery Act (RCRA) of 1976:* This legislation provides guidelines for the identification, control, and regulation of hazardous wastes by companies and state governments. The $1.6 billion Superfund, mentioned above, was created by Congress in 1980. It provides for the cleanup of chemical spills and toxic waste dumps. Chemical, petroleum, and oil firms' taxes help keep the Superfund going, along with U.S. Treasury funds and fees collected from pollution control. One in four U.S. residents lives within four miles of a Superfund site. It is estimated that 10,000 sites still need cleaning, and it may cost $1 trillion and take 50 years to complete this work.[94]
- *Chemical Safety Information, Site Security, and Fuels Regulatory Relief Act of 1999:* It created standards for storing flammable fuels and chemicals.

THE ETHICS OF ECOLOGY

Advocates of a new environmentalism argue that when the stakes approach the damage of the earth itself and human health and survival, the utilitarian ethic alone is an insufficient logic to justify continuing negligence and abuse of the earth. For example, Sagoff argues that cost-benefit analysis can measure only desires, not beliefs. In support of corporate environmental policies, he asks:

> Why should we think economic efficiency is an important goal? Why should we take wants and preferences more seriously than beliefs and opinions? Why should we base public policy on the model of a market transaction rather than the model of a political debate? . . . [E]conomists as a rule do not recognize one other value, namely, justice or equality, and they speak, therefore, of a "trade-off" between efficiency and our aesthetic and moral values. What about the trade-off between efficiency and dignity, efficiency and self-respect, efficiency and the magnificence of our natural heritage, efficiency and the quality of life?[95]

This line of reasoning raises questions such as these: What is human life worth? What is a "fair market" price or replacement value for Lake Erie? The Atlantic Ocean? The Brazilian rain forests? The stratosphere?

Five arguments from those who advocate for corporate social responsibility from an ecology-based organizational ethic include the following:

1. Organizations' responsibilities go beyond the production of goods and services at a profit.

2. These responsibilities involve helping to solve important social problems, especially those they have helped create.

3. Corporations have a broader constituency than stockholders alone.

4. Corporations have impacts that go beyond simple marketplace transactions.

5. Corporations serve a wider range of human values than a sole focus on economic values can capture.[96]

Although these guidelines serve as an ethical basis for understanding corporate responsibility for the environment, utilitarian logic and cost-benefit methods will continue to play key roles in corporate decisions regarding their uses of the environment. Also, judges, courts, and juries will use cost-benefit analysis in trying to decide who should pay and how much when settling case-by-case environmental disputes. Some experts and industry spokespersons argue that the costs of further controlling pollutants such as smog outweigh the benefits. For example, it is estimated that the cost of controlling pollution in the United States has exceeded $160 billion.[97] A World Health Organization study has estimated that air pollution will cause 8 million deaths worldwide by 2020.[98] How many lives would justify spending $160 billion annually? While some benefits of controlling pollution have been identified, such as the drop in emissions, improvement of air and water quality, cleanup of many waste sites, and growth of industries and jobs related to pollution control (environmental products, tourism, fishing, and boating), it is not clear whether these benefits outweigh the costs.[99] Measuring environmental costs and benefits is, as noted above, difficult. One question sometimes asked regarding this issue is, Would the environment be and have been better off *without* the environmental laws and protection agencies paid by tax dollars? An innovative way of integrating ethics and marketing is discussed in the following section.

GREEN MARKETING, ENVIRONMENTAL JUSTICE, AND INDUSTRIAL ECOLOGY

An innovative trend in new ecology ethical thinking is linking the concepts of green marketing, environmental justice, and industrial ecology.[100] Green marketing is the practice of ". . . adopting resource conserving and environmentally-friendly strategies in all stages of the value chain."[101] The green market was estimated at 52 million households in the United States in 1995. One study identified trends among consumers who would switch products to green brands: 88 percent of consumers surveyed in Germany said they would switch, as would 84 percent in Italy and 82 percent in Spain.[102] Companies are adopting green marketing as a competitive advantage and are also using green marketing in their operations: for example, packaging materials that are recyclable; pollution-free production processes, pesticide-free farming, and natural fertilizers.

Environmental justice is "the pursuit without discrimination based on race, ethnicity, and/or socioeconomic status concerning both the enforcement of existing environmental laws and regulations and the reformation of public health policy."[103] Linking environmental justice to green marketing involves identifying those companies that would qualify for visible, prestigious awards—as the Eddison Award—for producing the best green products. To win the award, companies would demonstrate that they had, for example, (1) produced new products and product extensions that represented an important achievement in reducing environmental impact, (2) indicated where and how they had disposed of industrial and toxic materials, and (3) incorporated recycling and use of less toxic materials in their strategies and processes.

The green marketing and environmental justice link to industrial ecology is made in the long-range vision and practice of companies' integrating environmental justice into sustainable operational practices on an industrywide basis. Industrial ecology is based on the principle of operating within nature's domain—that is, nothing is wasted or forever discarded; everything is recycled.

RIGHTS OF FUTURE GENERATIONS AND RIGHT TO A LIVABLE ENVIRONMENT

The ethical principles of rights and duties regarding the treatment of the environment and multiple stakeholders are (1) the rights of future generations and (2) the right to a livable environment. These rights are based on the responsibility that the present generation should bear regarding the preservation of the environment for future generations. In other words, how much of the environment can a present generation use or destroy to advance its own economic welfare? According to ethicist John Rawls, "Justice requires that we hand over to our immediate successors a world that is not in worse condition than the one we received from our ancestors."[104]

The right to a livable environment is an issue advanced by Blackstone.[105] The logic is that each human being has a moral and legal right to a decent, livable environment. This "environmental right" supersedes individuals' legal property rights and is based on the belief that human life is not possible without a livable environment. Therefore, laws must enforce the protection of the environment based on human survival. Several landmark laws have been passed, as noted earlier, that are based more on the logic related to Blackstone's "environmental right" than on a utilitarian ethic.

VALUE-BASED STAKEHOLDER MANAGEMENT PRACTICES AND THE ENVIRONMENT

New assumptions and practices driving corporate changes toward the environment include the following: (1) The international community, led by Europe, is embracing laws that establish supply chain "environmental management systems" to protect the environment. Instead of setting up environmental, health, and safety (EH&S) functions in organizations, new business and supply chain models are invented that integrate environmental sustainability into core organizational design, production, financial, and marketing strategies and systems.[106] (2) A green market, discussed above, is emerging. Rising energy costs create incentives to design and sell more energy-efficient products. Shareholders see environmental efficiency standards as a competitive advantage for increasing revenues. Governments and nonprofits are developing eco-labeling and certification programs (e.g. ISO 14000 environment standards, EPA's Energy Star Program, Germany's Blue Eagle Program), enabling firms to use these certifications to advertise environmentally superior manufacturing processes. (3) Entrepreneurs and corporate leaders are developing innovative environmentally friendly strategies for humanitarian motives to protect and sustain the ecological system; Tom's of Maine, Ben & Jerry's, Shell, and Hewlett-Packard are only a few examples.

Hewlett-Packard's (HP's) historical movement across the responsibility spectrum in addressing its concern for the environment is instructive. In the 1980s, HP took a pollution control and prevention approach by using *risk management* and facility improvement to reduce toxic materials and emissions in its operations. In the 1990s, the company shifted its focus to *product stewardship* and developed a function that tracked and managed global regulatory compliance issues, customer inquiry response systems, public policy, green packaging, and other product life cycle issues. At the turn of this century, HP is focusing on *sustainability;* that is, it is developing technologies

FIGURE 5.7	5 STAGES OF ENVIRONMENTAL CORPORATE COMMITMENT		
Stage	Manager Mindset	Resource Commitment	Top-Level Support & Involvement
1. Beginner	Environmental management unnecessary	Minimal resource commitment	No Involvement
2. Firefighter	Environmental issues addressed when necessary	Budgets for problems as they occur	Piecemeal Involvement
3. Concerned citizen	Environmental management is a worthwhile function	Consistent yet minimal budget	Commitment in theory
4. Pragmatist	Environmental management is an important business function	Generally sufficient funding	Aware and moderately involved
5. Proactivist	Environmental management is a priority item	Open-ended funding	Actively involved

SOURCE: Adapted from Christopher B. Hunt and Ellen R. Auster, "Proactive Environmental Management: Avoiding the Toxic Trap," *Sloan Management Review*, Winter 1990, p. 9. Permission granted by the publisher. Copyright 1990 by the Sloan Management Review Association. All rights reserved.

that positively impact the environment. The firm is also integrating environmental sustainability into its business strategy.[107]

RECOMMENDATIONS TO MANAGERS

Boards of directors, business leaders, managers, and professionals should ask four questions regarding their actual operations and responsibility toward the environment:

1. How much is your company really worth? (This question refers to the contingent liability a firm may have to assume depending on its practices.)
2. Have you made environmental risk analysis an integral part of your strategic planning process?
3. Does your information system "look out for" environmental problems?
4. Have you made it clear to your officers and employees that strict adherence to environmental safeguarding and sustainability requirements are a fundamental tenet of company policy?[108]

Using the answers to these questions, an organization can determine its stage on the corporate environmental responsibility profile (see Figure 5.7).

REFLECTIONS AND PERSONAL LESSONS ON FORD'S PINTO FIRES

The last chapter ended with a provocative case highlighting some of the sordid events in the history of the Pinto fires problem. As the authors have indicated in this chapter, I was involved with this infamous case in the early 1970s. They have asked me to reflect on lessons learned from my experience.

I take this case very personally, even though my name seldom comes up in its many recountings. I was one of those "faceless bureaucrats" who is often portrayed as making decisions without accountability and then walking away from them—even decisions with life-and-death implications. That characterization is, of course, far too stark and superficial. I certainly don't consider myself faceless, and I have always chafed at the label of bureaucrat as applied to me, even though I have found myself unfairly applying it to others. Furthermore, I have been unable to walk away from my decisions in this case. They have a tendency to haunt—especially when they have had such public airings as those involved in the Pinto fires debacle have had.

But why revisit 20-year-old decisions, and why take them so personally? Here's why: because I was in a position to do something about a serious problem . . . and didn't. That simple observation gives me pause for personal reflection and also makes me think about the many difficulties people face in trying to be ethical decision makers in organizations. It also helps me to keep in mind the features of modern business and organizational life that would influence someone like me (me of all people, who purposely set out to be an ethical decision maker!) to overlook basic moral issues in arriving at decisions that, when viewed retrospectively, look absurdly easy to make. But they are not easy to make, and that is perhaps the most important lesson of all.

THE PERSONAL ASPECT

I would like to reflect on my own experience mainly to emphasize the personal dimensions involved in ethical decision making. Although I recognize that there are strong organizational influences at work as well, I would like to keep the critical lens focused for a moment on me (and you) as individuals. I believe that there are insights and lessons from my experience that can help you think about your own likely involvement in issues with ethical overtones.

First, however, a little personal background. In the late 1960s and early 1970s, I was an engineering/MBA student; I also was an "activist," engaged in protests of social injustice and the social irresponsibility of business, among other things. I held some pretty strong values, and I thought they would stand up to virtually any challenge and enable me to "do the right thing" when I took a career job. I suspect that most of you feel that you also have developed a strongly held value system that will enable you to resist organizational inducements to do something unethical. Perhaps. Unfortunately, the challenges do not often come in overt forms that shout the need for resistance or ethical righteousness. They are much more subtle than that, and thus doubly difficult to deal with because they do not make it easy to see that a situation you are confronting might actually involve an ethical dilemma.

After school, I got the job of my dreams with Ford and, predictably enough, ended up on the fast track to promotion. That fast track enabled me to progress quickly into positions of some notable responsibility. Within two years I became Ford's vehicle recall coordinator, with first-level responsibility for tracking field safety problems. It was the most intense, information-overloaded job you can imagine, frequently dealing with some of the most serious problems in the company. Disasters were a phone call away, and action was the hallmark of the office where I worked. We all knew we were engaged in serious business, and we all took the job seriously. There were no irresponsible bureaucratic ogres there, contrary to popular portrayal.

In this context, I first encountered the neophyte Pinto fires problem—in the form of infrequent reports of cars erupting into horrendous fireballs in very low-speed crashes and the shuddering personal experience of inspecting a car that had burned, killing its trapped occupants. Over the space of a year, I had two distinct opportunities to initiate recall activities concerning the fuel tank problems, but on both occasions, I voted not to recall, despite my activist history and advocacy of business social responsibility.

The key question is how, after two short years, could I have engaged in a decision process that appeared to violate my own strong values—a decision process whose subsequent manifestations continue to be cited by many observers as a supposedly definitive study of corporate unethical behavior? I tend to discount the obvious accusations: that my values weren't really strongly held; that I had turned my back on my values in the interest of loyalty to Ford; that I was somehow intimidated into making decisions in the best interest of the company; that despite my principled statements, I had not actually achieved a high stage of moral development; and so on. Instead, I believe a more plausible explanation for my own actions looks to the foibles of normal human information processing.

I would argue that the complexity and intensity of the recall coordinator's job required that I develop cognitive strategies for simplifying the overwhelming amount of information I had to deal with. The best way to do that is to structure the information into cognitive "schemas," or more specifically "script schemas," that guide understanding and action when facing common or repetitive situations. Scripts offer marvelous cognitive shortcuts because they allow you to act virtually unconsciously and automatically, and thus permit you to handle complicated situations without being paralyzed by needing to think consciously about every little thing. Such scripts enabled me to discern the characteristic hallmarks of problem cases likely to result in recall and to execute a complicated series of steps required to initiate a recall.

All of us structure information all of the time; we could hardly get through the workday without doing so. But there is a penalty to be paid for this wonderful cognitive efficiency: we do not give sufficient attention to important information that requires special treatment because the general information pattern has surface appearances that indicate that automatic processing will suffice. That, I think, is what happened to me. The beginning stages of the Pinto case looked for all the world like a normal sort of problem. Lurking beneath the cognitive veneer, however, was a nasty set of circumstances waiting to conspire into a dangerous situation. Despite the awful nature of the accidents, the Pinto problem did not fit an existing script; the accidents were relatively rare by recall standards, and the accidents were not initially traceable to a specific component failure. Even when a failure mode suggesting a design flaw was identified, the cars did not perform significantly worse in crash tests than competitor vehicles. One might easily argue that I should have been jolted out of my script by the unusual nature of the accidents (very low speed, otherwise unharmed passengers trapped in a horrific fire), but those facts did not penetrate a script cued for other features. (It also is difficult to convey to the layperson that bad accidents are not a particularly unusual feature of the recall coordinator's information field. Accident severity is not necessarily a recall cue; frequently repeated patterns and identifiable causes are.)

THE CORPORATE MILIEU

In addition to the personalized scripting of information processing, there is another important influence on the decisions that led to the Pinto fires mess: the fact that decisions are made by individuals working within a corporate context. It has escaped almost no one's notice that the decisions made by corporate employees tend to be in the best interest of the corporation, even by people who mean to do better. Why? Because the socialization process and the overriding influence of organizational culture provide a strong, if generally subtle, context for defining appropriate ways of seeing and understanding. Because organizational culture can be viewed as a collection of scripts, scripted information processing relates even to organizational-level considerations. Scripts are context bound; they are not free-floating general cognitive structures that apply universally. They are tailored to specific contexts. And there are few more potent contexts than organizational settings.

There is no question that my perspective changed after joining Ford. In retrospect, I would be very surprised if it hadn't. In my former incarnation as a social activist, I had internalized values for doing what was right as I understood righteousness in grand terms, but I had not internalized a script for applying my values in a pragmatic business context. Ford and the recall coordinator role provided a powerful context for developing scripts—scripts that were inevitably and undeniably oriented toward ways of making sense that were influenced by the corporate and industry culture.

I wanted to do a good job, and I wanted to do what was right. Those are not mutually exclusive desires, but the corporate context affects their synthesis. I came to accept the idea that it was not feasible to fix everything that someone might construe as a problem. I therefore shifted to a value of wanting to do the greatest good for the greatest number (an ethical value tempered by the practical constraints of an economic enterprise). Doing the greatest good for the greatest number meant working with intensity and responsibility on those problems that would spare the most people from injury. It also meant developing scripts that responded to typical problems, not odd patterns like those presented by the Pinto.

Another way of noting how the organizational context so strongly affects individuals is to recognize that one's personal identity becomes heavily influenced by corporate identity. As a student, my identity centered on being a "good person" (with a certain dose of moral righteousness associated with it). As recall coordinator, my identity shifted to a more corporate definition. This is an extraordinarily important point, especially for students who have not yet held a permanent job role, and I would like to emphasize it. Before assuming your career role, identity derives mainly from social relationships. Upon putting on the mantle of a profession or a responsible position, identity begins to align with your role. And information processing perspective follows from the identity.

I remember accepting the portrayal of the auto industry and Ford as "under attack" from many quarters (oil crises, burgeoning government regulation, inflation, litigious customers, etc.). As we know, groups under assault develop into more cohesive communities that emphasize commonalities and shared identities. I was by then an insider in the industry and the company, sharing some of their beleaguered perceptions that there were significant forces arrayed against us and that the well-being of the company might be threatened.

What happened to the original perception that Ford was a socially irresponsible giant that needed a comeuppance? Well, it looks different from the inside. Over time, a responsible value for action against corporate dominance became tempered by another reasonable value that corporations serve social needs and are not automatically the villains of society. I saw a need for balance among multiple values, and as a result, my identity shifted in degrees toward a more corporate identity.

THE TORCH PASSES TO YOU

So, given my experiences, what would I recommend to you, as a budding organizational decision maker? I have some strong opinions. First, develop your ethical base now! Too many people do not give serious attention to assessing and articulating their own values. People simply do not know what they stand for because they haven't thought about it seriously. Even the ethical scenarios presented in classes or executive programs are treated as interesting little games without apparent implications for deciding how you intend to think or act. These exercises should be used to develop a principled, personal code that you will try to live by. Consciously decide your values. If you don't decide your values now, you are easy prey for others who will gladly decide them for you or influence you implicitly to accept theirs.

Second, recognize that everyone, including you, is an unwitting victim of his or her own cognitive structuring. Many people are surprised and fascinated to learn that they use schemas and scripts to understand and act in the organizational world. The idea that we automatically process so much information so much of the time intrigues us. Indeed, we would all turn into blithering idiots if we did not structure information and expectations, but that very structuring hides information that might be important—information that could require you to confront your values. We get lulled into thinking that automatic information processing is great stuff that obviates the necessity for trying to resolve so many frustrating decisional dilemmas.

Actually, I think too much ethical training focuses on supplying standards for contemplating dilemmas. The far greater problem, as I see it, is recognizing that a dilemma exists in the first place. The insidious problem of people not being aware that they are dealing with a situation that might have ethical overtones is another consequence of schema usage. I would venture that scripted routines seldom include ethical dimensions. Is a person behaving unethically if the situation is not even construed as having ethical implications? People are not necessarily stupid, ill-intentioned, or Machiavellian, but they are often unaware. They do indeed spend much of their time cruising on automatic, but the true hallmark of human information processing is the ability to switch from automatic to controlled information processing. What we really need to do is to encourage people to recognize cues that build a "Now Think!" step into their scripts—waving red flags at yourself, so to speak—even though you are engaged in essentially automatic cognition and action.

Third, because scripts are context bound and organizations are potent contexts, be aware of how strongly, yet how subtly, your job role and your organizational culture affect the ways you interpret and make sense of information (and thus affect the ways you develop the scripts that will guide you in unguarded moments). Organizational culture has a much greater effect on individual cognition than you would ever suspect (see Chapter 9).

Last, be prepared to face critical responsibility at a relatively young age, as I did. You need to know what your values are and you need to know how you think so that you can know how to make a good decision. Before you can do that, you need to articulate and affirm your values now, before you enter the fray. I wasn't really ready. Are you?

SOURCE: Dennis A. Gioia.

The stages range from Beginner (who shows no involvement and minimal resource commitment to responsible environmental management) to Proactivist (who is actively committed and involved in funding environmental management).

Finally, managers and professionals can determine whether or not and to what extent their company's environmental values are reflected in these three ethical principles, quoted from the article "Toward a Life Centered Ethic for Business."[109]

> The Principle of Connectedness. Human life is biologically dependent on other forms of life, and on ecosystems as a whole, including the non-living aspects of ecosystems. Therefore, humans must establish some connection with life itself and respect that life itself exists because living things exist in some state of cooperation and coexistence.
>
> The Principle of Ecologizing Values. Life exists itself in part because of the ecologizing values of linkage, diversity, homeostatic succession, and community. There is a presumption that these values are primary goods to be conserved.
>
> The Principle of Limited Competition. "You may compete (with other living beings) to the full extent of your abilities, but you may not hunt down your competitors or destroy their food or deny them access to food. . . . You may compete but may not wage war."[110] [We would add to the last sentence, "without just cause."]

SUMMARY

A general stakeholder map with the moral stakes of different constituencies was introduced, followed by an excerpt from the DoubleClick case to illustrate the challenges corporations face in managing social responsibility in the marketplace. Several corporate crises since the 1970s were summarized to reinforce the size of the stakes companies face when managing their products: for example, Dow Corning's silicon breast implant problems, Tylenol's poisoning episode, the diet drug fen-phen fiasco, and the Bridgestone/Firestone-Ford Explorer tire crisis. A discussion of reputable and socially responsible companies, as perceived and ranked by the public and the Domini 400 Social Index, followed.

The corporation as social and economic stakeholder was discussed from the perspectives of the social contract and covenantal ethic. Corporate social responsibility was also discussed from a pragmatic social power view. Corporations' philanthropic responsibilities were then summarized.

A major issues management approach from Chapter 2 explains and illustrates other methods for identifying environmental trends and organizational readiness in order to prevent potential crises from occurring. The issues management process adds to the stakeholder analysis not only by identifying issues but also by prioritizing them and by detecting and resolving potential or existing business-related crises. Brainstorming, creating best- and worst-case scenarios, and doing probability and impact analyses are prevention strategies several companies include in their issues management approach.

Corporate responsibility toward consumers was presented by explaining these corporate duties: (1) the duty to inform consumers truthfully, (2) the duty not to misrepresent or withhold information, (3) the duty not to unreasonably force consumer choice or take undue advantage of consumers through fear or stress, and (4) the duty to take "due care" to prevent any foreseeable injuries. However, the "due care" principle has several problems from a corporation's perspective. The use of a utilitarian ethic was discussed to show the problems in holding corporations accountable for product risks and injuries beyond their control.

The free-market theory of Adam Smith was summarized by way of explaining the market context governing the exchange of producers and buyers. Several limits of the free market were offered—namely, imperfect markets exist, the power between buyers and sellers is not symmetrical, and the line between telling the truth and lying about products is very thin. Economist Paul Samuelson's "mixed-economy" perspective was introduced to offer a more balanced view of free-market theory and of the unrealistic demands often placed on corporations in marketing new products.

Nevertheless, businesses have legal and moral obligations to provide their consumers with safe products without using false advertising and without doing harm to the environment. The complexities and controversies with respect to this obligation stem from attempts to define "safety," "truth in advertising," and levels of "harm" caused to the environment. The Federal Trade Commission's guidelines for on-line marketing show that this agency has considerable power and legitimacy in informing the public about ads; it also serves as a useful watchdog on corporate advertising and product regulation. Arguments for and against advertising were presented, with problematic examples of false advertising from the food and tobacco industries highlighted.

Product safety and liability were discussed through the doctrines of negligence, strict liability, and absolute liability. The Johns-Manville asbestos crisis was presented as an example. The legal and moral limits of product liability were summarized. Presently, states are moving to limit punitive damages in product liability cases, and tort reform is predicted to change the direction of product liability litigation toward more protection for manufacturers than for injured consumers.

Corporate responsibility toward the environment was presented by showing how air, water, and land pollution is a serious, long-term problem. Federal laws aimed at protecting the environment were summarized. Increasing concern over the destruction of the ozone layer, the destruction of the rain forests, and other environmental issues has presented firms with another area where economic and social responsibilities must be balanced. Innovative concepts and corporate attitude changes were discussed. Green marketing, environmental justice, and industrial ecology principles are being practiced by a growing number corporations, particularly in Europe—especially since green products and clean manufacturing processes (and certifications) offer competitive advantage. A recent innovative move by some corporations is to include environmental safety practices in the strategic, enterprise, and supply chain dimensions of industrial activities and practices. Hewlett-Packard was discussed as an example. A diagnostic (Figure 5.6) enables a company to identify its stage of social responsibility toward the environment.

QUESTIONS

1. Read the DoubleClick case at the end of the book. Do you believe consumer privacy issues as this case illustrates present any serious ethical issues for consumers? Explain.

2. Which of the corporate crises summarized at the beginning of the chapter were you unfamiliar with? Do you believe these crises represent business as usual or serious breakdowns in a company's system? Why?

3. After reading the Johns-Manville, Exxon *Valdez,* and Dow Corning cases, identify some ways these crises could have been (1) avoided and (2) managed more responsibly after they occurred.

4. What was your score on the Rank Your Organization's Reputation quiz in the chapter? After reading previous chapters in this book, how would you describe the "ethics" of your organization toward its customers and stakeholders? Explain.

5. Do you believe the covenantal ethic and social contract views are realistic with large organizations like Exxon and Citibank or federal agencies like the FTC and the Department of Defense? Why or why not? Explain.

6. Are there ethical principles of advertising that apply to consumers in all cultures and countries? Explain.

7. What is the free-market theory of corporate responsibility for consumers, and what are some of the problems associated with this view? Compare this view with the social contract and stakeholder perspectives of corporate social responsibility.

8. Is the "mixed economy" perspective more useful for you than the free-market theory? Which theory holds more promise of an "equal playing field" for buyer and manufacturer/seller? Explain.

9. Identify arguments for and against questionable ethical advertising. Which do you not agree with? Explain.

10. Describe an advertisement in the media that you believe is unethical. Explain your argument.

11. What is the four-step process developed by Justice Powell to determine whether commercial speech in advertising can be restricted or banned?

12. What constitutes "unreasonable risk" concerning the safety of a product? Identify considerations that define the safety of a product from an ethical perspective.

13. Explain the differences among the doctrines of negligence, strict liability, and absolute liability. What do you believe should be the "limits" to the product liability doctrine? Explain.

14. Identify moral arguments for corporate responsibility toward the environment. Do you believe trees, lakes, oceans, and animals should have rights? Explain.

15. Do you believe the environment (air, water, and land) is in trouble from human pollution, or do you believe this is "hype" and exaggeration from the press and scientists? Explain.

16. Explain several innovative ways corporations can help preserve the environment in their operations.

EXERCISES

1. Identify a recent example of a corporation accused of false or deceitful advertising. How did it justify the claims made in its ad? Do you agree or disagree with the claims? Explain.

2. In a few paragraphs, explain your opinion of whether advertising is a valid or legitimate industry.

3. Can you think of an instance when you or someone you know was affected by corporate negligence in terms of product safety standards? If so, did you communicate the problem to the company? Did it respond to the complaint? Characterize the response. How could or should the company have responded differently?

4. Do you believe cigarette, cigar, and pipe smoking should be banned from all public places where passive smoking can affect nonsmokers? Explain. Use the following (or other) Websites to argue your position: www.cdc.gov; www.tobacco.org; www.thetruth.com; www.trytostop.org; www.cancer.org; www.getoutraged.com.

5. Find a recent article discussing environmental damage caused by a corporation's activities. Recommend methods the firm in the article should employ to reduce harmful effects on the environment.

6. Find a recent article discussing an innovative way in which a corporation is helping the environment. Explain why the method is innovative and whether you believe the method will really help the environment or will only help the company promote its image as a good citizen.

ETHICAL DILEMMA

ETHICAL? OR ENTRAPMENT?

My job requires that I lie every day I go to work. I work for a private investigations agency called XRT. Most of the work I do involves undercover operations, mobile surveillances, and groundwork searches to determine the whereabouts of manufacturers that produce counterfeit merchandise.

Each assignment I take part in requires some deception on my part. Recently I have become very conscious of the fact that I frequently have to lie to get a lead to obtain concrete evidence for a client. I sometimes dig myself so deeply into a lie that I naturally take it to the next level without ever accomplishing the core purpose of the investigation.

Working for an investigative agency engages me in assignments that vary on a day-to-day basis. I choose to work for XRT because it is not a routine 9–5 desk job. But to continue working for the agency means I will constantly be developing new and untruthful stories. And the longer I decide to stay at XRT, the more involved the assignments will be. To leave would probably force me into a job photocopying and filing paperwork once I graduate from college.

Recently I was given an assignment which I believed would lead me to entrap a subject to obtain evidence for a client. The subject had filed for disabilities on workers' compensation after being hit by a truck. Because the subject refused to partake in any strenuous activity because of the accident, I was instructed to fake a flat tire and videotape the subject changing it for me. Although I did not feel comfortable engaging in this type of act, my supervisors assured me that it was ethical practice and not entrapment. Co-workers and other supervisors assured me that this was a standard "industry practice," that we would go out of business if we didn't "fudge" the facts once in a while. I was told, "Do you think every business does its work and makes profits in a purely ethical way? Get real. I don't know what they're teaching you in college, but this is the real world." It was either do the assignment or find myself on the street—in an economy with no jobs.

QUESTIONS

1. What is the dilemma here, or is there one?

2. What would you have done in the writer's situation? Explain.

3. React to the comment, "Do you think every business does its work and makes profits in a purely ethical way? Get real. I don't know what they're teaching you in college, but this is the real world." Do you agree or disagree? Why?

4. Describe the ethics of this company.

5. Compare and contrast your personal ethics with the company ethics revealed here.

EMPLOYEE STAKEHOLDERS
AND THE CORPORATION

The workforce continues to change, as the following quote by R. McCormick indicates:

> Success in business, in the 21st century, will depend on success in hiring and training and promoting a diverse workforce and vendor list in what is left of the 1990s. As we enter this next century, 80% of small businesses will be owned by women . . . more than half the stock in American corporations is owned by women. There are some 49 million Americans identified as having disabilities. The spending power of African-Americans, Asian-Americans and Hispanic-Americans is approaching $800 billion. Senior citizens—another $800 billion. Among gays and lesbians, 1 in 4 households earns more than $100,000 a year. Meanwhile, the number of new workers is declining. The Department of Labor says growth of the work force in the 15 years from 1990 to 2005 will be 12% slower than in the previous 15 years. Furthermore, new workers want more than "a job." They want respect. Understanding. They want coworkers to accept them and share their values.[1]

This chapter begins by addressing the changing characteristics of the workforce in the United States. What is different about the workforce, and how does this affect the corporation's ethical responsibilities? What, if anything, binds employees to their companies? What is the changing nature of the employer-employee social contract? How has this contract changed historically? Then, the rights and responsibilities of employers and employees are briefly discussed to offer a perspective on what each party can expect from the other. Problems of discrimination in the workplace and affirmative action legislation are then examined. The text addresses the question: What is illegal and unethical regarding workplace discrimination? Sexual harassment and the law are defined. Recommendations for organizations and individuals for preventing and dealing with this problem are discussed. Finally, we address issues surrounding whistle-blowing versus loyalty to the firm. What are the boundaries of employee loyalty? When do employees have the right or obligation to "blow the whistle" on the company?

6.1 EMPLOYEE STAKEHOLDERS: THE WORKFORCE IN THE 21ST CENTURY

Information technology and the Internet continue to revolutionize business paradigms and processes, as discussed in Chapter 1. Industries and companies are downsizing, restructuring, merging, and reinventing their businesses. Mid-level management layers are diminishing. Functions are being eliminated and replaced by online automation and networked infrastructures. Knowledge workers with technological and people skills must manage processes and themselves in cyberspace with speed, efficiency, and accuracy.

Within the context of the so-called "digital economy," the following changes with employees and professional stakeholders occur[2]:

- A shift to knowledge work, which increases the potential for satisfying work but heightened stress.
- The concept of "a job and career for life" is dead or dying. Professionals are changing careers five to eight times on average during their working lives.
- Compensation, income, and the social distribution of benefits in the "new economy" are shifting. Decreases in income are occurring among middle- and low-level professionals, with the exception of highly skilled knowledge workers, who are in high demand.
- Quality of work life is not inherent or guaranteed in the uses of technology. In one worse-case scenario, Thomas Malone of MIT stated that all work relationships could possibly be mediated by the market, with every employee functioning as a company in shifting alliances and ventures.[3]

Five other predicted trends in the work-life landscape of employees include[4]:

1. Demographics will drive a growing focus on family, personal and spiritual matters. Employees want balance in their lives. 82% of men

age 21 through 39 now offer family as their top priority. Aging baby-boomers desire less "overwork."

2. Employees will demand that employers make alternative schedules that work. Women attorneys, for example, who cannot obtain more part-time and flextime work arrangements are beginning to quit their jobs in law firms. Almost 40% of women attorneys who left firms over a 2-year period stated that outdated policies and attitudes regarding part-time work were prejudices and obstacles. Demands of raising families and taking care of aging parents and burnout contribute to the demand for flextime and part-time.

3. Internet-age values will take deeper root in the workplace. Many post–dot-com workforce practices and values continue to influence organizational behavior and policies, e.g., fluid working styles, short-term rewards for performance, and quick readiness to change jobs if their values and needs are not fulfilled.

4. The growth in New Age employee benefits will slow in a back-to-basics trend. Companies are cutting many perks that flourished during the previous economic boom, such as health and wellness programs and subsidized cafeterias, according to the Society for Human Resource Management.

5. It will get harder to tell work and home lifestyles apart. Sixty percent of employees reported that they spend 25% of each workday on personal matters, e.g., doctor appointments. Ford Motor Company, along with other corporations, supports the blending of work, family, and personal lives as a workplace strategy.

THE CHANGING WORKFORCE

The workforce in the United States is changing in ways that also affect management practices and ethical issues. Several demographic trends that were predicted for "workforce 2000" have been and are being realized.[5] The workforce is aging; managerial leadership positions are more difficult to fill; women entrants are increasing in number, with a mix of advances but with continued salary inequality; workforce cultures are mixing, as are values and potential value conflicts; the education gap in the workforce continues; the level of education lags in the United States compared to other countries; the number of workers with disabilities is expanding; and gay couples, still denied legal marriage in all states but one, are denied family health care insurance in most companies. The ethical implications of these changes for corporations are discussed in this chapter after the major trends are summarized.

THE AGING WORKFORCE. The workforce is aging. By 2015, nearly 20% of the U.S. workforce will be 55 years old or over, up from 13% in 2001. In 2001, the number of workers who are age 40 and older surpassed the number of those who are younger than age 40 for the first time. At the same time, those aged 16 to 24—the babybusters (who were born after the boomers)—make up 16% of the workforce, a proportion that continues to decrease. The seniors, older than age 55, represent about 13% of the workforce. Japan was the first nation ever with a population in which the average age is 40. By 2020, 6 out of 10 Japanese workers will be retired.

One result of the population growth slowdown is that the number of managerial leadership positions will outstrip available talent. As baby boomers age and retire, the number of managerial positions required is predicted to increase by 20% from 2000 to 2010, while U.S. demographic projections indicate a drop of 15% in the number of workers aged 35 to 44 (the pool from which these positions are filled) during this period. The executive recruitment war is predicted to ensue.

WOMEN IN THE WORKFORCE.   Women represented 46.6% of the workforce in 1999. This figure is projected to reach 47.5% in 2008.[6] Two thirds of the new entrants between 1985 and 2000 were women. Three fourths of all working women will be in their childbearing years. Women with children less than 6 years old represent the most rapidly increasing segment of the workforce. Women hold 49.5% of managerial and professional specialty positions. Of members of boards of directors, 12.5% are women; 4.1% of top earners are women. Two women were *Fortune 500* CEOs in 2000.

GAY MARRIAGES AND WORKFORCE RIGHTS.   On July 1, 2000, Vermont was the first state to grant, under the "civil unions" law, same-sex couples the same rights and responsibilities as married couples. Only Denmark, Norway, Sweden, Germany, and France have similar systems. This law is only valid and recognized in Vermont. While legally binding, same-sex–marriage health plans and other financially shared benefits are not guaranteed under the civil unions law. (A poll conducted in May 2001, showed that 51% of Vermonters favored the repeal of civil unions).[7]

THE INCREASING CULTURAL MIX.   By 2080, people of color will make up more than 27% of the U.S. population and 15% of the U.S. workforce. Census figures from the year 2000 show that the Hispanic population grew 58%, to 35.3 million people, since 1990 and is now the largest minority. Hispanic Americans outnumber blacks in Florida and make up one third of California's population. Also, for the first time, Americans had the option of identifying themselves as belonging to more than one race. Seven million people, 2.4% of the nation, described themselves as multiracial[8] This cultural mix is becoming increasingly evident in the workforce.

EDUCATIONAL WEAKNESSES AND GAPS.   The dichotomy in the educational levels of those in and entering the workforce is growing, and the number of less-educated entrants is increasing. (In the mid-1980s, 86% of 25- to 29-year-olds had graduated from high school, but in 1988, 20 million functionally illiterate people were living in the United States.) Of the 18- to 21-year-old population, 13.6% did not complete high school. Moreover, the United States has lost its international lead in educating workers for a knowledge-based economy. The Organization for Economic Cooperation and Development (OECD) analyzed the results of an 18-nation literacy survey conducted from 1994 to 1998 among high school graduates who were 16 to 25 years old. The results showed that 59% of Americans (the worst underachievement rate among 18 countries surveyed) failed to read well enough "to cope adequately with the complex demands of everyday life."[9]

MAINSTREAMING DISABLED WORKERS. Hiring and mainstreaming qualified disabled workers is increasing in importance because of the combined effects of the shrinking and aging of the workforce. A survey by the International Center for the Disabled found that two thirds of the working-age disabled were not in the workforce, although a "large majority" said they preferred to work.[10] Disabilities affect a large percentage of the workforce. Disabilities are categorized as permanent (for example, physical disabilities), temporary (such as those resulting from injury or stress), and progressive (for example, AIDS, alcohol and drug addiction, cancer). According to these definitions, disabled workers number into the millions. The exact rate of unemployment among disabled workers is unknown, because it is difficult to determine who is disabled and whether or not what they do fits the government's definition of employment.[11]

ISSUES AND IMPLICATIONS OF WORKFORCE CHANGES

These trends in the workforce necessitate accommodation from managers and employees. Moral and legal conflict will likely increase in workplace situations if responsible and proactive leadership, policies, and training are not planned and implemented with regard to the following:

1. *Age discrimination*: Companies can respond to aging and younger employees with fairness by implementing programs to accommodate skill training and mentoring. "Reverse mentoring" is occurring in some companies, in which younger, more technically savvy employees mentor and train older professionals.

2. *Sexual harassment:* More women are speaking out under the protection of Title VII of the amended Civil Rights Act, which is discussed in Section 6.5 of this chapter. Sexual harassment continues to be reported across industries, including in outstanding companies, such as Wal-Mart. Moreover, men's sex harassment charges regarding male bosses account for 13.5% of all charges brought in 2000 to the U.S. Equal Employment Opportunity Commission, compared to about 7% in 1991.[12] Diversity training programs are now offered in many larger reputable U.S. firms.

3. *Health care provisions:* Companies must work with a range of stakeholders, including government, community, and employees, to deal

with the increasing health care costs for aging baby boomers. These issues become more acute during economic recessions and in industries striving to maintain market competitiveness.

4. *Educational challenges*: A major stake here is the competitiveness of the U.S. in the global economy. Deficiencies in the American educational system are recognized by federal and state governments. The need for technologically knowledgeable workers is another major concern. Also, a gap exists in the workforce between highly and poorly educated professionals. Highly educated workers demand more involvement and autonomy, less supervisory control, more information, more career opportunities, and rewards commensurate with performance. Less-educated workers require more training, education, supervision, and structured opportunities to improve their productivity and increase their mobility. This educational mix strains personal, moral, and managerial-employee relationships unless training programs continue to be made available.

5. *Paradigm shift toward a new "work-life" model:* As more dual-career and child-rearing couples enter the workforce, conflicts and problems evolve over roles and responsibilities as families cope with workplace demands. Working family models illustrating these tensions have evolved over decades. Four such models, which are summarized in Figure 6.1, include: (1) an early model depicting complete separation of work and family life and issues, in which men worked and women maintained the family; (2) an overlapping model of "work" and "family life" spheres in which the boundaries were still fuzzy, but roles were recognized as being interrelated; (3) a model that defined multiple roles and responsibilities, including "his work," "her work," and "family" obligations, which, like the previous two models, was based on scarcity and zero-sum assumptions (i.e., a fixed number of resources that resulted in win-lose situations) regarding the allocation and use of resources and responsibilities at home and at work; and (4) the work-life systems model the most recent one, which assumes a systems perspective in which roles and responsibilities are not seen as competitive, isolated, or overlapping in undefined ways between family members, and the organization and community are built into individual and family responsibilities, which are shared to optimize the well-being of the entire system (company, employees, and families). In the fourth model, the emphasis also shifts from individual and family to include workplace needs, values, and aspirations; job conditions; and quality of life. Company policies are recognized as part of the work-life equation. The company becomes the context for assuming more policy responsibility and providing resources to assist families and communities. Xerox and Fleet Bank corporations are experimenting with this model, as are other companies that offer "family-friendly" places to work.[13]

| FIGURE 6.1 | EVOLUTION OF WORK AND FAMILY LIFE SYSTEMS MODELS |

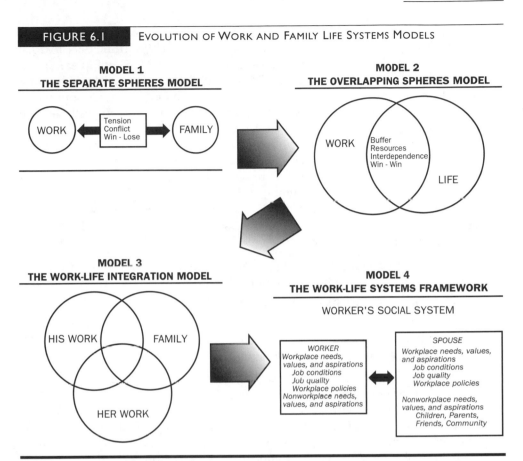

SOURCE: Adapted with permission from Barnett, R. (Mar. 1999). A new work-life model for the twenty-first century. *Annals of the American Academy of Political and Social Science, 562,* 143–158.

In a work-life systems model, policies accommodate flextime and part-time arrangements.

ADVANCEMENT OF WOMEN IN THE WORKFORCE

In 1999 the Financial Women's Association surveyed female senior executives in brokerage, investment, banking, and consulting businesses, with an average of 20 years in a job, and found that the executives believed the following situations are better today than they were 3 to 5 years ago: (1) worksite programs and benefits that balance work and families (52%), (2) workforce diversity (49%), (3) number of women on *Fortune 500* company boards (44%), (4) breaking through the glass ceiling (41%), (5) finding mentors to advance careers (34%), and (6) comparable pay for men and women doing comparable work (34%).[14] Also, the percentage of corporate women officers in America's 500 largest companies increased by 11.9% from 1999 to 2000 (1,622 out of 12,945). Women represented 4.1% (93 of 2,255) of top earners in 2000, up 3.3% from 1999. Also, 6.2% (154 of 2,488) of individuals holding top-level positions, including chair, CEO, vice chair, COO (chief operating officer), SEVP (senior executive vice president), and EVP (executive vice president), are women, a 5.1% gain from 1999 to 2000.[15]

Businesses owned in 2001 by women numbered 9 million and employed 27 million people, with sales of $3.6 trillion. Catalyst, a New York-based working women's organization, surveyed 461 female top executives, with the title of vice president or higher, at the 1,000 largest U.S. companies to determine the three highest-ranking barriers to advancement for women. This study was noted as the first large-scale study of women in senior management.[16] The findings follow:

- 52% believed male stereotyping and preconceptions of women were primary factors in holding women back.

- 49% believed exclusion from informal networks of communication was a primary reason.

- 47% chose their own lack of general management or line experience as a primary barrier to advancement.

In a parallel study of *Fortune 500* and *Service 500* chief executives, of whom 99% were men, only 25% of male chief executives cited male stereotyping and preconceptions of women as a top factor for holding women back. Fifteen percent believed that exclusion from informal networks was a primary barrier to women's advancement. Eighty-two percent said the most serious deterrent to women's advancement was lack of general management or line experience. The conclusion to the study pointed out the gender gaps in the male corporate culture and what female executives and companies must do to bridge this gap.

With the assistance of affirmative action laws, women have made significant strides over the past 30 years. The number of women getting "in the door" has increased. In 1972, women comprised 38% of all U.S. civilian workers; by 1980, this had risen to 42.4%, and by 1994, to 46%. In 1983, women held 40.9% of all managerial and professional jobs, and a decade later this had climbed to 47.8%.[17]

CHANGING WORKFORCE VALUES

What really motivates professionals? From a poll taken by the Radcliffe Public Policy Center and Fleet-Boston, the following values were identified[18]:

- Competitive pay
- Benefits and opportunities to improve skills
- A fair deal in seeing that the company keeps its promises

- A feeling of being valued
- Decent relationships at work, especially with immediate bosses

From surveying 350 managers and human resources professionals, Jamieson and O'Mara identified the following work-related values that were considered most important for "workforce 2000":

- Recognition for competence and accomplishment
- Respect and dignity
- Personal choice and freedom
- Involvement at work
- Pride in work
- Quality of lifestyle
- Financial security
- Self-development
- Health and wellness

With which of these values do you identify? What other values that are not listed here motivate you? Underlying individuals' values are a host of other background factors that influence perceptions, beliefs, and behaviors.

Next, we look at generational values as another way of understanding the workforce and its diversity. Place yourself into the designated generation where your age fits and decide whether or not and if so to what extent your values and beliefs are influenced by generational factors.

GENERATIONAL VALUE DIFFERENCES

Generational analysis looks at differences among world views, attitudes, and values of generations of Americans. Large differences in the generations from World War II to the present in the U.S. population have had a substantial influence on government, corporate, and workplace policies. This information, while subjective, is used to develop workplace strategies, and to evaluate ethical principles and beliefs of different groups in the workforce.[19] The following brief summary of five generations' dominant value orientations highlight some of these differences.

GI GENERATION (BORN 1901–1925). This generation survived the Great Depression and served in World War II. Members of this generation are church-goers and belong to clubs and professional organizations. They express rugged individualism but are members of many groups. They tend to believe in upward mobility, civic virtue, and the American Dream.

SILENT GENERATION (BORN 1926–1945). This generation was too young to fight in World War II. They were influenced by the patriotism and self-sacrifice of the GI generation, from whom they did not wish to differentiate themselves. Their dominant principles are allegiance to law and order, patriotism, and faith.

BABY BOOMERS (BORN 1945–1964).   This is currently the most powerful demographic generation, with 76 million members. They have led and set trends in society. They distinguish themselves from the former generations by assuming debt. Their "buy now, pay later" belief characterizes their instant gratification practices. They can be moralistic, but they question authority and the moral and ethical principles of institutions. They do not "join" or sacrifice personal pleasure for the good of the group or collective. They mix and match religious traditions and avoid the dogma and teachings of single religions.

GENERATION X (BORN 1965–1981).   Known as the "baby busters," this generation has 41 million members. Sandwiched between the two larger generations, they feel demographically overlooked. They came from a time of high national debt and bleak job markets, and were labeled as the "McJob" generation—a phrase referring to holders of low-level, entry-level jobs. This generation generally believes that they will get less materially than the boomers. Insecurity is a dominant theme for X-ers, who value close friends and virtual families more than material success. They, like the boomers, are also suspicious of institutions. They experience their journey through life as one that changes rapidly and continuously.

GENERATION Y (BORN 1982–2003).   The millenial generation numbers about 60 million. It is the second largest generation since the boomers. They have grown up with television, computers, instant messaging, and new technologies, just as the boomers grew up with the telephone. Y-ers don't want to be associated with X-ers, whom they believe are selfish and complaining and the least heroic generation—a bunch of slackers. Y-ers started growing up with a strong job market. They are ambitious, motivated, extremely impatient and demanding, and have a sense of entitlement. From a manager's viewpoint, they require "super-high maintenance," since they are "on fast forward with self-esteem." They often expect office cultures to adapt to them. With these attitudes, they generally require coaching, rigorous feedback, and smaller and more realistic goal setting, with deadlines and increasing responsibility.

From the employer's perspective, integrating individual and group differences in the workforce requires, as mentioned earlier, leadership, planning, new policies, and training. In larger, more complex organizations, providing education and training to integrate the workforce is a necessity.[20] Stakeholder and value-based leadership approaches, as discussed and illustrated in Chapter 4, also provide strategies for assessing and integrating stakeholder differences as organizational assets.

The social contract between employers and employees continues to evolve. Chapter 4 discussed the nature of voluntary, value-based relationships between employer and employees. The following section looks at the changing historical and legal relationships, rights, and obligations between employee stakeholders and employers.

6.2 THE CHANGING SOCIAL CONTRACT BETWEEN CORPORATIONS AND EMPLOYEES

The social contract that has historically defined the employee/employer relationship is known as *the employment-at-will (EAW) doctrine*. This doctrine remains the dominant view of the employment relationship in the U.S., although parts of the doctrine have eroded since its inception. This implied legal agreement has been in effect since 1884, when the *Payne* v. *Western A.R.R. Co.* judgment ruled that "all may dismiss their employees at will, be they many or few, for good cause, for no cause, or even for cause morally wrong without being thereby guilty of legal wrong."

Essentially, the EAW doctrine can be defined as "the right of an employer to fire an employee without giving a reason and the right of an employee to quit when he or she chooses." [21] If employees are unprotected by unions or other written contracts, they can be fired, according to this doctrine.

The EAW doctrine evolved as part of the laissez-faire philosophy of the Industrial Revolution. Between the 1930s and 1960s, however, exceptions to the doctrine appeared. Federal legislation since the 1960s has been enacted to protect employees against racial discrimination and to provide rights to a minimum wage, to equal hiring and employment opportunities, and to participation in labor unions.

The vast majority of states have an at-will provision in their legislative laws. In California, it is easier to terminate an employee than it is in New York. Some states have other obligations that must be addressed by employers, like good faith or fair dealing practices. [22]

Since the 1970s, state court decisions have limited the EAW doctrine. Specifically, state courts have upheld employees' rights to use legal action against their employers if an employee termination violated "public policy" principles; examples include (1) if employees were pressured to commit perjury or fix prices, (2) if employees were not permitted to perform jury duty or file for workers' compensation, (3) if employees were terminated because they refused to support a merger, and (4) if employees reported alleged employer violations of statutory policy (whistle-blowing).

An important 1981 California Appeals Court decision, *Pugh* v. *See's Candies, Inc.*, ruled that, in a noncontractual employment arrangement, an implied promise from the employer existed. The employer could not act arbitrarily with its employees regarding termination decisions when considering the following factors: (1) duration of employment, (2) recommendations and promotions received, (3) lack of direct criticism of work, (4) assurances given, and (5) the employer's acknowledged policies. [23]

FIGURE 6.2	EMPLOYEE CONTRACT UNDER THE EAW DOCTRINE

READ CAREFULLY BEFORE SIGNING:
I understand that refusal to submit to the testing noted [elsewhere] or a positive drug screen result will eliminate any consideration for employment.

I also certify that the statements and information furnished by me in this application are true and correct. I understand that falsification of such statements and information is grounds for dismissal at any time the company becomes aware of the falsified notification. In consideration of my employment, I agree to conform to the rules and regulations of the company and acknowledge that my employment and compensation can be terminated, with or without cause, and with or without notice, at any time, at the option of either the company or myself. I further understand that no policy, benefit or procedure contained in any employee handbook creates an employment contract for any period of time and no terms or conditions of employment contrary to the foregoing should be relied upon, except for those made in writing by a designated officer of the Company.

I agree and hereby authorize XYZ, Inc. to conduct a background inquiry to verify the information on this application, other documentation that I have provided and other areas that may include prior employment, consumer credit, criminal convictions, motor vehicle and other reports. These reports may include information as to my character, work habits, performance, education and experience along with reasons for termination of employment from previous employers. Further, I understand that you may be requesting information from various Federal, State and other agencies which maintain records concerning my past activities relating to my driving, credit, criminal, civil and other experiences as well as claims involving me in the files of insurance companies. I authorize all previous employers or other persons who have knowledge of me, or my records, to release such information to XYZ, Inc. I hereby release any party or agency and XYZ, Inc. from all claims or liabilities whatever that may arise by such disclosures or such investigation.

_____   _____
Date of Application   Signature of Applicant

Although the EAW doctrine has undergone change, it remains the cornerstone of U.S. labor law, as is illustrated in Figure 6.2. States vary on the application of the EAW doctrine, but the U.S. Eighth Circuit Court of Appeals has favored employers. The federal court has stated that it will not act as a "superpersonnel board" of a company. Figure 6.2 is a copy of a contract an employee must sign before beginning work at this reputable company in Massachusetts. It is an example of a strongly worded EAW-oriented contract.

At issue in the EAW doctrine is the continuing debate over the nature of property and property rights. Each organization defines property rights and responsibilities offered to managers and employees, such as severance payments, pensions, stock options, access to resources, and golden parachutes. Employers also view employees' labor, time, and effort as part of their property. At issue in the EAW doctrine is whether an employee's education, skills, and other intangible assets are seen as the employee's "property," and if so, whether employees have certain rights regarding these assets. Due process is one such right that accompanies the EAW doctrine.[24]

The debate will continue over whose "property" and rights take precedence and whose are violated and on what grounds between employer and employee, especially in disputed firings that do not involve clear legal violations of employee rights, such as blatant discrimination. One scholar has noted that:

> The present-day debate revolves mainly around utilitarian issues. To what extent is the welfare of society advanced by preserving or limiting the traditional prerogatives of employers? Employers typically favor employment at will not because they want to fire without cause but because they would rather avoid the need to account for their personnel decisions in court and face the possibility of stiff punitive awards. Even advocates of greater employee protection recognize the dangers of the courts becoming too deeply involved in business decision making.[25]

The next section presents employee rights and employer responsibilities and offers recommendations to managers for avoiding arbitrary termination decisions.

6.3 EMPLOYEE AND EMPLOYER RIGHTS AND RESPONSIBILITIES

The EAW doctrine was a transition from a feudal European governance context to a contemporary U.S. pluralistic setting. Employee rights in the workplace also continue to evolve. Changing social, political, legal, and technological forces present new issues, opportunities, and controversies between employee rights and corporate duties.

In a market economy, employer and employee rights and responsibilities are based on contrasting (sometimes conflicting) assumptions and values. Employers control private property and proprietary rights over their intellectual property, as noted earlier. Employees claim their constitutional rights to individual freedom, liberty, and control over their private lives. Employers try to maximize productivity and profits, to sustain financial growth and stability, to minimize costs, to improve quality, to increase market share, and to stabilize wages. Employees seek to increase their wages and benefits, to improve working conditions, to enhance mobility, and to ensure job security. No perfect boundary exists between employer and employee rights in a capitalist market economy.

Before discussing specific rights and responsibilities between employers and employees, this section begins by defining "rights" and two premises based on this definition. Then two organizing concepts that underlie employee rights are suggested: balance and governmental rights. The concept of balance is based on utilitarian ethical reasoning and that of moral entitlement is based on Kantian nonconsequentialist reasoning. Although these concepts are not mutually exclusive, it is helpful to understand the logic behind them in order to argue their merits and shortcomings as they apply to specific workplace controversies.

MORAL FOUNDATION OF EMPLOYEE RIGHTS

The ideal relationship between employer and employees is one based on mutual respect and trust. Trust generally leads to open communication, which, in turn, provides an environment of collaboration and productivity. In many companies, this is, unfortunately, not the case. Power and authority relationships between employers and employees are, by definition, asymmetrical. Employees are generally, as stated by J. Rowan, in a "comparatively inferior bargaining position with respect to their employers. This inequity opens up possibilities for various sorts of exploitation, such as inadequate compensation, discrimination, and privacy invasions, all of which have been known to occur." Rowan also notes that "employee rights are complex, in that managers, as a prerequisite for making ethically sound decisions, must assess which alleged employee rights are legitimate . . . and must weigh them against the rights of those in other stakeholder groups."[26] From these observations, a definition of "rights" is offered.

A right can be understood as a "moral claim." A right is moral when it is not necessarily part of any conventional system, as are legal rights. A right is a claim because it corresponds with a duty on the part of the person against whom the right is held. For example, I claim that I have a right to be safe in my workplace. I hold this claim against my employer, since the employer has the duty to provide me with this safety. Under particular circumstances, my moral claim can be argued and disputed. It may not be an absolute claim.

The moral foundation for employee rights is based on the fact that employees are persons. One generic right that all persons have is a right to freedom, including the concept of negative freedom (i.e., the right not to be coerced or inhibited by external forces.) Regarding employees, this right to freedom is a claim "that when managers choose to hire employees, they must bear in mind that they are dealing with persons, and the (positive and negative) freedom of their employees is therefore to be respected."[27] The second generic right of employees is the right to well-being. This right follows from individuals' having interests, which are preconditions for pursuing goals. Interests and the pursuit of goals are morally important because they are not satisfied when a person does not have well-being. When employees cannot satisfy their job-related goals, interests, and requirements because of work-related conditions, an employee's right to well-being may have been violated. With regard to these arguments on the moral foundation of employee rights, Sanford Jacoby has noted, "Employees should at all times be treated in a way that respects them as persons."[28] We might add that the same observation holds true for employers; they also should be treated with respect as individuals.

THE PRINCIPLE OF BALANCE IN THE EMPLOYEE AND EMPLOYER SOCIAL CONTRACT AND THE REALITY OF COMPETITIVE CHANGE

As common law and custom have evolved from the EAW doctrine to implied employee rights, employers have the opportunity to consider more than stockholder and financial interests when dealing with employee stakeholders. As argued in Chapter 4, a values-based stakeholder management perspective views the employee-employer relationship from a "win-win" foundation. Both employers and employees act from a base of values. When the values of an organization align and draw on the values of employees, innovation, productivity, and individual, as well as corporate, development can occur. In a high-growth competitive environment in which intellectual skills, flexibility, and speed of work are emphasized, traditional views of company ownership and employee loyalty change. The evolving social contract between employers and employees still recognizes employers' power over their physical and material property, but the contractual relationship between employer and employee aims in principle at *balance*, mutual respect, integrity, and fairness. The employer's interest in operating the business as she or he determines can and should be balanced against the employee's welfare, interests, and willing contribution to add value. This is especially the case when employee talent and competitive skills are at stake. Although employers generally have more power than employees in the contractual relationship, employees in the United States, for example, are still citizens under the protection of the Constitution. Employees must also balance their self-interests and motivations with the needs of the organization to succeed, which is necessary for the organization provide employment.

It is interesting to note that the principle of balance in the employer-employee relationship has been historically prevalent in some of the developed Asian countries, such as Japan, South Korea, Singapore, and Taiwan. In Japan, in particular, the Confucian tradition of harmony has underscored the cooperative relationship between unions and companies.[29] European countries, including Germany and France, have also enacted laws that protect employee benefits and welfare. Some of these countries have traditions that include socialism and strong populist social policies.

The employee-employer social contract must also be viewed in the context of changing national and global competition, technology innovations and the information revolution, and growth of the service sector. The U.S. industrial landscape began shifting in the 1970s when Japanese competition swept the electronics and automotive sectors, in particular. American consulting and corporate responses to Japan's global dominance during this period included total quality management, followed by re-engineering, and more recently, the uses of information technology and the Internet to transform business processes and ways of doing business. Consolidations in and across industries, massive downsizing, the increased size and scope of mergers and acquisitions, and a shift to a service-oriented economy all continue to affect employer-employee relationships. The principle of balancing the interests of stakeholder with stockholder and employer with employee is part of the stakeholder management perspective, as discussed in Chapter 4. This perspective takes on increased importance as a viable approach for understanding and dealing with numerous groups inside and outside the corporation within turbulent, changing market environments.

RIGHTS FROM GOVERNMENT LEGISLATION

Employee rights are based on principles determined by law. Certain *government rights* (federal, state, and local) of the employee are not negotiable in written or implied contracts: for example, rights related to the minimum wage; sexual harassment; discrimination based on race, creed, age, national origin, gender, or disability; and the right to assemble. Although employee rights based on certain legislation are not always negotiated according to employer-employee self-interests, these rights can be disputed, depending on circumstances. Reverse discrimination, to be discussed later, is one such example. While private corporations are the property of the owners, certain employee legal rights are still within a corporation's boundaries.

RIGHTS AND RESPONSIBILITIES BETWEEN EMPLOYERS AND EMPLOYEES

Employers and employees have rights and responsibilities each should honor with respect to the other. This section discusses these mutual responsibilities, some of which stem from each party's rights by law and legislation, while others are based on ethical principles. As discussed in Chapter 4, a values-based, stakeholder management approach views the employer-employee relationship as one grounded on mutual trust and reciprocal responsibility. While laws and legislation serve the purpose of protection for both parties, without trust that is demonstrated in fair and equitable treatment of basic rights and responsibilities, one or both parties stand to lose. Nevertheless, not all employers or employees have a personal, professional, or organizational ethic that respects the other's rights in all situations. Historical attitudes, negative prejudices, and stereotypes sometimes surface in institutionally unjust practices toward individuals and groups. For these reasons, ethical and legal rights and responsibilities must be written, made part of employee training, and reinforced in company codes, leadership examples, and organizational best practices to be effective. When voluntary trust and mutual respect fail and harm is done to employers or employees, the legal system can be evoked.

EMPLOYER RESPONSIBILITIES TO EMPLOYEES

Employers are obliged to pay employees fair wages for work performed and to provide safe working conditions. Take a look at and answer the questions

WHOSE RIGHTS? WHO SHOULD PAY? San Francisco Mayor Willie Brown signed the measure that the Board of Supervisors voted in favor of by a vote of nine to two that mandates the city to pay up to $50,000 for municipal workers' and employees' sex changes. The city is the first U.S. city to do so. Minnesota had sex-change benefits but disallowed them in 1998 (*USA Today*, May 1, 2001, 3A).

QUESTIONS

1. Do you agree with this measure? Why or why not? Please explain.

2. On what ethical grounds would you either justify or reject the measure? Explain.

in the box entitled, "Whose Rights? Who Should Pay?" After you have answered and discussed the questions, what, if anything, did you learn about your and other classmates' values and beliefs regarding employee-employer responsibilities and obligations?

FAIR WAGES. Fair wages are determined by factors such as what the public and society support and expect, conditions of the labor market, competitive industry wages in the specific location, the firm's profitability, the nature of the job and work, laws governing minimum wages, comparable salaries, and the fairness of the salary or wage negotiations.[30] As will be discussed in Section 6.4, fair wages for comparable jobs held by men and women are not always paid.

SAFE WORKING ENVIRONMENT. Employers also are obliged to provide workers with a safe working environment and safe working conditions. The Occupational Safety and Health Administation (OSHA) and federal laws and regulations provide safety standards and enforce employer institution of the company's own safety standards. The problems of employers providing—and of employees accepting—safe working environments stem from (1) lack of knowledge and of available, reliable information about levels of health risks; (2) lack of appropriate compensation proportional to the level of occupational risk; and (3) employees accepting known risks when the employer does not offer any safer alternatives.[31] When the option is employment versus no employment, workers, especially in low-income, noncompetitive employment regions, often choose jobs with hazardous risks to their health or life.

Employers, then, should pay competitive wages commensurate with the occupational risks associated with a profession, job, or work setting. For example, race car drivers would not be expected to receive the same pay as college professors. Employers also are expected to provide full information on the risks and health hazards related to the work, products, and working environments to all employees exposed to those risks. Finally, employers also should offer health insurance programs and benefits to employees exposed to workplace hazards. Not all employers meet these obligations.

WORKING CONDITIONS THAT EMPOWER EMPLOYEES. While employers are not required by law to offer employees working conditions that provide meaningful tasks and job satisfaction, doing so can lead to increased performance, job satisfaction, and productivity. Employees work most productively when they can participate in the control of their tasks, when they are given responsibility for and autonomy over their assignments, and when they are treated with respect.[32] Quality of work life (QWL) programs that provide employees with more autonomy, participation, satisfaction, and control in their work tasks have demonstrated positive results.[33] Many companies are organizing self-designing work teams, quality circles, and learning communities to tap into employee creativity and abilities. As noted in Chapter 4, there is an increase in companies offering opportunities for employees to practice their own religious and spiritual rituals during the work day. Employers and employees both gain when personal and organizational needs are met. Working environments that can provide conditions for this alignment are increasing.

EMPLOYEE RESPONSIBILITIES TO EMPLOYERS

Employees are responsible for fulfilling their contracted obligations to the corporation; for following the goals, procedural rules, and work plans of the organization; for offering competence commensurate with the work and job assignments; and for performing productively according to the required tasks. Other responsibilities include timeliness, avoiding absenteeism, acting legally and morally in the workplace and while on job assignments, and respecting the intellectual and private property rights of the employer.

CONFLICTS OF INTEREST. Employee responsibilities to employers become complicated when conflicts of interest appear, that is, when an employee's private interests compete or are not aligned with the company's interests. More obvious conflicts of interest arise in a number of situations, such as taking or offering commercial or personal bribes, kickbacks, gifts, and insider information for personal gain.

The so-called gray areas are more problematic for determining whose interests are violated at the expense of others: for example, an employee quits a firm, joins a competitor, and then is accused by the former employer of stealing proprietary property (that is, passing on intellectual property, sharing trade secrets, or offering a competitive advantage by divulging confidential information). Whose interests are violated?[34] Some courts have used a "balancing model" based on utilitarian logic to resolve trade-secret-protection cases; that is, an employee's interest in mobility and opportunity is weighed against the employer's right to decide the extent of protection given to confidential information. For example, the following three criteria have been used to decide whether trade secrets have been divulged by employees:

1. True trade secrecy and established ownership must be shown.
2. A trade secret must have been disclosed by an employee, thus breaching a duty of confidentiality.
3. The employer's interest in keeping the secret must outweigh the employee's interest in using the secret to earn a living and the public's interest in having the secret transmitted.

Courts also use other considerations in these types of rulings (for example, contract obligations, promises made, truthfulness, confidentiality, and loyalty). The point here is that as technology and expertise become more sophisticated and as employee mobility—and downsizing—increase, workplace and courtroom criteria regarding the proof of conflict of interest also grow more complicated. Although a utilitarian model is used to help determine conflict-of-interest court cases, such as trade secrecy, ethical principles such as rights, duty, and justice also remain essential considerations for determining right and wrong; violations of loyalty, confidentiality, or truthfulness; and harm done to either employers or employees.

EMPLOYEE RIGHTS IN THE WORKPLACE

Labor, along with money and materials, is considered capital in a free-market system. However, labor is not the same as materials and money; labor also means human beings who have general constitutional rights that should not be relinquished between working hours.[35] However, clashes of interests and of stakes between employee rights and management demands frequently occur. The boundary between an employer's private property and an employee's individual rights is often blurred in everyday experience. Understanding employee rights is part legal and part ethical because these rights must be viewed and interpreted within corporate policy, procedures, and particular circumstances. In some instances, there are clear violations of an employee's rights; other times there are "gray," or uncertain, areas. When employees and employers cannot agree on whose rights are seriously violated, third-party negotiation, arbitration, and even settlement may be required. This section presents major types of employee rights in the workplace:

- The right not to be terminated without just cause
- The right to due process
- The right to privacy
- The right to know
- The right to workplace health and safety

- The right to organize and strike
- Rights regarding plant closings

These rights become even more important in a society that rapidly transforms technological and scientific inventions into part of the human workplace environment.

JUST CAUSE TERMINATION. Employees have a right not to be terminated arbitrarily or without just cause, even in a free-market economy.[36] Under conditions of volatile economic downturns, mergers and acquisitions, new start-up failures (as with the "dot-com bubble burst"), and massive negative profit margin shifts in industries, it is often not difficult for employers to claim "just cause." As a principle, it also has been argued that workers should have three rights regarding work to maintain self-respect:

- The right to employment
- The right to equal opportunity
- The right to participate in job-related decisions[37]

These rights are less entitlements than goals and depend on market conditions. Just cause termination is problematic when other forms of employer discrimination are determined, such as discrimination in age, gender, disability, race, national origin, and other Title VII areas. For example, an Ohio jury awarded a 68-year-old woman $30.6 million in an age discrimination lawsuit after a jury ruled that the company violated her rights by refusing to give her another job within the company when it terminated her from her management position.[38]

DUE PROCESS. Due process is one of the most important underlying rights employees have in the workplace, because it affects most of their other rights. Due process refers to the right to have an impartial and fair hearing regarding employers' decisions, procedures, and rules that affect employees. As applied in the workplace, due process essentially refers to grievance procedures.

At a more general level, due process rights protect employees from arbitrary and illegitimate uses of power. These rights are based on the Fifth and Fourteenth Amendments of the Constitution, which state that no person shall be deprived of "life, liberty, or property, without the due process of law."

Patricia Werhane[39] states that the following corporate procedural mechanisms are needed to ensure employees' right to due process:

- Right to a public hearing
- Right to have peer evaluations
- Right to obtain external arbitration
- Right to an open, mutually approved grievance procedure

The right to due process applies to other employee rights, such as those involving privacy; safety and health; safe working environment; holding meetings and gatherings; and hiring, firing, and other human resource decisions.

RIGHT TO PRIVACY.   Employees' right to privacy remains one of the most debated and controversial rights. It raises these questions: Where does the employer's control over employee behavior, space, time, and property begin and end? What freedoms and liberties do employees have with employer property rights? What rights do employers have to protect their private property, earnings, and costs from employees? The U.S. Constitution does not actually refer to a person's right to privacy; the working definition of employees' right to privacy has come to mean "to be left alone." Privacy in the workplace also can refer to employees' right to autonomy and to determine "when, how, and to what extent information about them is communicated to others."[40]

The extent of an employee's privacy in the workplace remains an unsettled area of controversy. The definition of what constitutes an employee's privacy is still somewhat problematic, including the notion of psychological privacy (involving an employee's inner life) and the notion of physical privacy (involving an employee's space and time).[41] In the 1965 *Griswold* v. *Connecticut* case, the Supreme Court ruled that the Constitution guarantees individuals a "zone of privacy" around them into which the government cannot intrude. Proponents of this definition argue that this zone includes personnel records and files and protection against polygraph and psychological testing and surveillance in the workplace. The ruling also is intended to protect employees in their after-work activities; their need for peace and quiet in the workplace; their dress, manners, and grooming; and their personal property in the workplace. Identifying this "zone of privacy" has proved complicated, especially in cyberspace and the use of technological surveillance.

TECHNOLOGY AND EMPLOYEE PRIVACY.   While employee privacy rights remain largely undefined regarding uses and abuses of emerging technologies in the workplace, the following main types of court-upheld privacy violations and permissible employee privacy inquiries can serve as guidelines. Court-upheld privacy violations include:

1. Intrusion (locker room and bathroom surveillance)
2. Publication of private matters
3. Disclosure of medical records
4. Appropriation of an employee's name for commercial uses
5. Eavesdropping on employee conversations and retrieving or accessing employee E-mail (if unauthorized)

Permissible employee privacy inquiries include:

1. Criminal history inquiries
2. Credit history inquiries
3. Access to medical records[42]

POLYGRAPH AND PSYCHOLOGICAL TESTING. Employers are particularly concerned about employee privacy rights regarding testing. Polygraph and psychological testing and other related techniques that many managers would like to use to prevent and detect crime in the workplace may constitute violation of employee rights. Workplace theft has been estimated by the U.S. Department of Commerce to cost in excess of $40 billion a year in the United States.[43] Here are some of the issues surrounding the use of polygraphs and psychological testing:

1. These tests are not reliable or valid; they are only indicators.
2. The tests, to some extent, can be manipulated and influenced by the operators.
3. The tests may include irrelevant questions (such as those pertaining to gender, lifestyle, religion, and after-work activities) that invade a person's privacy.
4. Employees do not have control over the test results or how the information is used.

Researchers in the field of honesty testing have concluded that only 1.7% (at worst) to 13.6% (at best) of such tests are accurate.[44]

WORKPLACE SURVEILLANCE. Surveillance of employees at work (that is, employers using technology to spy on and invade workers' privacy) is also a subject of concern. Software programs are used to monitor workers who use computer terminals.[45] Employers can detect the speed of employees' work, number and length of phone calls made and received, breaks taken, when machines are in use, and so on. Although some form of work-related monitoring is certainly legal and even necessary, the ethical issues that the American Civil Liberties Union (ACLU) raises are the possible invasion of employee privacy and fair treatment. What type of information does an employer have a right to, and what effects do stress and anxiety from monitoring have on employee welfare? The Electronic Communications Privacy Act renders electronic eavesdropping through computer-to-computer transmissions, private videoconferences, and cellular phones illegal.

A study released by the Society for Human Resource Management, a trade association in Alexandria, Virginia, showed that 80% of the organizations in the study used E-mail. Only 36% of those groups had policies concerning E-mail use and only 32% had written privacy policies. The issue of individual employee privacy remains somewhat undefined in the workplace.[46]

INTERNET USE IN THE WORKPLACE. This is another undefined area regarding employee use of technology that requires the employer's development of "appropriate use policies," or AUPs. Millions of messages are estimated to pass through the Internet every hour. In 2000, an estimated 7 trillion messages traveled through cyberspace. Jo Tucker, head of labor and employment practices at Morrison and Foerster, a law firm based in Irvine, California, stated that "if a worker is using a computer in a company office, on company time, privacy is what the employer says it is."[47] Without AUPs, Internet use in the workplace remains a guessing game between employer and employee. An employee Internet use policy depends on the company, its corporate culture, and the nature of its business. The policy must have the involvement and endorsement of top-level leadership. Monitoring capability, with employee awareness, must also accompany the policy. As J. Martin states, "A clear AUP policy effectively removes employee expectations of privacy on the Internet, eliminating potential lawsuits."[48] All use policies should also be spelled out clearly with no ambiguities, with simple, easy, enforceable rules. Part of such a policy involves the security of data for the entire company, since the reputation of the system and violations of it involve not only employees but all stakeholders. A policy on Internet use can help companies in the following ways: (1) Save employee work time, (2) prevent tying up phone lines and computer disk space that could be used for vital company business, (3) prevent exposing sensitive company data stored on computers to outside attack, and (4) prevent creations of conditions that enable employee harassment of each other and, ultimately, of the company.

Guidelines offered to employers regarding employee privacy include:

- Inform employees not to assume privacy in the workplace.
- Require employees to acknowledge the company's privacy policy in writing.
- Use private information only for legitimate purposes.
- Limit access to private information about employees to only those with a need to know.
- Secure employee medical records separately from other personnel files.
- Obtain signed permission releases and waivers before using an employee's name or photograph in any commercial advertisement, promotional material or training film.[49]

DRUG TESTING AND PRIVACY RIGHTS.   Privacy is also an issue in drug testing. Advocates for employee drug testing argue that company health costs and costs associated with sick and lost (nonproductive) days are affected when employees contract serious diseases, such as AIDS, or suffer from drug and alcohol addiction. Also, in industries (such as the airline industry or nuclear plant operations) where drug abuse can cost the lives of innocent people, screening drug abusers is viewed as in the public interest. Those who oppose forced employee drug testing argue that the practice violates employees' rights to due process and privacy.

The following guidelines can be used by companies for policy development in drug-testing programs:[50]

1. Tests should be administered only for jobs that have a clear and present potential to cause harm to others.

2. Procedural testing limitations should include previous notice to those being tested.

3. Employees tested should be notified of the results.

4. Employees tested should be informed that they are entitled to appeal the results.

5. The employer should demonstrate how the information will be kept confidential (or destroyed).

Four steps managers can take to develop corporate policy guidelines to prepare for privacy regulation in general are[51]:

1. *Prepare a "privacy impact statement."* This analysis of the potential privacy implications should be taken as part of all proposals for new and expanded systems.

2. *Construct a comprehensive privacy plan.* The privacy impact statement provides the input for planning; the plan specifies all that has to be achieved.

3. *Train employees who handle personal information.* Make employees aware of protecting privacy and of the particular policies and procedures that should be followed.

4. *Make privacy part of social responsibility programs.* Keep organizational members informed about company plans regarding privacy issues, with or without regulatory pressures.

GENETIC DISCRIMINATION. Should employers perform DNA testing on employees when several areas of discrimination could surface? Two examples are: (1) Employment based on a person's predisposition to a disease could negatively and unfairly affect hiring, firing, and benefits; and (2) insurance companies that could obtain an employee's genetic information would also be able to deny a person certain benefits. One lawsuit, settled in April 2001, was filed against Burlington Northern Santa Fe Railway Company, in Fort Worth, Texas. The railroad agreed to stop genetic testing. Testing had been required for those employees who filed claims for carpal tunnel syndrome.

The Genetic Nondiscrimination in Health Insurance and Employment Act was introduced by Senator Thomas Daschle of South Dakota and Congresswoman Louise Slaughter from New York in 2001. This Act would prevent genetic testing of employees. President Bush's reported interest regarding genetic discrimination has been on placing a cap on damages that might arise from such lawsuits, although he did sign legislation in 1997, while he was governor of Texas, that prohibited genetic discrimination in employment and group health plans.[52] The testing and use of genetic information of employees remains to be fully defined and enforced in the workplace and in legislation.

THE RIGHT TO KNOW AND WORKPLACE HEALTH AND SAFETY. Every employee is entitled to a safe, healthy workplace environment, because one of ten employees in private industry suffers from an industrial accident or disease while working. Information about unsafe, hazardous workplace conditions and some form of protection from these hazards are needed.[53] Employees have a right to know the nature and extent of hazardous risks to which they are exposed and to be informed and trained about and protected from those risks. Right-to-know laws have been passed in 20 states since the mid-1980s.

The Occupational Safety and Health Administration (OSHA) is the federal agency responsible for researching, identifying, and determining workplace health hazards; setting safety and health standards; and enforcing the standards. These remain major tasks. Critics of OSHA claim they are too overwhelming for one agency to monitor and execute effectively. The missions and budgets of government regulatory agencies—including OSHA—are also a function of the politics of the governing administration and Congress.

SMOKING IN THE WORKPLACE: WHOSE RIGHTS? Should smoking be completely banned in all workplaces in the United States? Because it has been proved that smoking causes cancer, should nonsmokers have a right to nonexposure to smoke? Whether and to what extent smoking should be restricted and banned in the workplace remains a controversial topic among major stakeholders. Among stakeholders who argue and lobby against smoking in the workplace are the Environmental Protection Agency (EPA), OSHA, and ASH (Action on Smoking and Health—the powerful national antismoking group). Pro-smoking advocates include the tobacco industry and its lobbying group, the Tobacco Institute, and the Bakery, Confectionery, and Tobacco Workers union. OSHA has not been able to place an absolute ban on smoking in all workplaces to date, even though tobacco has been shown to be one of the leading causes of death. The issue reflects societal habits and attitudes and the politics and economics of the industry.

Consider these facts. It is estimated that 28% of Americans age 18 and over are smokers. Approximately 80% of workers are protected to some extent by a workplace policy, and nearly half of all indoor workers are employed in smoke-free workplaces. Twenty states and the District of Columbia have laws that restrict smoking in private-sector workplaces.[54] Almost 75% of 1,794 facility managers in a survey claim they ban or segregate smoking in their workplaces.[55] One of OSHA's strategies has been to link smoking in the workplace to indoor air-quality problems and pollution and to legislate against it. The Clean Air Act is one such move to further restrict indoor smoking in public facilities. Employers need to keep track of laws and regulations that affect employee rights regarding smoking in the workplace.

THE RIGHT TO ORGANIZE AND FORM UNIONS. Workers have a right to organize, just as owners and managers do. Individuals, as workers and citizens, have the right of free association to seek common ends. This also means employees have a right to form unions. Although unions have a right to exist, they have no special rights beyond those due organizations with legal status.[56]

PLANT CLOSINGS AND EMPLOYEE RIGHTS. Companies have the right to relocate and transfer operations to any place they choose. If firms can find cheaper labor, raw materials, and transportation costs, lower taxes, no unions, and other business advantages for making a profit elsewhere, they often close plants and move. Companies also close plants because of loss of competitiveness, financial losses, and other legitimate economic reasons. The ethical questions posed to corporate managers regarding plant closings are: What rights do the employees who are affected by the closing have? What responsibilities does the company have toward the affected communities, and even toward the national economy?

Since August 1988, companies with more than 100 employees must by law give 60-day notice to workers before closing. Employees also have moral rights—to be treated fairly, equally, and with justice—when companies decide to relocate or close. Employees have the right to be compensated for the costs of retraining, transferring, and relocating; they have rights to severance pay and to outplacement and support programs that assist them in finding alternative employment; and they have the right to have their pension, health, and retirement plans honored.[57]

Employees also should be given the right to find a new owner for the plant and to explore the possibility of employee ownership of the plant before it is closed.[58] These rights extend beyond workers and include the welfare of the communities where the plant operated. Plant closings affect jobs, careers, families, and the local tax base and can even negatively affect the regional and national economies, when sizable operations are shut down or moved abroad.

Whatever the motivations for corporate closings or transfer of facilities, the rights of employees and local community groups stand, even though these rights are often negotiated against the utilitarian interests of corporations in specific economic contexts.

THE FAMILY AND MEDICAL LEAVE ACT. The Family and Medical Leave Act (FMLA) was enacted into law in 1993, eight years after it was introduced in Congress by Christopher Dodd, William Clay, and Patricia Schroeder. The final rules were established in 1995. The FMLA entitles eligible employees to a maximum of 12 weeks of unpaid leave per year for the birth or adoption of a child, to care for a spouse or immediate family member with a serious health condition, or when an employee is unable to work because of personal illness. The 12 weeks need not be used consecutively because intermittent leave or reduced work schedules are allowed under the act. To be considered eligible, an employee must have been employed for a continuous 12-month period and for at least 1,250 hours during the year preceding the leave.

Companies that employ at last 50 people within a 75-mile radius are mandated to offer such leave. The employer is required to maintain any preexisting health coverage during the leave. Once the leave is concluded, the employee must be reinstated to the same position or an equivalent job. An equivalent position must have the same pay, benefits, working conditions, authority, and responsibilities.

Employers have the right to request a 30-day advance notice for foreseeable absences and may require employees to present evidence to support medically necessary leave. Employers may request employees to obtain a second medical opinion at the employer's expense. Employers may deny reinstatement of employment to "key employees." Such employees must be among the 10% highest paid company employees, and their absence must have a serious economic impact on their organization. It is the duty of employers to inform employees of their status as "key employees" when they request a leave.

Major problems with the FMLA, from employees' experience, have been serious illnesses (e.g., *Price* v. *City of Fort Wayne*); from employers' perspective, rising health and company costs; and, from government's viewpoint, administrative requirements (e.g., *Viereck* v. *City of Gloucester City*). Employers often unintentionally violate the sometimes confusing and contradictory FMLA.[59] The courts have also tended to rule in favor of employees who have less serious and even minor illnesses. Finally, based on a 7-year study of more than 7,500 adults, it was found that

> the burden of not having a national or state-by-state family paid leave policy
> falls heaviest on the middle class and the working poor. While 40% of
> Americans in the top quartile of income lacked a sick leave policy at work, 54%
> of Americans in the second quartile, 63% in the third quartile, and 76% of work-
> ers in the bottom quartile lacked sick leave . . . . While 41% of working parents
> in the top quartile of income have 2 weeks or less of sick leave and vacation
> leave, 57% of parents in the second quartile, 68% in the third quartile, and an as-
> tounding 84% in the bottom quartile had 2 weeks or less of sick and vacation
> leave.[60]

6.4 DISCRIMINATION, EQUAL EMPLOYMENT OPPORTUNITY, AND AFFIRMATIVE ACTION

It is difficult to imagine that throughout most of the 19th century, women in America could not vote, serve on juries, issue lawsuits in their own name, or initiate legal contracts if they lost their property to their husbands. In an 1873 Supreme Court decision, *Bradwell* v. *Illinois,* a woman had "no legal existence, separate from her husband, who was regarded as her head and representative in the social state."[61]

It is also difficult to imagine the legal status of black people in the United States in 1857. In the Dred Scott case, one of the opinions of the Supreme Court considered blacks as "beings of an inferior order . . . and so far inferior that they had no rights that the white man was bound to respect."[62]

More recently, discrimination has surfaced in a number of categories. Racial profiling remains an issue. Black individuals are more likely to be stopped and arrested by police than whites. Income disparities between whites and minorities continue to rise. The average income of a black family was 65% of a white family income; in 1994, that percentage was 63%.[63] The ratio of women's annual pay to men's for full-time employment was 83.8 cents on the dollar during the last decade. Women still make, on average, 76 cents on the dollar for comparable work compared with men.[64] It is against this background that the doctrines, laws, and policies of discrimination, equal opportunity, and affirmative action must be considered.

DISCRIMINATION

Discriminatory practices in employer-employee relationships include unequal or disparate treatment of individuals and groups.[65] Unequal or preferential treatment is based on irrelevant criteria, such as gender, race, color, religion, national origin, or disability. Systematic and systemic discrimination is based on historical and institutionally ingrained unequal and disparate treatment against minorities, the disadvantaged, and women.

Examples of contemporary and systemic discrimination in employer-employee relationships are found in practices such as recruitment, screening, promotion, termination, conditions of employment, and discharge.[66] These practices are attributed to closed employment systems and practices resulting from seniority systems, "old boy networks," and arbitrary job classifications. Recruiting procedures that are biased toward certain groups and that do not openly advertise to minority groups are discriminatory. Screening practices that exclude certain groups and that use biased tests or qualifications are discriminatory. Promotion procedures that have "glass ceilings" (that is, invisible discriminatory barriers to advancement) for women and minority groups are discriminatory.[67] Seniority tracks that favor white males or other groups over minorities or women are discriminatory. Terminating employees on the basis of sex, age, race, or national origin is discriminatory. Since September 11, 2001, Middle Eastern individuals have faced greater discrimination in the U.S.

EQUAL EMPLOYMENT OPPORTUNITY AND THE CIVIL RIGHTS ACT

Title VII of the Civil Rights Act of 1964 makes discrimination on the basis of gender, race, color, religion, or national origin in any term, condition, or privilege of employment illegal. The law prohibits discrimination in hiring, classifying, referring, assigning, promoting, training, retraining, conducting apprenticeships, firing, and dispensing wages and fringe benefits. The Civil Rights Act also created the Equal Employment Opportunity Commission (EEOC) as the administrative and implementation agency to investigate complaints that individuals submit. The EEOC negotiates and works with the Justice Department regarding complaints; however, the EEOC cannot enforce the law except through grievances.

The Civil Rights Act of 1991 extended, for the first time, punitive damages to victims of employment discrimination. This law states that job bias on the basis of gender, disability, religion, or national origin will be punished as severely as job discrimination based on race. It also makes it easier for job-bias plaintiffs to win lawsuits. This legislation shifts the legal burden of proof to the employer, who must defend any intentional or unintentional employment bias, especially if the practice in question has a "disparate impact" on minorities or women. Under this law, the employer must demonstrate that the alleged discriminatory act is "job-related for the position in question and consistent with business necessity."[68] "Job-related" and "business necessity" are undefined and are determined by the courts. The act specifies that employers with more than 500 employees could be liable for up to $300,000 in compensatory and punitive damages. Smaller companies are liable for less, depending on the number of workers they employ.

The Equal Employment Opportunity Act of 1972 amended the 1964 act to empower the EEOC to enforce the law by filing grievances from individuals, job applicants, and employees in the courts. All private employers with 15 or more employees fall under the jurisdiction of the revised act, with the exception of bona fide tax-exempt private clubs. All private and public educational institutions and employment agencies are covered by the law. Labor unions (local, national, and international) with 15 or more members are included. Joint labor-management committees that administer apprenticeship, training, and retraining programs are also under this law's jurisdiction.

There were 58,124 charges filed through Title VII in 2000, which resulted in recovery of $149 million in monetary benefits to workers who had been discriminated against.[69]

AGE AND DISCRIMINATION IN THE WORKPLACE

The Age Discrimination in Employment Act (ADEA) of 1967, revised in 1978, prohibits employers from discriminating against individuals based on their age (between ages 40 and 70) in hiring, promotions, terminations, and other employment practices. In 1987, ADEA again was amended when Congress banned any fixed retirement age. The EEOC also issued a final rule in 2001 that aimed at prohibiting contracts requiring terminated employees to give back severance benefits if they challenged their terminations under the ADEA. "The new regulation takes effect at a time when several large corporations have announced significant layoffs. In recent years, companies have increasingly tried to tie severance deals during mass terminations to waivers of ADEA rights, as many employees who lose their jobs in such actions are over 40 and covered by the statute."[70]

Age discrimination also applies to younger individuals. Hanigan Consulting Group of New York surveyed 170 recent graduates, some scheduled to receive master's and doctoral degrees. The firm found that some applicants were asked questions that clearly violated antidiscrimination laws; for example, Do you intend to get married and have children? What will your boyfriend think of you working long hours? How old are you? Are you married? The basic guideline, according to a Boston attorney with Seyfarth, Shaw, is "if the question is not business-related and there is no legitimate business reason for asking it, then do not ask it."[71]

COMPARABLE WORTH AND EQUAL PAY

The Equal Pay Act of 1963, amended in 1972, prohibits discriminatory payment of wages and overtime pay based on gender. The law, in large part, is based on the doctrine of "comparable worth." This doctrine and the Equal Pay Act hold that women should be paid wages comparable to men who hold jobs that require equal skill, effort, and responsibility and that have the same working conditions. Women generally are paid 76 cents for each dollar men earn in the marketplace. This law addresses this inequity and also applies to executive, professional, sales, and administrative positions. In 2000, President Clinton failed to get the Paycheck Fairness Act into legislation. That act would have enabled the EEOC to collect and monitor data on pay and compensation from employers based on gender, race, and national origin. Fines could have been levied against companies with unequal pay scales. The Republican-led Congress would not have likely passed the act had it been proposed by the Clinton Administration.[72] While glass ceilings and lower wages for comparable work prevail in the U.S. workplace for women, other gains have been made, as previously discussed.

AFFIRMATIVE ACTION

Affirmative action programs are a proactive attempt to recruit applicants from minority groups to create opportunities for those who, otherwise, because of past and present discriminatory employment practices, would be excluded from the job market. Affirmative action programs attempt to make employment practices blind to color, gender, national origin, disability, and age. Although the doctrine of equal opportunity states that everyone should have an equal chance at obtaining a job and a promotion, affirmative action goes further. For example, Richard DeGeorge stated, "Affirmative action implies a set of specific result-oriented procedures designed to achieve equal employment opportunity at a pace beyond that which would occur normally."[73] Affirmative action programs were designed to set goals, quotas, and time frames for companies to hire and promote women and minorities in proportion to their numbers in the labor force and in the same or similar occupational categories within the company.

Courts have supported and eroded affirmative action approaches in the Civil Rights Act. Because of the changing social, political, and demographic landscape in the U.S., different membership on the Supreme Court, and evidence of reverse discrimination, changes in affirmative action law are occurring. Affirmative action remains a controversial topic and policy. Individuals' rights are violated when affirmation action programs seek to protect particular groups. Also, in a market economy where individual achievement based on merit is encouraged and rewarded, it seems unfair that arbitrary quotas should supercede those who do excel. On the other side of the controversy are advocates of affirmative action who claim that the playing field still is not level in U.S. corporate, educational, and other institutions whose officers select, hire, reward, and promote based on race, gender, national origin, ability, and other biases.

Four arguments that have been offered to explain and summarize affirmative action as it applies to hiring, promotions, and terminations are:

1. Affirmative action does not justify hiring unqualified minority group members over qualified white males. All individuals must be qualified for the positions in question.

2. Qualified women and minority members can be given preference morally, on the basis of gender or race, over equally qualified white males to achieve affirmative action goals.

3. Qualified women and minority members can be given preference morally over better-qualified white males, also, to achieve affirmative action goals.

4. Companies must make adequate progress toward achieving affirmative action goals even though preferential hiring is not mandatory.[74]

Take a look at and answer the questions in the feature box entitled "Leveling the Playing Field For Whom?" Discuss your answers with the class. Read the next section on ethics and affirmative action. What are the ethical principles underlying your answers to the questions? Explain.

ETHICS AND AFFIRMATIVE ACTION

The ethical principles behind affirmative action are often debated. Affirmative action as a doctrine is derived from several ethical principles that serve as bases for laws.

First, the *principle of justice* can be used to argue for affirmative action, by claiming that because white males have historically dominated and continue to unfairly dominate the highest paying, most prestigious employment positions in society, members of groups who have been excluded from comparable employment opportunities because of past and present discriminatory practices deserve to be compensated through affirmative action programs embodied in equal opportunity laws. Opponents of affirmative action argue that it is unfair and unjust that the distribution of benefits be based only on a few categories (race, sex, ethnicity) rather than on achievement or other criteria.

Second, a *utilitarian principle* can be used to support affirmative action by claiming that such programs help the majority of people in a society. Opponents argue that affirmative action cannot be shown or proven to work or that its benefits exceed its costs.

The number of Hispanic American freshmen entering the University of California in fall 2001 increased by 18.2% and the number of Asian American students increased by 8.7%. The increases were due in part to changes in the SAT-I exam that de-emphasized verbal and math areas and by giving added weight to the SAT-II exam, which is based more on specific subjects, such as biology, history, and foreign language, and is considered to be less culturally biased. Affirmative action criteria were therefore redesigned to give minorities an advantage. On the SAT-II, Asian and Hispanic American students have an advantage over blacks because the foreign language tested on the examination is spoken at home. The university's diversity entrance policy also promises that the top 4% of graduating seniors at each high school are guaranteed admission.

QUESTIONS

1. Should affirmative action be geared mainly toward a group, such as African Americans, that has an historic grievance of slavery and institutional segregation? Take a position and justify it.

2. Should a university promote diversity across racial and ethnic boundaries, including immigrants, even if blacks are disadvantaged as a result? Take a position and justify it.

3. Are white students discriminated against by these policies? Note that in the 1978 Bakke decision, Supreme Court Justice Lewis F. Powell, Jr., wrote, "The atmosphere of speculation, experimentation and creation—so essential to the quality of higher education—is widely believed to be promoted by a diverse student body." Take a position and justify it.

4. What is your solution or remedy to solve the problem in college admissions policies for minorities who suffer from past discrimination, such as blacks, and ongoing discrimination, such as immigrants and blacks?

SOURCE: Steven Holmes, "Leveling the Playing Field, but for Whom?" *New York Times*, July 1, 2001, 6.

Finally, using a *rights principle*, proponents of affirmative action can argue that protected groups have a right to different treatment because these groups have not had equal or fair access to benefits as other groups have. In fact, the rights of minorities, women, and other underprivileged groups have been denied and violated regarding access to education, jobs, and other institutional opportunities. Opponents using the rights principle argue that the rights of all individuals are equal under the law. The controversy continues as the economic, social, political, and demographic environments change.

REVERSE DISCRIMINATION: ARGUMENTS AGAINST AFFIRMATIVE ACTION

Arguments against affirmative action are directed toward the doctrine itself and against its implementation of quotas. The doctrine has been criticized on the grounds that nondiscrimination requires discrimination (that is, reverse discrimination). Reverse discrimination is alleged to occur when an equally qualified woman or member of a minority group is given preference over a white male for a job or when less qualified members of an ethnic minority are given hiring preference over white males through a quota system. Affirmative action, opponents argue, discriminates against gender and race, that is, white males. Some even say affirmative action discriminates against age: white, middle-aged males.

Another major argument against affirmative action says that individuals are held responsible for injustices for which they were not and are not responsible. Why should all contemporary and future white males, as a group, have to compensate for discriminatory practices others in this demographic category once committed or now commit?

Although these claims have some validity, proponents of affirmative action argue that injustices from discrimination have been institutionalized against minority groups. It happens that white males continue to benefit from the competitive disadvantages that past and present discriminatory practices have created for others. To compensate and correct for these systemic disadvantages based on race, gender, and other irrelevant (i.e., not related to employment) characteristics, social affirmative action goals and programs must be implemented. Still, the law is not a perfect means to correct past or present injustices. People of all races will continue to be hurt by discrimination and reverse discrimination practices. In the meantime, the court system will continue to use civil rights laws, affirmative action guidelines, and moral reasoning to decide on a case-by-case basis the justice and fairness of employment practices.

The following discussion is a summary of four notable Supreme Court cases and one U.S. Circuit Court case that illustrates how affirmative action and discrimination issues have been addressed.

SUPREME COURT RULINGS AND REVERSE DISCRIMINATION

THE *BAKKE* CASE. Allan Bakke, a white male, sued the Regents of the University of California at Davis because he was denied admission to the medical school in 1973. He sued on the basis of reverse discrimination. Bakke charged that the university gave preferential treatment to less qualified applicants who belonged to minority groups. Of 100 places in the entering class of 1973, 84 were open for competitive admission; 16 places were given preference to candidates who belonged to minority groups. In 1978, the Supreme Court ruled, in a five-to-four vote, in favor of Bakke. The decision argued against strict quotas but upheld the criterion of race as a consideration in admissions policies. The ruling sent the message that quotas based on race were illegal when no previous discrimination had been proved. However, quotas could be used to offset inequalities as part of settlements when previous discrimination was shown.[75]

THE *WEBER* CASE. Brian Weber, a white male, sued his employer, Kaiser Aluminum and Chemical Corporation, and the Steelworkers Union because he had been discriminated against by his exclusion from a quota-regulated training program. Weber won the case at the lower District Court and at the Court of Appeals. However, in 1979, the Supreme Court, in a five-to-two vote, overturned these decisions (*Weber* v. *Kaiser Aluminum and Chemical Corporation*). The Court ruled that blacks can be given special consideration for jobs that have been held predominantly by whites and that affirmative action programs rectify "manifest racial imbalances." The message the Supreme Court sent to employers was that reverse-discrimination charges should not prevent them from implementing affirmative action programs. In this case, white citizens were not displaced or hurt because of the quota-based training program.

THE *STOTTS* CASE. Carl Stotts, a black district fire chief in Memphis, sued the Memphis Fire Department in a class-action suit in 1977, charging that the department discriminated against him and other black citizens in its policy of "last hired, first fired" (or LIFO, which is an acronym for "last in, first out"). The city announced layoffs in 1981 because of a budget deficit. It implemented the layoffs with a union-negotiated seniority policy. Stotts won at the District Court level but lost in an appeal by the city of Memphis and the labor union in the Supreme Court in 1984. The majority vote in the Supreme Court ruled that bona fide seniority systems are protected under the 1964 Civil Rights Act and could not be disrupted, especially during layoff periods. The ruling, in effect, sent a message to employers that bona fide seniority systems are blind to skin color.

THE *ADARAND CONSTRUCTORS* V. *PENA* CASE. The Court's attitude on minority preference programs has begun to change. In 1995, its ruling in *Adarand Constructors* v. *Pena* effectively eliminated mandatory special consideration of contracts of minorities. The case questioned the legality of a federal mandate that required at least 10% of federally funded highway projects to go to businesses owned by minorities or women. The majority opinion, written by Justice Sandra Day O'Connor, states that all racial classifications must be held to rigorous judicial standards, whether passed by Congress or the states, and must be narrowly tailored to advance governmental interests. This overrules the previous 1990 decision that allowed Congress to mandate a program specifically designed to increase the number of minority broadcasters. In *Missouri* v. *Jenkins,* the Supreme Court reviewed a federally directed racial integration program that required the state of Missouri to spend more than $200 million a year to improve inner-city schools. The Court ruling did not dismantle the program but questioned the methods used to measure its progress.

THE *HOPWOOD* V. *TEXAS* CASE. A U.S. Circuit Court ruled that the University of Texas could not use race as a determining factor for admissions. In this case, several white students sued the school when they were not admitted because of the school's policy to admit a certain number of nonwhite students. This ruling opened the door for other educational systems to re-evaluate their admission quotas. It also may have the potential to limit admission policies that consider the racial diversity of students. If this case affects other educational institutions, affirmative action policies could be questioned in business as well. Presently, it is not easy to predict the outcome. The issue remains: Is the playing field level or not in the U.S. regarding race?[76]

THE *GRUTTER V. UNIVERSITY OF MICHIGAN LAW SCHOOL* CASE. A federal judge in Detroit ruled in March of 2001 that the race-conscious admissions system in the University of Michigan's law school is unconstitutional. "All racial distinctions are inherently suspect and presumptively invalid. Whatever solution the law school elects to pursue, it must be race-neutral," wrote Judge Bernard Friedman of the United States District Court in Detroit. This case represents a continuing push to ban the use of race in admissions policies, initiated in 1995 when the University of California Regents banned the asking for racial identity on admissions applications. That decision influenced a Federal Court of Appeals decision in 1996 to also ban the practice of asking for racial identity in Texas, Mississippi, and Louisiana. Since then, voters in California and Washington have not accepted affirmative action in state contracts and educational settings.[77]

Affirmative action has come under attack since 1991. The Supreme Court has moved toward a more conservative stance with the appointment of Clarence Thomas and David Souter in 1990. While the Court has not ended affirmative action, it did establish a "strict scrutiny" standard, making it more difficult for current affirmative action programs to be enacted. Further evidence that the Supreme Court has moved toward more conservative positions was their 1997 refusal to hear an appeal by opponents of Proposition 209, the California ballot that amended the state's constitution to prohibit preferential treatment on the basis of race and color by state agencies.[78]

These laws certainly are not inclusive of all the equal-opportunity legislation or federal policy directives passed and amended from the 1960s through the 1990s, but they represent some of the prominent ones. Laws alone cannot, nor perhaps should they, guarantee or equalize employment opportunities, fairness, and justice to members of groups that have been discriminated against historically and that experience bias currently. Stereotypes and biases can be manipulated through subtle, legal means, such as in the ways job descriptions and evaluations are written and carried out, by the types of qualifications included in job descriptions, in advertising methods for jobs, and by other exclusionary conditions and practices of employing and terminating people. Still, equal opportunity laws and their enforcement change and evolve in free-market systems and representative democracies. As the consensus opinions of voters and power blocs change, so do laws and policies. Laws set social goals. The pursuit or abandonment of those goals depends on their perceived value and utility by the majority of voters, or, in other instances, the courts. It is impossible to separate the politics and economics from the judicial and legislative processes in a capitalistic, representative democracy.

6.5 SEXUAL HARASSMENT IN THE WORKPLACE

Sexual harassment was not a specific violation of federal law before 1981. It now may be difficult to imagine flagrant acts of sexual violation against women, but as recently as 20 years ago, when women worked in mines, they, like their male counterparts, were stripped and soaked in axle grease in a primitive hazing ritual, and then, unlike the male employees, the women were tied to wooden supports in spread-eagle positions.[79] The Senate hearings on sexual harassment charges against Supreme Court nominee Clarence Thomas awakened public and corporate concern about sexual harassment in society and the workplace. In addition, the overt sexual harassment of female U.S. Navy professionals also has brought attention to this issue. Although sexual harassment can be and is committed by both men and women, it is more often women who are the unwilling victims.

Sexual harassment remains among the most prominent civil right issues in the workplace. There were 15,836 sexual harassment charges filed with the EEOC or state agencies in 2000 with $54.6 million paid in monetary benefits (not including monetary benefits obtained through litigation). As noted earlier, 13.6% of those charges were filed by men, compared to 9.1% in 1992.[80] TWA recently agreed to pay $2.6 million to settle a sexual harassment suit filed in 1998. The suit is one of the largest in New York State. The company will pay $1.5 million to nine women who worked in ground traffic control, passenger service, and maintenance. The *New York Times* reported that three women "accused three high-level managers of egregious sexual harassment that included groping and verbal abuse." Lawyers for the women said that the airline did nothing about repeated complaints taken to different levels of management before the suit was filed.[81]

WHAT IS SEXUAL HARASSMENT?

The Supreme Court ruled in 1986 that sexual harassment is illegal under Title VII of the 1964 Civil Rights Act and that when a "hostile environment" is created through sexual harassment in the workplace, thereby interfering with an employee's performance, the law is violated, regardless of whether economic harm is done or whether demands for sexual favors in exchange for raises, promotions, bonuses, and other employment-related opportunities are granted.[82]

Under Title VII, the EEOC guidelines (1980) define sexual harassment as follows:

> Unwelcome sexual advances, requests for sexual favors, and other verbal or physical conduct of a sexual nature constitute sexual harassment when (1) submission to such conduct is made either explicitly or implicitly a term or condition of an individual's employment, (2) submission to or rejection of such conduct by an individual is used as the basis for employment decisions affecting such an individual, or (3) such conduct has the purpose or effect of unreasonably interfering with an individual's work performance or creating an intimidating, hostile, or offensive working environment.

The courts have defined sexual harassment as conduct ranging from blatant grabbing and touching to more subtle hints and suggestions about sex. Forms of sexual harassment include the following[83]:

- Unwelcome sexual advances
- Coercion
- Favoritism
- Indirect harassment
- Physical conduct
- Visual harassment (For example, courts have ruled that sexual harassment was committed when graffiti were written on men's bathroom walls about a female employee and when pornographic pictures were displayed in the workplace.)

WHO IS LIABLE?

The EEOC guidelines place absolute liability on employers for actions and violations of the law by their managers and supervisors, whether or not the conduct was known, authorized, or forbidden by the employer. Employers also are liable for coworkers' conduct if the employer knew, or should have known, of the actions in question, unless the employer shows, after learning of the problem, that the company took immediate and appropriate action to correct the situation. Employers may be liable for harassment of nonemployees under the same conditions as those stated for coworkers.[84]

Moreover, under EEOC guidelines employers are responsible for establishing programs (and standards) that develop, train, and inform employees about sanctions and procedures for dealing with sexual harassment complaints (see Figure 6.3). It is in the employer's economic and moral interest to institute such programs, since courts mitigate damages against companies that have harassment prevention and training programs. Some of the leaders in establishing sexual harassment policies and programs are Nynex, AT&T, DuPont, Corning, and Honeywell, to mention only a few.

TANGIBLE EMPLOYMENT ACTION AND VICARIOUS LIABILITY

A currently prominent feature of harassment cases is the concept of "tangible employment action," which Supreme Court Justice Anthony Kennedy described as "hiring, firing, failing to promote, reassignment with significantly different responsibilities or a decision causing a significant change in benefits."[85] An employer's defense against claims of harassment has been created in cases in which a hostile environment was evident but no tangible employment action occurred. In the Supreme Court decision in the case *Burlington Industries* v. *Ellerth,*

> Kimberly Ellerth's harasser threatened to take steps against her if she didn't comply with his wishes. Since he never carried out the threat, Ellerth's

---

| FIGURE 6.3 | SAMPLE CORPORATE SEXUAL HARASSMENT POLICY |

1. Sexual harassment is a violation of the corporation's EEO policy. Abuse of anyone through sexist slurs or other objectionable conduct is offensive behavior.
2. Management must ensure that a credible program exists for handling sexual harassment problems. If complaints are filed, they should receive prompt consideration without fear of negative consequences.
3. When a supervisor is made aware of an allegation of sexual harassment, the following guidelines should be considered:
   a. Obtain information about the allegation through discussion with the complainant. Ask for and document facts about what was said, what was done, when and where it occurred, and what the complainant believes was the inappropriate behavior. In addition, find out if any other individuals observed the incident, or similar incidents, to the complainant's knowledge. This is an *initial* step. In no case does the supervisor handle the complaint process alone.
   b. If the complaint is from an hourly employee, a request for union representation at any point must be handled as described in the labor agreement.
   c. The immediate supervisor or the department head and the personnel department must be notified *immediately*. When a complaint is raised by, or concerns, an hourly employee, the local labor relations representative is to be advised. When a complaint is raised by or concerns a salaried employee, the personnel director is to be advised.
4. The personnel department must conduct a complete investigation of the complaint for hourly and salaried employees. The investigation is to be handled in a professional and confidential manner.

SOURCE: Based on the General Motors corporate policy on sexual harassment.

employment status was not negatively affected. However, her harassment was severe and pervasive, and Burlington was held liable for that instead.[86]

Severe and pervasive harassment that has no tangible employment action characterized another case, *Faragher* v. *City of Boca Raton*. In this case, it was determined that

lifeguard Beth Faragher had been repeatedly harassed by two male supervisors for several years. She complained to other beach supervisors, but to no avail. Attorneys for the city argued that she had not complained to authorities at a high enough level. This defense laid the foundation for another key concept the Court stressed: "vicarious liability."[87]

Employers, under this concept, could be liable for harassment if it is committed by anyone present in the workplace and if it is brought to the attention of any manager or supervisor. Employers are liable for harassment by anyone who is present in the workplace (coworkers, customers, vendors), if the employers know or should have known about the harassment. Moreover, employers are liable for harassment by all supervisors, whether the employer knew about the harassment or not. This represents a significant change in sexual harassment liability.

EMPLOYER GUIDELINES WITH EXTENDED LIABILITY RULINGS. Employers should:

- Exercise reasonable care to prevent and correct for any harassment. There should be an anti-harassment policy and a complaint procedure present, made known to every employee, readily available, and used in training. The EEOC enforcement guidelines provide an excellent source of training materials.
- Quickly and effectively address all harassment complaints.[88]

INDIVIDUAL GUIDELINES. Although sexual harassment often occurs as part of a power issue, i.e., people in more-powerful positions exert pressure over people in less-powerful posts, a frequent observation is that men and women tend to see sexual harassment differently. This certainly does not justify legally or morally unwelcome sexual advances. It does suggest, however, that employers need to provide adequate education, training, and role-playing between the sexes so that gender differences in perceptions and feelings on what constitutes sexual harassment can be understood. Some practical guidelines that employees (men, in this instance) can use to check their motives and behavior regarding sexual harassment include the following:[89]

- If you are unsure whether you have offended a woman, ask her. If you did offend her, apologize, and don't do it again.
- Talk over your behavior with noninvolved women and with men you can trust not to make a mockery of your concerns.
- Ask yourself how you would feel if a man behaved toward your daughter the way you feel you may be behaving toward women.
- Ask yourself also if you would act this way if the shoe were on the other foot, if the woman were your boss or if she were physically stronger or more powerful than you.
- Most of all, don't interpret a woman's silence as consent. Silence is, at least, a "red light." Through silence, a woman may be trying to send you a signal of discomfort.
- Be very certain that your comments or behaviors are welcome, and if they are not, stop them.

SEXUAL HARASSMENT AND FOREIGN FIRMS IN THE UNITED STATES

Two foreign companies operating in the United States have reacted differently to sexual harassment charges; this is a perilous area where the law and societal norms are rapidly changing. These companies' reactions have exposed them to increased liability. One of the firms, Astra, a Swedish pharmaceutical firm, fired its CEO of the U.S. subsidiary and two other top

FIGURE 6.4	SURVEY OF HARASSMENT AND DISCRIMINATION LAW		
Jurisdiction	**Prohibitions on Employment Discrimination**	**Prohibitions on Sexual Harassment**	**Legal Basis**
Argentina	Yes	Yes, by judicial ruling	Section 16, Argentine Constitution
Australia	Yes	Yes	Race, Sex, and Disability Acts
Belgium	Yes	Yes	Article 10, Belgian Constitution; Royal Decree of September 19, 1997
Brazil	Yes	No	Article 5, Brazilian Constitution; Section 461, Brazilian Labor Code
Canada	Yes	Yes	Human rights laws of each province
Chile	Yes	Yes	Article 19, Constitution; Article 2, Labor Code
Colombia	Yes	No	Article 53, Constitution; Article 10, Labor Code
Czech Republic	Yes, by judicial decision	No	Decision No. 13/94, Constitutional Court
Egypt	Yes	No, except by extension of Civil Code	Article 40, Constitution
France	No	Yes	Article L 122-46, French Labor Code; Article 27, Law of December 31, 1992
Germany	No	Yes	Section 2, Article 31, Constitution; Disability Act; Employee Protection Act
Hong Kong	Yes	Yes	Sex Discrimination Ordinance; Disability Discrimination Ordinance
Hungary	Yes	No	Article 5, Hungarian Labor Code
Ireland	Yes	Yes	Employment Equality Act
Italy	Yes	Yes, by judicial decision	Law No. 125 of April 10, 1991
Japan	Yes	Yes	Equal Employment Opportunity Act
Mexico	No	Yes	Section 153, Mexican Penal Code
Netherlands	Yes	Yes	Article 3, Dutch Labor Conditions Act; Article 7, Dutch Civil Code
People's Republic of China	Yes	No	Article 12, Labor Law of the PRC (1995)
Philippines	No	Yes	Republic Act 7877 (1995)
Poland	Yes	No	Articles 32 and 33, Constitution; Labor Code

Republic of South Africa	Yes	No	Act No. 66, South African Labor Reform Act of 1995
Russia	Yes	No	Russian Labor Law of 1995
Singapore	Yes; age only	No	Retirement Act
Spain	Yes	Yes	Articles 9, 14, and 35, Spanish Constitution; Section 34.3.95 of Spanish Employment Act
Sweden	Yes	Yes	The Act on Equal Opportunities at Work
Switzerland	No	Yes	Article 3, Law on Equal Treatment of Women and Men
Taiwan	No	Yes	Article 83, ROC Social Order Maintenance Act
Thailand	Yes	Yes	Constitution; Labor Protection Act
Ukraine	Yes	No	Article 42, Labor Code of the Ukraine
United Kingdom	Yes	Yes	Sex, Race, and Disability Discrimination Laws
Venezuela	No	Yes	Law on Violence Against Women and Family

SOURCE: Adapted with permission from Gerald Maatman, Jr. "Harassment, discrimination laws go global." *National Underwriter*, September 11, 2000, 3.

managers. The other company, Mitsubishi, has denied all charges, has maintained that EEOC is wrong, and has mounted a full-scale public relations campaign to discredit complainers. Both companies lacked one of the most basic requirements consultants recommend: a clear and strong written policy on sexual harassment.[90]

Companies have the obligation of training and supporting their employees who work and conduct business internationally on harassment and discrimination laws. "When in Rome, do as the Romans do" does not mean do nothing, act immorally, or act from your own intuition as an employee representing your company. As Figure 6.4 illustrates, many countries have specific laws on employment discrimination and sexual harassment. Some are not the same as in the U.S. For example, Venezuela, as of January 1, 1999, has a new employment discrimination statute that prohibits sexual harassment and punishes this crime by a prison term from 3 to 12 months. The offender must also pay the victim twice the amount of economic damage in regard to lack of access to positions, promotions, or job performance that resulted from the sexual harassment.[91] Louise Simms, the MBA student from the opening story in Chapter 3, may now have more information to research before approaching her employer and potential client.

6.6 WHISTLE-BLOWING VERSUS ORGANIZATIONAL LOYALTY

The decision to become a whistleblower frequently requires breaking with the very group that we have viewed as critical to our financial success if not our very survival. The decision entails destabilizing one's life and placing all of the essential underpinnings of our financial security and the security of those who depend on us at total risk. It is easy to understand that such a decision is accompanied by a good deal of anxiety and stress.[92]

Among all of the rights discussed in this chapter, one of the most valued by a U.S. citizen is the freedom of speech. But how far does this right extend into the corporation, especially if an employee observes an employer committing an illegal or immoral activity that could harm others? What are the obligations and limits of employee loyalty to the employer? Under what, if any, circumstances should employees blow the whistle on their supervisors, managers, or firms?

Whistle-blowing is "the attempt of an employee or former employee of an organization to disclose what he or she believes to be wrongdoing in or by the organization."[93] Whistle-blowing can be internal (reported to an executive in the organization), external (reported to external public interest groups, the media, or enforcement agencies), personal (harm reportedly done only to the whistle-blower), and impersonal (harm observed as done to another).[94] Whistle-blowing goes against strong U.S. cultural norms of showing loyalty toward an employer and colleagues and avoiding the "snitch" label. However, strong cultural norms regarding fairness, justice, a sense of duty, and obedience to the law and to one's conscience also exist. A moral dilemma can occur when a loyal employee observes the employer committing or assisting in an illegal or immoral act and must decide what to do. The whistle-blower may not only lose his or her job but may also experience negative and damaging repercussions in his or her profession, marriage, and family life. Dr. Jeffrey Wigand, head of research at Brown and Williamson Tobacco Company from 1989 to 1993, testified that this company knew and controlled nicotine levels in its products. His testimony, along with that of others, helped the government initially win a substantial lawsuit against the tobacco industry. As the film, *The Insider*, accurately documented, Wigand paid an enormous personal price as a witness.[95] Karen Silkwood, the now classic example of one person's bold attempt to share inside information, may have been murdered for blowing the whistle on the Kerr-McGee plutonium company:

> Karen Silkwood was killed on November 12, 1974, at 28 years of age while driving to meet a reporter from the New York Times with documentation about plutonium fuel rod tampering at the Kerr-McGee uranium and plutonium plants in Cimarron, Oklahoma.[96]

The second edition of Richard Rashke's book, *The Killing of Karen Silkwood* (Cornell University Press, 2000) recounts the story in detail.

Not all whistle-blowers undergo such traumatic fates as the two examples offered here. Michael Haley, a Federal Bank Examiner, won $755,533 in back-pay, future loss of income, and compensatory damages under the federal whistle-blower statute and another amended federal statute. He had worked as a bank examiner for the Office of Thrift Supervision (OTS), starting in 1977. He inspected OTS-regulated banks, evaluating the soundness of their operations. He was terminated after he reported violations in federal banking laws and regulations regarding a forced merger.[97]

Under what conditions is whistle-blowing morally justified? DeGeorge[98] discusses five conditions:

1. When the firm, through a product or policy, will commit serious and considerable harm to the public (as consumers or bystanders), the employee should report the firm.

2. When the employee identifies a serious threat of harm, he or she should report it and state his or her moral concern.

3. When the employee's immediate supervisor does not act, the employee should exhaust the internal procedures and chain of command to the board of directors.

4. The employee must have documented evidence that is convincing to a reasonable, impartial observer that his or her view of the situation is accurate and evidence that the firm's practice, product, or policy seriously threatens and puts in danger the public or product user.

5. The employee must have valid reasons to believe that revealing the wrongdoing to the public will result in the changes necessary to remedy the situation. The chance of succeeding must be equal to the risk and danger the employee takes to blow the whistle.

The risks to whistle-blowers can range from outright termination to more subtle pressures, such as strong and hidden criticisms, undesirable and burdensome work assignments, lost perks, and exclusion from communication loops and social invitations.[99] Although 21 states have laws protecting corporate and governmental whistle-blowers from reprisal, experience shows that the government's actual protection to whistle-blowers, even if after resigning or being fired they are reinstated with back pay and compensation for physical suffering, is weak because of the many subtle forms of retaliation, such as those just listed.[100]

WHEN WHISTLE-BLOWERS SHOULD NOT BE PROTECTED

The most obvious condition under which whistle-blowers should not be protected is when their accusations are false and their motivation is not justifiable or accurate.

The following instances show when whistle-blowers should not have freedom of speech against their employers:

- When divulging information about legal and ethical plans, practices, operations, inventions, and other matters that should remain confidential and that are necessary for the organization to perform its work efficiently

- When an employee's personal accusations or slurs are irrelevant to questions about policies and practices that appear illegal or irresponsible

- When an employee's accusations do not show a conviction that a wrongdoing is being committed and when such accusations disrupt or damage the organization's morale

- When employees complain against a manager's competence to make daily work decisions that are irrelevant to the legality, morality, or responsibility of management actions

- When employees object to their discharge, transfer, or demotion if management can show that unsatisfactory performance or violation of a code of conduct was the reason for the decision[101]

FACTORS TO CONSIDER BEFORE BLOWING THE WHISTLE

Whistle-blowing is a serious action with real consequences. It often involves a decision to be made among conflicting moral, legal, economic, personal, family, and career demands and choices. No single answer may appear. A stakeholder analysis and questions can help the potential whistle-blower identify the groups and individuals, stakes, priorities, and trade-offs when selecting among different strategies and courses of action.

The following 12 guidelines offer factors[102] that a person should consider when deciding whether to blow the whistle on an employer:

1. Make sure the situation warrants whistle-blowing. If serious trade secrets or confidential company property will be exposed, know the harm and calculated risks.

2. Examine your motives.

3. Verify and document your information. Can your information stand up in a hearing and in court?

4. Determine the type of wrongdoing and to whom it should be reported. Knowing this will assist in gathering the type of evidence to obtain.

5. State your allegations specifically and appropriately. Obtain and state the type of data that will substantiate your claim.

6. Stay with the facts. This minimizes retaliation and avoids irrelevant mudslinging, name-calling, and stereotyping.

7. Decide whether to report to internal contacts or external contacts. Select the internal channel first if that route has proven effective and less damaging to whistle-blowers. Otherwise, select the appropriate external contacts.

8. Decide whether to be open or anonymous. Should you choose to re-main anonymous, document the wrongdoing and anticipate what you will do if your identity is revealed.

9. Decide whether current or alumni whistle-blowing is the best alter-native. Should you blow the whistle while you are an employee or resign first? Resigning should not be an automatic option. If the wrongdoing affects others, your decision is not only a personal one, but also you are fulfilling moral obligations beyond your own welfare.

10. Follow proper guidelines in reporting the wrongdoing. Check forms, meeting deadlines, and other technicalities.

11. Consult a lawyer at every step of the way.

12. Anticipate and document retaliation. This assists your effectiveness with courts and regulatory agencies.

MANAGERIAL STEPS TO PREVENT EXTERNAL WHISTLE-BLOWING

Managers have a responsibility to listen to and respond to their employees, especially regarding the observations of and reporting of illegal and im-moral acts. Chapter 4 discussed mechanisms such as "ethics offices," om-budsperson programs, and peer review programs. These are part of a corpo-ration's responsibility to provide due process for employees to report personal grievances, to obtain effective and just resolution of them, and to report the wrongdoings of others, including the employers. Four straightfor-ward and simple steps management can take to prevent external whistle-blowing are:[103]

1. Develop effective internal grievance procedures and processes that employees can use to report wrongdoings.

2. Reward people for using these channels.

3. Appoint senior executives and others whose primary responsibilities are to investigate and report wrongdoing.

4. Assess large fines for illegal actions. Include executives and profes-sionals who file false or illegal reports, who knowingly market dan-gerous products, or who offer bribes or take kickbacks.

Preventing, reporting, and effectively and fairly correcting illegal and im-moral actions, policies, and procedures are the responsibilities of employers and employees. Management cannot expect employees to be loyal to a com-pany that promotes or allows wrongdoing to its stakeholders. Whistle-blowing should be a last resort. A more active goal is to hire, train, and pro-mote morally and legally sensitive and responsive managers who communicate with and work for the welfare of all stakeholders.

SUMMARY

The demographics of the workforce at the beginning of the 21st century continue to change. These changes include the aging of employees, the "shrinking" of the workforce, an increasing number of women and minority entrants, the demand for work-life balance from singles and dual-career families, the gap in educational levels, a greater demand for the skills of disabled workers. These changes in the composition of the workforce signal changes in work-related values and motivations. Corporations and managers can expect moral tensions to rise regarding issues such as age discrimination, health care needs, conflicting communication, generational differences, and requests for more balance and flexible work schedules. "One size fits all" management techniques do not work.

The social contract between corporations and employees is changing. The original employment-at-will doctrine has been replaced by the doctrine of implied employee rights; still, the EAW policy is not dead. Many firms, large and small, use this policy—some explicitly, others less visibly. Two underlying concepts of employee rights are balance and governmental rights.

The nature of legal and moral relationships between employers and employees is also changing. Recent court decisions have backed down in supporting racial affirmative action practices. Although EEOC policies and affirmative action practices remain a part of federal law, some states are showing less acceptance of these laws and procedures. Current and future issues related to sexual harassment and reverse discrimination will continue to shape legal and moral guidelines for corporations. Conflicts regarding due process, privacy, and other employee rights issues will continue to be resolved through court cases and legislation; their resolution will influence corporate policies in the future.

Sexual harassment laws and guidelines for employers and employees and the moral dilemma of organizational loyalty versus personal ethics will always be important issues. The justification for whistle-blowing and guidelines for potential whistle-blowers must be considered by employees before blowing the whistle and by corporations to prevent external whistle-blowing.

QUESTIONS

1. Identify five major trends in the changing demographics of the workforce. Can you think of other changes now occurring in the workforce?

2. Identify moral tensions and conflicts associated with the changes you gave in question 1.

3. What are major factors an employer should consider to avoid arbitrarily terminating an employee?

4. What does the term *moral entitlement* mean as it relates to employee rights? Give an example. Do you agree that employees have moral entitlements to some rights in the workplace? Explain.

5. What are some procedural mechanisms that ensure an employee's right to due process?

6. What are some changes that have occurred as a result of the Civil Rights Act of 1991?

7. Do you believe there is now an "equal playing field" regarding access to educational institutions, jobs, and other employment opportunities for all individuals and groups in the United States? Explain. Do you believe women should still be a protected group under Title VII of the Civil Rights Act? Explain. Do you believe minorities of different races in the U.S. other than Caucasian should still be protected? If so, which group(s)? If not, explain why not.

8. What are some arguments for and against "reverse discrimination"? Is the "playing field" in U.S. corporations more level now?

9. Describe criteria used to determine whether verbal or physical actions constitute sexual harassment. What are some specific types of sexual harassment? Have you been sexually harassed in a work setting? Can you describe what happened and the outcome?

10. What should employees expect from their employers and their companies now in terms of rights and obligations? Explain. Is loyalty to an employer a "dead" or "dying" concept now? Why or why not?

11. Do you believe whistle-blowing is justifiable in corporations? Why or why not?

12. Should corporate managers prevent whistle-blowing? Why or why not? Explain.

13. How can employers prevent whistle-blowing?

EXERCISES

1. Identify an example in the recent news of a court decision relating to discrimination or reverse discrimination. Briefly describe the case and the outcome. What are the implications of this decision for employers and other stakeholders? Do you agree with the outcome? Explain.

2. Select an employee right in the workplace from the chapter. Give an example, based on your own outside reading or experience, of a case involving this right. Was it violated? How? What was the outcome? What should the outcome have been? Why?

3. Identify an example from your own experience of discrimination or sexual harassment. Did this experience influence your view of affirmative action or employee protection programs? If so, how?

4. Write a paragraph or two describing a situation from your experience in which you felt justified that you had cause to blow the whistle. Did you? Why or why not? Under what circumstances do you feel whistle-blowing is justified?

5. Briefly interview three people you know from three different generations discussed in the chapter. Ask open-ended questions about how they feel about the nature of their work, employer, and job. Find out whether or not and why they are satisfied with their work and job. Ask what their expectations are from their employer and job. Ask what they desire from work and a job. Summarize your findings. Then, determine in your brief summary whether or not and why generational differences and values affected your interviewees' answers.

6. Create a "for" and "against" set of arguments regarding the "employment-at-will" doctrine in the present economic and demographic environment. After you make a complete set of arguments, which position do you support? Did your views change after this exercise? Why or why not?

ETHICAL DILEMMA

CHEATING OR LEVELING THE PLAYING FIELD?

PART I

During one of last year's midterm examinations in my finance class, I was faced with my first ethical dilemma in college. My friend and I were studying for the exam when he explained that he was going to punch the formulas into his calculator. He said that he has attention deficit hyperactivity disorder (ADHD) and that it was very difficult for him to remember formulas. I shrugged off the suggestion in the hope that he would exclude me from his decision. A few days later, during the examination, I looked around and noticed that he was not the only one who had entered the formulas in their calculators. My first reaction was "damn, maybe I could have done the same thing." Then I remembered how the professor had told us that this was not allowed and that we had all signed onto the college's "honor code" system, which stated that we would not cheat and that we would report those who did. It was at that moment that I realized I was faced with a dilemma: to tell or not to tell. I violated the honor code if I kept silent; I violated my friend's trust if I told. After all, I thought, he did have ADHD. Shouldn't he be given a break? Also, I didn't want to tell on so many students. I'm not a police officer.

QUESTION

What would you have done in this situation and why? Answer this question before continuing.

PART II

I chose to continue taking the test without telling the professor that students were using their calculators to "remember" their formulas. When I arrived at class next week, the professor had a sad look on his face because the class average for the examination was only 72% correct. There was only one person who received an A. Surprise, I was the A student! I was one of the few who had not cheated, and I got the highest grade in the class. Not only did I get the highest grade, but I finished the semester with a grade well above the curve. At the semester's end, I reflected on the cheating incident. Had I chosen to tell the professor, one of two things could have happened: 1) The class would have had to take a make-up examination, or 2) several of my classmates would have received a 0, or have been punished in some way. (It's also possible that my A may not have counted because all the exams were trashed.) In fact, by my not telling, I ended up being able to capitalize on the other students' not studying. Had I blown the whistle, we may all have been required to take the test over, and, yes, I would have gotten an A; however, the curve would have been more narrow. This way, as I see it, I won and the others got their "just rewards," even though they cheated and I did, by default, violate the honors code.

QUESTIONS

1. Do you agree with this student's logical thinking and his ethical reasoning? Explain.

2. What do you believe should have happened (if anything) to the student in this situation? Explain.

3. What would you have done differently and why? Justify your answer.

7

THE GLOBAL ENVIRONMENT, STAKEHOLDER MANAGEMENT, AND MULTINATIONAL CORPORATIONS

7.1 THE CONNECTED GLOBAL ECONOMY AND GLOBALIZATION

The global environment consists of a dynamic set of relationships among companies, financial markets, cultures, political ideologies, government policies, laws, technologies, and numerous stakeholder interests. The terrorist attack on New York City's World Trade Center and the Pentagon, which left almost 4,000 American and international victims dead and missing, quickly demonstrated that the global environment and economy also comprise a human community—economically, politically, and emotionally. Fear, sadness, empathy, anger, pride, and loss were commonly shared emotions across geographies and cultures as the news broke on cable and network channels. Eighty international governmental leaders responded, expressing sympathy and support to the Bush administration. As one writer noted, "The imperatives of making money, of guessing what the Federal Reserve will do and how the markets will react, of assessing whether a recession is now more likely, of estimating insurance company losses or airline passenger levels, paled in significance. Who cared?"[1] The following excerpts illustrate the multidimensional connectedness of global and national stakeholders and stakes in the wake of this crisis.

■ "[T]he aftershocks of the worst terrorist attack in U.S. history hit the world yesterday. . . . Major central banks pumped more than $80 billion into financial markets to prevent gridlock. Finance ministers from the U.S., Japan, Germany, Italy and other leading industrialized nations tried to calm mounting fears that the attack could tip the world into outright recession."[2] As a result of the attack, the Dow Jones index of European blue chips plunged 6.1 percent; the London index, 5.7 percent; the Paris index, 7.4 percent; the Frankfurt index, 8.5 percent; and the Sao Paulo index, 9.2 percent, to name a few.

■ "'A full-blown global recession is highly likely. . . . The rest of the world, which has been in recession, will suffer more. Since the global economy is interwoven through trade and investment, all of us will be worse off,' Sung Won Shon, chief economist for Wells Fargo, stated. 'If the U.S. takes a bigger hit, then of course it will drag down everything else,' said Nariman Behravesh, chief economist for DRI-WEFA. 'The level of uncertainty that this act will bring will not be limited to the U.S.,' said Anthony Chan, chief economist for Banc One Investment Advisors. 'All over the world we will see that uncertainty will rise and with that will come diminished growth. The fact that such terrorist acts came in [waves] does suggest that anything resembling normalcy will take quite some time to regain.' 'No one knows what this means for the United States, the G7 [group of industrialized nations], for anyone, except that some kind of inflection point in history seems almost certain to be defined by this event,' said Carl Weinberg, chief economist for High Frequency Economics.'"[3]

■ "The insurers expect huge claims. Some of them estimated yesterday that they may end up paying $30 billion to $40 billion, or at least twice as much as in the worst previous insurance disaster in the United States, Hurricane Andrew in 1992. These payments would include coverage for the cost of the World Trade Center itself, for those who died and for extra expenses and lost income for individual businesses."[4]

■ Reactions from around the world reflected the tragedy: NATO invoked a mutual defense clause with the 19-member alliance for the first time; "an armed attack" against any of the allies in Europe or North America "shall be considered an attack against them all." Britain, France, Israel, the West Bank and Gaza, Syria, South Africa, Nigeria, North Korea, Russia, and other countries, in addition to the United Nations, the World Bank, and the World Trade Organization, joined in condemning this act of terrorism and in offering condolences for the victims and different forms of assistance.[5]

■ "'The notion of business as usual in America is suspended until further notice,' says Ian Mitroff, crisis management consultant. . . . 'This is a case where emotions have to take precedence over profits.'"[6]

■ "[M]ultinational corporations that do business in the [Middle East] said they were making sure that their employees were safe. But few plan to remove Americans working in the Mideast or make changes to their business. Still, as the Bush administration prepares to respond to what officials have called an act of war, companies operating in nations that may have sheltered, supported or fostered the people behind the attacks could face pressure from customers or from Washington to pull out."[7] Some of the companies that do business in the Middle East and that may be affected include Exxon Mobil, Chevron, Fluor (a multinational construction firm), Credit Suisse First Boston, Colgate-Palmolive, Procter & Gamble, Gillette, Coca-Cola, and Unilever. Multinationals are sometimes pressured to take a moral position, as well as a political and business position, and decide whether or not to leave a country during times of war or other highly charged controversies or crises, such as the killings in China's Tiananmen Square in 1989 or during South Africa's apartheid policy.

Different nation-states and regional stakeholders will be engaged in this continuing political crisis—"war," according to President Bush—which may require years to resolve. The economic, cultural, environmental, and human benefits and costs will be determined as events unfold.

This chapter continues by defining globalization and the changes driving this process. The competitiveness of global companies is then discussed, followed by a presentation of the "different faces of capitalism" across regions. Multinational corporations (MNCs) as stakeholders, MNC and host-country relationships, and issues related to these relationships are presented. We conclude by identifying international decision-making methods from a stakeholder management perspective.

GLOBALIZATION AND THE FORCES OF CHANGE

Globalization involves the integration of technology, markets, politics, cultures, labor, production, and commerce. Globalization is both the process and the result of this integration. The global economy is estimated at $33 trillion. While globalization has facilitated economic growth over several decades, this process is also vulnerable to the forces in the environment discussed above and in Chapter 1 and has experienced sluggish growth at the turn of the new millennium.[8] The most recent threat to economic stability and growth is global terrorism. Nevertheless, the technological, cultural, production, and political factors to date, along with the forces summarized below, continue to drive the globalization process. Some of the forces that have accelerated globalization include the following:

- The end of communism has allowed the opening of closed economies.
- Information technologies and the Internet have accelerated communication and productivity within and across companies globally. Today it is fairly easy for any company to globalize using the Internet.

GLOBAL
BRAINPOWER

"At 23, Naren is on the fast track. A recent computer science graduate from one of the best schools in India, Naren is a hotshot programmer at Bangalore-based Infosys Technologies Ltd. . . . Programmers like Naren, 'twentysomething' and ambitious, are hotter than Indian curry in a market that can't seem to churn them out fast enough. Starting salaries average $4,500 a year, high by Indian standards, but about one-tenth of what comparable U.S. programmers earn. With a relatively small market, at around $500 million a year, India's software business is mushrooming. . . . And in a survey of Indian information technology companies, 42% expect India's worldwide market share to grow to six times its current size in the next three to five years. It is no longer only the low-end legacy system jobs that are migrating to such countries as India. Work involving relational databases, C++, computer-aided software engineering tools, object-oriented programming, multimedia, networking and some niche market applications are starting to go over

the satellite to India. In some cases, U.S. companies are shipping all their development work overseas."[1]

"[India's] universities and technical training institutes churn out an estimated 178,000 qualified software engineers every year. If they practiced their trade at home, India's shortage of programmers—estimated at 145,000 and growing—would be wiped out within a few months. . . . Every year, some 15% of India's experienced software engineers pack their bags to chase opportunities in America, the UK, Germany, France, Italy, Australia, Japan, and the Middle East. . . . Fully four out of every 10 Indian software developers are now working in the U.S. . . ."[2]

NOTES

1. Moshavi, S. (1994). Selling shares in India Inc. *Business Week* (Special Issue), 60.

2. Kapoor, S. (Dec. 15, 2000). Subcontinental drift: India's I.T. aspirations are threatened as prized engineers emigrate. *AsiaWeek: Technology Trends*, 1.

■ Entrepreneurship and entrepreneurs are more mobile, skilled, intelligent, and thriving worldwide, as the "Global Brain Power" feature box indicates.

■ Free trade and trading agreements among nations open borders: among them are the European Union (EU)—(see Figure 7.1 for a list of these countries); the North American Free Trade Agreement (NAFTA), which encourages large and small businesses to operate in Canada and Mexico; the Association of Southeast Asian Nations (ASEAN), which helps emerging companies to compete with European and U.S. firms; and the World Trade Organization (WTO), which accepted China starting in 2002 and which provides a framework that "creates stability and predictability so that investors can, with more security, plan their activity. . . ."[9] Global trade has tripled over the past 25 years.

FIGURE 7.1	15 EUROPEAN UNION COUNTRIES

- The World Bank and the International Monetary Fund (IMF) offers a conduit for needed capital to flow to countries participating in building the global economy.
- As they grow and spread, transnational firms also open new markets and create local employment across the globe. International

professionals with industry experience are running U.S. companies such as General Electric, British Petroleum Amoco, Ford, Gerber, Coca-Cola, and Heinz, to name only a few.

■ A shift to service economies and knowledge workers using technologies has also propelled innovation and productivity worldwide.

■ Global political forces have, until the World Trade Center attack, contributed to peace and economic stability. "Global terrorism," international foreign policy, and responses to such acts can disrupt and slow economic and business growth. Acts on the scale of the World Trade Center attack represent multidimensional underlying problems that involve economic, political, social, and ethical issues.[10] There were 423 terrorist attacks in 2000—200 hundred directed at the United States—compared with 392 total attacks in 1999. The U.S. State Department lists over 40 terrorist groups in the world, ranging from Europe to the Middle East, Philippines, and Japan.[11]

An estimated 40,000 to 100,000 multinational companies are doing business across national boundaries and contributing to the global economy. It is likely these numbers will increase. Where there are new markets, companies will be created and go.[12]

GLOBALIZATION: MANAGING COMPETITIVENESS

Michael Bonsignore, former CEO of Honeywell, describes the "global connectivity" underlying his firm's 85 years of operating experience in 100 countries in the box on page 261. Honeywell's 120,000 employees, carrying on 13 global lines of business with over $24 billion in sales, succeed, he states, because ". . . we've made it our business to also understand our markets, our people, our customers and the countries and cultures in which we operate." Bonsignore emphasizes the social issues and diversity of stakeholders involved in managing competitiveness and social responsibility globally.

Small and large companies like Honeywell must maintain competitiveness to grow and be profitable. Sustaining shareholder value in the global economy is a responsibility of global firms. As Bonsignore notes, "Global corporations exist first and foremost as profit-making ventures. . . . Having said that, we see that one of the by-products of economic globalization is the movement toward more open societies that value the power of the individual."

Some of the major competitive success factors driving firms like Honeywell in the global economy include these:

1. The best talent is recruited at all levels in a company locally and globally.

2. High-quality, innovative products are designed, manufactured, and delivered to world markets at competitive costs. An example is Dell Computer's integrated model of collapsing the supply and value

MICHAEL BONSIGNORE, FORMER CEO OF HONEYWELL

"If I am an internationalist—and I am—it is in part, because Honeywell has been operating in the international arena for more than 85 years. I spent a number of years in Brussels as president of Honeywell Europe. I've also traveled to nearly all of the 100 countries in which Honeywell does business. . . . Our recent merger with AlliedSignal has created a diverse global enterprise of 120,000 employees doing business around the world with sales of nearly $24 billion last year. . . . As our integration took place, we formed 13 distinct global lines of business that develop, manufacture and distribute products and provide services to customers worldwide. . . . And like most companies that understand both the value and price of globalization, we're succeeding because we've made it our business to also understand our markets, our people, our customers and the countries and cultures in which we operate. . . . There is a profound game changer challenging Honeywell and every corporation today that I call global connectivity. . . . In the 'physics' of globalization, for every action there is now a chain reaction of consequences—much like this Rubik's cube. Each move we make affects another block, another pattern, another side. Likewise, a business decision in one country can affect a worker, a market, a government or a culture a world away. . . . Every global stakeholder from the smallest government to the largest labor union to the loudest street protester is part of this chain reaction linked through trade, tradition, and, now, technology. . . . I also believe, however, that the world's stakeholders are not nearly as far apart as it might seem at times. Listen to these two quotes, 'Ending child prostitution, slavery, debt bondage, pornography is one of the most urgent demands of our times.' And the second, 'Children must not be subjected to slavery, bondage, prostitution, drug trafficking and extremely hazardous forms of work'. . . . So, let me propose three actions that may help us do a Brief Manifesto for Global Economic Engagement. First, let us commit to a social compact for global prosperity. Social issues like health, education, the environment, and the growing gap between rich and poor create their own chain reactions that impact governments, markets, and global companies just as they impact individuals. . . . [I]f business is to play this essential social role, it must do so in the proper environment, which brings me to the second point of this Manifesto. Governments must assure an ethical and accountable global economic environment. . . . They must demand transparency and accountability from all stakeholders—business, labor, NGOs [non-governmental organizations] and themselves. . . . The third challenge in this manifesto is movement toward more open, free market societies. Global corporations exist first and foremost as profit-making ventures. . . . Having said that, we see that one of the by-products of economic globalization is the movement toward more open societies that value the power of the individual."

SOURCE: "Global connectivity: For every action there is a chain reaction" by Michael Bonsignore in *Vital Speeches of the Day*, July 15, 2000, volume 66(19), pp. 603-606. Reprinted by permission of City News Publishing and Michael Bonsignore, former CEO, Honeywell International.

chain from customer order to on-demand production of product and delivery.

3. Just-in-time manufacturing allows the transformation of innovative ideas into commodities. Robotics, computer-aided design, materials management, and flexible manufacturing technologies also keep inventories down, while decreasing error rates and increasing profit.

4. Web-based technologies connect customers with products, reducing transaction costs and product delivery time. Ford's Web-based extranet cuts costs and facilitates suppliers' and vendors' bidding for service contracts without going through middle managers. Web-based technologies also facilitate collaboration, commerce, and productivity among buyers, sellers, customers, employees, and teams within and between companies. B2B (business-to-business), B2C (business to customers), and C2C (customers to customers) technological exchanges eliminate overhead and grow and expand business's reach.

5. The new product patents and innovation that result when firms proactively use their local industrial infrastructures and resources (suppliers, related companies, research universities, and scientific, technical and managerial capital) enable regional and global competitive advantage.[13]

6. Mergers, acquisitions, and strategic alliances between multinational and national firms increase the reach and scope of services and products across geographies. Mergers and acquisitions (M&As) reached a new record in 2000, having increased for nine consecutive years. M&A volume was 9,566, a 3 percent increase from 1999, with total volume of $1,326 trillion.[14]

Global competitiveness is also enhanced when companies (1) operate on the imperatives of continuous quality improvement, responsiveness, speed, and loose-knit and entrepreneurial structures and (2) collaborate and partner with customers in local markets, global suppliers, competitors, and venture capitalists to access and capture new markets. Gary Hammel and Patricia Seybold, contemporary strategy and marketing experts, argue that the strategy and customer "revolution" involves companies opening themselves to new voices, passions, people, and ideas, while enabling customers to help define and drive solutions that meet their needs.[15]

"SMART GLOBALIZATION"

Some multinationals have experienced notable failures in their attempts to grow big and fast in developing countries. AT&T did not meet its promise of executing 20 ventures in China. Enron Corporation's $4 billion Indian power plant investment also did not work. General Motors' planned Asiawide network of auto plants based on its $1.2 billion plant in Shanghai failed. Moreover, "Exxon, Mobil, Cargill, Freeport-McMorRan, and Royal Dutch/Shell became targets of local uprisings over oil, mining, and other projects in Indonesia, India, and Nigeria."[16] A lesson learned: "Being first and biggest in an emerging market isn't always the best way to conquer it. A better tactic: Learn local cultures—and build a presence carefully Whirlpool, Citibank, and Kodak have pursued global competitive tactics that set a standard for growing in developing nations: (1) Methodically build a presence from the ground up instead of planning megaprojects, takeovers, and acquisitions. Partner with a savvy local business professional who has a factory and build from his or her strengths. (2) Do extensive homework before starting a business in the developing country by consulting with and learning from local stakeholders: entrepreneurs, bureaucrats, government officials, and grassroots social groups. (3) Forget about targeting the richest 10 percent of the global population and then marketing to them. There is an international market of 4 billion people who earn less than $1,500 annually. They are the source of future growth, even though few now can afford a PC, car, or mortgage. (4) Introduce and help stimulate product use with local populations. Hewlett-Packard offers computer literacy programs from Central Asia to Africa—serving commercial and social need programs simultaneously.

Several companies are using "smart globalization" practices. Whirlpool works with local distributors in China. The firm's machines have been modified for local tastes, and its basic models now use 70 percent of the same parts. The company expects that demand abroad will grow 17 percent to 293 million units through 2009, while flattening in the United States. Citibank in Banglalore, India, works with mid-sized companies to establish retail bank accounts for all their employees—from janitors to top officials—with a $22 deposit. A card is issued for accessing cash, getting loans, and paying bills at local ATMs. In three years, the company has gained 200,000 retail customers, while doubling its base in India to $10 million. Noted strategist C. K. Prahalad notes, "The next round of global expansion is as much about imagination as about resources. Putting a billion dollars down does not involve imagination. With the mistakes of the '90s behind them, the winners will approach the world in a smarter way."[17]

WORLD'S MOST ADMIRED COMPANIES: BEST PRACTICES

The Hay Group annually produces a peer-interviewed and -ranked list of the world's most admired firms for *Fortune* Magazine. Hay Group vice presidents Mel Stark and William Alper led this survey in 2000. The top 25 companies, listed below, were ranked on "best practices" of global competitiveness. Overall, the survey results showed that the most admired companies (1) set more challenging goals, (2) link executive compensation more closely to the completion of the goals, and (3) are more oriented toward long-term performance.[18] *Fortune* Magazine's list of the 25 "World's Most Admired Companies" for 2000, as compared to 1999, includes:

1. General Electric (ranked 1 in 1999)
2. Cisco Systems (8)
3. Microsoft (2)
4. Intel (4)
5. Wal-Mart Stores (7)
6. Sony (14)
7. Dell Computer (9)
8. Nokia (N/A)
9. Home Depot (20)
10. Toyota Motor (16)
11. Southwest Airlines (22)
12. Lucent Technologies (11)
13. Goldman Sachs Group (N/A)
14. Berkshire Hathaway (5)
15. Coca-Cola (3)
16. Charles Schwab (3)
17. Johnson & Johnson (17)
18. Citigroup (25)
19. Ford Motor (15)
20. Pfizer (13)
21. Merck (10)
22. Walt Disney (21)
23. American Express (19)
24. United Parcel Services (39)
25. Enron (N/A)

The other significant practices of these companies include the following:

- While 80 percent of the companies surveyed use profits as a measure of their success, these firms use broader, return-based methods of measurement—that is, equity, capital, assets, and shareholder value—more than their peers were likely to use. Most admired companies are more likely to measure their performance on customer- and employee-based measurements than peers. These measurements focus on growth, customer loyalty, and collaboration. "Almost 60% of the Most Admired Companies rely on customer indicators like satisfaction, loyalty, and market share. Only 38% of their peers do. And 40% of Most Admired Companies chart retention, career development, and other employee-oriented measurements; that's more than triple the percentage of companies that didn't make the list."[19]

- Senior leaders in these firms were more involved in goal-setting activities than their counterparts in other companies. Ninety percent of CEOs participated in goal setting in the most admired companies, compared with 71 percent at other firms. Also, 27 percent of the boards of directors were involved in goal-setting activities in these firms, compared with 15 percent in peer organizations. These results indicate that a wider range of stakeholder concerns is involved in goal-setting activities than just financial performance—for example, human concerns, shareholder value, employees, and customers.

- British Oil BP Amoco charts the progress of its "people" in qualitative performance measurements that include innovation, mutual trust and respect, teamwork, and diversity.

Globalization, then, has been created and sustained by the expansion and integration of markets, information technologies (especially the Internet), competitive company practices, production methods, and the forces described earlier. Standards of living have been increased, jobs created, new products and patents introduced, and cross-border capital and money flows expanded.

Not all regions and countries have been winners in the globalization process. The countries of the First World—the more advanced industrialized countries—have reaped the major benefits, that is, higher standards of living and increased trade, gross national product (GNP), and gross domestic product (GDP). Singapore, Hong Kong, Taiwan, Korea, India, and several Latin American countries are integrating into the global economy as well. The Second World countries—former communist nations under the previous Soviet Union and China—continue to struggle out of their planned economies. The poorest Third World countries, which include all of sub-Saharan Africa and much of the Middle East, South Asia, and Central and South America, continue to struggle with poverty. Criticisms of globalization are discussed below.

Issues with Globalization: The Dark Side

It is difficult to determine whether the process of globalization is the cause or effect of the forces driving this phenomenon. The process of globalization may be producing "losers" (i.e., countries that cannot share in the wealth- and health-generating processes, activities, and outcomes of globalization because they are either excluded from or ignored with respect to the positive side of globalization—for example, technology development and use, education, and economic development).

Critics generally argue that globalization has caused, or at least enhanced, the following problems: crime and corruption; drug consumption; massive layoffs that occur when companies move to regions that offer cheaper labor; decreases in wages; the erosion of individual nations' sovereignty; and the Westernization (led by Americanization) of culture, standards, and trends in entertainment, fashion, food, technology, move star role models, ways of living, and values. We will discuss some of these issues related and attributed to globalization.

CRIME AND CORRUPTION. "In Eastern Europe, traffickers ship girls through the Balkans and into sex slavery. Russians launder money through tiny Pacific islands that have hundreds of banks but scarcely any roads. Colombian drug barons accumulate such vast resources that they can acquire a Soviet submarine to ship cocaine to the United States. . . . [I]t is clear that the globalization of crime is a logical outcome of the fall of Communism. Capitalism and Communism, ideologies that served as intellectual straitjackets for Americans and Soviets allowed them to feel justified in unsavory proxies to fight their cold war."[20] The Global Trends 2015 Report estimates that corruption costs $500 billion annually, 1 percent of the global economy. The report also stated that in the illegitimate economy, narcotics trafficking has projected annual revenues of $100 to $300 billion. Auto theft in Europe and the United States is estimated to net $9 billion, and the sex slave business projects $7 billion. Every third cigarette exported is sold on the black market.[21] The Corruption Perception Index—based on the perceptions of ordinary citizens, business leaders, and experts and developed by the nonprofit group Transparency International—shows that the most corrupt countries in 2001 were Bangladesh, Nigeria, Uganda, Indonesia, Kenya, Cameroon, and Bolivia. The United States moved down to 17th place. Almost two-thirds of the countries scored less than 5 from a "clean" 10 score. See Figure 7.2 for recent survey results of the global country corruption index. Interesting to note that some of the industrialist leading nations did not rank at the top for non-corrupt activities.

ECONOMIC POVERTY AND CHILD SLAVE LABOR. "Among countries, the big losers are in Africa, south of the Sahara. They are not losing, however, because they are being crushed by globalization. . . . [T]hey are losing because they are being ignored by globalization. They are not in the *global economy*. No one in the global business community wants anything to do with countries where illiteracy is high, where modern infrastructure (telecommunications, reliable electrical power) does not exist, and where social chaos reigns. Such countries are neither potential markets nor potential production bases."[22] The gap in per capita GDP between the richest and poorest countries in the world is about 140:1. This gap will increase as the shift from industrial- to knowledge-based economies continues to occur. "Any Third World country that wants the benefits of globalization has to get itself organized to acquire those technologies."[23]

Regions of the Ivory Coast of Africa (e.g., Logbogba, Sinfra, Soubre) continue to attract child labor traffickers (those who buy, enslave, and sell children to work on industrial projects and plantations, like cocoa and chocolate production). Annual wages paid for children under the age of 14 are around US $135 to US $165. Poverty is dire in this region. A broad UNICEF estimate is that there are 200,000 children worldwide who are victims of traffickers every year. Ivory Coast law permits children over 14 to work if the work is not dangerous and they have parental consent.[24]

The Third World includes not only all of sub-Saharan Africa, but also most of the Middle East and much of South Asia and Central and South America. "Hunger is common; disease is rampant; infant mortality is high; life expectancy is short."[25] Notable economists from the Group of Eight (leading industrial countries) conclude that solutions to Third World poverty must include ". . . systematic attempts to change incentives at every level in the global system—from the gangsterish Third World governments that exploit their citizens to the international institutions that prop them up through continued lending."[26]

THE GLOBAL DIGITAL DIVIDE. The world is being dividing by technology. One-third of the world's population is disconnected from and has no access to the Internet. This fact continues to broaden the divide between the have's

FIGURE 7.2	THE 2001 CORRUPTION PERCEPTION INDEX*

Rank	Country	Score	Rank	Country	Score
1	Finland	9.9	34	Slovenia	5.2
2	Denmark	9.5	35	Uruguay	5.1
3	New Zealand	9.4	36	Malaysia	5.0
4	Iceland	9.2	37	Jordan	4.9
5	Singapore	9.2	38	Lithuania	4.8
6	Sweden	9.0	39	South Africa	4.8
7	Canada	8.9	40	Costa Rica	4.5
8	Netherlands	8.8	41	Mauritius	4.5
9	Luxembourg	8.7	42	Greece	4.2
10	Norway	8.6	43	South Korea	4.2
11	Australia	8.5	44	Peru	4.1
12	Switzerland	8.4	45	Poland	4.1
13	United Kingdom	8.3	46	Brazil	4.0
14	Hong Kong	7.9	47	Bulgaria	3.9
15	Austria	7.8	48	Croatia	3.9
16	Israel	7.6	49	Czech Republic	3.9
17	United States	7.6	50	Colombia	3.8
18	Chile	7.5	51	Mexico	3.7
19	Ireland	7.5	52	Panama	3.7
20	Germany	7.4	53	Slovak Republic	3.7
21	Japan	7.1	54	Egypt	3.6
22	Spain	7.0	55	El Salvador	3.6
23	France	6.7	56	Turkey	3.6
24	Belgium	6.6	57	Argentina	3.5
25	Portugal	6.3	58	China	3.5
26	Botswana	6.0	59	Ghana	3.4
27	Taiwan	5.9	60	Latvia	3.4
28	Estonia	5.6	61	Malawi	3.2
29	Italy	5.5	62	Thailand	3.2
30	Namibia	5.4	63	Dominican Republic	3.1
31	Hungary	5.3	64	Moldova	3.1
32	Trinidad & Tobago	5.3	65	Guatemala	2.9
33	Tunisia	5.3	66	Philippines	2.9

continued

FIGURE 7.2	CONTINUED

Rank	Country	Score	Rank	Country	Score
67	Senegal	2.9	80	Pakistan	2.3
68	Zimbabwe	2.9	81	Russia	2.3
69	Romania	2.8	82	Tanzania	2.2
70	Venezuela	2.8	83	Ukraine	2.1
71	Honduras	2.7	84	Azerbaijan	2.0
72	India	2.7	85	Bolivia	2.0
73	Kazakhstan	2.7	86	Cameroon	2.0
74	Uzbekistan	2.7	87	Kenya	2.0
75	Vietnam	2.6	88	Indonesia	1.9
76	Zambia	2.6	89	Uganda	1.9
77	Cote d'Ivoire	2.4	90	Nigeria	1.0
78	Nicaragua	2.4	91	Bangladesh	0.4
79	Ecuador	2.3			

*The lower the ranking, the less corruption.

SOURCE: "U.S. Rank Drops in Latest Corruption Perception Index" from Business & Management Practices. Reprinted with permission from Transparency International.

and the have-not's and between the First and Third World countries. Less than 1 percent of on-line users live in Africa. Less than 5 percent of computers are connected to the Internet in developing countries. The developed world has almost 50 phone lines for every 100 people, compared to 1.4 phones per 100 people in low-income countries. Countries excluded from the global economy are those that cannot and do not build access to the Internet. Wireless technologies offer encouraging signs for Third World country access to First World technologies.[27]

WESTERNIZATION (AMERICANIZATION) OF CULTURES. Globalization has brought "Americanization" (some critics say imperialism) to other cultures through fast food commerce (McDonald's, the *Fast Food Nation* phenomenon discussed in Chapter 5, and Starbucks, for starters). The Internet has brought instant exposure to all forms of American culture: entertainment, films, news, music, and art. Values and ways of living underlie these influences and are not welcome in many countries—France, China, Singapore, and countries in the Middle East to name a few.

"Affluenza" is a society's "sickness," a "disease" experienced through materialistic overconsumption.[28] Countries like the United States can experience affluenza from so much economic prosperity and access to products and services. Compared to poorer countries, and even some European countries, the U.S. consumption of energy, food, housing space, and other indicators of standard of living is questionable according to critics of globalization.

The World Trade Center attack emphasized America's image and influence abroad, particularly in the Middle East. Journalists and the media asked, "Who Hates the U.S.? Who Loves It?"[29] One article noted, "Take Iran. In the 1960s the writer Jalal Al-e Ahmad identified what he called a cultural 'illness' that had stricken the country's cities and towns. He coined a new word to describe it: gharbzadegi—'Westsicken-ness,' or 'Westoxication.' He mourned the villager who 'in search of work flees from the village to the town so he can drink Pepsi-Cola and eat a five-rial sandwich and see a Brigette Bardot film. . . .' Two decades later, the elimination of 'Westoxication' was a central goal of Ayatollah Ruhollah Khomeini. Now Osama bin Laden is accusing Saudi Arabia of becoming Westoxicated by allowing American military forces on its soil."[30] The article continued: "An important feature of this complicated landscape is a broad chasm between the way Americans see themselves and the way they are seen. . . . A good deal of the struggle is over something that has long troubled traditional societies: the invasion of their cultures by powerful outside influences, forces like social mobility and cosmopolitan thinking that can undermine the authority of clans and religious elders, kings and dictators. Americans sometimes call the new influences freedom. Older societies have other names."[31]

LOSS OF NATION-STATE SOVEREIGNTY. Critics are protesting that globalization also erodes the ability of governments to protect the interests of their citizens against more powerful multinational corporations. At conflict are the benefits of economic globalization and the laws and institutions within these nations' own boundaries. Part of the debate centers around the argument that market forces are global and must be dealt with by global businesses.

There is also tension over sovereignty between nations and multinationals regarding power and influence. An example is the rejection of the proposed merger between General Electric and Honeywell by the European Commission's antitrust authorities. The merger, it was argued, would have left public interest behind, since these companies bring different legal and regulatory traditions across the Atlantic. Questions raised included, "What right does the European Commission have telling two American companies what they can and cannot do . . . especially when its decision conflicts with the decision reached by the relevant American authority? Sure, [the United States] supports the rule of law, but whose law? Aren't [U.S.] antitrust laws, which reflect our strong market tradition, superior to Europe's, which tend to reflect a strong statist tradition?"[32]

These arguments diminish when evidence is provided that multinationals do not, cannot, and do not claim to protect citizens during wars and regional conflicts; collect taxes; distribute benefits; build roads and infrastructure; care for the environment; or protect the rights of individuals, groups, and the elderly. In fact, governments subsidize and support companies when needed. The terrorist attack on the World Trade Center left the U.S. airlines with an estimated $4.88 billion loss for the month of September. The Congress supplied a $15 billion bailout package to alleviate this loss. Other industries (e.g., railroad, automobile, agribusiness, aerospace) have also been subsidized by government funds. Still, it is argued that ". . . globalization will continue to chip away at the power of the nation state. As the Europeans know from their experience over the last 50 years, surrendering some degree of national autonomy is a natural and inevitable concomitant of growing economic interdependence."[33] The degree to which nation-states share and/or give up power, influence, and sovereignty to global companies —and the types of power, influence, and sovereignty they do give up or share—is and will be a continuing subject of debate. The subject of the power and influence of global capitalism, discussed below, is in part related to the debate on globalization.

7.2 CAPITALISM: ONE SYSTEM WITH DIFFERENT FACES

Capitalism is a worldwide system.[34] Multinationals, for example, operate in that system without complete regard for traditional political, economic, or social boundaries. The economies of capitalist nations are intricately interconnected through the processes of globalization, discussed above, even though their systems of capitalism vary.

Capitalism can be defined as an economic system whose major portion of production and distribution is in private hands, operating under what is termed a *profit* or *market system*. Key components and features of capitalism follow:

1. *Companies.* Capitalism permits the creation of companies or business organizations that exist separately from the people associated with them. Large companies such as Exxon, AT&T, Ford, and IBM are, in fact, incorporated businesses, or corporations.

2. *Profit motive.* A second characteristic of capitalism lies in the primary motive of companies and other capitalists: to make a profit. The profit motive implies and reflects a critical assumption about human nature: Human beings are basically economic creatures who recognize and are motivated by their financial self-interests.

3. *Competition.* Capitalism and competition are interchangeable concepts. Competition keeps the prices of desired goods from escalating and discourages individual greed. Although capitalism generally has been regarded as a monolithic system, evidence shows that with the end of communism, several forms of capitalism are emerging.[35]

The Faces of Global Capitalism

From the 1760s to the 1830s, steam engines, textile mills, and the Enlightenment drove the Industrial Revolution. The years between 1880 and 1930 were shaped by the spread of electric power, mass production, and democracy. The twenty-first century has already brought simultaneous upheavals in politics, technology, and economics and the development of different forms of international capitalism. Underlying these unprecedented changes lies one powerful idea: openness and increasing transparency. Many governments are pursuing liberal economic policies. Multinational corporations are accelerating the exchange of innovations across open borders. Global investors are pressuring companies to open their books. Populations are generally demanding stronger political and civil rights, with the exception of those authoritarian societies that are controlled by extreme fundamentalist ideologies that support closed societies.

On a global scale, freer trade encourages growth by providing entrepreneurs from major economies with access to larger markets, as discussed earlier. Open trade also spurs the growth of new technologies and manufacturing techniques. General Electric operates factories and power plants in Mexico and India. Microsoft and other high-tech and software firms receive nearly 50 percent of their revenue from international sales. Xerox adopted its Japanese division's technology for designing and manufacturing copying machines in the United States and used this alignment to distribute products in Japan. Emergent systems of international capitalism are developing, and some are experimental. These systems are being documented and studied. They will evolve as trade, global economies, politics, technologies, and strategic business alliances change. Figure 7.3 illustrates four emerging international types of capitalism.

The four "faces of capitalism" discussed next are consumer, frontier, producer, and family capitalism. These forms of capitalism are absolute models; they require additional research and validation. This section is presented to stimulate further discussion and investigation of the evolution of capitalism across regions and countries.

Consumer Capitalism. Consumer capitalism is represented by the United States, Britain, Canada, and Australia and can be characterized as having a laissez-faire, profit-oriented ideology. Competition is also a central driving element of this form of capitalism. Governments generally take a hands-off approach to regulating business, although their involvement depends on the political party in power and economic conditions. For example, the government's role in Canada's economic system differs from that in the United States. The U.S. system currently appears more seamless with regard to its trade boundaries.

The downsides of consumer capitalism include institutionalized income inequality, typically low savings rates, and a weak central government, although this characteristic depends on the country. It is interesting to note that before the so-called dot-com crash, consumer capitalism in the United States

FIGURE 7.3   THE GLOBAL FACES OF CAPITALISM

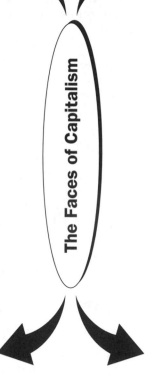

Consumer Capitalism

U.S., Britain, Canada, Australia

Traits: Laissez-faire, open borders, small government, profit mentality

Potential problems: income inequality, low savings rate, weak central governments

Producer Capitalism

Germany, France, Japan, Mexico

Traits: Emphasizes production, employment, statist policies

Potential problems: Fraying of social safety net, slowing innovation, consumer dissatisfaction

The Faces of Capitalism

Family Capitalism

Taiwan, Malaysia, Thailand, Indonesia

Traits: Created by Chinese diaspora, extended clans dominate business and capital flows

Potential problems: Creating modern corporate organizations and money markets

Frontier Capitalism

China, Russia

Traits: Government pursues for-profit business activities, entrepreneurial class sprouts

Potential problems: Must establish rule of law and open borders, curb criminality

SOURCE: From "The Triple Revolution" by Christopher Farrell. Reprinted from the 1994 issue of *Business Week*, Special McGraw-Hill Companies Bonus Issue, 16, by special permission. Copyright © 1994 by The McGraw-Hill Companies, Inc.

was also termed "IPO (initial public offering) capitalism." The IPO markets in the early to mid-1990s helped fuel innovations that continue to transform the U.S. economy into one of the world's productivity powerhouses. Forces behind the technologically driven IPO capitalism are risk-taking entrepreneurs and attractive Internet, software, and wireless technologies. Backing these entrepreneurs are some of the most sophisticated capital markets in the world. Since the dot-com crash, venture capital continues to drive innovative new company growth, but not with the previous irrational exuberance, when investment money chased new ideas without regard to sound profit projections.

Innovators also are reshaping old-line industries, such as the airline, steel, telecommunications, and retailing industries. Web-based enterprise software applications are combining "bricks and mortar" with "clicks and mortar" technologies that streamline operations and enhance productivity. New business models that drive new products and markets continue to shape American and global capitalism.

A downside of the IPO aspect of consumer capitalism is "boom and bust" economic cycles that create jobs and economic opportunities quickly and then result in a disappearance (or transformation) of growth into layoffs, dips, and crashes in financial markets, as we have recently experienced.

FRONTIER CAPITALISM. Frontier capitalism is a new, experimental, and entrepreneurial system of economic activity. China and Russia are evolving these systems of capitalism from former communist ideologies. Rules, infrastructures, and discipline are at first absent, but develop with experience. Frontier capitalism has emerged in stretches of the former Soviet Union, China, parts of Latin America, and Vietnam. Corruption and criminal activity are often rampant; violence erupts regularly; legal systems are weak; and scams abound. The risks to life and limb are present. The winnings can be great for those willing to take these risks, but danger awaits those who take uncalculated risks.

Sustained growth in these systems requires more than reckless risk taking. Eventually, frontier economies need large capital infusions from outsiders, individual investors, corporations, and banks. To make the leap to the next stage of growth, these economies have to begin "civilizing." That is, they have to put in place an array of laws and institutions ranging from effective judiciaries to functioning financial markets. In the twenty-first century, economies such as Russia's and China's may be well on their way toward making those changes.

Frontier capitalism evolves in the following stages:

Stage one: Statist economies collapse or fade away. Black marketers profit enormously, while some become gangsters. Government corruption spreads.

Stage two: Small-scale entrepreneurs, often financed by family loans, flourish. The rule of law remains weak, but businesspeople start creating their own rules of commerce.

Stage three: Economic growth is brisk, but hard to measure. Financial markets begin to evolve, tapping savings and attracting foreign institutional investors. Clearer legal codes appear.

PRODUCER CAPITALISM. Producer capitalism is based on controlled production, employment, and statist policies governed by top-down central bureaucracies. Countries such as France and Japan symbolize producer capitalism. In France, the Ecole Nationale d'Administration is an institution of more than 100 students. It is the training ground for the brightest technocrats, who run ministries, manage companies, and in general run the centralized economy. Many of France's leaders of producer capitalism were educated in this institution.

France's "hypereducated" technocrats realize that the statist system has become a serious economic handicap. The state has wasted resources on ill-conceived ventures in computers and high-definition television. The state's overbearing role is also a constraint for potential foreign partners. For example, Renault's planned merger with Sweden's Volvo was a casualty of France's rigid system of doing business.

The French practice of blurring the line between public and private is under intense attack. A series of investigations is probing corruption at the highest level of French public life. Nonetheless, economic efficiency is gradually replacing political goals in France's economy. Socialist leaders began the change in the 1980s by introducing the profit motive at state companies, a revolutionary notion at places such as Renault, whose raison d'être has been to provide jobs.

Producer capitalism, unlike consumer capitalism, can be a rigid system. "Customer focus" is not at the center of supply and demand. Producers and corporations determine price, quantity, availability, and access to consumer markets and products.

FAMILY CAPITALISM. Family capitalism is found in Taiwan, Malaysia, Thailand, Indonesia, and to some extent Japan. Japan's *keiretsu* (corporate structure) system is actually an outgrowth of family capitalism, a system in which extended families and clans bond together into interlocking cross-company and industry networks to provide capital, investment, and resources and to share risk in order to grow wealth and business opportunities. The Japanese system has also been described as "alliance capitalism."[36] Like the *chaebols* (conglomerates) in South Korea, Japan's *keiretsu* represent a sophisticated outgrowth of what started as family and informal networks. Japan's integration into the global economy is progressing. International firms are entering and doing business in Japan.

In family capitalism, the family and clan elders traditionally set the interwoven business, cultural, social, and infrastructural rules that govern the structure and functioning of businesses. Trust, loyalty, blood relationship, and dedication are the glues that bind the business together in this system. A hindrance to this system is the creation of modern companies that need to grow to the next level of globally sophisticated competitors, where blood ties may not be the most advantageous factors in moving ahead. Also, family-based and traditional rules and customs dictate decisions. Lack of openness to innovation and to new alliances can present obstacles to expansion of this form of capitalism. Another downside of this system of capitalism is the possibility of corruption and monopolistic control that excludes innovation and outside influences and invites unlawful activities.

METACAPITALISM

MetaCapitalism is a concept that applies to the massive business and economic transformation resulting from the exponential growth of several factors we have discussed: business-to-consumer, e-business, use of the Internet, globalization of the world economy, reliance on technology for management, and restructuring of companies over the past 20 years.[37] While some claims in Means and Schneider's book *MetaCapitalism* appear overstated, many of the ideas and principles are worth noting. For example, the critical success factors for "winning and growing" in a global MetaCapitalism system cut across the capitalist systems discussed above and may very well represent many of the drivers that promote globalization:

- Strong infrastructure network that is relatively easy to use but requires the political will to liberalize policies and provides easy access for a country's businesses and consumers.

- Local capital markets that are fully integrated into worldwide capital markets and accessible by network from any point globally.

- Low levels of economic nationalism and minimal restrictions on inflow and outflow of goods, information, and services.

- Open internal capital markets through which investment capital can freely flow to ventures providing a high return rate to economies integrated into MetaMarkets. If capital flows are prevented by public policy or cartel-like corporate alliances, MetaCapitalism will be restricted and not occur. "MetaCapitalism is about business, but it is also very powerfully about the interface between government and business—and people's lives and welfare are at stake."[38]

The authors of *MetaCapitalism* predict that those countries "relatively prepared" for MetaCapitalism include the United States, United Kingdom, France, Italy, and Benelux. Those that will have a "difficult transition" include Germany, Japan, China, Indonesia, and Malaysia. Countries that have "major opportunities" include Russia, India, Singapore, Taiwan, and those of Eastern Europe. Countries that have an "uncertain" status are Brazil, Mexico, and Korea.[39] Unfortunately, the authors do not address the ethical, social, or stakeholder side of doing business successfully in a global MetaCapitalist system.

AMERICAN CAPITALISM AND MANAGEMENT

CULTURAL CONTEXT. The United States is a country of countries. Garreau[40] argued that historically and culturally North America is made up of nine nations. As such, the United States is an ethnically diverse society where distinctive traditions and customs coexist and share the following common values: individualism, self-reliance, self-discipline, a Protestant-influenced work ethic, the value of private property, and the belief in fairness and individual rights. Some argue that the Protestant work ethic has undergone significant change. Preoccupation with the self has developed into narcissism, and justice is being defined as fairness.[41]

Individual rights and ownership of private property are at the center of the U.S. value system. The Declaration of Independence focuses on rights as *inalienable.* Ownership of private property reinforces individualism in the social fabric. Americans also value family and collective membership. Group membership, however, is based more on voluntarism than on cultural norms.[42] A distinction, for example, between U.S. and Japanese values is that Japan is essentially a group-oriented culture, whereas American values center on self and individualism. These value differences are reflected in the way U.S. businesses reward and recognize entrepreneurs and inventors. Knowledge as it is patented and protected legally is the private property of the individual, not of the society, as is the case with Japan. In Japan, the individual is not considered the focal point of industrial innovation or success.

SOCIOPOLITICAL AND GOVERNMENTAL CONTEXT. The United States is a pluralistic political and government system. The Constitution grounds ultimate authority in the people and separates power among the executive, legislative, and judicial branches of government. Within this pluralistic system, the government, businesses, and unions share power and solve problems through adversarial relationships. Cooperation continually must be negotiated through advocacy, argument, and special-interest and political-action-group lobbying.

Competition and fragmentation are built into the system, the very infrastructure of government and politics. Federal and state governments compete over the power of budgets, policies, and resources. For example, the national government lacks an industrial policy for the country, so the states develop their own and compete with each other for domestic and foreign investment. Iowa during the 1980s used tax incentives to persuade Japanese auto manufacturers to build and operate along Interstate 75. During that same period, Detroit automakers unsuccessfully lobbied the president to adopt a broad national industrial policy to limit Japanese auto imports and manufacturing in the United States. To compare, while Japan has operated in global markets through a united front of governmental, union, and *keiretsu* cooperation and strategies, the United States has until recently tended to operate in a piecemeal, state-by-state, and corporation-by-corporation manner. More recently, megamergers, acquisitions, and global strategic alliances of U.S.-based and other multinational corporations have blurred corporate, state, regional, and national boundaries.

U.S. CAPITALISM. United States capitalism is based on the ideology of "free-market enterprise." Large corporations in the past have embodied U.S. business wealth and success and therefore have defined the rules of the capitalist system. Such corporations obtain equity capital from private investors and capital markets. These institutions compete among themselves and with the government for funds. Unlike in Japan, U.S. banks are not permitted to buy stock in corporations; this helps to prevent conflicts of interest. Also unlike in Japan, the government is more often than not the watchdog and regulator of business growth and activity—not the strategic partner. The U.S. corporation, then, must depend on the attractiveness of its stock on the open market to survive and succeed.

Because most of the largest corporations sell shares to the public, the stock market defines the health of a firm. The trading price of a company's shares also determines the company's ability to obtain capital and resources to grow and innovate. Corporations, then, walk a tightrope between their debt and equity in their capital structure. "A highly leveraged company is more risk prone and must pay a higher cost for funds unless its growth prospects are phenomenal and investors are willing to assume above-average risks."[43]

Consequently, U.S. corporations are continuously monitored by the public and shareholders. Because it relies on companies' stock trading prices, quarterly earnings reports, and profit-and-loss statements and on financial markets' perceptions of companies, U.S. capitalism is characterized as short-term oriented and price sensitive. For American managers, unlike their Japanese counterparts, this means short-term planning, investing, and strategies are the rules and boundaries managers must operate under. Global competition and the changing nature of international markets represent mixed forms of capitalism.

U.S. MANAGEMENT PRACTICES. The U.S. management system is not a single system. American entrepreneurs have not followed—and probably will not follow—any single set of rules for borrowing, inventing, investing, or doing business. However, a historical background of management systems and thought exists that, again, large and traditional corporations have embodied.

Although entrepreneurial firms differ from larger, older ones and although a variety of management systems and changing styles exist in the United States, certain generalizations still can be made about American management practices because these practices have been historically grounded in the country's dominant value system, sociocultural context, business/ government relationships, and form of capitalism. These generalizations represent a profile of U.S. business practices through the 1980s and mid-1990s, and some still exist:

1. Short-term time, profit, planning, and strategy horizons;
2. Individual decision making, responsibilities, performance, and rewards;
3. Managers who are understood, trained, and treated as professionals separate from but based on a specific knowledge base;
4. Outcomes as a focus over processes, measured and monitored by short-term financial tools;
5. Specialized and vertical career paths;
6. Individual career development.[44]

U.S. management practices also have been greatly influenced by the school of scientific management, proposed by Frederick Taylor (1947). Taylor separated managers from workers and viewed managers as professionals; he articulated a logic for making and maintaining a division of labor and chain of command; he based building organizational structures on carrying out separate tasks; and he defined work and management so that both could be measured and executed "scientifically," in a cost-benefit, compartmentalized, individualistic, and piecemeal way.

The legacy of scientific management is the "stovepipe" organization, with isolated, specialized management functions. The artificial division of worker from manager, the top-down decision making, and the eventual need for unions to advocate benefits for workers alienated from management and economically disadvantaged also were set in motion. Productivity was defined apart from the enterprise's mission and more on an individual piece-rate basis. Attention to process was lost. These components of U.S. management are being ripped apart by global competition and by the changing rules of knowledge technology as it replaces the assembly line.

TWENTY-FIRST CENTURY U.S. CAPITALISM AND MANAGEMENT PRACTICES. Many elements of the U.S. capitalist system described above persist—for example, a short-term emphasis on financially measured corporate growth and returns. Innovation funded by venture capital remains a key ingredient of U.S. capitalism. However, older companies are also incorporating Web-based technologies in order to globalize and extend marketing, sales, and production functions. The U.S. legal system has not substantially changed, although depending on the president and Congress in power, antitrust and other corporate laws can be interpreted and enforced differently. The George W. Bush administration, for example, has shown more laxness in enforcing Microsoft's antitrust findings than the Clinton administration. The U.S. adversarial system of pluralistic competition and governance is still intact. The relationships among governments, businesses, and unions are also still politically adversarial in nature.

FIGURE 7.4	DEMING PRINCIPLES

1. Create constancy of purpose. Strive for long-term improvement more than short-term profits.
2. Adopt the new philosophy. Accept as gospel the need for total quality with no tolerance for delays and mistakes.
3. Cease dependence on mass inspection. Build quality into the process and identify and correct problems early rather than late.
4. End the practice of awarding business on price tag alone. Don't purchase from the cheapest supplier. Build long-term relationships based on loyalty and trust.
5. Improve constantly and forever the system of production and service. At every stage of the process, strive to continually improve and satisfy internal as well as external customers.
6. Institute training and retraining. This includes continual updating and training in statistical methods and thinking.
7. Institute leadership. Remove barriers that prevent employees from performing effectively, and continually provide the resources needed for effectiveness.
8. Drive out fear. People must believe it is safe to report problems or mistakes or to ask for help.
9. Break down barriers among departments. Promote teamwork and communications across departments, and provide common organizational vision.
10. Eliminate slogans, exhortations, and arbitrary targets. Supply methods, not just buzzwords.
11. Eliminate numerical quotas. Quotas place a limit on improvement and are contrary to the idea of continuous improvement.
12. Remove barriers to pride in workmanship. Allow autonomy and spontaneity. Abandon regular performance reviews.
13. Institute a vigorous program of education and retraining. This is similar to point 6 but is meant to highlight a philosophy that people are assets not commodities.
14. Take action to accomplish the transformation. Provide access to top management, an organization structure, and information that allows the other 13 points to be adhered to on a daily basis.

SOURCE: Reprinted from *Out of the Crisis* by W. Edwards Deming by permission of MIT and the W. Edwards Deming Institute. Published by MIT, Center for Advanced Educational Services, Cambridge, MA 02142. Copyright © 1986 by The W. Edwards Deming Institute.

More significant changes have occurred in U.S. management practices. As noted at the outset of the chapter, competitive practices have changed and are accelerated by the following:

- *Information technologies*: These include information and process technologies, implementation of total quality management, continuous improvement, and just-in-time inventory and techniques for getting product ideas to market in one-third less time. The now deceased quality guru Edward Deming lives on through his now classic quality management principles. Figure 7.4 summarizes Deming's principles, which have gained greater importance for knowledge workers using information technologies.

- *"Communities of creation"*: As organizations become more electronically networked, there is an open system for sharing individual knowledge, information, and distributed innovation (research and development) among external and internal groups. IBM and Linux have developed an open, cooperative approach to Web marketing and technology transfer. Communities of expertise are formed through electronic networks to solve problems, innovate, and create new marketing and selling opportunities.[45]

■ *Alliances*: American firms have used mergers and acquisitions, joint ventures, strategic alliances, and consortia to form *keiretsu*-like coalitions and thus to extend their market share and their geographic reach, breadth, and depth. Toyota and General Motors constructed a Chevrolet Nova plant in California. Texas Instruments bought out Sony's share of four major plants in Japan that produced semiconductors. Merck, Eli Lilly, and Bayer have cross-licensing agreements on their newest drugs. These companies share innovations, advertising, and the fixed costs of research and development.[46] *Shared leadership, expertise, virtual collaboration*, and *the creation of customer value* are ingredients for successful alliances. Global teams and leaders are successfully learning to collaborate electronically and face-to-face across geographies. Making strategic alliances work requires focusing on customer value, while sharing knowledge and skills at all levels of expertise.[47]

September 11, 2001: A Turning Point?

While U.S. companies and institutions have experienced long-term success, now the United States and its system of capitalism face perhaps the most significant challenges since the country's founding: Can the country and its institutions effectively cooperate with and integrate their values and practices (economic, political and foreign policy, business, social, technological, and legal) into the religiously, ideologically, and economically diverse regions of the world? This is a question not only for U.S. systems of governance and capitalism, but also for all members of the global community. The September 11 events emphasized that competitiveness is predicated and embedded in ethical, moral, and human values and rights worldwide. First World countries face the challenges of assisting less-wealthy nations and regions in developing economically, educationally, and politically to legitimately compete in the global economy. The dark side of globalization has another face and set of multidimensional realities and issues added. As discussed in Chapter 1, the rules for business engagement are even more pronouncedly interconnected with moral, political, legal, and foreign policy areas.

The next section transitions to a discussion of multinational enterprises as stakeholders in the global environment and in host countries. Since these very large firms extend across national boundaries and are economically stronger than many countries, questions are raised regarding the ethical uses of their power and influence as well as the benefits they produce.

7.3 MULTINATIONAL ENTERPRISES AS STAKEHOLDERS

Multinational enterprises (MNEs) are corporations that "own or control production or service facilities outside the country in which they are based."[48] MNEs also are referred to as global, transnational, and international companies.[49] No distinction is made here among these names.

Companies go global to enhance profit by creating value, building and increasing markets, and reducing costs. Costs are reduced by locating and using raw materials, skilled labor, land, and taxes at lower costs. Value can also be added by joint venturing with other national and regional partners who have market reach, global skills, experience, and resources. Xerox's global strategy in the 1960s took it from a high-cost, low-quality company to a low-cost, higher quality, more innovative firm when it partnered with Fuji to introduce its products in Japan. The joint venture created Fuji Xerox. The Japanese engineers, as it turned out, transformed Xerox's copying machines and manufacturing process in the 1980s. These moves eventually kept the parent Xerox alive, since IBM, Canon, and other competitors had taken market share. Xerox's market share had fallen by over 40 percent.[50]

POWER OF MULTINATIONAL ENTERPRISES

Although MNEs often reflect and extend their home nation's culture and resources, many are powerful enough to act as independent nations. This section focuses on MNEs as independent, powerful stakeholders, using their power across national boundaries to gain comparative advantages, with or without the support of their home country. Common characteristics MNEs share include (1) operating a sales organization, manufacturing plant, distribution center, licensed business, or subsidiary in at least two countries; (2) earning an estimated 25 to 45 percent of revenue from foreign markets; and (3) having common ownership, resources, and global strategies.[51] Since MNEs often span nations, governments, and different types of businesses and markets, their operations are based on a shared network of strategies, information and data, expertise, capital, and resources.[52] MNEs have become the most strategically powerful stakeholders in the race to compete and dominate global industry market shares. "Privately held multinational corporations now represent many of the largest economic entities on Earth, larger than most countries, amounting to about thirteen of the fifty largest economic entities, and about forty-eight of the largest one hundred. Multinational businesses have the ability to avoid or to hamper legal enforcement on certain occasions—by withdrawal or by threatening withdrawal from economically dependent nations."[53] In 1995, almost 70 percent of world trade was controlled by 500 corporations. One percent of all multinationals own half the total stock of foreign direct investment. About one-third of the

FIGURE 7.5	WORLD'S LARGEST COMPANIES				

Search Rank	Company	Revenues ($ millions)	Profits ($ millions)	Assets ($ millions)	Stockholders' Equity ($ millions)	Employees
1	Citigroup	111826.00	13519.00	902210.00	66206.00	237500
2	General Electric	129853.00	12735.00	437006.00	50492.00	341000
3	Bank of America Corp.	57747.00	7517.00	642191.00	47628.00	142724
4	J.P. Morgan Chase	60065.00	5727.00	715348.00	42338.00	98240
5	ING Group	71195.87	11075.20	610407.61	23728.25	92650
6	Exxon Mobil	210392.00	17720.00	149000.00	70757.00	99600
7	HSBC Holdings	48632.77	6632.36	674380.60	45608.41	161624
8	BP	148062.00	11870.00	143938.00	73416.00	107200
9	DaimlerChrysler	150069.70	7295.36	187086.44	39815.27	416501
10	Deutsche Bank	67133.24	4502.53	882540.76	25826.55	98311

$3.3 trillion in goods and services transaction that took place in 1990 occurred with a single firm.[54]

Honeywell, as noted earlier, operates in more than 100 countries and has 120,000 employees and 13 global lines of business with over $24 billion in sales. The world's largest companies are shown in Figure 7.5. They include Citigroup, General Electric, Bank of America, J.P. Morgan, ING Group (Netherlands), Exxon Mobil, HSBC Holdings (UK), BP (UK), Daimler-Chrysler (Germany), and Deutsche Bank (Germany). Note that half of these firms are U.S. based.

Figure 7.6 lists the 10 largest non-U.S. MNEs and their revenues and profits for 2001: DaimlerChrysler A.G., Royal Dutch/Shell Group, BP, Mitsubishi, Toyota, Mitsui & Company, Itochu, Total Fina Elf S.A., Nippon, and AXA. Figure 7.7 lists the top 10 U.S. exporters: Exxon Mobil, General Motors, Ford, General Electric, IBM, AT&T, Verizon, Philip Morris, Boeing, and Hewlett-Packard. Revenues and profits are listed in both figures, illustrating the economic power these preeminent global firms display.

The dominant goal of MNEs is, as noted earlier, to make a profit and take comparative advantage of marketing, trade, cost, investment, labor, and other factors. At the same time, MNEs assist local economies in many ways, as will be explained. The ethical questions critics of MNEs have raised are reflected in the following statement by the late Raymond Vernon, noted Harvard professor and international business expert: "Is the multinational enterprise undermining the capacity of nations to work for the welfare of their people? Is the multinational enterprise being used by a dominant power as a means of penetrating and controlling the economies of other countries?"[55]

FIGURE 7.6	THE 10 LARGEST NON-U.S. MNES	
	Profits ($ millions)	Revenues ($ millions)
1. DaimlerChrysler A.G.	7,295.4 % change from 1999: 19.0	150,069.7 % change from 1999: −6.2
2. Royal Dutch/Shell Group	12,719.0 % change from 1999: 48.2	149,146.0 % change from 1999: 41.6
3. BP	11,870.0 % change from 1999: 137.0	148,062.0 % change from 1999: 77.2
4. Mitsubishi Corporation	833.0 % change from 1999: 256.4	126.579.4 % change from 1999: 7.5
5. Toyota Motor Corporation	4,262.6 % change from 1999: 16.7	121,416.2 % change from 1999: 5.0
6. Mitsui & Company, Ltd.	466.6 % change from 1999: 45.5	118,013.7 % change from 1999: −0.5
7. Itochu Corporation	637.7 % change from 1999: N/A	109,756.5 % change from 1999: 0.6
8. Total Fina Elf S.A.	6,380.4 % change from 1999: 293.5	105,856.6 % change from 1999: 135.3
9. Nippon Telegraph and Telephone Corp.	4,197.3 % change from 1999: N/A	103,234.7 % change from 1999: 10.3
10. AXA	3,607.9 % change from 1999: 67.4	92,781.6 % change from 1999: 5.9

SOURCE: From www.fortune.com, 7/23/01. © 2001 Time Inc. All rights reserved. Reprinted by permission. All companies are identified as either an "international public company" or a "multi-national public company."

The next subsection addresses these questions in a discussion of the mutual responsibilities and expectations of MNEs and their host countries.

MISUSES OF MNE POWER

Crises since the birth of the multinational corporation after World War II have raised international concern over the ethical conduct of MNEs in host and other countries. Most recently, the Ford-Bridgestone/Firestone tire crisis was international in nature. These companies were not forthright early on with their consumers about defects known by the companies. Union Carbide's historic chemical spill disaster in Bhopal, India, resulted in thousands of deaths and injuries and alarmed other nations over the questionable safety standards and controls of MNE foreign operations. Nestle's marketing of its powdered infant milk formula that resulted in the illness and death of a large number of infants in less-developed countries raised questions about the lack of proper product instructions issued to indigent, less-educated consumers. (Nestle's practice resulted in a boycott of the company from 1976 to

FIGURE 7.7	THE TOP 10 U.S. EXPORTERS	
	Profits ($ millions)	**Revenue ($ millions)**
1. Exxon Mobil	17,720.0 % change from 1999: 124.0	210,392.0 % change from 1999: 28.4
2. General Motors	4,452.0 % change from 1999: −25.8	184,632.0 % change from 1999: 4.6
3. Ford Motor	3,467.0 % change from 1999: −52.1	180,598.0 % change from 1999: 11.1
4. General Electric	12,7350.0 % change from 1999: 18.8	129,853.0 % change from 1999: 16.3
5. International Business Machines	8,093.0 % change from 1999: 4.9	88,396.0 % change from 1999: 1.0
6. AT & T	4,669.0 % change from 1999: 36.2	65,981.0 % change from 1999: 5.8
7. Verizon	11,797.0 % change from 1999: 180.8	64,707.0 % change from 1999: 95.1
8. Philip Morris Companies Inc.	8,510.0 % change from 1999: 10.8	63,276.0 % change from 1999: 2.5
9. Boeing	2,128.0 % change from 1999: −7.8	51,321.0 % change from 1999: −11.5
10. Hewlett-Packard	3,697.0 % change from 1999: 5.9	48,782.0 % change from 1999: listed as N/A

SOURCE: From www.fortune.com, 7/23/01. © 2001 Time Inc. All rights reserved. Reprinted by permission.

1984.) Also, the presence of MNEs in South Africa raised criticisms over the role of large corporations in actively supporting apartheid or government-supported racism. Because MNEs had to pay taxes to the South African government and because apartheid was a government-supported policy, MNEs —it is argued—supported racism. Several U.S.-based MNEs that operated in South Africa witnessed boycotts and disinvestments by many shareholders. Many MNEs, including IBM and Polaroid, later withdrew. Post-apartheid South Africa has seen the reentry of companies from all countries. Another long-standing moral issue is the practice of MNEs of not paying their fair share of taxes in countries where they do business and in their home countries. Through transfer pricing and other creative accounting techniques, many MNEs have shown paper losses, thereby enabling them to avoid paying any taxes.

Critics claim that many multinational corporations are not fulfilling their part of the implicit social contract discussed in Chapter 6. Some of these critics include Richard Barnet and John Cavanagh in their book *Global Dreams*, David Korten in *When Corporations Rule the World*, Tom Athanasiou in *Divided Planet: The Ecology of Rich and Poor*, Paul Hawken in *The Ecology of*

Commerce, and William Greider in *One World, Ready or Not*.[56] Multinationals' practices subject to criticism include committing corporate crimes, exerting undue political influence and control, determining and controlling plant closings and layoffs, and damaging the physical environment and human health. Evidence regarding these claims showed, for example, that 11 percent of 1,043 MNEs studied were involved in one or more major crimes over a 10-year period. The crimes included foreign bribery, kickbacks, and improper payments. A small sample of those firms included American Cyanamid, Anheuser-Busch, Bethlehem Steel, Allied Chemical, Ashland Oil, and Beatrice Foods. Large corporations (along with trial lawyers and labor unions) also have immense influence through political action committees (PACs). The organization Common Cause noted that the majority of soft money contributions to both American parties in 1999 came from corporate business interests. With regard to plant closings and "downsizings," critics are concerned that some MNEs are more concerned with a particular profit margin than with their share of responsibility to community and society. After all, taxpayers support roads and other external conditions that allow corporations to operate in a country. While corporations are not expected to be a welfare system for employees, critics note that large companies are expected to share in the social consequences of their actions, especially when, for example, plant-closing decisions are made to reap the benefits of cheaper labor in another country. Finally, there is historical evidence that several large corporations have harmed the physical environment and the health of their employees and local communities. Classic crises cases discussed in Chapter 5 regarding asbestos manufacturing, oil spills, chemical plant explosions, toxic dumping, and industrial air pollution demonstrate corporate misuses of the environment in recent history. The external and human costs that communities, governments, the environment, and taxpayers have had to pay for these misuses of power are documented.

In the following sections, two perspectives regarding global corporations' responsibilities—that of the MNE and that of the host country—are discussed.

MNE PERSPECTIVE

"A rising tide lifts all ships." MNEs enter foreign countries primarily to make profit, but also to create opportunities host countries would not have access to without these companies. While MNEs benefit from international currency fluctuations, available labor at cheaper costs, tax and trade incentives, and the use of natural resources, and gain access to more foreign markets, these companies benefit their host countries through foreign direct investment and in these ways:

- Hire local labor
- Create new jobs
- Co-venture with local entrepreneurs and companies

- Attract local capital to projects
- Provide for and enhance technology transfer
- Develop particular industry sectors
- Provide business learning and skills
- Increase industrial output and productivity
- Intensify competition in the country by introducing new products, services, and ideas
- Help decrease the country's debt and improve its balance of payments and standard of living

Moreover, MNEs open less-developed countries (LDCs) to international markets, thereby helping the local economy attract greatly desired hard currencies. Also, new technical and managerial skills are brought in, and local workers receive training and knowledge. Job and social-class mobility is provided to inhabitants.[57] Some MNEs also establish schools, colleges, and hospitals in their host countries. For example, while Nike has been criticized for its international child labor practices, it is also true that by contracting with factories abroad, it has helped employ over half a million workers in 55 countries. Eighty-three percent of Nike's workforce in Indonesia is women who would not otherwise be employed.[58] Another company, Patagonia Inc., gives 1 percent of its annual sales to environmental groups and gives employees up to two paid months off to work for nonprofit environmental groups. The company also routinely permits independent human rights organizations to audit any of its facilities. The company participates in the Apparel Industry Partnership (AIP) to set standards to expose and monitor inhumane business practices in their industry. Cadbury's is another example of a company that practices high ethical standards abroad. In India, the company hired local workers and instilled new work-related ethical values in its plant.[59]

The MNE must manage overlapping and often conflicting multiple constituencies in its home- and host-country operations. Figure 7.8 illustrates some of the major environments and stakeholder issues the MNE must technically and ethically balance and manage in its foreign location. From the MNE's perspective, managing these stakeholder issues is difficult and challenging, especially as the global economy presents new problems.

MNE executives and other managers also complain of what they consider unethical practices and arbitrary control by host-country governments. For example, local governments can and sometimes do the following:

- Limit repatriation of MNE assets and earnings
- Pressure and require MNEs to buy component parts and other materials from local suppliers
- Require MNEs to use local nationals in upper-level management positions
- Require MNEs to produce and sell selected products in order to enter the country

FIGURE 7.8   MNE STAKEHOLDER MANAGEMENT, ENVIRONMENTAL ISSUES, AND ETHICAL CONCERNS

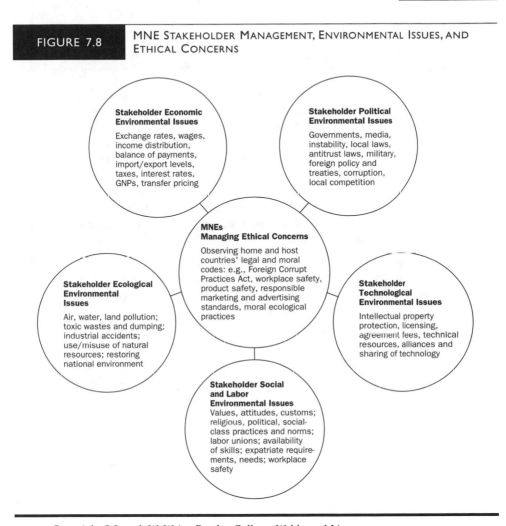

Stakeholder Economic Environmental Issues

Exchange rates, wages, income distribution, balance of payments, import/export levels, taxes, interest rates, GNPs, transfer pricing

Stakeholder Political Environmental Issues

Governments, media, instability, local laws, antitrust laws, military, foreign policy and treaties, corruption, local competition

MNEs Managing Ethical Concerns

Observing home and host countries' legal and moral codes: e.g., Foreign Corrupt Practices Act, workplace safety, product safety, responsible marketing and advertising standards, moral ecological practices

Stakeholder Ecological Environmental Issues

Air, water, land pollution; toxic wastes and dumping; industrial accidents; use/misuse of natural resources; restoring national environment

Stakeholder Technological Environmental Issues

Intellectual property protection, licensing, agreement fees, technical resources, alliances and sharing of technology

Stakeholder Social and Labor Environmental Issues

Values, attitudes, customs; religious, political, social-class practices and norms; labor unions; availability of skills; expatriate requirements, needs; workplace safety

SOURCE: Copyright © Joseph W. Weiss, Bentley College, Waltham, MA.

- Limit imports and pressure exports
- Require a certain amount or percentage of profit to remain in or be invested in the country

Finally, MNEs always face the threat of expropriation or nationalization of their operations by the host government. More recently, MNEs must assume high-stakes risks, liabilities, and responsibilities in the area of safety since September 11, 2001. The airline industry in particular has been hit very hard by this unpredictable crisis. The crisis itself, along with the "fallout" over laxness in safety standards and enforcement, has taken a heavy toll on all U.S. and most international carriers. The price of doing business safely has escalated.

HOST-COUNTRY PERSPECTIVE

Six criticisms of the presence and practices of MNEs in host and other foreign locations are discussed here.

1. MNEs can dominate and protect their core technology and research and development, thus keeping the host country a consumer, not a partner or producer. The Brazilian government, for example, has counteracted this by having entry barriers and laws that, since the 1970s, have protected against the complete control of its own electronics industries by foreign manufacturers. It is also argued (or feared) that Japan's MNEs could in the long term dominate certain critical industries (such as the electronics industry and perhaps the automobile industry) in the United States and use American labor more as assemblers than as technology R&D partners.

2. MNEs can destabilize national sovereignty by limiting a country's access to critical capital and resources, thereby creating a host-country dependency on the MNE's governments and politics.

3. MNEs can create a "brain drain" by attracting scientists, expertise, and talent from the host country.

4. MNEs can create an imbalance of capital outflows over inflows. They produce, but emphasize exports over imports in the host country, thereby leaving local economies dependent on foreign control.

5. MNEs can disturb local government economic planning and business practices by exerting control over the development and capitalization of a country's infrastructure. Also, by providing higher wages and better working conditions, MNEs influence and change a country's traditions, values, and customs. "Cultural imperialism" is imported through business practices.

6. MNEs can destroy, pollute, and endanger host-country and LDC environments and the health of local populations. For example, the mining of and dangerous exposure to asbestos continue in some LDCs and in Canada.

Obviously, these criticisms do not apply to all MNEs. These criticisms represent the concerns of host-country and LDC governments that have suffered abuses from multinationals over the decades. Tensions in the relationships between MNEs and host countries and other foreign governments will continue, especially in the least-developed settings. Whenever the stakes for both parties are high, so will be the pressures to negotiate the most profitable and equitable benefits for each stakeholder. Often, it is the less-educated, indigent inhabitants of LDCs who suffer the most from the operations of MNEs.

More global companies are beginning to self-monitor and contribute to host-country education, consumer awareness, and community programs (e.g., Shell has written a primer on human rights with Amnesty International; Hewlett-Packard offers consumer education programs and computer training in host countries.

7.4 MNE GUIDELINES FOR MANAGING MORALITY

Guidelines for managing international ethical conduct have received detailed attention and effort over the past four decades in the areas of consumer protection, employment, environmental pollution, human rights, and political conduct.[60] The driving forces behind the development of these published guidelines, or universal rights, include the United Nations, the International Labor Office, the Organization for Economic Cooperation and Development (OECD), the CERES Principles on the Environment, the Conference Board, and the Caux Round Table Principles for Business.

The underlying normative sources of the guidelines that these global organizations developed include beliefs in (1) national sovereignty, (2) social equity, (3) market integrity, and (4) human rights and fundamental freedoms.[61] DeGeorge specifically offers the following guidelines that multinationals can use in dealing with less developed countries:

1. Do no intentional harm.
2. Produce more good than harm for the host country.
3. Contribute to the host country's development.
4. Respect the human rights of their employees.
5. Respect the local culture; work with, not against, it.
6. Pay their fair share of taxes.
7. Cooperate with the local government to develop and enforce just background institutions.
8. Majority control of a firm includes the ethical responsibility of attending to the actions and failures of the firm.
9. Multinationals that build hazardous plants are obliged to ensure that the plants are safe and operated safely.
10. Multinationals are responsible for redesigning the transfer of hazardous technologies so that such technologies can be safely administered in host countries.[62]

Other recent developments involving global companies and business ethics include the following: (1) Global companies are developing and using core principles relevant to their business practices; (2) codes of ethics with minimum social responsibility standards (e.g., gender discrimination and environmental responsibility) are being adopted and employees trained on them; and (3) a broad consensus for ethical requirements is being articulated. The Conference Board, a global network of businesses, academic institutions, governments, and non-governmental organizations (NGOs) in over 60 countries, is working to define global business practice standards, core principles for doing business across cultures, and the requirements for the support of and cooperation between business and nonbusiness institutions.[63]

Some classic guidelines that continue to influence policies and practices of global companies are presented next. The following MNE guidelines are summarized under the categories of employment practices and policies, consumer protection, environmental protection, political payments and involvement, and basic human rights and fundamental freedoms.[64]

Employment Practices and Policies

- MNEs should not contravene the workforce policies of host nations.

- MNEs should respect the right of employees to join trade unions and to bargain collectively.

- MNEs should develop nondiscriminatory employment policies and promote equal job opportunities.

- MNEs should provide equal pay for equal work.

- MNEs should give advance notice of changes in operations, especially plant closings, and mitigate the adverse effects of these changes.

- MNEs should provide favorable work conditions, limited working hours, holidays with pay, and protection against unemployment.

- MNEs should promote job stability and job security, avoiding arbitrary dismissals and providing severance pay for those unemployed.

- MNEs should respect local host-country job standards and upgrade the local labor force through training.

- MNEs should adopt adequate health and safety standards for employees and grant them the right to know about job-related health hazards.

- MNEs should, minimally, pay basic living wages to employees.

- MNEs' operations should benefit the low-income groups of the host nation.

- MNEs should balance job opportunities, work conditions, job training, and living conditions among migrant workers and host-country nationals.

Consumer Protection

- MNEs should respect host-country laws and policies regarding the protection of consumers.

- MNEs should safeguard the health and safety of consumers by various disclosures, safe packaging, proper labeling, and accurate advertising.

Environmental Protection

- MNEs should respect host-country laws, goals, and priorities concerning protection of the environment.

- MNEs should preserve ecological balance, protect the environment, adopt preventive measures to avoid environmental harm, and rehabilitate environments damaged by operations.

- MNEs should disclose likely environmental harms and minimize the risks of accidents that could cause environmental damage.

- MNEs should promote the development of international environmental standards.
- MNEs should control specific operations that contribute to the pollution of air, water, and soils.
- MNEs should develop and use technology that can monitor, protect, and enhance the environment.

Political Payments and Involvement
- MNEs should not pay bribes or make improper payments to public officials.
- MNEs should avoid improper or illegal involvement or interference in the internal politics of host countries.

Basic Human Rights and Fundamental Freedoms
- MNEs should respect the rights of all persons to life, liberty, security of person, and privacy.
- MNEs should respect the rights of all persons to equal protection of the law, to work, to choice of job, to just and favorable work conditions, and to protection against unemployment and discrimination.
- MNEs should respect all persons' freedoms of thought, conscience, religion, opinion and expression, communication, peaceful assembly and association, and movement and residence within each state.
- MNEs should promote a standard of living to support the health and well-being of workers and their families.
- MNEs should promote special care and assistance to motherhood and childhood.

Frederick[65] states that these guidelines should be viewed as a "collective phenomenon," since all do not appear in each of the five international pacts they originated from: the 1948 United Nations Universal Declaration of Human Rights, 1975 Helsinki Final Act, 1976 OECD Guidelines for Multinational Enterprises, 1977 International Labor Organization Tripartite Declaration of Principles Concerning Multinational Enterprises and Social Policy, and 1972 United Nations Code of Conduct on Transnational Corporations.

The guidelines serve as broad bases that all international corporations can use to design specific policies and procedures; these corporations can then apply their own policies and procedures to such areas as "[c]hild care, minimum wages, hours of work, employee training and education, adequate housing and health care, pollution control efforts, advertising and marketing activities, severance pay, privacy of employees and consumers, information concerning on-the-job hazards. . . ."[66]

Managing ethically in the international marketplace requires corporate self-regulation as well as the involvement of external governments, legislation, NGOs, and other human rights and monitoring groups, including the media, to protect the rights of all stakeholders, including consumers and private citizens, as we discuss below.

7.5 STAKEHOLDER MANAGEMENT: ETHICAL INTERNATIONAL DECISION-MAKING METHODS

"You are a manager of Ben & Jerry's in Russia. One day you discover that the most senior officer of your company's Russian venture has been 'borrowing' equipment from the company and using it in his other business ventures. When you confront him, the Russian partner defends his actions. After all, as a part owner of both companies, isn't he entitled to share in the equipment?"[67] These and so many other international business situations confront managers and professionals with dilemmas and gray areas in their decision making. As one author noted, "Global business ethics has now become 'the ultimate dilemma for many U.S. businesses.'"[68]

"Transnationals operate in what may be called the margins of morality because the historical, cultural, and governmental mores of the world's nation-states are not uniform. There is a gray area of ethical judgment where standards of the transnational's home country differ substantially from those of the host country. . . . [T]here is yet no fixed, institutionalized policing agency to regularly constrain morally questionable practices of transnational commerce. Moreover, there is no true global consensus on what is morally questionable."[69] Scholars and business leaders agree that solving ethical dilemmas that involve global, cross-cultural dimensions is not easy. Often there are no "quick fixes." Where other laws, business practices, and local norms conflict, the decision makers must decide, using their own business and value judgments. Ethics codes help, but decision makers must also take local and their own company's interests into consideration. In short, there is no one best method to solve international business ethical dilemmas. From a larger perspective, external human rights and corporate monitoring groups are also needed to inform and advise corporations before dilemmas occur about human rights and methods that can prevent abuses of local workers and private citizens. In this section, several guidelines are discussed to complement principles and "quick tests" presented in Chapter 3.

CONTEXT OF GLOBAL ETHICAL DECISION MAKING

DeGeorge offers five broad "lessons" about business ethics from his work in this field.[70] These lessons are paraphrased here, since they apply in the context of international ethical decision making:

1. Business ethics is here to stay, it isn't a fad: ". . . the general population, workers' groups, environmental activists, and human

rights watchers are all putting pressure on companies to act as ethics demands. . . ."

2. Ethical people are necessary but not sufficient. Company board chairs, CEOs, and those leaders who set the tone for the company have to "walk the talk," or "their workers will do as their leaders do and not as they say."

3. Ethical structures count. Corporations can be structured to reward either ethical or unethical and amoral behavior. The better companies structure and reinforce ethical behavior.

4. Ethical problems are industrywide and often reflect inadequate laws or corrupt governments. Country and national legislation is necessary to protect workers, consumers, and the environment and to help businesses develop.

5. Industry and company legal and ethical self-regulation is necessary, but insufficient at the international level. Additional background institutions and nations must join the effort to agree on what acts are legal and illegal internationally. Bribery, for example, is one example of a practice that countries and institutions agree is illegal.

EXTERNAL CORPORATE MONITORING GROUPS

Corporations and their leaders are ultimately responsible for articulating, modeling, and working with international stakeholders to enforce legal and ethical standards in their firms as they do business around the world. Many do. However, as noted earlier, gray areas and lack of universal laws and norms leave loopholes that companies and local groups might use as competitive, but harmful, cost-saving advantages (e.g., not providing even "living wages" to the poor women and children they employ, polluting the environment, and using undue political influence to beat out competition). Numerous international groups[71] that work with and monitor MNEs regarding human rights include—but are not limited to—Amnesty International (promotes and advocates human rights), OECD (developed Guidelines for Multinational Enterprises), International Labor Organization (publishes and works in the area of human rights), NGOs (combat corruption, assure adequate labor conditions, and establish standards for economic responsibility), Transparency International (monitors and publishes the international Corruption Perception Index), Apparel Industry Partnership (AIP, which develops codes of conduct regarding child labor practices and working conditions related to "sweat shops" and subcontractors), and The Round Table (an executive group formed in Switzerland that published the noted Caux Principles and works with other international business professionals on developing and implementing universal ethics codes). These groups work with, and some are composed of, MNE executives, governments, legislators, local citizenry, and other stakeholders worldwide to inform, monitor, and assist MNEs with ethical global business practices.

INDIVIDUAL STAKEHOLDER METHODS FOR ETHICAL DECISION MAKING

Individual employee and professional stakeholders—when confronted with ethical dilemmas, conflicting norms, and potentially illegal acts in international situations, like the case of Louise in Chapter 3—can use several guidelines. DeGeorge[72] offers the following tactics for solving ethical dilemmas internationally:

1. Do not violate the very norms and values that you want to preserve and that you use to evaluate your adversary's actions to be unethical. Seek to pursue with integrity economic survival and self-defense tactics. Winning a tactical battle unethically or illegally is not the goal.

2. Use your moral imagination, since there are no specific rules for responding to an ethical opponent. Stakeholder analysis can help. Explore different options. Use literature, stories, and lives of heroes and saints for creative responses instead of rules.

3. Use restraint and rely on those to whom the use of force is legitimately allocated when your response to immorality involves justifiable force or retaliation. Use minimal force that is justified as the ultimate solution, realizing that force is a reaction to unethical acts and practices.

4. Apply the principle of proportionality when measuring your response to an unethical opponent. The force you use should be commensurate with the offense, the harm suffered, and the good to be gained.

5. Use the technique of *ethical displacement* when responding to unethical forces. This principle consists of searching for clarification and a solution to a dilemma on different, higher levels than the personal (e.g., as discussed in Chapter 1, look at the problems from these levels: international, industry, organizational, structural, and national or legislative policy).

6. Use publicity to respond to an unethical practice, adversary, or system. Corruption, unethical and illegal practices and actions, operates best in the dark. Using publicity judiciously can mobilize pressures against the perpetrators.

7. Work jointly with others to create new social, legal, or popular structures and institutions to respond to immoral opponents.

8. Act with moral courage and from your values, personally and corporately.

9. Be prepared to pay a price, even a high one. Innocent people sometimes must pay costs that others impose on them by their unethical and illegal activities.

10. Use the principle of accountability when responding to an unethical activity. Those who harm others must be held accountable for their acts.

Solving a moral dilemma in an international context is not easy. These guidelines offer interrelated strategies to help in the decision-making process.

Four Typical Styles of International Ethical Decision Making

George Enderle[73] identified four distinctive international ethical decision-making styles that companies often use when making decisions abroad: (1) *Foreign Country style*: a company applies the values and norms of its local host—"When in Rome, do as the Romans do"; (2) *Empire style*: a company applies its own domestic values and rules; this can be an imperialistic practice; (3) *Innerconnection style*: a company applies shared norms with other companies and groups; national identities and interests are transcended and blurred, as when states make commercial decisions and rely on NAFTA or the EU members to offer agreed-on processes and solutions; and (4) *Global style*: a company abstracts all local and regional differences and norms, coming up with a more cosmopolitan set of standards and solutions for its actions in the host country.

The Foreign Country and Empire styles have obvious drawbacks in reaching ethical decisions. The Foreign Country style may result in gross injustices and inequities that are inherent in the norms adopted. Some local country norms and business practices, for example, do not prohibit child labor. The second style is a form of imperialism that disregards local norms and practices. The Global style, seemingly the "right answer," also presents problems. This style imposes its own interpretation of a "global morality and truth" on a host culture and norms. The Global style can also suffer from shortcomings shared by the Foreign Country and Empire styles. The Interconnection style "acknowledges both universal moral limits and the ability of communities to set moral standards of their own. It balances better than the other types a need to retain local identity with the acknowledgment of values that transcend individual communities. The drawbacks of this style are practical rather than moral." Companies and individual employees usually do not have quick or direct access to a commonly shared local, national, and international source to advise on a particular issue. Of the four styles, the Interconnection style appears to be less arbitrary and absolutist.[74] Another option is creative ethical navigation (which Donaldson and Dunfee term "integrative social contract theory" or ICST). This is not really a "style" of decision making; rather, it is the process of a decision maker navigating among "hypernorms," company interests, and local norms, as explained below.

HYPERNORMS, LOCAL NORMS, AND CREATIVE ETHICAL NAVIGATION

It would be helpful to have a set of norms that everyone agreed on. *Hypernorms* represent such an ideal. "Hypernorms are principles so fundamental that, by definition, they serve to evaluate lower-order norms, reaching to the root of what is ethical for humanity. They represent norms by which all others are to be judged."[75] Hypernorms relate to universal rights: for example, the right not to be enslaved, the right to have physical security, the right not to be tortured, and the right not to be discriminated against.[76] However, the problem even with hypernorms is that when "rights," local traditions, country economic systems, or business practices conflict, decisions have to be made; in such cases, it is necessary for a manager or professional to use his or her hypernorms as a starting principle, but then to be creative in considering the local context and competing norms. Reaching a win-win situation without violating anyone's norms is an ideal goal. An example of such a troublesome gray area, along with a suitable solution, is offered by Donaldson and Dunfee:

> Consider another situation confronted by Levi-Strauss, this time involving hypernorms connected with child labor. The company discovered in the early 1990s that two of its suppliers in Bangladesh were employing children under the age of fourteen—a practice that violated the company's principles but was tolerated in Bangladesh. Forcing the suppliers to fire the children would not have insured that the children received an education, and it would have caused serious hardship for the families depending on the children's wages. In a creative arrangement, the suppliers agreed to pay the children's regular wages while they attended school and to offer each child a job at age fifteen. Levi-Strauss, in turn, agreed to pay the children's tuition and provide books and uniforms. This approach allowed Levi-Strauss to uphold its principles and provide long-term benefits to the host country.[77]

Figure 7.9 illustrates Donaldson and Dunfee's "Global Values Map," which portrays the zones groups may consider to creatively navigate among and reach agreement on competing norms and business practices.[78] At the center of the figure are "hypernorms," which are basic values acceptable to all cultures and organizations. The next concentric circle represents "consistent norms," which are culture-specific values, but still consistent with both hypernorms and other legitimate norms. Ethical codes of companies, such as Johnson & Johnson's Credo, are examples of consistent norms. Moving away from the center of the circle to the outer circle, one encounters inconsistent norms, which may conflict with hypernorms and/or local business practices. Outside the concentric circle are illegitimate norms—values or practices that transgress hypernorms (e.g., exposing workers to asbestos or other carcinogens). In the "moral free space," a company can creatively explore unique solutions that satisfy all parties.

The example above of Levi-Strauss illustrates a process using Figure 7.9. Levi-Strauss had to decide among a "hypernorm" (child labor is wrong), its

FIGURE 7.9 GLOBAL VALUES MAP

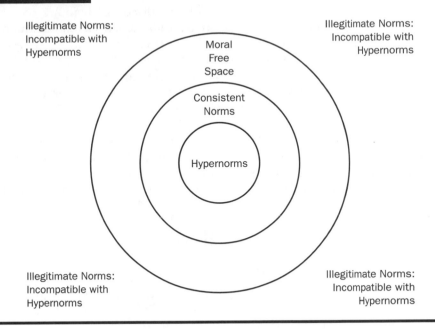

SOURCE: Reprinted by permission of *Harvard Business Review* from "Ties that bind: A social contract approach to business ethics" by T. Donaldson and T. Dunfee. Copyright © 1999 by the Harvard Business School Publishing Corporation.

own company norms ("consistent norms"—children cannot be hired or used by company suppliers), and Bangladesh suppliers' child labor practices ("illegitimate norms") to reach an agreement that would benefit the children and their families. Levi-Strauss entered the "moral free space" and worked out what seems to have been a "win-win" situation for all parties involved—and an arrangement that brought no harm to any party.

Finding such creative solutions to international moral dilemmas involves balancing and combining business pressures, legal enforcement, and political will. A company attempting to make tough decisions with local groups could also seek to do so with the cooperation of other companies, local government officials, or even an external human rights group as the Interconnectedness style of decision making would suggest. The ultimate decision may very well entail *no compromise* after reflecting on the situation, the hypernorm, and a company norm. Still, the methods discussed here can enable a decision maker—individual or global or company team—to look for options without getting trapped into blind absolutes, amoral gray zones, or relativism. Entering "moral free space" requires flexibility and negotiating. The embedded process in Figure 7.9 also enables a company or individual decision maker to use the principles and quick tests discussed in Chapter 3.

VALUE-BASED STAKEHOLDER MANAGEMENT

The international decision-making methods discussed here are consistent with and add an important dimension to a value-based stakeholder management approach. Mapping and understanding the stakeholders, stakes, and interests, as well the issues to be addressed, are steps that can be taken initially, before approaching the ethical part of solving dilemmas. Also, having an identifiable set of values (personal, professional, and company) from which to negotiate with other cultural and country norms is important; otherwise, individuals and teams are left at their own risk (and ultimately the company's) to solve questionable issues. The more aligned a company and its members are around a set of core ethical values, the more guidance professionals have in negotiating tough choices. Still, solving international ethical dilemmas requires flexibility, wise judgment, and sound moral imagination.

SUMMARY

The global environment consists of a dynamic set of relationships among companies, financial markets, cultures, political ideologies, government policies, laws, technologies, and numerous stakeholders, as the brutal attack on New York's World Trade Center demonstrated.

There are estimates of between 40,000 to 100,000 multinational companies doing business across national boundaries and contributing to the global economy. It is likely these numbers will increase. Where there are new markets, companies will be created and go.

Globalization is the integration of technology, markets, politics, cultures, labor, production, and commerce. Globalization is both the process and the result of this integration. The global economy is estimated at $33 trillion.

Forces that have accelerated globalization include the end of communism and the opening of closed economies; information technologies and the Internet, which accelerate communication and productivity within and across companies globally; entrepreneurship and entrepreneurs who are more mobile, skilled, intelligent, and thriving worldwide; free trade and trading agreements among nations; the flow of money through the World Bank and the International Monetary Fund (IMF), which offers a conduit to bring needed capital to countries participating in building the global economy; the growth and the spread of transnational firms, which open new markets and create local employment; a shift to service economies and knowledge workers using technologies, which has also propelled innovation and productivity worldwide; and global political forces that have, until the World Trade Center attack, contributed to peace and economic stability. Given the attacks on September 11, 2001, and the threat of other organized attacks on individual, country, and corporate interests in all countries, a question asked is, Will globalization and accelerated business integration across national borders be slowed and negatively affected, or rejuvenated through new alliances?

Major competitive success factors driving firms like Honeywell in the global economy include (1) recruiting the best talent at all levels in a company locally and globally; (2) designing, manufacturing, and delivering high-quality innovative products to world markets at competitive costs; (3) shifting to service economies and knowledge workers using technologies, which has also propelled innovation and productivity; (4) developing just-in-time manufacturing capability, which transforms innovative ideas into commodities; (5) using robotics, computer-aided design, materials management, and flexible manufacturing technologies, which also keep inventories down, while decreasing error rates and increasing profit; (6) employing Web-based technologies that connect customers with products and reduce transaction costs and product delivery time, such as B2B (business-to-business), B2C (business to customers), and C2C (customers to customers) technological exchanges, which eliminate overhead and expand business's reach.

"Smart globalization" strategies and processes that several companies are using include the following: (1) methodically building a presence from the ground up instead of planning takeovers and acquisitions; (2) doing extensive homework before starting a business in a developing country by consulting with and learning from local stakeholders; (3) forgetting about targeting the richest 10 percent of the global population and marketing to the 4 billion people internationally who earn less than $1,500 annually and are the source of future growth; and (4) introducing and helping to stimulate product use with local populations.

The "dark side of globalization" includes such issues as corporate crime and corruption, child slave labor, Westernization (Americanization) of values, the global digital divide, and loss of nation-state sovereignty.

Capitalism as a global system is also "one system with different faces." Four "faces of capitalism" are emerging in the global economy: consumer, producer, family, and frontier capitalism. Each system has different characteristics and problems. MetaCapitalism is a concept related to globalization. Countries that succeed in the emerging MetaCapitalist system demonstrate the following success factors: a strong infrastructure network and easy access for a country's businesses and consumers; local capital markets that are fully integrated into worldwide capital markets; low levels of economic nationalism; and minimal restrictions on inflow and outflow of goods, information, and services. MetaCapitalism is about business, but it is also very much about the interface between government and business, where people's lives and welfare are at stake. While MetaCapitalism as a concept is somewhat exaggerated, the success factors that contribute to countries' long-term success in the global economy are noteworthy.

American capitalism and management were characterized in the 1980s and 1990s by the following characteristics: short-term time, profit, planning, and strategy horizons; individual decision making, responsibilities, performance, and rewards; managers who are understood, trained, and treated as professionals separate from but based on a specific knowledge base; outcomes as a focus over processes, measured and monitored by short-term financial tools; specialized and vertical career paths; and individual career development. Recent changes in American management practices include the use of information and process technologies; implementation of customer-centered total quality management, continuous improvement, and just-in-time inventory; and electronic networking of organizations through shared systems, enabling an increase in market share through joint research and development; mergers and acquisitions, joint ventures, strategic alliances, and consortia.

The power of multinational enterprises (MNEs) or global companies lies in their size, economic prowess, and ability to locate and operate across national borders. MNEs offer benefits to their host countries by employing local populations, investing capital, co-venturing with local entrepreneurs and companies; providing enhanced technology; developing particular industry sectors; providing business learning and skills; and increasing industrial output and productivity.

MNEs also abuse their power by committing corporate crimes, exerting undue political influence and control, determining and controlling plant closings and layoffs, and damaging the physical environment and human health. Guidelines drawn from over four decades' worth of international agreements and charters were summarized to illustrate a consensus of host-country rights that have been used to help MNEs to design equity into their policies and procedures.

Finally, ethical decision-making methods were presented for companies, teams, and individuals working in international settings. A creative model was summarized enabling companies to reach agreements among conflicting hypernorms (universal rights), consistent norms (company ethics and values codes), and illegitimate norms. Being able to balance local cultural norms, a company's norms, and competing business practices involves creative and responsible navigation and decision-making skills based on personal, professional, company, and universal values.

Questions

1. Describe the emerging competitive global business environment and the forces that define it. What is different about the changing global environment?

2. Define "globalization." What are some of the forces driving this process?

3. Identify several factors that contribute to the global competitiveness of companies. How have U.S. corporations become more competitive? Give some examples.

4. Select two global companies mentioned in this chapter and locate their corporate Websites. Find their codes of conduct or ethics statements. Download these and evaluate whether or not they serve any practical purposes or help meet the companies' social responsibility goals and why.

5. Explain what the "dark side of globalization" means. Offer some examples. Was the September 11, 2001, attack one of these dark sides? Explain.

6. Identify and characterize four forms of capitalism. What are some competitive and moral advantages and disadvantages of each in the global marketplace? Why?

7. Characterize the U.S. system of capitalism. What are strengths and weaknesses of this "U.S. capitalism"?

8. Explain the differences in perception and experience with regard to moral issues for (a) a host country viewing an MNE and (b) an MNE viewing a host country. Which perspective are you more inclined to support or sympathize with? Why?

9. Find an example from the media of an international dilemma a company has had in a host country and apply the process of the "Global Values Map." Evaluate how well you believe the process could have worked in the example you found.

EXERCISES

1. Argue and defend your positions on the following statements:
   (a) Only one system of world capitalism really exists, even though it may be practiced differently regionally.
   (b) To succeed, globalization must involve justice and fairness practices from First World countries toward Third World nations and peoples.
   (c) The U.S. management system does not and need not include ethics.
   (d) MNEs cannot financially afford to follow the guidelines in Section 7.4; it would be too costly for them.
   (e) When two MNEs are both right on a controversial issue—for example, violation of patent or intellectual property rights—ethics should be avoided, and other, more concrete issues should be used to resolve the dispute.

2. Identify and describe from the media a dispute between (a) two multinational corporations and (b) a multinational corporation and a nation.

3. Answer these questions for 2(a) and (b): Who is right and who is wrong? Why? How would you propose to resolve the dispute? Include a moral perspective in your answer.

ETHICAL DILEMMA

JANE'S NEW ASSIGNMENT

You (Jane) are a 29-year-old single woman who has an MBA and has been working in your current marketing position for a year. Your firm has recently opened a new pilot branch in Moscow. The CEO of your company believes there are real growth opportunities for your firm's products in that region and also wants visibility there. The company has decided to launch a small office there for visibility as well as to introduce the product. You are one of the most outgoing and talented marketing professionals in your firm. It is believed that you'll make a positive impression and represent the company well. There is a small community of American business professionals there who will assist you.

Country values there are very different from what you are accustomed to. You overhear a discussion between two of your male colleagues who were recently in that country completing arrangements for the office. One says, "Jane's going to have some interesting challenges with the men she has to do business with. . . . It's like the Wild West." The other answered, "Yeah, she's got some real surprises coming." Your research suggests that country laws and norms on issues you take for granted (like women's rights and sexual harassment) are not well defined.

You have a conflict over wanting to advance with your company, but not wanting to take this assignment. You are aware that the CEO has his mind set. In fact, you've already had a discussion expressing your concerns and fears. He brushed your issues aside when he told you earlier, "Jane, try it. You need the international exposure and experience." The second time you approached him with your concerns, he blurted out, "Look, Jane. I understand your concerns, but this is important to me and our company. There are some people there who can help you. I know it's going to be a challenge. But after a couple of years, you'll thank me." You still don't feel right.

QUESTIONS

1. What do you do, and why?

2. If you do decide to go, what specific preparations should you make?

3. If you decide not to go, draft out the dialogue you would have with your CEO.

ETHICAL DILEMMA

WHO'S TRAINING WHOM?

You are attending a sexual harassment training seminar for local managers in your company's branch office in a Middle Eastern, predominately Muslim country. You were flown over with the trainers to observe their techniques and become familiar with the training materials, since you, as a new human resource staff member, would be expected to give this course. The course has been a success for managers in the United States. The same materials have been perfected and are being used in the United States. The instructors call on local Muslim managers (men and women) to role play and openly share stories about sexual harassment that involved them or that they had heard about. Near the end of the half-day session, several of the host country employees uncharacteristically walk out. The trainers are dazed and become upset.

QUESTIONS

1. What do you think went wrong?

2. What would you do in this case if you were one of the trainers?

3. Read the epilogue below, then return and answer this question: "Assume the trainers have been briefed on the research you just read. Who should do what, if anything, with the Muslim managers after this cultural mishap? Why?"

EPILOGUE

"In 1993, a large U.S. computer-products company insisted on using exactly the same sexual harassment exercises and lessons with Muslim managers halfway around the globe that they used with American employees in California. It did so in the name of 'ethical consistency.' The result was ludicrous. The managers were baffled by the instructors' presentation, and the instructors were oblivious of the intricate connections between Muslim religion and sexual manners.

"The U.S. trainers needed to know that Muslim ethics are especially strict about male/female social interaction. By explaining sexual harassment in the same way to Muslims as to Westerners, the trainers offended the Muslim managers. To the Muslim managers, their remarks seemed odd and disrespectful. In turn, the underlying ethical message about avoiding coercion and sexual discrimination was lost. Clearly sexual discrimination does occur in Muslim countries. But helping to eliminate it there means respecting—and understanding Muslim differences."

SOURCE: Donaldson, T., Dunfee, T. (Summer 1999). When ethics travel: The promise and peril of global business ethics. *California Management Review 41(4)*, 60.

8

BUSINESS ETHICS
IN THE TWENTY-FIRST CENTURY

8.1 A PERSPECTIVE ON BUSINESS AND ETHICS SINCE SEPTEMBER 11, 2001

War changes everything. The September 11, 2001, attacks on the World Trade Center and the Pentagon in New York City and Washington, D.C., represent a turning point for the United States, the global community, and globalization. The unexpected, sudden loss of innocent lives sent a message to all nations and individuals: No country or person is secure from "terrorist" attack. As this crisis transforms into a new type of war, several different issues have emerged. These are issues that have ethical, economic, legal, social, and political consequences that are all global in scope: (1) the vulnerability of nation-states, including all leading industrialized countries; (2) security as a national and global priority; (3) information monitoring, profiling, and privacy on an unprecedented scale; (4) religious, ideological, and racial stereotyping; and (5) whether or not this is and will be a "just war."

VULNERABILITY OF NATION-STATES: SHIFTING COALITIONS AND COLLABORATION

Beyond the grief for the lives lost, the September 11 attack brought down the symbol and center of the global financial community and damaged the image of one of the world's most powerful military planning machines. The vulnerability of the United States, the world's preeminent superpower, and other nation-states was sharply exposed. At stake are the very physical security and survival of civilians and democratic societies as we know them. The Bush administration's clear and unequivocal message that all nations would have to decide whether they were on the side of (and would harbor) Osama bin Laden and the Al-Qaeda network or whether they would join the U.S.-led anti-terrorist campaign also created a platform for a new global coalition. Russia, China, Pakistan, Uzbekistan, Iran, Syria, and other Muslim nations, for example, agreed to support the United States in its campaign. President Putin of Russia continued lobbying for admission into NATO. President Bush also endorsed a Palestinian state.[1]

This coalition-building activity brought a new, perhaps temporary, awakening: "It is no exaggeration to say that the events of Sept. 11 may be delivering what Peter the Great, the empress Catherine and President Boris N. Yeltsin could not: a Russian state anchored solidly in the West for the first time in a millennium. By shattering the notion of a sole American superpower that could single-handedly build global stability and prosperity, those events may have removed the biggest obstacle to Russia's final integration with the West."[2] These budding—and perhaps temporary and shifting—new alliances bring several questions: Whose national values and local norms, belief systems, and customs will be subordinated and emphasized when and if the issues and stakes change in the war? What will be the economic, political, and social costs required to sustain these alliances? Whatever pattern emerges from the continually shifting coalitions, the initial U.S.-led alliance is unprecedented and could lead to a new chapter on globalization in terms of trade, economic assistance, military cooperation and peace agreements.

NATIONAL AND INDIVIDUAL SECURITY: THREATS OF BIO- AND CYBERTERRORISM

The scope and scale of the issue of national and individual security are another result of the attack. Bin Laden and the Al-Qaeda network publicly declared that no American would be safe until Middle Eastern people were safe.[3] This is a physical threat that the U.S. intelligence agencies took seriously. In effect, bin Laden waged war on every country where American interests and citizens are found. The threat of possible biological, chemical, and Internet terrorism is one of global proportion. The delivery of anthrax to several U.S. companies demonstrates the seriousness of this threat.

American institutions, infrastructure, and government are not prepared for such attacks: "'For bioterrorism, the No. 1 inadequacy, if you had to rank them, is the inadequacy of our public health infrastructure,' said Senator Bill Frist, Republican of Tennessee. 'That is a product of about 15 years of neglect. . . . At the same time, there are holes in the federal bureaucracy, where two important health positions remain unfilled: commissioner of food and drugs and director of the National Institutes of Health. The FDA will play a crucial role in the development of vaccines or treatments for use in the event of a biological attack, but President Bush and Senator Edward M. Kennedy . . . have been unable to agree on an acceptable nominee.'" Federal spending to fight terrorism has increased 50 percent in five years. Spending to fight weapons of mass destruction—nuclear, biological, and chemical—has increased at an even faster rate.[4]

The threat of cyberterrorism is equally important for the United States and the international community. Consider this: "One of the first moves in America's new war on terrorism took place Sept. 5, six days before the attacks on the World Trade Center and the Pentagon. The target: a Richardson, Texas company called InfoCom that hosts Arabic Websites. An 80-man terrorism task force launched a three-day raid, crashing 500 Internet sites, freezing bank accounts, and copying information from the company's hard drives. . . . While government officials aren't saying whether the Texas raid and the attacks on New York and Washington intersect, the Feds have become increasingly worried about terrorism's links to the computer world. After the Sept. 11 attacks, Defense Secretary Donald Rumsfeld included cyberterrorism among the potential threats that "are front and center to us. . . ."[5] Neil Livingston, CEO of GlobalOptions, a risk-management firm comprised of ex-FBI and Navy SEALs, stated, "The most devastating scenarios we look at today that are not chemical, biological, or radiological tend to be cyber-attacks."[6] Moreover, "[c]omputer-security experts say that the country's technostructure is vulnerable to attacks that could cripple corporate America, cause billions of dollars in business losses, and disable the global positioning satellite (GPS) system, potentially wreaking havoc in the skies."[7]

While measures have and continue to be taken to provide security from physical, bio- and cyberterrorism, there are no guaranteed safeguards. Microsoft's top information-security executive, an Army Reserve special agent, was called to Washington to assist. He headed a four-year-old Information Systems Security Association composed of Fortune 500 members who share on a real-time basis cybersecurity information with rival firms in their industry.[8] Measures being considered to gear up for a bioterrorist attack include the following:[9] (1) Develop cutting-edge diagnostic tools that can identify anthrax, smallpox, and other biowarfare agents in blood samples. (2) Develop master plans to coordinate government agencies during bioterror crises. Legal and social problems would be addressed; responsibility roles would be assigned; who would get life-saving doses of scarce antibiotics would be determined; how doctors would be shielded from malpractice suits if they let patients die in a triage situation would be identified. (3) Organize fire-brigade-like teams of hospital workers and staff nationwide who are trained and ready to respond to bioterrorist attacks on the population. One survey showed that 20 percent of hospitals already have such plans for dealing with chemical attacks. (4) Quickly increase the federal government's pharmaceutical stockpile of vaccines and antibiotics to contain outbreaks of biochemical attacks in multiple cities simultaneously.

INFORMATION MONITORING, PROFILING, AND PRIVACY: COST OF FREEDOM?

"After Sept. 11 . . . everything . . . changed. A New York Times/CBS News poll at the end of September found that 8 in 10 Americans believe they will have to give up some of their personal freedom to make the country safe from terrorist attacks."[10] Visionics, a New Jersey company, is an industry leader in the science of biometrics, ". . . a method of identifying people by scanning and quantifying their unique physical characteristics—their facial structures, for example, or their retinal patterns. Visionics manufactures a face-recognition technology called FaceIt, which creates identification codes for individuals based on 80 unique aspects of their facial structures. . . . FaceIt can instantly compare an image of any individual's face with a database of the faces of suspected terrorists, or anyone else."[11] Joseph Attick, Visionics CEO, has proposed wiring up Reagan National Airport and others throughout the United States to create a "watch list." He suggests the newly created "Homeland Security" czar and organization control the national biometric network platform and coordinate it with local police forces.

A similar system has been installed in England—and criticized for its lack of reliability as a deterrent to local and would-be criminals. Another criticism of the use of these biometrics systems relates to the power and discretion given to the person who controls access to the network of intimate images. One observer of a surveillance system in England notes, "During my time in the control room, from 9 p.m. to midnight, I experienced firsthand a phenomenon that critics of CCTV [closed circuit television] surveillance have often described: when you put a group of bored, unsupervised men in front of live video screens and allow them to zoom in on whatever happens to catch their eyes, they tend to spend a fair amount of time leering at women."[12] Other concerns include the following: How many of these will be installed, how long, and where? What are the limits of the results of these systems? Who decides? What happens to individual rights and procedural justice with the widespread use of such systems?

The CEO of Visionics argues that his technology is an alternative to racial and ethic profiling. He also argues that if faces in the biometric database can be limited to known terrorists, the issues of profiling can be controlled. To date, however, existing biometric databases in the United States and England cannot restrict face recognition to known terrorists—who also can disguise themselves to go undetected by such systems.

DIVERSITY, TOLERANCE, AND STEREOTYPING

Related to racial profiling is the issue of lack of tolerance for ethnic, religious, and ideological diversity—especially for Muslims, many of whom are stereotyped as "terrorists." The problem of racial profiling and discrimination was and may continue to be problematic after September 11. Suspects—

Middle Eastern-looking men—were taken off Northwest Airlines and other carriers in September and held for no observed offense or crime; several passengers simply felt uncomfortable with these individuals on board. The attorney general of the state in which the incident occurred threatened to file suit against Northwest Airlines unless officials apologized for the unjustified action. President Bush has been visible and vocal about respecting Muslim and Muslim American citizens' rights during this crisis. At the same time, President Bush and members of his cabinet asked Americans to be vigilant and to report any suspicious activities they see. There are thin lines separating perception, prejudice, and discrimination.

Still, Muslims have been harassed and beaten. For example, 67 attacks on Muslim students and individuals were reported in Tampa, Florida, from September 11 through early October. Muslim-owned small businesses have been burned and vandalized. Reminiscent of the internment and treatment of 110,000 Japanese Americans in U.S. camps during World War II, and of the surveillance and blacklists of suspected American "Communists" during Senator Joe McCarthy's era, profiling by race, religion, or ideology can result in serious violations of human rights.

COURAGE, COMPASSION, AND COMMUNITY

The courage, sacrifice, compassion, and sense of community shown by those involved directly and indirectly during and after the September 11 attacks are documented on Websites, during CNN news broadcasts, and in the print media. New York firefighters and police officers and the airline crewmembers and passengers on Flights 11, 93, and 175 became international heroes.

Scott McNealy, CEO of Sun Microsystems, discovered another dimension of his employees after the attack:

> It would be hours before McNealy started to hear scattered reports from his employees. Each report brought a sigh of relief as more and more Sun employees became safely accounted for. While many fortunate refugees from the collapsed skyscrapers were able to retreat to the safety of their homes and families, McNealy's troops were treated to a quick hug from coworkers, a shower and perhaps a bite to eat before heading back out to help Sun's Trade Center clients with their servers. Whether it was retrieving data or ordering new computer workstations for emergency trading rooms in New Jersey, the same Sun employees who could easily have been part of the death toll were now attending to their jobs just hours after black clouds enveloped lower Manhattan. McNealy could not say enough about the character, fortitude and resilience of his employees. "The amazing thing is that they don't even feel like the victims. And yet they were the victims," McNealy recounted. "I'm blown away by them."[13]

Altruism in the face of this crisis was and is demonstrated and witnessed.

Is This a "Just War"?

War brings death and destruction to both victor and vanquished. For the United States and its allies, the justification of this war includes self-defense, retribution, and future protection. The "global war on terrorism," like any war, raises the issue of social justice with specific reference to "collateral damage"—unintended harm done to civilian victims from bombing and those made refugees. As will be discussed, "just wars" should be justified.

Killing innocent people as "collateral damage" is unjust. Creating refugees of innocent people is also unjust. In wars, however, collateral damage happens. A utilitarian ethic is often used. Innocent people will be killed and misplaced in order to save greater numbers later. The issue of creating refugees was complicated with regard to the Afghan people. Twenty years of war, drought, and a worsening economy under the Taliban regime have created unbearable hunger, poverty, and death among the population. Before this war, 4 million Afghans depended on food from the United States for 80 percent of their diet. Since the war began, it is estimated that 8 million will require food to stay alive as the number of refugees increases daily. The United Nations has sought $584 million in donations to limit their misery and exodus from their homes and camps.[14] Food and grain donated by the United States to the United Nations World Food Program was keeping 26 million Afghans alive before this war started. In 2001, the United States provided 304,010 tons of food to Afghanistan, 438,400 tons to Ethiopia, 350,005 tons to North Korea, 288,510 tons to Kenya, and 137,429 tons to Eritrea.[15] A complicating problem is not being able to ensure that food provided by international agencies like the UN and countries like the United States gets to those in need. Smugglers, warring tribal groups, and warlords often intercept food and other relief items. Beyond this issue is that of ensuring the viability of Afghanistan's next "government."

Ethical questions asked in defending this (and perhaps an extended war) as a "just war" include the following: What are the clear objectives of this war, and can these objectives be defended morally? Can this war be "won"? What would "victory" be for America and its allies? Will individual privacy rights and free speech be curtailed by national security measures, i.e., military tribunals, profiling, and new surveillance? Have all feasible options for settling the issues underlying the attacks and this brand of terrorism with all parties been identified and used? Whose rights can be rectified and how by this war? Where does revenge end and justice begin? Who will protect the survivors, that is, civilian populations in affected countries, during this and the next phase of this war? Finally, are there ways of achieving peaceful coexistence in this continuing war that are based on educational, humanitarian, and political reforms rather than on the use of violence and war? Can these means be nonpartisan, non-ideological, non-nationalistic, and global perspectives and terms that all parties can agree on? To what extent, if any, is U.S. foreign policy responsible for conditions related to any aspects of this war?

8.2 EMERGING MACRO-ETHICAL ISSUES IN THE TWENTY-FIRST CENTURY

Significant issues that involve business and ethics in the foreseeable future include

- "First and Third World" divides: economic, technological, political, and ideological
- The human genome project, cloning, and the issue "What is the human self?"
- The environment as free-market commodity or sustainable stakeholder
- The future of globalization

Each of these issues is discussed in turn.

FIRST AND THIRD WORLD DIVIDES: ECONOMIC, TECHNOLOGICAL, POLITICAL, AND IDEOLOGICAL

Economic, technological, political, and ideological forces combine to increase the divide between First and Third World countries. A persuasive argument could be made that these so-called divides, taken together, provide some of the sources of "global terrorism." Sub-Saharan Africa and most of the Middle East, South Asia, and Central and South America constitute "Third World" countries. As noted in Chapter 7, the gap in per capita gross domestic product (GDP) between the richest "First World" countries and the poorest "Third World" countries is about 140:1. Technologically, less than 1 percent of on-line users live in Africa. Less than 5 percent of computers are connected to the Internet in developing countries. The developed world has almost 50 phone lines for every 100 people, compared to 1.4 phones per 100 people in low-income countries—also noted in Chapter 7.

Several factors are both the cause and the effect of these divides; for example, there is corruption in all countries. Third World nations have suffered the most from political and economic corruption, since it impedes the development and distribution of resources for creating wealth at all levels of society: jobs and mobility. Corruption costs $500 billion annually—1 percent of the global economy—as noted in Chapter 7. In the illegitimate and black market economies, narcotics trafficking has projected annual revenues of $100 to $300 billion. Second, more multinational enterprises (MNEs) could play a developmental role, contributing more to host countries whose resources have been freely used for decades. MNEs can help by offering more opportunities in education, job training and creation, technology transfer, and assistance in developing infant industries. For example, Unilever (a multibillion-dollar multinational with over 300,000 employees in 100 countries) produces foods, fish, chemicals, and household products. Its corporatewide initiative "The Triple Bottom Line"[16] changed its definition of organizational effectiveness from "economic value added" to a triple bottom line that measures performance based on economic, ecological, and community assets, liabilities, and profits/benefits and losses.[17] Finally, many countries are shut out of the economic and technological benefits of twenty-first-century global capitalism and globalization because they are governed by dictators who do not make human rights a priority or highly value human life. Currently, the following organizations are working with multinational corporations and host governments toward promoting human rights: Amnesty International, Organization for Economic Cooperation and Development (OECD, which provides Guidelines for Multinational Enterprises), International Labor Organization, NGOs (non-governmental organizations), Transparency International (which monitors and publishes the international Corruption Perception Index), Apparel Industry Partnership (AIP), and The Round Table in Switzerland.

Politically, Western industrialized companies have a diplomatic as well as an economic, technological, and humanitarian responsibility to take a global perspective toward integrating Third World, and heretofore "hostile," regimes into the First World network of economical and political development. The Cold War is not over when Western countries and blocs continue to "take sides," polarizing internal Third World country crises by helping to create and support regimes and then turning against them when they become corrupt dictatorships, as has previously happened. The ethical challenge for First World countries involves balancing and weighing principles of justice and rights among all countries and regional interests in a global economy.

THE HUMAN GENOME PROJECT, CLONING, AND THE ISSUE "WHAT IS THE HUMAN SELF?"

Other significant developments on the horizon are the commercial and medical uses of DNA and biotech discoveries. On June 26, 2000, Francis Collins, director of the National Human Genome Research Institute, and J. Craig Venter, head of the biotechnology company Celera, announced the completion of the first draft of the genetic information in our chromosomes, which "spelled out sequences of DNA."[18] Ethically, the uses of the human genome project, once completely finished, signal a range of concerns that were raised at the BIO 2000 Conference, held in Boston in the spring of 2000 and attended by over 10,000 scientists and businessmen. Over $8 billion was raised on the stock market in 2000 by businesses related to research on and potential uses of biogenetic engineering.[19] Over 1,500 protesters, who included "farmers, consumers, geneticists, public-interest lawyers, and disabled and indigenous people from several states and countries," also showed up at a nearby "counter-conference," which they termed Biodevastation 2000.

The counter-conference attendees protested lack of public involvement and insufficient government oversight regarding the rapid research-to-commercialization of genetic engineering breakthroughs. One company president at the conference stated, "If we are successful, everything will change—our health, our food, ourselves." A protester, Brian Tokar of the Institute for Social Ecology, stated at the counter-conference, "The biotechnology industry is making decisions that affect all life on Earth, and they're doing it behind closed doors. They have no right to control our seeds, our genes, and our future."[20]

Farmers filed a class-action suit against Monsanto, the large company that has dedicated its mission to genetic research with crops, arguing that the firm has not properly tested its biogenetics methods and that the company is trying to monopolize the seed industry. The Alliance for Bio-Integrity in Iowa also filed suit against the Food and Drug Administration, alleging that it misrepresented risks and violated federal law requiring that safety be demonstrated before marketing occurs. On the other side of this particular part of the debate, food industry representatives argue that they have tested their product for years and that 90 percent of today's cheeses are made purer by using a "GM enzyme rather than the scrapings from calves' stomachs."[21] Still, the possibility exists for "germ-line interventions, in which genetic modifications would be passed on to children." Also, "[u]sing genetics for human enhancement rather than therapeutics poses huge dilemmas," argues Eric Parens, an associate at the Hastings Center in Garrison, New York. He also has said that "no institution in the US today is constituted as a forum for discussing such big-picture issues. . . . The risks are huge. I'm surprised by how little attention these developments have received. . . . Nobody is educating people, and it's crucially important that we have a public conversation."[22] Other critics of genetic engineering and human cloning argue that the vision promised by this science is against nature's and God's design— humans should be able to get sick, grow old, and die. A counterargument to this charge is this: "Evolution perfects nothing; it is a tinkerer, not an engineer. The dream of perfect health is specious. New forms of disease will continue to emerge as bacteria and viruses evolve, genes mutate and our environment changes. We can no more eradicate all disease than control the evolution of all life."[23] Still another related aspect of this debate is the issue over human cloning. Dolly the Scottish sheep was cloned after 227 attempts. Presently, "[t]he success rate for all cloning experiments is only a few percent."[24] Still, attempts are moving forward by some scientists to clone humans. Panos Zavos of the University of Kentucky and Severino Antinori, the Italian fertility doctor, are trying to clone a human baby over the next few years. Part of the ethical and theological issue centers on humans taking the power and responsibility to create—worse, to duplicate an already existing —human life. One argument countering this ethical charge is that while it may be possible to create a physical replica of a person, it is not possible to replicate a human *self*. "The essence of the self then is information—information embodied in that flux of flowing matter called life, partly inborn, partly acquired through experience. As the ancients guessed, the soul is immaterial and potentially immortal. . . ."[25] Not all critics would agree.

The stem-cell debate addresses the question of whether scientists should be permitted to use embryonic stem cells as treatments for an unlimited number of human diseases (such as Parkinson's and Alzheimer's) and as replacements for poorly functioning or life-threatening human organs. Stem cells are unspecialized human cells that are capable of developing into any kind of tissue or cell that can be used to replace and/or treat illnesses. One ethical aspect of this debate is whether or not stem cells from unborn fetuses should be used, especially if the life of a fetus is threatened. The question then becomes at what point an embryo is considered a human life. Another issue is, What would prevent unborn fetuses' stem cells from being sold on a market (even a black market) to those willing to pay? This has already happened with kidneys. Also, would stem cells be in demand for customers who were not ill, but who wished to reap whatever physical benefits stem cells could provide? The issue then develops legal, legislative, and enforcement dimensions of international proportion. Currently, the use of federal funds for stem-cell research on a limited number of stem-cell "lines" that already exist is at the legislative level of the issue life cycle (as discussed in Chapter 2).[26]

The scientific breakthroughs discussed here also echo the issue of whether society is creating a "Brave New World," as Aldous Huxley wrote in 1932. In that book, Huxley warned of a futuristic society where pain, sickness, unhappiness, and even humanity are replaced by a somewhat draconian portrayal of science. Based partly on Huxley's thinking, in this age of genetic engineering and human cloning, two ethics collide: the "sanctity-of-life ethic" and the "quality-of-life ethic." The sanctity-of-life ethic is characterized by those who advocate against the promises, uses, and consumption of bioengineered and other genetically altered and newly created products, services, and treatments. The quality-of-life ethic is characterized by those who advocate the opposite.[27] It may be simplistic and even unrealistic to divide ethics and individuals or groups into these dichotomous categories. At the same time, it is may also be a useful exercise to ask which of the two categories you would use to categorize your own beliefs regarding issues about genetically engineered food, treatments, medicines, and other possibilities for altering and extending human life.

THE ENVIRONMENT: FREE-MARKET COMMODITY OR SUSTAINABLE STAKEHOLDER?

Whether the next or later generations will be able to breathe, drink water, and eat from the earth is a debated issue for the future that is also surfacing now. As stated in Chapter 5:

> A time existed when corporations used the environment as a free and unlimited resource. That time is ending, in terms of international public awareness and increasing legislative control. The magnitude of environmental abuse, not only by industries but also by human activities and nature's processes, has awakened

an international awareness to protect and save the environment. At risk is the most valuable stakeholder, the earth itself. Depletion and destruction of air, water, and land are at stake in terms of natural resources. Consider the destruction of the rain forests in Brazil; the thinning of the ozone layer above the earth's atmosphere; climatic warming changes from carbon dioxide accumulations; the smog in Mexico City, Los Angeles, and New York City; and the pollution of the seas, lakes, rivers, and groundwater supplies contaminated from toxic dumping; the survival of Florida's Everglades national park. At the human level, environmental pollution and damage cause heart and respiratory diseases and lung and skin cancer. Registered voters stated that the most important environmental problems facing the nation were: Air pollution 26%, Unsafe drinking water 11%, Water pollution 11%, Toxic/hazardous waste 10%.[28]

There is evidence that governments, nations, and many corporations have contributed and are contributing to an ecology ethic that respects the environment as a sustainable, valued resource. At the 1997 Earth Summit Plus Five conference, representatives from 170 countries evaluated the need for economic development of poor nations while protecting the environment for future generations. The nations that met in Kyoto, Japan, in 1997 signed an international treaty on global warming and other agreements to protect the environment (the United States was the only country not to sign some of these agreements). Evidence shows that as the world population grows, the rate of growth lessens. Efforts have been made to reduce the deterioration of and restore the ozone layer. Global organizations that observe, meet with, and assist companies and governments to develop, implement, and monitor standards to protect the air, water, and land from pollution include the World Bank, the World Commission on Environment and Development, NGOs (non-governmental organizations, discussed earlier), the World Business Council for Sustainable Development, the World Industry Council for the Environment, the International Chamber of Commerce, and the International Organization for Standardization (ISO).[29] Still, the issue for many companies and nations remains: What ethic do companies use in the actual policies and practices toward the environment? Environmental ethics is not based on the Western philosophy of control over the environment or on the dualism and separation between humans and nature. Rather, an emerging view holds that ". . . human society is part of an integrated ecosystem and that humans have ethical obligations toward nature."[30] Since most companies, and governments, use a profit-based and utilitarian ethic in deciding what and how many resources to exploit, an ecology ethic toward the environment represents a radical departure in thinking and decision making. As discussed in Chapter 5, many firms have adopted green marketing and environmental justice with a profit ethic.

Finally, managing environmental stakeholders is a necessary part of doing business responsibly for companies who are serious about "doing good while doing well." One study[31] of 6 UK water and electricity companies showed that while none of the companies had a systematic stakeholder approach that included all potential environmental groups, the "green stakeholders"—especially the Environmental Protection Agency and those stakeholders with an institutional power base with governmental legislation and environmental and industry regulation—were accorded increasing importance in political discourse. Customers and the general public were also found to be important as sources for corporate social legitimacy whose influence ". . . was more long term and based on voice, rather than the potential for direct retaliation." Including key stakeholders who affect business and "green" decisions is a necessary part of managing the environment responsibly.

THE FUTURE OF GLOBALIZATION

The September 11 attack has had and may have one the most profound impacts on globalization to date. John Gray, a professor at the London School of Economics, pessimistically declared that the era of globalization is finished after September 11: "The entire view of the world that supported the markets' faith in globalisation has melted down . . . Led by the United States, the world's richest states have acted on the assumption that people everywhere want to live as they do. As a result, they failed to recognise the deadly mixture of emotions—cultural resentment, the sense of injustice and a genuine rejection of western modernity—that lies behind the attacks on New York and Washington . . . The ideal of a universal civilisation is a recipe for unending conflict, and it is time it was given up."[32] Counterarguments to this claim include the following: ". . . Western governments do a poor job of explaining and defending globalisation—so poor as to breed disaffection with democratic politics."[33] Also, ". . . what about the view that globalisation is a kind of cultural conquest? This too is plainly wrong. Under a market system, economic interaction is voluntary. This is the market's greatest virtue, greater by far than its superior productivity. So there is no reason to fear that globalisation itself threatens traditional non-western cultures, such as Islam, except in so far as individual freedom threatens them. McDonald's does not march people into its outlets at the point of a gun. Nike does not require people to wear its trainers on pain of imprisonment. If people buy those things, it is because they choose to, not because globalisation is forcing them to."[34]

The magnitude of the economic process in globalization between the United States and Europe prior to September 11 illustrates only part of the economic growth that is at stake since the attack:

> Total U.S. direct investment in Europe amounted to $520 billion, more than 60% of all foreign direct investment in the U.S. While in 1999, $68 billion flowed from the U.S. to the EU in direct investment, the flow from the EU to the U.S. was over $235 billion and as a result our economic ties are strong and getting stronger. Now French, German, British, Dutch, Belgian, Spanish, and Italian companies are prominent in America. Indeed in America today, one in 12 factory workers is employed by one of the 4,000 European-owned businesses active in the U.S.[35]

If the productive processes of globalization are to survive and thrive in the twenty-first century, the so-called Second and Third World countries must be listened to and included into economic world trade and planning organizations. Political stability is a prerequisite for economic growth. A human rights ethic must become global in practice. One author stated, "We know that our ancestors were social beings long before they were human beings, and could not have developed the abilities and capacities of human beings if they had not been social beings first. In any case we are not, now, isolated individuals. If we consider people living together in a community, it is less easy to assume that rights must be restricted to rights against interference. We might, instead, adopt the view that taking rights to life seriously is incompatible with standing by and watching people die when one could easily save them. . . ."[36] The "dark side" of globalization identified in Chapter 7 will also continue to exert influences on the other processes: global crime and corruption, child labor, the drug trade, the unwelcome export of Western culture and values to other cultures, and tensions over terrorism and nation-state sovereignty. After the September 11 attack, a major part of and threat to globalization is the ideological divide between fundamentalist movements that misinterpret Islam for political reasons and the West. The following questions may provide clues that can help close this divide: What countries and groups continue to be left out of the global political, economic, technological, and wealth-generating activities and why? What human and moral issues need to be addressed to bridge the divides between the First and Third World nations that inhibit the positive aspects of globalization?

Positive developments that could emerge from the September attack are, as noted earlier, new alliances, trading partners, an openness to religious diversity, and the integration of previous political adversaries that may form a new world order with even more dramatic global growth. The future development of globalization will depend in large part on how issues from the dark side of globalization will be addressed and solved and by whom.

8.3 THE TECHNOLOGY REVOLUTION AND ETHICS

"A Verizon switching office that handled 200,000 telephone lines and 3 million data lines was severely damaged by the attack. Its office represented 40 percent of lower Manhattan's phone lines and 20 percent of the New York Stock Exchange's phones, according to Associated Press reports. WorldCom and Sprint, which operate much of the Internet's 'backbone' infrastructure, also lost hundreds of high-bandwidth data lines that had passed under the World Trade Center. . . . But the Internet itself remained strong, as data was routed around the damaged switches and transmission lines, taking alternate paths exactly as its designers intended. . . . For businesses, that amounts to a ringing endorsement of Internet-based communications.

Executives who pooh-poohed instant messaging in the past may find themselves relying on it now, particularly in emergencies where other forms of communication have been shut down or damaged beyond immediate repair. . . ."[37]

The technology revolution led by the Internet and digital and wireless technologies has created change in almost every dimension of society: communication, science, medicine, politics, commerce, law, education, productivity, work, and professions. And during crises, as the above excerpt shows, Internet and wireless technologies can prove to be vital.

Technologies have also reconfigured our use of time: We can now work and do commerce on a 24-7-365 cycle. Earlier chapters discussed how technology and the Internet have accelerated business productivity, competitiveness, and growth globally. Globalization and capitalism have been enhanced by information technologies: financial markets, trading and currency exchanges, and capital flows are no longer limited by time of day or time zones; intranets and extranets enable buying, selling, and brokering of products and services among companies, vendors, suppliers, customers, and strategic alliances. New companies (portals, media firms, e-commerce firms) have been created, as have new professions—Web designers, information technology consultants, and database and content managers, to name a few). Advances in DNA, genetics, and stem-cell research are aided by information technologies, as are new medical procedures. Politically, the Internet creates information-sharing communities and, as such, enhances conditions for democratizing closed societies as well as mobilizing political groups.

ETHICAL ISSUES

New technologies present ethical problems and issues as well as opportunities. Possible scientific and "Brave New World" misuses of technology were discussed above. For individual citizens and employees, technology also poses issues relating to privacy, individual rights, and personal safety. Consider these three scenarios:[38]

> *Scenario #1:* "A 31-year-old single mother in Lanham, Md., had her government-mandated Social Security number hijacked by a thief who created a false identity, ran up huge bills, and ruined the woman's credit."

> *Scenario #2:* "President Bush has sent his last e-mail, concerned that anything he might write online to a friend or family member could be obtained by the media under public-records laws."

> *Scenario #3:* "At the Colorado Neurological Institute, the majority of people in a Huntington's disease support group declined to undergo genetic tests for fear that the results would end up in records that could affect their health-care coverage or employment prospects."

What do these three situations have in common? "The justified fear that information intended for one purpose (a Social Security account number, a private e-mail, a medical diagnosis) could be taken out of context, used for some other purpose and then cause lasting harm to the person who 'owns' the information. . . ."[39]

The myth that "information and computing are amoral" was presented in Chapter 1, where it was noted that ". . . information and computing have a dark side: information about individuals can be used as 'a form of control, power, and manipulation.' "[40] Also, with open access to information, the following issues arise: the violation of privacy, children being exposed to pornography and stalking, consumers becoming an easier target for fraudulent advertising and selling practices, and the pirating of intellectual property. DeGeorge observed that truth and accuracy must be protected and guarded, ". . . falsehood, inaccuracy, lying, deception, disinformation, misleading information are all vices and enemies of the Information Age, for they undermine it. . . . [F]raud, misrepresentation, and falsehood are inimical to all of them."[41]

A related issue in cyberspace is that of censorship versus free speech. The Telecommunications Competition and Deregulation Act, signed into law in February 1996, has an "indecency" provision that makes graphic displays of sex and nudity on the Internet illegal. Supporters of the legislation claimed it is necessary to protect children, while civil libertarians say the Internet should have no more restrictions on free speech than books have. Several groups, including the American Civil Liberties Union and the Electronic Frontier Foundation, challenged the "indecency" law in court.

Another censorship problem is: Who sets the limits for the context of information? Especially of concern are pornography and gambling. States such as Nevada, in which gambling is legal, introduced on-line gambling services. Censoring cyberspace is a difficult endeavor, especially on a global scale. Although governments' efforts to legally impede the spread of "indecent" content on the Internet have begun, the issues have yet to be settled among stakeholders.

In the United States, an amendment to the telecom-reform legislation would make it a crime to knowingly transmit "indecent" materials over the Net. The punishment: $100,000 and two years in jail. As the Internet industry is embroiled with regulation and censorship, children are being targeted in a very different way. In fact, children's advocacy groups have called on the federal government to regulate the growing volume of cyberspace marketing aimed at children. The Center for Media Education, a public-interest organization, targeted 32 snack-food, toy, entertainment, and on-line computer service companies that sell products or services for children. The report stated that the companies are using the Internet's World Wide Web and other interactive computer sites to communicate with unsuspecting youngsters—as young as four years old. The companies also obtain personal information about children and make aggressive pitches to children for their products. Children's advocacy groups have called for strong governmental and industry actions to set standards governing on-line marketing aimed at children. The idea is not to ban ads for children on the Internet, but to make it a safer place for child viewers. This same argument holds true not only for marketing, but also for on-line Websites that take more from consumers of all ages than they are aware of and, if they were aware, are willing to give.

Senator Ernest Hollings, a Democrat from South Carolina, stated at a July, 2001 hearing on Internet privacy that Internet privacy legislation should be based on the definition of fair information practices formulated by Robert Pitofsky (former Federal Trade Commission chairman): "(1) providing notices to consumers about a company's privacy policies; (2) obtaining consent from consumers to share information; (3) giving consumers access to information collected about them; and (4) ensuring the security of consumers' personal information."[42]

Stephen Keating, executive director of the Denver-based Privacy Foundation, identified weak areas of on-line privacy protection and suggested five ways to solve privacy issues on the Internet.[43]

1. *Research on privacy issues from the perspectives of computer science, law, and business ethics is needed.* Keating argued that there are not enough available facts about privacy implications of the Internet and other two-way communication technologies (e.g., TV set-top boxes and wireless phones) for consumers to make informed judgments. Research has barely scratched the surface on medical records privacy, broadband privacy and the economics of privacy.

2. *Review of government data is required.* The privacy standards of government agencies need review. The Social Security Administration, created in 1936, is a prime example. "Social Security numbers have become a skeleton key—seemingly available to anyone—to unlock our credit and financial records and wreak havoc. The solution is so basic that it will probably never be enacted: return the Social Security number to its original purpose, as an identifier for retirement accounts and as an identifier for reporting income to the Internal Revenue Service. If we want to create a national numbering system for citizens, then we should have that debate openly and publicly. It shouldn't be done on the sly, through a system like Social Security numbering that is rife with abuse," states Keating.[44]

    Another area of concern is the judiciary. There is a proposal that, if passed, would put most court documents online through a system called PACER. If divorce lawsuits and bankruptcy records, for example, are put on the World Wide Web for data brokers to "slice, dice and sell," that would a significant privacy violation. Keating has suggested that the Administrative Office of the Courts form a national commission to study this subject before moving forward.

3. *Clear disclosure will help.* A sentence from a privacy policy of a popular retailer's Internet site states in very fine print: "We also use personally

identifiable and aggregate information for a variety of marketing and promotional purposes. For instance, we use what we have learned about your preferences to alert you to new areas when you return to our Web site, or to help us or our business partners target advertising or product placements to your particular interests." This is complicated and confusing, Keating observes. He proposes that companies use "straight talk" for consumers so they can decide if they wish to do business with the company and allow them to use their information.

4. *Common sense can be used.* Common sense is not used. Keating offers the example of workplace surveillance. "There seems to be a 'don't-ask-don't-tell' policy among employers and employees, by which some employers secretly monitor the e-mail and Internet use of employees but it's never discussed until something bad happens and people get fired," Keating notes and goes on to recommend that "[e]mployers should disclose up front what they're monitoring and why. Employees should make it their business to know what's allowed and what's not."

5. *Fair information practices should be created.* A 1973 government report, Keating wrote, identified many standards to protect an individual's use of personal information, which also included a prohibiting against "secondary use"—". . . which is personal information collected for one purpose that is instead used for another purpose without the person's consent. Secondary use is why we shouldn't allow our driver's license pictures, for example, to be sold by the state to data brokers without our consent—no matter how worthy the goal."[45] Secondary use is a good and fair standard that could be used with other privacy problems. Fair information practices based on reasonable, common-sense standards are needed for individual privacy protection on the Internet.

Employers are also challenged to develop fair and reasonable standards for employees' workplace use of the Internet. Such standards and practices should be based on current research regarding Internet use in the workplace, laws and government guidelines, and common sense that clearly articulates management's expectations and policies, while respecting employees' rights as corporate and constitutional citizens.

8.4 THE CHANGING WORKFORCE

The changing nature of the workforce and related issues affects employers, employees, and other stakeholders. Current and projected changes in the workforce that were discussed in Chapter 6 are briefly referenced here, along with ethical implications.

A Workforce Faces Crisis

The September 11 attack and aftermath provide one of the most vivid profiles of the demonstrated values of a wide cross-section of senior executives and employees of every rank and level in public and private organizations across industries—not only in New York City, but internationally.
American executives and employees who survived the attack in New York
showed courage, compassion, responsibility, and community in the face of
crisis. Many professionals and employees who faced death—often their
own—then grief, and destruction around them continued to meet the challenges at hand, while helping others. One example among many illustrates the values professionals demonstrated following the September 11
attack:

> The world's two largest insurance brokers, while still reeling from the loss of
> their employees at the World Trade Center September 11, said last week that
> they are committed to meeting clients' needs and resuming normal business
> operations. For the past week, the primary focus at Marsh & McLennan Cos. Inc.
> and Aon Corp. has been on searching for missing employees and on comforting
> and assisting family members and other employees affected by the catastrophe.
> . . . Late last week, Marsh was missing 313 of the approximately 1,900
> employees who either worked at or were visiting 1 World Trade Center, where
> Marsh Inc. occupied floors 93 through 100. Aon, which occupied floors 92 and 98
> through 105 of 2 World Trade Center, is missing approximately 200 of its 1,146
> employees who were in the South Tower when it was struck by United Airlines
> 767 at the level of about the 87th floor.[46]

Kenneth J. LeStrange, chairman of Aon Risk Services Cos. Inc., said during an interview from Aon's temporary client service center, set up in mid-
town Manhattan, "We remain very committed to our clients, as well as very
saddened by the loss of our employees," "We never lost sight of their
needs."[47]

Philosopher and consultant Peter Koestenbaum reflected on the crisis
this way:

> Yesterday we thought: "Those brokers up in the towers are my competitors. They
> make more money than I do. I am going to beat them in the competition for
> clients' funds!" Today, we are confronted with the thought: "Now they are dead,
> and their offices are pulverized. Some jumped out of windows." Today, it's
> obvious that what matters is our common humanity, not that we are adversaries
> in the marketplace. How twisted have our values become that we forgot this for
> a moment? The world hasn't changed from self-sufficiency to dependency. No.
> We have changed from who we pretended to be to who we truly are. . . . The
> shock of death exists to teach you that your first decision—and there is no
> other—is to commit yourself to the creation of an ethical world, a civilized
> existence, a moral order. Am I an ethical person, first and foremost, always and
> with no exceptions? How can I, even for a moment, bypass this weighty cross-
> examination?[48]

A WORKFORCE IN TRANSITION: BETWEEN OLD AND NEW ECONOMIES

The American workforce also continues to experience a paradigm shift between the so-called old and new economies. The effects of integrating information technology into work and work life are not trivial:

> There is a shift to knowledge work which increases the potential for satisfying work but also heightened stress. The concept of "a job and career for life" is dead or dying. Professionals are changing careers 5 to 8 times on average during their working lives. Compensation, income, and the social distribution of benefits in the "new economy" are shifting. Decreases in income are occurring at mid and lower level professions with the exception of high skill, high demand technologies. Quality of work life is not inherent or guaranteed in the uses of technology. In one worse case scenario, Thomas Malone of MIT stated that all work relationships could possibly be mediated by the market with every employee functioning as a company in shifting alliances and ventures.[49]

Moreover, demographics will drive an increasing focus on family, personal, and spiritual matters. Employees want balance in their lives. Of men age 21 through 39, 82 percent now offer family as their top priority. Aging baby boomers desire less "overwork." Employees will demand that employers make alternative schedules that work. Demands from the "sandwiched generation" (i.e., those raising families while taking care of aging parents) and also from burnout contribute to the demand for flextime and part-time. Internet-age values will take deeper root in the workplace. Many post dot-com workforce values will continue, such as fluid working styles, short-term rewards for performance, and quick readiness to change jobs if their values and needs are not fulfilled. The growth in New Age employee benefits will slow in a back-to-basics trend. Companies are cutting many perks that flourished during the previous economic boom—health and wellness programs and subsidized cafeterias, according to the Society for Human Resource Management. It will get harder to tell work and home lifestyles apart. Sixty percent of employees reported they spend 25 percent of each workday on personal matters (e.g. doctor appointments). Ford Motor Company, along with other corporations, supports the blending of work, family, and personal lives as a workplace strategy.

A sample of expectations and American workforce values taken from interviews during this paradigm shift includes:

- Competitive pay
- Benefits and opportunities to improve skills
- A fair deal in seeing that the company keeps its promises
- A feeling of being valued
- Decent relationships at work, especially with immediate bosses
- Recognition for competence and accomplishment

- Respect and dignity
- Personal choice and freedom
- Involvement at work
- Pride in work
- Quality of lifestyle
- Financial security
- Self-development
- Health and wellness

THE AGING WORKFORCE

"By 2015, nearly 20% of the U.S. workforce will be 55 years old or over, up from 13% in 2001. In 2001, those who are 40 and above will surpass those under 40 for the first time. At the same time, those aged 16 to 24—the baby-busters (those born after the boomers)—will make up 16 percent of the workforce and will continue to decline. The seniors—those over age 55—will represent about 13 percent of the workforce. It is interesting to note that Japan is the first nation ever with a population that has an average age of 40. By 2020, 6 out of 10 Japanese will be retired." The aging of the "baby boom" generation, combined with the relatively low supply of younger entrants to the labor market, presents problems for future leadership of many corporations. The demand for technology-savvy and competent workers will continue the trend toward hiring and outsourcing professionals. Pressure for training existing professionals in new technologies will also continue.

Value shifts in the aging population are also surfacing. For example, health and wellness programs, retirement planning, and reward systems that provide more flex-time arrangements are getting more attention. Also, an increase in the demand for young workers will lead to an increase in the demand for those professionals who are available, increasing numbers of women, international professionals, and workers with disabilities. Companies will need to institute adequate training programs to develop necessary skills in a labor pool that will probably lack many specific skills. This change in demand also will lead to increasing competition for entry-level workers. Restructured compensation packages will be required to respond to the needs and values of young and other nontraditional workers. Dependent care and family responsibilities also will appear as dominant concerns for a growing majority of the workforce. All of these changes will pressure established values and stakeholders' rights.

WOMEN IN THE WORKFORCE

"Women represented 46.6% percent of the workforce in 1999. This figure is projected to reach 47.5% in 2008. Two-thirds of the new entrants between 1985 and 2000 were female. Three-fourths of all working women will be in their childbearing years. Women with children under six years old represent the most rapidly increasing segment of the workforce. 49.5% of managerial and professional specialty positions are women. 12.5% are on boards of directors. 4.1% are top earners. Two were Fortune 500 CEOs in 2000." As a result, corporations hoping to attract and retain qualified female employees will need to address issues relevant to women in particular. Some of these will include changes in the measurements of success, as more females reach the executive level; changes in leave and flex-time policies to accommodate family responsibilities; benefit requirements of single mothers, women in dual-career families, and women without children; emphasis on child care; and availability of flexible or home-based positions. Questions and issues of "fairness" in work policies, procedures, and decisions among single and married employees, and employees with children, are also likely to continue.

ETHNIC AND CULTURAL DIVERSITY IN THE WORKFORCE

"By 2080, more than 27 percent of the U.S. population will be nonwhite; nonwhite people will make up 15 percent of the U.S. workforce. 2000 census figures show that the Hispanic population grew 58 percent to 35.3 million people since 1990, now at near parity with blacks." Hispanics outnumber blacks in Florida and make up one-third of California's population. "For the first time, Americans had the option of identifying themselves as belonging to more than one race. Nearly 7 million people, or 2.4 percent of the nation, described themselves as multiracial." These changes are challenging companies to integrate varieties of values, norms, and lifestyles. Corporations will need to adopt many new policies and procedures in order to meet this challenge. These may include providing cultural awareness training, redesigning jobs and establishing training to compensate for language barriers, establishing reward systems and promotion possibilities that correspond to different value systems, developing new and improved methods for dealing with cultural diversity, and perhaps formally recognizing managers who are successful at integrating a diverse workforce.

In addition to race, national origin, gender, and age diversity, employers are also facing issues regarding the recognition of same-sex marriages, with accompanying rights and employer obligations (such as insurance and other benefits).

WORKERS WITH DISABILITIES

A diminishing traditional labor pool will continue to precipitate the need to tap into currently available resources. The population of workers with disabilities has remained largely underused, but an increasing future demand is predicted for skills this group offers. Workers with disabilities typically have had problems finding and maintaining jobs even though legislation has been enacted to protect their rights. This is due in large measure to distorted perceptions of their skills and a lack of support for those who attempt to fit into rigid corporate cultures. Corporations will need to continue to implement policies to assist and support both workers with disabilities and nondisabled workers in the effort to integrate the workforce. The following initiatives will need to be implemented: career development programs for persons with disabilities, employee assistance programs, flexible hours and working conditions, and programs with community, state, and health care providers for education and resources for effectively integrating persons with disabilities into the workforce.

THE EDUCATION GAP IN THE WORKFORCE

The dichotomy in the education levels of those in and those entering the workforce is growing. The number of less-educated entrants is also increasing. For example, in the mid-1980s, 86 percent of 25- to 29-year-olds had graduated from high school; but in 1988, 20 million functionally illiterate people were living in the United States. Of the 18- to 21-year-old population, 13.6 percent did not complete high school. This disparity divides the workforce into two segments: (1) the highly educated middle-aged employees, who will demand a challenging, semiautonomous, and performance-based environment, and (2) the less-educated employees, who will require structured special training. Companies will need to sponsor programs within the community to facilitate appropriate training. Business leaders and companies are already working with legislators, private education foundations, competitive private school certification programs, and school system administrators and educators to increase the quality and standards of education.

The task of managing and working with a wide range of professional needs, values, and ethical standards will continue to challenge corporations in the future. On-line training, face-to-face training, and coaching programs will continue to flourish as managers and professionals work internally to integrate their diversity while competing externally.

8.5 STAKEHOLDER MANAGEMENT AND ETHICAL NAVIGATION

The legitimacy of U.S. business institutions is founded on the notion that the free-market system operates to provide value to society and to serve the public good. The historical role of business initially was to maximize profits in order to effect greater economic welfare for the general public. It was believed business fulfilled its social and economic responsibilities through the "invisible hand" working in the market system.[50] The underlying public support for business as a legitimate institution stems from that perception. Although a time existed when the moral obligations of corporations were taken for granted and were assumed to be fulfilled when economic functions were achieved, that time is past. September 11 opened up the gates and blurred the invisible boundaries between emotions and intellect, ethics, politics, security, and international interests with business at the local level.

A stakeholder, value-based management perspective holds that the legitimacy, power, and long-term success of a company depend on the extent to which it serves the public through its economic competitiveness and innovativeness, while meeting moral obligations to its stakeholders. These are not mutually exclusive goals. Business executives demonstrated a high level of moral sensitivity and responsiveness after the September 11 attack. For example, U.S. markets and the financial system rallied because of dedicated workers who showed a sense of duty to the welfare of the country as well as to their own interests. This was the response of most businesses in the country.

The stakeholder management view acknowledges the integration of the corporation's economic and competitive imperatives with its moral priorities of serving the public good through, for example, the responsible design, manufacture, and distribution of products and services and the concern for the welfare of its stakeholders. Attention to these moral as well as business concerns is essential to the firm's long-term survival, reputation, and relationship with its buying public. This view also recognizes that firms should not destroy the environment while using its resources. Nor should firms produce dangerous products that can harm and even kill consumers over time while creating and satisfying temporary needs.

Issues that businesses should, we argue, prioritize in the twenty-first century include their economic, political, and moral obligations toward a wide range of stakeholders. For example, some of the predominant issues include:

- Ensuring the safety and security of employees
- Resolving national trade rivalries and respecting human rights internationally, as well as helping host economies and workers where business is conducted
- Prioritizing consumer protection and product safety
- Preventing environmental pollution and depletion of the ozone layer and natural resources
- Actively using economic influence and investments to alleviate domestic and international social injustices
- Providing healthy working environments
- Providing policies and procedures that prevent discrimination within the organization
- Being a good societal and global citizen, as reflected in policies and actions taken toward all stakeholders

ETHICAL LEADERSHIP IN AND AMONG COMPANIES

Ethical principles and practices in business start with the top leaders. Their values model behaviors for others in the organization. The corporate culture also mirrors these values that underlie business practices. The development and implementation of ethical values through codes, ethics training courses, ethics offices, sexual harassment programs, and ombudsperson and peer review programs provide the concrete blocks that build long-term stakeholder relationships based on principles of fairness.[51] Seven recommendations for integrating ethical codes of conduct and practices into real-time corporate strategies, culture, and values are as follows:

1. Confidentiality should not be so restrictive that it prohibits employees from consulting with internal personnel regarding ethical questions.

2. A fair and objective hearing process should follow any report of an ethical problem or conflict.

3. Assurance should be given to all employees that their rights with respect to discrimination and to adequate notice and compensation in the event of a layoff will be protected.

4. In order to facilitate open communication and clarify expectations, employee rights and terms of employment should be clearly stated in codes of conduct and ethics codes.

5. Executive support of the code of conduct should be demonstrated in the form of clear sanctions against those who violate it.

6. Conflicts of interest revolving around ownership interest in related concerns need to be addressed, as these conflicts can cloud judgments.

7. Consider any external ethical codes of conduct that influence employees in the corporation, and design the corporate code so it does not conflict with these.

NAVIGATING ETHICS IN THE GLOBAL BUSINESS ENVIRONMENT

The international environment and community became local and blurred as of September 11, 2001. While the number of multinational firms operating in the global marketplace today has set the stage for increasing interdependencies, every professional traveling and doing business abroad is now required to understand the new complexities involved in doing business abroad. The overlap of ideology, ethics, safety, and politics with business imperatives is evident. Globalization that integrates multinational with national corporations, and international interests with local concerns, provides new business and economic opportunities and increased risks for conflicts between companies and professionals with differing values and moral codes of conduct.

This is especially true given the context of shifting regional alliances and blocs in which business occurs: for example, the integration of old and new political alliances in the Middle East after September 11, the continuing integration of European countries and the Commonwealth of Independent States (formerly the U.S.S.R.), and the inclusion of China into the World Trade Organization. Stakeholder and value-based management views also became global in scope after September 11.

Buller, Kohls, and Anderson[52] define ethics to include "both the moral codes and values used in the reasoning process as well as the decisions and the behaviors that result from them." Their goal is to define and achieve a global *level of consensus* among international parties regarding the rightness or wrongness of particular acts, policies, and decisions. The authors suggest that the following four interrelated dimensions (individual, corporate, societal, and global) strongly influence each other. The ethics of an individual, for example, is greatly influenced by ethical standards common to his or her society and corporate environment. Likewise, although corporate ethics largely reflects the society where the organization is operating, individuals within the organization also bring their own perspectives and ethical beliefs into the firm.

The concept of global ethics is even more complex because people and institutions reflecting different individual, corporate, and societal ethical standards interact. The higher the degree to which nations and multinational enterprises share values, beliefs, and opinions regarding ethical conduct for specific issues, the greater everyone's ability and opportunity to establish global ethical guidelines should be. The challenges are learning (1) to become aware of value and perceptual differences across cultures at all levels and (2) to become competent in negotiating differences into consensual agreements.

Using universal ethical principles is necessary but not always sufficient for resolving local conflicts of interest where two or three "right" ways seem to conflict. Universal ethical principles (i.e., hypernorms, as discussed in Chapter 7) can help stakeholders negotiate consensus across individual, corporate, and societal levels (e.g., acknowledging that an ecology policy should be designed to protect natural forests and bodies of water). Identifying agreed-on hypernorms can also help raise awareness of the harmful effects of well-intended local interests on a larger number of people. However, hypernorms or "global ethics" alone usually does not dissuade stakeholders from wanting their share of benefits from a decision. For this reason, resolving moral dilemmas requires thinking globally, while solving problems locally.

THINK GLOBALLY, ACT LOCALLY

Resolving ethical dilemmas both locally and internationally involves creative and critical thinking, collaboration, and sound ethical judgment, as discussed in Chapter 7. A trend in corporate training and business ethics, as discussed in this book, is toward value-based management of stakeholder relationships, which are grounded on developing trust and a high level of informal communication between individuals and teams. While companies generally identify universal ethical principles and values to ground employees' decisions, the changing complexities and turbulence in international environments require "outside the box" thinking to reach practical, good business decisions that are morally defensible. Gray decisional areas can quickly become dilemmas and even crises. It is therefore helpful for companies and professionals to form relationships with their stakeholders and to understand and share those values that ultimately define the parameters of business decisions. Toward this end, professionals can use these key stakeholder management principles to navigate ethics while still responding to profit imperatives:

- Articulate independent, responsible *choices* compatible with the corporation's and other stakeholders' values and missions in unclear and poorly defined gray decision areas.

- Understand *the uses and limits of responsible corporate power* in developing autonomous business relationships and making tough decisions. Know what the senior officers' and managers' guidelines, thoughts, and recommendations are in these areas.

- Maintain *responsibility in flexible business relationships*, while balancing profit with different ethical imperatives. Find out what dilemmas others in the company have experienced and how they effectively solved difficult problems. Develop a repertoire of company success stories and creative problem-solving techniques.

- Negotiate among cross-cultural values, interests, and expectations, while maintaining one's core values and business commitments. First, it is necessary to *be familiar with the cultural norms, traditions, and business practices of the region, country, and group with which business is being conducted.* Japanese, Chinese, North Americans, Latin Americans, Russians, and Arabs all have different values, styles, views of relationships, and understandings of time.[53] Understanding the differences is a first step.

- *Become familiar with conditions and techniques regarding when or when not to negotiate.* Ellen Raider offers conditions for determining when to "negotiate, bargain, or just take-it-or-leave it."[54]

- Buller, Kohls, and Anderson[55] present seven approaches for dealing with cross-cultural conflicts, which are summarized in the box on page 331. Although these approaches are not new, they illustrate starting points for discussing the choices a corporation or party has for solving and resolving conflicts.

- *Listen to and assertively communicate the "best interests" of all parties* when required in a negotiation without sacrificing one's ethical position. Four simple but effective principles in the book *Getting to Yes* are helpful[56]:
  (1) Separate the people from the problem;
  (2) Focus on interests, not positions;
  (3) Generate a variety of possibilities before deciding what to do;
  (4) Insist that the result be based upon some objective standard.

Being aware of and using skills for effectively negotiating and managing morality in business transactions increase in importance as professionals

<table>
<tr><td>

7 CONFLICT RESOLUTION TECHNIQUES

</td></tr>
</table>

1. Avoidance. This technique is used when the conflict is relegated to a background position and is not dealt with directly. If one party is in a significantly stronger bargaining position, avoidance as a negotiation and conflict-resolution strategy may be used to prevent the occurrence or further escalation of ethical conflicts.

2. Forcing. When one party imposes its will on another, this technique can be helpful. Many multinational corporations have been accused of disrespecting and intruding on host-country cultures. Host-country governments, such as India, Brazil, and Spain, have responded in the past by forcing restrictions on MNEs' profits, such as by requiring that profits stay in the country and by limiting technological manufacturing. Forcing is a high-risk strategy in the international arena and should be considered only when the situation, people, and interests require it. Some critics argue the U.S. government should use this tactic more often with Japan regarding trade policies. The United States, it is argued, has negotiated with Japan from a position of weakness and has not identified what long-term stakes the U.S. government really needs in order to bargain.

3. Education/Persuasion. This technique employs a specific means of relating the values of one party's perspectives in order to persuade the other to adopt its position. Multinationals have educated host-country employees on the values and uses of new technologies, and MNEs have learned from host governments how to share resources and help develop local economies.

4. Infiltration. This technique is an often slow process of introducing others to one party's ethic. Infiltration can result in wide acceptance of particular ideas if they hold some appeal for these individuals. Infiltration is often used unintentionally rather than strategically. For example, many former Soviet bloc countries are pursuing market economies based on their interactions with and evolving desires for Western societal structures and values. As Western market-oriented nations penetrate these economies, infiltration of marketing concepts and methods occurs.

5. Negotiation/Compromise. This technique is used when the ethical conflict presents a severe obstacle to productivity. Resolution through negotiation often will lead to compromise on both sides. Although negotiation/compromise may allow the business transaction to occur, it often can leave both sides feeling the underlying issue was never resolved.

6. Accommodation. With this technique, either party may find it beneficial to adopt the ethic of the other and may do so with little, if any, resistance. Accommodation requires patience, "give-and-take," and listening.

7. Collaboration. When implementing this technique, both parties would discuss the conflict and attempt to reach a mutually beneficial solution. Willingness to learn, to change attitudes, and to renegotiate interests is vital for collaboration. This is the most desired form of conflict resolution because it deals directly with the source.

Buller, K., Kohls, J., Anderson, K. (1991). The challenges of global ethics. *Journal of Business Ethics, 10,* 767-775.

gain independence, autonomy, authority, and control in dispersed organizations and international situations. Navigating between an organization's and other stakeholders' imperatives and interests is part art, part learned techniques, and—more often than not—involves a person's and an organization's beliefs, values, and moral imagination. Ethical decision making and business practices are inseparable.

SUMMARY

September 11, 2001: A Turning Point

September 11, 2001, is a turning point for the United States and the global community. As the crisis transforms into a new type of war, several issues have emerged that have ethical, economic, legal, social, and political consequences: (1) the vulnerability of nation-states, including all leading industrialized countries, in the twenty-first century; (2) security as a national and global priority; (3) information monitoring, profiling, and privacy concerns on an unprecedented scale; (4) religious, ideological, and racial stereotyping; and (5) whether or not this is a "just war."

The vulnerability of the United States, the world's preeminent superpower and of other nation-states was exposed. At stake are the very physical security and survival of civilians and democratic societies as we have known them.

The scope and scale of the issue of national and individual security are another result of the attack. The threat of possible biological, chemical, and Internet terrorism is one of global proportion. American institutions, infrastructure, and government are not prepared for such attacks. The threat of cyberterrorism is equally important for the United States and the international community.

Visionics, a New Jersey company, is an industry leader in the science of biometrics, ". . . a method of identifying people by scanning and quantifying their unique physical characteristics—their facial structures, for example, or their retinal patterns." A similar system has been criticized for its lack of reliability as a deterrent to local and would-be criminals. Another criticism of these types of systems relates to the power and discretion given to the person who controls access to the network of intimate images. Other concerns include the following: How many of these will be installed, how long, and where? What are the limits of the results of these systems? Who decides? What happens to individual rights and procedural justice with the widespread use of such systems? At the same time, this technology may serve as an alternative to racial and ethnic profiling. If faces in the biometric database can be limited to known terrorists, the issues of profiling can be controlled. To date, however, biometric databases in the United States and England cannot restrict face recognition to known terrorists.

Related to electronic profiling is the issue of racial and religious profiling and discrimination—especially for Muslims, some of whom are being stereotyped as "terrorists" after September 11. There are thin lines separating perception, prejudice, and discrimination.

The aftermath of the attack also revealed the courage, sacrifice, compassion, and sense of community of all those involved directly and indirectly. Business leaders and employees went beyond "the call of duty" in helping others, including their businesses. New York firefighters and police officers and the airline crew members and passengers on Flights 11, 93, and 175 became international heroes. Altruism in the face of crisis was demonstrated and witnessed.

The "global war on terrorism" raises the issue of whether this phase and the possible expansion are and will be a "just war." What are the objectives and limits of this war, and can these be defended morally? Can this war be "won"? What would "victory" be for America and its allies? Will individual privacy rights and free speech be curtailed by national security measures, i.e., military tribunals, profiling, and new surveillance? Have all feasible options for settling the issues underlying the attacks and this brand of terrorism with all parties been identified and used? Whose rights can be rectified and how by this war? Where does revenge end and justice begin? Should the terror escalate to a large-scale biochemical attack on the United States and other countries in which a large number of fatalities occur, the "just war" debate may shift to a war based on survival.

OTHER FUTURE ISSUES

Other significant issues that involve business and ethics in the foreseeable future include "First and Third World" divides, economic, technological, political, and ideological; the human genome project, cloning, and the issue "What is the human self?"; the environment as free-market commodity or sustainable stakeholder; and the future of globalization. If the productive processes of globalization are to survive and thrive in the twenty-first century, the Second and Third World countries must be listened to and included in world trade and economic planning organizations. Political stability is a prerequisite for economic growth.

New technologies present ethical problems and issues as well as opportunities for the future. Possible scientific and "Brave New World" misuses of technology were discussed. For individual citizens and employees, technology also poses issues relating to privacy, individual rights, and personal safety.

Current and projected changes in the workforce that were discussed in Chapter 6 were briefly referenced here, along with ethical implications. The September attack showed that many professionals and employees who faced death—often their own—then grief, and destruction around them continued to meet the challenges at hand, while helping others. A different face of the American workforce emerged after the attack. At the same time, many professionals began to reassess their values and meaning regarding work, family life, and purpose.

There is also a shift to a service-oriented economy and knowledge work resulting in part from the increased use of technologies. This shift increases the potential for satisfying work but also heightens stress. The concept of a "a job and career for life" is dead or dying. Professionals are changing careers five to eight times on average during their working lives. Compensation, income, and the social distribution of benefits in the "new economy" are shifting. Decreases in income are occurring at mid- and lower-level professions with the exception of high-skill, high-demand technologies. Quality of work life is not inherent or guaranteed in the uses of technology. The aging of the workforce, the inclusion of women and persons with disabilities in the workforce, the growing gap in education between groups of workers, and the need to integrate diverse groups of workers are trends that continue to present problems and opportunities. Innovation and competitive advantage come from a diverse workforce; integrating diversity also creates conflict and demands costs.

Finally, the chapter closed with a review of the stakeholder management approach and the negotiating skills required to navigate the complex environments resulting from September 11 and from continued globalization. Conditions for determining whether and when to bargain, negotiate, or "take it or leave it" in international situations were presented, along with seven conflict resolution tactics.

The stakeholder management view acknowledges the integration of the corporation's economic and competitive imperatives with its moral priorities of serving the public good through, for example, the responsible design, manufacture, and distribution of products and services and the concern for the welfare of its stakeholders. Attention to these moral as well as business concerns is essential to the firm's long-term survival, reputation, and relationship with its buying public. This view also recognizes that firms should not destroy the environment while using its resources. Nor should firms produce dangerous products that can harm and even kill consumers over time while creating and satisfying temporary needs. Navigating between an organization's and other stakeholders' interests requires creativity, moral resourcefulness, and negotiation skills.

QUESTIONS

1. Identify major issues resulting from the September 11 attack that were discussed in this chapter. Then update and identify two or more issues that have evolved from these events.

2. Describe specifically how the September 11 attack and its aftermath have or have not affected your beliefs, values, behaviors, and ethics.

3. Address the issues below, which were discussed in this chapter. Be clear and support your arguments in responding to each:
   - First and Third World economic, technological, political, and ideological "divides" must be closed before processes of globalization can continue to develop and grow.
   - As a result of the genome project and continued breakthroughs in human cloning and bioengineering, identical human beings will be produced.
   - Describe your beliefs regarding the "sanctity-of-life" versus the "quality-of-life" ethics with regard to human cloning and bioengineered food.
   - The "dark sides" of globalization can never be eradicated or "solved"—to say they can be would be equivalent to saying "evil" can be eliminated from life.
   - The increased stress and negative effects on individuals and professionals created by information technologies, wireless technologies, and the Internet are greater than the resulting benefits and increased quality of life.
   - Electronic monitoring, profiling, and biometrics (scanning and quantifying all people by their unique physical features) should be done in all cities and towns and become an ongoing method used by the FBI, CIA, and local law enforcement officers to check everyone in public places to identify possible terrorists and even those who have committed criminal offenses.

4. What are the advantages and disadvantages for a company to create and use a "global set of ethics"? What is your own belief about doing this? Explain.

5. Identify three trends that are changing the workforce. Of the trends discussed in this chapter, which add the most value, no value, or the least value in terms of creativity, innovation, and productivity? What is another trend you observe occurring in the workforce? Explain it.

EXERCISES

1. Having read this chapter, as well as related sources on business, ethics, the environment, and organizations, draft a one-page briefing you would give a chief executive officer (CEO) of a mid-sized company who wishes to know trends and issues that would help her now and in her planning for the future of her company. She also wants any insights about "business ethics" you can offer that she could use in her own thinking as a leader and in her firm.

2. Draft a statement identifying the effects you see the September 11, 2001, attacks have had on business practices and business ethics.

CASES

CASE 1
MICROSOFT: INDUSTRY PREDATOR
OR FIERCE COMPETITOR?

INTRODUCTION

On April 28, 2000, the Justice Department (under the Clinton administration) and 19 states formally asked a federal judge to split Microsoft into two competing companies to impede its dominance in the PC software market. Microsoft will appeal the decision. Fast forward to October 15, 2001: "Another mediator has been appointed to try and settle on sanctions Microsoft will accept in its ongoing antitrust case brought by the US Government [under the Bush administration]. An arbitration specialist, Eric Green, a Boston University professor, was appointed by the judge in the case. He has until November 2, 2001, to come up with a solution. If Green can't get the two sides to come together, District Judge Colleen Kollar-Kotelly said she would hold hearings starting 11 March on the penalties" (Wall Street Journal Interactive Website, World Reporter 2001). On October 31, 2001, a settlement was reached. Microsoft won and gave up some practices considered monopolistic. Highlights of the settlement will be discussed in this case. What led to Microsoft's future business stakes being openly decided by the U.S. judicial system?

Microsoft was one of the most influential software companies of the twentieth century. The company was founded by Bill Gates, Paul Allen, and several other friends to fill a niche in the personal computer (PC) operating system and software business. The phenomenal growth of this company did not happen by luck. Events that led the Department of Justice (DOJ) and 19 state attorneys general to file class action lawsuits against Microsoft for illegally bundling its Internet Explorer with Windows 95 are still controversial. When Judge Thomas Penfield Jackson released his finding on November 5, 1999, declaring Microsoft's monopoly in the PC industry, the company's business practices once again were under scrutiny. Even with changes in politics (President Clinton to President Bush) and Attorneys General (Reno to Ashcroft), as well as judges (Jackson to Kollar-Kotelly), Microsoft still is not completely "off the hook." If a settlement can be reached without going back to court, market watchers and competitors will still keep an eye on the company's business practices. If Microsoft goes back to court, some observers believe the company will not be "punished" as severely as Judge Jackson had desired, but its business practices could be constrained. (Or could they?)

THE ROAD TO MONOPOLY

Microsoft enjoys a monopoly in the market for Intel-compatible PC operating systems. No products currently in the market or anticipated in the near future can be substituted for the Intel-compatible operating system without incurring substantial costs. Three facts bolster the previous arguments offered by DOJ and Judge Jackson that Microsoft exerted monopoly power in the market for PC operating systems: market share, high barriers to entry, and lack of viable alternatives.

Microsoft maintains a dominant and increasing market share for Intel-compatible PC operating systems. In each of the last 10 years, Microsoft has had a 90 percent market share in operating systems for Intel-compatible PCs. In the last two years, Microsoft's market share has stood at 95 percent and is expected to increase even further. Microsoft has effectively argued that it has just been successful and competitive.

HIGH BARRIERS TO ENTRY. Microsoft has managed to maintain its monopoly in PC operating systems because of persistent high barriers to entry for competing operating systems. Consumer interest is based on the ability of the operating system to run software applications needed in the present and in the near future. Consumers also prefer an operating system that has several software vendors' applications in different software categories. Microsoft has over 70,000 software applications written for it.

LACK OF VIABLE ALTERNATIVES. The fixed costs of developing software applications are high, while the margins for selling software applications are low. Producing software to run on multiple operating systems is time consuming and expensive. Software developers produce software for an operating system that has the largest installed base of users. A goal is quick recovery of net costs. Windows has the largest market share for PC operating systems. Software developers profit by producing applications for Windows.

EXAMPLES OF HIGH BARRIERS TO ENTRY. Two examples illustrate the difficulty in overcoming Windows' dominant market share and applications. In 1994, IBM introduced the OS/2 warp operating system. IBM spent tens of millions of dollars on attempts to get software developers to produce applications for OS/2. But IBM was unsuccessful, and by 1996, OS/2 supported only 2,500 applications, with 10 percent of the market for Intel-compatible PC operating systems. IBM realized it could not generate enough software applications for OS/2 to make it a viable alternative to Windows. IBM marketed OS/2 as a specialized operating system that does not compete head to head with Windows.

Apple's Mac OS operating system also does not compete effectively with Windows. Although Mac OS has over 12,000 applications written for it, consumers still lack adequate software options compared with the number of applications written for Windows. Consumers could not rely on Mac OS as a replacement for Windows.

EXAMPLES OF NONCOMPETITIVE OPERATING SYSTEMS. Barriers to entry do not prevent Microsoft's competitors from attracting consumer interest, nor do the barriers prevent software vendors from making a profit. The high barriers to entry do, however, prevent competing operating systems from drawing a large percentage of users away from Windows. There are several operating systems on the market today that serve niche markets but do not pose a direct threat to Microsoft's Windows. Be Inc. sells an Intel-compatible operating system that is designed to support multimedia functions. The operating system supports 1,000 software applications and has an installed base of 750,000. Be OS's market share is minuscule compared to Windows', and it is marketed as a complement to Windows rather than a substitute. Be OS is loaded alongside Windows on a computer, and users must take steps to enable Be OS.

Another PC operating system on the market today is the Linux open-ended operating system, which has an estimated 15 million or more users. Linux programs run on servers and not PCs. Linux was created and is updated by a global network of software developers who freely contribute their labor. There are only a limited number of software developers willing to convert applications to Linux, and it does not pose a significant threat to Windows' market position yet. Several software developers have announced plans to develop software for Linux, but a majority have not followed through, although IBM has endorsed and uses Linux. Consumers have shown little desire to abandon Windows, with its reliable development support, in favor of Linux and its uncertain future.

STRATEGIC ALLIANCE PARTNERS OR HOSTAGES TO MICROSOFT?

Several companies that transacted business with Microsoft testified that they acquiesced to Microsoft's dominance in the market because Microsoft's corporate practices intimidated and threatened them. How? Companies claimed that Microsoft forced them to freeze the development of software applications that directly competed with Microsoft's software products by threatening to change technologies so non-Microsoft applications, chips, and systems would be incompatible with Microsoft's. On the other hand, Microsoft argued that its cross-marketing agreements with firms are based on industry standards contracts that were legal and competitive.

INTEL. By early 1995, Intel Architecture Labs was in the advanced stage of development of its Native Signal Processing (NSP) software, which would provide Intel microprocessors with substantially superior video and graphics quality. Microsoft was alarmed, as Intel's development of software for non-Microsoft operating systems had the potential of weakening the barrier to entry that protected Microsoft's monopoly power.

During the first week of July, at a meeting between Gates and Andrew Grove (then CEO of Intel), Gates tried to talk Grove into not shipping NSPs and decreasing the number of people working on software at Intel. In a meeting between Gates and Grove in August of 1995, Gates informed Grove that Microsoft would withdraw its support of the next generation of microprocessors if Intel continued to develop platform-level software that competed with Windows. Intel was in an awkward situation; if Microsoft did not support Intel chips and told its OEMs likewise—and if Microsoft made the chips incompatible with Windows—Intel would have had a tough time selling its PC microprocessors. Faced with this threat, Intel stopped the development of platform-level interfaces.

APPLE. QuickTime (QT) was Apple's software for creating, editing, publishing, and playing back multimedia content. Apple's versions of QT run on MAC OS and Windows, which competed with Microsoft's multimedia DirectX. QT has the capability of running across platforms. Microsoft therefore considered QT a potential threat to its applications barrier to entry. Microsoft, from mid-1997 to 1998, tried to stop Apple from producing a Windows 95 version of its multimedia software.

Microsoft informed Apple that if it did not stop marketing the multimedia software with a platform for content development, Microsoft itself would enter the authoring business in order to ensure that those writing multimedia content for Windows 95 would concentrate on Microsoft's APIs instead of Apple's. Microsoft further informed Apple that if Apple developed and marketed its authoring tools, Microsoft would render the technologies in those tools incompatible with Apple's tools. Furthermore, whatever means and resources were needed to make sure that the developers used Microsoft's tools would be invested.

In June 1998, Microsoft met with Apple to persuade Apple to stop the development of multimedia software for Windows. A few weeks after the meeting, Apple rejected Microsoft's proposal. Microsoft's main aim was to deter the development of multimedia software that would run across platforms.

IBM. During the summer of 1994, IBM informed Microsoft that IBM wanted the same favorable terms that it gave Compaq for licensing Microsoft's OS products. Compaq, it seemed, paid the lowest rate in the market and had strong marketing and technical support from Microsoft. Microsoft asked IBM to enter into a "Frontline Partnership," which was prevalent between Microsoft and Compaq. If IBM accepted the terms, it meant that it would have to abandon its own operating system.

At an industry conference in November 1994, Microsoft and IBM met, and IBM rejected the terms. IBM then went on to acquire Lotus Development Corporation. Lotus, according to Microsoft, was a middleware threat. Lotus offered users a common interface across platforms. At this time, IBM was in negotiations with Microsoft for a Windows 95 license. After IBM's acquisition of Lotus, there was trouble in paradise. On July 20, 1995, three days after IBM announced its intention of installing SmartSuite—which directly competed with MS Office—Microsoft informed IBM that it was ceasing negotiations with IBM for the licensing of its Windows 95 and refused to release the "golden master" code of Windows 95. Microsoft stated that it first wanted to settle the ongoing audit of IBM's previous royalty payments to Microsoft for different OS systems. IBM needed the code for its product planning and development. With this type of ultimatum, the company would lose the "back-to-school" season. Finally, 15 minutes before the start of Microsoft's official launch event on August 24, 1995, Microsoft granted IBM a license to pre-install Windows 95. On the same day, IBM paid Microsoft $31 million to close the issue of the audit. (IBM missed the back-to-school season market and lost substantial revenue.)

SUN'S IMPLEMENTATION OF JAVA TECHNOLOGIES.   Sun's (Java Technology's) aim was to permit applications written in Java language to run on a variety of platforms with minimal porting. More applications would be written for operating systems other than Windows if developers found it easier to port their applications to different operating systems. The ultimate ambition of Sun was to have the Java technology be an end-user-oriented application written cross-platform. If this were to happen, the applications barrier to entry would be diminished. By late spring of 1996, Microsoft was concerned about Java's potential. In May 1995, Netscape agreed to include the Java runtime environment with every Navigator, and this soon became the main mode by which Java was placed on the PCs of Windows users. This laid the foundation for a non-Microsoft OS to emerge as an acceptable substitute for Windows.

MONOPOLY POWER THROUGH PRICING?

Microsoft charged different OEMs different prices for Windows. The pricing strategy was dependent on the extent to which the OEMs act in accordance with Microsoft's terms. Of the five largest OEMs, Gateway and IBM have not always complied with Microsoft's terms and pay higher prices than Compaq, Dell, and Hewlett-Packard, who have had less problematic issues with Microsoft.

The Windows license conditions curbed OEMs from promoting software that would weaken the applications barrier to entry. Lower prices were charged to OEMs who ensured that their machines were powerful enough to run Windows NT for Workstations.

When Microsoft launched Windows 98, it did not consider other vendors' prices for competing operating systems. In a competitive market, a firm pays close attention to what other firms are charging for competing products. Microsoft conducted a study in November 1997, which found that Microsoft could have charged $49 for a Windows 98 upgrade. Microsoft chose instead to charge the revenue-maximizing price of $89.

Microsoft's alleged monopoly power in pricing was demonstrated when Microsoft raised the price it charged OEMs for Windows 95 to the same level charged for Windows 98 just before it released Windows 98. In a competitive market, one could expect the price for an older operating system to decrease. Microsoft's primary concern was getting OEMs to ship the new operating system. It is highly unlikely that Microsoft would have imposed price increases if it were concerned that OEMs might shift business to competing operating systems.

MICROSOFT'S PERSPECTIVE. Microsoft has argued that its agreements, contracts, and pricing have evolved with the fast-moving pace of the PC and software industry. Prices in this industry fluctuate widely. Microsoft acknowledges that while it has been a leader in the PC and software areas, it is not the only dominant player. It is only one of over 10,000 companies in the United States and overseas. IBM, Hewlett-Packard, Sun Microsystems, Apple, and AOL (now AOL Time-Warner) remain active competitors in an industry with $1 trillion in revenues (Microsoft claims its revenues are less than 1 percent of this).

BUNDLING: COMPETITIVE STRATEGY OR MONOPOLY PLOY?

Microsoft used bundling (i.e., combining new or untested, and even weaker, products with market leading name brands) as a strategy by distributing its Web browser Internet Explorer (IE) free with its Windows 95 and 98 operating systems. Microsoft required PC makers to accept IE as a condition of receiving Windows. Through this practice, consumers were automatically introduced to IE exclusive of any other browser, most notably Netscape Navigator, which was the market leader at the time. Microsoft viewed Netscape Communications Corp. of Mountain View, California, as a competitor after Netscape declined to collaborate with Microsoft on a browser deal that would have left Netscape with a narrow niche market for its product. The rationale behind the bundling strategy was that Netscape's browser could be developed as a platform to be used as an alternative to the Windows operating system. Therefore, it was considered a threat. Had Netscape Navigator been allowed to compete freely and succeed, application writers would no longer have had an incentive to write only for Windows. Consequently, the applications barrier to entry for smaller operating systems would have disappeared. Microsoft tied Explorer to Windows to avert that threat, while preserving its existing monopoly.

With Microsoft's operating system running on about 85 percent of personal computers in the United States, distributing Internet Explorer in this way potentially constituted an unfair advantage. This practice was considered by the U.S. Department of Justice (DOJ) under President Clinton and by Judge Jackson as a use of monopolistic power to stifle competition. The primary charge against Microsoft by DOJ involved tying a product that is a potential substitute for the monopoly product. DOJ requested Microsoft to include and incorporate Netscape's browser into its Windows system.

MICROSOFT'S PERSPECTIVE.   From Microsoft's perspective, customers were just given another option (IE) without paying for it—the same strategy (a "product design" decision, as Microsoft vice president James Allchin stated) as giving away free software as a way to win over customers—a standard industry practice. Customers did not and do not have to adopt and use IE; they can delete it from their operating system. Also, Netscape is available to customers through Microsoft's Windows operating system.

Microsoft also claimed that DOJ's request to force Microsoft to include Netscape Navigator, a competitor's product) in its operating system was like forcing Coca-Cola to distribute Pepsi or McDonald's to sell Burger King or Wendy's hamburgers or Sears to provide floor space for Wal-Mart products. In direct testimony, an MIT economist, Richard Schmalensee, argued that Netscape's browser's market share was related to the superiority of Microsoft's IE—"A rising tide lifts all ships" argument.

BROWSER BATTLE: INTERNET EXPLORER VERSUS NETSCAPE NAVIGATOR

The events that led to DOJ's finding that Microsoft engaged in the monopolistic practice of bundling started as soon as Netscape released Navigator (on December 15, 1994) and it received dramatic acceptance by the public. Microsoft, critics claimed, was alarmed and feared that the enthusiastic acceptance of Navigator could embolden Netscape to develop its browser into an alternative platform for applications development. By late spring of 1995, Microsoft executives expressed deep concern (as internal memos revealed) that Netscape was pursuing a multiplatform strategy where the underlying operating system's applications development tools would be released. Netscape was moving its business in a direction that could diminish the applications barrier to entry that existed with Microsoft's Windows.

TALKS WITH NETSCAPE.   The first response by Microsoft was to persuade Netscape to structure its business so that the company would not distribute platform-level browsing software for Windows. So long as Navigator was written for Windows 95 and relied on Microsoft's Internet-related APIs instead of exposing its own, developing for Navigator would not mean cross-platform development, a potential Windows competitor. The meeting with Netscape executives in June 1995 was intended by Microsoft to make a deal that would limit Navigator's development.

Microsoft made it clear that it would be releasing its own browser for Windows 95 based on its own platform-level Internet technologies, and if Netscape marketed browsing software for Windows 95 based on different technologies, Netscape would be considered a competitor, not a partner. If

Netscape agreed to the deal, it would acquire preferential treatment with access to technical information. Although both sides left the meeting agreeing to keep the channels of communication open, Microsoft's Thomas Reardon convinced CEO Bill Gates that Netscape would compete with almost all of Microsoft's platform-level Internet technologies. In July of 1995, the effort to reach a strategic agreement with Netscape failed.

Netscape continued to request the applications development tools despite having declined the special relationship with Microsoft. It was not until three months later, in October, that Microsoft released the tools to Netscape. Microsoft gained an edge in releasing Windows 95 with its browser, Internet Explorer, in August 1995, significantly ahead of Navigator's release. Netscape was therefore excluded from the holiday sales. This alleged monopolistic tactic, combined with the bundling of IE with Windows 95 at no cost to consumers, gave Microsoft power to reduce Navigator's market share and make consumers use their browser over Netscape's.

Since 1996, a dramatic increase has occurred in new usage of Internet Explorer. Despite the fact that most users considered Netscape Navigator a superior product compared to the initial release of Internet Explorer, users continued to use IE at Netscape's expense. According to estimates that Microsoft executives cited to support their testimony in the trial, and those on which Microsoft relied in the course of its business planning, the shares of all browser usage enjoyed by Navigator and Internet Explorer changed dramatically in favor of Internet Explorer. This happened after Microsoft began its campaign to protect the applications barrier to entry. From January 1997 to November 1997, Navigator's share fell from 80 to 55 percent, while IE's share rose from 5 to 36 percent. By April 1988, IE's usage was above 55 percent, and Navigator's was at 40 percent. An internal Microsoft presentation concluded that many customers see IE and Navigator as parity products, providing no strong reason to switch. The fact that IE experienced such a dramatic increase in usage share was a result of Microsoft's practice of bundling IE with its Windows operating system.

One interpretation and argument of these events and relations is as follows: Microsoft not only prevented Navigator from lowering the applications barrier to entry, but also did considerable damage to Netscape's business. An opposing argument is this: Microsoft's IE helped open up the entire market for browsers, which in effect helped Netscape's browser increase market share. Netscape originally lost market share because IE became a preferred product over Netscape Navigator. The market determines winners and losers.

Looking Back: Judge Jackson's Ruling

On November 5, 1999, U.S. District Judge Jackson released his finding of fact, which declared that Microsoft routinely used its monopoly power to crush competitors; he portrayed the software giant as nothing less than a social menace. On November 19, Judge Jackson appointed Richard Posner as the mediator and urged both Microsoft and the DOJ to settle the case outside of court. Although Judge Jackson released only the finding of fact on November 5, Microsoft is facing at least six other lawsuits as the result of the finding of fact—California: class action suit; Ohio: $10 billion class action suit; Louisiana: Class action suit; Orange County, California: private suit seeking class action status; New York: private suit seeking class action status; and Birmingham, Alabama: private suit seeking class action status. "Taming Microsoft may require the ultimate penalty. The trick will be to also promote innovation." Richard Posner failed to effectively arbitrate this case. No agreement could be reached by the parties involved. Now it's arbitration expert Robert Green's turn. First, let's look back.

WHAT WOULD A "BREAKUP" HAVE MEANT FOR MICROSOFT?

Horizontal Breakup. Microsoft could have been broken up into three companies—one with operating systems, another with application software, and a third with the Microsoft Internet businesses. But this proposal falls short of the key goal of any remedy: to create competition in the market for operating systems. The horizontal breakup would keep the Microsoft operating system intact as a monopoly company. Microsoft might intentionally have placed several experts in different groups to keep knowledge flowing across the three companies and continue to rule the software industry as three companies.

Vertical Breakup. The second scenario would mandate a "Baby Bells" vertical breakup. "Microsoft would be divided in three with each company getting a third of the assets in every line of business. This approach would improve competition, but it would be a logistical nightmare. Worse, it could fracture the Windows Standard. Critics fear that this would ultimately increase the price for consumers." With this scenario, Microsoft could potentially have placed all of its best programmers, analysts, and managers in one company and slowly phased out the other two companies. Over time, Microsoft would probably have become one company again. However, this scenario could have hurt the consumer if different versions of Microsoft software started to appear with different standards. For the vertical and horizontal breakups, Microsoft reacted to both the scenarios even before the fruition. On November 21, 1999, Microsoft had an executive reorganization of the company. Microsoft proclaims that this reorganization had nothing to do with mediation. "Part of this reorganization, I think, is to make the breakup more difficult," said Rob Enderle, an analyst at Giga Info-nation Group, in Santa Clara, California. "Richard Poser has a background as a conservative jurist which suggests he may be more inclined to coax the DOJ away from dramatic remedies than urging Microsoft toward them." "I think Posner will find a violation of the [Sherman Antitrust Act of 1890] but will try to suggest a mild remedy," said Robert Lande, professor of Law at University of Maryland.

Windows Auction. The third scenario would have been to have a Windows auction. "Getting a major computer company such as Sun Microsystems or IBM to buy a license to Windows would have created a new competitor in the operating systems market. But it is unlikely that any company would want to take on the challenge, which would require huge investments in product upgrade to keep up with Microsoft." This action would have splintered Windows. This scenario would have been theoretically possible, but not practically feasible. First, a buyer is required who would invest a large amount of capital to keep up with Microsoft's upgrades. Second, it is almost impossible to lure away any top programmer of Microsoft's operating system. "Why? Windows has millions of lines of code, and all of the programmers who understand how it all works live in Seattle and their average salary is $400,000 and they don't want to move," says Michael H. Morris, vice president and general counsel of Sun Microsystems Inc.

*Open Source Licensing.*Microsoft could have been forced to publish its source code to Windows with a provision allowing other companies to create clones. Software companies that create applications that run on Windows could have gotten a boost: The code would have put them on an equal footing with Microsoft's own applications writers. A problem: Pirates might make illegal copies of Windows. Open source is a potential hazard for millions of consumer and business users. Hackers could obtain a copy of the source code and potentially violate the security of all users. Users could also be denied support from Microsoft.

*Close Supervision.*The last scenario is to keep closer watch over the company's practices. "Rather than changing the way Microsoft is structured or how it does business, the government would establish rules of behavior aimed at curbing the company's abusive conduct. This would cover contracts with other companies and pricing, among other things. Critics say there are two problems with this approach: First, it already failed. Microsoft signed a consent decree in 1991 that forbade it from engaging in certain anticompetitive practices. Also, a behavioral approach could make the government permanent overseer of Microsoft."

FAST FORWARD

Since Judge Jackson's term and decisions, Microsoft has fared better. While a breakup is not on the table, the question of whether and how to address some of Microsoft's alleged monopoly business practices is the subject of settlement talks. Industry changes and the economic conditions since September 11, 2001, may well have a bearing on the case. First, Microsoft is not the only giant around now. AOL's purchase of Netscape Communications Corp. and the merger of AOL Time-Warner indicate that competition in the industry is alive and well. In addition, mergers and acquisitions, shifting alliances, and consolidations have been occurring in most industries at breakneck speed. The antitrust laws will have to run to keep pace with this rate, scale,

Timeline: September 30, 1997–Present

September 30, 1997	Microsoft releases Internet Explorer 4.0.
October 20, 1997	DOJ sues Microsoft for violating a 1995 court order.
December 11, 1997	Judge Jackson issues an injunction barring Microsoft from bundling IE with Windows 95.
December 15, 1997	Microsoft files an appeal with the U.S. Court of Appeals.
January 11, 1998	DOJ asks court to fine Microsoft $1 million a day for continuing to ship Windows 95 with IE.
January 22, 1998	Microsoft and DOJ settle on contempt charge.
February 2, 1998	Court of Appeals sets April 21 to begin oral argument.
May 5, 1998	Microsoft asks Court of Appeals to rule that IE should not be removed from Windows 98.
May 12, 1998	Court agrees that decision on December 11 does not apply to Windows 98.
May 18, 1998	20 states sue Microsoft.
May 21, 1998	Microsoft asks judge to delay hearing.
May 22, 1998	Judge sets September as the court date.
June 23, 1998	Five computer executives complain to the Senate Judiciary Committee.
July 28, 1998	Microsoft countersues the 20 states.
August 11, 1998	Judge Jackson rules that pretrial needs to be open.
August 19, 1998	Federal court of appeals rules that pretrial interview should be closed.
August 25, 1998	U.S. checks if Microsoft put illegal pressure on Intel and Apple.
September 8, 1998	Microsoft wants the case to be dismissed.
September 11, 1998	Both Microsoft and DOJ ask for three weeks' delay.
September 14, 1998	Judge refuses to throw out both cases.
October 1, 1998	Microsoft IE overtakes Netscape in the market place.
October 9, 1998	Court agrees to delay until October 19, 1998.
October 19, 1998	The trial begins at the E. Barrett Prettyman Courthouse in Washington D.C.
August 10, 1999	Microsoft and DOJ submit their findings of fact.
September 10, 1999	Revised finding of fact was submitted.
September 21, 1999	Closing argument of the trial.
November 5, 1999	Judge Jackson releases his finding of fact.
April 28, 2000	DOJ and 17 states ask a federal judge to split Microsoft into a Windows operating system company and a content company for the PC and Internet.
June 28, 2001	The Washington D.C. Circuit Court reverses the breakup order and upholds Judge Jackson's finding that Microsoft illegally defended its Windows monopoly.
August 24, 2001	District Judge Coleen Kollar-Kotelly picked at random to handle the case.

continued

	CONTINUED
September 6, 2001	DOJ says it does not seek a breakup but wishes a quick remedy. It does not pursue the claim that Microsoft illegally bundled its Internet Explorer with Windows.
October 15, 2001	Judge Kollar-Kotelly appoints arbitration specialist Eric Green, a Boston University professor, to the case. He is given until November 2, 2001, to come up with a settlement solution.
October 31, 2001	A settlement is reached with nine of eighteen states dissenting. Greater freedom is given to PC makers to install non-Microsoft software on new machines and to remove competing Microsoft features, like Internet browsers.

and scope of change. Also, the industry is rapidly changing. Currently, Microsoft has moved into integrating digital music and photography technology. It is also adding on-line services to Windows. RealNetworks is one of Microsoft's next competitors. Microsoft's vision has shifted from Gates's 1975 announcement of "A computer on every desk and in every home" to "Empower people through great software anytime, anyplace, and on any device." Microsoft is enlisting companies now to enable its forthcoming media player software to record music in the MP3 format and play DVD movies. Still, one question that will be relevant to the settlement talks and to Microsoft's continued operations is, Who are its stakeholders, and how will they be affected and treated?

MICROSOFT'S STAKEHOLDERS

Microsoft is a publicly traded company owned by shareholders. The shareholders could be negatively impacted depending on the final outcome of the antirust case. If Microsoft were to lose its monopoly in PC operating systems, it would be expected that its profits might also diminish. Also, the uncertainties of the outcome of the antitrust case could affect the price of Microsoft stock in the near term. Microsoft employs several thousand people whose jobs could be affected by the outcome of the court case or even a settlement. Microsoft gave an aggressive but inconsistent and unconvincing defense to the government's charges. With the Clinton administration out and the Bush team in, the company may have a better chance of settling this case.

The media are another important stakeholder. The media consist of newspapers, magazines, television, radio, and the Internet. The media have provided significant coverage of the antitrust case, and their coverage could affect public opinion regarding Microsoft. With the "New War on Terrorism," the media have devoted their attention to breaking stories and facts. Microsoft is, at least in the near term, out of the media sights.

Individual PC users and customers are perhaps the most important stakeholders of Microsoft. Most PC users are satisfied with Microsoft's operating system. Microsoft has made the PC operating system very affordable for the average person to own. The company has also provided a standard platform for running software applications. Individuals and corporate PC users are more concerned with ease of use, standardization, innovative technologies, and price—all which Microsoft continues to provide.

Partners and competitors could be affected by the outcome of the settlement. A competitor of Microsoft in one market could also be a customer of it in another market. For example, AOL uses Microsoft's Internet Explorer, while AOL competes directly against Microsoft's Internet service. Since AOL's merger with Time-Warner, Microsoft does not look like the only giant in this industry anymore. Computer manufactures like IBM, Compaq, and Dell might continue to get operating systems from Microsoft. IBM, AOL, and Sun Microsystems provided testimony that was very helpful in proving DOJ's case. It is uncertain whether these firms would now be helped or hurt by a settlement that limited Microsoft's reach. Several computer software and hardware companies earlier formed an alliance against Microsoft in the antirust case. Since the antitrust decree by Jackson, the economy has experienced a significant downturn. The technology sector has suffered from the economic slump in general and from the dot.com bust in particular. Now, with the war on terrorism, Microsoft's market leadership may be needed as a catalyst for the U.S. as well as the global economy.

The presently nonexistent, invisible next competitor to Microsoft is perhaps the stakeholder with the most, theoretically, to lose. Potential competitors to Microsoft who may be shut out of a market that is dominated by imposed barriers to entry are the ones that the antitrust laws were designed to protect and give opportunity to enter markets. Microsoft advocates might counter this argument by claiming that they continue to acquire new companies and innovative groups that add value to their business and the markets they serve. (It is, however, curious to note that Netscape was not one of those bright stars for Microsoft.)

OCTOBER 31, 2001 SETTLEMENT

On October 31, 2001, a settlement was reached between Microsoft, the DOJ, and eight of the eighteen states. Essentially, the settlement gave PC makers more freedom to install non-Microsoft software on new machines. Also, PC makers could remove user access to competing Micosoft features like Internet browsers. Retaliation against companies that take advantage of these freedoms is banned. The settlement prohibits exclusive contracts; moreover, Microsoft must disclose design information to hardware and software makers to enable the manufacture of products that run compatibly with Windows (Wilke 2001). California, Connecticut, and Iowa led the dissenting nine states in requesting tougher provisions. Judge Kollar-Kotelly asked the dissenting states for their proposals and scheduled more hearings for March

2002. Before March, there is a mandatory public-comment period along with a court hearing that permits people a last chance to have a voice on U.S. v. Microsoft.

EPILOGUE

Whether Microsoft was and continues to be a fierce competitor or an industry predator depends on point of view—and ultimately on what the court and arbitrators decide. Defenders of the company's practices argue that government should not get involved, since it does not really understand the industry and cannot predict or dictate competitive practices in a rapidly changing industry, and that constraining Microsoft, a global leader in innovation, would also constrain multiple related and dependent industries. Opponents to Microsoft's practices argue that if Microsoft's monopolistic practices are not curtailed, new companies competing to develop technologies for the Internet will be invisibly confined, made to service Microsoft's technologies, bought out, or never allowed to enter the market in the first place.

QUESTIONS FOR DISCUSSION

1. Is Microsoft guilty of being a monopoly? Explain.
2. What are the major issues in this case? How have these issues evolved?
3. Identify the stakeholders and their stakes in this case.
4. Do you agree or disagree with the legal and court decisions made to date in the case? Explain.
5. How have the environments (see Chapter 1) changed in this case? Explain.
6. How has Microsoft's competition changed since this case?
7. Suggest a settlement to the case. Should Microsoft be punished? How?
8. What are the lessons from this case and since this case?

SOURCES

Bank, D., Clark, D. (July 23, 1999). Microsoft broadens vision statement to go beyond the PC-centric world. *Wall Street Journal*, A3.

Barrett, R. (Nov. 29, 1999). *Interactive Week, 6(49)*, 401.

Becker, G. (April 6, 1998). Let the marketplace judge Microsoft. *Business Week*, 26.

Bork, R. (May 22, 1998). The most misunderstood antitrust case. *Wall Street Journal*, A6.

Bork, R. (Nov. 8, 1999). Manager's journal—US vs. Microsoft: Judge Jackson's finding of fact—A predatory monopoly. *Wall Street Journal*, A50.

Defendant Microsoft Corporation's Answer to the Complaint Filed by the U.S. Department of Justice, United States of America v. Microsoft Corporation, United States District Court for the District of Columbia, No. 98-1232 (TPJ), July 28, 1998; and Defendant Microsoft Corporation's Answer to Plaintiff States' First Amended Complaint and Counterclaim,

State of New York v. Microsoft Corporation, United States District Court for the District Court of Columbia, No. 98-1232 (TPJ), July 28, 1998.

France, M., Burrows, P., Himelstein, L., Moeller, M.. (Nov. 22, 1999). Does a breakup make sense? *Business Week*, 28.

Jackson, T. P. (Nov. 5, 1999). United States of America v. Microsoft Corporation, CA 98-232, Findings of Fact, 1–141.

Kerber, R. (April 29, 2000). U.S. asks judge to break up Microsoft. *Boston Globe*, A-1, A-12.

Lohr, S., Harmon, A.. (Jan. 28, 1999). Microsoft executive defends folding browser into Windows. *New York Times*, C2.

Mediator to sort out Microsoft/DoJ battle. (Oct. 15, 2001). Newswire (VNU), VNU Business Publications, Ltd. Source: World Reporter, *Wall Street Journal*.

Microsoft PressPass. (July 25, 1998). Competition in the software industry, January 1998. http://www.microsoft.com/presspass/doj/1-98whitepaper.htm.

Microsoft PressPass. (Dec. 18, 1998). Fact vs. Fiction, 3. http://www.microsoft.com/presspass/fvsf.htm.

Rill, J. (Nov. 20, 1997). Why Bill Gates is wrong. *Wall Street Journal*, A22.

Schmalensee, R., Direct Testimony, in the United States District Court for the District of Columbia, United States of America Plaintiffs v. Microsoft Corporation Defendant, Civil Action No. 98-1232 (TPJ), January 13, 1999, p. 322.

Shiver, J., Jr. (Dec. 8, 1998). United front cracks in case against Microsoft. *Los Angeles Times*, C1.

Technology briefing software: Microsoft's new MP3 venture. (July 17, 2001). *New York Times*, 6.

Weil, N., Hancy, C. (Dec. 6, 1999). DOJ appoints adviser as Microsoft reshuffles. *Infoworld*, 21(49), 3.

Wilke, J. (Nov. 9, 2001). Negotiating all night, tenacious Microsoft won many loopholes. *Wall Street Journal*, A1, A6.

CASE 2
DOW CORNING CORPORATION AND SILICONE BREAST IMPLANTS

On May 15, 1995, after years of controversy surrounding silicone breast implants, Dow Corning Corporation (DDC)—a joint venture of Dow Chemical and its parent company, Corning Incorporated—filed for Chapter 11 bankruptcy protection. Richard Hazelton, the CEO of DCC, explained the decision: "It became clear to Dow Corning that to continue our current course ultimately would make it impossible to either resolve this controversy responsibly or remain a healthy company. A Chapter 11 reorganization will bring closure and preserve underlying business."[1]

BACKGROUND: MARKET OPPORTUNITIES, COMPETITIVE PRESSURES, INTERNAL COMPANY QUESTIONS

Dow Corning Corporation was a start-up venture between Dow Chemical and Corning in 1943. As an incubator, the goal of DCC was to create and market a new material—silicone. While the company later proved successful, with almost 10,000 employees and revenues in excess of $2 billion, it did so with the support of Dow Chemical and Corning, both looking for promising profits from the new venture.[2]

The first silicone gel implant took place in 1964. Since that time, "about two million women nationwide have received breast implants, most of them for cosmetic reasons."[3] Although the majority of these women were satisfied with the implants, "a small minority of recipients in both Canada and the United States have complained that the implants have ruptured, allowing gel to leak into the breast cavity and migrate to other parts of the body. Some women maintain that implant problems cause pain in the chest, arms, and back, as well as debilitating autoimmune diseases such as rheumatoid arthritis. Some also complain that scar tissue formed around the implants, causing a hardening of the breasts."[4]

While the silicone gel breast implants were believed by scientists at DCC to have been safe for humans, internal memos suggest that competitive pressures and a lack of attention to some animal tests and personnel complaints short-circuited safety issues for business reasons. Competitors had by 1975 already cut DCC's market share in this area by a third. To counter the competition, DCC wanted to rush its new product, flo-gel, to market by June 15. Projected annual sales were 50,000. An internal memo, dated January 31, 1975, stated, "17 weeks, 121 days, 2,904 hours, 174,240 minutes."[5]

Gel-bleed (the seepage of silicon modules through the plastic container that housed the new liquid gel) was so evident that the implants had a noticeable greasy, even oily, sensation when handled. In an internal memo dated May 2, 1975, sales managers stated that the implants on display at a trade show "were bleeding on the velvet in the showcase."[6] Even members of mammary task force that had been established by DCC in January 1975 expressed concern over problems that gel-bleed might cause in humans.

Animal studies conducted on rabbits in February 1975 showed that inflammation occurred. A test on dogs also showed that gel had leaked internally. Thomas Talcott, a product engineer with the implant team, argued for more study because of his concern that a ruptured implant sac in a human could cause health risks. When his arguments were ignored, he resigned. The flo-gel went to market in the fall of 1975. A disgruntled and angry sales force started fielding complaints from plastic surgeons over gel-bleed, leaking gel, and ruptured implants. An internal memo from a sales professional stated to his superior, "To put a questionable lot of mammaries on the market is inexcusable. I don't know who is responsible for this decision but it has to rank right up there with the Pinto gas tank."[7]

One of the first lawsuits filed was by a woman who "claimed that a silicone breast implant manufactured by DCC caused her to contract a disabling immune-system disorder. The case, brought in 1989 by Mariann Hopkins, was among the first breast-implant lawsuits. In 1991, a federal jury in San Francisco had ordered Dow Corning to pay Hopkins $840,000 in compensatory damages and $6.5 million in punitive damages. The award at the time was the largest ever in a breast-implant case."[8] Dow Corning claimed that this award "triggered the explosion of breast-implant litigation. . . .

State and federal courts have been inundated with cases . . . against all manufacturers of mammary prostheses in which plaintiffs claim whatever injury, disease or illness from which they suffer is causally related to their implants."[9]

In response to the litigation, DCC, Bristol-Myers Squibb Co., and Baxter Health Care Corp. attempted to handle the individual suits together in a class action suit. These companies agreed to pay $4.25 billion to women who contended that implants caused illness. The settlement was designed to provide women with net payments ranging from $105,000 to $1.4 million, depending on their physical condition and age. These amounts could be reduced if an unexpected number of women registered to participate and if companies refused to pay more. Women would have an opportunity to leave the settlement if payments were reduced, although such actions could possibly have jeopardized the entire settlement idea.[10] "The settlement contributions would be based on each manufacturer's market share, litigation exposure, and ability to defend the claims, with Dow Corning paying $2 billion, Bristol-Meyers $1.5 billion, and Baxter $556 million."[11] The manufacturers also had the ability "to drop out if a certain number of victims chose not to participate. Each manufacturer would be left to their own discretion to determine if the number of participants was significant."[12] The manufacturers were trying to push this class action settlement knowing that "if the cases are all tried together . . . every recipient in a successful suit would probably get a small settlement, much less than the multimillion dollar awards that a handful have gotten."[13]

Many people feel DCC threatened bankruptcy early on to scare women into opting to join the class action suit. The various methods used by manufacturers to get women to join the suit were not completely successful, however, as "more than 11,300 women rejected the $4.25 billion settlement. Those women have reserved their right to sue implant manufacturers individually."[14] These individual lawsuits, coupled with the difficulties DCC experienced in coming to agreement with so many other women, led to DCC's filing for Chapter 11. "The bankruptcy filing signaled the breakdown in an attempt by Dow Corning and three other corporate defendants to funnel claims through a no-fault facility somewhat similar to the still-unresolved problem of asbestos cases in the 1980's."[15]

ENTER THE ATTORNEYS

As DCC and the other manufacturers learned, when a crisis arises due to product liability, it is not easily resolved. "The difficulties were legion. Among the women involved, there was a wide range of consequences and varying degrees of certainty about the link between implants and subsequent medical difficulties. The intensity of the pursuit varied from lawyer to lawyer, and the willingness of parties to settle changed with time, making patterns of settlement difficult to establish."[16] Two Houston attorneys in particular campaigned through public ads to solicit women who had experienced problems with gel implants. These attorneys kept their clients away from the class action suit in order to have each person appear before the manufacturer, a judge, and a jury. The lawyers won $25 million in their first trial against Bristol-Myers Squibb. These attorneys at one point had over 2,000 individual cases lined up for adjudication. They were obtaining settlements of $1 million per case with fees of 40 percent per settlement.[17] It can be argued that this factor—that is, the continuing success of the attorneys at persuading juries of the fate of injured women who were not properly informed of the gel's dangers and potential risks—put Dow Corning's president and executives in the position of having to declare bankruptcy.

DCC provides a compelling modern-day example of the close relationship that developed between product liability suits and Chapter 11 filings, an issue that Congress must finally address. "If bankruptcy is now the ultimate limit on liability, what figure short of that can Congress agree on to avoid the danger implicit in Dow Corning's case: that an otherwise viable business, and the jobs that go with it, might go down the drain of tort practice."[18]

THE FINANCIAL PICTURE

In order to fully understand the financial implications that silicone has had for DCC, it is essential to note the sales and reported earnings of DCC and its parent companies, Corning Inc. and Dow Chemical.

In 1967, just after the first silicone implant surgery, DCC reported sales of $102 million. By 1970, sales had climbed to $140.3 million on earnings of $13.8 million. By 1980, DCC's reported sales soared to $681.5 million, while earnings rose to $73.9 million. An estimated 150,000 million individuals annually sought implants for augmentation or reconstruction.[19] In Boston, the surgical fees for an implant could run from $2,000 to $5,000, according to Dr. Sharon Webb, a plastic surgeon at the Faulkner Breast Center. Anesthesia and hospitalization could add another $2,000 to the tab.[20]

The sales growth of DCC significantly enhanced its two parent companies, Corning Inc. and Dow Chemical. In 1970, Corning Inc. reported sales of $593 million on earnings of $39.5 million. This figure rose to $1,529.7 million in 1980 on earnings of $114.7 million. A similar impact was seen on overall sales for Dow Chemical, with reported sales of $1,911 million in 1970 on earnings of $103 million. These figures rose to $10,626 million in sales on earnings of $805 million in 1980.

The 1980s saw continued growth in the breast implant market. This growth led DCC's reported sales of $901.1 million on earnings of $95.2 million in 1985. "By the middle of the decade, surgeons were performing more than 130,000 breast implant operations every year. The average patient was a college educated woman in her early thirties, who was married and had two children."[21] By 1990, DCC had reached sales of $1,718.3 million on earnings $171.1 million. Corning Inc.'s sales were $2,940.5 million on earnings of $292 million; and Dow Chemical reported sales of $19,773 million on earnings of $1378 million.

Unfortunately for DCC, as discussed earlier, the company soon found itself at the center of one of the largest product liability suits in American history. The suits caused DCC's litigation expenses to rise sharply. Reported litigation expense was $25 million in 1991. This figure rose to $69 million in 1992, and, by 1993, DCC reported spending over $640 million in litigation. In 1993, DCC reported sales of $2,043.7, while actually losing $287 million dollars. DCC had 1994 sales of $2.2 billion but reported a $6.8 million loss, which it attributed to the expense of the breast implant claims.[22]

DCC's financial outlook appeared grim. Merrill Lynch estimated that DCC would earn $8.20 per share in 1995 (down from the earlier estimate of $9.00 per share) and $9.15 per share in 1996 (down from the earlier estimate of $9.50 per share).[23] Merrill Lynch also reduced the five-year earnings per share growth rate for DCC to 0%.[24]

A HISTORICAL PERSPECTIVE

In 1976, the federal government passed an amendment to the federal Food, Drug, and Cosmetic Act, which provided stricter reporting and inspection standards for all new medical devices. At this time, there were 1,700 types of devices on the market, many of them containing silicone. Through a grandfather clause, these devices were allowed to remain on the market with minimal Food and Drug Administration (FDA) review. A manufacturer simply filed a "510(k)" form informing the FDA of the new product and its similarity to an existing product already on the market. In 1996, the FDA acknowledged that there were 58,000 medical devices, many containing solid silicone, that entered the market through this 510(k) process.[25]

It was almost 12 years before further government attention was given to the breast implant controversy. "A Public Citizen, physician Dr. Sydney Wolfe, said in a petition, '. . . an increasingly larger pool of women is being created who may, in the prime of their lives, ultimately develop chronic illness, disfigurement and disability because of the implants (silicone).'"[26] Dr. Wolfe began to publicly attack manufacturers and plastic surgeons for downplaying the potential health risks. Opponents of Dr. Wolfe agreed with Bruce Hansel, a biochemist and bioengineer at the Emergency Care Research Institute (ECRI), a watchdog group that had been tracking silicone-containing medical devices. Hansel stated, "'You can nit-pick anything to death. There will never be a perfect biomaterial,' but 'I would say that silicone in my view is probably the biomaterial of the 20th century. It is the best biomaterial we have going for us now.'" "Manufacturers continue to deny a link between such illnesses of the human immune system and breast implants, but various doctors have concluded that such causation exists."[27]

As a result of conflicting expert medical data and opinions, the FDA once again became involved in the breast implant controversy. The agency announced, in November of 1988, that although manufacturers could continue to produce breast implants, they would have to provide more detailed information on the safety concern for a 1991 investigation. Unfortunately, the

1991 investigation proved uneventful. Although the FDA panel cited the overall lack of safety data, it did not move to ban the sale of breast implants. The panel noted testimony from cancer patients (and their psychological benefits from the implants) as an integral part of their decision.

Finally, in 1992, after DCC was ordered to pay $6.5 million in punitive damages to a breast implant claimant, FDA Commissioner David Kessler announced a 45-day moratorium on the sale of silicone implants.[28] "Since April 1992, the FDA has banned breast implants for cosmetic purposes and allows them only for reconstructive breast surgery as part of the controlled clinical studies."[29] This was the last significant act by the federal government in the breast implant controversy.

As illustrated, the swirling controversy in the DCC case can be summarized as whether or not the silicone gel breast implants cause medical disorders in women who have had implant surgery. By 1991, "the FDA had received 2,500 reports of illnesses or injuries associated with the implants, which have been used in one million women. But the degree of risk was unclear because extensive research had not been done." As pressures mounted regarding the product's safety, Dow adamantly "denied any link between the implants and illness."[30] Moreover, "rather than wait for results from the [FDA] research, Dow undertook to determine the safety of silicone gel implants."[31] The Dow study of silicone implants in March 1993 "reported that the silicone gel in the implants altered the immune systems of laboratory rats . . . but [rats] are more susceptible to inflammatory reactions than humans."[32]

The Controversy

Women who have had medical problems with their implants allege, with their doctors' support, that the following medical disorders were present: autoimmune disease, breast cancer, arthritis, abnormal tissue growth, scleroderma, lupus erythematosus, fatigue, and nerve damage. Still, DCC has maintained the safety of the implants, stating "plaintiffs [the women] claim that whatever injury, disease or illness from which they suffer is causally related to their implants."[33]

Numerous studies, including the Mayo Clinic Study, the University of Southern California Study, and a French International Study, reported similar results. The French Ministry said that an analysis of international research "showed that the risk of contracting autoimmune diseases and cancer after the implantation of silicone breast implants was no greater than in the general public."[34] Scientists involved "noted that no study could completely dismiss the possibility that breast implants contributed to medical disorders." The degree of safety may never be completely known, but as of 1995, "about 5% of the two million American women with silicone implants have demanded compensation for side effects."[35]

THE RIGHT TO KNOW

"Dow Corning has actively covered this issue up," said Dr. Wolfe, who is director of the Public Citizen Health Research Group in Washington. "They are reckless and they have a reckless attitude about women."[36] Wolfe continued, "DCC was only thinking of themselves when they 'repeatedly assured women and their doctors that the implants were safe'[37] while keeping 'guard over hundreds of internal memos that suggested that some of Dow Corning's own employees have long been dissatisfied with the scientific data on implants.'"[38]

The release of these internal memos suggests that Dow has long known of major problems with the silicone implants it has marketed since 1975. The following are highlights from a sample of the memos to and from Dow scientists:

Jan. 28, 1975: Memo from Arthur H. Rathjen, chairman of the Dow
implant task force, as Dow rushed a new implant to market: "A
question not yet answered is whether or not there is excessive bleed
[leakage] of the gel through the envelope. We must address ourselves
to this question immediately. . . . The stakes are too high if a wrong
decision is made. . . ."

Sept. 15, 1983: Memo from Bill Boley: "Only inferential data exists to
substantiate the long-term safety of these gels for human implant
applications. . . ."

April 10, 1987: Memo to Rathjen and others suggesting that Dow was
considering a study to review 1,250 implant recipients: "The cost of
this data is expected to be minimal, less than $10 million." The study
never took place.[39]

In response to these memos, Dow Corning stepped up an ad campaign that it had started in the fall of 1991. In newspapers across the country, DCC urged women with questions about implants to call a company hotline. The ads said that instead of "half-truths," callers would receive information based on 30 years of valid scientific research. But when some women called, they were told that the implants were "100 percent safe." Shortly afterward, the FDA warned Dow Corning that some of the information on its hotline was "false or used in a confusing or misleading context."[40]

An ethical issue at hand, however, is not only whether the implants do or do not cause harm to patients, but also that DCC failed to inform stakeholders and clients that some of their employees felt there was reason for concern about safety. Failure to accurately and timely inform consumers of questionable product uses violated the right of these women to know. "If you do not have data on the range of risks and problems, you are not free to choose, you are free to be ignorant. Informed consent requires both information and choice. Since the companies have not supplied the information, this is a dubious choice."[41]

AFTERMATH

In June of 1994, DCC began to make announcements that it may have to declare bankruptcy if too many women opted out of the $4.25 billion settlement. These comments "led some financial analysts to suggest that the chairman (Keith McKennon made the statements) was trying to 'scare' women into joining the settlement, which could potentially save the company millions of dollars in litigation fees." DCC and the other manufacturers involved in the case have attempted to make the settlement appear generous on their part, but "it is hardly the simple and generous solution described. In reality, the payout to each woman would depend on the total number of claims filed and could decrease dramatically as the number of plaintiffs climbs. And the rights of women to drop out of the plan and seek their own settlements would actually be sharply curtailed. Thousands of sick women could lose their legal access to any compensation altogether. 'This is not insurance,' Norman D. Anderson, a Johns Hopkins University professor stated, who has treated hundreds of patients with problems related to silicone implants, 'This is pennies-on-the-dollar reimbursement.'"[42]

When DCC felt it had become financially overburdened with the trials, it followed through on the threat and filed Chapter 11. This was "a move that threaten[ed] to unravel a $4.25 billion breast implant settlement and has frozen thousands of individual lawsuits. The company's Chapter 11 filing was akin to protective bankruptcy-filing steps taken by big companies in other important product liability cases, which delayed payments to recipients for years. Under Chapter 11, a company gets a reprieve from bills while it works out a way to pay creditors and survive as a healthy business."[43]

DCC may have modeled its behavior after its parent company, Dow Chemical Corporation. In an attempt to avoid litigation, Dow Chemical Corporation has maintained that it was not aware of DCC's research activities in silicone. Dow Chemical Corporation was initially dismissed from the case until "a federal judge reinstated Dow Chemical as a defendant in thousands of breast implant lawsuits, raising the possibility of new negotiations in a landmark product liability settlement. . . . The ruling 'means Dow Chemical can no longer sit on the sidelines and pretend it is not a player in this litigation.'"[44]

Judge Arthur Spectors approved in December 1999 "Dow Corning's $4.5-billion reorganization plan, including $3.2 billion to settle claims brought by silicone gel breast implant recipients. The remaining $1.3 billion will be paid to commercial creditors, in part through a $900 million–$1 billion bond issue."[45] Spectors's ruling enabled Dow Corning to emerge from bankruptcy, even though appeals were expected. The company still had to resolve 170,000 implant recipients' product liability claims. "The proposed settlement plan, which represents an agreement between 94% of the plaintiffs and the company, would protect Dow Corning and third parties such as Dow Chemical from future lawsuits. . . . It would also pay $2,000–$300,000 to plaintiffs, depending on their medical condition."[46]

Plaintiffs agreed in the settlement to waive punitive damages. Dow Corning established a cap of \$400 million to settle claims by plaintiffs "who choose the plan's litigation provision[,] . . . an option for women who do not agree with the settlement offer. The only appeals that could prevent the plan from going forward are challenges to the settlement amount or to the third-party release provision, says Barbara Houser, Dow Corning's lead bankruptcy attorney."[47]

FINAL THOUGHTS

DCC's silicone breast implant troubles occurred in a free-market, capitalist society. A free market encourages innovation, but it can also lead to corporate manipulation and to the introduction of dangerous products into the market. Marcia Angell, a physician and executive editor of *The New England Journal of Medicine*, concluded in her book *Science on Trial: The Clash of Medical Evidence and the Law in the Breast Implant Case*[48] that "[o]nly by relying on scientific evidence can we hope to curb the greed, fear and self-indulgence that too often govern such disputes. This is the lesson of the breast implant story." Charles Rosenberg, professor of history and sociology of science at the University of Pennsylvania, argued in a *New York Times* review of Dr. Angell's book that "it is difficult to share her hope that scientific evidence can or will translate easily or naturally into social policy. She is dismayed, for example, that regulations 'should be influenced by political and social considerations.' Yet this is the way our system works. In most policy matters, scientific evidence is only one among a complex assortment of factors that interact to produce particular decisions."[49] A careful reading of the events, stakeholders, and outcomes in the silicone breast implant controversy reveals the social, economic, legal, and political—as well as scientific—factors involved: "the practice of Federal regulation, the relationship between science and courts, the lack of consistently enforced professional standards in law, medicine and journalism."[50] A major lesson from this case also involves the role of the plaintiffs. The Houston lawyers' relentless pressure with inconclusive medical facts on Dow Corning, along with their courtroom successes, demonstrates that "facts" alone are insufficient factors in determining truth.

QUESTIONS FOR DISCUSSION

1. Identify major stakeholders and stakes in this case. Who gained and lost in this case?

2. Was the Dow Corning Corporation justified in considering bankruptcy? Why or why not?

3. What are the ethical issues and principles involved in this case? Who has acted the most responsibly? The least? Explain. Who in this case was at fault? Support your answer.

4. Evaluate the statement of Dr. Angell, "Only by relying on scientific evidence can we hope to curb the greed, fear, and self-indulgence that too often govern such disputes [referring to disputes raised in this case]. This is the lesson of the breast implant story." Do you agree? Is this the major or the only lesson from this case? Explain.

Sources

Associated Press. (April 12, 1994). 5 firms join implant settlement. *Boston Globe*, 44.

Associated Press. (July 21, 1994). Firms may face thousands of suits. *Boston Globe*, 19.

Associated Press. (Aug. 5, 1994). FDA is petitioned to outlaw saline-filled implants. *Boston Globe*, 17.

Associated Press. (Sept. 2, 1994). Judge finalizes $4.25B settlement from breast implant maker. *Boston Globe*, 3.

Associated Press. (Sept. 16, 1994). Women rejecting implant award. *Boston Globe*, 79.

Associated Press. (Feb. 15, 1995). Couple wins $5.2M in breast implant case: Dow Chemical faulted. *Boston Globe*, 88.

Associated Press. (March 1, 1995). France readmits breast implants. *Boston Globe*, 4.

Associated Press. (March 29, 1995). Dow freed from suit. *Boston Globe*, 14.

Associated Press. (April 26, 1995). Company reinstated in implant lawsuit. *Boston Globe*, 7.

Associated Press. (May 11, 1995). Jury selection is halted over an implant and Dow Corning denies trying to influence liability. *Boston Globe*, 14.

The best-laid ethics programs. (March 9, 1992). *Business Week*, 67-69.

Breast implant makers prepare $4B settlement. (March 7, 1994). *National Underwriter*, 6.

Burton, T. (July 1994). Adding insult to injury. *Progressive*, 28-30.

Carelli, R. (Jan. 10, 1995). Justices uphold breast implant award. *Boston Globe*, 10.

Chisholm, P. (March 9, 1992). Anatomy of a nightmare: Dow Corning fights a public outcry. *Maclean's*, 42–43.

Dow Chemical not liable in implant case. (March 30, 1995). *Facts on File*, Medicine and Health, 233.

Dow Corning announces medical silicone resins. (May 30, 1994). *Chemical & Engineering News*, 9.

Dow Corning down for the count: A new high flier for Boeing. (May 21, 1995). *Boston Globe*, 48.

Dow Corning mulls over filing for bankruptcy. (June 20, 1994). *Chemical & Engineering News*, 8.

Facts on File. (Dec. 31, 1994). 992.

Facts on File. (Feb. 9, 1995). 88.

Facts on File. (March 2, 1995). 154.

Foreman, J. (Jan. 13, 1992). Implants: Is uninformed consent a woman's right? *Boston Globe*, 1.

Foreman, J. (Jan. 19, 1992). Women and silicone: A history of risk. *Boston Globe*, 1.

Foreman, J. (Jan. 25, 1992). Safety of solid silicone at issue. *Boston Globe*, 1.

Foreman, J. (May 15, 1992). Lawyers fight over limits of implant trials. *Boston Globe*, 25.

Foreman, J. (June 17, 1994). Breast implant study criticized timing, funding of report at issue. *Boston Globe*, 4.

Foreman, J. (Nov. 20, 1994). Dec. 1 deadline to join implant lawsuit. *Boston Globe*, 6.

Grimmer, L. (Nov. 3, 1992). Silicone-gel implant records altered, company admits. *Boston Globe*, 3.

Haney, D. Q. (Dec. 21, 1994). Harvard doctors quit implant study, citing conflict. *Boston Globe*, 35.

Implant makers near a deal. (Feb. 21, 1994). *Business Insurance*, 1, 51.

Lehr, D. (Sept. 10, 1993). 4.75B accord eyed on breast implant plaintiffs, manufacturers agree on compensation fund. *Boston Globe*, 1.

McCarthy, M. (April 2, 1994). U.S. breast implant agreement. *Lancet*, 7.

Neuffer, E. (March 20, 1992). Maker quits implant market: Dow Corning cites drop in sales, sets up fund. *Boston Globe*, 1.

New York Times. (May 15, 1995).

New York Times. (May 16, 1995). 1.

Strategic withdrawal. (March 30, 1992). *Time,* 51.

Wall Street Journal. (May 15, 1995). 2.

Wall Street Journal. (May 16, 1995). 1.

Warrick, Earl L. (1990). *Forty Years of Firsts: The Recollections of a Dow Corning Pioneer.* New York: McGraw-Hill.

CASE 3

THE "ALMOST CRISIS": INTEL'S PENTIUM CHIP PROBLEM

Intel Corporation develops, manufactures, and markets integrated circuit components. These complex components are constructed from small pieces of silicon composed of numerous transistors that perform electronic circuit functions. Silicon chips are essential for processing information in computers worldwide. Intel began its venture in the microprocessing business when it was created in 1968 by Robert Noyce, Gordon Moore, and Andrew Grove.

Andrew Grove became the president and chief operating officer of Intel in 1979, at which time he focused Intel on a mission to take 2,000 new customers away from Motorola Inc. Intel surpassed this goal. One of the new customers, IBM, chose Intel's 8088 chip as the brain of its first PC. Intel has not looked back since. It is at the top of the computer chip industry. Throughout the 1980s, Intel solidified its hold on the market. Intel rapidly became an $11.5 billion corporation.

Intel Corporation is a company with a progressive management philosophy that strives toward success through an empowered team approach. At Intel, even the chief executive officer (CEO) occupies a cubicle, sitting among staff at the Silicon Valley–based company. Intel takes pride in its ability to promote internal feedback flexibility. All employees express opinions on any decision or action taken within the company by notifying the involved individual, including the CEO and upper management.

The company has been a dominating force in the computer microprocessing industry and has managed to remain ahead of its competitors in most facets of the processing chip industry. Andrew Grove claimed that the open, proactive environment Intel promoted enabled the company to leap ahead of its competitors.

CHIP POWER

In March 1994, Intel released a microprocessor expected to bring the computer industry to the next level. The microprocessing chip was labeled the Pentium chip. The goal was to replace 486 models by becoming the fastest information processor in the market. Responding to the imminence of the IBM PowerPC chip, Intel outpaced its competitors by introducing the

Pentium product to the computer industry two months ahead of the projected release date.

Computer producers driven by the potential of the new chip rushed to design and develop machines to accommodate the chip. Dell, AST, Hewlett-Packard, NEC, and Digital were among the companies that launched computer processing units to either coincide with the Pentium introduction or accommodate the chip shortly after its introduction. Noticeably, Compaq, then an extremely important player in the production of computers, did not act immediately meet this need and stated its belief that Intel's movement into this area was unnecessary and, at the very least, premature.

In a market where speed is a competitive advantage, Intel insisted that all PC software operated more effectively on a Pentium processor. Independent tests by the National Software Testing Labs (NSTL) confirmed the discernible speed advantages of the Pentium chip. NSTL ran tests on Windows applications such as Microsoft Word, Microsoft Excel, and Lotus 123. The Pentium processor outpaced 486 DX2s, the market's leading chip, by roughly 40 percent. Programs that relied on intensive graphics ran smoother and quicker on the Pentium chip. These programs took advantage of the Pentium's floating point unit (FPU). (The FPU is the part of the microprocessor responsible for performing complicated mathematical functions.)

Intel pointed to the speed advantage of the Pentium chip, using the 3D Home Architect program from Broderbund. Using this program, Pentium users could bring up three-dimensional home designs twice as fast as those using a 486 processor.

Intel planned to be the first into the market with its new chip in order to take advantage of the consumer fever for the newest technological advance. In an interview with America Online, Andrew Grove commented on the exponential need to be first into the market with an advanced processor in order to be successful. Intel had commanded 80 percent of the microprocessor market. Prior to the release of the Pentium chip, concern was growing over the impending introduction of the PowerPC chip, produced collectively by IBM, Apple Computers, and Motorola. This chip would present the first significant challenge to Intel products—and it was to be headed by IBM, an important customer of Intel microprocessors. Realizing the consequences of the impending situation, Grove spearheaded an Intel effort to accelerate product development and increase capacity to manufacture the Pentium chip. Intel began a new procedure of overlapping new product development to meet its needs for accelerated production. Grove stated and believed that "[p]roducts are what made this business."

THE RACE BEGAN

Intel began rigorously testing the Pentium chip toward the end of 1993, with the hope of releasing the chip early in the coming year. After the March 1994 rollout, the company continued testing, hoping to catch mistakes in order to correct future Pentium editions. The Intel labs were running tests 24 hours a day. Finally, in July 1994, after nearly two trillion random test calculations, Intel discovered a bug in the chip's FPU. The Pentium chip bug affected certain high-precision division problems and would not have an effect on the majority of Pentium users. The error, which occurred when dividing particular rare combinations of numbers, appeared in the 4th to the 19th decimal places. It seemed a minor problem unless the chip was used for designing bridges and homes, where high degrees of accuracy are necessary to ensure safety.

THE HIDDEN FLAW

Intel considered this flaw not serious enough to notify customers and decided to promote the chips. On October 30, 1994, a mathematics professor from Lynchburg College, Thomas Nicely, sent an e-mail to several colleagues notifying them that answers provided through calculations from Pentium-based PCs were flawed. One of the corresponding colleagues posted the letter on CompuServe's on-line service. Eventually the letter was copied onto the Internet.

INTEL'S CRISIS MANAGEMENT STRATEGY

The following week the first press release acknowledging the existence of the chip flaw was published in *Electrical Engineering Times*. Intel attempted to prevent further escalation of this problem by offering to replace the chips to the customers, with one catch. The customer had to prove to Intel that he or she used the PC in such a way that it would be affected by the flaw. This crisis management strategy proved damaging. Home users were outraged by Intel's arrogance; they believed the company's attitude insinuated that the company understood its customers' needs better than they did. Public outcry toward the company surfaced through numerous Internet communications and in thousands of phone calls complaining about the stance taken by Intel. Momentum built through the media. A feeding frenzy began over Intel's lack of concern for its customers.

Intel tried to initiate further damage control by explaining the rarity of the effects of this flaw. According to Intel reports, the typical computer user would encounter a wrong answer as a result of the flaw once every 27,000 years. At this juncture, Intel made the decision to stop selling the defective chip, and attempted to calm computer producers by informing them that it was correcting the Pentium. Consumers' concerns persisted, and published stories continued to surface about the Pentium chip.

IBM's ROLE

Intel's Pentium crisis reached its apex when IBM guaranteed replacement of Pentium chips for any customer that requested it. IBM went a step further toward promoting its image as a company that would respond to the needs of its customers by refusing to ship Pentium-based PCs. Researchers for IBM claimed that the flaw could come into play once every 24 days for individuals that routinely used their PCs to make thousands of spreadsheet calculations a day. IBM would continue to make the Pentium-based computers and sell them to customers that insisted on operating the machines.

Many industry analysts believed IBM's concerns were based its desire to gain an advantage within the chip market. Following IBM's actions, the Gartner Group, a prominent consulting firm, recommended to its clients that they delay large-volume purchases of Pentium-based PCs. Reactions on Wall Street were negative, and Intel stock dropped 2⅜ points.

INTEL CONCEDES

Intel finally capitulated to customer anger over its restrictive replacement policy and promised to replace at no cost any Pentium chips—no questions asked. Intel added a public apology for problems the flawed chips had created and for the company's inappropriate actions.

Intel continued to sell the updated chip. The decision to bow to consumer demands was made on December 20, 1994, approximately two months after the first public discovery of the flaw. By that time, Intel's stock had fallen 3.6 percent since the public became aware of this issue.

As a result of the Pentium chip situation, Intel recorded a loss of $475 million within the fourth quarter of 1994. Profits were dramatically affected in the fourth quarter, and project projections remained lower through the first quarter of 1995, compared to the previous level in the second quarter of 1994. However, profit projections showed a rise throughout 1995, beyond the first quarter. An estimated 1.5 million flawed chips were on inventory at the time Intel stopped selling them. These chips were transported to a warehouse where they remain. The cost of that inventory constituted nearly half of Intel's losses.

Andrew Grove conceded, "Sometimes you need a real jolt to realize a reality has kind of happened around you. We have to learn some skills that are second nature to others."

This episode certainly has taught Intel that the demographics within the PC market's customer base have moved away from businesses and have gone toward home users. PC sales passed car sales in 1993 and are gaining on television sales. The irony of the business today is that the more sophisticated the technology becomes, the more likely it is to be in the hands of a novice. Case in point: In the last quarter of 1994, more PCs based on the Pentium chip were purchased by individual consumers than by businesses. The progression of the market in the future will be a test of Intel's ability to manage its customer base.

AFTERMATH

According to reports after this event, Intel's business survived the Pentium crisis and regained its stellar reputation through sales of the corrected chip.

Prices on all Pentium models were cut from 7 to 40 percent to win a larger stake in the market.

The proportion of the flawed microprocessors returned has been much smaller than anticipated. Individual consumers comprised approximately two-thirds of the estimated 5.5 million owners of flawed chips, and only 1 to 3 percent have returned the chips. The corporate customers have returned their faulty Pentium chips at a 25 percent rate. Overall, the returns have been close to 10 percent, with over a half million chips having been returned to Intel.

Lessons Learned

Based on the results of the returns to Intel, customers' concerns over the defect in the chips were not the driving force behind the Pentium crisis. "They've had [PC makers] by the short hairs," says management consultant Rich Bader, who ran Intel's small retail operation in Oregon in the mid-1980s. "They treat the consumers with a very similar philosophy."

Intel realized the change within the market structure and recognized that future dealings with individual consumers must be handled differently, as compared with the way it dealt with larger corporate business clients in the past. The overwhelming movement toward home computers has awakened Intel's understanding of a changing customer base. Intel has begun to develop a customer service strategy and has made strides in areas that have previously been foreign to the company. Marketing has further thrust the company closer to its customer base by concentrating on an advertisement campaign revolving around the slogan "Intel Inside." This approach is new for microprocessor producers and has surprised the computer producers. Most of Intel's rivals do not advertise in this manner and leave marketing to the manufacturer of the finished product. Intel has also recently begun to realize that being closer to the customer can at times be frightening. The necessity of understanding the consumer's point of view has caused Intel to create a telephone hotline to answer any questions concerning the Pentium component.

The Pentium ordeal proved to be the first major usage of the Internet by consumers to express dissatisfaction with a company and its product. The Internet currently has over 169.4 million users—and is growing (Nielsen Net Ratings, 2001). The Internet proved to be the accelerant of the Intel crisis. Andrew Grove got the message.

Questions for Discussion

1. What went wrong with the Pentium chip? What events and pressures led to the "almost crisis"?
2. Describe Intel's crisis management strategy. Did it work? Explain.
3. Using one of the crisis management frameworks in Chapter 2 of the text, explain the events in this case.

4. What were the "lessons learned" in this case? Do you agree? (Were there other lessons? If so, describe them.)

NOTES AND SOURCES

Are you ready for a Pentium Power chip? (Nov. 21, 1994). *Business Week*.
Big Blue chews up Intel chip. (Dec. 12, 1994). *Time*.
Despite furor, most keep their Pentium chips. (April 13, 1995). *Wall Street Journal*, B1-2.
The education of Andrew Grove. (Jan. 16, 1995). *Business Week*.
Interview with Andrew Grove. (June 29, 1994). *America On Line*.
Here's how. (April 1995). *PC World*.
Intel, Fay beyond the Pentium. (Feb. 20, 1995). *Business Week*.
Intel takes a bullet—and barely breaks stride. (Jan. 30, 1995). *Business Week*.
The lurking "time bomb" of the Silicon Valley. (Dec. 19, 1994). *Business Week*.
Nielsen Net Ratings. At http://www.nielsen-netratings.com/hot_off_the_net.jsp. Accessed
    Dec. 10, 2001.
Pentium: A house divided. (March 1995). *PC World*.
Top of the news. (June 1994). *PC World*.

CASE 4
WHAT'S WRITTEN VERSUS WHAT'S REALITY: ETHICAL DILEMMAS IN A HI-TECH PUBLIC RELATIONS FIRM

INDUSTRY AND COMPANY OVERVIEW

The goal of public relations (PR) is to make desired targets aware of clients and products. Through relationships with the media—press, television, and Internet—as well as stock market analysts, client and product awareness is broadened. Articles in trade magazines and newspapers, television interviews, tradeshow bookings, promotional tours, and general market research on clients and their competitors are the stock and trade of this business. Consultative strategies on the launch of initial public offerings (IPOs), timing and marketplace, corporate branding, and crisis management, as well as C-level (CEO, CFO, CAO, CIO) media training sessions, are some higher-level offerings of PR agencies.

The nature of the PR industry is competitive, individualist, and "catty." Agencies compete for qualified staff, as well as clients, and are quick to bad-mouth their competitors. There is very little loyalty in this industry. Staff are quick to "agency hop," leave for a competing agency offering them more money, and "client hop," leave the agency to work for a client. Title inflation and pay inflation flourish in this individualist culture. As a mediocre staff person hops up the corporate ladder, title and pay grow. Eventually, it is discovered that this person is overpaid and underqualified; then he is blackballed. Word spreads rapidly throughout the industry that this individual is no good, making it very difficult for him to progress further in his career.

Additionally, agencies are eager to "client swap," terminate their relationship with an existing client if a competitor offers the agency more money. The client with the biggest budget wins, regardless of contractual obligations.

The nature of the PR professional is not reported favorably. An article in *PRWEEK*, a major PR trade publication, reported that 25 percent of all PR pros admit lying (*PRWEEK*, May 22, 2000). In order to advance their careers or their client's business, PR professionals may resort to lying. The culture of this industry is individualistic and egotistic.

PRI (Public Relations, Inc.) is an actual, medium-to-large PR agency located in the northeastern United States. PRI specializes in PR consulting for hi-tech companies. The name PRI is a disguise.

Seven Common Ethical Dilemmas

This case focuses on common ethical dilemmas. Our dilemmas are based on real, everyday dilemmas that PR professionals face in a real PR agency. Seven reoccurring dilemmas that PR professionals struggle with frequently are the following:

1. Client noncompete agreement
2. Client confidentiality: insider information
3. Integrity of client information
4. Employee poaching
5. Friends and family stock gifting
6. Unrealistic financial forecasting
7. Promised versus realized employee benefits

Several vice presidents and senior vice presidents at PRI were consulted to identify and validate these dilemmas, and to discuss real-life outcomes when their own professional ethics are challenged.

Ethical Dilemmas: Up Close and Personal

Each of the ethical dilemmas, which have occurred (and still occur) at PRI, is identified with an example. First, the written "policy" regarding the practice is identified. Then, an example of the dilemma is given, followed by the result or what actually happened. Finally, comments and afterthoughts regarding the dilemma are offered.

#1 Client Noncompete Agreements.   Contracts between the agency and the client specifically state that the agency will not solicit or accept work from a competitor during the term of the contract. If the agency wants to pursue a competitor, it should end the relationship prior to making contact with the competitor. Of course, this is a gamble, so PR agencies rarely follow this clause if the competitor has more money to spend.

What's Written

- Noncompete clause in contract: "PRI will not solicit or accept work from a competitor during the term of this contract."

Dilemma

- You have a long-standing relationship with Client G.
- This client is very demanding, and the staff on the account are unhappy.
- One of your staff has told you that he has a contact inside Client M, a more desirable client, but a competitor of Client G.

Reality: What Happened

- Client M was contacted, pitched, and won. Upon Client M's contract signature, PRI notified Client G that the relationship would be terminated.

Comments and Afterthoughts

This is commonplace in the PR industry. The client with the biggest budget wins; there is no client loyalty. In turn, there is very little agency loyalty. A company may burn through three agencies in one year. There is a disincentive, or "hassle factor," as well as a cost factor in switching agencies. Bringing an agency "up to speed" on a company's business and strategy can be time consuming.

#2 CLIENT CONFIDENTIALITY: INSIDER INFORMATION. Highly confidential client information is shared with PR agencies in an effort to place clients and their products in the best strategic position. Once the client-agency relationship is terminated, all documents containing confidential information are returned to the client. However, the staff cannot simply erase the information they have absorbed while working for that client. Because PR professionals gain domain expertise by working on clients within the same industry, they are frequently asked to pitch competitors of their current clients. Then, if the pitch is won, their current client is terminated and the PR pro is assigned to the new competing client. Below is an example of a dilemma that occurred with the "Ford" and "Chevy" of hi-tech clients.

What's Written

- Clause in the contract: "PRI will keep confidential all client information for the term of this contract."

Dilemma

- Because you have industry-specific experience (you worked on Client G), you have been placed in charge of the Client M account.
- You know that Client G is developing a new product that could clobber Client M's product.

Reality: What Happened

- Client M was not told the confidential information.
- Due to the financial impact of the competition, Client M reduced its marketing budget.

Comments and Afterthoughts

We are not aware of any breach of confidentiality at PRI. However, that does not mean that it does not occur. The guideline for this decision is whether or not your client is so unscrupulous that it would appreciate this kind of information. Sharing this kind of information is a double-edged sword; the client may be concerned that you would share its trade secrets and pull the business. Therefore, the motivation for keeping information confidential is often not an ethical decision, but a financial decision.

#3 INTEGRITY OF CLIENT INFORMATION. PR professionals rely on client-supplied information. The information is then passed on to the media for broadcast or publication. It is not the responsibility of the PR agency to research the accuracy of client-supplied information. However, the blame can fall on the agency when things go wrong. What follows is an article where a PR agency was blamed for publishing misinformation.

> Client's counterfeit biography hurls Horn Group into the headlines, by Aimee Grove. SAN FRANCISCO: Pitching a CEO's credentials in a rags-to-riches tale is a tried-and-true PR tactic. But what if a client's head honcho lied on his resume, approved a press-kit bio constructed around these falsehoods, then turned around and pinned the blame on the PR firm when the media uncovered the truth? That's exactly what happened to The Horn Group, which found itself in Bay Area headlines last week when the CEO of client Luna Information Systems tried to finger them for circulating "An Entrepreneur's Story"—press materials containing exaggerated and unfounded claims about his background and education. [*PRWEEK*, July 25, 2000]

The CEO told Horn Group that he was a graduate of Harvard Business School and played professional soccer for eight years. All this was false.

But how can a PR pro question a client on the truth or accuracy of information without offending the client in this egotistical industry?

What's Written

- As a PR professional, you are not required to check the accuracy of the information provided by your client.

Dilemma

- Client L is releasing a new product: *Printer 2000*.
- Your client has provided you with some product specifications that sound fabulous, almost "too good to be true."
- You have already lined up some great press opportunities and will lose them if you delay the release.

Reality: What Happened
- PRI questioned the information and gave up some of the press opportunities.
- The client was extremely offended and threatened to fire PRI.
- Client L's information was published and was wrong.

Comments and Afterthoughts
This is a balance among losing press arrangements, offending clients, and covering the agency's reputation. This is a judgment call with no guidelines.

#4 EMPLOYEE POACHING. Contracts between the agency and the client specifically state the client will not solicit any employees of the agency during the term of this contract. Knowing that this statement alone will not deter solicitation, the agency includes additional language: If the client solicits and hires any employees from PRI, the client must pay 50 percent of the employees' current salary. As headhunters charge fees up to 35 percent, the 50 percent acts as a disincentive. However, in a booming economy, clients are willing to spend more to get the right person for the job. Paying the 50 percent fee for a known quantity is more efficient than paying 35 percent for a bad or mediocre hire. Employees of the agency develop strong relationships with their clients as part of their job. If a client offers them a higher paying, more prestigious job, it is tough to pass up the opportunity.

What's Written
- Included in the client contract is this clause: "If Client L solicits and hires any employees from PRI, Client L must pay 50 percent of employees' current salary."

Dilemma
- You have a great relationship with your client, Client L, and have secretly contemplated working at Client L.
- Client L has mentioned that there is a position available that you would be "perfect" for . . . but that the 50 percent fee is a lot of money.

Reality: What Happened
- Together, employee and Client L approached PRI's CEO.
- The 50 percent fee was waived in exchange for increased business for PRI.

Comments and Afterthoughts
This is a win/win situation—and is rare. There are three clients that currently owe PRI fees for employee recruitment. Since the client relationships have been terminated, PRI has little leverage for collection. Legal suits have been filed in these three cases.

#5 FRIENDS AND FAMILY STOCK GIFTING.   As the clients of PRI are dot.coms and hi-tech companies hiring PRI to assist them in their IPO launches, as well as general PR, the offering of friends and family (F&F) stock to the agency and its employees is common. To avoid conflicts of interest, PRI has a "Just Say No" policy to stock. This policy is more to protect the firm from legal liability of conflicts than to act ethically. Clients not offering F&F stock may try to claim that they were not given the same level of service, interview opportunities, press coverage, and so on as clients who contributed stock.

What's Written
- PRI has a "Just Say No" policy to F&F stock.

Dilemma
- You have a long-standing relationship with Client I.
- This client is launching its IPO next month; the IPO is expected to be very successful.
- Knowing your policy, Client I offers F&F stock for your spouse.

Reality: What Happened
- No stock was accepted.

Comments and Afterthoughts
We are only aware of this case because the employee informed PRI. There may be many cases that PRI is unaware of.

#6 UNREALISTIC FINANCIAL FORECASTING.   The senior management team is recognized and rewarded for business growth, organic growth of existing clients' accounts, and new clients. In order to appear heroic, many of the senior managers are overly conservative (that is, they sandbag or low ball) in their forecasts of clients' planned spending with the agency. Then when actual revenues are higher than originally planned, the senior manager looks like a hero and is awarded a bonus accordingly.

What's Written
- Forecast accurately for the good of the company.

Dilemma
- Your bonus is based on increased activity from the annual forecast of the organic growth of existing clients (as well as new business).
- All your clients have increased their budgets for next year.
- If you claim this in the 2002 forecast, you will need to grow the business even more over the year to realize your bonus.

Reality: What Happened
- Sandbagging!
- Results: A scramble to hire more staff, inappropriate expense planning, and overall inaccurate information for decision making.

Comments and Afterthoughts

The rewards system needs to be changed to encourage the behavior that is desired, accuracy in forecasting.

#7 PROMISED VERSUS REALIZED EMPLOYEE BENEFITS. This is a dilemma of culture conflict. As in many companies, PRI has a "face-time" culture. The senior leaders paid their dues by working long hours and expect their junior staff to do the same. Although PRI presents itself as a results-oriented agency, the "face-time" culture dominates. Additionally, there are political battles among some of the senior leaders. This conflict filters down to middle management and below. How can a middle manager lead his or her staff with fairness without limiting his or her own advancement?

What's Written

- PRI offers a new FlexTime Condensed Work Week available to all employees, with manager approval (created by HR).

Dilemma

- Your boss does not support this plan and has an adversarial relationship with the head of HR.
- A staff member has requested a condensed work week.
- You know that approving this request may be a career limiting move (CLM) for both you and the staff person, in this "face-time" culture.

Reality: What Happened

- The manager encouraged the staff person to wait 90 days and see how other staff are managing their workload on this plan.
- The manager suggested to the boss that the staff person participate in the FlexTime plan as a show of support for the CEO (self-promotion).
- The boss said, "NO!"

Comments and Afterthoughts

Employee participation in this FlexTime program is less than 5 percent. The corporate culture is contra to a traditional 40-hour week, much less a flexible 40-hour week. The regular week is 50+ hours of face time.

PRI's ETHICAL PROFILE

LEADERSHIP. The managers at PRI relate to their constituencies from an amoral orientation. They often act without concern for the consequences of their actions for other stakeholders. With amoral management, although there may not be willful wrongdoing, no thought is given to the morality of actions (Weiss, 1998, 80).

The manipulator style is based on a "ends justifies the means" ethic (ibid., 114). The egotistic nature of the culture feeds into this style of leadership.

Motivations driving managers' actions include power, the ego, and economics. It has a short-term focus and lacks trust or long-term relationship-building qualities. The second style is the professional manager. In this style, managers and organizational executives set the ground rules and ethics that govern the manager's behavior (ibid., 115). The strong influence of culture on this style can lead to problems in a company like PRI.

CULTURE. The culture in this industry and at PRI is individualistic and egotistical. The industry is also very competitive in nature. There is little loyalty, either between agencies and clients or between employees and their agencies. This culture does not encourage professionals to act in an ethical manner. As was mentioned in the industry overview, 25 percent of all PR professionals admit to lying (*PRWEEK*, May 22, 2000).

STRUCTURE. PRI has several locations throughout the world and is one branch of a larger network of PR firms worldwide. Consequently, the company has a divisional structure. The divisions operate in a fairly decentralized manner. Decentralized structures tend to encourage more unethical behavior among employees than structures that are more centralized and controlled (Weiss, 1998, 111).

CONTROL SYSTEMS. The contracts that exist between agencies and clients comprise one system that is put in place to govern the behavior of the two parties. The contracts are typically prepared by the PR agency. Some clauses can be very specific and detailed when that is in the best interest of the agency. For example, in the employee poaching dilemma, the contract states not only that the client will not solicit any employees of the agency during the term of the contract, but also that "if the client solicits and hires any employees from PRI, the client must pay 50 percent of the employees' current salary." In other cases, when there is not such a specific benefit to the agency, wording in the contract if often vague. In the client confidentiality dilemma, the contract states that "PRI will keep confidential all client information for the term of this contract." In this example, nothing is said to indicate that the information should be kept confidential when the contract expires or is terminated. This, and other similar vague clauses, can leave employees to face ethical dilemmas regarding appropriate behavior.

Although there are contracts governing the relationship between agency and client, there are no clear written policies for the employees. A clear set of guidelines could help employees understand the agency's expectations regarding the appropriate decisions when faced with common ethical dilemmas.

As the unrealistic financial forecasting dilemma described, there is a reward system in place for agency employees. Company reward systems can have a profound influence on employee behavior. Companies should evaluate their reward systems carefully to make sure that they reinforce the behaviors that are desired. In this case, the structure of the reward system has negative consequences in that it encourages managers to make overly conservative forecasts. The result is the inability of the firm to gather accurate information for planning and decision making.

IMPACT OF THESE FACTORS ON EMPLOYEE BEHAVIOR. The relationship among these factors at PRI influences the actions and behaviors of employees. The decentralized structure and lack of clear policies encourage a climate that allows immoral activities, especially when there are strong pressures to increase profits. An incentive system driven by numbers encourages shortcuts around responsible decisions. The amoral orientation of the culture and leadership creates an environment that essentially condones immoral actions. PRI is not alone in facing these problems. These are common reasons why managers may compromise their ethics (ibid., 112).

CLOSING THOUGHTS

It is highly unlikely that PRI's leadership could or would be able to overcome the industry and company barriers to create a truly high-ethics environment (ibid., 121) at PRI. The owners and top managers actually do not want their employees to act with any absolute sense of what is right and wrong. They do want employees to use a "reasonable person" approach to decision making when faced with ethical dilemmas. PRI's leaders would, in all likelihood, advocate for a combination of amoral leadership styles along with utilitarian and ethical relativism as the common ethical decision-making mode. This combination leaves space for individual entrepreneurial, competitive interpretation regarding what the "right decision" would be in a particular situation.

In the meantime, there are actions the agency can take to help employees resolve ethical dilemmas. A set of guidelines could be developed to help people do "the right things" in very gray areas—especially in addressing the common ethical dilemmas faced in this industry. Top managers should also lead by example and make sure that their behavior is consistent with the behavior they desire from their employees. The reward system should be reevaluated to make sure it rewards the desired results without creating other dilemmas for the agency. In summary, the agency should try to implement some small measures that achieve the desired results, which do not always clash with the highly competitive industry culture.

REFERENCES

Grove, A. (July 25, 2000). Client's counterfeit biography hurls Horn Group into the headlines. *PRWEEK.*

PR pros admit lying. (May 22, 2000). *PRWEEK.*

Weiss, J. W. (1998). *Business Ethics: A Stakeholder and Issues Management Approach,* 2nd ed. Fort Worth, TX: Dryden Press.

QUESTIONS FOR DISCUSSION

1. Do you agree with the "Closing Thoughts"? Why or why not? Explain.

2. How would you conduct yourself regarding each of the seven dilemmas if you were a PRI employee? Explain.

3. How would you "fit" working at PRI? Do your "ethics" match the company's? Explain.

4. What issues would *you* likely face as a leader (either CEO, CFO, or CIO) at PRI? Explain.

5. Do PRI's leaders face the same ethical tensions and consequences as its lower-level employees? Explain.

6. As an ethics consultant, what specifically—if anything—would you recommend to the PRI leadership regarding the ethical dilemmas it continually faces? Explain.

CASE 5
MERRILL LYNCH'S ENTRY INTO ON-LINE TRADING

INDUSTRY OVERVIEW

On-line trading is a technology that allows individuals to trade securities and bonds over the Internet without going through a traditional broker. The emergence of this technology opened up a host of controversies and heated debates. The number of customers and stakeholders mushroomed before the "Internet bubble" burst, the economy took a drastic downturn, and technology stocks plummeted. September 11 also hit the company hard: "The outlook remains uncertain for many securities in the current market environment, including Merrill Lynch. Equity markets have been volatile since the Sept. 11 attack and few firms have wanted to conduct merger and acquisitions in their uncertain environment. At the same time, many consumers are shaken daily by reports of anthrax scares or the possibility of additional terrorist attacks. In the third quarter, Merrill Lynch's commissions declined 25.9% to $1.2 billion, down from $1.6 billion a year ago and $1.4 billion in the second quarter. Revenue from principal transactions declined 35% to $759 million, down from $1.1 billion a year earlier and $911 million in the second quarter"(Bray, 2001).

Consumers and institutions will continue to trade (buy and sell) stocks, bonds, and other financial options on the Web. On-line trading will suffer economy swings and crises, as will other businesses, but this business is believed to be here for the long term: "Assets held in online brokerage accounts are predicted to grow from $1.1 trillion in 2000 to $3.2 trillion in 2004, according to the eInvesting Report released in November 2000 by eMarketer.

Compare that to the $9.6 billion in FDIC insured deposits in 1999, of which pure Internet banks accounted for only 2%. How does online brokerage growth continue despite the fact that recent market volatility has resulted in a real dip in online trading transactions? The secret of success is fairly simple—brokers have learned to stay nimble "(Berstel, 2001).

Beginning as an Internet game of sorts, on-line trading has evolved into a combination of services offered by some firms—like Merrill Lynch. When on-line trading first appeared, however, Merrill Lynch was not an early adopter. It wasn't consistent with its vision, image, strategy, and structure; therefore, it wasn't on the company's radar screen.

When on-line trading first became possible, a negative image also came along: On-line trading was widely publicized as "day trading." Burton G. Malkiel, author of *A Random Walk down Wall Street,* described it best when he said, "Day-trading involves the pursuit of short-term profit through quick in and out trades, sometimes over the period of just a few minutes. For day traders the long term means later in the afternoon. These traders usually liquidate their positions at the end of each day."

On-line trading provides liquidity to the market, making the market more efficient by narrowing bid-ask spreads. Day traders try to exploit small differences in market-maker prices, pouncing on pricing anomalies by market-makers who do not react quickly enough to changing information. On-line trading also allows individuals to choose to exercise autonomy over their financial destiny rather than giving control to brokers and professional money managers.

INNOVATOR'S DILEMMA

At the beginning of Internet trading, traditional brokerage houses, like Merrill Lynch, Morgan Stanley, and PaineWebber, were assaulted by upstart e-brokers like E*Trade, Ameritrade, and Charles Schwab. First entrants into any new business field focus on creating an Internet brand identity. Merrill Lynch entered this arena after the pioneers blazed the trail.

Merrill Lynch's goal was to balance the interests of its army of full-service brokers with on-line trading firms that first gained ground by offering rock-bottom commissions. Merrill Lynch, when first deciding whether or not to enter the field, was faced with the "Innovator's Dilemma," a problem described by Clayton Christensen at Harvard Business School. He argued, "When successful companies are faced with a big technological leap that transforms their markets, all choices are bad ones." Doing nothing is not an option, as Merrill Lynch & Co. and other established outfits have learned. Facing a major innovation like the Internet with a head-in-the-sand strategy can maintain profits in the short run. In the long term, however, market share and profits are going to be eaten away by low-cost upstarts.

THE DECISION TO GO ON-LINE

The Internet has already changed the brokerage industry. Web-based financial transactions are now changing banks and blurring boundaries between financial institutions. The Internet effectively eliminates or reduces the need for intermediaries because information is readily available and customers can quickly compare broker commissions and services. This increased transparency is eroding profit margins and customer bases of established brokerage houses like Merrill Lynch and Prudential Securities. Morgan Stanley analyst Henry McVey expects the average industry commission to fall from $80 in 1998 to $28 in 2003, a decline of 65 percent.

Merrill Lynch, for three years, watched from the sidelines as the competitive landscape in the retail brokerage industry shifted. Once thought to be a temporary fad, on-line trading revolutionized the industry, and Merrill scrambled to regain its footing. E*Trade went public in August 1996 and several other on-line brokers followed suit soon after, so what took Merrill so long? Merrill had to first overcome strong cultural barriers that were preventing a smooth transition to the new business model.

Profit margins were being squeezed as on-line brokers slashed commissions to gain market share from full-service firms. In 1999, Merrill Lynch finally decided to embrace on-line trading in two stages. First, in May 1999, Merrill introduced a new fee structure that allowed unlimited trading for an annual fee of about 1 percent of total assets ($1,500 minimum) rather than a per trade commission. Then, in December 1999, Merrill Lynch launched its long-anticipated on-line trading product, *Merrill Lynch Direct*, with commissions of $29.95 per trade, matching Charles Schwab's rates.

Aside from the immediate concern over commission price compression, a more far-reaching industry shift made it clear that Merrill Lynch could no longer delay entering the on-line trading wars. Consumers were rapidly changing the way they do business. An October 1998 study by Britain Associates estimated that 58 percent of over roughly 30 million Internet households used the Internet to research stocks, bonds, and mutual funds. Another study, conducted by Cyber Dialogue, showed that Internet users are financially savvy. They have a high awareness of a variety of on-line services and a particularly high "conversion rate" for on-line trading, nearly 27 percent. The conversion rate is measured by the number of people using a product as a percentage of the people aware of the product (McVey, 1999, 44). Given this revolutionary paradigm shift, with the swiftness and magnitude of its acceptance, Merrill Lynch had no choice but to embrace a business model compatible with the so-called new economy.

MERRILL'S ON-LINE STRATEGY

Merrill's on-line strategy involved four key strategic areas: attract more customers with on-line services, integrate on-line services with the existing brokerage model, translate the experience and knowledge of employees into on-line content, and rethink every business function from research to asset management.

With the launch of Merrill Lynch Direct on December 1, 1999, Merrill offered expanded service in order to compete with other on-line investment centers. Merrill offered brokerless trading with a discounted fee of $29.99 per stock trade, access to Merrill's IPOs, real-time positions and pricing for entire portfolios, stock search engines, greater access to Merrill research, detailed account information, and portfolio management tools. In order to compete with the likes of Yahoo!, Merrill Lynch Direct also offered links for on-line shopping, auctions, and news. This strategy was planned to retain existing customers as well as attract a broader base of new customers.

An issue that Merrill had to address in its strategy was its heavy-fixed cost structure. The broker's fee of $140.00 a trade was now considered extremely high, given the low on-line fees. Merrill's $29.95 on-line fee is also considered high compared to the fees of its on-line competitors. But along with Merrill's $29.95 trading fee came their brokers' research and knowledge, a service that an on-line firm could not claim. Merrill's brokers, or financial consultants as the firm refers to them, are high-profile brokers who are known for their excellent advice and research.

STRATEGIC PARTNERSHIPS

Merrill also formed partnerships and began investing in companies in order to expand its on-line technology reach. Some of these include marketing and content partnerships with Microsoft Network, Medialink, Dow Jones, and Intuit. Merrill is heavily investing in alternative electronic trading systems, known as electronic communications networks (ECNs), such as Archipelago, Bloomberg, and TradeWeb, which are competing with NASDAQ and the New York Stock Exchange (NYSE). To keep pace with technology innovations and development, Merrill also formed partnerships with AT&T and Cisco Systems, to name a few.

To shift from a high-cost "bureaucracy" to a lower margin on-line business, Merrill attempted to leverage the knowledge from its best brokers and research groups to provide on-line content and research. Merrill's on-line strategy bumped up against its older strategy of maintaining 17,000 registered brokers. The company's ads during its on-line start-up phase stressed that its existing offices and brokers would not be going away with the advent of its on-line service offering. But it was unclear how Merrill would lower costs without downsizing while it continued to invest heavily in technology. Nor had Merrill completed "rethinking" the rest of its business and how that would fit into the new world of on-line brokerage. The fit of Merrill's on-line service with the company's overall strategies remained vague, probably because it was still playing catch-up with the rest of its competitors.

Merrill's challenges were daunting when you consider that they were shifting their entire corporate strategy while dealing with fierce competition, attempting to lure the "common investor" (new territory), and keeping pace with technology and industry changes. Merrill's brokers had influence within the company and with investors. They were content to continue to react and adapt to the new changes. Several experts had their doubts about whether Merrill had the management or the will power to execute its transformation. However, where there's market share and money to be made, there's a way.

REPUTATION COUNTS

Merrill Lynch's reputation helped with its transition on-line. "There is a certain amount of security people feel when people deal with Merrill Lynch or a full-service brokerage firm." Schwieterman states. This is an advantage Merrill has over the pioneers of on-line trading such as E*Trade. Merrill Lynch offering on-line trading has broadened its distribution. This should help stem the outflow of assets to on-line firms and provide Merrill with the next generation of investors. Merrill can now focus on its advisors and not "stock jockeys" for gaining new clients and retaining the present ones. The brokers will become advisors to the clients.

COMPETITORS. The days of loyalty to brokers have evolved through self-instructed, independent customers trading their stocks on-line to a full range of services where brokers can also help, especially during economic downturns, when bonds become more attractive than stocks. The roles of retail brokerage firms and brokers have and still are evolving as competitors arise and economic conditions continue to change. Discount brokerage firms and full-service firms are incorporating on-line trading to keep afloat in the Internet era. The Charles Schwabs and PaineWebbers of the business that once ridiculed on-line trading are leading the chase. Fidelity charged $14.99 for on-line trades. E*Trade dropped its fee to $4.95 per trade in 2000 to attract high-volume trading. Top-tier full-service firms such as DLJdirect were competing by offering after-hours trading. According to BankBoston Robertson Stephens analyst Scott Appleby, Internet trading in 1999 accounted for close to 40 percent of all retail transactions and about a half a million trades a day (Broker, 1999). The fine lines distinguishing discount, full-service, and on-line brokerage firms were blurring then and continue to overlap.

CONSUMERS, The Internet has become a powerful tool in consumers' personal financing. Consumers now have the ability to open accounts, check balances, and transfer funds between accounts in privacy at their leisure. On-line accounts save customers money on the traditional brokerage fees and commissions to the brokers. With the frantic competition for on-line dollars, accounts are now selling for as little as $5.00 per trade and an average of about $15.00, compared to the average full-service firm's cost of $120.00. Along with pricing, firms are also competing for services, after-hour trading, ECNs, financial planning, and more.

As Merrill Lynch is increasing its presence in on-line trading, its competitors—DLJdirect and Morgan Stanley Dean Witter, to name a few—are also involved in the on-line race. With the definition lines blurred, the competition on-line is still being sorted out by the market and economic conditions. Who is gaining and sustaining clients? At the beginning of the on-line trading race, it was the firms that offered more to their clients at their Website. The game is evolving to include not only the firms with this advantage, but also those firms that can offer deeper services such as advising during crises and economic downturns.

The on-line threat of Schwab to Merrill Lynch is Schwab's ability to leverage both the power of the Internet and its network of 340 brick-and-mortar customer centers and 7,000 brokers. David Pottruck, president of Charles Schwab & Co., reported in 1999 that his company does not intend to let the need for personal interaction get lost on the Internet. In 1999, he increased his branches by 10 percent. Pottruck was quoted: "A significant number of people are more comfortable starting an investment relationship in person, even if they later choose the phone or web as the primary method of communication" (Goldfield, 1999). These attributes have brought in clients' assets faster than any other discount or full-service brokerage in America. With one-fourth the work force and one-tenth the revenues of Merrill Lynch, Schwab has a larger stock capital market capitalization than Merrill had at that time (Lim, 1999).

CUSTOMERS. On-line trading was in 1999 perceived as the exclusive realm of seasoned investors and bold brokers. But that image has given way to reality. Although only a few years old (since its start in the mid-1990s), on-line investing has become increasingly popular with the everyday "average" citizens. This class of citizen, according to Paul Kelly, professor of finance at New York University's Stem Business School, includes "college students, house wives, grandparents and those who are learning about and experiencing the stock market for the first time in their lives" (Lim, 1999).

Millions of Americans have come to expect the convenience of electronic stock trading and a range of other services: banking, paying bills, planning calculators, and obtaining quotes and other information, even advice. Armed with Pentium III processors and cutting-edge financial software (often provided when one joins an on-line trade service like Ameritrade, E*Trade, and Charles Schwab), clients view themselves as the epicenter of the on-line trading market. "It is easier than ever to buy and trade stocks with the advent of online investing," says Andrew M. Brooks, vice president in charge of equity trading at T. Rowe Price in Baltimore, Maryland. "Where before a lot of people may have been discouraged or intimidated to utilize a traditional brokerage house, you now have the ability to download whatever research you need and invest within the privacy of your home" (Goldfield, 1999).

Still, about half of all U.S. households do not own stocks or mutual funds. But the half that do are using the Internet and were in 1999 opening roughly 17,000 accounts every business day.

In an effort to capture a portion of the growing segment of households delving into on-line trading, firms began charging a fraction of the trading fees that full-service firms such as Salomon Smith Barney, Morgan Stanley Dean Witter, and PaineWebber charged. These fires were commanding fees of $100–$200 a trade. In contrast, Charles Schwab, a leader in on-line broker services, charged about $30.00 for each Internet trade, while Ameritrade charged as little as $8.00. American Express even offered commissionfree trades to its on-line customers.

These low prices attracted increasing numbers of Americans to on-line investing in the late 1990s. On-line trading also gave the average American a sense of autonomy and importance. "Online trading is a boon to the investor who wants inexpensive trades and control over their own portfolio," William Doyle, an analyst at Forrester Research in Cambridge, Massachusetts, said. "This is the perfect way to become involved in the market as long as you're willing to put time into researching your investments."

Merrill Lynch started on-line trading for about 55,000 U.S. clients in March of 1999 with so-called wrap accounts, which charge annual fees for money management services based on the level of account assets. Merrill Lynch is still navigating its on-line strategy so that more customers see and can take advantage of a wider array of products for the first-time or inexperienced investor. (Merrill does manage 3.2 percent of U.S. households' financial assets.)

According to a 1999 published report, "The Bumpy Ride to Bigger, Better, Cheaper, Faster," a financial services memorandum published by Henry H. McVey (Oct. 12, 1999), on-line trading services are the wave of the future. "We believe the introduction of online trading was the right move for Merrill Lynch," says McVey. "Research estimates that by 2003, 40% of retail brokerage assets will have moved online compared to 3.3% today. In our opinion, broadening its distribution should help stem the outflow of assets to other online brokerage firms and provide Merrill with access to the next generation of investors."

"Online trading is one of the most dramatic forces reshaping the market today," says David Cushing, director of research at ITG Inc., a research and trading company that runs a trade-matching service. "Traditional and electronic brokerages must acknowledge a growing customer base created through the Internet generation. This involves a corps of first-time investors who are looking for a service that provides them with all the background they need to invest like the big boys."

FEDERAL REGULATIONS AND THE SEC. Until recently, the Securities and Exchange Commission (SEC) has allowed on-line brokerage firms to regulate themselves. The speed at which changes have been occurring as a result of technology has not allowed the SEC its usual time to observe and make judgments. The SEC, however, is stepping up the pace at which it observes, researches, comments on, and proposes regulations around on-line trading. A report released by SEC Commissioner Laura Unger represents over 10 months of work in researching the impact of technology and on-line trading. Although the report does not introduce specific proposals on regulations for on-line brokers, it does make several "recommendations" on how brokerage firms, the SEC, and other regulators can manage the on-line brokerage industry.

The report addresses several issues facing consumers and brokerage firms with on-line trading. Perhaps one of the biggest issues that may face Merrill and Internet-based trading firms is suitability obligations. In essence, suitability refers to the blurring of the fine line between securities recommendations and order taking on the Web. As Internet trading companies, service providers, and brokerage companies serve up more research and investment information over the Web, the question of what constitutes financial advice becomes complicated for the SEC and regulators. The information provided by Websites could become the focus of investor-arbitration complaints and lawsuits when investments go bad.

One of the recommendations calls for Web brokers to provide the public with more information about technical problems, contingency plans, and server outages. There has been a growing concern among industry experts and SEC regulators over companies' ability to handle the capacity of new on-line brokers. Many on-line brokers have been plagued by slow performance and temporary outages, while some advertising would lead consumers to believe trades can be executed as quickly as a click of a mouse. Most brokerage firms do not feel the need to provide the public with information about their outages. "We don't think it's the right kind of information to provide to the public at large," states Michael Hogan of Dudirect. Part of the problem is identifying the source of the outage, which can oftentimes be a problem from the Internet service provider versus the actual brokerage company. The recommendations clearly indicate that new rules from industry regulators may be required to force companies to inform brokers and consumers of outages during trading hours.

The issue of outages also becomes a fundamental issue related to the heavy spending in advertising where the SEC is concerned whether these companies are simultaneously spending enough on their computer systems to support the number of new customers brought in by the advertising.

The SEC report also comments on several other issues such as privacy rights for Web investors, hidden fees and fees charged by the NYSE, and financial discussions over Internet chat rooms. Regulators are concerned over the fees charged to brokers by the NYSE, especially given the potential for the NYSE to become a for-profit company and attempt to sell its services and information, which could sharply increase fees for consumers. The proliferation of ECNs will further complicate and revolutionize the on-line trading arena. ECNs are on-line alternative trading forums that compete with traditional trading auction houses such as the NYSE. The SEC has approved and recognized ECNs. The implications for brokers and floor traders from companies such as Merrill and the NYSE will further revolutionize the securities and brokerage industries. Whether brokers and floor

TIME LINE

Year	Event
1867	First stock-quote ticker installed
1871	Stock "specialist" role created on the NYSE floor; enables continuos trading on each stock
1878	First telephone installed on NYSE
1903	NYSE moves to current site
1915	Charles Merrill and Edmond Lynch company born
1934	U.S. Securities and Exchange Commission created
1971	Electronic NASDAQ market created as a rival to NYSE
1982	First 100-million-share day on NYSE
1982	William Porter formed TradePlus on-line
1982	First on-line service, "Tickerscreen" by Max Ule
1983	TradePlus enables customers to access market information and conduct trades during market hours; also offers 24-hour portfolio management capability—pricing $195 signing subscription fee and $15 dollars for each 1-hour connection time
1987	TradePlus reported their server in use every minute; on-line usage increasing
1991	Porter started E*Trade Securities, offering free information and flat-rate pricing fees
1992	Average daily NYSE volume reaches 200 million shares
1994	2 million customers between E*Trade and TradePlus
1995	Multimedia PCs bundling sound, video, and modems; E*Trade drops fee to $19.95
1995	Merrill Lynch acquires Smith New Court to become the largest equity organization in the world with unsurpassed research, trading, and sale capabilities
1996	E*Trade drops prices with competition of Charles Schwab Online brokerage
1997	Merrill Lynch's total assets in private client accounts reach the $1 trillion mark
1997	Stock trading allowed in increments of sixteenths instead of eighths, narrowing down the "spread" specialists and dealers take from investors to trade
1997	E*Trade direct site on-line at Yahoo
1999	NYSE and NASDAQ announce step toward becoming publicly traded companies themselves, to raise capital to expand electronic trading capabilities
1999	Merrill Lynch announces new model for on-line trading for unlimited advantage accounts for individual investors; commissions are $29.95
1999	Numerous brokerages offer extended trading hours for individuals
2000	Merrill takeover of Herzog Heine Geduld
2001	January/February Merrill Lynch expands Web services due to customer demand; on-line brokerages continue to take the lead over on-line banks in customer popularity
2001	September 30, after the attack, Merrill's headquarters (4 and 2 World Financial Centers) inaccessible; operated from backup offices; Merrill cut 2,300 employees in the third quarter

traders will be eliminated altogether and some form of hybrid will evolve will be known only in time.

The SEC report may be only a first step towards future regulatory changes. There is no question, however, that the industry will continue its revolution, and you can bet that the SEC and other regulators will play a hand in molding the future.

THE FUTURE IS NOW

While Merrill continues to reinvent itself, the changes in the financial services industry and on-line trading will also continue to evolve at a rapid pace. To date, Merrill seems to have successfully adapted to the blurring effect of on-line trading. Merrill's bureaucratic culture has so far been able to withstand the speed at which on-line trading has revolutionized the industry. Its on-line services have attracted new customers without cannibalizing its existing base.

A current trend toward mergers and acquisitions in financial services, especially between banks and on-line businesses, has been fueled by brick-and-mortars seeking "market-makers." Merrill recently succeeded in the takeover of Herzog Heine Geduld. If this trend continues, some of Merrill's on-line competitors (Ameritrade, E*Trade, and others) may become part of its business. Merrill recently invested $25 million in an ad campaign (print, TV, radio) aimed at capturing investors in a downturn economy who need advice as well as Internet convenience. Steve Martin's voice was used in the following ad description:

> In a radio spot, Mr. Martin says he has always stuck with stocks because bonds are "boring." But after the rough period in the market, he consulted his Merrill Lynch adviser, who recommended diversifying into fixed-income securities. "I was like, fixed-income securities, great. Just so I don't have to buy any bonds," Mr. Martin says with enthusiasm. "That's when he told me that bonds and fixed-income securities are pretty much the same thing."
>
> The moral of the story: Don't turn your back on bonds. "If you're embarrassed, just call them fixed-income securities. It's way more impressive." The campaign represents something of a shift for Merrill Lynch. Responding to investor demand for online trading, the firm two years ago promoted a plan enabling investors to invest online, by phone or with a broker, for one set fee. In this campaign, Merrill Lynch's toll-free phone number is displayed before its Internet Web-site address, an obvious toning down of the emphasis on online trading.

QUESTIONS FOR DISCUSSION

1. What was Merrill Lynch's "innovator's dilemma," as described in this case, when it faced going into the on-line brokerage business?

2. What delayed Merrill Lynch from being a pioneer in on-line brokerage services? What caused the company to move in that direction? What is

Merrill Lynch's present strategy in using the Internet for brokerage services?

3. What were the issues raised in the case? How have these issues changed?

4. What ethical questions or issues are raised in this case? Explain.

5. What is your opinion or belief about on-line brokerage services? Does it verge on gambling? Is it a service every customer should have access to? What are the risks, if any, of on-line brokerage services?

REFERENCES

Advertising—New Merrill ads advise: Buy bonds and diversify. (July 9, 2001). *Asian Wall Street Journal*, 9.

The architect of Merrill's digital future. (Nov. 15, 1999). *Business Week*, 264.

Berstel, J. (Jan./Feb. 2001). Learning from online brokerage firms. *Bank Marketing, 33(1)*, 18.

Merrill Lynch readies online trading. (Feb. 18, 1999). *Bloomberg News*.

Bray, C. (Oct. 19, 2001). Merrill Lynch's net plunges over 50% following attacks—Expenses tied to U.S. tragedy total $53 million, firm says. *Wall Street Journal*, 9.

Broker, K. (Dec. 20, 1999). They want you wired! *Fortune*, 113.

Buckman, R. (Feb. 17, 1999). Schwab clients increase activity in online trading. *Wall Street Journal*, C11.

Buckman, R. (March 28, 1999). New SEC report details "suitable" online trading. *Wall Street Journal*, C1.

Business Week Online. (Nov. 10, 1999).

Can Merrill be a maverick? (June 14, 1999). *Business Week*, 46.

Cerne, F. (Aug. 1999). Investing in the future. *Bank Technology News*, 10–11.

Dugan, I. (Nov. 18, 1999). Online trading fees headed lower: Rivalry amongst Internet brokerages will force commissions cuts, analysts say. *Washington Post*, E10.

Everybody is talking about suitability in qualifying online investors—Except online firms. (Oct. 18, 1999). *Securities Week, 26(42)*, 1.

An explosive increase in online stock trading. (Dec. 22, 1998). *Bloomberg News* Website.

Financial companies look for partners in the brave new world. (Nov. 22, 1999). Associated Press Newswires.

Frederick, J. (July 1, 1999). Why online brokers can win the Web war: Full-service firms are finally fighting back, but their hearts aren't in it. *Money*, 103.

Goldfield, R. (Nov. 22, 1999). Drop in online trading expected to be fleeting. *Business Journal, Portland*, Industry News Columns.

Grasso is left to arbitrate. (Nov. 15, 1999). *Wall Street Journal*, A1.

Gutner, T. (Nov. 15, 1999). The e-bond revolution. *Business Week*, 270.

Internet trading services and the burgeoning home market. (Nov. 10, 1999). *Business Week Online*.

Lee, C. (Oct. 11, 1999). New E*Trade ad jabs as online competition heats up. Dow Jones News Service.

Lim, P. (Oct. 28, 1999). Broker wars: The battle heats up, Schwab, Merrill plans blur industry lines. *Los Angeles Times*, C1.

MacKintosh, J. (Oct. 9, 2000). Online banks increasingly move from clicks back to bricks. *Financial Times* (London), 30.

Marjanovic, S. (Feb. 22, 1999). Merrill Lynch buying Internet savvy but says it won't go discount route. *American Banker*, 1.

McVey, H. (Oct. 12, 1999). The bumpy ride to bigger, better, cheaper, faster. *American Investment Research*.

Meet the dinosaurs of the NYSE: Will the "faster, better, cheaper" world of electronic trading make floor specialists extinct? (Nov. 15, 1999). *National Post.*

Merrill commission cut triggers Wall Street upheaval. (June 30, 1999). *Australian Banking & Finance,* 12.

Merrill gives you a bargaining chip. (Sept. 20, 1999). *Business Week,* 154.

Merrill Lynch offers online trading to select customers. (Nov. 27, 1999). Associated Press Online.

Merrill Lynch and the online trading phenomenon. (Oct. 1999). Business Today.Com/Associated Press.

Morgenson, G. (April 19, 1999). Hidden costs of online trading. *New York Times,* sec. 3, p. 1.

The next step in the e-bond revolution. (Nov. 15, 1999). Wall Street Journal Online.

Online trading: It's not just for professionals anymore. (April 29, 1999). New York Times Online.

Phipps, M. (June 1, 1999). A gaining net: Between the humor and the hype, what does the online trading trend mean for the financial intermediary? *Financial Planning,* 142–145.

Quinton, B. (Oct. 25, 1999). Speeding time to [stock] market. *Telephony,* 16.

Regnier, P. (Sept. 1999). Schwab vs. Merrill Lynch. *Money,* 42–44.

Santoli, M. (July 19, 1999). Hitting the wall. *Barron's,* 19.

SEC chief says no moratorium on ECNs, expanded trading ours. (Oct. 19, 1999). *Dow Jones Business News.*

Simon, R., Buckman, R. (Nov. 15, 1999). E-broker outages are difficult to track. *Wall Street Journal,* C1.

Simon, R., Gasparino, C. (Oct. 19, 1999). Full-service brokers complicate the online world. *Wall Street Journal,* C1.

Sorkin, A. (Oct. 11, 2000). Deutsche Bank offers to buy National Discount Brokers. *New York Times,* 14.

Sugawara, S. (Dec. 8, 1999). Market data fees an online bonanza. *Washington Post,* EO2.

US brokers. (Oct. 18, 2000). *Financial Times Limited* (London), 28.

CASE 6
FLEET BANK/BANKBOSTON MERGER: CULTURE CLASH: BACK TO THE FUTURE

After taking over the smallish Industrial National Bank in 1982 and changing its name to Fleet, Terrence Murray went on a two-decade acquisition binge that made it the biggest bank in New England and the seventh-biggest bank in the country. The latest purchase came in October, 2001 when Fleet gobbled up New Jersey's Summit Bancorp. The $7.4 billion acquisition makes Fleet the biggest bank in New Jersey and augments its recently aggressive moves into the New York City market. Now, though, Murray is telling anyone who will listen that he has changed his stripes. Fleet is out of the merger-and-acquisition game and focusing on internal growth, he has said repeatedly. . . . "When you want to get big fast, you have to do it through acquisitions," Murray said. "We did that, and now we're adjusting our priorities." Like most of its brethren in the banking world, Fleet has had a moderately difficult time [in 2000]. Problem loans have risen as the economy has fallen, and Fleet's formerly turbocharged capital markets division has seen its revenue hit by the stock-market pullback. (Nelson, May 2001)

COMPANY/INDUSTRY BACKGROUND

BANKBOSTON. BankBoston—one of the nation's oldest commercial banks-was founded in 1784 as Massachusetts Bank. It has undergone numerous mergers and acquisitions—for example, First National Bank of Boston, Old Trust Company, Baybank, and Bank of Boston. Prior to the most recent merger with Fleet Bank, BankBoston had become not only the oldest commercial bank, but also New England's only global bank with full-service banking in Latin American markets. Under the leadership of Charles Gifford, the bank's "assets totaled $75.7 billion, 428 branches, 1,589 ATMs, and over 25,000 employees" (Inside BankBoston: Facts and Figures, 1). Its services targeted primarily individual consumers and businesses in New England. Financial solutions were also offered to corporations and governments nationally and internationally through First Community Bank.

FLEET BANK. Before the merger with BankBoston, Fleet was the nation's sixth largest commercial lender and the leading New England small business lender. Under the leadership of Terrence Murray, Fleet's "assets totaled $185.3 billion, and had over 30,000 employees" (Fleet.com). Fleet's products include consumer, government, private, and mortgage banking; corporate finance; commercial real estate; credit cards; investments; and foreign trade.

SOVEREIGN BANK. Sovereign Bank, which is primarily a thrift bank, operates in retail and small business lending. Dating back 124 years, Sovereign established itself as a leader—"$35 billion in assets, and is the 27th largest financial institution" (Sovereign Bank: Investor Relations, 1). Sovereign currently has over 600 community banking offices located in Delaware, New Jersey, Connecticut, New Hampshire, Rhode Island, and Massachusetts and has 4,000 employees. As a result of the merger, Sovereign has acquired over 268 branches.

MERGER HISTORY

MERGER NEGOTIATIONS. Fleet has been on an aggressive acquisitions campaign for several years and is continuing. The bank's leadership has global ranking, financial assets and monetary gain in mind for its shareholders. This strategic path, which has an entrepreneurial, external focus, can pressure internal managers, employees, operations, and procedures to bend under the rapid wealth-creating pace.

In November 1998, Terry Murray, the head of Fleet Financial Group, and Chad Gifford, the head of BankBoston, began talks with top executives to determine if a successful merger might be in their future.

As merger negotiations finally approached, solutions were reached through difficult decisions. Terrence Murray, it is believed, kept his current salary from 1999, $992,000, as well as a $3.4 million bonus. Gifford was to make an equal amount, and he would trade his current stock for 300,000 shares of restricted stock after the merger closed. At that point, the shares were worth approximately $13.2 million (Browning, July 9, 1999). Gifford was scheduled to also donate at least 75,000 of his shares to a charity. Terrence Murray would become chairman of the board and chief executive officer, and Chad Gifford would be president and chief operating officer. Murray planned on retiring at the end of 2001, at which time Gifford would replace him as the CEO. To secure Gifford's current and future position, an 80 percent supermajority by the board of directors—which consists of 22 members, 12 from Fleet and 10 from BankBoston (see Figure 1)—would be required to remove Gifford from his position. In March of 1999, the final decision was made. Fleet Bank would purchase BankBoston for $16 billion.

MERGER APPROVAL. The federal government approved the merger on September 7, 1999. As a stipulation of the merger, both banks were required to divest themselves of branches, accounts, and other operations to comply with state and federal regulations. Sovereign Bancorp purchased 278 branches and other selected assets from Fleet and BankBoston. Approximately 28 additional branches were sold to community banks such as Eastern Bank, Cape Cod Bank and Trust, and Rockland Trust.

FleetBoston was officially formed on September 30,1999. The members of the board of directors finalized the merger as well as the organizational structure (see Figures 1 and 4) and publicized the new creation on October 4, 1999.

Within the first month of the merger, the company's earnings rose 41 percent, to $711 million, with dividends increasing by 11 percent (http://fleet.com/fbth.html). As of 2000, Fleet Boston started joint ventures with several big-name companies, and as of March 22, 2000, the new company entered the New York Stock Exchange. On March 27, 2000, the Sovereign divestiture was complete.

TIMEFRAME AND FINANCIAL RESULTS OF MERGER. The actual merger of BankBoston and Fleet offices took place in three phases. During Phase One, the BankBoston sites in Massachusetts and southern New Hampshire became Fleet. This process was completed during the weekend of May 13, 2000. Phase Two included BankBoston's western Massachusetts branches, as well as ATM locations, which were converted to FleetBoston. This was completed during the weekend of July 7, 2000. Phase Three included the conversion of the Connecticut BankBoston branches to FleetBoston. This during the weekend of September 8, 2000. (See Figure 2.)

The FleetBoston merger brought together over $170 billion in assets, 55,000 employees, 20 million customers worldwide, 1,250 branches, and over 3,400 ATMs in the Northeast. It will be the eighth largest bank holding company in the nation and the third largest in the Northeast, and it will remain headquartered in Boston.

FIGURE I	BOARD OF DIRECTORS

Members of the Board/Present Position	Original Affiliation
Terrence Murray Chairman and CEO FleetBoston Corporation	Fleet
Charles K. Gifford President and Managing Director FleetBoston Corporation	BankBoston
Joel B. Alvord President and Managing Director Shawmut Capital Partners	Fleet
William Barnet President and Chief Executive Officer William Barnet & Son	Fleet
Daniel Burnham Chairman and Chief Executive Raytheon Company	BankBoston
Paul Choquette Chairman and CEO Gilbane Building Group	Fleet
John Collins Chairman and CEO The Collins Group	Fleet
William Connell Chairman and CEO Connell Limited Partnership	BankBoston
Gary Countryman Chairman Liberty Mutual Insurance Company	BankBoston
Alice Emerson Senior Advisor President Emerita/Wheaton College/The Andrew Mellon Foundation	BankBoston
James Hardymon Retired and CEO Textron Inc.	Fleet
Marian L. Heard President and CEO United Way of Massachusetts Bay	Fleet
Robert Higgins President, Commercial and Retail Banking Fleet Boston Corporation	Fleet
Robert Kavner General Partner Idealab	Fleet

continued

FIGURE I   CONTINUED

Thomas May Chairman and CEO NSTAR	BankBoston
Donald McHenry University Research Professor of Diplomacy Georgetown University	BankBoston
Henrique De Campos Meirelles President, Global Banking and Financial Services FleetBoston Companies	BankBoston
Michael Picotte President and CEO The Picotte Companies	Fleet
Thomas Piper Lawrence Fouraker Professor of Business Administration Harvard University School of Business Administration	BankBoston
Thomas Quick President and COO Quick and Reilly/Fleet Securities	Fleet
Francene Rodgers CEO Work Family Directions, Inc.	BankBoston
John Rowe Chairman, President, CEO Unicom Corporation	BankBoston
Thomas Ryan Chairman and CEO CVS Corporation	Fleet
Paul Tregurtha Chairman and CEO Mormac Marine Group and Moran Towing	Fleet

When the merger was finalized, each of the former CEOs commented on its position. Terrence Murray, chairman and CEO of Fleet, stated, "This strategic alliance will create a New England based world class financial services institution that can grow and compete in the global financial services institution." Chad Gifford, former CEO of BankBoston and current COO of Fleet, stated, "Relying on each other's complementary strengths, we will be able to further enhance and diversify our range of financial products. These innovations combined with a talented and dedicated workforce and a healthy earnings mix will result in a powerful global financial institution with strong ties to this region" (Business Wire, Sept. 7, 1999).

FIGURE 2	TIMELINE

Date	Event
Nov. 1998	CEO of Fleet and CEO of BankBoston begin private talks.
Dec. 1998–Feb. 1999	Top executives from each company meet to see if they would all get along.
March 1999	Decision was made to merge the banks, and the board of directors was chosen.
Aug. 11, 1999	Shareholders voted to accept the merger.
Sept. 7, 1999	Fleet and BankBoston received federal approval for merger.
	• As a result of the merger, both banks are required to sell branches, accounts, and other operations to comply with state and federal regulations. This process is known as divestiture; it helps to ensure competition and customer choice within the market.
	• Sovereign Bancorp is to purchase 278 branches and other selected assets from Fleet and BankBoston. Approximately 28 additional branches will be sold to community banks within the region: Eastern Bank, Cape Cod Bank and Trust, and Rockland Trust.
Sept. 30, 1999	Fleet and BankBoston merge.
Oct. 4, 1999	FleetBoston Corporation names board of directors (13 Fleet members; 11 BankBoston members; Fleet, Terrence Murray—CEO; Bank Boston, Chad Gifford—COO, CEO by end of 2001).
Oct. 18, 1999	Unsettled market gives rise to concern among investors per a Quick and Reilly survey.
Oct. 20, 1999	Earnings rise 41 percent to $711 million; dividends increase by 11 percent.
March 3, 2000	FleetBoston Financial launches on-line investing game for children on its Fleet Kids Website—teaches principles for stock picking.
March 13, 2000	New on-line payment processing center.
March 22, 2000	FleetBoston now listed on New York Stock Exchange.
March 27, 2000	Internet broker SURETRADE to offer wireless securities trading.
March 27, 2000	Completed divestitures to Sovereign (Phase 1).
April 14, 2000	Free admission for 1.5 million New York City students and their families to Metropolitan Museum.
April 11, 2000	Opening day for Fleet Financial.
May 13, 2000	Phase 1—BankBoston sites become Fleet in Massachusetts and southern New Hampshire; bank accounts are rolled over to Fleet Financial.
June 5, 2000	Fleet announces $2 billion initiative for women business owners and entrepreneurs.
June 21, 2000	Fleet ranked as "Best place to work for IT professionals."
June 26, 2000	Fleet completes divestitures to Eastern Bank and Cape Cod Bank and Trust.
June 27, 2000	Fleet provides $200 million in financing Staples.

continued

FIGURE 2	CONTINUED
June 29, 2000	Fleet and Disney announce Website agreement.
July 2, 2000	Fleet announces $600 million initiative to accelerate investments in low-moderate income businesses.
July 7, 2000	Phase 2—Branches and ATM locations transferred to Fleet locations in western Massachusetts.
July 17, 2000	Fleet net income up at $847 million, operating expenses up 15 percent from prior year.
July 18, 2000	Fleet joined with Ariba to offer on-line *BQB* procurement solutions
Sept. 8, 2000	Phase 3—Connecticut Bank Boston accounts will switch to Fleet

MERGING CULTURES: BLUE BLOOD WITH BLUE COLLAR

Fleet and BankBoston comprised two very dissimilar business cultures. Whereas BankBoston's culture has been characterized as "blue-blooded," Fleet's culture was known as "blue collar." BankBoston's headquarters remained in the Boston area for years, and it has since shown its commitment to the New England area as well as to its other customers. Besides the physical atmosphere, BankBoston has also had notable differences in relation to its *leaders and management styles*. Charles Gifford invested considerable time in the bank since he joined the company in 1966. Chad can be described as a "people person," committed to ensuring customer service. Sources from FleetBoston stated: "Chad was a very open, and approachable guy. He openly communicates with the employees, and is visible in all aspects of his position." (See Figure 3 for interview questions).

BankBoston was devoted to developing a high level of *employee morale*, while simultaneously providing the highest level of customer service to all of its clients, both large and small. The bank has been a supporter of the local arts programs, such as the BankBoston Celebrity Series and the BankBoston Pavilion. In addition, BankBoston has focused on community reinvestment, pouring money into many underserved communities.

Fleet Bank is widely known for being very profit driven. Its former president and CEO, Terrence Murray, was quite the opposite of Gifford in terms of personality and leadership style. From speaking with Fleet employees, the following is said of Murray: "Terry was not a man of the people. He was more of a dealmaker, and talked more among his peers rather than the bottom line employees. He is also more profit driven and geared towards shareholder value, at any means necessary, even at the expense of the employees and customers."

Fleet's *strategic goals* differed from those of BankBoston in that its main priority was to increase its profits, it used extremely aggressive behavior in its cost-cutting strategies, and it oftentimes was viewed as the "predator" or "bad partner." Another source noted: "Employees are treated with ruthlessness,

FIGURE 3	INFORMATION GATHERING—BANKBOSTON & FLEET

1. What was the leadership strategy or structure of your organization before the merger?

2a. What was the culture of your organization before the merger?

2b. How has it changed?

3. What committees or teams were formed to prepare for the merger? What issues were addressed by these teams?

4a. Who was identified as being affected by the merger?

4b. What was done to prepare them for the merger? What types of communications were used?

5a. What changes needed to be made to your systems for the merger?

5b. Were the changes that were needed successfully accomplished?

6. What changes were made to your workforce?

7a. What has been successful in regard to the merger?

7b. What has been problematic in regard to the merger?

8a. What/who has the merger helped? What still has to be done?

8b. What will give you more power to deal with issues, good or bad?

9. What control systems are in place to address issues? Do associates of each former organization still tend to handle issues differently? How so?

10. Do you have a code of ethics or mission statement from your former organization? Do you have a code of ethics or mission statement from the new organization, FleetBoston?

they are there only to get the job done, no matter what the costs." It is interesting to note that Fleet's former symbol portrayed three sails, which were later referred to as shark fins, due to the company's ruthless business practices.

When asked about organizational culture in general, a former BankBoston employee currently at Fleet said: "The culture at BankBoston was very informal. People were encouraged to try tasks outside their job description. However, the atmosphere became more formal, more 'silo' oriented, and employees stayed within their job description." In addition, another former BankBoston employee currently at Sovereign responded to the same question by stating: "The culture was 'warm and fuzzy' among Human Resources. HR was so busy trying to please and hand hold everyone that they lost sight of the goals at hand. The BankBoston culture focused on customer service. Trying to please everyone will not work in a large organization." Finally, another cultural difference could be found in the expressed and sponsored interests of the banks. While BankBoston's interests included the arts, Fleet was highly involved with sporting events. These interests reflect the blue-blood and blue-collar artifacts of the two cultures.

CULTURE CLASHES: EMPLOYEE PERSPECTIVES

BankBoston and Fleet employees played a large role in administering strategic information and making significant decisions. From interviews with former BankBoston and Fleet managers, it can be observed how the two cultures initially clashed.

Fleet Bank was focused on cost savings and driven by quarterly earnings and shareholder value. As quoted by a strategic development representative: "Do whatever it takes to create shareholder value even at the expense of employees and customers." At the opposite end of the spectrum, BankBoston's focus was on generating revenues in such a way that customers and employees benefit most. Reducing costs by the most effective means available was also part of this focus. As stated earlier, the leadership at BankBoston prior to the merger was very customer oriented. Within the organization, the structure was built on team implementation and team building within divisions. As a former BankBoston employee stated: "The CEO of the organization was a person you could go up to and say hello without feeling intimidated." Employees actually felt a part of the team. In terms of the actual atmospheric differences between Fleet and BankBoston, a BankBoston employee states: "The culture of BankBoston was cozy."

Another notable difference in culture, noted by the director of Human Resources (HR) for FleetBoston, was the ethical decision making and general decision processes. BankBoston was more focused on ascertaining how one felt about a decision and then choosing an action course that best fit the customers' and employees' needs, whereas, Fleet's stand was to "just get it done." A strategic development officer of Fleet Bank said: " Fleet was more focused on making decisions quickly and speedy. Even if the decision was wrong, just make it."

PEOPLE ISSUES IN PREPARING FOR THE MERGER

OVERVIEW OF OBJECTIVES. More preparation was needed during the pre-merger stage in terms of preparing people, including both customers and employees. Management focused on five major objectives of the merger:

- Create a dynamic forward-looking company that can compete with the upper-tier financial services companies.
- Grow and provide value-added products and services to wholesale and retail customers.
- Preserve the New England headquarters.
- Have an abiding commitment to support employees and communities.
- Create a greater value for shareholders.

Based upon the major objectives of the merger, a core set of objectives guided the entire integration process. Following are these six:

- Achieve target expense savings.
- Identify revenue synergies.
- Maintain earnings and revenue momentum.

- Design and implement a new organizational structure.
- Staff the organization with a diverse, qualified workforce.
- Make fair and objective decisions.

To prepare for the merger, both banks tried to focus on critical issues that needed to be addressed to ensure the success of the merger. Some of the issues included the following: maintaining a disciplined approach and correctly estimating the resources needed in both the systems and the people, communicating truthfully with employees and customers, fully understanding the differences in the culture of both banks, and focusing on the positive aspects of each institution. While focusing on employees, the banks needed to design and support a fair selection process and create programs that offered at least minimal support for employee orientation. In spite of these efforts, decisions were made too quickly because of the imposed "as-is" Fleet culture. Results of many of the decisions were unsuccessful—especially those related to issues regarding employee and customer communications as well as policy choices.

MERGER TEAMS

Different cross-functional and functional-area-specific teams were created to deal with merger issues that arose. The teams addressed integration schedules and personnel problems in particular. Various teams were assembled to address other issues such as deciding what new benefit plans to offer, facilitating publications with information about the merger, and dealing with employees that would be severed from the organization. HR played a major role in supporting the functional integration teams. HR also assisted with the design of an effective end-state organization that was based on operating models from both BankBoston and Fleet Bank. In the actual reorganization, HR needed to ensure that the most qualified people were selected for the organization as well as ensuring that all HR policies and practices necessary for the successful implementation were in place.

COMMUNICATION.   The teams in charge of facilitating publications were responsible for various levels of communication. They facilitated publications such as merger bulletins that kept employees up to date on issues related to the merger. News bulletins and stories from the local network news also kept employees informed of the merger. Voice-mails and e-mails were sent to employees to notify them of the newscasts, as well as to clarify the issues raised. Question-and-answer (Q&A) sessions were held in the year prior to the completion of the merger. In one department, only two Q&A sessions were given. Managers were then left with the task of dealing with all of the other issues and rumors that came up through the year. Many managers felt that their time was not well spent, and because of that, they had to focus on the people issues, which were important, but left them with less time to actually "do their job." After the merger was finalized, the communication quickly dwindled. Employees, primarily former BankBoston employees, were frustrated and unaware of what was going to happen next. Advertising and mailings were sent to customers to notify them of changes and the dates when those changes would be occurring.

TO RETAIN OR SEVER EMPLOYEES?   A team was established to deal with the employees at all levels that were being severed. This team provided literature and employment counseling from staff inside as well as from professionals outside of the organization. A program was designed to help employees with résumé creation and interviewing skills. Services were also provided to help employees with analyzing their existing skills to help them possibly choose another career path.

For the "survivors"—employees who stayed—incentive packages were offered that would provide the best of each benefit package. After speaking with a former BankBoston employee, it was learned that various tactics were used to eliminate employees who were no longer needed. For example, a former BankBoston employee's boss was fired, and a new manager was brought in to find every mistake made and then turn it into a "situation" that required documentation. For those employees targeted to stay, the best features of each company including a few added incentives—for example, health coverage for extended families (including unmarried domestic partners)—were offered. Also, $5,000 in assistance was provided to parents in adoption processes, and two days off with pay for full-time employees who participated in community volunteer programs was also offered. Hefty parachute retirement programs for the top-level management were also given.

To decide on the workforce that would stay, the organization was broken down into divisions where the managers did skills assessments of their employees. After the skills assessments were completed, the decision was made to retain an employee for a job in the new organization, sever him or her immediately and provide a severance package, or put him or her into an employee pool that would be interviewed by Sovereign Bank. Employees were told after these decisions were made where they stood. Some were informed about their new job, and others were severed immediately. The group in the "employee pool" was frustrated, since they faced an uncertain future. After the interview process with Sovereign Bank, the employees were either hired or considered no longer eligible for the FleetBoston severance package. Some employees chose to leave. As a result of this process, many former BankBoston employees distrusted Fleet. Many were informed that after a "grace" period, Fleet Bank would terminate them and not offer the severance package that was originally offered.

CUSTOMER OPINIONS.   The corporate customers of both BankBoston and Fleet Bank seem satisfied with the results of the merger. They have found an abundance of services to be available that previously did not exist. Retail customers, on the other hand, openly expressed displeasure with lack of service after the merger. For many, fees have risen and customer service has fallen. Massachusetts's retail customers seemed to be much less satisfied than in other states. According to the revenue-driven Fleet Bank, the fee structure was raised because most customers who kept low balances in their accounts also used the bank more often—causing increased expenses for the bank. As stated by an HR representative: "These customers are also the people who do not like change and cannot see beyond their immediate needs to the broader picture of what is happening."

Customers were in fact an important part of the merger in that they were major stakeholders with respect to the success or failure of the corporation. Because of customer reactions to the merger, many employees left the new FleetBoston. Customer complaints were very frequent due to lack of communication, higher bank rates with no warning, lost payments, nonworking ATMs, and accounts being switched to other banks without approval. Fleet-Boston tried to address these issues by offering a 1-800 Help Line; however, calls went unanswered or were put on hold indefinitely.

Fleet also faced a class action lawsuit from 1990 with Fleet mortgage customers. The issue involved Fleet's failure to pay property tax and homeowners' insurance premiums for which there was escrow. Many customers received a notice that their property would be sold at auction. There was also another situation in which clients were made to file Chapter 13 because Fleet could not account for payments. Some customers had to wait over two years for a response from the former Fleet.

SUMMARY.   There are different reviews regarding the success of the merger. Many employees were happy, while many were extremely dissatisfied. (It is not possible to put numbers or percentages on these views.) A similar situation existed with customers as well. The media also pressured Fleet Boston, making it extremely difficult for the bank to achieve a successful image from the merger. Several negative issues were displayed on local Massachusetts TV stations. The media reflected dissatisfied customers who openly complained. Employees who were dealing with their own adjustment and who said they "just wanted to get on with their jobs" constantly had to handle customer complaints. Employees in general seemed to be in a state of flux, not quite knowing where they fit into the new organization. Complicating postmerger adjustments were diminished communications from management. "The idea seems to be that everything will work itself out," said one mid- level bank manager.

ETHICAL ISSUES

Several ethical issues were raised concerning the implications of the merger, particularly for the primary stakeholders—shareholders, customers, employees, and management. For example, the question surfaced, "Who has the merger actually helped?" Many employees were offered severance packages to leave. However, just as many employees complained that they were being forced out of the company by management and made to work in environments that compelled a person to leave rather than stay. Shareholders seemed to be satisfied with the long-term prospects. Customers continued complaining, since they were in fact not being served well.

| FIGURE 4 | FLEET BOSTON HIERARCHY |

As a footnote, "[I]n 1999, [Massachusetts State Senator Dianne Wilkerson] pushed state and federal regulators to allow the Boston Bank of Commerce to buy bank branches being sold as part of the Fleet Bank-BankBoston merger. According to the State Ethics Commission, her actions violated state law because she made no written public disclosure of her consulting contract with the Bank of Commerce" (Klein, 2001). In 2001, the Commission fined Wilkerson for not properly reporting that a bank she lobbied for as a state senator was paying her more than $20,000 a year as a consultant. (Ibid.)

STRUCTURE

The hierarchy of Fleet Boston looks like that of most large corporations (Figure 4), with the shareholders at the top. Shareholder opinions were taken into consideration, as was shown in a court hearing in July 1999, as a part of the merger approval process. However, Fleet had been criticized regarding this hearing because it appeared that it paid the expenses of the big supporters and did very little for the shareholders that had been unhappy with it in the past.

The board of directors composed the next level of the organization and was split evenly between former BankBoston and Fleet employees. (See Figure 1.) With Murray as CEO of Fleet Boston, there was likelihood that Fleet's management style, which appeared utilitarian, would be followed, as compared to BankBoston's, which could also be considered utilitarianism, but also was combined with universalism. Fleet Bank was utilitarian in that it calculated and weighed the costs versus benefits; critics contended that management looked only at their own costs versus benefits, not those of all of their stakeholders. BankBoston was utilitarian in that it also weighed costs versus benefits in its financial decisions. Universalism was a part of its management style since BankBoston tried to treat all people with respect and seemed to look at how consequences of a decision would affect its stakeholders. It also identified stakeholders and customers who were at risk and tried to implement solutions that would benefit them. An example was their dedication to community reinvestment, investing in Latin America and different community arts programs. These contrasting styles stand out in the comments made by Gifford and Murray when the merger was made final.

STRUCTURE COUNTS. This type of hierarchy (Figure 4) allows more ethical behavior due to the centralization of management. Everyone is watching over each other's shoulders. A survey from the Wall Street Journal suggested that structure does affect ethical behavior (Weiss, 1998, 110). Fleet Boston is highly structured. Whether or not this degree of centralization, with a high-profit strategic orientation, will lead to more or less ethical behavior toward stakeholders will be a topic of future observation.

When employees were questioned about the actual merger, the blame for the numerous unethical issues and strategic goals in relation to employee severance pay and the dissatisfied customers seemed to lie heavily in the business practices implemented by the leadership, namely, upper management and the two CEOs, Gifford and Murray. The merger has helped top executives in terms of salary increases. Aside from the CEOs of the company, "What has the merger done to help anyone?" asked one manager. The bank has created more frustration and fees for its external customers. From an internal perspective, it appears the employees were still in a state of flux after the merger. This is in part an expected occurrence.

OTHER PRACTICES AND POTENTIAL ISSUES. As a perceived result of management's strategic goals, the issue of banking fees in relation to other financial intermediaries has come into play concerning ethical business practices by Fleet. Many customers feel that the leadership has "raised the bar." For example, Fleet's high banking fees could cause other companies to also charge higher—some say "unfair"—rates. Another employee noted, "If Fleet can charge 75 cents for something, Citizens Bank (another local bank) could go to 50 cents without anybody even noticing."

Many also feel that this merger has resulted in a rather "forced" transition in terms of banks to choose from. Because BankBoston and Fleet were two of New England's largest banks, customers feel as if this severely limits their selection of financial institutions. Representatives from the strategic development department of FleetBoston noted in an interview that the director felt that management created the most successful, ethical merger possible in terms of meeting the needs of the commercial bankers. However, other employees observed that certain issues were not handled as well in relation to the average retail customer. In addition, the representative stated that the commercial bankers are Fleet's main priority, rather than the retail sector.

Because commercial bankers bring more money to the facility, Fleet Boston's main objective was to provide them with an increased diversified product line, as well as added services, through this merger. When questioned about the ethicality behind this method of doing business, the response was: "The revenues are still high, therefore, the situation cannot be as bad as the media and retail customers, primarily in Massachusetts, are making it" (personal interview with author).

Overall, the leaders of the merger have benefited quite well. The most notable areas in terms of ethical issues tended to stem from Fleet's side of business, as opposed to BankBoston's. As with most mergers, problems generally do arise with respect to mismanagement. However, as another employee stated, "Is it really ethical to allow problems to persist in hopes that unwanted employees as well as customers with low cash balances eventually disappear?" Management did not address these problems after the merger.

With most mergers, there generally is only a 50 percent chance that a merger will be truly successful (Buono, Bowditch, 1989, 262). The success or failure of mergers is oftentimes due to the people involved in the merger. There is usually a focus on technical issues that need to be solved for the merger to be successful and less of a focus on the employee issues. This is due in part to the ease in making a decision about technical issues; there is the correct process that is followed to reach the conclusion, a series of steps that are followed. With people issues, it is different; there is no standard way to deal with them, and there is no "quick fix." The employee issues need just as much focus as the technical issues. The initial reaction of employees in horizontal mergers is that they are losing their company, a company that they personally associated with, and they immediately see the overlap of jobs and changes that will be made to internal structures.

In this situation, it seems as if Fleet and BankBoston did truly try to address all of the issues that would arise with their employees. They formed many groups, internal to functional areas as well as cross-functional, that addressed most of the issues. The employees who were severed were specifically addressed, and communications were many. These two banks did address the organization issues that arose during the merger but possibly may have stopped too soon. The thought now seems to be that everything is fine, and the people issues will work themselves out. The communications and merger teams need to be continued into this postmerger phase.

To employees, especially former BankBoston employees, there seem to be too many unknowns. These "unknowns" often lead to uncertainty—"Where do I fit? or "Will I really have my job in a month?"—allowing them to focus only on their present situations. These employees will focus on how the situation will affect them and will be unable to clearly focus on their job while losing trust in their new organization.

The effects of these "unknowns" could lead to absenteeism and a higher rate of voluntary turnover, time lost in the workplace due to internal debating, a lower level of commitment to the organization, and a lower level of customer service. Employees will also follow the lead of the actions of their leaders and management staff. If the perception is a low level of management or control, the levels of productivity may decrease. Often employees and managers will become more out for themselves, in the hopes that that will increase their value to the firm, and focus less on their jobs or subordinates. There is less of a team-building atmosphere present. The occurrences of whistleblowing often increase after mergers, and associates are out for themselves, trying to prove their own values and self-worth over the "other" employees from the "other" organization.

The above issues will ultimately lead to higher corporate expenses and decreased revenues. Employees could take "shortcuts" and increase mistakes in their work. Absenteeism and turnover could rise, creating higher levels of stress for the employees still working and increased time and cost in hiring new people. Employees that voluntarily leave will most likely be those with higher skills that are not afraid of another position somewhere else. Fleet Boston now needs to address the employee issues that are facing it postmerger. The "we versus them" attitude needs to be eliminated. Employees need to begin working together towards a common goal.

From the customer's perspective, most feel there has been a major lack of communication and little concern for the customers. There have been complaints from many of the customers, as mentioned above. Yet 96 percent of dissatisfied customers do not complain, they just take their money elsewhere and spread the word to their friends and colleagues (Buono, Bowditch, 1989, 234). Imagine how many dissatisfied customers really exist! There have been mergers continuously throughout the past few years, and customers rarely know what bank will be buying out their account next.

BACK TO THE FUTURE?

"FleetBoston Financial Corp. nearly doubled the size of its retail mutual fund division [on June 4, 2001,] buying what's left of Liberty Financial Cos. in a deal worth more than $1 billion. The deal, which was announced after the stock markets closed, will add more than 70 mutual funds . . . to Fleet's portfolio" (Nelson, June 2001).

Fleet has almost $56 billion in retail assets under management. The purchase of Liberty Financial adds $50 billion. With institutional and private banking assets, Fleet's holdings increase from $125 billion to $170 billion. This acquisition also increases Fleet's mutual fund sales staff from 30 or 40 people to over 250. The in-house analysts also double from 10 to 21. There are now overlapping areas that will experience layoffs—primarily back-office positions. "The idea is to build on what we have and become a major factor in the business," said Keith Banks, chief executive officer of Fleet Asset Management. "The goal is to become a top 20 player in the world." (Ibid.)

If the merger process described in this case is any indication of how future workforces, cultures, and strategies will be handled by Fleet Boston, there may reason to be concerned not only about daily operating procedures, but also about stakeholder management and ethics.

QUESTIONS FOR DISCUSSION

1. How do the strategy and goals of Fleet's leaders influence individual mergers such as the one described here?

2. Evaluate the process and results of this merger.

3. What ethical concerns should an objective observer be watching with regard to Fleet's internal and external business practices? Why?

4. Should the merger have been planned and conducted differently? How? Why?

5. Do the "ends justify the means" for all stakeholders when a company like Fleet adds vast wealth to its shareholders from its acquisitions and impressive global ranking as a financial institution? Explain.

SOURCES

Blake, F. (BankBoston/FleetBoston). (July 27, 2002). Personal interview.

Boston Globe. (Jan. 1, 1999–present). LEXIS-NEXIS Academic Document—all articles relating to merger.

Boston Herald. (Jan. 1, 1999–present). LEXIS-NEXIS Academic Document—all documents relating to merger.

Browning, L. (March 16, 1999). Fleet Boston/making the deal work. *Boston Globe,* A1.

Browning, L. (July 9, 1999). Heir apparent Gifford to gain kingly bundle after Fleet merger. *Boston Globe,* C1.

Buono, A., Bowditch, J. (1989). *The Human Side of Mergers and Acquisitions: Managing Collisions Between People, Cultures, and Organizations.* San Francisco: Jossey-Bass.

Cannata, R. (BankBoston/FleetBoston). (August 2000). Personal interview.

Dahle, C. (Sept. 1999). Merger she wrote. Fast Company Online, http://www.fastcompany.com/online/27/toolbox.html.

Fleet and Bank Boston unveil employee benefits package. (Sept. 29, 1999). *Business Wire.*

Fleet Boston Corporation names board of directors. (Oct. 4, 1999). *Business Wire.*

Fleet news. www.fleet.com.

Fuller, K. (Fleet Bank). (July 26, 2000). Personal interview.

Healthy ever after—supporting staff through merger and beyond. www.hawnhs.hea.org.uk/publications/trusts/healthy/healthy.html.

Inside BankBoston: Facts and figures. www.bankboston.com.

Klein, R. (Sept. 14, 2001). Ethics panel fines Wilkerson, finds she didn't properly report her ties to bank. *Boston Globe,* B3.

Nelson, S. (May 22, 2001). After growth years, bank looks inward. *Boston Globe,* E14.

Nelson, S. (June 5, 2001). Fleet buys Liberty in deal worth $1b; 70-fund addition seen doubling size, boosting stature of retail division. *Boston Globe,* D1.

Peck, L. (Human Resources Director/Strategic Development, FleetBoston). Personal interview.

Sleek, S. (July 1998). Some corporate mergers, like marriages, end up on the rocks. *APA Monitor, 29(7),* http://www.apa.org/monitor/jul98/merger.html.

Sovereign Bank: Investor relations. www.sovereignbank.com.

Tokarz, L. (BankBoston/Sovereign Bank). (August, 2000). Personal interview.

Weiss, J. (1998). *Business Ethics: A Stakeholder and Issues Management Approach,* 2nd ed. Fort Worth, TX: Dryden Press.

CASE 7
IN THE BEGINNING, NAPSTER: KILLER APP OR ILLEGAL WEAPON?

Pandora's box was opened with the help of Websites like Napster and Gnutella, companies that introduced peer-to-peer (P2P) networks, which have changed the way we use the Internet. The P2P application creates an environment where millions of users can share various types of files, including files that hold a copyright, such as music files called MP3s. During the relatively short time since inception, Napster rapidly became one of the most popular P2P applications, amassing a file-sharing community that originally had over 38 million registered accounts. The research firm Media Metrix first discovered the application on almost 10 percent of American computers connected to the Internet. Another research firm, NetRatings, first found Napster on slightly more than 6 percent of Internet-connected computers in the United Kingdom and Germany.[1]

Napster.com and Gnutella.com originally provided their services and interface programs to make the exchange of MP3s more straightforward and convenient. This convenience started the controversy over the legality of using other owners' music without permission. With the continuous improvement of Internet connectivity and speed, users were unrestricted and able to copy limitless files for free.

THE TECHNOLOGY BEHIND THE P2P APP(LICATION)

The P2P application creates a marketplace where users can pick and choose what they wish and exchange files directly and promptly without the dependence of a centralized mediator. P2P file-sharing technology shortcircuits the need for accessing a large centralized marketplace where information is gathered, stored, and controlled by one party.

There are several variations of P2P applications. Napster.com originally provided a directory of MP3s where users could download music without charge from another user's PC. This was accomplished through various filesharing protocols. Gnutella was also a freely distributed network software that used similar file-sharing protocols. Gnutella, however, did not maintain a centralized directory or index. Gnutella users were able to share MP3s as well as pictures, documents, and proprietary software, for example, Windows 2000.

The P2P application utilizes what is known in the communications industry as TCP/IP. TCP/IP stands for transmission control protocol/Internet protocol and is the most widely used Internet protocol for the transmission of data. Data is first broken down into many packets of information and then transferred along a medium to its destination. Each client/server, while connected to the Internet, begins the transfer of data by calling upon a file transfer protocol (FTP). FTP is used in conjunction with TCP/IP to communicate with the destination client/server and, in this manner, transfers data at

| FIGURE I | TRANSFER PROTOCOL (FTP) |

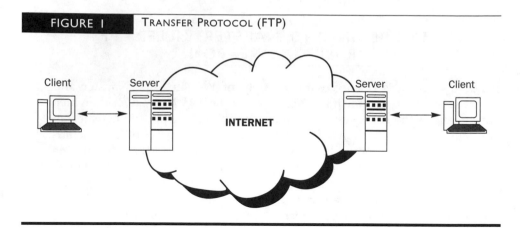

speeds equal to the slowest connection. A simple diagram of the connection and transfer is shown in Figure 1.

The communication link between each client and server is typically a modem connection, which transmits and receives at speeds up to 56 kbps. This speed infers that 56,000 bits of information are sent per second. In communications engineering, 1 kilobyte is equal to 1,024 bytes. However, we will illustrate how long it takes to transfer an MP3 file using 1 kilobyte as 1000 bytes. Also, 1 byte consists of 8 bits. The MP3 files that are shared between P2P users using applications such as Napster are roughly 3 megabytes long. Using a 56-kbps connection, we can see that a 3-megabyte file will transfer in approximately

$$\frac{3 \text{ megabytes}}{56 \text{ kbps}} = \frac{3 \text{ megabytes} \times 8 \text{ bits}}{56 \times 1000 \text{ bits}} = \frac{24,000,000}{56,000} = 428.6 \text{ seconds}$$

Therefore, it takes roughly 7 minutes for each 3-megabyte MP3 file to be downloaded—assuming there is no other traffic on the Internet and errors do not occur during the transmission. A smart estimate is to add 25 percent to the calculated time, which gives us an average transmission time of 9 minutes for each MP3 file. Faster connection speeds like T3, T1, and DSL download files almost 100 times faster than 56-kbps connections. Connection speeds are the backbone of the file-sharing phenomenon. The faster the Internet connection is, the faster files are downloaded. Without these speeds, too much time would be consumed in downloading files.

BRIEF HISTORY

The P2P application—first called file transfer protocol (FTP)—was developed at MIT in 1971. This early program, however, was limited in usefulness because it required the user to know the exact file name before the file could be found.[2] Several incremental changes were made throughout the seventies and eighties, and then, in 1990, Alan Emtage at McGill University in

Montreal developed a program he called "Archie." Archie worked like a search engine as it regularly downloaded indexes of public FTP host computers and file names. Archie was limited to querying file names containing search key words. In October of 1993, Archie evolved into Aliweb, which allowed Webmasters to include an index of URL keywords that allowed more than just the file name to be queried.[3] The new generation of FTP programs is much more advanced and user friendly. Sean Fanning, a 19-year-old college dropout, developed the most recognizable FTP, Napster. His program had the recording industry pursuing FTP regulation for files that hold copyrights. Justin Frankel and his fellow programmers at Nullsoft, an AOL company, have created a new file-sharing protocol called Gnutella that utilizes limitless P2P exchanges of all file types.

Docster is a new P2P application that uses technology similar to Napster. However, instead of the MP3s being queried, specific text documents will be targeted and exchanged. This site will work like a virtual library.[4] Another P2P start-up gaining respectability is Lightshare Inc. It plans on using the P2P application to directly connect users who want to buy and sell merchandise through an auction format similar to eBay.[5] These are two examples of the aggressive evolution of P2P applications.

STAKEHOLDERS AND STAKES

GOVERNMENT/COURTS. The U.S. government, its courts, and a host of lawyers who first represented Napster will soon set forth statutes and precedents that will govern how file-sharing applications function in the future. The U.S. Constitution gave Congress the responsibility for protecting copyrights: "Congress is to promote the progress of science and useful arts by securing for a limited time to authors and investors the exclusive right to their respective writings and discoveries."[6] As a result, the government and the courts are major stakeholders regarding any issue concerning copyrights. A central issue for the government is maintaining a balance between the rights of the content owners and promoting the common good of society by allowing the free flow of ideas and information. From the 1909 Copyright Act to the 1992 Audio Home Recording Act (AHRA), technology developed in accordance with the laws and acts associated with copyrights. Napster interrupted the process. At issue was how to address the disruptive technology of Napster and other similar applications that impinged on others' property rights. The courts had to consider (1) how to address the fact that millions of users were in violation of copyright laws, (2) how to protect the intellectual property and rights of the copyright holders, and (3) how to harness this technical ability to freely and easily access and then share vast amounts of information without restraint.

USERS. The users of P2P applications are anyone and everyone connected to the Internet who want to search for information, songs, and documents. "47% of college students are spending more time on the Internet than one year ago, and digital music is becoming a regular part of that experience."[7]

Searching for information on the Internet is also more commonplace. Methods for searching for information are more innovative and have expanded into areas more technical than the simple HTML documents.

Questions that originally surrounded the security of P2P applications were concerned with "Should I be worried about the potential hazards of giving anyone access to my computer?"[8] Users were—and are—more reluctant to join the file-sharing phenomenon if speeds are too slow. At many colleges, where Internet and Networking hardware was newer and faster, students flocked to join the frenzy caused by P2P networks. Consequently, bandwidth of college networking systems was inundated with file sharing and exchanging—so much so at one time that "[t]hirty-four percent of 50 U.S. colleges and universities have banned students from using Napster Inc.'s song-swap service on their campuses."[9]

Despite ongoing P2P concerns regarding security and legality, 57 percent of college students were using Napster on a regular basis, and 63 percent of students were spending more time listening to downloaded music than one year ago.[10] Users of P2P applications also originally had concerns about paying a price to share files over the Internet. P2P companies like Napster eventually had to change their freewheeling practices and accommodate copyright holders to avoid legal issues.

RIAA/ARTISTS—COPYRIGHT HOLDERS. The file-sharing technology developed by Napster and Gnutella impacted several groups in society differently, most notably the music industry. Dr. Dre, a concerned music artist, recently summed up his feelings toward Napster this way: "I'm in the business to make money, and Napster is —ing that up!"[11] The British Music Rights (an organization for composers, songwriters, and publishers) asked society to "[r]espect the value of music."[12] Besides popular artists such as Metallica, Britney Spears, and Dave Matthews, other lesser-known songwriters and composers who were not in the public eye depended upon income from their work to continue making music. Besides individual artists or groups, the corporations that offer financial and marketing support to recording artists and songwriters were also affected.

Warner Brothers Music, Sony, Bertlesmann Music Group (BMG), Universal, and EMI Group Plc, who are all members of the RIAA, recently settled lawsuits with MP3.com for distributing copyrighted materials without their consent over the Internet. MP3.com Inc. agreed to pay $53.4 million in damages to Universal and $20 million each in damages to Warner, BMG, EMI, and Sony.[13] Hillary Rosen, president of the Recording Industry of America (RIAA), said the recording industry lawsuit against MP3.com was "never about stifling the technology or putting this company out of business, but rather about protecting the copyright owners' and artists' rights to be compensated for their works."[14]

After the settlement with MP3.com, the focus was no longer on who will distribute the music over the Internet, but rather how. Like Dr. Dre and other musical groups, the RIAA has expressed financial concerns about the potential threat song-swapping applications create. The identical plaintiffs who filed lawsuits against MP3.com filed lawsuits against Napster, claiming the music-sharing application encourages copyright infringement by facilitating the exchange of songs over the Internet for free. Forrester, an Internet research group, predicted that free music services and file-swapping technologies like this would make up a major part of the annual two billion pounds ($3 billion) in lost music sales expected globally by 2005.[15]

BMG delayed its lawsuit against Napster and created a strategic alliance that requires Napster to change its business model to comply with copyright laws by creating a secure trading environment where users pay an unspecified fee to share/swap songs. Under the terms of the agreement, BMG will provide a loan to Napster to develop this service, which can later be converted into shares. While Napster and BMG have not disclosed the terms of the agreement, speculation persists that BMG loaned upwards of $30 to $50 million to develop the subscription-based service.[16] The alliance between these two groups marks the first step toward creating a P2P environment where all parties are happy.

In a survey that was conducted by MSNBC, users were asked whether or not they would be willing to pay to use Napster. Seventy percent of the 17,633 people who responded said they would not be willing to pay.[17] Andrea Schmidt, president and chief executive of BMG's e-commerce group expects 80 percent of Napster's estimated 38 million users worldwide to pay about $15 per month to subscribe to Napster.[18]

BMG was the first corporation to adopt Napster's file-sharing application. Limp Bizkit was one of the first musical groups to adopt Napster and its file-sharing service. The band's lead singer, Fred Durst, publicly supported Napster, saying the file-sharing service "provides an amazing way to market and promote music to a massive audience."[19] He also went on to say that Napster provides a great forum for fans to sample an album before buying it. Courtney Love, another recording artist, had this to say about Napster:

> Stealing our copyright provisions in the dead of night when no-one is looking is piracy. It's not piracy when kids swap music over the Internet using Napster. There were one billion downloads last year but music sales are way up, so how is Napster hurting the music industry? It's not. The only people who are scared of Napster are the people who have filler on their albums and are scared that if people hear more than one single they're not going to buy the album."[20]

Lars Ulrich, the drummer for the popular rock band Metallica, on the other hand, sued Napster for copyright infringement. He claimed Napster's service of sharing MP3s was "trafficking stolen goods."[21] Ulrich, like most of the recording industry, was threatened by Napster's reach.

The file-sharing issues surrounding the music industry and Napster have passed through a political and highly publicized phase. Gnutella allowed users to swap/share JPEGs or pictures. Several users shared pictures of landscapes and towering mountain ranges; others shared pornographic pictures that are illegal for children and underage teenagers to view.

Besides the ethical issues of trading porn over the Internet, there were financial ramifications where the P2P application could impact the $10 billion a year porn industry's revenues.[22] Just as Napster originally affected the recording industry's revenues, the book and movie industries shared the same negative financial impact. It was believed—feared by many—that file-sharing technology would be available that enabled DVDs and book transcripts to be traded like music . . . without the copyright holder ever knowing.

VENTURE CAPITALISTS. Napster, Inc., in its early phase closed a $15 million Series C venture capital funding round. The round was led by Hummer Winblad Venture Partners, with additional investments from Angel Investors LP and other existing investors. As part of the investment in Napster, Hummer Winblad partners Hank Barry and John Hummer joined the board of directors and Hank Barry assumed the role of interim CEO.[23] BMG then reportedly invested upwards of $30 to $ 50 million as part of its strategic alliance with Napster. Each of these investors stood to lose substantial funds if Napster could not create a P2P business model that generated revenue. On the other hand, if that business model was successful, each of the investors stood to be the first P2P multimillionaire. That was then.

COMPETITION. The P2P technology proposed a different approach for finding and acquiring content from the Web, compared to the centralized e-commerce models like eBay, Amazon, and Yahoo. The P2P service offers a decentralized marketplace, where users can trade information or products without the need of a third party. eBay's centralized server acted like a virtual auction house that brought both buyers and sellers together to trade merchandise on-line. Unlike Lightshare's P2P application, eBay's auction service required users to register and leave extensive personal information with the site. What attracted buyers and sellers to eBay's service was the ease of use and the global reach customers had to buy and sell goods and services. Transactions are monitored and aided by the site, which is part of the service for which users paid. The P2P technology would still allow users to buy or sell merchandise, but it promises in its early days to eliminate the middleman and fee that eBay normally charges. Also, the search engine interfaces like Yahoo and Google have extraordinary reach over the Web, but these are limited to the visible parts of the network. They do not have capabilities to access all servers and personal computers like P2P technologies. With the decentralization of the P2P technology, the need for centralized servers to store information, as noted earlier, decreases and is replaced by the direct communication between users.[24] Thus, the role of mediators such as eBay and Yahoo is possibly threatened.

As more information about P2P networks becomes available, some predict that more users could migrate from a centralized marketplace like eBay to a more decentralized marketplace like Napster. Decreases in usage would, it is thought, trigger a drop in financials for sites such as eBay that once held

$2.8 billion in gross merchandise and had $227 million in net revenues.[25] Yahoo, once at the top of its competitive game, reported $1 billion in revenues.[26] Looking back, neither Yahoo nor eBay was threatened by this technology. Other forces in the environment intervened on the dot.coms in harsher ways.

PC MAKERS/ISPs. The P2P network impacted not only the recording industry and moviemakers, but also PC makers and Internet service providers like DELL and AOL, respectively. To use services like Napster or Gnutella, users had to own a PC, and they also had to be connected to the Internet. According to PC Pitstop, a start-up that provided on-line analysis of PC problems, 30 percent of the 45,482 PCs it examined had the Napster application on it, which was more popular than Quicken (23%) and closing in on Netscape (34%). AOL and other high-speed Internet companies stood to gain from Napster as well. AOL's reported 7 million unique IP addresses per day a few years ago. Napster originally reported approximately 6 million unique IP addresses per day, according to its then CEO Hank Barry.[27]

FINAL THOUGHTS: PROMISES AND ILLUSIONS

The Napster controversy set off an unprecedented flurry of publicity for a company that had no source of revenue. Potentially, Napster might have made money through subscription fees, advertising income, and the outsourcing of its technology to other companies. A *New York Times* article characterizes another chapter in the life of Napster:

> Even though the music industry succeeded last summer [2001] in shutting down the free music file-sharing service Napster, other services—like Kazaa, Aimster and Napigator—are filling the Napster vacuum. (No longer able to support file swapping, Napster is still used by people to chat online with friends or listen to music files.) In some ways, the Napster alternatives may be harder for the music industry to thwart. Of the nine alternative services that Jupiter tracks, several use the same file-sharing format—meaning that users of one service can share files with people using another, according to Aram Sinnreich, a Jupiter analyst. So recording companies, which have already filed lawsuits against two of the newer services, may have a tough time keeping the music from flowing.[28]

If the middleman can be avoided in any business transaction, it is usually in the best interest of the parties exchanging goods or services to do so—if it is legally and ethically accomplished! P2P applications created by Napster and Gnutella have raised several issues that added a new chapter in technology and created turmoil legally and ethically for a number of other stakeholders.

The new players who are emerging with P2P network technologies must look at all stakeholders and issues surrounding their product before implementing a business model. Eventually, a P2P environment may exist where users feel comfortable trading files and copyright holders are compensated fairly and swiftly. However, Napster showed that even with a killer app and disruptive technology, there are few free lunches and illusions about making money illegally, especially when the stakes are so high.

QUESTIONS FOR DISCUSSION

1. What are the major issues in this case?
2. Who are the stakeholders, and how have they changed since Napster's beginning?
3. What were the stakes for the different constituencies in this case during this time?
4. Describe the ethics of the different stakeholders in this case.
5. Why didn't Napster succeed in the marketplace as first intended?
6. What would you have done differently if you had been Napster's business leaders? At what point in the case? Why?

CASE 8
TROUBLE IN PARIS: EURODISNEY'S EXPERIMENT

Disneyland Paris parent EuroDisney is awaiting French government approval to build a second theme park, to the tune of $705 million, right next to its existing pioneer. Once a sniffed-at symbol of U.S. cultural imperialism, Disneyland Paris now is Europe's top vacation destination (12.5 million visitors in 1998) and a touchstone for other theme park companies who see the Old World as their profit-rich new world. (della Cava, 1999).

Now a success, EuroDisney's first experiment in Paris had rocky start. Transplanting an established, highly successful American company's vision, mission, culture and values, and business model "as is" provides a lot of lessons about doing business abroad.

On January 1,1994, Michael Eisner, chairman and chief executive officer of Walt Disney Company (WD), discovered that he had become the latest casualty of Disney's European theme park, EuroDisney (ED). Excluding stock options, Eisner had averaged an annual income of $7.5 million per year since 1989, which included a $750,000 salary plus a bonus equal to 2 percent of the amount by which the company's net income exceeded a return on stockholders equity of 11 percent. (Eisner did not receive a bonus for fiscal 1993, Disney's worst performance in years.)

Regarded as the unchallenged leader of WD, Eisner faced a demanding board of directors in 1994. Stockholders wanted answers on poor stock showings. Bondholders were threatening to take legal actions. For the first time since Eisner took over, the Disney magic and image were faltering, and his job was on the line.

Eisner's problems stemmed from the failures of ED, which lost $900 million in fiscal year 1993. Moreover, ED's first quarter 1994 estimates were worse than the previous year's. WD's 1993 net profit was $300 million with ED; without ED, WD's profit would have been $1.2 billion.

Eisner did not need his Harvard law degree to know that he needed a solution to ED's financial crisis. In an effort to reach a solution, he threatened to close down ED if an agreement with creditor banks was not reached on a financial rescue plan by March 31, 1994. Eisner, WD, the French creditor banks, and the French government were braced for hard negotiations that would determine the future of this venture.

BACKGROUND

Walt Disney, the founder of Disney, declared that his first park in Anaheim was "The happiest place on Earth." By the early 1980s, WD had maintained a squeaky clean image, consistent but mediocre earnings, and a growing presence abroad. It had built large additions to its domestic parks and studios and had successfully opened a profitable theme park in Japan.

In 1984, Disney hired a new CEO, Michael Eisner. Eisner and many of his own handpicked executives set out immediately to "remake" the company by increasing profits domestically.

Eisner's domestic strategy worked to the delight of shareholders. WD's stock soared every year (increasing by a 20 percent return on investment). The 1992 annual report to shareholders reflected management's pride in Disney's growth and earnings. Eisner pointed out the success stories in animation, films, and studios and the continued success of the theme parks in Orlando, Anaheim, and Japan. He even bragged about ED, "the most beautiful park and hotels we have ever developed—somewhat expensive but still fantastic!" He stated, "During a year of continued worldwide economic downturn, how many companies were fortunate to grow at 28 percent?"

EURODISNEY PLANNING

Eisner was determined to exploit the European market by taking slim royalties. The ED plan called for a 5,000-acre lot, 5,200 hotel rooms, an amusement park and parking complex, a golf course, office space, 580 homes, and MGM studios. The projected cost was $4.5 billion. The creation of 11,000 jobs was also planned.

France won the bid to house ED over Spain late in 1985. France provided tax breaks and guaranteed the improvement of the surrounding infrastructure and the building of special rail lines. In addition, France provided the lowest interest loans, along with a financial deal that largely insulated WD from risk. Access to larger airports with a central European location was also offered. In return, the French socialist government would prove, before its upcoming elections, that it was a "modern" government that was receptive to private enterprise—and 11,000 jobs. When the final contract was signed, the French government included a clause that constrained WD to respect the French culture.

WD planned on making ED a sister company. Stock was offered to finance its creation. WD planned on using the stock revenue along with bank capital to build phase one—everything but the MGM studios. WD then planned on issuing convertible bonds to finance phase two: the MGM studios.

ED anticipated 11 million visitors in 1992, of which 50 percent were projected to be French. WD set the admission fee at $40 for adults and $27 for children—30 percent higher than the Disney World fee in Florida. ED estimated the average visitor would spend $33 per day on food and souvenirs. These numbers were based on the park's central location, vast and elegant hotels (like the Newport Bay Club, which operated at above 76 percent occupancy), and—most important—the popular Disney name.

ED also used its Japanese park as a guide in planning the French venture. The elimination of trade and travel barriers during the anticipated unity of the European Community further increased ED's optimistic expectations. Although an economic recession occurred after these optimistic projections-and before the park opened—the Disney corporation remained upbeat about meeting its projections.

ED supported its popularity and French cultural ties by pointing out that "Le Journal de Mickey Mouse" had been a long-running French story, read by millions of French children since 1934. ED also enjoyed the top rating for family programming in France. In addition, Disney's video *Jungle Book* achieved world record sales in the European Community. ED intended to use the current Disney theme, which referenced the world of dreams and childhood. The cast of characters, led by Mickey Mouse, Donald Duck, and Snow White, remained the same.

ORGANIZATION

ED was given the status of an independent company. Banks and investors would put up approximately $3.6 billion to finance the private enterprise. Walt Disney would pay only $200 million, most of which was a 49 percent share of the new company. This 49 percent was bought at a firesale price of $1.50 per share —outside investors purchased shares at the offered price of $11.50 per share. ED Chairman Robert Fitzpatrick and a host of other Walt Disney management members were assigned to the ED Management Team. The French and other Europeans comprised the remainder of the ED staff. With or without a profit, WD established for itself a royalty of 10 percent of ticket sales and 5 percent of merchandise sales.

CULTURAL CONTEXT

EuroDisneyland is similar to its U.S. counterparts in Florida and California, but because of critical press reviews, the Walt Disney Company carefully placed the park in a European cultural context. French was planned as the park's first language; English was the second language. Signs would be bilingual and multilingual. Some of the park's areas highlight French themes, such as Discoveryland, which is inspired by the work of the French science-fiction writer Jules Verne. Mickey Mouse and Donald Duck have French accents. The fairy-tale castle, the centerpiece of every Disney theme park, would be known as "Le Chateau de la Belle au Bois Dormant." Only the major attractions, such as the Pirates of the Caribbean and Adventureland, would be called by their English names.

Robert Fitzpatrick was promoted to the position of president of EuroDisneyland because of his knowledge of France, French, and French culture. Even Michael Eisner, chairman and chief executive officer of the Walt Disney Company, "found himself explaining to French visitors that 'Snow White' is a German fairy tale; 'Pinocchio' was written by an Italian; 'Cinderella' and 'Sleeping Beauty' were both written by Frenchman Charles Perrault; the characters Mary Poppins and Peter Pan are English." Against French culture was the ban on wine and beer in the park.

CULTURAL CONFLICT

From the beginning, ED was plagued with problems. Months before the opening of the theme park, members of the French intelligentsia and the Socialist establishment blasted the park as the latest example of American cultural imperialism. A Parisian theater director, Ariane Mnouchkine, was the first "to arms!"—"aux armes." "EuroDisneyland is a 'Cultural Chernobyl,'" she declared. Also, her colleague, Jean Cau of the Academie Francaise, wrote of "this horror of cardboard, plastic, atrocious colors, solidified chewing-gum constructions, and idiotic folk stories that come straight out of cartoon books for fat Americans. It is going to wipe out millions of children . . . mutilate their imaginations."

Only hours before the opening day, saboteurs blew up an electricity pylon and plunged the entire complex into darkness. On opening day, a new railway station remained empty as the staff struck in hopes of damaging EuroDisneyland's reputation.

Intellectuals were not alone in their cultural protest. EuroDisneyland's employees had to accommodate a conservative, professional look. It was this clear, all-American, 'Disney look' that brought scorn from the French. The French labor union, for example, complained that Disney's 13-page employee manual on dress and manners stripped the employees of their French individualism: "Men cannot have moustaches, beards or exposed tattoos, nor can they wear jeans. Women cannot wear any obtrusive jewelry (larger than two centimeters in diameter) nor have 'unusually colored' hair or long fingernails." Employees could not smoke or chew gum and had to use deodorant and wear "proper underwear." Workers had been quoted as telling tales of being "spied on" by undercover management operatives. The Magic Kingdom was quickly labeled "Mouseschwitz." Leftist magazine editors of *Le Nouvelle Observateur* went so far as to assign a reporter to infiltrate the EuroDisney organization as a job trainee "to expose the rot of American Imperialism." (The reporter not only was impressed and charmed by the operation, but also eventually wrote a positive article for EuroDisneyland. The story was published, suggesting that the reporter had been "brainwashed.")

Despite rigid appearance codes, the cleanliness and friendliness requirements worked because of rigorous training. Disney executives apparently had worked magic. Even the French intellectuals noticed the curious phenomenon of smiling faces and conviviality, which, they quoted, "unsettled home-grown visitors." Jenny Rees, a writer for the *National Review,* said, "I know France well; I have studied there and lived there. At EuroDisneyland, I heard uttered from French lips for the first time ever in my life, the words, 'You're welcome' and 'That's no trouble.'"

Hard Times

In April 1992, ED opened its gates for the first time. Advertising costs for the event totaled $110 million. The opening day ceremonies were broadcast to 30 countries. ED staged a giant parade before a soldout park. The stock price reached a high of $28.18 per share.

Attendance remained strong through the summer months. Hotel occupancy rates maintained a respectable 76 percent through September. However, merchandise sales had fallen more than 10 percent below expectations, and labor costs were almost 20 percent of revenue. In September 1992, Banque Paribus, the most influential bank in France, issued a "sell" recommendation for the ED stock, which then proceeded to nose-dive as the critical cold weather season began in late September. ED was not attracting the volume of French visitors returning from their typical August vacations.

Travel agencies and potential visitors complained aloud about high prices, but ED President Robert Fitzpatrick denied the claim. He publicly stated that ED represented a "good value," despite reports that visitors were taking as many rides as possible to get the most out of the admission fee while spending less on merchandise.

As attendance continued to plummet, the cast members' spirits deflated. Many jobs, both union and nonunion, were in jeopardy. The Newport Bay Club, the largest of the six hotels in Euro Disneyland and one of the largest in Europe, closed its 1,100 rooms until spring because of grim advance bookings. Park officials rationalized that it was closed because it was a "summer theme" hotel. The lack of "a sunshine experience" for ED visitors contributed to the attendance problems.

Reactions: Financial and Cultural

In January 1993, Disney reacted to the dismally low occupancy rates at their six resort hotels by cutting rates from $80 to $54 per night (for four people) at their least expensive properties, the Hotel Cheyenne and the Hotel Santa Fe. Prices at the luxurious Disneyland Hotel, Sequoia Lodge, and Newport Bay

Hotel ranged from $240 to $360 per night. In the first year of operation, EuroDisney's hotels operated at an occupancy rate of 55 percent against a forecasted 68 percent. According to most analysts, it was projected that the company would not break even anytime prior to 1997. Restaurants were also slashing meal prices in an effort to compete with fast-food providers.

In its first year of operation, EuroDisney's stock fell over 68 percent. Disney announced the delay of the Disney-MGM theme park in France until revenues were increased. The MGM park, similar to the one in Orlando, was projected to provide EuroDisney with a "second-gate appeal." Original plans for the EuroDisney complex include a park expanded to a size two-thirds that of Paris by 2017. Presently, all further expansion has been delayed indefinitely. EuroDisney continues discussion with creditor banks and its parent company over raising money to reduce debt and to begin the MGM Studios project.

As of 1993, the proposed attraction had already been halved to a $1.6 billion investment by dropping plans for two hotels and a water park. The loss through delay is felt by the French government due to lack of tax revenue received from road construction. EuroDisney announced that it was laying off 950 employees to help balance the budget. Management blamed the European recession, high interest rates, and the decline of several currencies against the French franc.

A major cultural change that occurred in June 1993 was the offering of beer and wine by several park restaurants. (Selling alcoholic beverages is forbidden in all other Disney theme parks.) The typical 90-minute, European-style, sit-down lunch did not appeal to the park's diverse clientele. Unpredicted, European customers preferred a 20-minute, American-style, eat-and-run lunch. Another unforeseen habit was that, unlike Americans who wander around with a hot dog in hand, Europeans eat at daily set times. Everyone converged upon restaurants at 12:30 P.M. for lunch.

Disney hotels were also told that Europeans did not prefer full breakfasts. Surprisingly, guests desired full-course, American-style breakfasts. The restaurants were caught trying to serve 2,500 breakfasts in a 350-seat layout.

The November 1993 report for EuroDisney's first fiscal year showed that the park lost more than $900 million and that its stock dropped to $7.00 per share—down from $30.00 prior to the park's opening. This move forced WD to call on its banks to restructure its debt. Michael Eisner followed with a December statement that the park might shut down while negotiations continued. Surprisingly, this rumor created a surge in bookings: people wanted to experience the park "before it closed."

In early February 1994, Moody's Investors Service Inc. lowered its rating on Disney's $1.8 billion of long-term debt securities from double-A-3 to single-A-1. "The New York based rating service said the downgrades reflect expectations that operations at the EuroDisney theme park near Paris will remain under pressure at least in the indeterminate term and that as a result, uncertainty over Walt Disney's future financial commitments to the project will increase its risk profile." Moody was concerned that the price reduction would create difficulties in maintaining revenue levels. In February 1994, EuroDisney's first quarter losses were 30 percent above those of the previous year.

Internally, the park operated more efficiently by decreasing the number of items available on the restaurant menus by half and by training staff who sell admission tickets in the morning to also sell tee-shirts in the afternoon. The number of gift store items was reduced from 30,000 to 17,111, and more of the proceeds were directed to the parent Walt Disney Company.

FAST FORWARD FIVE YEARS LATER

Assuming that the September 11 crisis and the continuing threats of terrorist attacks do not pose either real or perceived dangers of flying and being in large public places, "Disneyland Paris speaks volumes about the European appetite for theme parks," says Kieran Burke, chairman and CEO of Premier Parks. "This is a very important strategic market for us" (della Cava, 1999).

Major changes in European life have contributed to the success of U.S. theme parks in general and Disney in particular in Europe:

- Deregulation of European air travel has made flights more affordable.
- Construction of the Chunnel between England and France has facilitated unprecedented British mobility.
- Europeans have more leisure time—up to six weeks. This creates significant opportunities for those in the short-break holiday business.
- Europeans' "love affair with the USA" has accelerated a familiarity with U.S. theme parks. (Ibid.)
- Globalization of the holiday concept: Europeans who liked the theme parks in the United States now have them in their own countries.
- Branding works: The Disney "magic" as a name brand and concept has worked in Europe after adjustments were made in the theme park to accommodate cultural differences.
- EuroDisney aims at increasing marketing to attract more conventions. The company has sold land to a developer who plans to build a 900,000-square-foot U.S.-style mall two miles from the park. (Ibid.)

CULTURE STILL PLAYS

Europeans are still not ideal theme park visitors. They carry their own lunches and are not as "souvenir-crazy" as Americans or Japanese. Moreover, there is still a cultural sensitivity on the part of many Europeans. Disney learned this lesson soon after its 1992 launch in Paris when the park planner did not realize that most Europeans travel on tour buses—no provisions for a drivers' lounge were made. A boycott quickly changed that blindspot.

As also noted in the case, the French complained about the absence of wine, and the Germans were angered over the lack of beer. These oversights have been corrected. (The beer has a reduced-alcohol variant.) "You don't create an American park in a foreign country," says Tim O'Brien of Nashville-based *Amusement Business* magazine. "You use your know-how to build an American-style park in the heart of a European culture. There is a difference." (Ibid.)

QUESTIONS FOR DISCUSSION

1. Evaluate the WD executives' strategic assumptions and planning process for the Paris theme park.
2. What cultural clashes were not foreseen or planned?
3. Explain how a corporation's strategy should consider the culture of a project, using this case as an example.
4. Who is responsible for this park's financial success? Who pays if the park is unsuccessful?
5. What specifically should have been done differently before the park was opened to the public? Why?
6. Disney is building themes parks in other countries. Has the WD Company made similar cultural mistakes in other locations?

SOURCES

Cohen, R. (Nov. 21, 1993). The French, Disneyed and Jurassick, fear erosion. *New York Times*, E2.

della Cava, M. (Feb. 17, 1999). Magic kingdoms, new colonies theme parks are staking bigger claims in Europe. *USA Today*, 1D.

Gumbel, P. (Feb. 23, 1994). EuroDisney counts on Mary Poppins to tidy up mess at French resort. *Wall Street Journal*, A20.

Gumbel, P. (March 10, 1994). Fans like Euro Disney but its parent's goofs weigh the park down. *Wall Street Journal*, A1, A12.

Henderson, J., et al. (Aug. 1992). Euro Disney: oui or non? *Travel & Leisure, 80*, 114–115.

Liddle, A. (Nov. 23, 1992). Vivre le Mouse! Mickey takes on Europe. *Nation's Restaurant News*, 54.

Phillips, A. (May 3, 1993). Where's the magic? Problems plague Euro Disney's first year. *Maclean's*, 47.

Rees, J. (May 11, 1992). The mouse that ate France. *National Review*, 57–61.

Revel, J-F. (Nov. 1992.) Who's afraid of Mickey Mouse? *Current*, 31.

Rudolf, B. (March 25, 1991). Monsieur Mickey: EuroDisneyland is on schedule, but with a distinctive French accent. *Time*, 48–49.

Solomon, J. (Aug. 10, 1993). EuroDisney's attendance is disappointingly Mickey Mouse. *Journal of Commerce*, 9a.

Solomon, J. (Feb. 14, 1994). Mickey's trip to trouble. *Newsweek*, 34–39.

Solomon, J. (Feb. 11, 1994). Walt Disney's rating on long-term debt is lowered by Moody's. *Wall Street Journal*, C16.

Solomon, J. (July 18, 1993). When you wish upon a deficit. *New York Times*, 82.

Vaughan, V. (May 2, 1991). EuroDisney designers work to avoid culture clash. *Orlando Sentinel*.

CASE 9
GENERAL MOTORS VERSUS THE MEDIA,
DATELINE NBC

On Tuesday, February 9, 1993, Harry Pearce, chief counsel at General Motors (GM), listened to *Dateline NBC* co-anchors Jane Pauley and Stone Phillips as they read a carefully worded statement to their viewers. The statement was an apology for withholding information and making misrepresentations in a story aired on the November 17, 1992, show entitled "Waiting to Explode?" The statement was made as part of the settlement of a defamation suit that GM brought against the National Broadcasting Company (NBC) on the previous day. The suit against NBC was a result of evidence gathered on a test crash that the network aired in a November 17 segment. General Motors' lawyers had gathered significant evidence alleging that the crash had been rigged by the contractor and that this evidence was presented by Mr. Pearce in a 90-minute closed-circuit TV news conference from Detroit on February 8, 1993. The damaging evidence presented sent NBC executives and those of its parent company, General Electric, scrambling.

BACKGROUND

GM, a Big Three U.S. automaker, is based in Detroit, Michigan. Its sales for 1993 were $138 billion, which positioned the company then as number one.[1] The design of the GM model C/K truck's fuel tank was similar to those of Ford and Chrysler, which were mounted inside the cab, behind the seats, until federal regulations in 1973 forced the companies to relocate the tanks.[2] Ford and Chrysler responded by placing the fuel tank under the chassis separated by the steel frame. GM placed two 20-gallon fuel tanks on each side of the truck, outside the frame, in order to enlarge fuel capacity. The tanks were shielded only by the sheet metal of the body, instead of being protected by the steel frame of the truck.

The first sign that the tank design may have presented higher risks was noted in an internal memo dated September 7, 1970. The memo was issued by a GM safety engineer, George Carvill. He wrote: "Moving these side tanks inboard might eliminate most of these potential leakers."[3] A second memo, dated December 15, 1983, written by GM product analyst Richard Monakaba, sent a message similar to that in Carvill's memo. GM responded 18 years later by changing the design of the tanks, beginning in 1988, for only some models. The new design placed a single 34-gallon tank within the frame.

When staff did not act deliberately and quickly, the product liability cases began to increase against GM. Side impact crashes caused the pickups to explode. The company had been involved in 120 lawsuits stemming from the location of the gas tank. In the fall of 1992, consumer groups like the Center for Auto Safety (founded by Ralph Nader in 1970), the Institute for Injury Reduction, and the Consumer Federation of America began to pressure the

National Highway Safety Administration (NHTSA)—a regulatory agency in the U.S. Department of Transportation—to order a recall on the trucks. Clarence Ditlow, executive director of the Center for Auto Safety, stated, "It's the Ford Pinto all over again, only worse."[4] Through November 1992, the company had paid over $200 million to settle fuel tank–related cases.[5]

THE MEDIA IGNITE THE ISSUE

Dateline NBC, the television investigative reporting program, was the first network that showed a staged test crash of the GM C/K pickup. The film aired on November 17, 1992. The story was titled "Waiting to Explode?" Robert Read was the story producer, and Michele Gillen was the reporter. The segment opened with the story of Shannon Mosely, a 17-year-old high school student who was killed in 1989 when a drunk driver hit his 1985 GMC pickup and it burst into flames. Gillen then interviewed Byron Bloch, "auto safety expert."[6] Mr. Bloch stated, "The fuel bursts out of the tank and there is an immediate holocaust."[7] Clarence Ditlow stated in an interview, "These pickups are rolling fire bombs."[8] Additional statements on the danger of the truck were made by Ron Elwell, a former GM engineer, and Mick McBee, an attorney for a plaintiff in a lawsuit against GM. Representing GM in the story were Robert Sinkle, Jr., GM's director of engineering analysis, and Clinton Varner, an attorney for GM. Both noted that the general safety record of the C/K pickups was comparable to other models. The test crash footage followed, with Gillen delivering the following narrative while a video of the crash was played:

> To see for ourselves what might happen in a side impact crash, DATELINE NBC hired the Institute for Safety Analysis to conduct unscientific crash demonstrations. In our demonstration, unlike GM tests, the fuel tank was filled with real gasoline. In one crash, at about 40 miles per hour, there was no leakage and no fire. But in the other, at around 30 miles per hour, look what happened. At impact, a small hole was punctured in the tank. According to our experts, the pressure of the collision and the crushing of the gas tank forced the gasoline to spew from the gas cap. The fuel then erupted into flames when ignited by the impacting car's headlight. The pickup's tank did not split open. If it had, the fire would have been much larger.[9]

The video of the crash was a dramatic illustration of a side impact collision. The test crash was conducted on October 24, 1992, on a deserted road in Indiana. The test crash was overseen by Bruce Enz, vice president of a company called The Institute for Safety Analysis (TISA.) This company, which "specializes in investigating and testifying the causes of accidents and injuries,"[10] showed two driverless Chevy Citations that were sent into the side of two C/K pickups. The first test crash resulted in a small fire; the second crash, at a higher speed, had no fire. "The NBC people were clearly disappointed"[11] says Mr. Enz. The show's producer presented a different version—a close view of the first crash, showing a fiery crash and explosion, even at a slower impact speed collision. The NBC video segment was damaging to GM. Media attention regarding the safety of the pickup mounted. On December 8, 1992, NHTSA opened a formal investigation on the GM truck in an attempt to respond to pressure from consumer groups.

THE CONTROVERSY ESCALATED

General Motors vigorously defended the safety of the pickup. The company noted that the trucks passed the traffic-safety administration's 20-mph side-impact crash tests and that GM had also conducted its own crash tests at 50 mph. GM argued that the risk of explosion from a side-impact crash with its pickups, though higher with some types of vehicles, was about average compared with most other vehicles. National Highway Traffic Safety Administration (NHTSA) statistics showed that for each year in which a person drove a heavy pickup, the odds of dying in an accident were[12]

Dodge	1 in 8,606
Ford	1 in 6,916
GM	1 in 6,605
All passenger cars	1 in 6,053

If NHTSA had forced GM to recall its questionable trucks, analysts estimated the cost at between $300 million and $1 billion to recall the 5 to 6 million C/K model pickups that were on the road.[13]

GM RESPONDED

After the *Dateline NBC* story aired, GM, led by Harry Pearce, began to vigorously respond to the critics. GM immediately asked NBC for test data and a chance to examine the trucks used in their crash. NBC delayed on giving the data. Its executives stated that the vehicles ". . . have subsequently been junked and are no longer available for inspection by anyone."[14]

On January 11, 1993, William O'Neill, head of North American Public Relations at GM, received a tip from a witness at the TISA test crash that the crash had been rigged. O'Neill began an investigation into the facts of the test crash. The trucks were subsequently found in a junkyard near the crash site. The tanks were missing. GM obtained video footage from witnesses of the crash that showed the planting of two model rocket motors next to the gas tank—rigged to ignite any fuel. GM also discovered that the tanks were overfilled, having an extra 5 gallons over normal capacity. These facts, along with an improper gas cap that the previous owner says in a sworn statement he used, caused the gas to spill from the tank. Using the wreckage of the trucks and the obtained video, GM contested the speed of the test and noted that what the program described as "around 30 mph"[15] was at least 39 mph. Also, the test had announced impact at "about 40 mph,"[16] but it was found to have been at least 47 mph.

During the process of gathering evidence against NBC, GM lost the lawsuit filed by the parents of Shannon Mosely, the boy who was described in the *Dateline NBC* story. On February 4, 1993, a jury in the Georgia court awarded the parents $4.2 million in compensatory damages and $101 million in punitive damages. On February 8, 1993, Harry Pearce, in a closed-circuit news conference, presented the evidence that GM had gathered on the test crash to its employees, to dealers, and to NBC executives. On the same day, GM filed a defamation suit in Indiana against NBC. The initial response of NBC President Michael Gartner was to defend "the segment as 'fair and accurate' and accuse GM of trying to divert attention from its truck problem."[17] On February 9, 1993, faced with indisputable evidence and the possible loss of its share of GM's $500 million a year television advertising budget, NBC settled the suit by agreeing to issue an apology on *Dateline NBC* that night and to compensate GM $2 million for the cost of its investigation.

This fiasco by NBC is not an isolated incident. What happened with GM is not uncommon between the TV networks and automobile companies, but the publicity and outcome are unprecedented. GM is, however, the first company to fight back against the so-called expert testing and win. Although GM won an apology and a $2 million settlement, the victory would serve as a precedent and send a louder message to the media.

GM's Postscript

On February 10, 1993, GM removed its advertising from NBC News programming. William O'Neil stated that GM did "not feel we wanted to advertise in a negative environment. We believe the environment on NBC's news programs is negative."[18] On February 11, GM removed its ban and accepted NBC's apology.

On March 2, 1993, Michael Gartner, president of NBC News, resigned under pressure from the *Dateline NBC* scandal. On March 11, 1993, GM filed for a retrial in the Shannon Mosely case. On March 22, 1993, the findings of an independent investigation conducted by attorneys Robert S. Warren and Lewis B. Kaden on the incident noted "that senior NBC News employees made 'serious flawed judgements' when producing "[19] the story. The report also blamed Michael Gartner for failing to properly investigate the affair sufficiently. Also on March 22, Jeff Diamond, the executive producer of *Dateline NBC*; David Rummell, the senior producer; and Robert Read, the story producer, all resigned under heavy pressure.

In April 1993, the NHTSA asked GM to voluntarily recall the pickups. GM refused, claiming the trucks were as safe as rivals' models. On November 3, 1993, a Texas state court cleared the way for a settlement with 650,000 GM truck owners in Texas. The settlement called for GM to issue $1,000 coupons toward the purchase of a new GM truck. On November 18, 1993, the Transportation Department announced that Transportation Secretary Federico Pena would decide on the government's next course of action. On December 16, 1993, "[a] Federal judge in Philadelphia approved a class-action settlement that required General Motors to give as much as $6 billion in coupons to owners of GM pickups with side-mounted gasoline tanks."[20]

QUESTIONS FOR DISCUSSION

1. What, if any, effect did this case have on your opinions of and attitudes toward the media? Explain. Do you believe this was a rogue incident, or does it represent an occurrence that the public should be concerned about regarding the media as a persuasive force in society? Explain.

2. Who are the major stakeholders, and what are their stakes in this case?

3. Why did *Dateline NBC* act as it did in this case? What were its motives?

4. Was GM without fault? If so, why? If it was at fault, explain.

5. Was justice served to NBC in this case? Explain.

6. Did the federal judge in Philadelphia treat GM fairly? Why or why not?

CASE 10
STELLA LIEBECK VERSUS THE MCDONALD'S CORPORATION: PRODUCT (FOR JUDICIAL SYSTEM) LIABILITY?

In August 1992, 81-year-old Stella Liebeck pulled up to McDonald's drive-through window in Albuquerque, New Mexico, to purchase a cup of coffee. Stella was a frequent customer of McDonald's, one of the largest fast-food franchises in the world—with over eleven thousand restaurants serving over 22 million customers per day.

After buying a 49-cent cup of coffee, Stella Liebeck placed the coffee container between her legs, removed the lid, and proceeded to pull away from the drive-through window. As she drove away, coffee spilled. She suffered second and third degree burns on her inner thighs, buttocks, and groin area. Treatment of the injuries required hospitalization and surgery. Stella Liebeck asked McDonald's to reimburse her $11,000 for medical bills. McDonald's responded to Ms Liebeck's request by presenting her with a counteroffer of a lesser amount. Dissatisfied with that offer, Stella sought legal representation from a personal injury attorney, S. Reed Morgan and associates.

Morgan was familiar with this type of case and with the McDonald's Corporation. He had previously represented two other parties in separate lawsuits against McDonald's that involved injuries caused from hot beverage burns. Morgan's first run-in with McDonald's occurred in 1988, when he represented a 29-year-old woman in a suit for injuries received from hot coffee. The jury ruled in favor of the woman, who was awarded $27,000. Also, in 1992, Morgan represented a Santa Monica, California woman in a similar case against McDonald's; she won a settlement of $235,000.

S. Reed Morgan filed suit on behalf of Stella Liebeck (a former department store clerk who had never filed suit before), against the McDonald's Corporation, charging the company with "selling a defective product because it was unreasonably dangerous due to extreme temperatures, . . . failure to warn of extreme temperatures, . . . and breach of implied warranty of merchantability, because the coffee was not fit for human consumption."[1] Morgan and his associates sought an award of $300,000 for Stella for compensatory and punitive damages. In addition to the monetary award, Stella Liebeck requested that McDonald's print warning labels on its hot beverage containers.

During the trial, attorneys for Stella Liebeck argued that McDonald's was negligent in its failure to reduce the temperature of its coffee. According to Morgan, "McDonald's officials have known about hundreds of java-related injuries dating back to 1978, and could easily have solved the problem by serving their coffee at a lower temperature."[2] Testimony from an array of "burn" experts supported this argument. Morgan also argued that coffee brewed by home coffee-makers had an average temperature of 140 degrees, while McDonald's served its coffee at an average of 180 to 190 degrees. The temperature of the coffee that injured Stella Liebeck was estimated at approximately 170 degrees.

McDonald's countered by arguing that its coffee is served at between 180 and 190 degrees based on advice from a coffee consultant, who said that the beverage tastes best at that temperature.[3] Further supporting arguments came from Terry Dort, executive director of the National Council of Chain Restaurants, who stated, "Coffee in our industry is served between 180 and 190 degrees. This is what our manufacturers recommend and this is what our customers want."[4] McDonald's also testified that safety is always its number one priority and that the company had already printed warning labels on hot beverage containers before Stella's incident.

This was not the first time McDonald's had been sued for coffee burn injuries. The restaurant had received over 700 reports of coffee burns ranging from mild to third degree. Over $500,000 in claims related to scalding injuries had been settled.

THE VERDICT

In August 1994, almost two years after Stella Liebeck had been burned, an Albuquerque, New Mexico, jury decided in favor of the plaintiff. The jury awarded Stella Liebeck $2.7 million in punitive damages and $160,000 in compensatory damages—a sum in excess of the $300,000 originally sought. According to jurors, the unusually high punitive award not only was awarded for the injuries Stella Liebeck suffered, but also was intended to be a message to the fast-food industry to lower the temperature of the coffee.

Said one juror, "The coffee's too hot out there, this [just] happened to be Mc-Donald's."[5] McDonald's had little to say after the decision, but immediately filed an appeal, calling the punitive amount "excessive."

STAKEHOLDERS' REACTIONS

The response from the fast-food industry was mixed. The Popeye's fast-food franchise pulled coffee off its menus completely. Hardee's Restaurant, which was named two years earlier in a similar lawsuit and was ordered to pay a plaintiff over $150,000, announced it was considering issuing warning labels on containers and implementing more rigid training programs for employees on the safe handling of hot food and beverages.[6] "Because [of the jury's decision,] the public is more aware, [and] it is our belief that it will change the industry standard for serving coffee," said Maurice Bridges, spokesman for Hardee's Food Systems, Inc. "We are looking to raise the awareness internally and externally."[7] Wendy's International, Inc., temporarily removed hot chocolate from its menus as it tried to find a way to serve coffee at a reduced temperature. Wendy's felt that hot chocolate, which often ends up in the hands of children, did not require as high a temperature as coffee.[8]

While these chains reacted almost immediately to the initial *Liebeck* decision, the majority of fast-food chains took a "wait and see" approach. Burger King, Bruegger's Bagels, and Dunkin Donuts all said they serve their product within the industry standard temperature range of 180 to 190 degrees and are likely to continue to do so. "It's a difficult issue," said Steven Grover, assistant director of technical services, public health, and safety for the National Restaurant Association. "The expectation in our industry is that when customers order a hot cup of coffee, it should be hot. But then any beverage that is perceivably hot has the potential to hurt somebody. The restaurants are in a tough situation."[9]

The National Association of Trial Lawyers praised the jury's decision and the message it sent to fast-food restaurants. Russell F. Moran, an attorney and publisher of the *New York Jury Verdict Reporter*, stated, "People get upset when there are huge awards . . . like the woman burned by the McDonald's coffee . . . but you need to look beyond the facts, especially in this case. There were 700 incidents of prior notice. The fact is, the company was negligent . . . coffee doesn't have to be that hot."[10]

Punitive reform activists spoke out against the decision, citing it as one of the many "excessive jury verdicts and frivolous lawsuits that continue to plague the U.S. civil justice system, inhibiting the competitiveness of corporate America."[11] "If ever a single incident shows how badly we need tort reform, this does," said Terry Dort. "A $2.9 million decision points out how seriously flawed the [court] system is."[12] Still other reactions, such as one article written in the *Wall Street Journal*, questioned the common sense of the jurors. "We've often championed the common sense of the average citizen over a regulatory bureaucracy, but decisions like this make us scratch our heads."[13]

The decision came while at least two major pieces of legislation were being introduced to the Senate that would place strict limitations on punitive awards and place product liability cases under federal jurisdiction. The GOP's controversial Contract with America—led by Newt Gingrich—contained a proposal supported by the National Association of Manufacturers (NAM) that would limit damages in product liability cases to three times compensatory damages or $250,000, whichever is greater. Even more sweeping was the Lawsuit Reform Act of 1995, which capped punitive damages in *all* civil cases to $250,000 or three times economic damages, whichever is greater.

Critics of product liability reform, such as Ralph Nader, have asserted that "[the proposed product liability] legislation would be a monumental rollback of consumer protections that have taken years to develop. Once the scaffolding of Federalism develops around product liability, there will be no stopping the downward erosion of individual rights."[14]

FOLLOW-UP

McDonald's appeal of the $2.7 million punitive damages award was heard in September 1994. State District Judge Robert Scott responded by lowering the punitive award to $480,000, a figure he calculated by tripling the $160,000 in compensatory damages previously awarded by the jury. The judge's ruling did not affect the compensatory damages. The total award was $640,000.[15] Judge Scott said the new amount was appropriate for the "willful, wanton, reckless, and what the court finds as callous" behavior on the part of the fast-food company.[16]

McDonald's believed the settlement was excessive and immediately followed with a statement announcing it would appeal the decision. "Safety is always our first concern, and that is why we have 'hot contents' printed as a reminder on our cups," said Ann Connolly, spokeswoman for McDonald's. "We knew the initial damages awarded were excessive and unjustified, and yesterday the judge acknowledged that and agreed. But we feel they are still excessive, and will appeal this decision."[17] Attorneys for Stella Liebeck said they would appeal the judge's decision to reduce the award.

Before any appeal could be heard, both parties agreed to an out-of-court settlement of an undisclosed amount of money. As part of the settlement, however, McDonald's requested that neither Liebeck nor her attorney, Kenneth Wagner, speak about it.[18] Although the details of this request are unknown, attorneys for Stella Liebeck made public statements to the news media following the agreement, and Stella Liebeck appeared on the television news magazine *20/20* on April 28, 1995, to discuss her ordeal.

The fast-food industry found itself in an uncomfortable position from the attention of the *Liebeck* case. After the decision, representatives of the industry seemed relieved and even showed support for McDonald's. "At this point, I'll probably get together with managers and take a strong look at putting [coffee] back in the stores," said Greg Cutchall, president of Cutchall

McDonald's suffered substantial, but hardly outrageous, financial punishment for its irresponsible practices. Mrs. Liebeck was compensated for her injuries. And folks like me are less likely to get burned.

That's exactly how our legal system is supposed to work. That's also why the insurance, tobacco, and other major industries want to change it. They think it works too well.

The key is punitive damages—an unpredictable business expense for corporate misconduct. Corporations want Americans to think that huge punitive damages are awarded constantly, crippling businesses and raising consumer prices.

This is simply not true. Punitive damages are rare, especially in products liability cases. A Rand study showed that 47 percent are awarded in business-against-business litigation, versus less than 5 percent in products cases. And according to a study by Suffolk University law professor Michael Rustad, punitive damages were awarded in only 353 products liability cases (91 of them asbestos) between 1965 and 1990—an average of 14 per year or one per state every four years.

Most important, punitive damages bring safety. They have forced removal from the market of flammable children's pajamas, asbestos, tampons causing toxic shock syndrome, defective intrauterine contraceptive devices, and a host of hazardous drugs. They have forced car manufacturers to correct design defects like exploding gas tanks on Ford Pintos, slipping transmissions, and faulty minivan door latches.

In vetoing the products liability bill in 1996, President Clinton said arbitrary limits on punitive damages "would mean more unsafe products in our homes . . . [and] let wrongdoers off the hook."

Trial lawyers put our faith in the good judgment of juries. In cases where punitive damages may be applied, court instructions require jurors to use their good judgment—their common sense of right and wrong.

In America, a driver who kills someone can be imprisoned. But there are no prison terms for corporations that maim and kill. If a jury is convinced a corporate wrongdoer [20] has been so irresponsible that it deserves punishment, the idea of Washington politicians stepping in to say "no" is repugnant."

SOURCE: Source: Twiggs, H. (June 1997). How civil justice saved me from getting burned. *Trial, 33(1)*, 9.

Management Co., which franchises five Popeye's stores. "I consider it a moral victory for McDonald's."[19]

The case caused some franchises to review their procedures. According to Don Perry, a spokesman for the Atlanta-based Chik-Fil-A Inc., "Something of that scale captures your attention . . . we went through the process of doing some checks and going back to suppliers and asked them to advise us on their position for their own specifications and guidelines." He continued by stating, "In keeping with one of our major tenets of operations of continuous improvements, we are analyzing the whole process from a viewpoint of safety."

For the "wait and see" franchises, business returned to normal. Although many of these restaurants now have labels cautioning consumers about the "hot" contents of containers of coffee, tea, and hot chocolate, these beverages—including McDonald's coffee—continue to be served at the 180- to 190-degree industry standard.

QUESTIONS FOR DISCUSSION

1. Was McDonald's fairly treated by the courts, given all the facts in the case? Support your answer with case information.

2. Who are the stakeholders in this case? What are their stakes? Who won and who lost in this case?

3. Should the outcome of this case affect other beverage practices and standards of franchises like McDonald's? Why or why not?

4. Does the McDonald's case signal that strong product liability law and tort reform is needed in the United States, or does this case prove that justice is fairly served in a democratic, capitalist society? Explain your answer.

5. Respond to the reading in the box below: Do you agree with the statement or disagree? Justify your answer.

6. Would consumers be better served if there were fewer or no standards regarding franchise beverage temperatures? Explain.

7. Was McDonald's just giving the customers what they wanted, or was McDonald's manipulating consumer tastes? Explain.

8. Has this case made any difference in McDonald's coffee temperature and labels today? Explain.

BIBLIOGRAPHY

A case for iced coffee. (Aug. 26, 1994). *Wall Street Journal*, A10.

Coffee spill burns woman; jury awards $2.9M. (Aug. 19, 1994). *Wall Street Journal*, B3.

Howard, T. (Sept. 26, 1994). Judge slashes McD settlement to $480,000. *Nations Restaurant News*, 1, 4.

Howard, T. (Aug. 29, 1994). Jury "burns" McD in $2.9M verdict. *Nations Restaurant News*, 1, 55.

Howard, T. (Dec. 12, 1994). McD settles coffee suit in out-of-court agreement. *Nations Restaurant News*, 59.

Jost, K. (Jan. 1995). A changing legal landscape. *ABA Journal*, 14.

Labaton, S. (Feb. 19, 1995). G.O.P. preparing bill to overhaul negligence law. *New York Times*, 1, 24.

McDonald's coffee award reduced 75% by judge. (Sept. 15, 1994). *Wall Street Journal*, A4.

McDonald's settles lawsuit over burns from coffee. *Wall Street Journal*, B6.

Pick a number, any number. (Feb. 17, 1992). *Legal Times*.

Schine, E. (Sept. 5, 1994). McDonald's hot coffee gets her cool cash. *Business Week*, 38.

Sprunt, H. (Sept. 2, 1994). How hot is coffee that's not too hot. *Wall Street Journal*, A9.

When risk management fails. (Sept. 12, 1994). *Business Insurance*, 8.

Wojcik, J. (Feb. 6, 1995). Excessive punitive awards a matter of debate. *Business Insurance*, 1, 49.

CASE I I
COLT AND THE GUN CONTROL CONTROVERSY

On December 7, 1999, the Clinton administration announced its intention to join settlement negotiations between the gun industry and local cities and counties. The aim was to limit the flow of handguns to youth and criminals. In addition, the administration announced that if no visible progress was observed in the negotiations, it would file a nationwide class action lawsuit against the industry on behalf of the Department of Housing and Urban Development to seek compensation for lack of security and other costs associated with gun violence. How did the gun industry arrive at this predicament? Founded on the U.S. Constitution's Second Amendment right to bear arms, the gun industry has long served the public in supplying needed firearms. Now, the same industry is defending itself from its past supporters. Colt has a long, illustrious history as one of the largest and most innovative suppliers of firearms. If Colt cannot survive the numerous lawsuits it faces, its existence may be at stake.

HISTORICAL OVERVIEW

The success story of Sam Colt began with the issuance of a U.S. patent in 1836 for a Colt firearm equipped with a revolving cylinder containing five or six bullets. Only one- and two-barrel flintlock pistols were available before Sam Colt greatly increased firepower with his invention. The principle applied to both long arms and side arms and was remarkably simple. The idea, however, was not an instant success because many people still preferred the traditional flintlock musket or pistol. Sam Colt built his first plant in Patterson, New Jersey, and at age 22, he was the firm's chief salesman and new business promoter. He soon developed new products based on his principle: Gun powder and bullets were loaded into a revolving cylinder. The product generally performed very well. Sales, however, were disappointing despite the fact that the U.S. government purchased small quantities of the Colt ring lever rifle and Colt 1839 carbine. In 1842, because of the sluggish sales, the Patterson company, known as the Patent Arms Manufacturing Co., closed. It auctioned much of its equipment and began bankruptcy proceedings.

With his partner Samuel Morse, the inventor of the telegraph, Sam Colt started selling the U.S. government his ideas for waterproof ammunition. In 1855, with an initial issuance of 10,000 shares of stock, the firm was incorporated in Connecticut as the Clts Patent Firearms Mfg. Co. The company produced 150 weapons a day and was gaining a reputation for exceptional quality, workmanship, and design. Samuel Colt became one of the ten wealthiest businessmen in the United States. His estate was worth $15 million, which is equivalent to more than $300 million today.[1]

Before the official declaration of war, Colt supplied both the North and the South. After war was declared, Colt supplied only Union forces. In 1861,

Colt had annual earnings of about $250,000 and more than 1,000 employees. In 1862, Sam Colt died at the age of 47, having produced more than 400,000 weapons in his lifetime. Colt's strongest competitors for sidearms, rifles, and shotguns were Smith & Wesson, Remington, and Winchester.

FIREARMS EMERGE AS A NATIONAL ISSUE

Colt was a major producer and supplier of firearms during both World Wars and subsequent U.S. military actions. From 1901 to 1955, Colt faced and successfully dealt with the usual problems encountered by weapons manufacturers. Some issues that were successfully addressed were the need to rapidly increase production, as well as increase employment levels during wartime, and the subsequent need to sharply reduce employment after the war. After World War I, a new controversy, which could affect Colt and the entire gun industry for the rest of the century, emerged. The St. Valentine's Day massacre of 1929 brought the death toll in Chicago's underworld turf wars to 135 as gangsters battled over the profits of bootleg liquor during Prohibition. Realizing just how gruesome firearms could be in the hands of criminals, Americans started demanding the first national gun-control laws. But Congress moved cautiously, caught in a Second Amendment cross-fire argument over the right of gun ownership. It was a 1933 assassination attempt on President Franklin D. Roosevelt that prompted Washington to restrict the sale of sawed-off shotguns, machine guns and automatic weapons in 1934 and 1938. The National Firearms Act of 1934 aimed to cut down on ownership of machine guns and sawed-off shotguns by slapping a $200 tax on their purchase.[2]

In 1942, Colt more than tripled its workforce to 15,000 employees in three plants. After World War II, Colt was almost entirely dependent on government orders; as a result, sales fluctuated greatly. The Korean War temporarily boosted its earnings until 1952, but after the United States withdrew, Colt was in financial trouble. In 1955, Penn-Texas Corporation, one of the nation's first conglomerates, purchased the Colt Firearms Company.

Leopold Silberstein and his family took Colt Firearms into the Silberstein family of diversified companies as a wholly owned subsidiary. Four years later, in 1959, a group of investors took control of the company and changed the name to Fairbanks Whitney. In 1960, Colt achieved another milestone when it introduced the AR-15 semiautomatic rifle and the M-16 military fully automatic version. The Vietnam conflict again put heavy demands on Colt.

GUN CONTROL ACT

In 1964, the parent company decided to reorganize under the name Colt Industries and changed the firearms subsidiary's name to Colt's Inc., Firearms Division. The Gun Control Act of 1968 was passed following the assassinations of Martin Luther King Jr. and Robert Kennedy. Congress rushed to ban the sale of mail order guns and placed minimum safety standards on imported guns to raise their purchase price. No standards were adopted for U.S.-manufactured guns, however, and the law helped spawn a huge domestic gun industry that turned out cheap handguns, now known as "junk guns" and "Saturday night specials". This did not have much impact on Colt as most of its business still came from government contracts.

Through the 1970s and 1980s, Colt continued to expand its blackpowder line to include the famed Walker and the 1860 Army revolver. In the same year, however, Colt received a major setback when the government decided to replace the Colt .45 as the official sidearm of the armed forces. In 1990, the company was sold again to a coalition of private investors, the state of Connecticut, and union employees. The company was renamed Colt Manufacturing Company. The newly named company again brought new products to market: the Double Eagle double action pistol, the Colt Anaconda .44 Magnum double action revolver, and the redesigned Sporter rifle.

BRADY HANDGUN ACT OF 1993

The early nineties were eventful for Colt. It was forced to enter into Chapter 11 in 1992, and litigation commenced between Colt Manufacturing Co. and C.F. Intellectual Properties. The Brady Handgun Act of 1993 was introduced that year, which mandated a five-day waiting period and background check for persons buying handguns from retailers. The law followed the shooting of President Ronald Reagan and Press Secretary Jim Brady in 1981. More than 250,000 felons, fugitives, and others have been denied handguns since the law was enacted, but the country also witnessed an exponential growth in purchases at gun shows and flea markets, where background checks are not required. The act did not negatively impact Colt, since production increased in 1994 and 1995 over 1993 levels.

COLT AT THE MILLENNIUM

Colt may have started a new era of weapons technology when it began work with the National Institute of Justice on the "Smart Gun." This is a significant advancement in light of all the controversy surrounding recent gun violence, especially in high schools. Several new commercial products were introduced in 1997 and 1998. Colt scored again in 1998 when it won back its contract with the government to provide over 32,000 M-16 rifles and to update 88,000 M16A1 rifles for the U.S. Air Force. In addition, Colt acquired Saco Defense, which specializes in automatic weapons for the military.[3]

Since the 1929 St. Valentine's Day massacre, it has been estimated that the United States has been inundated with more than 20,000 gun laws on the state and federal books. The most significant of the federal laws have always followed in the wake of high-profile shootings. One of the more recent was the April 1999 high school massacre in Littleton, Colorado, which left 15 people dead. History repeated itself, and the Senate passed legislation in response to the shootings. However, Paul Blackman, who tracks gun legislation for the National Rifle Association, believes that "as far as crime is concerned, gun-control laws as a group are a total failure in affecting violence." However, David Bernstein of the Center to Prevent Handgun Violence claimed, "We think that the Brady Law was a major factor in reducing violence." Legislation such as the 1993 Brady Handgun Act prevented 250,000 felons and fugitives from purchasing handguns over the following five years. The following table illustrates this trend, showing that the total quantity of firearms manufactured decreased after the passage of the Brady Handgun Act.

Year	Firearms Manufactured
1986	~3.0 million
1989	~4.5 million
1991	~3.5 million
1993	~5.2 million
1994	~5.1 million
1995	~4.0 million
1996	~3.8 million
1997	~3.5 million

The Department of Justice agrees and credits recent gun-control laws, with an increase in firearm prosecutions, as a major reason for a 27 percent drop in gun-related crimes between 1992 and 1997.[4]

DEVELOPMENTS AFFECTING COLT AND THE GUN INDUSTRY

On October 30, 1998, New Orleans became the first city in the nation to file suit against the gun industry. Two weeks later, Chicago followed with a second lawsuit against the industry. The lawsuits claimed the industry failed to incorporate adequate safety systems into guns that would prevent widespread firearm misuse by unauthorized users. These lawsuits closely resemble the lawsuits brought against the tobacco industry. At first, the public considered tobacco-related diseases to be a result of choice made by the smoker. Little responsibility was attributed to the tobacco industry. After the deluge of state and city lawsuits against the tobacco industry, public views changed. Litigation caused a shift in public opinion and forced the tobacco industry to the bargaining table, where its executives finally acknowledged cigarette smoking was dangerous to health. Guns may become society's next tobacco controversy.[5]

LITIGATION

The litigation focuses on four choices that the firearms industry was alleged to have consciously made. First, it is alleged that the industry has focused all its design innovation efforts on making smaller and/or more powerful guns, while it has blocked installation of feasible safeties that would prevent thousands of unintentional shootings. Second, the industry's distribution system is being attacked because it is alleged that no controls exist and that the industry may even consciously target criminal markets, making it easy for criminals to obtain guns from the legal marketplace. Third, it is alleged that some gun manufacturers make high-firepower assault weapons that have no real sporting or self-defense use, but are more suited for criminals. Finally, it is alleged that the industry erroneously advertises that guns increase home safety, when evidence contradicts this message.[6]

Violence from firearms is without question a major problem in United States. More than 34,000 people were killed with firearms in 1996 (the most recent year for which statistics are available). This figure is second only to deaths related to motor vehicles, the most frequent cause of fatal injuries in the United States. Of these deaths, more than 14,300 were homicides, and about 18,100 were suicides, with more than 1,100 deaths caused by unintentional shootings. In addition, 1992 data shows that during that year approximately 99,000 individuals were treated in hospital emergency rooms for nonfatal firearm injuries, and 20,000 of these individuals were the victims of unintentional shootings.

The case of *Morial v. Smith & Wesson* was filed in New Orleans. The major issue was the promotion of safer gun designs. Recent data shows that 1 child is killed and at least 13 more are injured in unintentional shootings each day. The Center to Prevent Handgun Violence's Legal Action Project decided these occurrences are due to the negligence of the firearms industry, which should therefore pay damages. The lawsuit alleged that children are killed or injured with firearms in New Orleans because the gun manufacturers have not installed feasible internal locking devices that would prevent unauthorized use. The city is seeking unspecified damages for its costs in responding to this crisis.[7]

The *Morial* case was modeled after another lawsuit, *Dix v. Baretta USA Corp.*, filed by the Center and the Legal Action Project in 1994. This case was based on the unintentional shooting of a 14-year-old boy, Kenzo Dix, by his best friend. Kenzo was unaware that a bullet remained hidden in the pistol's chamber when he placed what he thought was an empty magazine in the gun. The lawsuit alleged that the pistol failed to include an internal lock that would prevent unauthorized users from firing the weapon. Therefore, the pistol was defectively designed. An argument was made that an internal locking device called "Saf-T-Lok" was available at the time and could have been adapted for the Baretta. The case alleged that Baretta rejected every safety idea sent to the company and made no effort to determine how serious a problem its guns presented to families, even after reports of unintentional shootings. This case is currently under appeal.[8]

A federal appeals court determined on October 16, 2001, that the Second Amendment does give individual citizens a right to own firearms. This ruling is expected to be influential in the continuing legal battle over the issue in the courts.[9] "Some legal experts who argue that the Second Amendment provides an individual right to firearms said the ruling was one of the most important ever on the issue. Eugene Volokh, a law professor at the University of California at Los Angeles, said the opinion would lay the groundwork for many other decisions that will analyze when gun control is permitted and when it is not."[10]

FIREARM COMPANIES AND INSURERS

More than 29 cities and counties have brought and are bringing lawsuits against the firearms industry. The gun companies' own insurers have notified their clients that they will not pay any large legal bills or any judgments associated with the lawsuits. Without the insurers, the firearms firms will be forced to defend themselves and therefore may be more likely to require bankruptcy protection or discontinue their business. In response to this threat, many gun companies are suing their insurers. Some of these lawsuits, such as *The National Shooting Sports Foundation v. Nationwide Mutual Insurance* in New Orleans, have already been successful. The judge ordered the insurer to pay.[11]

The consequences of the insurance issue will mean more expensive insurance for gun companies. Some gun-control advocates see this as another motivation to encourage companies to avoid litigation and make positive changes to their industry. According to Josh Horowitz, director of the Firearms Litigation Clearinghouse, the insurance problem is "one more thing to bring them to the settlement table."[12]

GOVERNMENT VERSUS FIREARMS INDUSTRY

The most recent and perhaps most potentially damaging lawsuit may come from the federal government. The Clinton administration, arguing that gun violence in public housing projects costs taxpayers too much money, was preparing to file a class action lawsuit against gun manufacturers. The Department of Housing and Urban Development would coordinate the action and might appear as a plaintiff on behalf of local authorities. No final decision, however, has been made to go forward. The idea is to put tremendous pressure on the industry to reach an agreement with the cities and states and make the following changes:

1. Crack down on gun sales to disreputable dealers,
2. Computerize gun inventories for easier tracking,
3. Manufacture safer guns, and
4. Discontinue advertising a particular kind of gun that is popular with criminals because it is fingerprint-proof.[13]

The gun industry has fought back and is not without its supporters. In response to the potential federal lawsuit, industry representatives are claiming the government has no grounds for an anti-gun suit. According to James P.

Dorr, an industry lawyer, "[T]to sue someone they have authorized to sell those products has no basis in law." Also, the Second Amendment Foundation is accusing the cities and states of trying to make firearms unavailable or unaffordable and is suing on these grounds. It is their position that anti-gun litigation is like "blaming the National Weather Service for storm damage."[14]

Colt has been portrayed by the media as discontinuing the handgun portion of its business in 1999 due to the financial implications of these and other pending lawsuits. This was not the case according to William Keys, CEO of Colt. "The lawsuits did not force us into this decision." The reality is that Colt would discontinue seven lines of handguns simply because they have not been selling the models. They would also slash 200 of the plant's 725 jobs with the hope of financially strengthening the company. Later in December of 1999, Colt contradicted this assertion in a letter to its shareholders by claiming, "We have had to face the harsh reality of the significant impact which our litigation defense costs are having on our ability to operate competitively in the marketplace."[15]

With all current lawsuits and the potential for a class action lawsuit by the U.S. government, Colt, as well as the rest of the gun industry, is in a fight for its survival. Colt does not have pockets as deep as those of the tobacco industry; therefore, it will need to be creative to forge reasonable settlements. Undoubtedly, some gun manufacturers will be driven out of business by the gun-control controversy. However, with its history and established reputation for supplying innovative firearms to the U.S. government, Colt just may have a chance to navigate its way through the minefield of lawsuits, especially while the Bush administration remains in the White House. However, it is not clear whether or not and to what extent this administration and the events after September 11, 2001, will have any effect on Colt's financial future.

TIMELINE: COLT AND THE GUN CONTROL CONTROVERSY

Date	Event
16-Oct-01	A federal appeals court rules that the Second Amendment gives individuals the right to bear arms.
08-Dec-99	Clinton and the Department of Housing and Urban Development prepare a national lawsuit for the violence and damage that guns have created in public housing projects.
12-Oct-99	In twin rulings, the Supreme Court lets stand laws barring nonviolent felons and those convicted of domestic abuse from possessing guns.
10-Oct-99	Faced with numerous handgun lawsuits, Colt Manufacturing Co. announces plans to curtail its retail gun business.
08-Oct-99	An Ohio state court judge throws out Cincinnati's lawsuit against the handgun industry. Cincinnati's city council later says it will appeal the ruling.

continued

███████████ CONTINUED

09-Sep-99   President Clinton announces a $15 million federal gun buy-back program.

12-Jul-99   The NAACP says it will sue handgun manufacturers, distributors, and importers, seeking restrictions on the marketing and sale of firearms.

20-May-99   By the narrowest of margins, the Senate passes a bill that approves locks on all new handguns and imposes tougher restrictions on gun show sales. The senators split 50-50, allowing Vice President Al Gore to use his constitutional power to break the tie in favor of the measure sponsored by Sen. Frank Lautenberg, D–N.J.

11-Feb-99   The Brooklyn jury in the *Hamilton v. Accu-tek* case determines that 15 of 25 handgun manufacturers negligently distributed their products.

27-Jan-99   Bridgeport, Connecticut, and Miami–Dade County, Florida, file separate suits against gun manufacturers to recover the costs they incurred due to gun violence.

04-Jan-99   A civil suit against gun manufacturers goes to trial in Brooklyn, New York.

05-Dec-98   President Clinton hails the new instant background checking system for gun purchases as a success, saying it has stopped 400 illegal buys. The National Rifle Association disputes the findings, saying the statistics are misleading.

01-Dec-98   National Rifle Association files a federal lawsuit to block the FBI from keeping records on gun buyers.

30-Nov-98   A nationwide system of instant background checks goes into effect, replacing the five-day waiting period on the purchase of handguns that was required in all states beginning in 1994.

17-Nov-98   A California jury dismisses a lawsuit against gun manufacturer Baretta. The family of a 14-year-old boy killed with a Baretta handgun by another boy sued the gun manufacturer for negligence.

13-Nov-98   President Clinton signs a measure to increase penalties for federal offenses committed with guns.

12-Nov-98   Chicago files a $433 million suit against gun shops, manufacturers, and distributors, claiming they conspired to provide guns to criminals by oversupplying local markets.

30-Oct-98   New Orleans sues gun manufacturers, trade associations, and local gun dealers to recover municipal costs associated with gun violence in the city.

01-Jul-98   The Senate defeats an amendment to require the sale of a trigger lock with every handgun sold in the United States.

21-Jun-98   The Justice Department reports that an estimated 69,000 handgun sales were blocked in 1997 by presale background checks. The rejections represented about 2.7 percent of the nearly 2.6 million applications for handgun purchases.

10-Jan-98   George Soros gives a $300,000 grant to ensure the *Hamilton* case gets into court.

17-Jul-97   The Florida Supreme Court affirms an $11.5 million jury verdict against Kmart for selling a gun to an intoxicated buyer who used it to shoot his estranged girlfriend.

27-Jun-97   The U.S. Supreme Court finds unconstitutional a portion of the Brady Handgun Violence Prevention Act requiring local law enforcement officials to conduct handgun background checks until a nationwide system is put in place.

continued

CONTINUED

05-Mar-96	In a novel ruling, Federal District Court Judge Jack B. Weinstein in Brooklyn, New York, says that victims of handgun violence may proceed with a lawsuit against the firearms industry to discover whether it failed to take adequate steps to prevent weapon sales to illegal buyers like teenagers. Several legal experts said the current case appeared to be the first that involves the industry's marketing practices.
01-Jan-96	Davis Industries files bankruptcy, alleging too many lawsuits.
01-Jan-95	Ms. Elisa Barnes files a lawsuit against the gun industry on behalf of Mrs. Hamilton. This case is known as the *Hamilton* case.
01-May-94	Pettit & Martin takes gun manufacturer to court.
28-Feb-94	Brady Handgun Violence Prevention Act, requiring a five-day waiting period for the purchase of a handgun, goes into effect.
30-Nov-93	The Brady bill is signed into law by President Clinton. The law was named after former White House Press Secretary James Brady, who was shot in the head during the 1981 assassination attempt on President Ronald Reagan. James Brady's wife, Sarah, heads Handgun Control Inc. (HCI), a highly influential 400,000-member organization that lobbies against gun ownership.
01-Jan-93	Shooting erupts in the law firm of Pettit & Martin, leaving several dead.
01-Jan-87	The Firearm Owners Protection Law repeals cross-state firearm sales prohibition (19- Jun-1968).
01-Jan-72	Alcohol, Tobacco, and Firearms (ATF) is created from a division within the IRS.
19-Jun-68	The Omnibus Crime Control & Safe Street Act, signed by President Johnson, prohibits firearm sales to criminals, fugitives, mentally incompetent persons, drug addicts, and illegal aliens. Cross-state firearm sales are also prohibited.
01-Jan-34	Federal controls are imposed on machine guns, sawed-off shotguns, and other dangerous devices by the National Firearms Act.
01-Jan-33	An assassination attempt is made on President Franklin Roosevelt.
01-Feb-14	The St. Valentine's Day massacre by underworld gangsters causes an uproar from citizens to curtail guns.
01-Jan-11	New York City passes the Sullivan law, which required a police permit for both owning and carrying a gun, after an attempted assassination of the governor of New York.

QUESTIONS

1. What is the controversy regarding "gun control" in the U.S.?
2. Who is "winning" (stands to gain) and who is "losing" (more likely to suffer) in this controversy?
3. Looking at the evolution of laws and litigation on gun control, what insights do you gain?
4. Are guns (firearms) a "dangerous" product like cigarettes? Explain.

5. Why has Colt managed to survive and succeed in its business? What does the company need to be concerned about now? Why?

6. Explain your position on private citizens being able to buy and use firearms.

CASE 12
WOMEN IN PUBLIC ACCOUNTING (AND OTHER PROFESSIONS): GENDER AND WORKPLACE OBSTACLES

The accounting profession has seen rapid growth in the percentage and number of women entering the profession over the past 15 years. However, this increase has not been appropriately reflected in the number of women who have penetrated the higher echelons of accounting firms, particularly the Big Six firms. Also, although a growing number of women are entering the profession, a significant number of women are leaving.

The retention of talented Certified Public Accountants (CPAs), many of whom are women, has become a critical issue for the Big Six. Firms allot a sizable amount of money to recruit, train, and develop CPAs. Deloitte and Touche noted that "companies that lose women employees recoup no long-term payback on their recruiting and training dollars, and there is no pot of gold at the end of the learning curve."[1] It is widely agreed that CPA firms that do not respond to the needs of increasing numbers of women will find themselves at a competitive disadvantage in the near future. As Joanne Alter observed, "Public accounting is a game of finding and keeping top talent. Half of that talent happens to be female. If we can keep these top people, we're at a competitive advantage."[2]

In 1977, 28 percent of all graduating accounting students were female. In 1991, that percentage increased to 50 percent.[3] By the year 2000, 60 percent of the entrants into the accounting profession will be female. However, in 1983, only 1 percent of partners and principals in what were then the Big Nine were women.[4] In 1990, the percentage had increased only to 3 percent, and was estimated to be about 5 percent in 1990 in the Big Six.[5]

Initially, one might conclude that the lack of women at the top may be the result of a time lag. It generally takes 10 to 12 years to be promoted to partner in the Big Six. Women began to permeate the profession just about 10 or 12 years ago. However, it does not appear that a time lag explains the low percentage of female partners. Accounting firms hired men and women in equal ratios during the 1980s; yet, after six to eight years, only two women remain for every three men in the same accounting class.[6] In addition, the American Women's Society of CPAs estimates that less than 20 percent of managerial positions are held by women; yet 40 percent of all women CPAs have been in the field for at least ten years.[7] In the CPA

Personnel Report, an annual survey of women in public accounting in 2001 found that 12.8 percent of partner-level positions at the nation's largest firms were occupied by women. This represents an increase of 11.7 percent over 2000. (Women's share of partnerships at large firms rises to 12.8%. Oct. 2001. *CPA Managing Partner Report* [Atlanta], 5.) These statements indicate the following: first, that women are leaving the profession after only a few years; and second, that those who stay are not being promoted at the same rate as men.

Until recently, there was little written on the issue of retention and promotion of women CPAs. However, during the last five years, an increasing number of surveys and articles have been published that address reasons why women are leaving the profession. There is also a growing awareness of this problem.

In 1984, the Accounting Institute of Certified Public Accountants (AICPA) Future Issues Committee identified the upward mobility of women in public accounting as one of the 14 major issues facing the profession. As a result, the Upward Mobility of Women Special Committee was formed and charged with identifying obstacles to the upward mobility of women CPAs and with recommending strategies to eliminate these obstacles in order to promote upward mobility of women in public accounting. This report was submitted to the AICPA Board of Directors in March 1988. Since then, several articles and studies have been published. Most of the literature appears in the national trade journals such as the *Journal of Accountancy* and the *Ohio CPA Journal*, as well as more regional publications.

ISSUES

The first issue raised is, Why are women leaving public accounting firms? One theory is that the profession is perceived by women to be irreconcilable with having a family. A 1989 New York Society of Public Accountants study demonstrated that 45 percent of more than 800 women CPAs surveyed found family responsibilities incompatible with their career in their present firm under its current policies.[8] Additionally, a 1988 survey conducted by the American Women's Society of CPAs suggested that the main reason women leave public accounting is scheduling demands that negatively impact their family life. Results from an industry survey showed that "about one third of the respondents indicated that their careers have had some adverse effect on either their marriages or on opportunities to marry . . . several [respondents] indicated that job considerations (such as overtime and stress) had influenced the decision not to have children."[9]

When the Management of Accounting Practice Committee of the AICPA asked a staff sample if they believed they could simultaneously attain partnership and be a parent, the results were startling. Eighty-one percent of the men surveyed said yes, while only 41 percent of the women said yes.

STRESS

Another factor that is thought to impact women CPAs' decision to leave public accounting is stress. A study published by the National Society of Public Accountants in 1983 found that women faced greater stress than men in the workplace. Women perceived that they were constantly being scrutinized by upper management—mainly male—and consequently they felt they had to perform better than their male counterparts.[10] The New York Society study found that an "estimated 49 percent of all women surveyed believed they were less accepted by partners than were males, while nearly half reported having fewer advancement opportunities than males."[11] This observation raises another issue: Are women in fact scrutinized more than their male counterparts; and are women discriminated against when considered for upper-level promotions?

OTHER OBSTACLES

It is helpful to examine the results of the study conducted by the AICPA's Upward Mobility of Women Special Committee. The Committee was composed of four men and four women. Their methodology included the following: review of relevant literature, analysis of statistics, interviews, distribution of questionnaires, and communications with other professional organizations.[12]

As previously mentioned, the Committee was charged with identifying the obstacles to women CPAs' upward mobility in public accounting. Having identified seven obstacles, the Committee stated that these were not unique to accounting, but rather were universal obstacles confronting women in the workplace in general.[13]

First, it was determined that outdated, negative ideas about women still exist in organizations. Often women are seen as dependents, not colleagues. Women are still referred to as "girls" or "ladies," and they are criticized for displaying traits such as aggressiveness, which is viewed as a positive trait in men. Overall, management tends to judge women as a group, while judging men as individuals.[14]

The Committee also identified a second obstacle, termed "the perception problem," in which employers deny that such attitudes still exist.

The third obstacle identified involved awareness of success criteria by women. The Committee felt that women receive less advice from superiors about how to achieve success within an organization. Women can identify personal traits required to succeed, but seem to have a hard time identifying the subtle criteria, such as visibility in the organization and projecting a successful self-image.

The fact that women still bear most of the responsibility for child care is also viewed as an obstacle. Marriage and family are viewed as a social asset for a man in an organization, yet these are considered a liability for women, and sometimes marriage and family can hinder advancement in a firm. Some women sense these obstacles and abandon getting married and having a family; others resent having to make such choices and leave public accounting instead.

NETWORKING

It was also noted that women do not participate as actively as men in professional organizations. Such networking can further careers through contacts.

Another obstacle that the Committee presented was the fact that some organizations appeared to have dating and marriage policies that discriminated unfairly against women.

Again, women face stress that results from facing all of the other obstacles. A woman still experiences more family pressures and organizational prejudice, and maintains the perception that, to succeed, her performance must exceed that of her male peers.

WOMEN IN OTHER PROFESSIONS

Many of the issues facing women in public accounting are not unique to the profession, but are experienced by women in the workforce in general. Literature on the subject of retention and promotion addresses women in the legal profession. In many ways, the accounting and legal professions are similar with regard to partnership structures and the increased entry of women into these fields in the past ten to fifteen years. Many of the issues faced by female lawyers are related to those experienced by women in public accounting. Many top law firms are increasingly facing the loss of talented women and are trying to address the situation.

Take the information technology (IT) industry. "According to the U.S. Bureau of Labor Statistics, the number of women computer professionals—computer-systems analysts, scientists and programmers—has grown to 710,000 in 2000 from 426,000 in 1990. However, the percentage of women in the profession has declined during the same years to 28.4% from 35.2%. Moreover, it appears that an increasing number of women are shying away from high tech. The most recent statistics from the U.S. Department of Education show that women received just 27% of computer-science degrees in 1998, down from 37% in 1984."[15]

Why is this the case? ". . . [F]rom a recent survey of women in high tech by Deloitte & Touche, the accounting firm, and pollster Roper Starch Worldwide: Three of every five women in IT would choose another profession if they could because of a perceived glass ceiling. Women surveyed by Deloitte and Roper say they're perceived as less knowledgeable and qualified than men. One woman surveyed says women have a tough time 'being taken seriously' in high tech. To advance in such a clubby atmosphere, women also must develop a rapport with their male bosses."[16]

A panel of female high-tech executives assembled by the Computing Technology Industry Association, based in Lombard, Illinois, were asked about the problem of women entering and staying in IT fields. Many women reportedly have misconceptions about high-tech careers. It seems they are afraid of getting stuck forever staring at a computer, writing lines of arcane programming code. "Women don't want to sit and talk to a computer," says Terry Taylor, a former senior vice president of field operations for Spherion Inc., a human-capital management company in Fort Lauderdale, Florida. "Women want more people interaction."[17]

Female professionals in general face a variety of challenges unique to their gender. Many of these are the result of generations of a male-dominated business world, a type of "old boy network." The passing of time is no longer an explanation for why women have not advanced in corporations. As one female executive in her mid-forties observed, "My generation came out of graduate school fifteen or twenty years ago. The men are now next in line to run major corporations. The women are not. Period."[18] A recent study by *Fortune* of the 1,000 largest U.S. industrial and service companies found that of the 4,012 people listed as the highest-paid officers and directors, only 19 were women. This is less than one-half of 1 percent. Although this is slightly higher that a similar study done in 1978, the results are hardly encouraging.

PRECONCEPTIONS AND POWER DIFFERENCES

The primary barriers to professional women are stereotyping and preconceptions. In a Fortune poll of 1,000 CEOs, 81 percent listed these factors as the main impediments to women's professional advancement. This is a subtle form of discrimination. For example, if one were to ask most male executives whether they were prejudiced against women, the answer would likely be no. However, when selecting an individual for a top job, males frequently choose men.

Corporate males are often uncomfortable dealing with women in the workplace. Negative feedback is often more difficult from men to women. One executive commented, "Men often worry women will run from the room in tears . . . they think they are yelling at their mothers or their wives . . . they just don't trust them as much as the guys with whom they talk football."[19] These stereotypes of women impede their success. For example, a strong male is seen as "aggressive" or "ambitious." An equally strong woman is often categorized as "abrasive" or even "bitchy." The same qualities in the different genders are regarded differently, especially by professional males in power.

THE PART-TIME STIGMA

Difficulties and disadvantages in climbing the corporate ladder are also encountered by professional women who have chosen to work part-time for a period of time. One law firm believed that promoting women who have worked part-time to partnership sent a message that the firm was not "demanding an equal commitment to the firm . . . [it] would be telling all of [its] associates that [it] no longer values motivation and dedication."[20] However, the firm also realized that "the rules must change because the game has changed."[21] Firms need to "redefine the word *commitment* to mean whatever it takes to meet client needs—not a particular number of hours spent at the office."[22]

Firms realize the investment in female employees. As one CEO affirmed, "It seems idiotic if we're investing in people but making it impossible for them to advance. Are we sending out signals that women need not aspire to the top?" One male executive noted that "the question should not be what's wrong with a woman who doesn't want to work twelve-hour days, but what's wrong with a man who does—and a culture that applauds, glorifies, promotes people who put their jobs before their families. . . . This penchant for promotions via overtime reflects an assumption that those willing to work long hours are the best and the brightest, but maybe the ones willing to work long hours are just the ones willing to work long hours. . . . What if we discover the answer to moving American commerce and industry ahead is finding those smart enough not to work twelve-hour days and turning the reins of business over to them?"[23]

RECOMMENDATIONS FOR CHANGE

Even though Deloitte & Touche reportedly plans to double the number of women partners in the U.S. firm by 2005, to 35 percent, up from the current 18%,[24] the issues identified above regarding the recruitment and retention of women in the accounting profession must be addressed by national and local associations as well as by the leading companies in the field that set the example and trends.

CHANGE SALARY DISPARITIES

 "The 2001 Salary Survey from CareerBank.com polled 1,500 accounting, finance and banking professionals on how much they make, what degrees they possess and why they left their last job. Among entry level accountants, 54% of women are making less than $30,000. The same percent of men are making between $30,000 and $70,000 per year."[25]

Moreover, the same survey found that of the entry- to mid-level staff accountants surveyed, the majority of men (70 percent) and women (85 percent) make between $30,000 and $50,000 annually.[26] "'In many cases, the Salary Survey shows a significant difference in the salaries of men and women even when they are at the same level on the corporate ladder,' said CareerBank president and chief executive Robert Epstein. 'Why are women so often making less than men in this profession? Why are men more likely to have an MBA?'"[27]

It was also found that 56 percent of those surveyed earned a bachelor's degree and 28 percent have a master's degree. Fifty-five percent of men and 57 percent of women completed undergraduate studies. Seventy percent of men have a master's degree, while only 30 percent of women have that degree. Thirty-one percent of respondents said that they left their last job because they were not earning enough; 30 percent said it was for a career change.[28]

Interestingly, the surveyors concluded, "We certainly don't know all of the answers to the questions raised by this survey, but we hope the results serve as a starting point for a discussion of these issues within the industry." (Ibid.) We suggest some recommendations below based on other surveys and studies in this area. Specific recommendations for the public accounting industry, in particular, are offered by the AICPA Special Committee. These recommendations may also apply to other professions. The Committee suggested that employers establish a mentoring process to encourage training and guidance of talented women. The Committee also recommended that open discussions be held by firms on the issue of upward mobility, that organizations rid their publications and policies of sexist materials and references, and that constructive steps to deal with pregnancy and child care issues be mandated.

The Committee's recommendations to women included increasing participation in the AICPA and state societies; becoming more involved in office activities, such as business luncheons and meetings with clients; and joining support groups.

Recommendations to the AICPA itself included monitoring trends and continuing to compile more information on the upward mobility of women CPAs. Also, appointing more women to AICPA committees, boards, and the Council, and studying and reporting on the effect of stress on female CPAs related to career advancement should be priorities.

CPA Rebeka Joy Maupin, in her article "Why Are There So Few Women CPA Partners?"[29] offers more in-depth explanations for women's problems in professions. She presents two types of perspectives used to account for the scarcity of women in partnership positions: the person-centered perspective and the situation-centered perspective.

THE PERSON-CENTERED VERSUS THE SITUATION-CENTERED PERSPECTIVE

The person-centered perspective suggests that female socialization in our culture encourages the development of personality traits and behavior patterns that are contrary to the demands of a managerial role. This view asserts that a man will be more committed to his work than a woman because a female is socialized to choose her family if a conflict arises. Furthermore, even if a woman makes an equal initial commitment, the many demands she faces, with more intensity than her male counterpart, may encourage her incapability of maintaining her commitment. Because of extended socialization, women often lack the requisite managerial skills and traits and behave in a different manner than men in managerial positions.

In contrast, the situation-centered perspective emphasizes that the characteristics of an organization shape and define a women's behavior on jobs. For example, when women are viewed as a token group in an organization, three negative outcomes result: (1) visibility, which creates perceived performance pressures on the token group, (2) contrast, which exaggerates the differences between the groups and results in isolation of the token group from nonwork activities; and (3) assimilation, where the dominant group (males) assigns stereotypes to the token group to accept them.

Maupin administered a survey to 700 AICPA members (350 men and 350 women), using a questionnaire describing these two separate explanations for the problem. The results illustrated that men disproportionately emphasized the person-centered perspective, assigning blame to women's personal and social traits. Women emphasized both perspectives, recognizing women's responsibility, as well as organizational responsibility, for the problem.

Those who subscribe to the person-centered explanation believe the solution lies with women. Those who aspire to top management might develop more "male-oriented" behavior patterns and suppress or eliminate attitudes and behaviors identified as "typically female." Women can be resocialized to compete with men on an equal basis if they are taught traditional male-oriented skills.

Disturbingly, some studies suggest that some women who have reached the upper echelons resemble males in power, demonstrating "old boy network" aggressiveness and dominance.

Maupin supports further exploration of the situation-centered hypothesis. She cites a need to "critically appraise current organizational barriers for women" and cautions that conforming to the person-centered perspective and acquiring the appropriate skills and traits "may do nothing to reduce the hostility that women face on the job or mitigate the fact that they may be in token positions."[30]

WHY CHANGE?

Many of the findings in Deloitte & Touche's (D & T) special report team bulletin "Women in the 90's: A Business Imperative" are still valid. In that issue, Ellen Gabriel, D & T's national director for the advancement of women, wrote that if firms do not see the ethical, legal, or moral arguments for advancing women, sheer business reasons should be enough. She stated that the combination of three factors—(1) the percentage of men available in labor pool is declining; (2) global businesses will continue to prosper, creating labor needs; and (3) low birth rates in the 1970s will result in a growth in the population of less than 1 percent per year through the following decades—should motivate firms to accommodate talented women and promote their retention.

SOLUTIONS?

First, it is imperative that firms recognize a problem exists and take steps to resolve it through formal programs. Much of the literature implies that the first step in creating a formal program is for firms to articulate a stated, solid commitment to support women employees and to seek solutions to their problems. The MAP survey mentioned earlier found that although half of the staff respondents to the survey favored the implementation of flex-time and sabbaticals for parents who opt to take a slower path to partnership, they would hesitate to take advantage of such programs for fear that it would still impact their advancement in the long run. The message is that even if employers establish policies to address women professionals' problems, companies must also assure employees that the organization supports these employees. Second, employers can survey employees to identify their needs and ask what would make it easier to continue working in the current organization. Third, flexible schedules such as part-time or work-at-home programs can be offered. Child care options can be provided. Concrete guidelines on advancement paths within the firm (i.e., partnership requirements) can be explicitly published. Mentor programs for women can be created. Delayed and nonpartnership tracks for those who may not be able to meet the traditional partner track advancement can be established.

Firms need to recognize the urgency of these problems and take concrete steps to help women in need and at risk. Companies can address these issues openly and offer comprehensive goals for advancement. Firms can no longer address these problems on a piecemeal basis because if follow-through is lacking, expectations are raised, then dashed.

The high turnover rate in public accounting costs firms money and resources. As noted by Big Six CPA firm Deloitte & Touche, companies willing to address these issues are finding the results worth the cost. All the differences that now hold women back in the corporate workplace are remedial—and at a cost that is infinitesimal compared with the devastating cost of continuing to bury their talent. As one female CPA stated in an interview, "In a ferociously competitive global economy, no company can afford to waste valuable brainpower, simply because it's wearing a skirt." However, in the meantime, in order to strive to achieve corporate advancements, women may have to follow what has, unfortunately, been the American female's formula for success: "Look like a lady; act like a man; work like a dog."

QUESTIONS FOR DISCUSSION

1. Why are there so few women CPA partners? Is this phenomenon unique to accounting firms?
2. What are some major obstacles that prevent women in public accounting and other professions from advancing to top-level positions?

3. Identify the person- and situation-centered perspectives regarding women's roles in the workplace. Comment on whether or not you find these perspectives of value, and why.

4. Discuss some solutions that companies and women can use to help advance their career paths to top-level positions.

5. Evaluate the validity of this statement as a success criterion from your perspective: "Look like a lady; act like a man; work like a dog."

6. Is there an "equal and level playing field" for women in most professions? Explain your point of view.

CASE 13
DOUBLECLICK'S BATTLE OVER ON-LINE PRIVACY

Ad sales house DoubleClick has signed up to the Safe Harbor agreement in the US as part of its ongoing efforts to repair an image damaged by claims over the company's privacy standards. Safe Harbor, a system designed to ensure US companies meet data protection standards laid down by the European Union, has only attracted around 100 members including Intel and Microsoft (Gale Group Inc., 2001).

INTRODUCTION

In the wake of the September 11 terrorist attacks . . . Privacy advocates have trouble mustering a case against government plans to intelligently link their databases with those of the State Dept. and the FBI to help prevent terrorist suspects from entering the country (*Business Week* Online, 2001). After September 11, how many Americans will really complain if they are thoroughly checked out before boarding an airplane? In the new America, no one can afford to be a privacy absolutist. That doesn't mean that the battle over privacy rights is over, however. In the next few months, the government will be making dozens of critical decisions about who has access to what data and how it will be scanned, sorted, and linked. That's why now, more than ever, it's essential to strike a balance between security and the right to be left alone (Black, 2001).

On June 14, 1999, DoubleClick Incorporated (http://www.doubleclick.com), a global Internet advertising solutions firm, announced its plans to acquire market researcher Abacus Direct (http://www.abacusonline.com) in a $1 billion stock swap deal. Under the terms of the agreement, e-commerce sites in DoubleClick's extensive network would be correlated with the names and addresses in Abacus's database of consumer catalog shoppers. The resulting database of several billion consumer profiles would link personally identifiable information, including names, addresses, and other personal details, with individual on-line and catalog buying habits. What followed the announcement was a storm of protest from consumer groups and privacy advocates from around the country and the international community. The ethical and legal implications pushed the issue to the forefront of the public's consciousness, resulting in a flurry of legal activity, including class action lawsuits and proposed state and federal legislation.

BACKGROUND

TECHNOLOGY. At the core of the privacy and consumer profiling issue is the underlying Internet technology that enables DoubleClick and competing Web-based advertisers to gather information about on-line consumers and use this data to deliver targeted advertisements. To gather personal information, DoubleClick uses cookies, small data files written to the users' hard drives by certain Websites when they are viewed in the users' browsers. These data files contain information that can be used by that site in order to track such information as passwords, sites that the user has visited, and the date that a user last viewed a particular page (http://coverate.cnet.com/Resources/Info/Glossary/Terms/cookie.html). Although cookies can be used for benign purposes such as keeping track of on-line purchases, DoubleClick and other advertisers read and write cookies on users' PCs when they visit Web pages containing one of their banner ads. This practice enables the advertisers to store the "clickstream" of user activities, showing exactly what sites consumers visit and in what order.

According to the *Wall Street Journal*, the ease by which advertisers obtain this information is a result of the Web's open structure. Originally designed to allow small groups of global scientists to share information, the Web has retained this open structure despite the technology's widespread proliferation, making user information intrinsically vulnerable.

PROPOSED MERGER. Prior to June of 1999, DoubleClick operated an advertising network of over 1,300 Websites. The company's DART system employed cookies to track users' Internet surfing habits in order to deliver targeted advertisements to consumers visiting sites within its network. According to DoubleClick's privacy policy posted on its Website, the company promised not to collect any personally identifiable information about consumers:

> DoubleClick does not know the name, email address, phone number, or home address of anybody who visits a site in the DoubleClick Network. All users who receive an ad targeted by DoubleClick's technology remain completely anonymous. Since we do not have any information concerning names or addresses, we do not sell or rent any such information to third parties. Because of our efforts to keep users anonymous, the information DoubleClick has is useful only across the DoubleClick Network, and only in the context of ad selection (Junkbusters, 2000).

On June 14, 1999, DoubleClick announced its intended merger with market researching firm Abacus Direct. As a result of the merger, the e-commerce sites in DoubleClick's advertising network could correlate the names and addresses of Internet consumers and the Abacus Alliance buying-habit database, which contains information from over two billion consumer catalog purchases. Prior to the merger, DoubleClick was able to identify a user with a DoubleClick cookie and send that user a targeted advertisement based on his or her Web-browsing activity. With the creation of the Abacus Alliance, DoubleClick would have a great deal more information about that user if he or she has given personal information to a member of the Alliance and could advise those companies to target the user with Internet ads instead of catalogs. Over the next several months, consumer groups and privacy advocates fervently protested the merger of the two companies, citing fears that DoubleClick could now correlate personal information with its 100 million cookies, creating a database with extensive personal information and violating consumers' on-line privacy.

Although DoubleClick does not inform users when they are sent a DoubleClick cookie unless their browser is preset to do so, consumers are able to opt out and receive a blank cookie through the company's Website. Because this blank cookie is not associated with any personal information, DoubleClick will not send these users targeted ads, nor will the company be able to identify these users on-line. Most on-line marketers have adopted a model called opt-in, which requires that the merchant obtain the consumer's explicit consent before gathering any personal information. Others, such as NetCreations, offer consumers an even more secure measure called the double opt-in. Under this scenario, the on-line marketer takes consent one step further by sending consumers e-mail messages confirming their requests.

In May 2000, DoubleClick took yet another step to protect its image and on-line users' privacy. It set up an independent board. The concept of an independent privacy body is nothing new to the private sector. Responding to harsh criticisms from consumers and the press, DoubleClick and Predictive Networks, a Massachusetts company that tracks Internet users and develops behavior models, both established independent privacy boards in May, 2000. Predictive's software was accused by The Wall Street Journal of pushing "digital eavesdropping to a new level."

The criticisms from the press were a wake-up call to Predictive Networks founder and CEO, Devin Hosea, who stated,"'Although we felt from a technical point of view that we were privacy-friendly, we hadn't done a good job telling the public that we were monitoring ourselves,' he says" (Black, 2001).

ISSUES

CONSUMER PRIVACY.   According to DoubleClick's new privacy policy, the company maintains that the correlation of the information collected by the advertiser's cookies and Abacus's database of off-line catalog purchases will be used for the sole purpose of targeting advertisements to specific households. DoubleClick has also stated that it will not associate any personally identifiable information regarding medical history, financial history, or sexual preference, nor will it profile children under the age of 13. However, these statements do not alleviate privacy advocates' concerns that the information collected about consumers will be used for purposes other than advertising. For example, such information would be fair game for a subpoena in a civil or criminal court case.

UNFAMILIARITY WITH TECHNOLOGY. Although DoubleClick and most other Internet advertisers who use cookies allow consumers to elect not to receive them, many Internet users do not understand the underlying technology. As a result, many consumers are unaware that when they make on-line purchases from companies within the DoubleClick network, their personal information may be shared with others in the company's vast database. Of particular concern is the use of third-party cookies. Most Internet users do not understand that banner ads from third-party advertisers may contain cookies from companies like DoubleClick. Although a company may post an elaborate privacy policy on its Website, this policy may not clearly state that third parties also may be using cookies to collect data about site visitors. "The analogy would be if Sears were to post a warning on its doors that surveillance cameras are used to deter crime and track down thieves, but the notice failed to mention that a vacuum cleaner company also has installed video cameras to monitor the habits of Sears' shoppers" (Goodin, 1999).

DECLINE IN E-COMMERCE. Consumers' lack of familiarity with Internet technology coupled with the negative media coverage of consumer profiling could lead to a decline in the growth of e-commerce. For example, a study conducted by research firm Jupiter Communications found that 64 percent of Internet users do not trust the sites they visit, regardless of whether or not those sites have posted policies on privacy. The same study states that the $40 billion in e-commerce sales projected for 2002 could be cut by almost 50 percent, or $18 billion, if consumers' privacy concerns are not alleviated (Goodin, 1999).

RESPONSE TO THE MERGER

CONSUMER ADVOCACY AND PRIVACY GROUPS. The announcement of DoubleClick's intended acquisition of Abacus Direct in a stock swap deal alarmed consumer advocacy and privacy groups. Critics contended that consumers should have more control over with whom their contact information is shared and how it is used, stating that self-regulation is ineffective. Jason Catlett, president of the privacy advocacy firm Junkbusters, commented, "This merger is the most dangerous assault against anonymity on the Internet since the Intel Processor Serial Number.[1] By synchronizing cookies with name and address from email, registrations and eCommerce transactions, the merged company would have a surveillance database of Orwellian proportions" (quoted in Junkbusters, 2000).

On June 21, 1999, privacy advocates sent an open letter to Kevin O'Connor, CEO of DoubleClick, and the CEO of Abacus, asking them to abandon the $1 billion proposed merger. The letter stated, "We write to urge you to abandon the proposed merger of your companies on the grounds that it would severely undermine the privacy of Internet users" (Marinaccio, June 21, 1999).

Consumer advocates sent a second letter to the stockholders of Abacus Direct on June 29, 1999, pleading with them to not to approve the merger on grounds that it could potentially violate international privacy protection laws. The letter cited a European Union privacy directive that prohibits the transfer of data from EU members to countries or companies that do not adequately protect personal data or obtain proper consent prior to sharing this data with others. The letter threatened, "Privacy International, a human rights organization based in London, now regards DoubleClick as an outstanding choice for its planned actions to enjoin illegal trans-Atlantic data flows" (Macavinta, June 29, 1999).

In July of 1999, a coalition of privacy advocates drafted a petition to the Federal Trade Commission (FTC), urging Congress to adopt legislation to protect consumers' fundamental privacy rights and safeguard their personal information on the Internet. Members of the group included the Center for Media Education, Electronic Privacy Information Center (EPIC), Junkbusters, Privacy Times, Privacy International, and Privacy Rights Clearinghouse. In response, the four-member commission of the FTC issued a report, recommending to Congress that no new legislation regarding Web privacy was necessary at the present time. According to the report, "Self-regulation is the least intrusive and most efficient means to ensure fair information practices, given the rapidly evolving nature of the Internet and computer technology" (Junkbusters, 2000). This report contradicted the FTC's statement one year earlier that it planned to desert the Clinton administration's position favoring industry self-regulation for the pursuit of legislation to ensure Internet privacy (*New York Times*, Sept. 21, 2000).

As a last-minute attempt to block the merger of DoubleClick and Abacus, in November consumer groups sent letters to "so-called socially responsible mutual funds" such as the Citizens Emerging Growth Fund, Dreyfus Third Century Fund, and Smith Barney Concert Social Awareness Fund, urging them to remove both companies from their portfolios. "Divest any holdings of DoubleClick and Abacus Direct as soon as possible. Add DoubleClick and Abacus to 'screening' lists of companies that are to be excluded from investment based on social criteria, specifically a disregard for human rights," the letter stated (quoted in Macavinta, Nov. 22, 1999).

On February 1, 2000, after the merger between DoubleClick and Abacus was completed and DoubleClick changed its privacy policy, The Center for Democracy and Technology (CDT) launched an e-mail campaign against DoubleClick. CDT encouraged consumers to e-mail complaints about the company's new privacy policy, allowing for the correlation of the company's cookies with personally identifiable information for DoubleClick and 60 of its major customers (Hansen, Feb. 2, 2000). Designed to raise consumer awareness about the profiling issue, the e-mail blast put both DoubleClick and its customers on the defensive.

One month later, CDT filed a report with the FTC, alleging potential privacy violations in DoubleClick's data collection practices. According to Ari Schwartz, a CDT representative, "Companies could be transporting information that could be possibly used by DoubleClick in a personally identifiable way without the companies' knowledge. [They] could be violating their own privacy policy without knowing it" (Hu, March 1, 2000).

DOUBLE CLICK/ABACUS DIRECT. In response to consumer groups' criticism upon the announcement of the DoubleClick/Abacus merger, DoubleClick CEO Kevin O'Connor stated that the company would continue to respect consumer privacy issues by giving people the option of removing themselves from the company's databases. Consumer groups requested that the company shift from an opt-out to an opt-in strategy; DoubleClick said it would listen to consumer concerns but was unlikely to change to opt-in status (Macavinta, June 14, 2000). According to Kevin Ryan, DoubleClick's president, there was little demand from consumers for prior consent. Of the 75 million people per month who viewed ads from the DoubleClick Network, approximately 30 of them chose to remove the DoubleClick cookie (Macavinta, June 15, 2000).

In order to fend off potential Internet privacy legislation, in July of 1999, DoubleClick and eight other leading Internet companies formed NetCoalition.com. The group, which also included America Online, Yahoo, and Amazon.com, formed to represent the interests of the Internet industry and attempt to influence potential legislation that would regulate the Internet and potentially curb growth (Reuters, July 12, 1999). As of October 6, 1999, there were over 75 pieces of legislation pending that would regulate the Internet in some way, most seeking to protect consumers. The majority of these bills had been referred to committees and stayed there (Goodin, 1999).

On November 8, 1999, Privacy & American Business, a nonpartisan think tank, released the results of a survey underwritten by DoubleClick regarding the effect of profiling on consumers. According to the study, "Personalized Marketing and Privacy on the Net: What Consumers Want," 61 percent of those surveyed were interested in receiving personalized banner advertisements. The study also found that approximately 60 percent would consent to having their off-line transactions used for targeted marketing purposes so long as they were adequately informed beforehand and given the opportunity to opt out if they did not agree (Macavinta, Nov. 8, 1999).

In order to defend itself against privacy critics, on December 9, 1999, DoubleClick named Josh Isay, then chief of staff to New York Senator Charles Schumer, director of public policy and government affairs. In this capacity, Schumer was to represent the company's legal interest, both domestically and globally, and coordinate the company's industry efforts on matters related to public policy (Balderama, Dec. 9, 1999).

Contradicting its early privacy statements, in January of 2000, DoubleClick announced that it was creating a network of Websites in order to track Internet users' shopping habits and personal data. According to the company's new privacy policy, DoubleClick would use this information to build a database of consumer profiles, including consumers' names; addresses; retail, catalog, and on-line purchase histories; and demographic data. The company's plans for the correlation of personal information confirmed consumer advocates' earlier fears.

In response to criticism and protests by consumer advocates, DoubleClick announced a series of steps to restore its reputation on February 14, 2000. DoubleClick launched an educational Website, www.privacychoices.org, to educate users about on-line privacy and simplify the company's opt-out process. The company also announced that it would accept advertisements only from companies with data collection policies (although it would not set guidelines for these policies) and that it would hire outside auditors to ensure that the company was complying with its own privacy standards. However, DoubleClick's initiatives were inadequate, according to privacy advocates. "DoubleClick is launching an advertising campaign because they're trying desperately to avoid legislation that would make it illegal to assign cookies without prior consent," said Mark Rotenberg, executive director of EPIC (Jacobus, Feb. 14, 2000).

LEGISLATION/LITIGATION. As a result of all of the consumer and media attention to on-line privacy, the FTC passed the Children's Online Privacy Protection Act (COPPA) on October 20, 1999, the first legislation enacted to protect consumer privacy on the Internet. Under the terms stipulated by COPPA, on-line advertisers will not be able to gather data about Internet users under the age of 13 without first obtaining written parental consent. Although the law was seen as a victory for privacy advocates, some raised concerns over the limited scope of the law. "Americans should not lose all privacy rights online the day they turn 13," said Catlett of Junkbusters (quoted in Junkbusters, 2000).

On November 8, 1999, the FTC scheduled a one-day hearing regarding the practice of on-line profiling. The hearing came in response to petitions from consumer and privacy advocacy groups stating that the data collection practices of companies such as RealNetworks and DoubleClick increased the probability of corporate abuse of consumer data (Hansen, Nov. 5, 1999). In his opening remarks, FTC Chairman Robert Pitofsky stated, "The use of conventional demographic information by advertisers to target consumers most likely to be interested in their products and services is a staple of the advertising industry and does not raise any eyebrows. Online profiling, however, looks like it may be a very different beast. On a personal level, I find this more than a bit disturbing." (Macavinta, Nov. 8, 1999).

On January 27, 2000, Hariett Judnick filed suit against DoubleClick in the California Superior Court of Marin County, accusing the company of "unlawfully obtaining and selling consumers' private information." The suit alleged that DoubleClick had represented to the general public that it was not collecting personal data and identifying information and that it considered consumer privacy issues to be of the utmost importance. The suit also alleged that the company had used its powerful cookie technology to create a "sophisticated and highly intrusive means of collecting and cross-referencing private personal information without the knowing consent of Internet users." The plaintiff's lawyers requested an injunction against DoubleClick that would stop the company from using cookies to collect personal information without first obtaining written consent from the consumer (Jacobus, Feb. 14, 2000). Several other class action lawsuits were also filed over the next several months.

As the profiling backlash gained momentum, Congress began to devote more attention to the issue. On February 10, 2000, Senator Robert Torricelli, D–N.J., introduced a bill that would require companies to obtain permission from consumers before collecting their personal information on-line. The senator's bill specifically targeted the use of cookies by on-line advertisers. According to Torricelli, "The fundamental right to privacy should not be sacrificed in the Information Age" (Jacobus, Feb. 11, 2000).

On February 14, EPIC filed a complaint with the FTC, charging DoubleClick with engaging in unfair and deceptive trade practices. EPIC asked that the advertising firm refrain from collecting personal information using cookies without first obtaining consumers' informed consent. The company also requested that the FTC assign civil penalties to DoubleClick, amounting to 50 percent of the company's revenue.

In addition to the FTC inquiry, Michigan Attorney General Jennifer Granholm filed a consumer protection lawsuit against DoubleClick on February 17, 2000, alleging that the company was in violation of Michigan's Consumer Protection Act. "Forget Big Brother. Truly Big Browser appears to have arrived in the form of an Internet corporate giant. Companies like DoubleClick take advantage of the technology to rob people of their privacy," said Granholm in a statement. On the same day, New York Attorney General Elliot Spitzer launched an informal inquiry into the company's data collection practices. As a result of the litigation, DoubleClick's stock price fell $15.75 to $90.75, down from an earlier high of $135 (Jacobus, Feb. 17, 2000). Separately, the attorneys general of New York, Connecticut, and Vermont filed suit against the on-line marketing engine.

CUSTOMERS. Fallout from DoubleClick's handling of the privacy issue continued in March of 2000 as the company's partners began to distance themselves from the on-line advertiser. AltaVista decided to limit the release of its customer information to DoubleClick, and Kozmo, an Internet home-delivery service, initiated steps to terminate its relationship with the company (Reuters, March 1, 2000). The Website drkoop.com also reevaluated its relationship with DoubleClick and opted to pull its advertisements from the company's network.

Also in March, DoubleClick customer Intuit discovered that information on the users of its Quicken Website had inadvertently been supplied to DoubleClick. Within two hours of the discovery, Intuit pulled the advertisements supplied by DoubleClick in Intuit's loan and mortgage sections because of the company's contract with the advertiser that prohibits them from gathering any personally identifiable data from Intuit's sites. Information that users had input into the mortgage and credit-assessment calculators on Quicken.com, including annual salary data and total assets, was being sent to DoubleClick. According to Richard Smith, an Internet security consultant, DoubleClick should have been able to notice this problem and been "more proactive about getting sites to fix it" (Junnarkar, March 2, 2000).

BLOCKING SOFTWARE COMPANIES. The growth of consumer privacy fears sparked by the DoubleClick media feeding frenzy created a market opportunity for software companies. Such companies began to develop programs to block advertisements and cookies sent by on-line marketers. On February 8, 2000, AdSubtract of Braintree, Massachusetts, announced the creation of AdSubtract SE, which specifically targeted ads and cookies assigned by DoubleClick. According to AdSubtract's president, Ed English, the company specifically targeted DoubleClick because it was "the most aggressive about profiling." Other companies developed blocking devices, including Junkbusters and Seimans' WebWasher program (Jacobus, Feb. 8, 2000).

COMPETITORS. In September of 1999, DoubleClick's competitor AdForce ran a series of ads with the tagline "You've just been Double Clicked," claiming that DoubleClick had supplied confidential information about its own customers to AdForce's competitors. DoubleClick filed suit over the advertisements. In response to the lawsuit, AdForce modified its ads but continued to run them. The lawsuit was subsequently settled with a stipulated injunction (Junkbusters 2000).

OrbDigital, an on-line ad-tracking company that does not use cookies, also used the backlash against DoubleClick and cookie technology as a marketing opportunity. OrbDigital ran a full-page advertisement in the *Wall Street Journal* with the tagline "Don't get caught with your hand in the cookie jar!" By positioning themselves as "privacy friendly," these competing on-line advertisers were attempting to distinguish themselves from DoubleClick in order to gain market share.

DOUBLECLICK POSTPONES PLANS

On March 2, 2000, DoubleClick yielded to the pressure from consumer groups, privacy advocates, possible legislation, and pending litigation and announced that the company would postpone its plans to correlate its cookies with the personal information from the Abacus database of consumer buying habits. DoubleClick CEO Kevin O'Connor explained that the decision was a response to the feedback the company had received from hundreds of consumers about the company's plan to create a database of consumer profiles containing personal information. "It is clear. . . . I made a mistake by planning to merge names with anonymous user activity across Web sites in the absence of government and industry privacy standards." At the time of the announcement, DoubleClick's stock was trading at $79.81, down from its earlier high of $135 on January 3 (Hansen, March 2, 2000).

On March 8, the company announced the hiring of two consumer advocates: Jules Polonetsky, consumer affairs commissioner to Rudolph Giuliani, mayor of New York City, and Bob Abrams, former attorney general of New York State. Polonetsky and Abrams were appointed DoubleClick's chief privacy officer and chair of the company's Privacy Advisory Board, respectively (Hu, March 8, 2000). The new staff members were expected to lead DoubleClick's ongoing on-line privacy efforts.

DoubleClick entered into settlement discussions with several states and the FTC over its method of on-line data collection. Michigan, New York, Connecticut, and Vermont held discussions with the company over alleged violations of consumer privacy. Both sides of the debate prepared proposals for "an Internet protocol that will address privacy concerns." All parties involved declined to describe the various settlement proposals, although DoubleClick continued to defend its business practices ("DoubleClick in settlement discussions," March 23, 2000).

NEXT STEPS FOR CONSUMER PRIVACY

The DoubleClick controversy has captured the attention of consumers, the media, and lawmakers alike. Although the Clinton administration favored self-regulation, the backlash over the DoubleClick/Abacus Direct merger prompted the introduction of new bills designed to protect consumer privacy. Such legislation can have widespread consequences for e-commerce as a whole. Certainly, the ramifications of the case are being felt across the industry. DoubleClick has stated that it will not correlate personal information with its cookies without government and industry privacy standards. Privacy policies have become standard for e-commerce companies. Software companies are scrambling to develop blocking software that will prevent cookies from targeting on-line consumers.

For example, in the summer of 2000, the World Wide Web Consortium (W3C) piloted a new technology standard that enabled Internet surfers to determine the amount of personal information they would release to Websites. The project, the Platform for Privacy Preferences (P3P), sets technical specifications that allow Internet users to specify their preferences in browser settings.

DoubleClick will have to wait and see whether legislation or industry standards will be introduced to regulate its ability to collect consumer information on-line. As noted in the opening statement, the company signed on in 2001 to the Safe Harbor agreement in the United States as part of ongoing efforts to control damage to its image, which was battered with claims regarding the company's privacy standards. Safe Harbor is a system designed to ensure that American companies meet data protection standards set by the European Union. The September 11 event and how the federal government handles privacy issues in general could affect the company's outlook and practices over this issue. For example, "[t]he Bush Administration also appears to be putting privacy concerns on the back burner. On Oct. 4, Timothy Muris, the new head of the Federal Trade Commission, which oversees privacy efforts in the commercial sector, announced that it would repeal calls for tough new privacy laws. Instead, it would focus on improving enforcement and educating the public" (Black, 2001). Regardless of the outcome, DoubleClick has forever changed the face of e-commerce.

QUESTIONS

1. Has DoubleClick acted responsibly and ethically or not? Explain.

2. What specifically do you recommend DoubleClick do, if anything, to protect consumers' privacy?

3. Identify DoubleClick's stakeholders and their stakes, as well as DoubleClick's stake.

4. Select an issues framework from Chapter 2, and identify the issues and how they have evolved for DoubleClick.

5. Do you believe from the case that DoubleClick could have done more on the privacy issue, considering what the national, state, and local governments require and what competitors in the industry have done? Explain.

6. Using what you learned from your answers to Questions 3 and 4, readdress Question 1. Is your answer to that question now still the same? Explain.

REFERENCES

A turning point for e-privacy. (March 4, 2000). Wired News, http://www.wired.com/news/print/0,1294,34734,00.html.

Adauction to change name, receive CMGI investment. (April 14, 2000). CNET News.Com, http://news.cnet.com/news/0-1007-200-1697744.html?tag=st.ne.1002.

Attorneys general strive for Net privacy, crime solutions. (March 24, 2000). Reuters. CNET News.Com, http://news.cnet.com/news/0-1005-200-1583993.html?tag=st.cn.1..

Are security fears running ahead of reality? (Feb. 28, 2000). CNET News.Com, http://news.cnet.com/news/0-1005-200-1558696.html?tag=st.ne.ni.rnbot.rn.

Black, J. (October 18, 2001). A federal privacy commission? That's right. *Business Week* Online, www.businessweek.com:/print/bwdaily/dnflas.../nf20011018_5933.htm, 1.

Blocking software firms to release new programs. (Feb. 8, 2000). CNET News.Com, http://news.cnet.com/news/0-1005-200-1544438.html?tag=st.cn.1..

Business Week Online. (Oct. 12, 2001). The immigration laws' bureaucratic Babel.

Consumer advocates to head DoubleClick privacy efforts. (March 8, 2000). CNET News.Com, http://news.cnet.com/news/0-1005-200-1566622.html?tag=st.cn.1..

Consumer group to fight DoubleClick deal. (June 14, 1999). CNET News.Com, http://news.cnet.com/news/0-1007-200-343608.html.

DoubleClick Gets Double Trouble with Database Plan. (March 6, 2000). *InformationWeek* Online, http://www.techweb.com/se/directlink.cgi?IWK20000306S0014..

DoubleClick held at arm's length by partners. (March 1, 2000). Reuters. CNET News.Com, http://news.cnet.com/news/0-1005-200-1561080.html?tag=st.cn.1..

DoubleClick in settlement discussions. (March 23, 2000). Bloomberg News. CNET News.Com, http://news.cnet.com/news/0-1005-200-1582990.html?tag=st.cn.1..

DoubleClick launches privacy education program amid criticism. (Feb. 14, 2000). CNET News.Com, http://news.cnet.com/news/0-1005-201-1549798-0.html?tag=st.cn.1..

DoubleClick matches Wall Street forecasts. (April 17, 2000). CNET News.Com, http://news.cnet.com/news/0-1005-200-1708626.html?tag=st.ne.1002.

DoubleClick not worried about privacy charges. (June 15, 1999). CNET News.Com, http://news.cnet.com/news/0-1007-200-343680.html?tag=st.cn.1..

DoubleClick postpones data-merging plan. (March 2, 2000). CNET News.Com, http://news.cnet.com/news/0-1005-200-1562746.html?tag=st.cn.1.

DoubleClick, Trans Union among Big Brother Award winners. (April 6, 2000). PrivacyPlace.Com., http://www.privacyplace.com/news/00news/04 April/04 06/bigbro.html..

DoubleClick wins for losing. (April 6, 2000). Wired News, http://www.wired.com/news/print/0,1294,35432,00.html.

Email marketers try new tactics for consumer attention. (Feb. 1, 2000). CNET News.Com, http://news.cnet.com/news/0-1005-200-1539071.html?tag=st.cn.1..

FTC investigates DoubleClick's data-collection practices. (Feb. 16, 2000). CNET News.Com, http://news.cnet.com/news/0-1005-200-1551521.html?tag=st.cn.1..

FTC opens inquiry into health care site privacy. (Feb. 18, 2000). CNET News.Com, http://news.cnet.com/news/0-1005-200-1553403.html?tag=st.ne.1005-203-1558696..

Gale Group Inc. (Aug. 30, 2001). http://www.galegroup.com, 14.

Goodin, D. (August 20, 1999). Online ads may track more than you know. CNET News.Com, http://news.cnet.com/news/0,10000,0-1005-200-346278,00.html, 3.

Hansen, E. (February 2, 2000). DoubleClick under email attack for consumer profiling plans. CNET News.Com, http://quicken.cnet.com/news/0-1—5-200-1539478.html.

Hu, J. Consumer group blasts DoubleClick in report to FTC. CNET News.Com, http://news.cnet.com/news/0-1005-200-1561502.html, 1, 2.

Internet firms join forces to shape Web. (July 12, 1999). Reuters. CNET News.Com, Intuit plugs leaks to DoubleClick. CNet.Com. (March 2, 2000). CNET News.Com, http://news.cnet.com/news/0-1007-200-1562341.html?tag=st.cn.1..

Is DoubleClick privacy plan adequate? (Feb. 14, 2000). CNET News.Com, http://news.cnet.com/news/0-1005-200-1549770.html?tag=st.cn.1..

Jacobus, P. (Feb. 11, 2000). "Cookies" targeted as Congress advocates address Net privacy. CNET News.Com, http//news.cnet.com/news/0-1005-200-1547443.html?tag-rltdnws, 3.

Junkbusters. (April 20, 2000). www.junkbusters.com.

Junnarkar, S. (January 28, 2000). DoubleClick accused of unlawful consumer data use. CNET News.Com, http://news.cnet.com/news/0-1005-200-1534533.html, 2.

Macavinta, C. (November 22, 1999). Privacy advocates rally against DoubleClick–Abacus merger. CNET News.Com, http://news.cnet.com/news/0-1005-200-1461826.html?tag=rltdnws, 2.

Marinaccio, W. (June 21, 1999). Privacy advocates blast DoubleClick merger. CNET News.Com, http://news.cnet.com/news/0-1005-200-343915.html, 1.

Michigan initiates DoubleClick inquiry. (Feb. 17, 2000). CNET News.Com, http://news.cnet.com/news/0-1005-200-1553030.html?tag=st.cn.1..

N.Y. Senate seeks to protect online privacy. (March 8, 2000). Reuters. CNET News.Com, http://news.cnet.com/news/0-1005-200-1567498.html?tag=st.cn.1..

Net companies join forces to influence lawmakers. (Oct. 6, 1999). Bloomberg News. CNET News.Com, http://news.cnet.com/news/0-1005-200-808878.html?tag=st.cn.1..

Online ads may track more than you know. (Aug. 20, 1999). CNET News.Com, http://news.cnet.com/news/0-1005-200-346278.html?tag=st.cn.1..

Online marketer gains second "profiling" patent. (Dec. 6, 1999). CNET News.Com, http://news.cnet.com/news/0-1005-200-1482304.html?tag=st.cn.1..

Privacy advocates target Abacus shareholders. (June 29, 1999). CNET News.Com, http://news.cnet.com/news/0-1005-200-344244.html?tag=st.cn.1..

Privacy fears raised by DoubleClick database plans. (Jan. 25, 2000). CNET News.Com, http://news.cnet.com/news/0-1005-200-1531929.html?tag=st.cn.1..

Privacy standard to get New York audition. (April 6, 2000). CNET News.Com, http://news.cnet.com/news/0-1005-200-1648391.html?tag=st.cn.1..

Probes are latest headache in e-commerce. (Feb. 16, 2000). CNET News.Com, http://news.cnet.com/news/0-1007-200-1551662.html?tag=st.cn.1..

Rights groups urge government to protect privacy. (Nov. 5, 1999). CNET News.Com, http://news.cnet.com/news/0-1005-200-1431252.html?tag=st.cn.1..

Senator says Web devices a target of consumer concern. (March 9, 2000). CNET News.Com, http://news.cnet.com/news/0-1006-200-1568396.html?tag=st.cn.1..

Short Take: DoubleClick appoints public policy director. (Dec. 9, 1999). CNET News.Com, http://news.cnet.com/news/0-1005-200-1489734.html?tag=st.cn.1..

Short Take: Net ad association to set wireless guidelines. (April 17, 2000). CNET News.Com, http://news.cnet.com/news/0-1004-200-1709973.html?tag=st.ne.1002.

Software makers see opportunity in privacy fears. (April 14, 2000). CNET News.Com, http://news.cnet.com/news/0-1005-200-1697590.html?tag=st.ne.1002.

States, federal government conduct DoubleClick probes. (Feb. 17, 2000). CNET News.Com, http://news.cnet.com/news/0-1005-201-1553056-0.html?tag=st.ne.1005-203-1566622..

Trustee reports on RealNetworks as FTC examines Net privacy. (Nov. 8, 1999). CNET News.Com, http://news.cnet.com/news/0-1005-200-1431844.html?tag=st.cn.1..

United States Department of Commerce, Secretariat on Electronic Commerce, Economics and Statistics Administration, Office of Policy Development. *The emerging digital economy II*, by David Henry, Patricia Buckley, Gurmukh Gill, Sandra Cooke, Jess Dumagan, and Dennis Pastore. Washington, D.C. (June 1999), http://www.ecommerce.gov/ede/.

NOTES

Chapter 1

1. Friedman, T. (2000). *The Lexus and the Olive Tree*, 17, 20, 24. New York: Anchor Books.
2. Nash, L. (1990). *Good Intentions Aside: A Manager's Guide to Resolving Ethical Problems*, 5. Boston: Harvard Business School Press.
3. Sources such as *The Wall Street Journal* and *USA Today* have reported and continue to report surveys on unethical behavior in organizations. Other sources reporting such unethical behavior include: Gordon, J., et al. (1990). *Management and Organizational Behavior*, 93. Boston: Allyn & Bacon; and Gordon, J. (1999). *Organizational Behavior*, 6th ed., 121–122. Upper Saddle River, NJ: Prentice-Hall.
4. An OfficeClick.com survey of some 148 secretaries found 47% have been asked to lie for bosses. *Wall Street Journal*. (Nov. 30, 1999). Section A, p. 1, col. 5.
5. Gordon et al. (1990); Gordon (1999).
6. Marchetti, M. (Dec. 1997). Whatever it takes. *Sales & Marketing Management*, 28–38.
7. Colvin, G. (March 6, 2000). The amazing future of business. *Fortune*, F6–F10.
8. Frooman, J. (1997). Socially irresponsible and illegal behavior and shareholder wealth. *Business & Society*, 36(3), 221–229.
9. Zemke, R. (May 1986). Employee theft: How to cut your losses. *Training*, 74–78.
10. KMPG Report. (Nov. 27, 1999). Managing ethics costs and benefits. *Ethics & Integrity*. See also www.kpmg.ca/ethics/vl/eth ben.htm.
11. Ibid.
12. Levering, R., Milton, M. (Jan. 10, 2000). The 100 best companies to work for. *Fortune*, 82–114.
13. Carroll, A. (1993). *Business & Society: Ethics and Stakeholder Management*, 3rd ed., 110–112. Cincinnati: South-Western.
14. Badaracco, J., Jr. (1998). Defining moments: When managers must choose between right and right, *Strategy and Business (1st qtr)*, 4–6.
15. Ibid.
16. Friedman, M. (Sept. 13, 1970). The social responsibility of business is to increase its profits. *New York Times Magazine*, 33.
17. Frooman.
18. Key, S., Popkin, S. (1998). Integrating ethics into the strategic management process: Doing well by doing good. *Management Decision*, 36(5), 331–338. See Colvin and Frooman. Also see Allinson, R. (1993). *Global Disasters: Inquiries into Management Ethics*. New York: Prentice-Hall; and Arthur, H. (1984). Making business ethics useful. *Strategic Management Journal*, 5, 319–333.
19. Senge, P. (1990). *The fifth discipline: The art and practice of the learning organization*, New York: Doubleday. Also see the following sources: In search of the holy performance grail. (April 1996). *Training & Development*, 26–32. Also see Covey, S. R. (1989). *The Seven Habits of Highly Effective People*. New York: Simon & Schuster.
20. DeGeorge, Richard. (1999). *Business Ethics*, 5th ed. Upper Saddle River, NJ: Prentice-Hall.
21. Stone, C. D. (1975). *Where the Law Ends*. New York: Harper & Row.
22. Buchholz, R. (1989). *Fundamental Concepts and Problems in Business Ethics*. Englewood Cliffs, NJ: Prentice Hall. For more information, see Buchholz, Rogene A. (1995). *Business Environment and Public Policy*, 5th ed. Englewood Cliffs, NJ: Prentice-Hall.
23. Newton, L. (1986). The internal morality of the corporation. *Journal of Business Ethics*, 5, 249-258.
24. Hoffman, M., Moore, J. (1995). *Business Ethics: Readings and Cases in Corporate Morality*, 3rd ed. New York: McGraw-Hill.
25. DeGeorge, Richard. (2000). Business ethics and the challenge of the information age. *Business Ethics Quarterly*, 10(1), 63–72.
26. Ibid.
27. Stone.
28. Carroll.
29. Stead, B., Miller, J. (1988). Can social awareness be decreased through business school curriculum? *Journal of Business Ethics*, 7(7), 30.
30. Jones, T. (1989). Ethics education in business: Theoretical considerations. *Organizational Behavior Teaching Review*, 13(4), 1–18.
31. Hanson, K. O. (Sept. 1987). What good are ethics courses? *Across the Board*, 10–11.

32. Kohlberg, L. (1969). State and sequence: The cognitive developmental approach to socialization. In Gosline, D. A. *Handbook of Socialization Theory and Research.* Chicago: Rand-McNally.

33. Jones, T. (1991). Ethical decision making by individuals in organizations: An issue-contingent model. *Academy of Management Review, 16(2),* 366–395.

34. Weaver, G., Trevion, L., Cochran, P. (1999). Corporate ethics practices in the mid-1990s: An empirical study of the *Fortune 1000. Journal of Business Ethics, 18,* 283–294.

35. Jones, 383, 391.

CHAPTER 2

1. Key, S. (1999). Toward a new theory of the firm: A critique of stakeholder "theory." *Management Decision, 37(4),* 319.

2. Preston, L., Sapienza, H. (1990). Stakeholder management and corporate performance. *Journal of Behavioral Economics, 19(4),* 373. See also: Evan, W., Freeman, R. (1988). A stakeholder theory of the modern corporation: Kantian capitalism. In Beauchamp, T. L., Bowie, N. E. *Ethical Theory and Business,* 3rd ed. Englewood Cliffs, NJ: Prentice Hall.

3. For a critique of the stakeholder theory, see Reed, D. (1999). Stakeholder management theory: A critical theory perspective. *Business Ethics Quarterly, 9(3),* 453–483.

4. Key.

5. Mitchell, R. B., Agle, B. R., Wood, D. (1997). Toward a theory of stakeholder identification and salience: Defining the principle of who and what really counts. *Academy of Management Review, 22(4),* 853–886. See also Key.

6. Bowie, N., Duska, R. (1991). *Business ethics,* 2nd ed. Englewood Cliffs, NJ: Prentice Hall; Frederick, W. (1994). From CSR1 To CSR2: The maturing of business and society thought. *Business & Society, 3(2),* 150–166; Bowen, H. (1953). *Social Responsibilities of Businessmen.* New York: Harper.

7. Clarkson, M. (Ed). (1998). *The Corporation and Its Stakeholders: Classic and Contemporary Readings.* Toronto: University of Toronto Press.

8. Freeman, R. E. (1984). *Strategic Management: A Stakeholder Approach,* 25. Boston: Pitman.

9. Frederick, W., et al. (1988). *Business and Society: Corporate Strategy, Public Policy, Ethics,* 6th ed. New York: McGraw-Hill.

10. Freeman, R. E. (1984). *Strategic Management: A Stakeholder Approach.* Boston: Pitman.

11. Savage, G., Nix, T., Whitehead, C., Blair, J. (1991). Strategies for assessing and managing organizational stakeholders. *The Executive, 5(2),* 61–75.

12. Jones, T. (1991). Ethical decision making by individuals in organizations: An issue-contingent model. *Academy of Management Review, 16(2),* 366–395.

13. Ibid.

14. King, W. (1987). Strategic issue management. In King, W., Cleland, D., eds. *Strategic Planning and Management Handbook,* 256. New York: Van Nostrand Reinhold; Buchholz, R. (1982). Education for public issues management: Key insights from a survey of top practitioners. *Public Affairs Review, 3,* 65–76; Brown, J. (1979). *This Business of Issues: Coping with the Company's Environment.* New York: Conference Board. Also see Carroll, A. B. (1989, 1983). *Business and Society: Ethics and Stakeholder Management,* 1st, 3rd eds. Cincinnati: South-Western.

15. Fink, S. (1986). *Crisis Management,* 15. New York: AMACOM.

16. Marx, T. (Fall 1986). Integrating public affairs and strategic planning. *California Management Review,* 145.

17. See Marx.

18. Fink, 20.

19. Matthews, J. B., Goodpaster, K., and Nash, L. (1985). *Policies and Persons: A Casebook in Business Ethics.* New York: McGraw-Hill.

20. Mitroff, I., Shrivastava, P., Firdaus, U. (1987). Effective crisis management. *Academy of Management Executive, 1(7),* 283–92.

21. Wartick, S., Rude, R. (Fall 1986). Issues management: Fad or function? *California Management Review,* 134–40.

22. Key.

CHAPTER 3

1. Nash, L. (Nov./Dec. 1981). Ethics without the sermon. *Harvard Business Review,* 88.

2. Velasquez, M. G. (1998). *Business Ethics: Concepts and Cases,* 4th ed. Englewood Cliffs, NJ: Prentice Hall.

3. Ibid.

4. Ibid.

5. Steiner, G. A., Steiner, J. F. (2000). *Business, Government, and Society: A Managerial Perspective,* 9th ed. Boston: McGraw-Hill.

6. Freeman, R. E., Gilbert, Jr., D. (1988). *Corporate Strategy and the Search for Ethics,* 36. Englewood Cliffs, NJ: Prentice Hall.

7. Ibid., 39.

8. Mill, J. S. (1957). *Utilitarianism.* Indianapolis: Bobbs-Merrill; Carroll, A. (1993). *Business and Society: Ethics and Stakeholder Management,* 2nd ed. Cincinnati: South-Western; Valesquez, M. G. (1992). *Business Ethics: Concepts and Cases,* 3rd ed. Englewood Cliffs, NJ: Prentice Hall.

9. Delong, J. V., et al. (March/April 1981). Defending cost-benefit analysis: Replies to Steven Kelman. *AEI Journal on Government and Society,* 39–43.

10. Hoffman, W. M., Moore, J. (1990). *Business Ethics: Readings and Cases in Corporate Morality*, 2nd ed. New York: McGraw-Hill.

11. Kelman, S. (January/February 1981). Cost-benefit analysis: An ethical critique. *AEI Journal on Government and Society*, 33–40.

12. Freeman and Gilbert.

13. Ibid.

14. Rawls, J. (1971). *A Theory of Justice*. Cambridge, MA: Harvard University Press.

15. DeGeorge, R. T. (1990). *Business Ethics*, 3rd ed. New York: Macmillan.

16. McMahon, T. (1999). Transforming justice: a conceptualization. *Business Ethics Quarterly*, *9(4)*, 593-602.

17. Ibid., 600.

18. McMahon.

19. Buono, A. F., Nichols, L. T. (1990). Stockholder and stakeholder interpretations of business' social role. In Hoffman, W. M., Moore, J. *Business Ethics: Readings and Cases in Corporate Morality*, 2nd ed. New York: McGraw-Hill.

20. L. Davis. (1976). Comments on Nozick's entitlement theory. *The Journal of Philosophy*, *73*, 839–842.

21. Krolick, S. (1987). *Ethical Decision-Making Style: Survey and Interpretive Notes*. Beverly, MA: Addison-Wesley.

22. Ibid.

23. Krolick, 18.

24. Krolick, 20.

25. Steiner and Steiner; Freeman and Gilbert; Mill; Carroll; Valesquez (1992). Based on Steiner and Steiner, and Carroll.

26. Freeman and Gilbert.

CHAPTER 4

1. Barnard, C. (1939). *The functions of the executive*, 259. Cambridge, MA: Harvard University Press; also see this classic work for an "institutional" view of organizations and leadership: Selznick, P. (1983). *Leadership in administration: A sociological interpretation*. Berkeley: University of California Press.

2. Collins, J., Porras, J. (1994). *Built to last: Successful habits of visionary companies*, 78. New York: Harper Collins.

3. Examples of resources for examining the ethical and stakeholder management of an organization's internal systems may be found in: Waddock, S., Smith, N. (2000). Relationships: The real challenge of corporate global citizenship. *Business and Society Review, 104(1)*, 47–62; Clarkson, M. (1995). A stakeholder framework for analyzing and evaluating corporate social performance. *Academy of Management Review, 20*, 91–117; Liedtka, J. (1998). Constructing an ethic for business practice: Competing effectively and doing good. *Business and Society 37(3)*, 254–280.

4. The term *stakeholder responsive corporations* is used in Svendsen, A. (1998). *The Stakeholder Strategy*. San Francisco: Berrett-Koehler. The concept of value-based management is found in Quinn, D., Jones, T. (1995). An agent morality view of business policy. *Academy of Management Review, 20(1)*, 22–42.

5. Does it pay to be ethical? (March/April 1997). *Business Ethics*, 14. Other studies cited that also support this assertion: Waddock, S., Graves, S. (1997). The corporate social performance–financial performance link. *Strategic Management Journal, 18(4)*, 303–319; Waddock, S., Graves, S. (1997). Quality of management and quality of stakeholder relations: Are they synonymous? *Business and Society Review, 36(3)*, 250–279; Waddock, S., Graves, S. (2000). Beyond built to last . . . stakeholder relations in built-to-last companies. *Business and Society Review, 105(4)*, 393–418.

6. Based on Svendsen, Table 1, 2.

7. Collins, *Built to last*, 78.

8. Based on Svendsen, 1–2.

9. Based on Svendsen, 73.

10. Svendsen, 70.

11. Based on Svendsen, 70.

12. Collins, J. *Good to Great*, New York: Harper Business, 2001, p. 20. Great companies include Abbott, Circuit City, Fannie Mae, Gillette, Kimberly Clark, Kroger, Nucor, Phillip Morris, Pitney Bowes, Walgreens, and Wells Fargo.

13. Foster, R., Kaplan, S. (2001). *Creative Destruction*. New York: Doubleday.

14. Foster and Kaplan, 9.

15. See note 5.

16. Waddock and Graves, 2000.

17. Ibid., 414.

18. Hyatt, J. (May 24, 2001). Dot-com survivors demonstrate law of creative reconstruction. *Boston Globe*, p. E4.

19. Svendsen refers to many company examples. Many Fortune 500 companies that are not built-to-last examples also use and depend on elaborate codes of ethics, ethical training programs, and different versions of stakeholder management; see Driscoll, D. M., Hoffman, W. (2000). *Ethics Matters*. Waltham, MA: Center for Business Ethics.

20. Nadler, D. (1998). *Champions of Change*. San Francisco: Jossey-Bass.

21. Anderson, C. (1997). Values-based management. *Academy of Management Executive, 11(4)*, 25.

22. See Driscoll and Hoffman; Svendsen; and Weaver, G., Trevino, L. (1999). Compliance and values-oriented ethics programs: influences on employees' attitudes and behavior. *Business Ethics Quarterly, 9(2)*, 315–335; Werhane, P. (1998). Moral imagination and the search for ethical decision making in man-

agement. *Business Ethics Quarterly, The Ruffin Series: Special Issue No. 1*, 75–98. For a discussion of fit between culture and ethics training programs, see Weaver, G. (March 2001). Ethics programs in global businesses: Culture's role in managing ethics. *Journal of Business Ethics, 30*, 3–15.

23. Based on Svendsen, 99–100.

24. Simison, R. (September 11, 2000). For Ford CEO Nasser, damage control is the new Job One. *Wall Street Journal*, A1.

25. Brelis, M. (November 5, 2000). Herb's way. *Boston Globe*, Florida. A more complete description of Kelleher's story and Southwest Airlines culture is found in O'Neill, M. (May 28, 2001). The chairman of the board looks back. *Fortune*, 63–76.

26. Brelis, F4.

27. Ibid.

28. Fulmer, R. (Winter 2001). Johnson & Johnson: Frameworks for leadership. *Organizational Dynamics, 29(3)*, 219.

29. Vaill, P. (1998). *Spirited Leading and Learning: Process Wisdom for a New Age*. San Francisco: Jossey-Bass; Novak, M. (1996). *Business as a Calling: Work and the Examined Life*. New York: The Free Press; Conger, J. (1994). *Spirit at Work: Discovering the Spirituality in Leadership*. San Francisco: Jossey-Bass. For an overview of a study on spirituality and corporate leadership, see Mitroff, I., Denton, E. (1999). *A Spiritual Audit of Corporate America: A Hard Look at Values in the Workplace*. San Francisco: Jossey-Bass/Pfeiffer. This section is also based on Weiss, J. (August 2000). New careers, leadership as calling and spirituality. Paper delivered at the Academy of Management annual meeting, Spirituality and Religion Interest Group, Toronto, Canada.

30. Frederick, W. (March, 2001). Review of Mitroff and Denton's *A Spiritual Audit of Corporate America: A Hard Look at Values in the Workplace. Religion and Society, 40(1)*, 118.

31. See Weiss (note 29) for sources and citations used here.

32. Havel, V. (1989). *Letters to Olga*, trans. P. Wilson, 232. New York: Holt.

33. Mitroff and Denton.

34. Mitroff and Denton.

35. Hitt, W. (1990). *Ethics and Leadership: Putting Theory into Practice*, 138–174. Columbus, OH: Batelle.

36. Gerth, H. (1946). *From Max Weber: Essays in Sociology*, trans. C. Wright Mills. Cambridge: Oxford University Press.

37. Drucker, P. (1978). *Management: Tasks, Responsibilities, Practices*. New York: Harper & Row.

38. Janis, I. (1972). *Groupthink: Psychological Studies of Policy Decisions and Fiascoes*. Boston: Houghton Mifflin.

39. Burns, J. (1978). *Leadership*. New York: Harper & Row; Hitt.

40. Hitt, 169.

41. Ibid.

42. See http://www.law.emory.edu/6circuit/oct97a0311p.06.html, *United States of America, Plaintiff (Appellee)* v. *Michael I. Monus, Defendant (Appellant)*, No. 95–4316; appeal from the United States District Court for the Northern District of Ohio at Cleveland, No. 93–00034. George W. White, Chief District Judge. Argued September 8, 1997; decided and filed October 21, 1997.

43. New York: Simon and Schuster, 1997.

44. For an account of the proceedings against Micky Monus, see http://www.emory.edu/6circuit/oct97a0311p.06.html. More on Al Dunlap can be found in: Byrne, J. (July 6, 1998). How Al Dunlap self-destructed. *Business Week*, 44–45; Norris, F. (May 18, 2001). They noticed the fraud but figured it was not important. *New York Times*, C1.

45. Driscoll and Hoffman, 68.

46. Strauss, G. (May 21, 2001). Many execs pocket perks aplenty. *USA Today*, 2A, 2B. Also available on USA Today.com and http://money.usatoday.com.

47. Conger, J., Lawler, E., III, Benson, G., and Finegold, D. (2000). CEO appraisal: Keys to effectiveness. *Global Focus, 12(2)*, 35-44.

48. Young, G. (March 2000). Boards of directors and the adoption of a CEO performance evaluation process. *Journal of Management Studies, 37(2)*, 277.

49. Hamel, G. (2000). *Leading the Revolution*, 204–205. Cambridge, MA: Harvard Business School Press.

50. Cusumano, M., Markides, C. (2001). Strategic thinking for the next economy. San Francisco: Jossey-Bass.

51. Hofer, C., Schendel, D. (1979). *Strategic Management: A New View of Business Policy and Planning*. Boston: Little, Brown.

52. Freeman, R. E., and Gilbert, D., Jr. (1988.) *Corporate Strategy and the Search for Ethics*. Englewood Cliffs: Prentice Hall.

53. Pastin, M. (1986). Lessons from high profit, high-ethics companies: An agenda for managerial action (Chapter 11), 218–228. In *The Hard Problems of Management: Gaining the Ethics Edge*. San Francisco: Jossey-Bass.

54. Deal, T., Kennedy, A. (1982). *Corporate Culture: The Rites and Rituals of Corporate Life*, 9–12. Reading, MA: Addison-Wesley.

55. Keogh, J., ed. (1988). *Corporate Ethics: A Prime Business Asset. A Report on Policy and Privacy in Company Conduct*. New York: The Business Roundtable.

56. Ibid., 45.

57. Weiss, J. (2001). *Organizational Behavior and Change*, 2nd ed., 236–333. Cincinnati: South-Western/ITP; Jones, G. (2001). *Organizational Theory*, 3rd ed., 63–92. Upper Saddle River, NJ: Prentice Hall.

58. Cullen, J., Victor, B., Stephens, C. (1989). An ethical weather report: assessing the organization's ethical climate. *Organizational Dynamics, 18,* 50–62.

59. Posner, B., Schmidt, W. (1984). Value and the American manager: An update. *California Management Review,* Spring, 202–216.

60. Ashkeas, R., Ulrich, D., Jick, T., Kerr, S. (1995). *The Boundaryless Organization.* San Francisco: Jossey-Bass.

61. Chan, K. (May 21, 2001). From top to bottom. *Wall Street Journal,* R12.

62. Brey, P. (1999). Worker autonomy and the drama of digital networks in organizations. *Journal of Business Ethics, 22(1),* 15–22.

63. Senge, P. (1990). *The Fifth Discipline.* New York: Doubleday.

64. Rosthorn, J. (September 2000). Business ethics auditing: More than a stakeholder's toy. *Journal of Business Ethics, 27,* 9–20.

65. Kim, W., Mauborgne, R. (2001). Strategy, value innovation, and the knowledge economy, 197–228. In Cusumano, M., and Markides, C. *Strategic Thinking for the Next Economy.* San Francisco: Jossey-Bass.

66. Ibid., 218.

67. Ibid., 222.

68. Donaldson, T., Preston, L. (1995). The stakeholder theory of the corporation: Concepts, evidence, and implications. *Academy of Management Review, 20,* 65–91.

69. Ansoff, H. (1965). *Corporate Strategy,* 38. New York: McGraw-Hill; Boatright, J. (1999). *Ethics and the Conduct of Business,* 3rd ed., Chapter 13. Upper Saddle River, NJ: Prentice Hall. This book also presents arguments for and against the stakeholder corporate model.

70. Driscoll, D., Hoffman, W., Petry, E. (1995). *The Ethical Edge,* 120. New York: MasterMedia Ltd.

71. Weaver, G., Trevino, L., Cochran, P. (February, 1999). Corporate ethics practices in the mid–1990s: An empirical study of the Fortune 1000. *Journal of Business Ethics, 18,* 3, 283–294.

72. Self-regulation future. (April 16, 2001). *Advertising Age, 72,* 16; Harker, D., Harker, M. (Dec., 2000). The role of codes of conduct in the advertising self-regulatory framework. *Journal of Macromarketing, 20, 2,* 155–166.

73. Brooks, L. (1989). Corporate codes of ethics. *Journal of Business Ethics, 8,* 117–129; Bowie, N., Duska, R. (1990). *Business ethics.* 2nd ed. Englewood Cliffs: Prentice Hall.

74. Frankel, M. (1989). Professional codes: Why, how, and with what impact? *Journal of Business Ethics, 8,* 109–115.

75. Harrison, J. (1999). Finding the ethics soft spots of a target. *Mergers and Acquisitions, 34,* 2, 8.

76. Frankel.

77. Somers, M. (2001). Ethical codes of conduct and organizational context: A study of the relationship between codes of conduct, employee behavior, and organizational values. *Journal of Business Ethics, 30,* 194.

78. Franchise association launches ombudsman program as key self-regulation component. (April 2001). *Franchising World, 33,* 36.

79. Campbell, K. (July 6, 2000). This is a job for . . . ombudsman writer of wrongs! *Christian Science Monitor, 15,* 15; Burd, S. (Oct. 8, 1999). U.S. Education Department introduces ombudsmans and 6 other top managers. *Chronicle of Higher Education 46,* A46; Ombudsman looks into supplier complaints. (Sept. 16, 1999). *Purchasing, 127,* 42.

80. Moriarity, S. (Dec. 2000). Trends in ethical sanctions within the accounting profession. *Accounting Horizons, 14,* 427–439.

81. Bhatia, A., Blackstock, S., Nelson, R., Ng, T. (Fall 2000). Evolution of quality review programs for Medicare: Quality assurance to quality improvement. *Health Care Financing Review, 22,* 69–74.

82. Shaw, C. (April 7, 2001). External assessment of health care. *British Medical Journal, 322,* 851–854.

83. See www.eoa.org for information on ethics programs and the Ethics Officer Association.

CHAPTER 5

1. *Wall Street Journal.* (May 18, 2000). M2 Presswire; Coventry, p.1. For other sources to this case excerpt, see the case references at the end of the text.

2. Lilly discloses e-mail addresses of Prozac patients. (July 6, 2001). *Boston Globe,* E2.

3. See Belsie, L. (Sept. 13, 2000). The rise of corporate apology: Bridgestone/Firestone's crisis reveals quickening cycle of accountability in era of Web and instant communication. *Christian Science Monitor,* 1.

4. The following excerpts are based on these sources: Geyelin, M. (Aug. 27, 2001). For Firestone, tire trial is mixed victory. *Wall Street Journal,* A3; Belsie, 1; Sissell, K. (Dec. 8, 1999). Judge approves Dow Corning bankruptcy plan. *Chemical Week,* 21; Bloomberg News. (May 17, 2001). Payout in 2001 in diet cases to be $7 billion. *New York Times,* C.7; Donaldson, T., Werhane, P. (1988). *Ethical Issues in Business: A Philosophical Approach,* 89–100, 414–414. Englewood Cliffs, NJ: Prentice-Hall; Barett. Dalkon Shield maker concedes possible user injuries. (April 3, 1985). *Dallas Times Herald,* A8; Buchholz, R. A. (1989). *Fundamental Concepts and Problems in Business Ethics.* Englewood Cliffs, NJ: Prentice Hall; Geyelin, M. (Nov. 12, 1991). Dalkon Shield trust lawyers draw fire. *Wall Street Journal,* B5; Matthews, J., Goodpaster, K., Nash, L. (1991). *Policies and Persons: A*

Casebook in Business Ethics, 2d ed. New York: McGraw-Hill; Weinberger, Romeo. (1989).

5. Viewpoint: beyond compliance: Social accountability can protect companies and profits. (April 13, 2001). *Asiaweek*, 1.

6. Carroll, A. (1991). The pyramid of corporate social responsibility: Toward the moral management of organizational stakeholders. *Business Horizons, 34(4),* 39–48.

7. Albinger, H., Freeman, S. (2000). Corporate social performance and attractiveness as an employer to different job seeking populations. *Journal of Business Ethics, 28(3),* 243–253; Fombrun C., Shanley, M. (1990). What's in a name? Reputation building and corporate strategy. *Academy of Management Journal, 33,* 233–258.

8. Social Investment Forum. (1998). Social Investment Forum announcement. Washington, DC.

9. Turban, D., Greening, D. (1997). Corporate social performance and organizational attractiveness to prospective employees. *Academy of Management Journal 40,* 658–672.

10. Wagner, C. (July/Aug., 2001). Economics: Evaluating good corporate citizenship. *The Futurist, 35(4),* 16.

11. Alsop, R. (2001). Corporate reputations are earned with trust, reliability, study shows. *Wall Street Journal,* www.reputations.com.

12. Ibid.

13. Hillman, A., Keim, G. (2001). Shareholder value, stakeholder management, and social issues: What's the bottom line? *Strategic Management Journal, 22,* 125.

14. Ibid., 136.

15. New economy, new social contract. (Sept. 11, 2000). *Business Week,* 182.

16. Ibid., 148.

17. Ibid.

18. Ibid.

19. Gordon et al.

20. Torabzadeh, K., et al. (1989). The effect of the recent insider-trading scandal on stock prices of securities firms. *Journal of Business Ethics, 8,* 303.

21. Nash, L. (1990). *Good Intentions Aside: A Manager's Guide to Resolving Ethical Problems,* 101. Boston: Harvard Business School.

22. Ibid., 104.

23. Bowie, N., Duska, R. (1990). *Business Ethics,* 2d ed., 34–37. Englewood Cliffs, NJ: Prentice Hall.

24. Davis, K., Blomstrom, R. (1966). *Business and Its Environment.* New York: McGraw-Hill.

25. Carroll, 43.

26. Faircloth, A., Boolinger, C. (Feb. 2, 1998). Fortune's 40 most generous Americans. *Fortune.*

27. Oomens M., van den Bosch, F. (1999). Strategic issue management in major European-based companies. *Long Range Planning, 32(1),* 49.

28. Elkington, J., Trisoglio, A. (Dec. 1996). Developing realistic scenarios for the environment: Lessons from Brent Spart. *Long Range Planning, 29(6),* 762–769; O'Malley, G. (1997). Issue management adds value at Weyerhaeuser. *Corporate Public Issues and Their Management, 21(18);* Anderson, D. (1997). Key concepts in anticipatory issues management. *Corporate Environmental Strategy, The Journal of Environmental Leadership.*

29. Lenz, R., Engledow, J. (1986). Environmental analysis units and strategic decision-making: A field study of selected "leading-edge" corporations. *Strategic Management Journal, 7(1),* 69–89; Oomens and Bosch, 52.

30. Oomens and Bosch, 52.

31. Ibid., 55.

32. Maignan, I. (2001). Consumers' perceptions of corporate social responsibilities: A cross-cultural comparison. *Journal of Business Ethics, 30(1),* 57–72.

33. Ibid., 69.

34. Velasquez, M. (1988, 1998). *Business Ethics Concepts and Cases,* 2d and 4th eds. Englewood Cliffs: Prentice Hall.

35. Velasquez, M. (2001). The ethics of consumer protection. In Hoffman, W., Frederick, R., Schwartz, M., eds. *Business Ethics,* 4th ed., 424. Boston: McGraw-Hill.

36. Buchholz, R. (July/Aug. 1991). Corporate responsibility and the good society: From economics to ecology. *Business Horizons,* 24; Holloway and Hancock. (1973). *Marketing in a Changing Environment,* 2d ed. New York: John Wiley and Sons.

37. Boatright, J. (1999). *Ethics and the Conduct of Business,* 3d ed., 273. Englewood Cliffs, NJ: Prentice Hall.

38. Szwajkowski, E. (Dec. 2000). Simplifying the principles of stakeholder management: The three most important principles. *Business and Society, 39(4),* 381. Other advocates of this interpretation of Smith's views include Bishop, J. (1995). Adam Smith's invisible hand argument. *Journal of Business Ethics, 14,* 165; Rothchild, E. (1994). Adam Smith and the invisible hand. *AEA Papers and Proceedings, 8(2),* 312–322; Winch, D. (1997). Adam Smith's problems and ours. *Scottish Journal of Political Economy, 44,* 384–402.

39. Szwajkowski, 381.

40. Bell, C. (April 3, 2001). Testing reliance on free market. *Boston Globe,* C4.

41. Ibid.

42. Samuelson, P. (1973). *Economics,* 9th ed., 345. New York: McGraw-Hill. This discussion is also based on Velasquez, 1998, 166–200.

43. Wright, J. (1996). *General Editory, The Universal Almanac*, 270. Kansas City: Andrews and McMeel.

44. Vranica, S. (June 15, 2001). Ad-spending growth is forecast to slow to 2.5% in 2001. *Wall Street Journal*, B6.

45. http://www.ftc.gov/bcp/online/pubs/buspubs/ruleroad.htm (Sept. 2000).

46. Hansell, S. (July 23, 2001). Pop-up Web ads pose a measurement puzzle. *New York Times*, C1.

47. Evangelista, B. (July 23, 2001). Byte-size movies. *New York Times*, E1.

48. Dobrzynski, J. (July 29, 2001). So, technology pros, what comes after the fall? *New York Times*, B1, B11.

49. Ibid.

50. http://www.ftc.gov/bcp/online/pubs/buspubs/ruleroad.htm (Sept. 2000).

51. Velasquez (1998), 343–349.

52. Post, J., Lawrence, A., Weber, J. (1999). *Business and Society*, 9th ed., 464. Boston: Irwin McGraw-Hill.

53. Noble, B. (Oct. 27, 1991). After terms of deregulation, a new push to inform the public. *New York Times*, F5.

54. Kranish, M. (July 29, 2001). Fat chance. *Boston Globe*, D1.

55. Schlosser, E. (2001). *Fast Food Nation*. New York: Houghton Mifflin.

56. Nagorski, A. (Feb. 26, 2001). Hold the French fries: A reasoned attack on the fast-food culture. *Newsweek*, 50; Schrader, M. (March 12, 2001). Survey of fast food in America presents one-sided, dark view. *Nation's Restaurant News*, 84; Schlosser, E. (March 2001). Fast food nation: The dark side of the all-American meal. *Food Management*, 13.

57. Post, Lawrence, and Weber.

58. http://www.msnbc.com/news/615678.asp?cp1=1, p. 2.

59. Jackson, D. (July 25, 2001). When death is the bottom line. *Boston Globe*, A19.

60. See Steiner, Steiner. (2000). *Business, Government, and Society*, 9th ed., 596. Boston: McGraw-Hill.

61. Cava, A. (Spring 2000). Commercial speech 1999: Significant developments. *Academy of Marketing Science Journal, 28(2)*, 316–317. For more detail and discussion on these issues and recent Court cases see Emord, J. (Spring 2000). Person v. Shalala: The beginning of the end for FDA speech suppression. *Journal of Public Policy & Marketing, 19(1)*, 139–143.

62. (January 1991). *Circulation*, 4.

63. Lee, D. (Dec. 2000). How government prevents us from buying safety. *Ideas on Liberty, 50(12)*, 32–33.

64. DeGeorge. (1990). *Business Ethics*, 3d ed., 182, 183. New York: Macmillan.

65. O'Donnell, J. (April 4, 2001). Cosco's history reads like a recipe for recalls/Company kept quiet. *USA Today*, B1.

66. Simplest e-mail queries confound companies. (Oct. 21, 1996). *Wall Street Journal*, B1, B9. See Post, Lawrence, and Weber, chapter 14, for a discussion of consumer affairs departments.

67. Payout in 2001 in diet cases to be $7 billion. (May 17, 2001). *New York Times*, C7.

68. Sook Kim, Q. (Feb. 7, 2001). Asbestos claims continue to mount—Did broker of settlements unwittingly encourage more plaintiffs' suits? *Wall Street Journal*, B1.

69. Des Jardins, J., McCall, T., eds. (1990). *Contemporary Issues in Business Ethics*, 255. Belmont, CA: Wadsworth.

70. See Posch, R. (1988). *The Complete Guide to Marketing and the Law*, 3. Englewood Cliffs, NJ: Prentice Hall; Sturdivant, F., Vernon-Wortzel, H. (1991). *Business and Society: A Managerial Approach*, 4th ed., 305. Homewood, IL: Irwin.

71. Carroll, 258; Des Jardins and McCall, 255.

72. Carroll, 259.

73. Editor. (June 19, 2001). Maljustice in the courts. *Boston Globe*, A14.

74. Geyelin, M. (Jan. 6, 1992). Law: Product suits yield few punitive awards. *Wall Street Journal*, B1.

75. Felsenthal, E. (June 17, 1996). Punitive awards are called modest, rare. *Wall Street Journal*, B4.

76. Geyelin, B1.

77. Bravin, J. (June 12, 2000). Surprise: Judges hand out most punitive awards. *Wall Street Journal*, B1.

78. Geyelin, B1.

79. Morrow, D. (Nov. 9, 1997). Transporting lawsuits across state lines. *New York Times*.

80. Ollanik, S. (Nov. 2000). Products cases: An uphill battle for plaintiffs. *Trial*, 20–28.

81. Shapo, M. Reeg, K. (Winter 2001). E-commerce and products liability: A primer on exposure at the speed of light. *Federation of Insurance & Corporate Counsel Quarterly* (Iowa City, Iowa), 73–98.

82. Pollution is top environmental concern. (Aug. 29, 2000). *USA Today*, D1.

83. Seabrook, C. (Aug. 17, 2001). Air pollution labeled a killer/Direct link to deaths, study claims. *Atlanta Constitution*, A3.

84. Steiner, R. (July 19, 2001). Does global warming really matter? *USA Today*, A15.

85. Ibid.

86. Water unsafe in much of world. (May 17, 2001). *USA Today*, A1.

87. Sampat, P. (July 2001). The hidden threat of groundwater pollution. *USA Today*, 28–31.

88. Woods, R. (Aug. 3, 2001). EPA estimates costs of clean water TMDL program.

Environmental News, EPA Headquarters press release, 1.

89. Bloom, G., Morton, M. (Summer 1991). Hazardous waste is every manager's problem. *Sloan Management Review*, 80.

90. Buchholz, R. (1992). *Business Environment and Public Policy: Implications for Management and Strategy*, 4th ed. Englewood Cliffs, NJ: Prentice Hall.

91. Marks, A. (Dec. 11, 2000). Cleaning up Hudson River: Who should foot the bill? EPA and GE wage a $460 million fight that may impact pollution cleanups nationwide. *Christian Science Monitor*, 2.

92. Armstrong, D. (Nov. 15, 1999). Toxic impact spreads far pollution at US bases worldwide. *Boston Globe*, A1:1.

93. Based on Steiner, Steiner. (1991). *Business, Government, and Society*, 3d ed., 591; and Steiner and Steiner (2000), 484–485.

94. Post, J., Lawrence, A., Weber, J. (2002). *Business and Society*,10th ed., 266. New York: McGraw-Hill.

95. Sagoff, M., ed. Des Jardins, J., McCall, J. (1990). *Economic Theory and Environmental Law in Contemporary Issues in Business Ethics*, 360–364. Belmont, CA: Wadsworth.

96. Buchholz (1991), 19.

97. Environmental Protection Agency. (1990). *Environmental Investments: The Cost of a Clean Environment*. Washington, DC: EPA.

98. Recer, P. A4.

99. Post, Lawrence, and Weber (2001), 272.

100. This section is based on Oyewole, P. (Feb. 2001). Social costs of environmental justice associated with the practice of green marketing. *Journal of Business Ethics, 29(3)*, 239–251.

101. Johri, L., Sahasakmontri, K. Green marketing of cosmetics and toiletries in Thailand. *Journal of Consumer Marketing, 15(3)*.

102. See Oyewole, 239.

103. Ibid., 240.

104. Velasquez, 1998, 292.

105. Blackstone, W. (1974). Ethics and ecology. In Blackstone, W., ed. *Philosophy and Environmental Crisis*. Athens: University of Georgia Press.

106. Rosen, C. (Spring 2001). Environmental strategy and competitive advantage: An Introduction. *California Management Review, 43(3)*, 8.

107. Preston, L. (Spring 2001). Sustainability at Hewlett-Packard: From theory to practice. *California Management Review, 43(3)*, 27.

108. Bloom and Morton, 83.

109. Freeman, R., Reichart, J. (2000). Toward a life centered ethic for business. *Society for Business Ethics, The Ruffin Series No. 2*, 154. Reprinted with permission of the publisher.

110. Quinn, D. (1992). *Ishmael*, 129. New York: Bantam Books.

CHAPTER 6

1. McCormick, R. (Dec./Jan., 2000/2001). Erasing the differences. *Executive Speeches, 15(3)*, 52.

2. Based on the discussion of Tapscott, D. (1996). *The Digital Economy*, 296–303. New York: McGraw-Hill; Washburn, E. (Jan./Feb. 2000). Are you ready for generation X? *The Physician Executive, 26(1)*, 51–56.

3. Tapscott, 301; Howe, N. (2000). *Millennials Rising*. New York: Vintage Books.

4. Shellenbarger, S. (Dec. 17, 2000). More relaxed boomers, fewer workplace frills and other job trends. *Wall Street Journal*, B1; Mui, N. (Feb. 4, 2001). Here come the kids: Gen Y invades the workplace. *New York Times*, sec. 9, p. 1, col. 3.

5. Shellenbarger, S. (May 23, 2001). Why many bosses need to alter their approach toward older workers. *Wall Street Journal*, A6; Stuller, J. (July 2000). Ready for the other millennium bomb? *Chief Executive*, 48–54; Lofgren, E. (Winter 1999). Workforce management is new discipline for the future. *Compensation & Benefits Management, 15*, 13–18; Watmon, I. (Feb. 15, 2001). MCA: The new workforce seeks freedom and security. A new report from the Management Consultancies Assocation. Jamieson, D., O'Mara, J. (1991). *Managing Workforce 2000: Gaining the Diversity Advantage*. San Francisco: Jossey-Bass; Did Mayor Willie Brown sign the measure that his San Francisco Board of Supervisors voted in favor of to pay $50,000 for municipal workers' sex changes? (May 1, 2001). *USA Today*, 3A.

6. U.S. Bureau of Labor Statistics. (1999). Employment and earning. January issues. Monthly labor review. At www.catalystwomen.org/press/factsheets/factscote00.html; Jamieson and O'Mara.

7. Miller, N. (June 17, 2000). For better, for worse. *Boston Globe Magazine*, 13.

8. Schmitt, E. (April 1, 2001). U.S. Now more diverse, ethnically and racially. *New York Times*, 18.

9. Mollison, A. (March 28, 2001). U.S. falling behind in educating workers. *Atlanta Constitution*, A12; also see www.oecd.org.

10. Arellano, K. (Sept. 4, 2000). Employers look to the disabled: Labor shortage creates opportunity, *Denver Post*, F1.

11. Ibid.

12. Abselson, R. (June 10, 2001). Men, increasingly, are the ones claiming sex harassment by men. *New York Times*, 1.

13. Barnett, R. A new work–life model for the twenty–first century. (March 1999). *Annals of the American Academy of Political and Social Science, 562*, 143–158.

14. Workplace better for women. (Sept. 8, 1999). *USA Today*, 1B.

15. www.catalystwomen.org/press/factsheets/factscote00.html, 1.

16. Dobrzynski, J. (March 4, 1996). The glass ceiling for corporate women made crystal clear once again. *International Herald Tribune*, 25; Sullivan, B. (Feb. 28, 1996). Breaking the glass ceiling slowly. *Chicago Tribune*, 3; Fitzgerald, T. (Feb. 4, 2001). Held back by glass border. *Boston Globe*, J1.

17. Shoa, M. (May 24, 1995). Working and coexisting affirmative action hasn't yet altered the balance of power in corporate America, but it has changed the working environment. *Boston Globe*, 1.

18. Shellenbarger (2000), B1.

19. Washburn, 51–56; Howe; Mui.

20. Weiss, J. (2000). *Organization Behavior & Change*, 2nd ed. South–Western College Publishing, 18–23.

21. Fulmer, W., Casey, A. (1990). Employment at will: Options for managers. *Academy of Management Review*, 4, 102.

22. Flynn, G. (2000). How do you treat the at–will employment relationship? *Workforce*, 79, 178–179.

23. Fulmer and Casey (1990), 102.

24. For a discussion of these issues, see R. Awney. (1920). *The Acquisitive Society*. New York: Harcourt, Brace & World, 53–55; C. Reich. (1964). The new property. *Yale Law Review; 73*, 733; also Supreme Court case *Perry v. Sindermann*.

25. Boatright, J. (2000). *Ethics and the Conduct of Business*, 3rd ed. New Jersey: Prentice Hall, 265.

26. Rowan, J. (April 2000). The moral foundation of employee rights. *Journal of Business Ethics, 24*, 355–361.

27. Ibid., 358.

28. Ibid.

29. Jacoby, S. (1995). Social dimensions of global economic integration. In Jacoby, S., ed. *The Workers of Nations: Industrial Relations in a Global Economy*. New York: Oxford University Press, 21–22. Also see Steiner, S., and Steiner, J. (2000). *Business, Government, and Society*, 9th ed. Boston: McGraw–Hill, 618–619.

30. Velasquez, M. (1998). *Business Ethics*, 4th ed. Upper Saddle River, NJ: Prentice Hall, 439, 440.

31. Ibid.

32. Hackman, R., Oldham, G., Jansen, R., Purdy, K. (Summer 1975). A new strategy for job enrichment. *California Management Review, 17*, 56–58.

33. Bjork, L. (March 1975). An experiment in work satisfaction. *Scientific American, 232(3)*, 17–23; also, Simmons, J., Mares, W. (1983). *Working Together*. New York: Knopf.

34. Beauchamp, T., Bowie, N. (1988). *Ethical theory and business*, 3rd ed. Englewood Cliffs, NJ: Prentice Hall, 264. Also see chapter 5 in the 6th edition (2001), published by Prentice Hall.

35. DeGeorge, R. (1990). *Business ethics*, 3rd ed. New York: McMillan; D. Ewing. (1977). *Freedom Inside the Organization: Bringing Civil Liberties to the Workplace*. New York: McGraw–Hill.

36. Beauchamp and Bowie (1988), 260, 261; Beauchamp and Bowie (2001), 369, ch. 6.

37. Meyers, D. (1998). Work and self–respect. In Beauchamp and Bowie (1988), 275–279; Beauchamp and Bowie (2001), 256–258.

38. Court of Common Pleas, Mahoning County, Ohio, No. 98CV1937, 2000; Anderson, T. (May 2001). Elsewhere in the courts. . . *Security Management, 45*, 105.

39. Werhane, P. (1985). *Persons, rights and corporations*. Englewood Cliffs: Prentice Hall, 118.

40. Des Jardins, J., McCall, J. (1990). A defense of employee rights. *Journal of Business Ethics, 4*, 367–376.

41. Ibid.

42. Zall, M. (May/June 2001). Employee privacy. *Journal of Property Management, 66*, 16–18.

43. Post, J., Lawrence, A., Weber, J. (1999). *Business and society*, 9th ed. Boston: McGraw–Hill, 378.

44. Dalton, D., Metzger, M. (Feb. 1993). Integrity testing for personnel selection: An unsparing perspective. *Journal of Business Ethics, 12(2)*, 147–156.

45. Carroll, A. (1993). *Business and society: Ethics and stakeholder management*, 3rd ed. Cincinnati: South-Western, 371, 372.

46. Samuels, P. (May 12, 1996). Who's reading your E–mail? Maybe the boss. *New York Times*, 11; also Guernsey, L. (Dec. 16, 1999). On the job, the boss can watch your every online move, and you have a few defenses. *New York Times*, G1, 3.

47. Martin, J. (March 1999). Internet policy: Employee rights and wrongs. *Human Resources Focus, 76*, 13.

48. Ibid.

49. Zall, 18.

50. Des Jardins and McCall, 204–206.

51. Goldstein, R., Nolan, R. (March/April 1975). Personal privacy versus the corporate computer. *Harvard Business Review, 53(2)*, 62-70. In addition to these guidelines, another source that provides drug testing guidelines is M. Bernardo. (1994). Workplace drug testing: An employer's development and implementation guide. Washington, DC: Institute for a Drug–Free Workplace.

52. Timms, E. (June 24, 2001). Bush campaigns to outlaw "genetic discrimination." *Boston Globe*, A5.

53. Des Jardins and McCall, 213.

54. Eisenberg, M., Ranger–Moore, J., Taylor, K., Hall, R., et al. (Feb. 2001). Workplace tobacco policy: Progress on a winding road. *Journal of Community Health, 26*, 1, 23.

55. Karr, A., Guthfield, R. (Jan. 16, 1992). OSHA inches toward limiting smoking. *Wall Street Journal*, B1.

56. DeGeorge, 322–324.

57. Velasquez, M. G. (1988). *Business ethics: Concepts and cases*, 2nd ed. Englewood Cliffs, NJ: Prentice Hall, 388; also see the 4th edition (1998), 463–467.

58. Carroll, 371, 372.

59. Fletcher, M. (May 21, 2001). Employee leave and law. *Business Insurance, 35*, 3.

60. Ibid.

61. Kanowitz, L. (1969). *Women and the law.* Albuquerque, NM: University of New Mexico Press, 36; also quoted in Velasquez (1988), 324; and Velasquez (1998), 387–392.

62. Fehrenbacher, D. (1978). *The Dred Scott case.* New York: Oxford University Press.

63. Velasquez (1998), 375.

64. Lewis, D. (Nov. 26, 2000). Revisiting equal pay. *Boston Globe*, G2.

65. Des Jardins and McCall, 377–382.

66. Feagin, J., Feagin, C. (1986). *Discrimination American Style*, 2nd ed. Malabar, FL: Robert Krieger, 23–33; Velasquez (1998), 391.

67. J. Krasner. (May 20, 2001). Hitting the glass ceiling. *Boston Globe*, G1.

68. Noah, T., Karr., A. (Nov. 4, 1991). What new civil rights law will mean: Charges of sex, disability bias will multiply. *Wall Street Journal*, 31.

69. U.S. Equal Opportunity Commission. Title VII of the Civil Rights Act of 1964. Charges: FY 1992–FY 2000, at http://www.eeoc.gov/stats/vii.html.

70. Excerpts from: Supreme Court opinions on limits of Disabilities Act. (Feb. 22, 2001). *New York Times*, A20.

71. Discrimination interviewer questions sometimes illegal. (May 20, 2001). *Boston Globe*, p. H2.

72. Lewis, G2.

73. DeGeorge, 322–324.

74. Ibid.

75. *Bakke* v. *Regents of the University of California.*

76. Mollins, C. (July 17, 1995). Shaky freedoms: The U.S. supreme court challenges liberalism. *McLean's*, 22; and Gwynne, S. (April 1, 1996). Undoing diversity: A bombshell court ruling curtails affirmative action, *Time, 147*, 54.

77. Wilgoren, J. (March 28, 2001). U.S. court bars race as factor in school entry. *New York Times*, http://www.nytimes.com/2001/03/28/national/28MICH.html.

78. Steiner and Steiner, 656.

79. Strom, S. (Oct. 20, 1991). Harassment rules often not posted. *New York Times*, 1, 22.

80. U.S. Equal Employment Opportunity Commission. Sexual Harassment Charges: EEOC & FEPAs Combined, FY 1992–FY 2000, at http://www.eeoc.gov/stats/harass.html.

81. Finkelstein, K. (May 25, 2001). TWA to pay $2.6 million to settle harassment suit. *New York Times*, B6.

82. Machlowitz, M., Machlowitz, D. (Sept. 25, 1986). Hug by the boss could lead to a slap from the judge. *Wall Street Journal*, 20; Wermiel, S., Trost, C. (June 20, 1986). Justices say hostile job environment due to sex harassment violates rights. *Wall Street Journal*, 2.

83. Hayes, A. (October 11, 1991). How the courts define harassment. *Wall Street Journal*, B1; Lublin, J. (October 11, 1991). Companies try a variety of approaches to halt sexual harassment on the job. *Wall Street Journal*, B1.

84. Mastalli, G. (1991). Appendix: The legal context. In Matthews, J., Goodpaster, K., Nash, L., eds. *Policies and reasons: A casebook in business ethics*, 2nd ed. New York: McGraw–Hill, 157, 158.

85. Long, S., Leonard, C. (Oct. 1999). The changing face of sexual harassment, *Human Resources Focus*, S1–S3.

86. Ibid.

87. Ibid.

88. www.blr.com is an excellent source of training for human resources employees and employers. This section is also based on the work by Long and Leonard.

89. Foreman, J., Lehman, B. (Oct. 21, 1991). What to do if you think you may be guilty of sex harassment. *Boston Globe*.

90. Johannes, L., Lublin, S. (May 9, 1996). Sexual-harassment cases trip up foreign companies. *Wall Street Journal*, B4.

91. Maatman, G., Jr. (July 2000). A global view of sexual harassment. *HR Magazine, 45*, 158.

92. Steeley, B. (Sept. 2000). Evaluating your client as a possible qui tam relator. *The Practical Litigator, 11(5)*, 15.

93. Hoffman, H., Moore, J. (1990). Whistle blowing: Its moral justification. In James, G. *Business Ethics: Readings and Cases in Corporate Morality*, 2nd ed., 332. New York: McGraw-Hill.

94. Ibid., 333.

95. The Brown & Williamson papers can be found at http://www.library.ucsf.edu/tobacco.

96. Sass, R. (2001). The killing of Karen Silkwood: The story behind the Kerr–McGee plutonium case. *Winter Relations Industrielles, 56*, 222.

97. *Haley* v. *Retsinas*, 1998 U.S. App. LEXIS 4654 (8th Cir. Ct., March 16, 1998), No. 97–1946; also see http://www.hrlawindex.com/articles/a/w_0525_9.html.

98. DeGeorge, 208–214.

99. Near, J., Miceli, M., Jensen, R. (March 1983). Variables associated with the whistle-blowing process. Working Paper Series 83–111, Ohio State University, College of Administrative Science, Columbus, 5. Cited in Carroll, 354, 355.

100. Carroll, 356.

101. Ewing.

102. See the Brown and Williamson papers.

103. Maatman, 158.

CHAPTER 7

1. Norris, F. (Sept. 13, 2001). A symbol was destroyed, not America's financial system. *New York Times*, C1.

2. The world braces for economic blows of attack. (Sept. 13, 2001). *Wall Street Journal*, A14.

3. Hager, G. (Sept. 12, 2001). Full global recession "highly likely." *USA Today*, 5B.

4. Treaster, J., Johnston, D. (Sept. 13, 2001). Billions of dollars in claims expected, but compensation could vary widely. *New York Times*, C1.

5. Reactions from around the world. (Sept. 13, 2001). *New York Times*, A17.

6. Strauss, G. (Sept. 12, 2001). Catastrophe suspends business as usual in USA. *USA Today*, 2A.

7. Barnes, J., Holson, L. (Sept. 14, 2001). Multinationals will protect workers, but plan to remain in hot zones. *New York Times*, A6.

8. Kahn, J. Andrews, E. (Aug. 20, 2001). World's economy slows to a walk in rare lock step. *New York Times*, A1.

9. Koppel, N. (Sept. 15, 2001). China in accord on entry to WTO. *Boston Globe*, C1.

10. Lacey, M. (May 1, 2001). Attacks were up last year, U.S. terrorism report says. *New York Times*, A14.

11. Facts on terrorism can be found on these Websites: www.fema.gov/library/terror.htm, http://usinfo.state.gov/topical/pol/terror/homepage.htm, and www.state.gov/s/ct/rls/2000.11.

12. Post, J., Lawrence, A., Weber, J. (2002). *Business and society*, 10th ed., 478. Boston: McGraw-Hill.

13. Porter, M., Stern, S. (Summer 2001). Innovation: Location matters. *MIT Sloan Management Review*, 42(4), 28–36.

14. *Mergerstat review 2001*, 1. (2001). Los Angeles: Mergerstat; also see mergerstat.com.

15. Hammel, G. *Leading the Revolution*, chapter 5. Boston: Harvard Business School Press, 2000;

16. Engardio, P., with Kripalani, M., Webb, A. (Aug. 17, 2001). Smart globalization. *Business Week*, 32. Quotes in this section are taken from this article.

17. Ibid.

18. Stein, N. (Oct. 2, 2000). Global most admired, measuring people power. At www.fortune.com.

19. Ibid.

20. Smale, A. (Aug. 16, 2001). The dark side of the global economy. *New York Times*, 3.

21. Ibid.

22. Thurow, L. (Aug. 7, 2001). Third World must help itself. *Boston Globe*, F4.

23. Ibid.

24. Onishi, N. (July 29, 2001). The bondage of poverty that produces chocolate. *New York Times*, 1.

25. Warsh, D. (July 29, 2001). The next 50 years. *Boston Globe*, E2.

26. Ibid.

27. Shadid, A. (Jan. 24, 2001). Third World nations threatened as digital divide grows, report says. *Boston Globe*, D2.

28. Post, Lawrence, and Weber, 485.

29. Sciolino, D. (Sept. 23, 2001). Who hates the U.S.? Who loves it? *New York Times*, sec. 4, p. 1.

30. Ibid.

31. Ibid.

32. Tyson, L. (July 14, 2001). The new laws of nations. *New York Times*, A15.

33. Ibid.

34. Shaw, H. W., Barry, V. (1995). *Moral issues in business*, 6th ed. Belmont, CA: Wadsworth.

35. Farrell, C. (1994). The triple revolution. *Business Week*, special issue 16.

36. Gerlach, M. (1992). *Alliance capitalism: The social organization of Japanese business*. Berkeley: University of California Press.

37. Means, G., Schneider, D. (2000). *MetaCapitalism*. New York: John Wiley & Sons.

38. Ibid., 177, 178.

39. Ibid., 179.

40. Garreau, J. (1981). *The nine nations of North America*. New York: Avon; Kahle, L. (1988). The nine nations of North America and the value basis of geographic segmentation. In *Regional cultures, managerial behaviors, and entrepreneurship: An international perspective*, edited by Joseph Weiss, 43–60. New York: Quorum Books.

41. Sethi, S., Nobuaki Namiki, N., Swanson, C. (1984). *The false promise of the Japanese miracle: Illusions and realities of the Japanese management system*, 104. Boston: Pitman.

42. Ibid., chs. 5, 6.

43. Ibid., 115–116.

44. Ouchi, W., Jaeger, A. (1978). Type Z organizations: Stability in the midst of mobility. *Academy of Management* Review, 3, 305–314.

45. Sawhney, M., Prandelli, E. (Summer 2000). Communities of creation. *California Management Review, 42(4)*, 1–31.

46. Lei, D., Slocum, J., Jr. (Winter 1991). Global strategic alliances: Payoffs and pitfalls. *Organizational Dynamics*, 17–29.

47. Judge, W., Ryman, J. (2001). The shared leadership challenge in strategic alliances: Lessons from the U.S. healthcare industry. *Academy of Management Executive, 15(2)*, 71-79.

48. United Nations. (1973). *Multinational corporations in world development*, 23.

49. Czinkota, M., Ronkainen, I. (1989). *International business*, 338. Chicago: Dryden.

50. Jacobson, G., Hillkirk, J. (1986). *Xerox: American Samurai*. New York: Macmillan, Collier Books.

51. Sturdivant, F., Vernon-Wortzel, H. (1990). *Business and society: A managerial approach*, 189–190. Homewood, IL: Irwin.

52. Vernon, R., Wells, L., Jr. (1986). *Manager in the international economy*, 5th ed., 2. Englewood Cliffs, NJ: Prentice Hall.

53. Palmer, E. (June 2001). Multinational corporations and the social contract. *Journal of Business Ethics, 31(3)*, 245.

54. Mayer, D. (Winter 2001). Community, business ethics, and global capitalism. *American Business Law Journal, 38(2)*, 215–260.

55. Vernon, R. (1971). *Sovereignty at bay*. New York: Basic Books.

56. Meyer, 215–260. Citations for the following section are also taken from Meyer.

57. Czinkota and Ronkainen, 346–347.

58. Akst, D. (March 4, 2001). Nike in Indonesia, through a different lens. *New York Times*, 3.

59. Beyer, J. (Sept. 1999). Ethics and cultures in international business. *Journal of Management Inquiry, 8(3)*, 287–297.

60. This section is based on Frederick, W. (1991). The moral authority of transnational corporate codes. *Journal of Business Ethics, 10*, 165–177.

61. Ibid., 168–169.

62. DeGeorge, R. Ethics in personal business—a contradiction in terms? *Business Credit, 102(8)*, 45–46.

63. Berenbeim, R. (Oct. 2000). Globalization drives ethics. *New Zealand Management, 47(9)*, 26–29.

64. Frederick,166–167.

65. Ibid., 167.

66. Ibid.

67. Puffere, S., McCarthy, D. J. (Winter 1995). Finding the common ground in Russian and American business ethics. *California Management Review, 37(2)*, 20–46. Donaldson, T., Dunfee, T. (Summer 1999). When ethics travel: The promise and peril of global business ethics. *California Management Review, 41(4)*, 45.

68. Davis, M. (Jan./Feb. 1999). Global standards, local problems. *Journal of Business Ethics, 20(1)*, 38.

69. Maynard, M. (March 2001). Policing transnational commerce: Global awareness in the margins of morality. *Journal of Business Ethics, 30, 17, 27*.

70. DeGeorge, R. (Sept. 2000). Ethics in international business—A contradiction in terms? *Business Credit, 102(8)*, 50–52.

71. Cattaui, M. (Summer 2000). Responsible business conduct in a global economy. *OECD Observer, Issue 221/222, 18–20*; Berenbeim, R. (Sept. 1, 1999). The divergence of a global economy: One company, one market, one code, one world. *Vital Speeches of the Day, 65(22)*, 696–698; Morrison, A. (May 2001). Integrity and global leadership. *Journal of Business Ethics, 31(31)*, 65–76; Palmer, E. (June 2001). Multinational corporations and the social contract. *Journal of Business Ethics, 31(3)*, 245–258.

72. DeGeorge, R. (1993). *Competing with Integrity*, 114–121. New York: Oxford University Press.

73. Referenced in Donaldson and Dunfee, 48.

74. Ibid.

75. Ibid., 63.

76. Donaldson, T. (1989). *The ethics of international business*, ch. 5. New York: Oxford University Press.

77. Donaldson and Dunfee, 62.

78. Ibid.

CHAPTER 8

1. Wines, M. (Sept. 30, 2001). An act of terror reshapes the globe. *New York Times*, 4B; Slavin, B. (Oct. 3, 2001). Bush expresses endorsement of Palestinian state. *USA Today*, 6A.

2. Wines, 4B.

3. Buildings . . . destroyed, thank God. (Text of Osama bin Laden's remarks aired on al-Jazeera, an Arab Gulf state television station, translated from Arabic.) (Oct. 8, 2001). *Boston Globe*, A2.

4. S. Stolberg, "Some Experts Say U.S. Is Vulnerable to a Germ Attack," New York Times, Sept. 30, 2001, A1, B3.

5. R. Behar, "Fear along the firewall," *Fortune*, Oct. 15, 2001, 145.

6. Ibid.

7. Ibid.

8. Ibid.

9. Stipp, D. (Oct. 15, 2001). Bioterror is in the air. *Fortune*, 154.

10. Rosen, J. (Oct. 7, 2001). A watchful state. *New York Times Magazine*, 93.

11. Ibid., 38.

12. Ibid., 92.

13. Veverka, M. (Sept. 24, 2001). The suicide attacks change everything. *Barron's, 82(39)*, 38.

14. Frantz, D. (Sept. 30, 2001). Refugees from Afghanistan flee out of fear and find despair. *New York Times*, B1, B7.

15. Slavin, B. (Oct. 4, 2001). Feeding Afghans is a battle in itself. *USA Today*, 4A.

16. Ibid.

17. Werhane, P. (2000). Exporting mental models: Global capitalism in the 21st century. *Business Ethics Quarterly, 10(1)*, 353–362.

18. Comfort, N. (Sept. 9, 2001). The stuff of life. *New York Times Book Review*, 23.

19. Lampman, J. (April 6, 2000). EnGENEering the future biotech revolution spawns vocal opposition, as science enters brave new world—With ethical debate trailing far behind. *Christian Science Monitor*, 11.

20. Ibid.

21. Ibid.

22. Ibid.

23. Comfort, 23.

24. Raymo, C. (March 20, 2001). Cloning and the human self. *Boston Globe*, C2.

25. Ibid.

26. Wolfson, A. (Jan. 24, 2001). Are you a person or a nonperson? The new bioethicists will decide. *Wall Street Journal*, A20. Wolfson is reviewing the book *Culture of Death* (Encounter, 2001) by Wesley Smith. This book uses the two ethics described above.

27. A. Wolfson, "Are You a Person or a Nonperson? The New Bioethicists Will Decide," Wall Street Journal, Jan. 24, 2001, A20. Wolfson is reviewing a book, *Culture of Death* (Encounter, 2001) by Wesley Smith. This book uses the two ethics described above.

28. See chapter 7 of this text for citations.

29. Velasquez, M. (1998). *Business Ethics*, 4th ed., ch. 11. Upper Saddle River, NJ: Prentice Hall.

30. Ibid., 256.

31. Harvery, B., Schaefer, A. (April 2001). Managing relationships with environmental stakeholders: A study of U.K. water and electricity utilities. *Journal of Business Ethics, 30(3)*, 243–260.

32. Is globalisation doomed? (Sept. 27, 2001). Economist.com, 1.

33. Ibid.

34. Ibid.

35. UK government: Britain, Europe and America—The challenge of globalization. (July 26, 2001). Coventry, 1.

36. Singer, P. (1979). *"Rich and Poor" in Practical Ethics*, 166. New York: Cambridge University Press.

37. Tweney, D. (Sept. 27, 2001). The Internet emerges as the most reliable way to communicate. *Business 2.0*, The DeFogger, Internet Communications, 1.

38. Keating, S. (April 15, 2001). In this age of the Internet and e-mail, we each face a battle to preserve our privacy. *Denver Post*, D1.

39. Ibid.

40. DeGeorge, R. (2000). Business ethics and the challenge of the information age. *Business Ethics Quarterly, 10(1)*, 63–72.

41. Ibid.

42. Senate holds hearing on Internet privacy. (Aug. 2001). ABA Bank Compliance, Washington, *22(8)*, 3.

43. Ibid.

44. Ibid.

45. Ibid.

46. Roberts, S. (Sept. 24, 2001). Marsh, Aon grieving but ready to serve. *Business Insurance, 35(39)*, 3, 39.

47. Ibid.

48. LaBarre, P., with Koestenbaum, P. (Oct. 21, 2001). Life after death. FastCompany.com, 1.

49. See section in Chapter 6 of this text on the workforce in transition.

50. Weaver, P. (1988). After social responsibility. In *The U.S. business corporation: An institution in transition*, edited by John Meyer and James Gustafson. Cambridge, MA: Ballinger.

51. Brooks, L. J. (1989). Corporate ethical performance: Trends, forecasts, and outlooks. *Journal of Business Ethics, 8*, 31–38.

52. Quoted in ibid., 31–38.

53. Glenn, E., Witmeyer, D., Stevenson, K. (Fall 1977). Cultural styles of persuasion. *International Journal of Intercultural Relations, 1(3)*, 7; Casse, P. (1982). *Training for the multicultural manager*. Yarmuth, ME: Intercultural Press. Also see Adler, N. (2002). *International dimensions of organizational behavior*, 4th ed., ch. 7. Canada: South-Western Thomson Learning.

54. Raider, E. (1982). Strategy assessment. In *International Negotiations*. Plymouth, MA: Situation Management Systems. According to Raider's framework, in any situation, when "strategy" is high, then it is important to negotiate; when strategy is considered of low importance, it may be more expedient to "take it or leave it"; when strategy is somewhere between high and low importance, then bargain. The same conditions hold true for the "value of the exchange," "relationship" involved, "commitment," and "time available"; that is, when each of these dimensions is high, very high, or very important, then it is best to negotiate. When the dimensions are low, very low, or unimportant, then it is better generally to take it or leave it. When the dimensions are somewhere between high and low, important and not important, then bargaining is suggested. When the dimension of "power distance" (i.e., the separation between your position, status, and authority and those of the other party) is very

low (i.e., you are both on the same level), it is better to negotiate. When it is very high, it is best to take it or leave it. Of course, knowledge of the situation, other parties, cultural context, and history of the issues and relationships is always a prerequisite for deciding whether or not, when, and how to maneuver. It is also important to *know and be able to use a range of conflict resolution techniques.* Many times conflict precedes or can occur during bargaining or negotiation.

55. Buller, K., Kohls, J., Anderson, K. (1991). The challenges of global ethics. *Journal of Business Ethics, 10,* 767–775.
56. Ury, W. (1993). *Getting to Yes.* New York: Penguin.

CASE 2

1. *Wall Street Journal,* May 17, 1995, A21.
2. Dow Corning Corporation. (Dec. 8, 1992). Dow Corning restructures medical materials product line. *Corporate News,* 2.
3. *Boston Globe,* Jan. 10, 1995, 10.
4. *Maclean's,* March 30, 1992, 39.
5. Cimons, M. (Jan. 17, 1992). Implant firm's memos linked to full FDA ban. *Los Angeles Times,* A32.
6. Ibid.
7. Byrne, J. (1996). *Informed Consent,* 78. New York: McGraw-Hill.
8. *Facts on File,* Feb. 9, 1995, 88.
9. *Boston Globe,* Jan. 10, 1995, 10.
10. *Boston Globe,* April 26, 1995, 7.
11. *Business Insurance,* Feb. 21, 1994, 1.
12. Ibid.
13. *Boston Globe,* May 15, 1992, 1.
14. *Boston Globe,* Jan. 22, 1995, 9.
15. *Boston Globe,* May 30, 1995, 14.
16. Ibid.
17. Nocera, J. (Oct. 16, 1995). Fatal litigation. *Fortune,* 78.
18. Ibid.
19. *Boston Globe,* April 16, 1992, 3.
20. *Boston Globe,* March 20, 1992, 1.
21. Redrawing the face of cosmetic surgery procedures. (July 22, 1986). *Washington Post,* 1.
22. *Boston Globe,* May 21, 1995, 48.
23. Global equity research: Dow Chemical. (July 24, 1995). *Merrill Lynch,* 2.
24. Ibid., 3.
25. *Boston Globe,* Jan. 25, 1992, 1.
26. *Boston Globe,* Aug. 5, 1994, 17.
27. *Progressive,* July 1994, 28–29.
28. *Wall Street Journal,* Jan. 7, 1992, B1.
29. *Chemical and Engineering News,* Feb. 21, 1994, 4.
30. *Boston Globe,* March 20, 1992, 16.
31. Ibid.
32. *Boston Globe,* May 5, 1993, 13.
33. *Boston Globe,* March 1, 1995, 4.
34. *Boston Globe,* Dec. 21, 1994, 35.
35. *Boston Globe,* March 1, 1995, 4.
36. *Maclean's,* March 9, 1992, 43.
37. Ibid., 42.
38. Ibid.
39. *Boston Globe,* Jan. 19, 1992.
40. *Maclean's,* March 9, 1992, 43.
41. *Boston Globe,* Jan. 13, 1992, 25.
42. *Progressive,* July 1994, 28.
43. *Boston Globe,* May 21, 1995, 48.
44. *Boston Globe,* April 26, 1995.
45. Sissell, K. (Dec. 8, 1999). Judge approves Dow Corning bankruptcy plan. *Chemical Week, 161(21),* 21.
46. Ibid.
47. Ibid.
48. New York: W. W. Norton & Co., 1996.
49. Rosenberg, C. (July 14, 1996). The Silicon Papers. *New York Times Book Review,* 10.
50. Ibid., 9.

CASE 7

1. Learmonth, M. (Oct. 31, 2000). Let the music play: Bertlesmann and Napster come together. http://www.thestandard.com.
2. http://www.landfield.com/rfcs/rfc959.html.
3. http://duke.usask.ca/~reeves/prog/geoe314/archie.html.
4. Chudnov, D. Docster: The future of document delivery? http://www.libraryjournal.com/docster.asp.
5. http://www.lightshare.com.
6. U.S. Constitution, Article I, Clause 8.
7. Napster University: File swapping and the future of entertainment. (Dec. 9, 2000). http://research.webnoize.com/item.rs?ID=9155.
8. http://gnutella.wego.com/go/wego.pages.page?groupId=116705&view=page&pageId=118401&folderID=118398&panelId=119597&action=view.
9. Gartner Group Inc. (Aug. 30, 2000). Napster banned at 34% of colleges. Reuters, http://msnbc.com/news/453430.asp.
10. Napster University.
11. Kover, A. (June 26, 2000). Napster: The hot idea of the year. *Fortune.* http://library.notherlight.com.
12. Musicians fight "free" Net music. (Nov. 27, 2000). Reuters, http://msnbc.com/news.
13. Caney, D. (Nov. 14, 2000). MP3.com, Universal settle for 53.4. Reuters, http://www.zdnet.com.
14. Musicians fight "free" Net music.
15. Caney.
16. Learmonth.
17. http://www.msnbc.com.
18. Kueffner, S. (Nov. 28, 2000). Bertlesmann is poised to unveil Napster plans. http://interactive.wsj.com.

19. Goodman, D. (April 25, 2000). Limp Bizkit backs Napster. Reuters, http://www.zdnet.com.
20. http://www.Napster.com/speakout/artists.html. (June 29, 2000).
21. Goodman.
22. Stein, J. (Sept. 7, 1998). Porn goes mainstream. *Time*, 54–55.
23. http://www.Napster/com/company.
24. Maney, K. (June 7, 2000). File sharing software may transform the next potential shift creates conflict, excitement about new uses. *USA Today*, 1B.
25. eBay Inc. Annual reports for 1999. http://eBay.com.
26. Yahoo Inc. Annual reports for 1999. http://Yahoo.
27. Yamamoto, M., Borland, J. (Oct. 26, 2000). A brave new—or old—world? http://CDNET.news.com.
28. Stellin, S. (Oct. 15, 2001). Napster's many successors. *New York Times*, 13.

CASE 9

1. Hardey, E. (April 25, 1984). The Forbes 500's annual directory. *Forbes*, 196.
2. McCarroll, T. (Nov. 30, 1992). Was GM reckless? *Time*, 61.
3. Ibid.
4. Ibid.
5. Ibid.
6. *Dateline NBC.* (Nov. 17, 1992). Transcript, 3.
7. Ibid.
8. Ibid., 4.
9. Ibid., 7.
10. Greising, D. (March 1, 1993). A safety expert under fire. *Business Week*, 42.
11. Ibid.
12. Thomas, R. (May 10, 1993). Just as safe at any speed. *Newsweek*, 52.
13. Treece, J. B. (Feb. 22, 1993). Now, the court of public opinion has GM worried. *Business Week*, 38.
14. Zine, K. (May 1993). Peacock eats crow. *Road and Track*, 35.
15. *Dateline NBC.* (Nov. 17, 1992). Transcript, 7.
16. Ibid.
17. Eastland, T. (May 1993). Keep on trucking. *American Spectator*, 54.
18. *Facts on File.* (Feb. 11, 1993).
19. *Facts on File.* (April 8, 1993).
20. Lavin, D. (Dec. 17, 1993). GM settlement of pickup suit backed by court. *Wall Street Journal*, A5.

CASE 10

1. Jury "burns" McD in $2.9M verdict. (Aug. 29, 1994). *Nations Restaurant News*, 1, 55.

2. McDonalds's hot coffee gets her cool cash. (Sept. 5, 1994). *Business Week*, 38.
3. Coffee spill burns woman; jury awards $2.9 million. (Aug. 19, 1994). *Wall Street Journal*, B3.
4. Jury "burns" McD in $2.9M verdict. (Aug. 29, 1994). *Nations Restaurant News*, 1, 55.
5. A case for iced coffee. (Aug. 26, 1994). *Wall Street Journal*, A10.
6. Jury "burns" McD in $2.9M verdict. (Aug. 29, 1994). *Nations Restaurant News*, 1, 55.
7. Ibid., 55.
8. McD settles coffee suit in out-of-court agreement. (Dec. 12, 1994). *Nations Restaurant News*, 1, 59.
9. Judge slashes McD settlement to $480,000. (Sept. 26, 1994). *Nations Restaurant News*, 4.
10. Excessive punitive awards a matter of debate. (Feb. 6, 1995). *Business Insurance*, 1.
11. Ibid.
12. Jury "burns" McD in $2.9M verdict. (Aug. 29, 1994). *Nations Restaurant News*, 55.
13. A case for iced coffee. (Aug. 26, 1994). *Wall Street Journal*, A10.
14. G.O.P. preparing bill to overhaul negligence law. (Feb. 19, 1995). *New York Times*, 24.
15. McDonald's coffee award reduced 75% by judge. (Sept. 15, 1994). *Wall Street Journal*, A4.
16. Judge slashes McD settlement to $480,000. (Sept. 26, 1994). *Nations Restaurant News*, 1.
17. Ibid.
18. McD settles coffee suit in out-of-court agreement. (Dec. 12, 1994). *Nations Restaurant News*, 1.
19. Judge slashes McD settlement to $480,000. (Sept. 26, 1994). *Nations Restaurant News*, 4.

CASE 11

1. History of Colt. www.colt.com/colt/htmi/iIa-historyofcolt.htn-d (official Colt Website).
2. Phinney, D. (June 11, 1999). When laws take aim at guns. ABC News.
3. Siebel, B. (1999). *City Lawsuits against the Gun Industry.* Center to Prevent Handgun Violence; History of Colt (Website).
4. Phinney.
5. Siebel.
6. Ibid.
7. Ibid.
8. Ibid.
9. Glaberson, W. (Oct. 17, 2001). Court says individuals have a right to firearms. *New York Times*, 14.
10. Ibid.
11. Walsh, S. (Nov. 26, 1999). Insurers are bailing out on the gun industry. *Washington Post*, A01.
12. Ibid.
13. Levin, M., Rubin, A. (Dec. 8, 1999). US to join legal fray against gun makers. *Los Angeles*

Times; Bloom, D. (Dec. 7, 1999). White House takes aim at gun makers. MSNBC News.

14. Levin and Rubin.

15. Colt's refutes Newsweek article. (Oct. 11, 1999). www.colt.com/colt/html/n news2; Levin and Rubin; Bloom.

CASE 12

1. Alter, J. (May 1991). Retaining women CPA's: Firms can benefit through programs that help keep talented female professionals. *Journal of Accountancy*, 50–55.

2. AICPA. (March 1988). Upward mobility of women. *Upward Mobility of Women Special Committee report to the AICPA Board of Directors.*

3. Borgia, C. R. (June 1989). Promoting women CPA's. *CPA Journal*, 38–45.

4. Deloitte & Touche. (April 1993). Women in the 90's: A business imperative. *Team Bulletin Special Report.*

5. Fierman, J. (July 30, 1990). Why women still don't hit the top. *Fortune*, 40.

6. Flynn, P. M., Leeth, J., Levy, E. (Winter 1996). The enduring gender mix in accounting: Implications for the future of the profession. *Selections*, 28–32. McLean, VA: Graduate Management Admission Council.

7. Hooks, K. I., Cheramy, S. J. (May 1988). Women accountants—Current status and future prospects. *CPA Journal*, 18–27.

8. King, T. T., Stockard, J. B. (June 1990). The woman CPA: Career and family. *CPA Journal*, 22–28.

9. Loveman, G. W. (Sept./Oct. 1990). The case of the part-time partner. *Harvard Business Review*, 12.

10. Marshall, M. H. Not by numbers alone: A new decade for women in the law. *New England Journal of Public Policy*, 107–118.

11. Maupin, R. J. (Nov.–Dec. 1991). Why are there so few women CPA partners? *Ohio CPA Journal*, 17–20.

12. Owen, E. (Nov.–Dec. 1991). Women in accounting: There is room at the top. *Ohio CPA Journal*, 10–14.

13. Parent, D. E., DeAngelis, C., Myers, N. R. (Feb. 1989). Parity for women CPAs. *Journal of Accountancy*, 72–76.

14. Sharpe, R. (March 29, 1994). Women in management: Family friendly firms don't always promote females. *Wall Street Journal*, B1.

15. Lancaster, H. (Aug. 14, 2001). Women try to break tech-glass ceiling—Number of female computer pros surged in past decade but many say they'd choose another career— Some executives say 'people jobs' can be attained once you've earned your stripes. *Wall Street Journal*, 19.

16. Ibid.

17. Ibid.

18. Ibid.

19. Personal interview conducted by the author, 2000.

20. Ibid.

21. Ibid.

22. Ibid.

23. Ibid.

24. Peterson, J. (June 20, 2001). Deloitte & Touche sets new goal for female partners. *International Accounting Bulletin* (London), 1.

25. Salary survey shows gender disparity. (May 21–June 3, 2001). *Accounting Today*, 9.

26. Ibid.

27. Ibid.

28. Ibid.

29. Maupin, R. J. (Nov./Dec. 1991). Why are there so few women CPA partners? *Ohio CPA Journal* (Columbus), *50(5)*, 17.

30. Ibid.

CASE 13

1. In January of 1999, Intel announced that its Pentium III chips would have unique identification numbers, which was regarded as a serious threat to consumer privacy. For more, see www.junkbusters.com/ht/en/enw.html.

INDEX